The Illustrated Encyclopedia of Recorded

OPERA

The Illustrated Encyclopedia of Recorded

OPERA

Peter Gammond

a Salamander book

Published by

H·A·R·M·O·N·Y B·O·O·K·S
NEW YORK

Harmony Books
A division of Crown Publishers, Inc.
One Park Avenue, New York, New York 10016
Published in Canada by
General Publishing Company, Limited

First published in the United Kingdom in
1979 by Salamander Books Limited

This book may not be sold outside the United States
of America and Canada.

© Salamander Books Ltd 1979
27 Old Gloucester Street
London WC1N 3AF
United Kingdom

Gammond, Peter.
The Illustrated Encyclopedia of Recorded Opera.
(A Salamander Book)
1. Operas—Discography. 2. Opera—Dictionaries.
I. Title.
ML156.4.046G29   782.1'03   79-17182
ISBN 0-517-53840-7

All correspondence concerning the content of this
volume should be addressed to Salamander Books Ltd.

Credits

Compiled by Peter Gammond
Opera entries by Peter Gammond and Burnett James
Singers' biographies by John Freestone

Editor: Trisha Palmer
Designers: Roger Hyde and Mark Holt
Picture research: Anne-Marie Ehrlich
Record sleeve photography: Bruce Scott
Filmsetting: Modern Text Typesetting, England
Colour reproduction: Process Colour Centre Ltd,
and Tenreck Ltd, England
Printed in Belgium by Henri Proost & Cie, Turnhout

Acknowledgements

The publishers would like to give special thanks to the
Classical Marketing/Promotion department of the
Decca Record Company Limited, London, for their
valuable assistance, and to Henry Stave & Co Ltd,
London, who kindly supplied record sleeves for
photography where these were unavailable
from the record companies listed below.

We would also like to thank the following record
companies who gave their permission to use
record sleeves as illustrations in this book:

CBS Records	EMI Records Ltd
Composers Recordings, Inc	Phonogram Ltd
Decca Record Co Ltd	RCA Ltd
Desto Records	Selecta (London)
Deutsche Grammophon	Unicorn Records Ltd

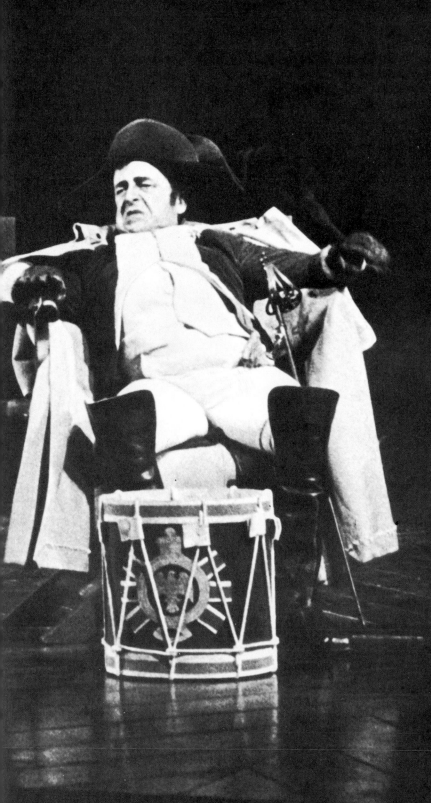

The Author

Peter Gammond, born in Northwich, Cheshire
in 1925, studied at Wadham College, Oxford
and is now Music Editor of the monthly
British magazine *Hi-Fi News*. He previously
held several posts in the musical world,
including those of Editor, *Audio Record Review*
from 1966 to 1970 and Music Editor with the
Decca Record Company from 1953 to 1959.

Since 1960 he has also worked in a freelance
capacity for various periodicals and newspapers,
among them the *Gramophone Record Review*
and *The Sunday Times*, and on BBC radio and
television. He is the author of 15 books on
music, notably *Music on Record* (four volumes,
1962-64, revised 1968), *Bluff Your Way in Music*
(1966), *One Man's Music* (1971), *Musical
Instruments in Color* (1975) and *Scott Joplin
and the Ragtime Era* (1975). Three further
titles are to appear in 1979.

He is married and lives in Shepperton, Middlesex.

Publisher's Note

Every care has been taken to ensure that record
catalogue numbers are correct and up to date
at the time of going to press. However, readers
are advised to consult current catalogues and
their local record dealer for the lastest information.

A cross-reference symbol ≫ is used throughout
the book after the names of those composers
who have their own main entry.

Contents

Pages 10-235

*The following 155 composers are
arranged in alphabetical order throughout the book*

Introduction

Any survey of opera has to impose some limitations on its content. We have allowed ours to take shape on the basis of it being a survey of 'recorded' opera, the recordings in this case being confined in practical terms to LP recordings that are, with a few exceptions, reasonably accessible to the general buyer. The LP age has, in fact, treated the opera collector well and it is fairly safe to say that it is hard to think of an important opera that has not been represented on record, if not complete then by some sample of its merits, during the last 20 years or so. Records come and go according to public demand, but a survey of the current catalogues reveals the availability of most of the accepted masterpieces of opera, and a good deal besides that we would not automatically expect to be there were it not for the dedicated enthusiasm for the subject shown by our record companies.

One of the major steps forward in the field of operatic recording came when Decca first gave the world a complete Wagner *Ring* cycle. Since then Philips, on a worldwide basis, have dedicated themselves to seeing that Berlioz has been thoroughly recorded and that even the most obscure Verdi operas have gradually been explored, and they are currently putting all the Haydn operas (once virtually unknown) onto record. EMI have been making available as much English opera as their budget will allow, with Decca seeing to it that virtually no work by the late Benjamin Britten was left without a hearing. We have *almost* ceased to grumble, not because there is nothing further to record, but because the record producers seem just as eager to fill all the gaps and we leave it to them to do their best for us as soon as possible.

The great operas, the staple classics, are well covered, in some cases to the point of over-indulgence. Of course, at any given time, with the present no exception, there are gaps. Some of these we have been able to cover by listing an American or Continental recording where no British issue was available. We have even fallen to the temptation of including some deleted recordings, hoping the enthusiast has a fair chance of picking up a second-hand copy. Some gaps we have not filled because once-popular works seem to have fallen by the wayside. New and important recordings will have appeared during and after production of this book, whose omission is regretted but unavoidable—eg Richard Strauss's *Die schweigsame Frau*.

Our coverage, then, has fundamentally been dictated by the presence of an operatic title in the present record listings, not only in the shape of a complete recording or substantial highlights but by virtue of any representation—even a single aria or just its overture. While it may not be a perfect guideline, it does seem logical to assume, in general, that if a work is of any commercial value somebody will have recorded it at some time or other. Which still leaves the enthusiast plenty of scope to say that innumerable items of genuine interest are unduly neglected.

Although it was my original intention to include as much light opera and operetta as possible, this proved impracticable owing to limitations of size. Generally stopping at the *opéra-comique* level of interest, there are one or two worthwhile exceptions, notably Johann Strauss, Jacques Offenbach and Arthur Sullivan, whose works have a weight of numbers and an importance that made them difficult to leave out.

I have also allowed the various degrees of availability (again with practical exceptions that dictated their own merits as the work progressed) to decide on the treatment each work gets. The plan basically is to give works that have a complete recording by a major company the full treatment: a full heading, giving number of acts, librettist, first performance and subsequent first performances in major cities (on a very selective basis); a full synopsis, act by act; a list of well-known arias; any notes of interest to that particular work beyond a general mention in the introductory sections on each composer; and a list of recordings deemed worthy of entry (and, again, not intended to be a complete listing) classified by the following symbols:
● = complete recording; ○ = abridged recording;
■ = highlights; □ = excerpt or excerpts; (d) indicates a deleted record. The book aims to be a guide to the availability of records rather than an arbiter of merit. But we have added a ★ to some records of outstanding merit, either to draw attention to them or, occasionally, to offer a choice among a generous selection of alternatives. Now and then a few guiding remarks are also added when a choice of recording is a matter of vital interest.

Where only highlights or excerpts are available a synopsis of the opera is not given but only such notes and comments as seem relevant; and where there are only isolated excerpts, only the normal heading is usually given. In practice this generally follows the whole contention of the book that importance is usually, though not inevitably, indicated by availability.

Peter Gammond

ADOLPHE ADAM
(b. Paris 24.7.1803; d. Paris 3.5.1856)

Adam's father, a musician, was reluctant to encourage him to enter the profession. Eventually he relented and the young Adam entered the Paris Conservatoire, where he studied under Boieldieu ». In his spare time he played in theatre orchestras and wrote some pieces for the music-halls, then in 1825 Boieldieu asked him to help with the orchestration of *La Dame Blanche*. This brought Adam to the attention of the Opéra-Comique, where his *Pierre et Catherine* was produced in 1829. Although Adam's music was mainly facile and only occasionally inspired, he nevertheless remains important as one of the few composers who bridged the gap between the opéra-comique and the operettas of Offenbach » and his successors. Berlioz » described Adam's music as "admirably suited to the requirements of the Opéra-Comique, for it is stylish, fluent, undistinguished and full of catchy little tunes which one can whistle on the way home". His light, vaudeville style was first seen in *Le Châlet* (1834) and his first full-length work, *Le Postillon de Longjumeau* (1836), has some excellent ensembles and one aria, listed below, which has remained popular with tenors. He was a prolific writer, eventually producing 24 operas, most of which are remembered today mainly for their catchy overtures. Ironically, his most popular work is not operatic, but the ballet *Giselle* (1841). In 1847 Adam founded the Théâtre National, and in 1849 became Professor of Composition at the Paris Conservatoire.

Le Postillon de Longjumeau
Opéra-comique in 3 Acts.
Text by Adolphe de Leuven and Léon Lévy Brunswick.
First performance: Paris (Opéra-Comique) October 13, 1836.

RECORDINGS:
Eurodisc 70657 (Ger) (d) ■
RIAS Chorus and Orchestra
c. Reinhard Peters
John Van Kestern (t)
Stina-Britta Melander (s)
Ivan Sardi (bs)
Ernst Krukowski (b)
Fritz Hoppe (bs)

HMV SLS5105 ☐
Angel S-3736 (3) (US)
Mes amis, écoutez l'histoire
Nicolai Gedda (t)

Le Toréador
Opéra-comique in 2 Acts.
Text by Thomas Sauvage.
First performance: Paris (Opéra-Comique) May 18, 1849.

RECORDINGS:
International 7.500 (Fr) ☐
Variations sur un thème de Mozart
Mado Robin (s)

Giralda
Opéra-comique in 3 Acts.
Text by Eugène Scribe.
First performance: Paris (Opéra-Comique) July 20, 1850.

RECORDINGS:
Decca SXL6422 ☐
London 6643 (US)
Overture
c. Richard Bonynge

La Poupée de Nuremburg
Opéra-comique in 1 Act.
Text by Adolphe de Leuven and Arthur de Beauplan.
First performance: Paris (Opéra-National) February 21, 1852.

RECORDINGS:
Decca SXL6422 ☐
London 6643 (US)
Overture
c. Richard Bonynge

Si J'étais Roi
Opéra-comique in 3 Acts.
Text by Philippe d'Ennery.
First performance: Paris (Théâtre-Lyrique) September 4, 1852.

RECORDINGS:
Decca ECS547 ☐
Overture
c. Jean Martinon

Decca SPA384 ☐
London STS-15021 (US)
Overture
c. Albert Wolff

DG 2548 260 ☐
Overture
c. Louis Frémaux

Far left: *Adolphe Adam, composer of 24 operas in the light French* opéra comique *vein, and of the ballet* Giselle.

Below: *Adam's* Si j'étais Roi *was one of those tuneful works in the* opéra-comique *tradition that led to the development of operetta. Its fantasy story offered a colourful production with designs by Nadar.*

EUGEN D'ALBERT
(b. Glasgow 10.4.1864; d. Riga 3.3.1932)

Son and pupil of dance composer and conductor Charles d'Albert, he studied piano at the National Training School in London. He also studied composition with Stainer, Prout and Sullivan » and continued his studies in Vienna where, for a time, he was a pupil of Liszt. D'Albert became well known as a pianist and, from 1907, was the Director of the Hochschule für Musik in Berlin. He wrote many operas, comic and serious, but *Tiefland (The Lowlands)* is the only one that is regularly heard today.

Tiefland
Opera in Prologue and 2 Acts.
Text by Rudolph Lothar, based on a Catalonian play 'Terra Baixa' by Angel Guimerá.
First performance: Prague (Neues Deutsches Theater) November 15, 1903.

Synopsis:
Prologue and Act 1   Pedro, a simple but contented mountain shepherd, is ordered down to the plains by his master Sebastian to marry Marta. Little does Pedro know that Marta has already been seduced by Sebastian, who intends to marry a rich widow but believes he can still keep Marta by marrying her off to Pedro, who will be easy to deceive. Sebastian forces Marta into the marriage but, believing Pedro has been paid to marry her, she refuses to sleep with him on the wedding night.
Act 2   Poor Pedro is perplexed at being made a figure of fun, and turns for sympathy to a child called Nuri. Marta, touched by Pedro's honesty and kindness, begins to love him. She confesses the truth about Sebastian and offers to kill herself, but Pedro forgives her and when Sebastian returns there is a fight and Sebastian is killed. The lovers now leave the sinful lowlands for the light and freedom of the mountains.

Well-known arias:
Prologue Zwei Vaterunser bet' ich (Pedro and Nando)
Act 1   Ich gruss' noch einmal meine Berge Wolfserzählung (Pedro)
Act 2   Hull' in die Mantille (Sebastian, Marta and Pedro)

Notes:
An opera in the grand manner and following a current fashion for naturalism, its real subject is a concern for the social evils of the growing towns as compared to the purer life of the country. It has a brilliantly colourful score and tenderly beautiful songs.

RECORDINGS:
Philips A00413/4L (d) ●
Vienna State Opera Chorus/Vienna Symphony Orchestra
c. Rudolf Moralt
Sebastian (b) Paul Schoeffler
Marta (s)   Judith Hellwig
Pedro (t)   Waldemar Kmentt

Deutsche Grammophon 19424 (d) ■
Deutschen Oper/Bamberg Symphony Orchestra
c. Hans Löwlein
Sebastian (b) Thomas Stewart
Marta (s)   Inge Borkh
Pedro (t)   Hans Hopf

Above: *Eugen d'Albert, composer of many operas of which* Tiefland *is the only one which remains popular.*

12

THOMAS ARNE
(b. London 12.3.1710; d. London 5.3.1778)

Intended for a legal career, Arne was educated at Eton and then apprenticed to a lawyer; but his inclinations were musical and he spent most of this time composing. He soon made his mark with a distinct vein of Englishness at a time when British music was all but submerged by the influence of Handel » and Italian opera. His writing has been described as having "an agreeable straight-forwardness and honourable simplicity". His reputation as a composer was established with the masque *Comus*, a setting of Milton's words written in 1738; and he achieved wide popularity with the masque *Alfred*, which contained the immortal song 'Rule, Britannia'. He was appointed resident composer at Drury Lane and started to produce his best operas after 1760 when he collaborated with Isaac Bickerstaffe on *Thomas and Sally*, followed by the ballad opera *Love in a Village* (1762). His most substantial and lasting opera was *Artaxerxes* (1762), which remained in the Covent Garden repertoire until the 19th century.

Thomas and Sally
Dramatic pastoral in 2 Acts.
Text by Isaac Bickerstaffe.
First performance: London (Covent Garden) November 28, 1760

Synopsis:

Act 1   While the fox-hunting Squire enjoys his gentlemanly pursuits, Sally pines at her cottage door for her absent sailor love, Thomas. Dorcas tries to persuade her to enjoy life and marry the Squire—without success. The Squire himself unsuccessfully tries to seduce her. He offers her riches but she prefers to remain faithful, virtuous and poor.

Act 2   Thomas returns and tells of his voyage. In the meantime the Squire and Dorcas are still scheming, but Sally remains true and repulses his advances. Thomas arrives on the scene just in time and sends the Squire packing. The lovers are re-united and Thomas praises the faithfulness of the 'British virgin'.

Notes:

Interesting as the first English opera to use clarinets in its scoring: an innovation probably due to the helping hand of J. C. Bach ». It also used recitative instead of dialogue—unusual at the time in English opera. The work once enjoyed great popularity.

RECORDINGS:
Pye Golden Guinea
GSGC14125 (d) ★ ●
Northern Sinfonia
c. Simon Preston
Sally (s)   Hazel Holt
Dorcas (m-s) Jean Temperly
Thomas (t)   Paul Taylor
Squire (t)   Philip Langridge

Artaxerxes
Opera in 2 Acts.
Text by Thomas Arne, translated from Metastasio's 'Artaserse'.
First performance: London (Covent Garden) February 2, 1762.

RECORDINGS: Decca SXL2256 □
Decca SET268/9 □   London 25232
London 1257 (2) (d)   or 1214 (2)
O too lovely   The soldier tir'd
Marilyn Horne (m-s)   **Joan Sutherland** (s)

The Cooper
Opera in 1 Act.
Text by Thomas Arne, based on 'Le Tonnelier' by Audinot and Quétant.
First performance: London (Haymarket) June 9, 1772.

RECORDINGS:
Saga XID5015 (d) ●
Intimate Opera Society

Left: *The popular Mrs Billington, who sang 'The soldier tir'd'.*   **Right:** *The eccentric but much-loved Thomas Arne.*

Below: Artaxerxes *was one of the few English operas of the time to achieve lasting success—with production troubles, however.*

DANIEL AUBER
(b. Caen 29.1.1782; d. Paris 12.5.1871)

Auber composed early in life, but for some years he followed a commercial career in London. He won attention as a composer by some attractive songs and his Cello and Violin Concertos (1804). His first opera, *L'Erreur d'un moment*, appeared in Paris in 1805, but he had little success in this field until 1820 when *La Bergère Châtelaine* was well received at the Opéra-Comique. In 1842 he became the Director of the Paris Conservatoire. He wrote 43 operas, now mainly remembered for their overtures and an occasional aria. He had a good technique and, like so many of the best French opéra-comique composers, wrote in a decidedly Mozartian vein. His most sparkling opera was *Fra Diavolo* (1830), while his *La Muette de Portici* (1828, also known as *Masaniello*) was his grandest, remaining popular till the end of the 19th century.

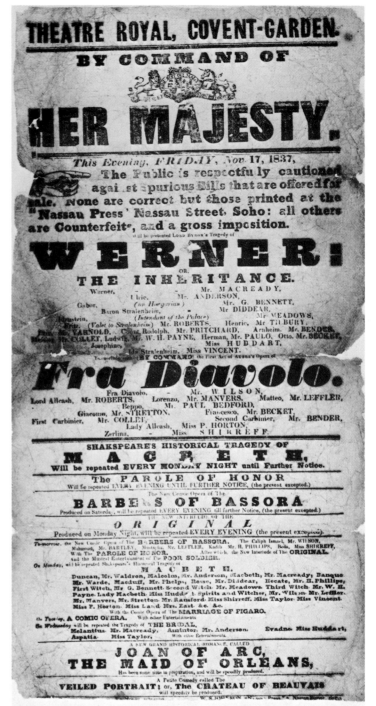

Above: *A caricature by André Gill of composer Daniel Auber.*
Right: *There was an enormous vogue for French opera in Victorian England, and Fra Diavolo received a Command Performance.*

La Muette de Portici (Masaniello)
Opera in 5 Acts.
Text by Eugène Scribe and Germain Delavigne.
First performance: Paris (Opéra) February 29, 1828.

RECORDINGS:

Decca ECS695 □	Decca SET268/9 □	Philips 6755 009 (Fr) □
Overture	London 1257 (2) (d) (US)	Overture
c. Albert Wolff	Ferme tes yeux	c. Paul Paray
	Marilyn Horne (m-s)	

Fra Diavolo
Opéra-comique in 3 Acts.
Text by Eugène Scribe.
First performance: Paris (Opéra-Comique) January 28, 1830.

RECORDINGS:

Decca ECS695 □	Decca SDD192 □	DG 2548 260 □
Overture	London STS 15217 (US)	Overture
c. Albert Wolff	Overture	c. Louis Frémaux
	c. Ernest Ansermet	
Philips 6755 009 (Fr) □	Decca SET454/5 □	
Overture	London 1286 (2) (US)	
c. Paul Paray	Quel bonheur	
	Joan Sutherland (s)	

Lestocq
Opéra-comique in 4 Acts.
Text by Eugène Scribe.
First performance: Paris (Opéra-Comique) May 24, 1834.

RECORDINGS:

Decca SXL6422 □
London 6643 (US)
Overture
c. Richard Bonynge

Le Cheval de Bronze
Opéra-féerique in 3 Acts.
Text by Eugène Scribe.
First performance: Paris (Opéra-Comique) March 23, 1835; revised as an opera-ballet, Paris (Opéra) September 21, 1857.

RECORDINGS:

Decca ECS695 □	Decca SXL6501 □
Overture	O tourment du veuvage
c. Albert Wolff	**Huguette Tourangeau** (m-s)
Philips 6755 009 (Fr) □	
Overture	
c. Paul Paray	

Above: *Design and costume for* Les Diamants de la Couronne.

Le Domino Noir
Opéra-comique in 3 Acts.
Text by Eugène Scribe.
First performance: Paris (Opéra-Comique) December 2, 1837.

RECORDINGS:

Decca ECS695 □	Decca SDD192 □
London STS-15021 (US)	London STS-15217 (US)
Overture	Overture
c. Albert Wolff	c. Ernest Ansermet

Les Diamants de la Couronne
Opéra-comique in 3 Acts.
Text by Eugène Scribe and Vernoy de Saint-Georges.
First performance: Paris (Opéra-Comique) March 6, 1841.

RECORDINGS:

Decca ECS695 □	Philips 6755 009 (Fr) □
Overture	Overture
c. Albert Wolff	c. Paul Paray

Marco Spada
Opéra-comique in 3 Acts.
Text by Eugène Scribe and Germain Delavigne.
First performance: Paris (Opéra-Comique) December 21, 1852; revised as a ballet in 1857.

RECORDINGS:

Decca SXL6422 □	Decca SXL6707 ●
London 6643 (US)	London 6923 (US)
Overture	Ballet version
c. Richard Bonynge	c. Richard Bonynge

Manon Lescaut
Opéra-comique in 3 Acts.
Text by Eugène Scribe, based on the novel by Provost.
First performance: Paris (Opéra-Comique) February 23, 1856.

RECORDINGS:

Voix de son Maître 167-14,056/8 (3) (Fr) ●	Voix de son Maître 065-14.121 (Fr) □
Chorus and Orchestra of French Radio	L'éclat de rire
c. Jean-Paul Marty	**Mado Robin** (s)
Mesplé/Orliac/Runge, etc.	

Decca SET454/5 □
London 1286 (2) (US)
C'est l'histoire amoureuse
Joan Sutherland (s)

JOHANN CHRISTIAN BACH
(b. Leipzig 5.9.1735; d. London 1.1.1782)

The youngest son of Johann Sebastian Bach and Anna Magdalena, he was taught music by his father and later by his elder brother Carl Philipp Emanuel Bach. In 1756 he went to Italy to study in Bologna where he wrote church music and was appointed organist at Milan Cathedral in 1760. He absorbed the strains of Italian opera, which clearly coloured his original Germanic traits, and had his first opera *Artaserse* produced in Turin in 1761. The following year he went to London, where he was to remain for the rest of his life—earning him the title of 'the English Bach'. In 1763 he produced his first opera for London, *Orione*, and was appointed music master to Queen Charlotte. His official position found him responsible for the Court visits of the Mozart family when they stayed in England from 1764-5, and he became a close friend and mentor of the young Mozart ». At the time of the visit there was a season of Bach's operas at the King's Theatre. One of the interests in Bach's operas of the time would be to assess their influence on the early Mozart operatic works; probably equal to the influence of his orchestral works on Mozart's style and instrumentation. Bach visited Mannheim in 1772 and Paris in 1778, where his last opera was produced.

La Clemenza di Scipione
Opera in 3 Acts.
Text by J. C. Bach and others.
First performance: London (King's Theatre) April 4, 1778. (Bach's fifth and last opera for the King's Theatre in the Haymarket).

RECORDINGS:
L'Oiseau-Lyre SOL317 □
Overture
c. Colin Davis

Below: *Johann Christian Bach, who came to be known as 'the English Bach'.*

MICHAEL BALFE
(b. Dublin 15.5.1808; d. Rowney Abbey, Herts 20.10.1870)

Son of a dancing master, he lived in Wexford, Ireland from 1810 where he studied the violin. In 1823 he went to London to study under C. E. Horn and played in the Drury Lane orchestra. He studied singing and composition, first appearing as a singer in Weber's » *Der Freischütz* at Norwich in 1824. After further singing studies in Rome and Milan, he went to Paris where he met Rossini » and in 1827 he appeared in *Il Barbiere di Siviglia*. His own first opera was produced in Palermo in 1830 and his first English opera, *The Siege of Rochelle*, at Drury Lane in 1835. In 1836 Malibran sang in his *The Maid of Artois*. He worked in Paris for several years, returning to London to produce his most popular work, *The Bohemian Girl*, in 1843. Achieved great popularity both as an opera-singer and composer, writing 29 operas in all before retiring to spend his last years farming in Hertfordshire.

The Bohemian Girl
Opera in 3 Acts.
Text by Alfred Bunn, based on a story by Cervantes as used in the ballet 'La Gypsy' by Vernoy de Saint-Georges.
First performance: London (Drury Lane) November 27, 1843.

Synopsis:
Act 1 Thaddeus, a Polish rebel, has escaped from the Austrian troops and joined a gypsy band led by Devilshoof. He saves Arline, the young daughter of Count Arnheim, from danger and is pardoned; but Devilshoof is arrested. He escapes and, in revenge, abducts Arline.
Act 2 Twelve years later, Arline has grown up and fallen in love with Thaddeus. The Queen of the Gypsies also loves him and tries to incriminate Arline by giving her a medal stolen from the Count's family. The medal is recognised and Arline is taken to the castle where her father identifies her by the old wound mark from her childhood escapade.
Act 3 Thaddeus implored Arline not to desert him but the Count cannot allow her to marry a vagabond. But Thaddeus is able to prove he is a nobleman and is married to Arline. At the wedding the Gypsy Queen and Devilshoof attempt to shoot Arline — but fail; and the festivities proceed.

Well-known arias:
Act 2 The heart bowed down (The Count)
I dreamt that I dwelt in marble halls (Arline)
Act 3 When other lips (Thaddeus)

Notes:
The lilting, memorable melodies and a generally uncomplicated score pleased the opera-going public of the day. Drawing-room piano stools were full of such songs by Balfe and others, who had evolved a popular English style based on Italian opera. The first night audience went mad with enthusiasm and the opera continued to run to packed audiences, creating a current craze for gypsy songs, novels and art. Balfe was paid £500 by Chappell & Co for the right to print and publish the opera's songs.

RECORDINGS:
HMV CSD3651 ■
c. Dr Havelock Nelson
Arline (s)   Veronica Dunne
Thaddeus (t)   Uel Deane
The Count (b) Eric Hinds

Decca SET247/8 □
London 2-1254 (2) (US)
I dreamt that I dwelt in marble halls
Joan Sutherland (s)

Above: Balfe's great success was The Bohemian Girl, *and parlour pianos of the day were well supplied with its music.*

The Daughter of St Mark
Opera Seria in 3 Acts.
Text by Alfred Bunn.
First performance: London (Drury Lane) November 27, 1844.

Synopsis:
Act 1 Catarina and Adolphe, a French knight, are to wed. They are welcomed by her uncle and guardian Andrea. Moncenigo, one of the dreaded 'council of Ten', arrives to tell Andrea that the wedding cannot proceed as it has been decreed that Catarina is to marry King Lusignano of Cyprus. The wedding is cancelled, leaving the families in a state of anger and perplexity.
Act 2 Andrea explains the situation to Catarina. She and Adolphe plan to elope but are overheard by Moncenigo, who tells Catarina that Adolphe will be assassinated if they proceed with their plans. To save Adolphe she tells him she no longer loves him; Adolphe is furious and says he will kill her proposed husband at the wedding. Catarina is taken away and Andrea is overcome with grief.
Act 3 Catarina and Andrea are in Cyprus and Moncenigo learns that Adolphe has also arrived on the island. He orders his death but Adolphe is helped by a masked nobleman who turns out to be King Lusignano. Catarina and Adolphe meet and are almost reconciled when Moncenigo returns and has them arrested, and prepares for their execution. He reports the

matter to the King, who receives Andrea and expresses his grief at the unhappiness that is being caused. Andrea reveals that Catarina's mother had a secret affair with Moncenigo, who is therefore Catarina's father. Lusignano pardons Adolphe and allows him to marry Catarina, while the scheming Moncenigo is banished.

Notes:

A typically involved plot used by Halévy in *La Reine de Chypre*, Donizetti in *Catarina Cornaro*, and others. Even in those days the story was criticised for its complicated absurdities but Balfe's music and reputation made the work palatable. Much work went into reviving the score for the recorded performance listed below.

RECORDING:
Rare Recorded Editions SRRE141/2 ●
c. Ken Jones
Gala Opera Group

Satanella, or The Power of Love

Opera in 4 Acts.
Text by Edmund Falconer and Augustus Harris.
First performance: London (Covent Garden) May 14, 1858.

Synopsis:

Act 1 On the eve of his marriage to Stella Count Rupert has lost his fortune in gambling. At his castle, where legend tells that one of his ancestors sold his soul to the Devil, he discovers a book containing magic words that allow him to summon up the fiend Arimanes who appears attended by a female demon, Satanella. Arimanes is annoyed and disguises Satanella as a page in order to ensnare Rupert but she falls in love with him.
Act 2 Rupert, possessed of his magical power, becomes wealthy. Stella still loves him, but he proposes to marry his foster-sister Lelia. Satanella has both ladies abducted and, disguised in a bridal dress, substitutes herself for Lelia. Rupert detects her at the altar, learns of Lelia's fate and rushes to her rescue.
Act 3 Arimanes, furious at Satanella's disobedience, threatens her with eternal damnation if she does not make Rupert his

slave in 30 days. She finds Rupert and Lelia at a slave-market in Tunisia and persuades him to sell his soul to her so that Lelia can be released. Rupert agrees and returns with his bride to the Castle.
Act 4 After 30 days Satanella returns to claim Rupert's soul. Lelia desires to share Rupert's fate and is about to stab herself. But Satanella tears up the contract and becomes the victim herself. She is, however, presented with a rosary, and when Arimanes comes to claim her, she braves the demons with the sacred relic and is saved by the power of love.

Notes:

In spite of its even greater absurdities, the opera became almost as popular as *The Bohemian Girl* and was played at Covent Garden until 1884 and by the Carl Rosa Opera as late as 1930. Again, Balfe's approachable music came to the rescue and the song 'The power of love' had astonishing popularity, remaining a favourite orchestral piece well into this century.

Well-known arias:

The power of love (Satanella)
The convent cell (Satanella)

RECORDINGS:
Rare Recorded Editions SRRE173/4 ●
Addison Orchestra
Amateur cast
c. Brian Galloway

Left: *Michael Balfe, Irish composer and singer.*
Below: *One of the 'hits' of the day was 'The power of love'.*

SAMUEL BARBER
(b. West Chester, Pa, USA 9.3.1910)

Leading American composer who studied at the Curtis Institute of Music in Philadelphia; graduated in 1932. A thoughtful, not particularly prolific composer, his style is a kind of 'moderate modernism'. He has written symphonies and other orchestral music, chamber music and songs, and is perhaps best known for his *Adagio for Strings*. He has been a close collaborator of Gian-Carlo Menotti », the librettist of his best-known opera *Vanessa*, and co-author of the mini-opera *A Hand of Bridge* (1960). For a third opera, *Antony and Cleopatra* (1966), Barber turned to a text based on Shakespeare.

Vanessa
Opera in 4 Acts.
Text by Gian-Carlo Menotti.
First performance: New York (Metropolitan Opera) January 15, 1958. Salzburg 1958.

Synopsis:
Scene: A Northern country, in the 1900s.
Act 1 Vanessa, a faded recluse, has shut herself away from the world with her niece, Erika, because of a disappointment in love. She awaits the return of her lover Anatol, who left her 20 years ago. Anatol does arrive, but he is not her old lover but his son.
Act 2 Anatol seduces Erika after Vanessa has fainted in disappointment; but he then turns to Vanessa, still an attractive middle-aged woman who is revived in visions of youth by the association.
Act 3 When the betrothal is announced at a ball, Erika, who is with child, goes out into the snow to end her life.
Act 4 She is rescued, has a miscarriage, renounces her claims on Anatol, and orders the house to be shut up again and settles down to wait for the return of love.

RECORDING:
RCA Red Seal RLO2094 (2) ●
RCA ARL2-2094 (2) (US)
(Original cast)
Metropolitan Opera Chorus and Orchestra
c. Dimitri Mitropoulos
Vanessa (s) Eleanor Steber
Erika (m-s) Rosalind Elias
Old Baroness (c) Regina Resnik
Anatol (t) Nicolai Gedda
Doctor (b) Giorgio Tozzi
Major-Domo (b) George Cehanovsky
Footman (t) Robert Nagy

A Hand of Bridge
Mini-opera.
Co-author Gian-Carlo Menotti.
First performance: New York 1960.
RECORDING:
Vanguard VSL11019 (d) ○
Symphony of the Air
c. Vladimir Golschmann
Patricia Neway (s)
E. Alberts (c)
W. Lewis (t)
P. Maero (b)

Antony and Cleopatra
First performance: New York (Metropolitan) 1966.
RECORDING:
RCA SB6799 (d) ■
RCA LSC-3062 (US)
New Philharmonic Orchestra
c. Thomas Schippers
Leontyne Price (s)

Right: *Samuel Barber.*

BÉLA BARTÓK
(b. Nagyszentmiklós, Hungary 25.3.1881; d. New York 26.9.1945)

Many of Bartók's compositions are among the central masterpieces of modern music, notably the six string quartets, the piano concertos, the *Music for strings, percussion and celeste*, the second *Violin concerto*, the *Concerto for Orchestra*. He was a dedicated collector of folk music, and in association with his friend and compatriot Zoltan Kodály » gathered an invaluable collection of Magyar folk songs and dances, the spirit of which infuses much of his own music. He wrote only one opera, but that one is full of his tough, uncompromising attitude and style, and though wanting in conventional 'action' is remarkable for its evocation of mood.

Duke Bluebeard's Castle (A Kékszakállú Herceg Vára)
Opera in 1 Act.
Text by Béla Balázs.
First performance: Budapest, May 24, 1918. Berlin 1929; New York 1952; London (Sadler's Wells) 1954.

Synopsis:
Scene and time: Both legendary.
A large gloomy Gothic-style room with no windows, a staircase and seven doors. Judith, Bluebeard's wife, has heard strange stories and is curious to know what lies behind the seven doors. She obtains the keys so that she can let in light and air. Behind five of the doors she finds blood on everything, on each successive evidence of his life and treasure. Behind the sixth door is water, the water of tears. Three beautiful women emerge, his former wives, representing the earlier phases of his life. Bluebeard tries to reassure Judith, swearing she is his final love. She frees the former wives and then, after pleading, dons his jewelled robe and crown and goes out through the seventh door, leaving Bluebeard once more alone.

RECORDINGS:
Decca SET311 ★●
London 1158 (US)
London Symphony Orchestra
c. István Kertesz
Bluebeard (bs) Walter Berry
Judith (m-s) Christa Ludwig

Hungaroton SLPX1148 ●
Budapest Philharmonic Orchestra
c. Janos Ferencsik
Bluebeard (bs) Gyorgy Mellis
Judith (m-s) K. Kasza

CBS 765181 ★●
Columbia M-34217 (US)
London Symphony Orchestra
c. Pierre Boulez
Bluebeard (bs) Siegmund Nimsgern
Judith (m-s) Tatiana Troyanos

Hungaroton LPX11001 (m) ●
Budapest Philharmonic Orchestra
c. János Ferencsik
Bluebeard (bs) Mihály Szekely
Judith (m-s) Klára Palánkay

Above: *Béla Bartók, photographed in New York shortly before his death in 1945.*

JACK BEESON
(b. Muncie, Indiana, 15.7.1921)

Beeson studied at the Eastman School of Music from 1939 to 1944 and with Béla Bartók » in New York 1944-5. He joined the Columbia University opera workshop in 1945 and the musical department soon after, becoming the MacDowell Professor of Music in 1967. He has been the recipient of various distinguished awards and is a prominent figure in various American musical organisations. Although not heard much outside the USA, his operatic output has been considerable, showing a strong dramatic sense and an ability to write expressively and attractively. He has been particularly successful in bringing American background and stories into his operas with strong characterisation of interesting figures. They include *Jonah* (1950), *Hello Out There* (1953), *The Sweet Bye and Bye* (1957), *Lizze Borden* (1965), *My Heart's in the Highlands* (1970) and *Captain Jinks of the Horse Marines* (1975).

Hello Out There
Chamber Opera in 1 Act.
Text by William Saroyan.
First performance: New York (Columbia University Opera Workshop) 1953.

Synopsis:
A young gambler is in jail in a small Texas town, accused of rape. He calls through the bars 'Hello out there' and a girl answers; at first she is suspicious but they become attracted. He plans to escape and go away with the girl, but the husband of the raped woman arrives and shoots him. The girl enters the jail to find him dying. She tries to prevent the body being taken away but is slapped and insulted by the rape victim and is finally left alone in the empty jail, calling 'Hello out there'.

RECORDING:
Desto DST-6451 (US) ●
Columbia Chamber Orchestra
c. Frederick Waldman
The Young Man
  (Gambler) (b) John Reardon
The Girl (s) Leyna Gabriele
The Husband (t) Marvin Worden

The Sweet Bye and Bye
Opera in 2 Acts.
Text by Kenward Elmslie.
First performance: New York (Juilliard School of Music) November 1957.

Synopsis:
The Lifeshine Flock, an evangelical sect, believe that their leader Rose Ora has drowned, but she has eloped with her lover Billy. Before they can marry, Rose is persuaded by Mother Rainey, who looked after her as a child, to rejoin the Flock, but is confronted by Billy and tells them that they must do without her. Again she and Billy plan their life together but Mother Rainey shoots him. The Sister Elect, eager to take over the Flock, denounces Rose, and she is left alone.

RECORDING:
Desto DC-7179/80 (2) (US) ●
Kansas City Lyric Theater Orchestra
c. Russell Patterson
Sister Rose Ora
  Easter (s) Noel Rogers
Sister Rees (s) Judith Anthony
Mother Rainey (m-s) Carolyn James
Sister Gladys (s) Paula Siebel
Brother Smiley (bs) Walter Hook
Billy Wilcox (t) Robert Owen Jones

Lizzie Borden
Opera in 3 Acts and an Epilogue.
Text by Kenward Elmslie, based on a scenario by Richard Plant.
First performance: New York (City Opera) March 25, 1965.

Synopsis:
Set in the Andrew Borden home in Fall River, Massachusetts in

Above: *Jack Beeson's Lizzie Borden was given its world première by the New York City Opera on March 25, 1965.*

the 1880s. The story avoids the melodramatic portrayal of the famous axe murders in detail but concentrates rather on the inner conflicts of personality in the Borden household. The final act ends before Lizzie has actually murdered her father. The Epilogue shows her several years later, still maintaining her religious affiliations while the children outside sing a taunting song about the murders.

RECORDING:
Desto DST-6455/6/7 (3) (US) ●
New York City Opera Chorus and
Orchestra
c. Anton Coppola
Andrew Borden (bs-b) Herbert Beatty
Abigail Borden (s) Ellen Faull
Elizabeth Andrew
  Borden (m-s) Brenda Lewis
Margret Borden (s) Ann Elgar
Reverend
  Harrington (t) Richard Krause
Captain Jason
  MacFarlane (b) Richard Fredricks

Captain Jinks of the Horse Marines
Romantic Comedy in 3 Acts.
Text by Sheldon Harnick, based on the play by Clyde Fitch.
First performance: Kansas City (Lyric Theatre) September 20, 1975.

Synopsis:
Jonathan Jinks and the opera star Aurelia Trentoni are in love, to the disapproval of Jinks's friend Charlie (who is jealous), his mother and Aurelia's uncle. Jinks is arrested for bribing an official while trying to speed Aurelia's luggage through Customs and misses his trial due to all the confusions, but Aurelia persuades the policeman who comes to collect him that he was helping her through an illness. In the end Jinks's mother and Aurelia's uncle relent, and all is well.

RECORDING:
RCA ARL2-1727 (2) (US) ●
Kansas City Lyric Theater Chorus/
Kansas City Philharmonic Orchestra
c. Russell Patterson
Colonel Mapleson Eugene Green
Willem Van Bleecker Brian Steele
Charles LaMartine Ronald Highley
Jonathan Jinks Robert Owen Jones
Mrs Greenborough Carolyne James
Aurelia Trentoni Carol Wilcox
Papa Belliarti Walter Hook
Mary Nancy Jones
Mrs Stonington Linda Sisney

LUDWIG VAN BEETHOVEN
(b. Bonn 16.12.1770; d. Vienna 26.3.1827)

Beethoven wrote only one opera, but that one occupied a great deal of his creative energies. It took nearly ten years of frustration and several versions before the masterpiece we know as *Fidelio* emerged. It was commissioned by Emanuel Schikaneder, the subject of Mozart's *Der Schauspieldirektor* and librettist of *The Magic Flute*, who was then a Viennese theatre manager. Opera was a fresh departure for Beethoven and he approached the project with misgiving. His models were, in the beginning, Méhul and Cherubini », but as the work progressed it soon passed out of the reach of such influences and became pure Beethoven, structurally and ethically. Beethoven was always on the lookout for the chance to write another opera, but he never found a suitable libretto. His demands were high: nothing frivolous or immoral, always something 'elevating'. Some ideas did inspire him—Goethe's *Faust*, *Macbeth*, even Alexander the Great—but apart from the occasional start nothing ever came from them.

Fidelio
Opera in 2 Acts.
Text by J. and G. Sonnleithner and G. F. Treitschke, after J. N. Bouilly.
First performance: Vienna (Kärntnertor) May 23, 1814.

Synopsis:
Scene: A fortress near Seville. Time: 18th Century.
Act 1 Disguised as a youth (Fidelio) Leonora obtains employment at the fortress as assistant to the chief jailer Rocco. So successful is her disguise that Rocco's daughter, Marzelline, falls in love with 'Fidelio', much to the disgust of Jacquino, her former suitor. Leonora's worst fears are soon realised: her husband, Florestan (friend of the Minister, Don Fernando and enemy of the tyrannical prison governor Don Pizarro) is languishing in a dark dungeon below. Pizarro has sworn revenge on Florestan for the latter's exposures of crimes and injustices. He learns that Don Fernando is on his way to make a surprise inspection of the prison, and so plans to murder Florestan before Fernando arrives. Pizarro tries to bribe Rocco to do the deed; he refuses, but agrees to dig the grave.

Act 2 Florestan in his dungeon is weak from thirst and starvation, and semi-delirious. He has a vision of Leonora as an angel. Rocco and Leonora enter and she manages to give Florestan food and drink, but without revealing her identity. Pizarro arrives and as he is about to kill Florestan, Leonora rushes between them declaiming, First kill his wife!' No sooner has the astonishment had time to register than the trumpet warning of Don Fernando's arrival sounds twice from the tower. Pizarro's scheme is in ruins and, as he and Rocco depart, Florestan and Leonora sing of their freedom. The scene changes to outside the prison, where Don Fernando lets Leonora unshackle Florestan's chains. The opera ends with general rejoicing.

Well-known arias:

Act 1 Mir ist so wunderbar (Quartet)
Ha! welch ein Augenblick (Pizarro)
Abscheulicher (Leonora)
O welche Lust (Chorus of prisoners)

Act 2 In des Lebens Frühlingstagen (Florestan)
O namenlose Freude (Florestan and Leonora)

Notes:

In its original form, under the title *Leonora* (which Beethoven himself always preferred) it was in three acts. On its first appearance in 1805 it suffered from the fact that Vienna was in occupation by Napoleon's troops and the consequent attentions of the censor, but it was also felt that the opera was not satisfactory; despite magnificent parts, it was too long and diffuse. After much haggling and resistance by Beethoven it was revised and reduced to two acts in 1806, but that failed too, making an almost total rewrite necessary. This was accomplished in 1814, producing the *Fidelio* we know and honour today. In all its forms it is basically a mixture of German *Singspiel*, retaining a certain amount of spoken dialogue, and *opera seria* (especially in the finely constructed second part).

RECORDINGS:
HMV SLS5006 (3) ★●
Angel S3625 (3) (US)
Philharmonia Chorus and Orchestra
c. Otto Klemperer
Leonora (s)   Christa Ludwig
Florestan (t)   Jon Vickers
Don Pizarro (b)   Walter Berry
Rocco (bs)   Gottlob Frick

HMV RL52 (2) (m) (d) ★●
Vienna State Opera Chorus/Vienna
Philharmonic Orchestra
c. Wilhelm Furtwängler
Leonora (s)   Martha Mödl
Florestan (t)   Wolfgang Windgassen
Don Pizarro (b)   Otto Edelmann
Rocco (bs)   Gottlob Frick

HMV SLS594 (3) ●
Angel S3773 (3) (US)
Chorus of German State Opera/
Berlin Philharmonic Orchestra
c. Herbert von Karajan
Leonora (s)   Helga Dernesch
Florestan (t)   Jon Vickers
Don Pizarro (b)   Zoltan Kélémen
Rocco (bs)   Karl Ridderbusch

DG Privilege 2705 037 (2) ●
Bavarian State Opera Chorus and
Orchestra
c. Ferenc Fricsay
Leonora (s)   Leonie Rysanek
Florestan (t)   Ernst Haefliger
Don Pizarro (b)   Dietrich Fischer-Dieskau
Rocco (bs)   Gottlob Frick

DG 2709 082 (3(●
DG 2709 082 (3) (US)
Vienna State Opera Chorus/Vienna
Philharmonic Orchestra
c. Leonard Bernstein
Leonora (s)   Gundula Janowitz
Florestan (t)   René Kollo
Don Pizarro (b)   Hans Sotin
Rocco (bs)   Manfred Jungwith

Cetra 'Opera Live' L066 (3) (US)
(r. 1956)●
West German Radio Chorus and
Orchestra
c. Erich Kleiber
Leonora (s)   Birgit Nilsson
Florestan (t)   Hans Hopf
Don Pizarro (b)   Paul Schoeffler
Rocco (bs)   Gottlob Frick

Decca SET272/3 (2) ●
London 1259 (2) (US)
Vienna State Opera Chorus/Vienna
Philharmonic Orchestra
c. Lorin Maazel
Leonora (s)   Birgit Nilsson
Florestan (t)   James McCracken
Don Pizarro (b)   Kurt Böhme

Decca SXL6276 ■
London 26009 (US)
(from above)

DG 2721 136 (3) ●
DG 2709 031 (3) (US)
Dresden State Opera Chorus and
Orchestra
c. Karl Böhm
Leonora (s)   Gwyneth Jones
Florestan (t)   James King
Don Pizarro (b)   Theo Adam
Rocco (bs)   Franz Crass

(A much recorded opera. Klemperer and Furtwängler are inspired; Karajan excellent all round; Bernstein probing; Maazel a brilliantly recorded average performance.)

HMV SXWD3032 (2) □
Seraphim S-60261 (US)
4 Overtures
c. Otto Klemperer

DG 2707 046 (2) □
DG 2707 246 (2) (US)
4 Overtures
c. Herbert von Karajan

Philips 6780 031 (2) □
4 Overtures
c. Kurt Masur

(NB: We have said that Beethoven wrote only one opera, but the original *Leonora* is sufficiently different to warrant consideration on its own. The score of the first Vienna (Theater an der Wien) production of 1805 has survived to achieve a modern recording):

HMV Angel SLS999 ●
Leipzig Radio Chorus/Dresden State
Opera Orchestra
c. Herbert Blomstedt
Leonora (s)   Edda Moser
Florestan (t)   Richard Cassilly
Don Pizarro (b)   Theo Adam
Rocco (bs)   Karl Ridderbusch

Top left: *Ludwig van Beethoven.*

Left: *Rene Kollo and Gundula Janowitz were Florestan and Leonora in the 1978 Fidelio recording, based on the Vienna State Opera production.*

Top: *Gwyneth Jones in a Covent Garden production of* Fidelio.

Top right: *Jon Vickers has twice recorded the part of Florestan. Photo: Angus McBean (EMI).*

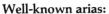

VINCENZO BELLINI
(b. Catania, Sicily 3.11.1801; d. Puteaux, France 23.9.1835)

With Donizetti » and Rossini », Bellini was one of the founders of modern Italian opera. His delicate, sensitive style was in complete contrast to Donizetti's easy-going facility and Rossini's muscular brilliance. It evolved out of the three central forces within him—Sicilian ancestry, delicate health, and short life. His ancestry undoubtedly had a major effect upon the development of his genius. His melody, subtly supported by extended harmony, was a true continuation of the Italian *bel canto* style. The element of *morbidezza* (a term derived from painting and signifying delicacy and gentleness rather than 'morbidity') is not only distinctive but exercised an important influence on several later instrumental composers, notably Chopin. There is nothing of the jocularity of Italian *opera buffa* in Bellini; still less the patriotic fervour found in most Italian composers, especially Giuseppe Verdi ». In many ways, though not in this, Bellini was the true precursor of Verdi in Italian opera, his integration of violent passion with lyric tenderness unquestionably anticipates his great successor. The generosity of a Sicilian nobleman enabled Bellini to study at the Naples Conservatoire, where he met Donizetti. Thereafter he produced a successful series of 11 operas, visiting several towns in Italy and also London and Paris for the occasions. It was after visiting London for a performance of *I Puritani*, his last work, that he went to Puteaux outside Paris, where he was taken fatally ill. His later operas were sung by some of the legendary singers in Italian opera, notably tenor Giovanni Battista Rubini, sopranos Giuditta Pasta and Giulia Grisi, baritone Antonio Tamburini and bass Luigi Lablache. He was unusually fortunate in having for all but three of his operas the collaboration of the outstanding librettist Felice Romani. In modern times, the two leading exponents of Bellini's music in the theatre and on record are the late Maria Callas and Joan Sutherland.

Above: *Vincenzo Bellini, one of the founders of modern Italian opera.*

Right: *A Royal Opera House presentation of Bellini's La Sonnambula.*

Adelson e Salvini
Opera in 3 Acts.
Text by Andrea Leone Tottola.
First performance: Naples (Teatrino del Collegio San Sebastiano) January 12, 1825.

RECORDING:
Philips 9500 203 □
Philips 9500 203 (US)
Ecco, signor, la sposa
José Carreras (t)

Il Pirata
Opera in 2 Acts.
Text by Felice Romani.
First performance: Milan (La Scala) October 27, 1827. London (King's Theatre) 1830; Paris 1832; New York 1832.

Synopsis:
Scene: Sicily. Time: 13th century.
Act 1 Scene 1: On the beach, the people pray for the safety of sailors during a storm; the Hermit Goffredo recognises his former pupil Gualtiero among the crew. The fact that they are pirates is concealed. Gualtiero is still in love with his former sweetheart Imogene who is about to offer hospitality to the shipwrecked mariners, according to custom. Imogene has been having a nightmare about Gualtiero and her husband, Ernesto. Scene 2: The pirates are drinking and singing. Gualtiero has kept apart from the throng; Imogene discovers his identity. He is upset to learn that she has married Ernesto during his absence, but she tells him she did so in order to save her father's life. Scene 3: Ernesto returns, with soldiers, from defeating some pirates. He enquires about the shipwrecked crew and is told by Itulbo (who is acting as captain to protect Gualtiero) that they come from Liguria. Ernesto orders them to be imprisoned, but Imogene succeeds in ensuring that they leave by dawn. Gualtiero tells Imogene he will come to her before leaving, but she pleads with him not to.

Act 2 Scene 1: Adele, Imogene's loyal attendant, tells her mistress that Gualtiero has sworn not to leave until he has seen Imogene. Ernesto charges his wife with still being in love with Gualtiero; she admits it, but argues that he knew about it before he married her. Ernesto is told that his rival is near; Imogene begs him not to make an issue of it, but Ernesto swears vengeance. Scene 2: Imogene comes to Gualtiero, but refuses when he begs her to run away with him. Ernesto enters, and to Imogene's distress the two men go off to fight. Imogene tells Adele she will part the duellists or die herself. Scene 3: Ernesto has been killed in the duel. Gualtiero surrenders and is led away to be tried, hoping Imogene may find a way to forgive him. She is haunted again by her nightmare, which seems to have come true. Gualtiero is condemned and Imogene swears she will die too.

Notes:
Romani's libretto is 'topped and tailed' by matter which does not appear in the opera. In the introductory material it is revealed that Gualtiero and Ernesto were on opposite sides in the struggle between Manfred and Charles of Anjou. After Charles's victory Gualtiero became a pirate, but his ships were defeated by Ernesto. At the end of the tale, the pirates try to rescue Gualtiero but when Imogene appears he sends them off and kills himself.

RECORDING:
HMV SLS953 (3) ●
Angel S3772 (3) (US)
Rome Radiotelevisione Chorus and Orchestra
c. Gianandrea Gavazzeni
Imogene (s)   Montserrat Caballé
Gualtiero (t)   Bernabé Marti
Ernesto (b)   Piero Cappuccilli
Adele (m-s)   Flore Rafanelli

La Straniera
Opera in 2 Acts.
Text by Felice Romani after a novel by C. V. P. d'Arlincourt.
First performance: Milan (La Scala) February 14, 1829.

RECORDING:
Decca SET268/9 □
London 1257 (2) (d) (US)
Un ritratto . . . Veggiam
Joan Sutherland (s)
Richard Conrad (t)

I Capuleti e i Montecchi

Opera in 2 Acts.
Text by Felice Romani after Matteo Bandello (c. 1480-1562) and, loosely, Shakespeare.
First performance: Venice (Teatro La Fenice) March, 1830. London 1833.

Synopsis:

Act 1 Despite peace moves by Romeo, leader of the Montagues, the feud between his family and the Capulets continues. Romeo has killed the son of Capellio, leader of the Capulets, in battle, and Tebaldo swears vengeance. Capellio wants an immediate marriage. Romeo comes disguised as the Montagues' ambassador, offering a peace to be sealed by his marriage to Giulietta, but the Capulets demand war and Romeo accepts that decision. Giulietta is in love with Romeo and laments his absence, but Lorenzo reveals that he is in Verona and brings him to her. Romeo wants them to run away together, but she will not desert her family. Romeo and his followers interrupt the wedding festivities of Tebaldo and Giulietta.

Act 2 Lorenzo proposes the use of a potion to make Giulietta appear dead in her family tomb, where she will be joined by Romeo. Romeo and Tebaldo meet and fight; the passing of Giulietta's funeral procession makes Romeo beg Tebaldo to kill him, but he refuses. At Giulietta's tomb, Romeo, grief-stricken, takes poison just as Giulietta awakens and tells him what has happened. Too late: Romeo dies and Giulietta kills herself. Both the Capulets and the Montagues blame Capellio.

RECORDING:

HMV SLS986 (3) ●
Angel SX3824 (US)
John Alldis Choir/New Philharmonic Orchestra
c. Giuseppe Patanè
Giulietta (s)   Beverly Sills
Romeo (m-s)   Janet Baker
Tebaldo (t)   Nicolai Gedda
Capellio (bs)   Roger Lloyd
Lorenzo (b)   Raimond Herincx

La Sonnambula

Opera in 2 Acts.
Text by Felice Romani after Eugène Scribe.
First performance: Milan (Teatro Carcano) March 6, 1835. London (Haymarket) 1831; New York 1835; London (Covent Garden) 1910; New York (Met) 1932.

Synopsis:

Scene: A Swiss village. Time: Early 19th century.

Act 1 At the betrothal celebrations of Amina and Elvino; Lisa, the local inn-keeper, is jealous as she is in love with Elvino herself. Count Rodolfo enters seeking memories of his happy childhood in the village. That night Amina, sleepwalking, enters his room, and Lisa rouses Elvino. Amina is awakened by the commotion and declares her innocence, but nobody believes her except Teresa, her foster mother.

Act 2 Elvino, believing the worst, promises to marry Lisa. Somnambulism is not a familiar subject to the simple villagers, who are bemused by Rodolfo's attempts at explanation. Lisa has dropped a handkerchief which has found its way into Rodolfo's room. When it is produced, Elvino again thinks he has been deceived. Rodolfo continues to protest Amina's innocence, but is still not believed until she re-appears, again sleep-walking, this time for all to see, crossing a dangerous bridge over a millstream and singing a sad lament of her innocence. Elvino sees the light, and all ends well.

Well-known arias:

Act 1 Care campagne . . . Coma per me sereno (Amina)
Sovra il sen la man mi posa (Amina)
Prendi l'anel ti dono (Elvino)
Vi ravviso (Rodolfo)
Son geloso dei zeffiro errante (Elvino)

Act 2 Ah! perchè non posso odiarti (Elvino)
Ah! non credea mirarti, si presto estinto, o fiore (Amina)
Ah! non giunge (Amina)

RECORDINGS:

Decca SET239/41 ●
London 1365 (3) (US)
Chorus and Orchestra of Maggio Musicale Fiorentino
c. Richard Bonynge
Amina (s)   Joan Sutherland
Elvino (t)   Nicola Monti
Lisa (s)   Sylvia Stahlman
Rodolfo (bs)   Fernando Corena

Decca SXL6128 □
London 25887 (US)
(from above)

Cetra Opera Live LP32 (3) (mono)
(r. 1955) ●
Chorus and Orchestra of La Scala, Milan
c. Leonard Bernstein
Amina (s)   Maria Callas
Elvino (t)   Cesare Velletti
Lisa (s)   Eugenia Ratti
Rodolfo (bs)   Giuseppe Modesti

Decca SXL6828 □
London 26437 (US)
Prendi l'anel ti dono
Joan Sutherland (s)
Luciano Pavarotti (t)

Decca SXL6192 □
London 25940 or 1214 (2) (US)
Ah! non credea mirarti
Ah! non giunge
Joan Sutherland (s)

HMV SLS5134 (3) ●
Chorus and Orchestra of La Scala, Milan
c. Antonio Votto
Amina (s)   Maria Callas
Elvino (t)   Nicola Monti
Lisa (s)   Eugenia Ratti
Rodolfo (bs)   Nicolas Zaccaria

Cetra LPC1240 (3) (mono) (d) ●
Chorus and Orchestra of Turin Radio
c. Franco Capuana
Amina (s)   Lina Pagliughia
Elvino (t)   Ferruccio Tagliavini
Rodolfo (bs)   Cesare Siepi
(Although a fallible old mono recording, this is perhaps the most stylish and elegant performance of all. Pagliughi and Tagliavini are irresistible, and the others are no way behind)

HMV ASD3535 (r. 1955) ■
Orchestra of La Scala, Milan
c. Tullio Serafin
Maria Callas (s)

HMV SLS5104 (2) □
Angel S-3696 (2) (US)
Ah! non credea mirarti
Ah! non giunge
Maria Callas (s)

Decca SXL 6690 □
London 26424 (US)
Ah! non credea mirarti
Ah! non giunge
Montserrat Caballé (s)

Norma

Opera in 2 Acts.
Text by Felice Romani after Louis Alexandre Soumet & Louis Belmontet.
First performance: Milan (La Scala) December 26, 1831. London (Haymarket) 1833; New York 1841; New York (Met) 1891 & 1927; London (Covent Garden) 1929.

Synopsis:

Scene: Gaul. Time: 1st century AD.

Act 1 Oroveso, the arch-Druid and father of Norma, a priestess, addresses the people and prays for victory over the Romans. Norma has had an earlier love affair with Pollione, the Roman pro-Consul, and borne him children; Pollione,

however, is now interested in the young priestess Adalgisa, though he fears Norma's vengeance. Adalgisa confides in Norma, after the latter has sung her great invocation to the rising moon, 'Casta diva'. When Adalgisa reveals the identity of the man she loves, the two realize they are in the same plight. **Act 2** Norma, distraught, is about to kill her sleeping children, but then sends her servant Clotilda to fetch Adalgisa to whom she gives the children, urging the young woman to take them with her when she goes with Pollione to Rome, for then she will herself die. Adalgisa begs Norma to live for the sake of the children and promises to try to return Pollione to Norma. Oroveso and the Druids inveigh against the Romans; Adalgisa wants to renew her vows but Pollione will have none of it. Norma leads a chorus of war; then Clotilda brings news that a Roman has been discovered in the temple. It is Pollione. Norma draws a dagger to kill him, but cannot. Pollione refuses to give up Adalgisa, so Norma orders her to be burnt. The pyre is prepared; but when she has to name the traitor, she says: 'It is I'. She goes into the flames and Pollione follows her to death.

Well-known arias:

Act 1 Meco all'altar di Venere (Pollione)
Casta diva (Norma)
Sgombra è la sacra selva (Adalgisa)
Va crudele, al dio spietato (Pollione)

Act 2 Mira, o Norma (Adalgisa)
Ah, del Tebro (Oroveso)
In mia man alfin tu sei (Norma and Pollione)
Qual cor tradisti (Norma and Pollione)
Deh, non volerli vittime (Norma)

RECORDINGS:
Decca SET424/6 ★●
London 1394 (3) (US)
London Symphony Chorus and Orchestra
c. Richard Bonynge
Norma (s)   Joan Sutherland
Pollione (t)   John Alexander
Adalgisa (m-s) Marilyn Horne
Oroveso (bs)   Richard Cross

London 26388 (US) ■
(from above)

Columbia 3C 163 00535/7 ●
(formerly Columbia SAX2412/4)
Angel S-3615 (3) (US)
Chorus and Orchestra of La Scala, Milan
c. Tullio Serafin
Norma (s)   Maria Callas
Pollione (t)   Franco Corelli
Adalgisa (m-s) Christa Ludwig
Oroveso (bs)   Nicolas Zaccaria

Angel S-35 666 (US) ■
(from above)

HMV SLS5115 (3) ●
Chorus and Orchestra of La Scala, Milan
c. Tullio Serafin
Norma (s)   Maria Callas
Pollione (t)   Mario Filippeschi
Adalgisa (m-s) Ebe Stignani
Oroveso (bs)   Nicola Rossi-Lemeni

Cetra Opera Live LP31 (3) (m) (r. 1955) ●
Chorus and Orchestra of La Scala, Milan
c. Antonio Votto
Norma (s)   Maria Callas
Pollione (t)   Mario del Monaco
Adalgisa (m-s) Giulietta Simionato
Oroveso (bs)   Nicola Zaccaria

RCA SER5658/60 ●
RCA LSC-6202 (3) (US)
Ambrosian Opera Chorus/London
Philharmonic Orchestra
c. Carlo Cillario
Norma (s)   Montserrat Caballé
Pollione (t)   Placido Domingo
Adalgisa (m-s) Fiorenza Cossotto
Oroveso (bs)   Ruggiero Raimondi

ABC ATS-20016 (3) (US) ●
Alldis Choir/New Philharmonic
Orchestra
c. James Levine
Norma (s)   Beverly Sills
Pollione (t)   Giuseppe di Stefano
Adalgisa (n-s) Shirley Verrett
Oroveso (bs)   Paul Plishka

Decca SET368/9 ○
London 1272 (2) (US)
Chorus and Orchestra of Accademmia
di Santa Cecilia, Rome
c. Silvio Varviso
Norma (s)   Elena Suliotis
Pollione (t)   Mario del Monaco
Adalgisa (m-s) Fiorenza Cossotto
Oroveso (bs)   Carlo Cava

Decca SET458 ■
(from above)

Decca SET456 □
London 26168 (US)
Duets (Rossini: *Semiramide*)
Joan Sutherland (s)
Marilyn Horne (m-s)

Right: *Giulia Grisi, the original Norma at La Scala, Milan, in 1831.*

Beatrice di Tenda
Opera in 2 Acts.
Text by Felice Romani.
First performance: Venice (Teatro la Fenice) March 16, 1833. London 1836. New York 1844.

Synopsis: Scene: Castle of Binasco. Time: 15th Century.
Act 1 Scene 1: Filippo Visconti, Duke of Milan, has left the festivities at the castle because they are run by his wife Beatrice, whom he no longer cares for. He prefers Agnese del Maino, but owes his position to his marriage. Scene 2: Agnese has sent a letter of assignation to Orombello, with whom she is in love. But Orombello is secretly in love with Beatrice, the Duchess, and reveals this when he meets Agnese. She is outraged and swears to ruin Beatrice. Scene 3: Beatrice is walking with her ladies in a grove. She is saddened by the turn things have taken, especially by the Duke's oppressive rule of her own people and by his apparent rejection of her affections. Agnese's brother Rizzardo enters with Filippo. Rizzardo wants to keep the Duke in his present mood of wanting to be rid of Beatrice. In a meeting between the Duke and Duchess, he accuses her of incitement to revolt and infidelity, which she firmly denies. Scene 4: Beatrice is lamenting her fate before the statue of her first husband, and begs his forgiveness. As she is saying that all have forsaken her, Orombello comes in and asserts that he at least is faithful to her. And so are her subjects, who will rise to defend her with him at their head. But this she sees as thoroughly dangerous, since they are rumoured to be lovers. He kneels before her and is discovered by Filippo, who has been brought in by Agnese; he thinks he has the proof he needs. In the final ensemble there is much protestation, but ultimately the Duke has his wife and Orombello taken off to jail.
Act 2 Scene 1: Poor Orombello is tortured and 'confesses' after initial resistance. Beatrice is condemned, despite Orombello's subsequent declaration that he confessed under torture and was lying. Filippo, however, is determined to press the charges, arguing, despite Beatrice's warning that Heaven is watching, that the law must take its course. Agnese, who has come to her senses when she realises what she has done, cannot move him. Beatrice refuses to confess, even under torture, but remains condemned. At first Filippo cannot sign the death warrant; but when news comes that a revolt is brewing outside, he signs it, saying it is all her fault and not his. Scene 2: Beatrice emerges

from solitary prayer to tell her ladies that God will judge and punish her husband and persecutors. Agnese confesses her sins, and Beatrice forgives her. As she goes to the scaffold, she asks for prayers for Filippo and Agnese rather than for herself, and then welcomes death as a triumph over the miseries of this world.

Well-known arias:
Act 1   Ah, non pensar che pieno sia (Agnese)
            Ma la sola, ohimé, son' io (Beatrice)
            Deh! se mi amasti un giorno (Beatrice)
Act 2   Qui m'accolse oppresso errante (Filippo)
            Angiol di pace (Orombello, Agnese & Beatrice)
            Ah! se un'urna (Beatrice)

RECORDINGS:
Decca SET 320/2 ●
London 1384 (3) (US)
Ambrosian Opera Chorus/London
Symphony Orchestra
c. Richard Bonynge
Beatrice (s)   Joan Sutherland
Filippo (b)   Cornelius Opthof
Orombello (t)   Luciano Pavarotti
Agnese (m-s)   Josephine Veasey

London 26140 (US) ■
(from above)

Decca SET 268/9 □
London 1257 (2) (d) US)
Angiol di pace
Joan Sutherland (s)
Marilyn Horne (m-s)
Richard Conrad (t)

Decca SET247/8 or SXL6192
or D69D3 □
London 1254 (2) or 25940 (US)
Ah! se un'urna
Joan Sutherland (s)

I Puritani (di Scozia)
Opera in 3 Acts.
Text by Count Carlo Pepoli after Francois Ancelot and Xavier Boniface Saintine, based on the play 'Old Mortality' by Sir Walter Scott.
First performance: Paris (Théâtre des Italiens), January 25, 1835. London (King's) 1835; New York 1844.

Synopsis: Scene: near Plymouth. Time: English Civil War.
Act 1   Within the Roundhead fortress. Preparations are going ahead for the wedding of Elvira, daughter of the Puritan Governor, General Lord Walter Walton (Gualtiero), to Sir Richard Forth, one of the generals. But Lord Walton withholds his permission because Elvira is in love with Lord Arthur Talbot (Arturo), a Cavalier, and at his instigation his brother, Sir George Walton, bids Elvira to prepare to marry Lord Arthur. Just before the wedding Queen Henrietta of France, widow of Charles I, is brought in a prisoner. She is to be put to death; but Lord Arthur, avowing his loyalty to the throne, plans to save

her, by having her put on Elvira's wedding dress — the only way, since Lord Walton has forbidden all others to leave the castle. But Elvira believes Lord Arthur is untrue to her, and loses her reason.
Act 2   Sir Richard (Riccardo) and Sir George (Giorgio) plan to avenge Elvira. Sir Richard has an order from Cromwell requiring the arrest and execution of Lord Arthur; however, Sir George, knowing from Elvira's behaviour that only the return of Lord Arthur will restore her sanity, asks Sir Richard to spare Lord Arthur's life. Sir Richard agrees, provided Lord Arthur is not captured fighting for the King.
Act 3   Lord Arthur has returned and during a storm seeks out Elvira. She at first believes it is a hallucination, but begins to regain her sanity after Lord Arthur has explained his dealings with the Queen. Soldiers seeking Lord Arthur draw near. He tries to escape with Elvira, but she, thinking he is deserting her again, has a relapse. Lord Arthur is arrested and Sir Richard tells him he is condemned to death. At these words Elvira is shocked back to sanity, and begs to die with him. But just in time a message comes from Sir Richard that the King is defeated, the war over and prisoners pardoned.

Well-known arias:
Act 1   Or dove fuggo . . . Ah, per sempre (Riccardo)
            A te, o caro (Arturo)
Act 2   Cinta di fiori (Giorgio)
            Qui la voce sua soave (Elvira, Giorgio and Riccardo)
Act 3   A una fonte afflitto e solo (Arturo and Elvira)
            Vieni fra queste braccia (Arturo and Elvira)

RECORDINGS:
Decca SET587/9 ●
London 13111 (3) (US)
Chorus and Orchestra of Royal
Opera House, Covent Garden
c. Richard Bonynge
Elvira (s)   Joan Sutherland
Arturo (t)   Luciano Pavarotti
Riccardo (b) Piero Cappuccilli
Giorgio (bs) Nicolai Ghiaurov
Gualtiero (b) Giancarlo Luccardi

Decca SET619 ■
(from above)

HMV SLS5140 (3) ●
Angel 3502 (3) (US)
Chorus and Orchestra of La Scala, Milan
c. Tullio Serafin
Elvira (s)   Maria Callas
Arturo (t)   Giuseppe di Stefano
Riccardo (b) Rolando Panerai
Giorgio (bs) Nicola Rossi-Lemeni
Gualtiero (bs) Carlo Forti
Enrichetta (s) Aurora Cattelani

ABC ATS-20016 (3) (US) ●
London Philharmonic Chorus
and Orchestra
c. Julius Rudel
Elvira (s)   Beverly Sills
Arturo (t)   Nicolai Gedda

Cetra Opera Live L052 (3) (m) ●
(r. Mexico City 1952)
Chorus and Orchestra of Palacio de
Bellas Artes
c. Guido Picco
Elvira (s)   Maria Callas
Arturo (t)   Giuseppe di Stefano

Decca SET259/61 (d) ●
London 1373 (3) (US)
Maggio Musicale Fiorentino
c. Richard Bonynge
Elvira (s)   Joan Sutherland
Arturo (t)   Pierre Duval

London 25922 (US) □
(from above)

Decca SXL6192 □
London 25940 (US)
Arias from Beatrice di Tenda/
Norma/I Puritani
Joan Sutherland (s)

Left: *Joan Sutherland in the Covent Garden production of Bellini's I Puritani.*

(Sir) JULIUS BENEDICT
(b. Stuttgart 27.11.1804; d. London 5.6.1885)

A naturalised English musician of German birth, Julius Benedict was a pupil of Hummel and Weber », met Beethoven », held appointments in Germany, worked in Italy and France and finally settled in London where he became an important musical figure. He was knighted in 1871. He was a prolific composer and an expert conductor. He wrote a number of operas, Italian and English, of which the agreeable *Lily of Killarney* is the only one to have retained any real currency.

The Lily of Killarney
Opera in 3 Acts.
Text by John Oxenford and Dion Boucicault, based on Boucicault's play 'Colleen Bawn'.
First performance: London (Covent Garden) February 8, 1862. New York 1868.

Well-known arias:
Act 1 The moon hath raised her lamp above (Hardress and Danny)
'Tis a charming girl I love (Myles)
Act 2 I'm alone (Eily)
Act 3 Eily Mavourneen (Hardress)

Notes:
The Lily of Killarney invokes a pleasant Irish quality, full of pleasant tunes and lively rhythms. The story is of suspicious goings-on in a rural setting, accusations of murder, and the expected happy ending. The well-known Irish drinking song 'Cruiskin Lawn' is also introduced.

RECORDINGS:
HMV CSD3651 ■
c. Dr. Havelock Ellis
Hardress Cregan (t) Uel Deane
Eily O'Connor (s) Veronica Dunne
Danny (b) Eric Hinds

EMI EMD5509 □
The moon hath raised her lamp above
Robert Tear (t)
Benjamin Luxon (b)

Below: *Benedict's* The Lily of Killarney, *produced at Covent Garden in 1862, was a great popular success, particularly through the duet 'The moon hath raised her lamp above'.*

RICHARD RODNEY BENNETT
(b. Broadstairs 29.3.1936)

Bennett studied at the London Royal College of Music with Lennox Berkeley and Howard Fergusson, and in Paris with Pierre Boulez, and has developed a prolific and varied career as a composer and pianist (including jazz). He has composed works in many different forms and has written successfully for films and television. A highly versatile musician, he uses serial as well as more traditional techniques with a clear individuality. He has written a number of operas, mostly to libretti by Beverley Cross. Major operatic works are: *The Mines of Sulphur* (first performed London, Sadlers Wells, 24.2.1965); *Victory*, from the novel by Conrad (London, Covent Garden 13.4.1970). Other operas are *The Ledge* and *A Penny for a Song;* and the children's opera *All the King's Men.*

All the King's Men
Opera for children.
Text by Beverley Cross.
First performance: Croydon (Fairfield Hall) 1970.

Synopsis:
Based on the siege of Gloucester in 1645, during the Civil War. The Royalists have a kind of 'secret weapon' for capturing the city, but the Parliamentarians find a way of destroying it.

RECORDING:
Abbey XMS703 ●
Trinity Boys Choir, Trinity School
Orchestra
c. David Squibb
Michael Flaxman
Paul Male
Jonathan Gaunt
Bill Tucker
etc, (all from Trinity School, Croydon)

Right: *Richard Rodney Bennett, a versatile composer successful in the film and television field.*

ALBAN BERG

(b. Vienna 9.2.1885; d. Vienna 24.12.1935)

Of the two most famous pupils of Arnold Schoenberg » (the other was Anton Webern, who wrote no opera), Berg showed more inclination to bridge the gap between the former tonal system and atonality leading to seriality. Berg was by nature an eminently warm and emotionally generous man; qualities which come through in his music, alongside and interwoven with the intellectual severity. His last completed work, the marvellous Violin Concerto, shows both aspects of his genius at their most creative. Of his two operas, the first, *Wozzeck*, is built on a form of extended tonality with clearly atonal passages, some in strict serial form; the second, *Lulu*, unfinished at his death, is more strictly serial, though still modified to Berg's expressive requirements. In both operas, individual sections are deliberately constructed to traditional absolute forms—*sonata, rondo, fugue, passacaglia, scherzo* etc. In *Wozzeck* the music is dedicated to the evocation of a great variety of moods, from the tenderest to the most violent and horrifying; in *Lulu* the effect is achieved by setting strictly formal music alongside passages which parody modern dance forms and idioms. Berg, a man

Below: Berg, the most approachable of the 'twelve-tone' composers.

Right: *A Royal Opera House production of Berg's Wozzeck, with Sir Geraint Evans.*

greatly loved and admired by all who knew him, died after a short but agonising illness on Christmas Eve, 1935, aged only 50. His loss to modern music remains incalculable.

Wozzeck

Opera in 3 Acts (of 5 scenes each).
Text by Alban Berg, based on the play by Georg Büchner
First performance: Berlin (State Opera) December 14, 1925. Prague 1926;
Philadelphia 1931; London (Covent Garden) 1952.

Synopsis:

Scene: German provincial town. Time: early 19th century.
Act 1 Five character sketches: (1) Suite. Wozzeck, the Captain's batman, is shaving his master, who chides Wozzeck for living with Marie and their illegitimate child. (2) Rhapsody. Wozzeck and Andreas are cutting wood in a field. Wozzeck, showing signs of mental instability, talks about ghosts and goblins. (3) Military march and Lullaby. Marie, at her window, watches a military band pass by and sings with it. The drum-major waves to her. She sings a lullaby to her child. Wozzeck appears but cannot linger, and Marie is frightened by his talk. (4) Passacaglia. The Doctor, who is carrying out experiments on Wozzeck, also chides the unfortunate soldier, and thinks he is going mad. (5) Andante affetuoso (quasi rondo). The drum-major makes a pass at Marie outside her house. She lets him in.
Act 2 Symphony in Five Movements: (1) Sonata. Wozzeck gives Marie all his money. She feels guilty about her infidelity. (2) Fantasy and Fugue. The Captain and Doctor tease Wozzeck about Marie and the drum-major, and are disturbed by his violent reaction. (3) Largo. In the street, Wozzeck hints to Marie that he knows about the drum-major. (4) Scherzo. Wozzeck sees Marie dancing with the drum-major in the beer garden. Soldiers and drunken workmen sing, and tease Wozzeck. The Fool talks to him about blood; he is becoming obsessed. (5) Rondo con introduzione. In the barracks the drum-major, drunk, boasts of his success with Marie. He and Wozzeck fight; Wozzeck is knocked down.
Act 3 Six Inventions: (1) Invention on a Theme. Marie reads the story of Mary Magdalen to her child, and prays for forgiveness. (2) Invention on one note. Wozzeck and Marie walk beside a pool. He cuts her throat. (3) Invention on a rhythm. At the inn, Wozzeck dances with Margaret. There is blood on his clothes. He flees. (4) Invention on a chord of six notes. Wozzeck returns to the pool and becomes haunted by visions of blood. He walks into the pool and drowns. (5) Invention on a quarter figure. Children playing in the street talk about Marie's death, and run off to see the body. Marie's own child doesn't understand, and continues to play by himself.

Notes:

Following in the footsteps of Schoenberg, Berg was less revolutionary and kept a more traditional musical feeling in his use of atonal and 12-note methods. In the case of *Wozzeck* there was immediate recognition of a masterpiece, and the work may be said to be the first major vindication of the whole school of atonal composition.

RECORDINGS:

DG 2707 023 (2) ●
DG 2702 023 (2) (US)
Berlin State Opera Orchestra
c. Karl Böhm
Wozzeck (b)   Dietrich Fischer-Dieskau
Drum-Major (t) Helmut Melchert
Andreas (t)   Fritz Wunderlich
Marie (s)   Evelyn Lear

CBS 77393 (2) ●
Columbia M2-30852 (2) (US)
Paris Opera Orchestra
c. Pierre Boulez
Wozzeck (b)   Walter Berry
Drum-Major (t) Fritz Uhl
Andreas (t)   R. Van Vrooman
Marie (s)   Isabel Strauss

Mercury 75065 (US) □
London Symphony Orchestra
c. Antal Dorati

Lulu

Opera in Prologue and 3 Acts (unfinished).
Text by Alban Berg based on dramas by Franz Wedekind.
First performance: Zurich, June 2, 1937. Venice 1949; Essen 1953.

Synopsis:

Scenes: German provincial town; Paris; London.
Time: end of 19th century.
Prologue: Animal trainer's troupe, with Lulu dressed as Pierrot but symbolising 'evil, seduction, murder.'
Act 1   Scene 1: Lulu is in costume, having her portrait painted in the presence of Dr Schön. The painter makes advances to Lulu after Schön has left with his son; Lulu's husband enters, finds her and the painter in a compromising position, collapses and dies. Scene 2: Lulu has married the painter; but the scene with the painter and her former husband is repeated, this time with Dr Schön. The painter kills himself: Lulu works on Schön, who had rescued her from penury as a child and who is infatuated with her. News comes of a revolution in Paris. Scene 3: Schön, in an effort to free himself of Lulu, has become engaged to another girl. Yet another of Lulu's admirers appears at the theatre where she is working; but she faints (because, she says, of having to dance in front of Schön's fiancée). She then forces Schön to break off his engagement.
Act 2   Scene 1: Lulu is married to Schön, but is now attracted to his son, Alwa. There is also the Countess Geschwitz who has lesbian designs on Lulu; and two more boys infatuated with her. Schön, maddened by jealousy, tries to force Lulu to shoot herself; but she shoots him instead, is arrested and imprisoned. Scene 2: The Countess has contrived to substitute herself for Lulu in prison. Lulu escapes and manages to reach Alwa. They make love on the same couch where Schön died.
Act 3   Scene 1: Paris. Lulu is the mistress of Count Casti Piani, who tries to make her enter a brothel by blackmailing her. She escapes in disguise. Scene 2: London. Lulu, penniless, is now a prostitute. Alwa, the Countess and others have followed her. Alwa is killed by one of Lulu's customers, the last of whom is Jack the Ripper, who then kills Lulu and also the Countess who tries to save her.

Notes:

Berg left *Lulu* unfinished at his death, having broken off to write his fine Violin Concerto. Acts 1 and 2 were complete and sketches for Act 3 existed, but not in sufficient detail to allow performances in the form Berg intended. After his death his widow asked Schoenberg » to complete the score but he refused, and thereafter she would allow no one to touch it. It was not until her death in 1976 that the work could be carried out and Berg's embryonic wishes realised, by the Austrian composer Friedrich Cerha; and this final version of the opera was given complete in Paris in March, 1979. Until then the last Act had been given in the form of the Lulu Symphony, as substitute (the text always existed; it was the music that was

incomplete). Now that we have at last heard the whole, some perspectives are adjusted, and the impression is reinforced that this is one of the major masterpieces of 20th century music. A recording was made from the Paris production under Pierre Boulez.

RECORDINGS:

DG 2709 029 (3) ●
DG 2709 029 (3) (US)
Berlin Opera Orchestra
c. Karl Böhm
Lulu (s)   Evelyn Lear
Dr Schön (b)   Dietrich Fischer-Dieskau
Countess (m-s) Patricia Johnson
Painter (t)   Loren Driscol
Alwa (t)   Donald Grobe

Decca SXL6657 □
London 26397 (US)
Symphonic Suite
Vienna Philharmonic Orchestra
c. Christoph von Dohnanyi

DG 2530 146 □
Symphonic Suite
London Symphony Orchestra
c. Claudio Abbado

Mercury 75065 (US) □
Symphonic Suite (*Wozzeck*)
London Symphony Orchestra
c. Antal Dorati

Decca D48D3 (3) ●
Vienna Philharmonic Orchestra
c. Christoph von Dohnanyi
Lulu (s)   Anja Silja
Dr Schön (b)   Walter Berry
Countess (m-s) Brigitte Fassbaender
Painter (s)   Horst Laubenthal
Alwa (t)   Josef Hopferwieser

DG recording (as yet unnumbered) due out in October 1979 ●
Chorus and Orchestra of Paris Opéra
c. Pierre Boulez
Lulu (s)   Teresa Stratas
Countess
  Geschwitz (m-s) Yvonne Minton
Painter (t)   Robert Tear
Dr Schön (b)   Frank Mazura
Alwa (t)   Kenneth Riegel
Animal Trainer (bs) Gerd Nienstedt
Jack the Ripper (bs) Frank Mazura
Marquis (t)   Helmut Pampuch
Negro (t)   Robert Tear

Philips ABL3394/6 (m) (d) ■
Columbia SL-121 (m) (d) (US)
Vienna Symphony Orchestra
c. Herbert Haefner
Ilona Steingruber (s)
Maria Cerny (m-s)
Otto Weiner (b)
etc.

Electrola SMA91711/3 (d) ■
Philharmonic State Orchestra, Hamburg
c. Leopold Ludwig
Anneliese Rothenberger (s)
Kersten Meyer (m-s)
Ernst Wendt (b)
etc

Below: *A scene from the recent complete Paris production of* Lulu.

HECTOR BERLIOZ
(b. Côte-Saint-André, Isère 11.12.1803; d. Paris 8.3.1869)

France's foremost composer was the son of a doctor who instilled in his son a lifelong enthusiasm for the Latin classics of literature, especially Virgil. Berlioz possessed a vivid dramatic imagination and a high order of original genius; yet he never made the best of either quality, and for many years Berlioz's genius was slenderly appreciated and little understood. Much of his work for the stage, and his many choral compositions, show Berlioz as an apostle of 19th century giganticism, fired by exalted visions of his vocation. He was also a gifted author and his criticisms and autobiographical writings are of permanent value. A master of orchestration (on which he wrote a famous treatise), Berlioz was also a master of a unique type of melody and a leading figure of the French Romantic movement. Yet his ingrained classicism resulted in an underlying purity of style that did much to counteract the natural excesses of romanticsm. He composed three operas, contrasted in style and subject matter, and two vocal/orchestral works that are sometimes admitted into the operatic canon though they were designed primarily as concert pieces and are nearer to cantata than opera, even though both have been adapted for the stage. The cause of all these compositions has been greatly advanced by high class modern recordings and the advocacy and insight of conductor Colin Davis. His orchestral music, notably the *Symphonie fantastique*, *Harold in Italy* and many overtures, and a number of choral/orchestral works (*Te Deum*, *Grand messe des morts*, *Symphonie funèbre et triomphale*) as well as the song cycle *Nuits d'été* are essential to a full understanding of his genuis.

Benvenuto Cellini
Opera in 2 (3) Acts.
Text by Léon de Wailly and August Barbier after the 'Memoirs of Benvenuto Cellini'.
First performance: Paris (Opéra) September 10, 1838. Weimar (Court Theatre) 1852; London (Covent Garden) 1853.

Synopsis:
Scene: Rome. Time: 16th century.
Act 1 Cellini, a sculptor, plans to elope with Teresa, daughter of the Papal Treasurer, Balducci, who disapproves of Cellini. But there is a rival for Teresa's hand, Fieramosca, another sculptor. Balducci, in an attempt to catch his daughter with Cellini, finds her with Fieramosca instead.
Act 2 (originally Scene 2 of Act 1) Cellini contrives to extract some money from the treasury by promising to finish his statue of Perseus by morning. But it is the evening of Shrove Tuesday and the carnival is in full spate (the famous Roman Carnival, familiar from the concert overture). To confuse Cellini,

Inset: *Hector Berlioz.*
Below: Benvenuto Cellini *at*   *Covent Garden, with Nicolai Gedda in the title role.*

Fieramosca goes out wearing the same disguise as him. There is a fight and the swordsman Pompeo is killed; Cellini escapes, but Fieramosca is arrested.

Act 3 (originally Act 2)   The Perseus statue remains unfinished. Cellini and Teresa try again to elope, but are again frustrated. Cardinal Salviati arrives to demand the work for which he has paid, and Cellini is accused of the murder the previous night. He is given until midnight to finish his work. Short of metal, he throws all his previous works into the crucible and completes Perseus, his masterpiece. He is saved, and wins the hand of Teresa.

RECORDINGS:
Philips 6707 019 (4) ●
Philips 6707 019 (4) (US)
Chorus of the Royal Opera House,
Covent Garden/BBC Symphony
Orchestra
c. Colin Davis
Benvenuto Cellini (t)   Nicolai Gedda
Giacomo Balducci (bs) Jules Bastin
Fieramosca (b)   Robert Massard
Pope Clement VII (bs) Roger Soyer
Teresa (s)   Christiane
                            Eda-Pierre
Pompeo (b)   Raimund Herincx
(This record uses a two-Act version
with later revisions, fully explained in
its accompanying booklet)

Decca SDD217 □
London STS-15031 (US)
Overture
c. Jean Martinon

HMV ASD3212 □
Angel S-37170 (US)
Overture
c. Andre Previn

Decca SXL6165 □
Overture
c. Ernest Ansermet

Decca ECS637 □
London STS-15145 (US)
Overture
c. Robert Denzler

Les Troyens
Opera in 2 Parts, 5 Acts.
Text by Hector Berlioz after Virgil's 'Aeneid'.
First performance: Part 1—Carlsruhe (in German) December 6, 1890; Part 2—Paris (Théâtre-Lyrique) November 4, 1863; complete—Carlsruhe December 5/6, 1890.

Synopsis:
Part 1
Scene: Troy. Time: Trojan War.
Act 1   The Greeks have left the Wooden Horse outside the walls of Troy. Cassandra foretells doom, but Aeneas has the horse brought into the city. He has terrified the people by telling them how the priest Laocoön, sensing danger, threw a spear at the horse and was devoured by serpents. This is taken as a sign of the wrath of the goddess Pallas Athene, but with the horse inside the walls there is rejoicing to the strains of the Trojan March.
Act 2   The ghost of Hector, Aeneas's close friend who was killed earlier in the war, appears to Aeneas in his tent outside Troy and warns him that the Greeks inside the horse have opened the gates and sacked the city, that King Priam is dead and that Aeneas should go with his son to found a new Troy in Italy. Aeneas leaves. Inside the city Cassandra stabs herself, urging the Trojan women to follow her example rather than fall into Greek hands.

Part 2
Scene: In and near Carthage. Time: After the war.
Act 3   A festival in honour of Dido, Queen of Carthage, and the building of the city. A hostile fleet appears. Aeneas, who has been in disguise, reveals himself and leads the Carthaginians to victory over the invaders.
Interlude: The Royal Hunt and Storm. Aeneas and Dido recognise their love.
Act 4   The victorious Aeneas returns to Carthage. There is concern that Dido's love for Aeneas is deflecting her from her public duties; even more that Aeneas, remembering the

Above: *Only in recent years have full performances and recordings of* Les Troyens *been attempted.*

Right: *A Covent Garden production of* Les Troyens *with Josephine Veasey as Dido.*

prompting of Hector's ghost, will soon leave again for Italy. There is a love duet, using words from Shakespeare's 'Merchant of Venice'.
Act 5   The Trojans are impatient to leave, fearful that delay will anger the gods. Aeneas decides to go, despite Dido, who begs him to stay. When he has gone Dido first orders the Carthaginians to pursue and destroy the fleet, then orders everything connected with the Trojan to be burnt. She has a funeral pyre built and stabs herself, prophesying that one day a son of Carthage will avenge her. A vision of Rome triumphant rises behind the flames.

RECORDINGS:
Philips 6709 002 (5) ★●
Philips 6709 002 (5) (US)
Wandsworth Schools Boys' Choir/
Chorus and Orchestra of the Royal
Opera House, Covent Garden
c. Colin Davis
Aeneas (t)   Jon Vickers
Dido (m-s)   Josephine Veasey
Cassandra (s)   Berit Lindholm
Chorebus (b)   Peter Glossop
Spirit of Hector (bs) Roger Soyer
Iopas (t)   Ian Partridge
Hecuba (m-s)   Elizabeth Bainbridge
Narbal (bs)   Roger Soyer
King Priam (bs)   Pierre Thau
Priam's Ghost (b)   Raimund Herincx

Philips 6500 161 ■
(from above)

HMV SXLP30248 □
Angel S-36695 (US)
Act 5, Scenes 2 and 3
Ambrosian Opera Chorus/ London
Symphony Orchestra
c. Sir Alexander Gibson
Janet Baker (m-s)
Bernadette Greevy (c)
Keith Erwen (t)
Gwynne Howell (b)

HMV ASD2276/7 (d) □
Seraphim S-60263 (US)
From Parts 1 and 2
Chorus and Orchestra of Paris
National Opera
c. Georges Prêtre
Régine Crespin (s)
Guy Chauvet (t)
Marie-Luce (c)

HMV SXLP30260 □
Royal Hunt and Storm
c. Sir Thomas Beecham

Columbia M-35112 (US) □
Royal Hunt and Storm
c. Daniel Barenboim

CBS 73085 (d) □
Columbia M-31799 (US)
Royal Hunt and Storm
c. Pierre Boulez

Decca SET392/3 □
Je vais mourir
Josephine Veasey (m-s)

Philips SAL3788 and 6500 774 □
Prelude to Part 2 (not in original score)
c. Colin Davis

Béatrice et Bénédict

Opera in 2 Acts.
Text by Berlioz, based on Shakespeare's 'Much Ado About Nothing'.
First performance: Baden-Baden August 9, 1862. Paris (Opéra-Comique) 1890.
Glasgow (in English) 1936; New York (concert performance) 1960.

Synopsis:

Act 1 Benedict, returning from the wars, meets Beatrice. He is a confirmed bachelor and intends to remain so, but Beatrice has other plans.

Act 2 Although Beatrice finds herself compelled to pursue Benedict she does not believe in matrimony either. Their mutual reluctance to become involved, each believing love to be a kind of weakness, is overcome by the irresistible attraction they have for one another, and in the end they have to give in to love and, like it or not, stand before the altar.

Notes:

The 15 scenes and 5 Acts are drawn mainly from the comic side of Shakespeare's play, the darker and more sinister elements largely by-passed.

RECORDINGS:

Philips 6700 121 (2) ●
John Alldis Choir/London Symphony Orchestra
c. Colin Davis
Beatrice (m-s) Janet Baker
Benedict (t) Robert Tear
Hero (s) Christiane Eda-Pierre
Ursula (c) Helen Watts
Claudio (b) Thomas Allen

L'Oiseau-Lyre SOL256/7 ★●
L'Oiseau-Lyre SOL256/7 (US)
St Anthony Singers/London Symphony Orchestra
c. Colin Davis
Beatrice (m-s) Josephine Veasey
Benedict (t) John Mitchinson
Hero (s) April Cantelo
Ursula (c) Helen Watts
Claudio (t) John Cameron
Don Pedro (b) John Shirley-Quirk
Someone (bs) Eric Shilling

L'Oiseau-Lyre SOL322 ■
(from above)

CBS 76522 □
Columbia M-34206 (US)
Dieu que viens-je d'entendre
Frederica von Stade (m-s)

La Damnation de Faust

Dramatic legend in 4 Parts.
Text by Berlioz and Almire Gandonnière after Gérard de Nerval's translation of Goethe's 'Faust', incorporating material from Berlioz's earlier 'Huit Scènes de Faust (1828).
First performance: Paris 1846. Stage version Monte Carlo 1893; Liverpool (in English) 1894; New Orleans and New York 1894.

Synopsis:

Scene: Hungary and Germany. Time: 16th century.

The first scene is set in Hungary, so that Berlioz can introduce the Rákoczy March. Otherwise it follows the Faust legend until the end, where Faust, instead of finding salvation, is confined to Hell (in 'Ride to the Abyss').

Notes:

La Damnation de Faust is not, strictly speaking, an opera but a dramatic cantata; it was, however, arranged for the stage by Raoul Gunsbourg and given at Monte Carlo in 1893. Although as a stage work it contravenes, in some respects, Berlioz's intentions, we include it briefly, especially since it has several fine recordings.

RECORDINGS:

Philips 6703 024 (3) ★●
Philips 6703 024 (3) (US)
Wandsworth School Boys' Choir/London Symphony Chorus and Orchestra
c. Colin Davis
Faust (t) Nicolai Gedda
Marguerite (s) Josephine Veasey
Mephistophélès (bs) Jules Bastin

DG Heliodor 2700 112 (3) ●
Elisabeth Brasseur Choir/Choeur Enfants RTF/Lamoureux Orchestra
c. Igor Markevitch
Faust (t) Richard Verreau
Marguerite (s) Consuela Rubio
Mephistophélès (bs) Michel Roux

DG 2709 048 (3) ●
DG 2709 048 (3) (US)
Tanglewood Festival Choir/Boston Boys' Choir/Boston Symphony Orchestra
c. Seiji Ozawa
Faust (t) Stuart Burrows
Marguerite (s) Edith Mathis
Mephistophélès (bs) Donald McIntyre

HMV SLS947 (3) (d) ●
Angel SCL-3758 (3) (US)
Orchestre de Paris
c. Georges Prêtre
Faust (t) Nicolai Gedda
Marguerite (s) Janet Baker (m-s)
Mephistophélès (bs) Gabriel Bacquier

Decca SXL6165 □
Hungarian March/Dance of the Sylphs/Minuet
c. Ernest Ansermet

LEONARD BERNSTEIN
(b. Lawrence, Mass. 25.8.1918)

Bernstein studied piano and composition at Harvard University and graduated in 1939, later attending the Curtis Institute of Music in New York. In 1941 he became assistant-conductor to Kussevitsky with the Boston Symphony Orchestra, after studying with him at the Berkshire Music Center at Tanglewood. The following year he became assistant to Artur Rodzinkski with the New York Philharmonic. In 1943 he was asked to substitute for Bruno Walter, who had been taken ill, and had a sensationally successful concert. He has had a very active career as a conductor (he became musical director of the NY Philharmonic in 1958) and an equally accomplished one as a pianist. Bernstein's busy life as conductor and musician has continually interrupted his preferred career as a composer. He wrote his *Jeremiah* symphony in 1942 and his *Second Symphony*, 'The Age of Anxiety', in 1943. He found his true *métier* in jazz-orientated music which bridged the gap between the serious and the popular world, such as he wrote for the ballets *Fancy Free* (1944) and *Facsimile* (1946). *Fancy Free* was adapted as a musical comedy *On the Town*, which was also filmed, and was followed by *Wonderful Town* in 1953 and the very successful *West Side Story* in 1957, also successful as a film. His operatic ambitions have yet to be properly fulfilled, but he went some way toward it with the strange and interesting *Trouble in Tahiti* (1952) and the delightful *Candide* in 1956, for which he also wrote the book. Other works include the film score for *On the Waterfront* (1954), the 3rd 'Kaddish' Symphony (1963), *Chichester Psalms* (1965) and a *Mass* (1971)

Trouble in Tahiti
Opera in 1 Act.
Text by Leonard Bernstein.
First performance: Waltham, Mass. (Brandeis University) July 1952. New York (television) 1952.

Synopsis:
In an American suburban home in the 1950s, Dinah and Sam are breakfasting to the sound of a jolly TV commercial. They quarrel as usual, then Sam leaves for work and broods in his office about his unhappy marriage. Dinah visits her psychiatrist. The couple meet at lunchtime but part with feeble excuses; then they tell of their wish for happiness, while the TV commercial continues its ironic comment. That afternoon, Sam plays handball while Dinah visits a clothes shop, where she tells the owner the story of a film she has seen, 'Trouble in Tahiti'. Although she denounces it as rubbish, she realises that it reflects her own frustration. She prepares dinner for Sam. Afterwards, they again lament their inability to make proper contact with each other, while the television plays the song 'Island Magic' from the film 'Trouble in Tahiti'.

RECORDING:
Columbia KM-32597 (US) ●
Columbia Wind Ensemble
c. Leonard Bernstein
Dinah (s) Nancy Williams
Sam (t) Julian Patrick

(A recording of the television version was once available on MGM E-3646 and HS-25020 (US))

Candide
Comic Operetta in 3 Acts.
Text by Lillian Hellman and Richard Wilbur, based on Voltaire's novel.
First performance: New York (Martin Beck Theater) December 1, 1956. London (Saville Theatre) 1959 New York 1974.

RECORDINGS:
CBS 61816 □
Columbia MS-6677 *or* MS-6988 (US)
Overture
c. Leonard Bernstein

Decca PFS4211 □
London 21048 (US)
Overture
c. Eric Rogers

HMV ASD2784 □
Angel S-37021 (US)
c. André Previn

Decca SXL6811 □
London 7031 *or* 2246 (2) (US)
c. Zubin Mehta

RCA SB6629 (d) □
RCA LSC-2789 (US)
c. Arthur Fiedler

(A recording of the original Broadway production was once available on Columbia OL5180 and OS-2350 (US), and of the London cast on Philips BBL7305)

Above: *The New York production of* Candide *(photo by Fred Fehl).*

FRANZ ADOLPH BERWALD
(b. Stockholm 23.7.1796; d. Stockholm 3.4.1868)

Berwald's works are gradually being rediscovered and found to be remarkably forward-looking for their period, romantic rather than classical in spirit. He became a violinist in the Royal Orchestra, having already started to compose before he went to study music in Berlin. He made two visits to Vienna, where he had more success with his music than in his homeland, eventually settling in Stockholm in 1849, becoming director of music at the University and Kappelmeister to the Swedish court. Berwald wrote a number of operas which have not yet become known beyond Sweden, including *Estrella di Soria* (1841), *Drottningen av Golconda* (1864) and two operettas. Even in their day they had little success, but the value of Berwald's other music suggests that they may be worth investigating.

Estrella di Soria
Opera in 4 Acts.
Text by Berwald.
First performance: privately (2 Acts only), Vienna 1841. Stockholm (Royal Theatre) April 9, 1862; Stockholm 1946.

RECORDINGS:
Nonesuch H-71218 (US) □
Overture and Polonaise
c. Sixten Ehrling

HMV SLS5096 (4) □
Overture
c. Ulf Björlin

Drottningen av Golconda
Opera in 4 Acts.
Text by Berwald.
First performance: Stockholm, April 1968.

RECORDINGS:
Nonesuch H-71218 (US) □
Overture
c. Sixten Ehrling

HMV SLS5096 (4) □
Overture
c. Ulf Björlin

Right: *Franz Berwald, contemporary of Schubert, whose operas are yet to be widely appreciated outside Sweden.*

GEORGES BIZET

(b. Paris 23.10.1838; d. Bougival 3.6.1875)

Bizet first learnt music from his parents: his singing-teacher father Adolphe Armand Bizet and his pianist mother, Aimée Léopoldine Joséphine Delsarte. Admitted to the Paris Conservatoire in 1848, he won second prize in the Marmontel piano class in 1851 and shared first prize the next year. His exceptional talents were widely recognised and he studied composition with Halévy ». He won the coveted Prix de Rome in 1857 after his operetta, *Le Docteur Miracle*, had been successful in a competition sponsored by Offenbach », tying with one by Lecocq. Both works were performed alternately at the Théâtre des Bouffes-Parisiens. After a visit to Rome in 1860 Bizet produced a series of works including operas, beginning with *Les Pêcheurs de perles* (1863). Another opera, *Ivan le Terrible*, written in 1865, was thought to have been destroyed by Bizet until its rediscovery in 1944. It was eventually produced in Germany (Württemberg) in 1946. (Bizet's engaging Symphony in C, written when he was still a student, was also thought to have been lost, but it was discovered in 1935, premiered the following year and has since become popular.) Other operas followed, including *La jolie fille de Perth* (after Sir Walter Scott) and *Djamileh* which failed when it was produced in 1872 — despite Bizet's high hopes. In 1875 he produced the masterpiece

upon which his fame most solidly rests: *Carmen*. At first, it received a mixed reception, but nowhere near the romantic legend that it was such a total failure it hastened Bizet's early death. That is pure sentimental imagination. Certainly Bizet died before his great opera had achieved world popularity; but from the beginning it had as many champions as detractors.

Carmen

Opera in 4 Acts.
Text by Henri Meilhac and Ludovic Halévy after the novel by Prosper Merimée. First performance : Paris (Opéra-Comique) March 3, 1875. Vienna (Court Opera) (in German) 1875; London (His Majesty's) (in Italian) 1878; New York (Italian) 1878.

Synopsis:
Scene: Seville. Time: c. 1820.

Act 1 A square in Seville: on one side a cigarette factory, on the other a military guardhouse. Micaëla is looking for her sweetheart Don José, bringing a message from his mother. The soldiers' flirting scares her off. The cigarette girls come out for a break. The guard changes, to the taunting of small boys. José learns that Micaëla is looking for him. Carmen enters, sings the *Habanera*, dismisses numerous suitors and incited by José's

indifference to her, flaunts herself in front of him and gives him a flower. Break over, the girls go back to work. Micaëla finds José and their brief talk makes him forget about the alluring gypsy. She leaves, and then Carmen is involved in a fight; Zuniga, officer of the guard, has her arrested and put in Corporal José's charge. She taunts him, singing the *Seguidilla*; he cannot resist, and allows her to escape. For that he is sent to prison.

Act 2 The tavern of Lillas Pastia. Carmen and gypsies are present. Zuniga is flirting. Enter Escamillo, the bullfighter, with his 'Toreador's Song'. All are fascinated, especially Carmen. But the smugglers want the soldiers distracted while they carry out a job. Don José comes in, his two-month sentence completed. Carmen has agreed to get José to join the smugglers, and entices him with gypsy song and dance. But the bugle sounds, recalling him to his post. He sings the 'Flower Song' and is about to go when Zuniga enters and makes a play for Carmen. José fights him, the smugglers return, hold Zuniga at gunpoint. Don José, knowing he has assaulted an officer, has no choice but to go with them.

Act 3 The smugglers' camp in the mountains. José, realising the fickleness of Carmen, is morose. Carmen and two gypsy friends are playing cards. Carmen turns up the Ace of Spades: the death card. The smugglers leave José on guard. Micaëla comes looking for him, doesn't see him and sings her song of love. Escamillo enters, in quest of Carmen. He and José fight, until the gypsies separate them. Escamillo invites them all to his next bullfight. Micaëla is discovered in hiding. José cares nothing for her love, but agrees to go with her when he learns his mother is dying.

Act 4 Outside the bullring in Seville. During the bullfight procession, Escamillo is with Carmen but she doesn't go in to watch the *corrida*. She is warned that José is near, with a knife. The shouts of the crowds and cheers for Escamillo sound from inside the bullring. Carmen and José meet: despite his pleadings she refuses to go with him. He stabs her, and the crowd pouring out of the bullring after Escamillo's triumph find José standing over Carmen's body.

Well-known arias:

Act 1 Avec la garde montante (Children and soldiers)
L'amour est un oiseau rebelle (Habanera) (Carmen)
Près des ramparts de Séville (Seguidilla) (Carmen)

Act 2 Les tringles des sistres tintaient (Carmen)
Votre toast je peux le rendre (Toreador's song) (Escamillo)
La fleur que tu m'avais jetée (Flower song) (Don José)

Act 3 Je dis que rien ne m'épouvante (Micaëla)

Notes:

Carmen has been damned as pseudo or bogus Spanish music. It is no such thing, and was never intended as such. It is French music evocative of Spain; and succeeds triumphantly. Many of the individual numbers, vocal and orchestral, such as the 'Habanera', the 'Seguidilla', the 'Toreador's Song, the 'Flower Song', the 'March of changing of the guard', and the Prelude, have gained universal currency outside the opera itself. There are also the two orchestral suites which are everlastingly popular. The problem of editions of *Carmen* is severe. Bizet wrote it with spoken dialogue; but later this was altered to sung recitatives by his friend Ernest Guiraud. This was the current version for a long time (except in Paris); but nowadays the spoken dialogue is, advantageously, usually restored. There are various editions and versions of this (notably by Oeser and by Choudens), and often a mixture of several. Of the recordings, Sir Georg Solti's (Decca) seems to reach the most satisfactory solution, the way to it lucidly explained by Sir Georg in the accompanying booklet. Beecham and von Karajan use the Guiraud edition; Abbado and Bernstein, one with spoken dialogue.

RECORDINGS:
Decca D11D3 (3) ★●
London 13115 (3) (US)
John Alldis Choir/Boys Chorus from Haberdashers School/London Philharmonic Orchestra
c. Sir Georg Solti
Carmen (m-s) Tatiana Troyanos
Don José (t) Placido Domingo
Micaëla (s) Kiri te Kanawa
Escamillo (b) José van Dam

Decca SET621 and SET622 □
(from above)

DG 2709 083 (3) ★★●
DG 2709 083 (3) (US)
Ambrosian Singers/London Symphony Orchestra
c. Claudio Abbado
Carmen (m-s) Teresa Berganza
Don José (t) Placido Domingo
Micaëla (s) Ileana Cotrubas
Escamillo (b) Sherrill Milnes

HMV SLS5021 (3) ★●
Angel S3613 (3)
Petits Chanteurs de Versailles/Chorus & Orchestra of Radiodiffusion Française
c. Sir Thomas Beecham
Carmen (m-s) Victoria de los Angeles
Don José (t) Nicolai Gedda
Micaëla (s) Janine Micheau
Escamillo (b) Ernest Blanc

HMV ESD7047 ■
Angel S-35818 (US)
(from above)

DG 2740 101 (3) ○
DG 2740 101 (3) (US)
Manhattan Opera Chorus/Children's Chorus/Metropolitan Opera Orchestra
c. Leonard Bernstein
Carmen (m-s) Marilyn Horne
Don José (t) James McCracken
Micaëla (s) Adriana Maliponte
Escamillo (b) Tom Krause

DG 2530 534 ■
DG 2530 534 (US)
(from above)

RCA SER5600/2 ●
Victor LSC-6199 (3) (US)
Vienna Boys Choir/Vienna State Opera Chorus/Vienna Philharmonic Orchestra
c. Herbert von Karajan
Carmen (m-s) Leontyne Price
Don José (t) Franco Corelli
Micaëla (s) Mirella Freni
Escamillo (b) Robert Merrill

RCA 2843 (US) ■
(from above)

HMV SLS952 (3) ●
Angel S-3767 (3) (US)
Paris Opera Chorus and Orchestra
c. Rafael Frühbeck de Burgos
Carmen (m-s) Grace Bumbry
Don José (t) Jon Vickers
Micaëla (s) Mirella Freni
Escamillo (b) Kostas Paskalis

HMV ASD2774 (d) ■
(from above)

HMV SLS913 (3) ○
Angel S-3650X (3) (US)
Duclos Chorus/Paris Opera Orchestra
c. Georges Prêtre
Carmen (m-s) Maria Callas
Don José (t) Nicolai Gedda
Micaëla (s) Andrea Guiot
Escamillo (b) Robert Massard

HMV ASD2282 ○
Angel S-36312 (US)
(from above)

Right: *A scene from the Bolshoi Theatre production of* Carmen *with Irina Arkhipova.*

Decca SET256/8 (3) ●
London 1368 (3) (US)
Chorus, Suisse Romande Orchestra
c. Thomas Schippers
Carmen (m-s) Regina Resnik
Don José (t) Mario del Monaco
Micaëla (s) Joan Sutherland
Escamillo (b) Tom Krause

Decca SXL6156 (d) ■
London 25924 (US)
(from above)

Decca PFS4204 (d) □
London 21055 (US)
Royal Philharmonic Chorus and Orchestra
c. Henry Lewis
Marilyn Horne (m-s)
Michele Molese (s)
etc.

HMV CSD1398 □
(in English)
Sadler's Wells Chorus and Orchestra
c. Colin Davis
(in English)
Patricia Johnson (s)
Ronald Smith (t)
Raimund Herincx (b)
Elizabeth Robson (s)

HMV SXLP30166 and P48 □
L'amour est un oiseau rebelle
Près des ramparts de Seville
Maria Callas (s)

Decca SDD222 □
London 26574 (US)
L'amour est un oiseau rebelle
Près des ramparts de Seville
Regina Resnik (s)

Decca SET520/1 □
London 1292 (2) (US)
L'amour est un oiseau rebelle
Près des ramparts de Seville
Régine Crespin (s)

Philips 6580 096 □
Philips 6570 107 (US)
Orchestral suites
c. Igor Markevitch

CBS 76587 □
Columbia M-34503 (US)
Orchestral Suites
c. Leopold Stokowski

Decca ECS755 □
London STS-15052 (US)
Orchestral Suites
c. Ernest Ansermet

HMV SXLP30276 □
Seraphim S-60134 (US)
Suite
c. Sir Thomas Beecham

(The above is a highly selective list in view of the numerous records of *Carmen* and excerpts from the opera that have been recorded.)

Above: *A costume for the First Sultana in* Djamileh, *designed by Multzer.*

Les Pêcheurs de Perles

Opera in 3 Acts.
Text by Michel Carré and Eugène Cormon.
First performance: Paris (Théâtre-Lyrique) September 30, 1863. Milan (in Italian) 1886; London (Covent Garden) 1887; Philadelphia (Italian) 1893.

Synopsis:

Scene: Ceylon. Time: Antiquity.

Act 1 The pearl fishers of Ceylon choose the season's king and priestess. The king is Zurga, the priestess remains unknown. Years earlier Zurga and Nadir were rivals for the hand of Léila. Now Nadir returns; the old rivalry is over, but Nadir recognises the priestess as Léila and confesses his continuing love.

Act 2 Léila's task as priestess is to protect the fishermen against the wrath of Brahma, whose high priest Nourabad is ever on the lookout. Léila is alone in the temple. Nadir comes to her and she warns him that if he is discovered it must mean death. In an impassioned duet they declare their lasting love. They are trapped by Nourabad, and Zurga vows vengeance on them both.

Act 3 Léila pleads with Zurga to spare Nadir, despite his anger and determination to go through with the execution. But Zurga's life was once saved by Léila, and in repayment he frees the lovers and they escape. The enraged fishermen fall on Zurga and stab him to death.

Well-known arias:

Act 1 C'est toi . . . Au fond du temple saint (Nadir and Zurga)
Je crois entendre encore (Nadir)
Le ciel est bleu (Chorus)

Act 2 Me voilà seul dans la nuit . . . Comme autrefois dans la nuit sombre (Léila)
De mon amie, fleur endormie (Nadir)
Dieu puissant le voilá (Léila and Nadir)

Act 3 L'orage c'est calmé—O Nadir, tendre amie (Zurga)

Notes:

This, Bizet's first full-scale opera, is lyrical in style, owing something to Offenbach and the French operetta tradition. He had not yet discovered the note of realism and the stylistic innovations which made *Carmen* so artistically important.

HMV SLS788 (2) ○
Angel S3603 (2) (US)
Chorus and Orchestra of the Paris Opéra-Comique
c. Pierre Dervaux
Leïla (s) Janine Micheau
Nadir (t) Nicolai Gedda
Zurga (b) Ernest Blanc
Nourabad (bs) Jacques Mars

HMV SLS5113 ○
Angel SX-3856 (2) (US)
Chorus and Orchestra of the Paris Opéra
c. Georges Prêtre
Leïla (s) Ileana Cotrubas
Nadir (t) Alain Vanzo
Zurga (b) Guillermo Sarabiax
Nourabad (bs) Roger Soyer

Decca SXL6267 □
London 25995 (US)
Me voila seul dans la nuit
Pilar Lorengar (s)

Decca SET454/5 □
Me voila seul dans la nuit
Joan Sutherland (s)

La Jolie Fille de Perth

Opera in 4 Acts.
Text by J. H. Vernay de St Georges and Jules Adenis after Scott.
First performance: Paris (Théâtre-Lyrique) December 26, 1867.

RECORDINGS:

Decca SXL6147 □	Decca SXL6637 □	DG 2535 238 □
Quand la flamme	Quand la flamme	DG 2535 238 (US)
Nicolai Ghiaurov (b)	**Joseph Rouleau** (bs)	Suite
		c. Jean Martinon

Philips 6580 174 □
Quand la flamme
Gérard Souzay (b)

Decca ECS801 □
London 6208 (US)
Suite
c. Ernest Ansermet

Djamileh

Opera in 1 Act.
Text by Louis Gallet.
First performance: Paris (Opéra-Comique) May 22, 1872. London (Covent Garden) 1893; Boston 1913.

RECORDING:
Decca SXL6501 □
Nour-Eddim, roi de Lahore
Huguette Tourangeau (m-s)

MARC BLITZSTEIN

(b. Philadelphia 2.3.1905; d. Fort-de-France, Martinique 23.1.1964)

Trained as a musician from boyhood, Blitzstein studied composition at the Curtis Institute in Philadelphia and piano in New York with Alexander Siloti. From 1926 he spent several years in Paris and Berlin, studying with Nadia Boulanger and Arnold Schoenberg ». Returning to New York, he lectured on avant-garde music and started his theatre writing by contributing a satirical one-act opera, *Triple Sec*, to the *Garrick Gaieties* in 1930. From this time he became a prophet of left-wing politics in America and made his music an instrument of political propaganda, starting with an oratorio *The Condemned* (1932) based on the famous Sacco-Vanzetti trial of the 1920s. In 1932 he travelled to Europe and the following year married the writer Eva Goldbeck. Her death in 1936 urged him into writing the music and text of the opera *The Cradle Will Rock* (1938), which strongly preached social revolution. Blitzstein's works hover on the borders between opera and 'musical', according to the viewpoint of the commentator, and are often dealt with in books covering the lighter vein; but they are certainly serious in intent. The next was *No For An Answer* (1941), which was banned for its radical viewpoint. He served in the Air Force during the Second World War. In 1946 he wrote a political ballet *The Guests*, and in 1949 came his most substantial 'musical play', *Regina*. In 1954 he wrote the text for an adaptation of Kurt Weill's » *The Threepenny Opera*, which had the longest run of any off-Broadway production up to that time. He was writing an opera, based again on the Sacco-Vanzetti case when while on holiday in Martinique he was attacked and beaten up by three sailors and died in hospital the following day. Regardless of political prejudice, Blitzstein was notable for dealing with problems of real life in his operas and for doing so with a clear understanding and use of the popular idioms of the day. *Regina*, sometimes described as a 'jazz opera', does in fact move near to the Broadway musical idiom, yet always in the manner of a pastiche rather than as a natural language. The waltz, the spiritual and the revivalist hymn are equally effectively employed, and there is an instrumental intermezzo that apes Gottschalk. Gilbert Chase has described *Regina* as an American type of opera; a viable work, a masterpiece of its kind.

The Cradle Will Rock

Musical drama in 10 Scenes.
Text by Marc Blitzstein.
First performance: New York (Windsor Theater) January 3, 1938.

Synopsis:

The action revolves around the efforts of a group of steel workers to create a union in Steeltown. Powerful members of the community use every device to try to defeat their efforts; Mr Mister, the capitalist who rules the whole town, compels the leaders of the town's various organisations to join a Liberty Committee whose aim is to destroy the union supporters. But the strength of the workers overcomes the power of capitalism, and the union is born.

Well-known arias:

Junior's gonna go to Honolulu (Editor Daily, Mister, Junior and
  Sister Mister)
Croon-spoon (Junior and Sister Mister)
The nickel under the foot (Moll)

Notes:

Blitzstein wrote the work at the suggestion of Bertolt Brecht, who was impressed by his music. Its first production in Washington (with John Houseman as producer and Orson Welles as director) was cancelled after pressure from government officials who objected to its left-wing views. Instead of the planned stage show it was put on in a nearby theatre in oratorio style, with Blitzstein accompanying at the piano and supplying a narration. This was so successful with its blend of torch songs,

tap dances and various other parodies that it continued in this shape for its New York production. The first performance with an orchestra was under Leonard Bernstein nearly a decade later in 1947, and it was revived on Broadway in 1960 and 1964. Virgil Thomson described it as 'the most appealing operatic socialism since *Louise*'. There was also a New York City Opera production in 1960.

RECORDING:
Composer Recordings SD-266 (2) (US) ●
Gershon Kingsley (dir. and piano)
Moll   Lauri Peters
Editor Daily   Dean Dittmann
Junior Mister   Joseph Bova
Sister Mister   Rita Gardner
Mister Mister   Gordon B. Clarke

Below: *Marc Blitzstein in London in 1945 where he wrote the words and music of* The Airborne *for the US Air Force.*

Regina

Musical drama in 3 Acts.
Text by Marc Blitzstein, based on Lillian Hellman's play 'The Little Foxes'.
First performance: New York (46th Street Theater) October 31, 1949.

Synopsis:
A declining family in the Southern States of America is gradually eliminated by every degree of avarice, ruthlessness and hate until only a single member, Regina Giddens, survives. Having destroyed all those around her, including her sick husband whom she allows to die of a heart-attack, she is able to take control of the lucrative family cotton-weaving business. But she finds herself lonely and haunted, bitterly hated even by her own daughter.

Notes:
The message in this opera is less blatantly driven home than in *The Cradle Will Rock*. The tragedy of Regina is allowed to make its own point in a carefully under-played drama. Again, ragtime, spiritual and popular song mingled with 'serious' musical influences make their point by their clever dramatic use at the right moment. Although it failed to become a popular success, it made a strong impression on thinking people. The work was taken into the New York City Opera repertoire in 1953.

RECORDING:
Odyssey Y3-35236 (3) (US) ●
New York City Opera Chorus and Orchestra
c. Samuel Krachmalnick
Regina Giddens (s) Brenda Lewis
Birdie Hubbard (s) Elisabeth Carron
Addie (c) Carol Brice
Horace Giddens (bs) Joshua Hecht

JOHN BLOW
(b. Newark, Nottinghamshire ?.2.1649; d. London 1.10.1708)

The teacher of Henry Purcell », Dr Blow was the composer of what may justly be called the first English opera, an honour frequently accorded to Purcell's *Dido and Aeneas*. Blow was probably educated first at the Magnus Song School in Newark. On the reconstitution of the Royal Chapel with the Restoration of Charles II, Blow became a chorister under Henry Cooke. He later became organist at Westminster Abbey, rejoined the royal service in 1669, being sworn as a Gentleman of the Royal Chapel in 1674 when he was also appointed Master of the Children of the Royal Chapel on the death of Pelham Humfrey. The same year Blow married the daughter of the Master of the Children of Westminster Abbey, Edward Braddock. His numerous compositions include many anthems, English and Latin services, various Welcome and other occasional songs and choral Odes, plus a few songs for theatrical productions.

Venus and Adonis

Masque for the Entertainment of the King. Prologue and 3 Acts.
Text by unknown author.
First performance: London (at Court), c. 1684 (date of composition uncertain, but after 1680).

Synopsis:
The delightful and stately Prologue leads into
Act 1 Venus and Adonis in love, with music both tender and strong. Venus then dispatches Adonis to show his skills in hunting, to the sound of a hunting chorus.
Act 2 Cupid and little cherubs are shown at play, tossing the alphabet across the stage (and the bar lines).
Act 3 Venus mourns the dying Adonis in a moving lament (foreshadowing Dido's Lament from Purcell's work). The masque ends with choral mourning and a final praise of Adonis.

Notes:
Venus and Adonis is described as a masque, but in every significant respect it is a mini-opera. It is not merely an important precursor of Purcell's masterpiece, but an original and memorable work in its own right.

RECORDING:
L'Oiseau-Lyre OLS128 (d) ○
London Singers/Chamber Orchestra
c. Anthony Lewis
Venus (s) Margaret Ritchie
Adonis (bs) Gordon Clinton
Cupid (s) Margaret Field-Hyde

Left: John Blow, English composer whose only opera, Venus and Adonis, *remains the work for which he is best known.*

Right: Plaque commemorating John Blow in Westminster Abbey, where he was organist for 15 years. He was buried close to Purcell, who was his pupil.

FRANÇOIS ADRIEN BOÏELDIEU
(b. Rouen 16.12.1775; d. Jarcy 8.10.1834)

After studying with the organist at Rouen, and producing his first opera there (libretto by his father, who was secretary to the Archbishop), he then went to the Paris Conservatoire where he became professor of piano and began to present a series of successful light operas, beginning with *La Famille Suisse*. He studied for a while with Cherubini », who chided him with winning a too easy success. In 1803 he went to St Petersburg as conductor of the Imperial Opera and wrote more operas himself. He returned to Paris in 1811 and repeated, even increased, his earlier triumphs. He was a master of the French *opéra comique* who never achieved, nor sought, the profounder regions of creative art; but his works are admirably written and gave enormous pleasure. Boïeldieu collaborated with various others (including Cherubini) on operas, but his best and most famous he did on his own. His best known and most durable opera is *La Dame blanche*; but *Le Calife de Bagdad*, *Jean de Paris* and others made him famous within and outside France.

Zoraime et Zulnar
Opera in 3 Acts.
Text by Claude Godard d'Aucour de Saint-Just.
First performance: Paris (Théâtre Favart) May 11, 1798.

RECORDING:
Decca SXL6531 □
London 6735 (US)
Overture
c. Richard Bonynge

Le Calife de Bagdad
Opera in 1 Act.
Text by Claude Godard d'Aucour de Saint-Just.
First performance: Paris (Théâtre Favart) September 16, 1800.

RECORDINGS:
Decca SXL6422 □
London 6643 (US)
Overture
c. Richard Bonynge

DG 2548 260 □
Overture
c. Louis Frémaux

Decca ECS547 □
Overture
c. Jean Martinon

Ma Tante Aurore
Opera in 3 Acts.
Text by Charles de Longchamps.
First performance: Paris (Opéra-Comique) January 13, 1803.

RECORDING:
Turnabout TV34222S ○
Philips 837.487 GY (Fr)
Paris ORTF Chamber Orchestra
c. Marcel Couraud
Julie (s)   Françoise Ogeas
Valsain (t)   Jean Mollien
Marton (c)   Berthe Kal
Prontin (t)   Bernard Plantey
Tante Aurore (m-s) Jeanine Collard

Angéla
Opera in 1 Act.
Text by G. Montcloux d'Epinay.
First performance: Paris (Opéra-Comique) June 13, 1814.

RECORDING:
Decca SET268/9 and SDD317 □
London 1257 (2) (d) (US)
Ma Fanchette est charmante
Joan Sutherland (s)
Marilyn Horne (m-s)

La Dame Blanche
Opera in 3 Acts.
Text by Eugène Scribe after Sir Walter Scott's 'The Monastery' and 'Guy Mannering'.
First performance: Paris (Opéra-Comique) December 10, 1825. Liège 1826; London (Drury Lane) (in English) 1826; New York 1927.

Synopsis:
Scene: Scotland. Time: 18th century.
Act 1   Georges Brown, an English soldier of mysterious (even to himself) background offers to take the place of tenant farmer Dickson who has been summoned to appear before the statue of the White Lady, guardian spirit of the Avenel family. The Avenel castle is to be sold next day because the Laird, a Jacobite, has had to flee with his family to France. Unlike Dickson, however, Brown does not take the White Lady business seriously.
Act 2   Gaveston, the Avenels' former steward, wants to buy the castle; but his ward Anna is determined he shall not. Brown appears and Anna sees a family likeness. She knows a secret about the Avenels. Also, she has been playing the part of the White Lady's ghost. She then recognises Brown as a young man she once nursed back to health. At the auction Brown, prompted by Anna, wins the castle with a huge bid.
Act 3   Brown is threatened with imprisonment if he does not meet the bid. But Anna reveals the secret, which is that the Avenel treasure is hidden in the White Lady statue. Dressed as the Lady, she gives it to Brown, who is revealed as the rightful Avenel heir. Gaveston tears away the White Lady's veil, and reveals Anna, to everyone's delight.

Notes:
The score contains traditional Scots tunes.

RECORDINGS:
Decca Ace of Diamonds
GOSR649/51 (d) ■
Chorus and Orchestra Raymond Saint-Paul
c. Pierre Stoll
Georges Brown (t) Michel Sénéchal
Anna (s)   Françoise Louvay
Gaveston (bs)   Adrien Legros
Dickson (b)   Aimé Doniat
Jenny (s)   Jane Berbié

Decca ECS547 □
Overture
c. Jean Martinon

DG 2548 260 □
Overture
c. Louis Frémaux

Below: *Portrait of François Boieldieu (1775-1834), opéra-comique composer.*

ARRIGO BOITO
(b. Padua 24.2.1842; d. Milan 10.6.1918)

A versatile man of the theatre, Boito is famous above all for his libretti, from Shakespeare, for Verdi's » two last masterpieces, *Otello* and *Falstaff*. (He also wrote a libretto from *Hamlet* for Franco Faccio (1840-1891). But he was also a composer in his own right, as well as a gifted conductor. His own operas make an oddly incongruous pair; they have little in common and the second, *Nerone*, was not produced until after his death and is little heard today. But the first, *Mefistofele*, based on Goethe's *Faust*, has remained popular.

Mefistofele
Opera in Prologue, 4 Acts, and Epilogue.
Text by Arrigo Boito.
First performance: Milan (La Scala) March 5, 1868. London (Her Majesty's) 1880; Boston (in English) 1880.

Synopsis:
Prologue 'In Heaven'. Mefistofele takes up a challenge that he can gain control of the soul of Faust, a 'madman for knowledge'. After that, a scherzo for cherubim and then a chorus of penitents from earth.
Act 1 Mefistofele enters Faust's study and makes the compact with him: his soul for an hour of total peace and knowledge.
Act 2 In a garden Faust and Margherita are shown to be in love. Mefistofele takes them to the Witches' Sabbath on the Brocken heights where Faust sees a vision of his beloved in chains.
Act 3 Margherita alone, forsaken and in prison is out of her mind. She dies; Faust can do nothing to help her.
Act 4 In a vision from the second part of Goethe's drama, the union of classical Greek and modern German culture and ideals is symbolised through the figures of Faust and Helen of Troy, with whom he falls in love, in the Vale of the Temple.
Epilogue Faust returns to his true nature, turns to religion, and will not fall into Mefistofele's trap. He dies a saved man.

Well-known arias:
Act 1 Dai campi dai prati (Faust)
Act 3 L'altra notte (Margherita)
Epilogue Giunto sul passo (Faust)

Notes:
The music of *Mefistofele* is complex, frequently contrapuntal, more intellectual than Italian audiences were accustomed to; there is little of *bel canto* style. It was a failure at first (partly through hostility to its composer) but was later revised and became successful. The Prologue and several of the individual numbers have gained great popularity, even though the opera as a whole is not quite so convincing. Oddly, the libretto is partly to blame; it shows little of the sure skill and theatrical aptitude of those he wrote for Verdi. All the same, it is an effective stage piece, several times recorded.

RECORDINGS:
HMV SLS973 (3) ●
Angel 3806 (3) (US)
Ambrosian Singers/Wandsworth School Boys' Choir/London Symphony Orchestra
c. Julius Rudel
Mefistofele (bs-b) Norman Treigle
Faust (t)   Placido Domingo
Margherita (s)   Montserrat Caballé
Wagner (t)   Thomas Allen
Marta (m-s)   Heather Begg

Angel S-37159 (US) ■
(from above)

Decca Ace of Diamonds GOS591/3
London 1307 (3) (US)
Chorus and Orchestra of Academia Santa Cecilia, Rome
c. Tullio Serafin
Mefistofele (bs) Cesare Siepi
Faust (t)   Mario del Monaco
Margherita (s)   Renata Tebaldi
Wagner (t)   Piero de Palma

Decca SET558 ■
London 26274 (US)
Chorus and Orchestra of Academia Santa Cecilia, Rome
c. Tullio Serafin
Cesare Siepi (bs)
Giuseppe di Stefano (t)
Renata Tebaldi (s)

Decca SXL 6305 □
London 26021 (US)
Rome Opera Orchestra
c. Silvio Varviso
Nicolai Ghiaurov (b)
Franco Tagliavini (t)

RCA AT31 □
RCA AT31 (US)
Prologue
Robert Shaw Chorale/Columbia Boy Choir/NBC Symphony Orchestra
c. Arturo Toscanini
Nicolai Moscona (bs)

DG 2707 100 (2) □
DG 2707 100 (2) (US)
Vienna State Opera Chorus/Vienna Philharmonic Orchestra
c. Leonard Bernstein
Nicolai Ghiaurov (bs)

HMV SLS869 □
L'altra notte
Maria Callas (s)

Decca SXL6548 □
London 26262 (US)
L'altra notte
Maria Chiara (s)

HMV SLS5051 (2) □
L'altra notte
Montserrat Caballé (s)

Above: *Arrigo Boito (1842-1918).*

Nerone
Opera in 4 Acts.
Text by Arrigo Boito.
First performance: Milan (La Scala) May 1, 1924. Rome 1928; Buenos Aires 1926.

Synopsis:
Scene: Rome. Time: 1st century.
Act 1 Nerone (Nero), full of guilt, comes to a place on the Appian Way to bury the ashes of his mother Agrippina, whom he has murdered. Simon Mago, the sorcerer, is there and sees the figure of Asteria, which appears to rise from the ground with her neck encircled by snakes. Above a crypt nearby, two Christians, Fanuèl and his sweetheart Rubria, see Simon as their arch enemy, but for the moment he has no hostile intention. He tries to win them over by promises of wealth and power.
Act 2 In his temple, Simon stages a great spectacle to make Nero believe he can perform miracles. But Asteria, playing the part of a goddess, is recognised by Nero who has Simon arrested. Simon has claimed he can fly and Nero throws him into prison, telling him to fly out if he can.
Act 3 Fanuèl and Rubria are gathered with other Christians when Asteria, having escaped from her prison, comes to warn them that Simon has been trying to buy his freedom by betraying the Christians. The guards arrive, and on orders from Fanuèl the Christians submit to capture.
Act 4 Nero has arranged games to entertain the people, with Christians as sacrifices. Simon has planned to burn Rome as an act of vengeance. Rubria, as a Vestal Virgin, pleads with Nero to spare the Christians; but he sends her into the arena. The games proceed; in the background Rome begins to burn. In the pit, or 'spoliarium' where the bodies of the Christian martyrs are thrown, Fanuèl and Rubria meet for the last time, confess their love and fidelity, and die.

RECORDING:
Cetra Opera Live LO56 (4) (r. 1957) ○
Chorus and Orchestra of San Carlo Opera
c. Franco Capuana
Nerone (Nero) (t) Mirto Picchi
Simon Mago (bs) Mario Petri

GIOVANNI BONONCINI
(b. Modena 18.7.1670; d. Vienna 8.7.1747)

The son of Giovanni Maria Bononcini (1642-1678), also a composer of some distinction, Bononcini studied with his father and with Paolo Colonna at Bologna, where he showed early signs of superior talent. He went first to Rome, where he began his operatic career, and then to Vienna, where he was court composer from 1700 until he left to return to Italy. He married, and in 1720 arrived in London where he remained for 12 years. During this period he was prominent in English musical life, receiving the patronage of several great families, including that of Marlborough. He was Handel's » chief rival on the London opera scene. A charge of faking an entry to the Academy of Ancient Music (he submitted work not his own) led to the end of his association with the Marlboroughs and his subsequent departure from London. The latter part of his life was spent in France and then in Vienna, where he died. There has been some doubt about the date of his death; it used to be given as 1755, the date given on a portrait. Whenever it was, by that time he was old and obscure.

Few of Bononcini's works for the theatre are heard today, with the exception of *Griselda*, though he was famous in his day and a musical power in several lands.

Griselda
Opera in 1 Act.
Text by Paolo Rolli from Apostolos Zeno.
First performance: London (King's Theatre), February 22, 1722.

RECORDINGS:
Decca SET352 (d) ●
London 1270 (US)
Ambrosian Singers/London
Philharmonic Orchestra
c. Richard Bonynge
Griselda (m-s)   Lauris Elms
Ernesto (s)   Joan Sutherland
Gualtiero (m-s)   Margreta Elkins
Almirena (s)   Monica Sinclair
Rambaldo (bs)   Spiro Malas

Decca Ace of Diamonds SDD317 □
Che giova fuggire—Troppo e il dolore
Joan Sutherland (s)

Decca SXL6650 □
London 26391 (US)
Per la gloria d'adorarvi
Luciano Pavarotti (t)

ALEXANDER BORODIN
(b. St Petersburg 11.11.1833; d. St Petersburg 28.2.1887)

The illegitimate son of a nobleman, Borodin was a scientist (chemist) as well as a musician. He studied in St Petersburg at the Academy of Medicine; then went to Germany where he met and married pianist Ektarina Protopopova. Studied composition with Balakirev and lectured at School of Medicine for Women. He composed three symphonies (the third unfinished), a number of orchestral and instrumental works, and one great opera, *Prince Igor*, (also unfinished at his death; completed by Rimsky-Korsakov » and Glazunov).

Prince Igor
Opera in Prologue and 4 Acts.
Text by Borodin from a draft by Vladimir Stassov.
First performance: St Petersburg November 4, 1890. Prague (in Czech) 1899; London (Drury Lane) 1914; New York (in Italian) 1915.

Synopsis:
Scene: Putivl and Polovtsian camp. Time: 12th century.
Prologue Despite an evil omen, Prince Igor and his son Vladimir Igorevich leave to fight the Polovtsian invaders. Prince Galitzky is left in charge.
Act 1 Galitzky is riding roughshod in Igor's absence, oppressing the populace and seducing the women. Yaroslavna, Igor's wife, tries to exercise restraining influence. News comes of a terrible defeat of the Russian armies; Igor and his son are prisoners.
Act 2 In the Polovtsian camp: singing and dancing in honour of their leader's daughter, Konchakovna. Igor is offered a chance to escape, but refuses. Vladimir falls in love with Konchakovna. Khan Konchak offers Igor freedom in return for a promise not to make war on the Polovtsians again; again Igor declines. They hold a grand banquet (Polovtsian Dances).
Act 3 Another Russian defeat puts the town of Putivl in danger of destruction. Igor now sees he must flee. He wants Vladimir to go with him; but Konchakovna begs to be allowed to go too, and raises the alarm when Vladimir refuses. Vladimir is caught but Igor escapes. Konchakovna and Vladimir are married.
Act 4 Yaroslavna mourns the destroyed Putivl. Igor returns and the people unite in renewed hope of victory.

Well-known arias:
Act 1   I hate a dreary life
   For long past.

Act 2   The prairie flower
   Daylight is fading
   How goes it, Prince?
   Polovtsian Dances
Act 3   I shed bitter tears

RECORDINGS:
Decca Ace of Diamonds GOS562/5 (4) ●
London 1501 (4) (d) (US)
Chorus and Orchestra of Belgrade
National Opera
c. Oscar Danon
Prince Igor (b)   Dushan Popivich
Yaroslavna (s)   Valeria Heybalova
Vladimir (t)   Noni Zhunetz
**Galitzky/
   Konchak** (bs)   Zharko Cvejic
Konchakovna (m-s) Melanie Bugerinovich

Decca SXL6263 □
London 6785 (US)
Overture/Polovtsian Dances/
Polovtsian March
c. Sir Georg Solti

RCA RL25098 □
RCA CRL3-2790 (3) (US)
Overture/Polovtsian Dances/
Polovtsian March
c. Loris Tjeknavorian

Philips 6582 012 □
Mercury 75016 (US)
Overture/Polovtsian Dances
c. Antal Dorati

CBS 79214 □
Columbia M3-34587 (2) (US)
Overture/Polovtsian Dances
c. Andrew Davis

Decca ECS757, SPA281 and SDD496 □
London 6212 (US)
Dance of the Polovtsian Maidens/
Polovtsian Dances
c. Ernest Ansermet

Decca PFS4189 □
London 21041 (US)
Dance of the Polovtsian Maidens/
Polovtsian Dances
c. Leopold Stokowski

HMV SXLP 30171 □
Dance of the Polovtsian Maidens/
Polovtsian Dances
c. Sir Thomas Beecham

Decca PFS4048 □
London 21003 (US)
Dance of the Polovtsian Maidens/
Polovtsian Dances
c. Stanley Black

Right: *A scene from Borodin's Prince Igor at the famous Bolshoi Theatre.*

Far right: *Fyodor Chaliapin in Prince Igor, a photograph from the Bakhrushin Theatre in Moscow.*

RUTLAND BOUGHTON

(b. Aylesbury 23.1.1878; d. London 25.1.1960)

Almost equally devoted to choral drama and socialism, Boughton cherished a dream of writing an English equivalent to Wagner's » *Ring* based on the Arthurian legend, and establishing an English Bayreuth at Glastonbury, where he directed the festival for a number of years. Neither dream was realised, but the conviction and dedication remained. A number of his works were produced at Glastonbury and elsewhere, but none have survived.

The Immortal Hour

Opera in 2 Acts.
Text by Boughton on plays by Fiona Macleod.
First performance: Glastonbury August 26, 1914. London 1922; New York 1926.

Notes:

The popular 'Faery Song' from this, his most successful, opera was for long a favourite with school choirs and tenors.

Right: *Rutland Boughton, who spent much of his career trying to establish an Arthurian music-drama tradition, on Wagnerian lines, at Glastonbury. The Immortal Hour is his best work.*

BENJAMIN BRITTEN

(b. Lowestoft 22.11.1913; d. Aldeburgh 4.12.1976)

After piano studies with Harold Samuel and composition with Frank Bridge, Britten won a scholarship to London's Royal College of Music. Prior to the Second World War some of his music was heard at various festivals, and during the early years of the war, while in America, he wrote his first opera, a light work with text by W. H. Auden on the subject of *Paul Bunyan* (this has recently been revived with great success and a recording is expected). His first notable success was with *Variations on a theme of Frank Bridge* which was heard at the Salzburg Festival in 1937 and astonished everyone with its novel sounds. The *Sinfonia da Requiem* (1940) and the *Serenade for Tenor, Horn and Strings* (1943) confirmed his reputation as one of the leading British composers of his time. Although he continued to write some orchestral, chamber and instrumental music, his reputation was chiefly to be founded on his special flair for setting words to music. He wrote many songs and song-cycles, and many choral works, but it is as a writer of opera that he will always be thought of first; not only the leading writer of English opera in his day, but arguably the greatest and most consistent composer in this field that we have produced. Major choral works and operas appeared regularly throughout his composing career and each one was eagerly awaited and rapturously received: *Peter Grimes* (1945); *The Rape of Lucretia* (1947); *Albert Herring* (1947); *Let's Make an Opera* (1949); *Billy Budd* (1951); *Gloriana* (1953); *The Turn of the Screw* (1954); *A Midsummer Night's Dream* (1960); *Owen Wingrave* (1970); *Death in Venice* (1973). In between came the Chester miracle play *Noye's Fludde* (1958); the church parables *Curlew River* (1964), *The Burning Fiery Furnace* (1966) and *The Prodigal Son* (1968); and the *War Requiem* (1962)—which are not dealt with in this volume.

Peter Grimes

Opera in Prologue and 3 Acts.
Text by Montagu Slater, based on a poem by George Crabbe.
First performance: London (Sadler's Wells) June 7, 1945. New York (Met) 1948.

Synopsis:
Scene: The Borough, a small fishing town on the East Coast.
Time: early 19th century.
Prologue An inquest is being held in the Moot Hall to examine the cause of the death at sea of Peter Grimes's apprentice. The townspeople are firmly convinced that Grimes is guilty, but the court acquits him, although with the advice that he must have a woman to take care of any boys he employs.
Act 1 With his bad reputation Grimes finds it difficult to get any help with his boat; but a new apprentice has been found and Ellen Orford offers to help by taking care of the boy. A storm begins to rage as the boy is brought to Grimes, who takes him home.
Act 2 Sunday is a day of rest for most, but Grimes makes it the first day of work for his new apprentice. The Church congregation, stirred by Bob Boles, Methodist preacher and fisherman, go along to Peter's hut to see what is happening. Grimes orders the boy to hide but while he is doing so he falls from the cliff and is killed on the rocks below.
Act 3 The crowd grows hostile when their suspicions are confirmed by finding the boy's shirt in the water. Captain Balstrode, who has tried to defend Peter Grimes, and Ellen persuade him to sail away from the town and sink his boat. Next day the overturned boat is seen drifting out at sea; but nobody is concerned.

Notes:
Few works have made a greater impact than *Peter Grimes*, either on stage or on record, with its stark realism and the power of its music in keeping with its grim setting. Outstanding features are the fine orchestral interludes, which are frequently played as individual items.

Above: *Benjamin Britten.*

RECORDINGS:
Decca SXL2150/2 ★●
London 1305 (3) (US)
Chorus and Orchestra of the Royal
Opera House, Covent Garden
c. Benjamin Britten

Peter Grimes (t)	Peter Pears
Ellen Orford (s)	Claire Watson
Captain Balstrode (b)	James Pease
Swallow—Mayor and	
lawyer (bs)	Owen Brannigan
Bob Boles (t)	Raymond Nilsson

Decca SXL2309 ■
London 26004 (US)
(from above)

Philips 6769 014 (3) ●
Philips 6769 014 (3) (US)
Chorus and Orchestra of the Royal
Opera House, Covent Garden
c. Colin Davis

Peter Grimes (t)	Jon Vickers
Ellen Orford (t)	Heather Harper
Captain Balstrode (b)	Jonathan Summers
Swallow (bs)	Forbes Robinson
Bob Boles (b)	John Dobson

Decca ECS712 □
Interludes and Passacaglia
c. Eduard van Beinum

Pye GSGC14059 □
Interludes and Passacaglia
c. Sir Adrian Boult

HMV ASD3154 □
Angel S-37142 (US)
Interludes and Passacaglia
c. André Previn

Decca SXL2189 □
London 6179 (US)
Interludes and Passacaglia
c. Benjamin Britten

CBS 76640 □
Columbia M-34529 (US)
Interludes and Passacaglia
c. Leonard Bernstein

HMV SXLP 30240 □
Angel S-36215 (US)
Interludes and Passacaglia
c. Carl Maria Giulini

RCA RL12744 □
RCA ARL1-2744 (US)
Interludes and Passacaglia
c. Eugene Ormandy

The Rape of Lucretia

Opera in 2 Acts.
Text by Ronald Duncan from the play by André Obey.
First performance: England (Glyndebourne) July 12, 1946. Basle 1947; New York 1949.

Synopsis:
Act 1 Rome under the rule of Tarquinius. During a rest between their distant battles, the soldiers wonder what their wives are doing back in Rome. Some are rather doubtful about their wives' faithfulness, but Collatinus is absolutely sure that his wife Lucretia is chaste and trustworthy. This arouses the lust of Tarquinius, who decides that he will make Collatinus a cuckold with the rest of them. Back in Rome all is peaceful as the city prepares to sleep. Tarquinius is heard approaching.
Act 2 Tarquinius rapes Lucretia in her bed. The next day she sends for Collatinus who arrives to find her dressed in mourning. She is so full of shame that she stabs herself and falls dead in his arms.

RECORDING:
Decca SET492/3 ★●
London 1288 (2) (US)
English Chamber Orchestra
c. Benjamin Britten

Collatinus (b)	John Shirley-Quirk
Tarquinius (b)	Benjamin Luxon
Lucretia (s)	Janet Baker
Chorus	Heather Harper and
	Peter Pears

Albert Herring

Comic Opera in 3 Acts.
Text by Eric Crozier.
First performance: Glyndebourne June 20, 1947. Hanover 1950; New York 1952.

Synopsis:

Act 1 In the small market town of Loxford in East Suffolk, it is
the tradition for a May Queen to be chosen from the virgins by a
committee and vetted by Lady Billows. But the committee is
unable to find anyone who qualifies and Police Superintendent
Budd suggests that they choose a May King instead. The only
youth who seems innocent enough is Albert Herring. He has,
however, been watching one Sid making love to one Nancy and,
feeling ashamed, he refuses the offer.

Act 2 Now the town is desperate. Sid tops up Albert's glass
with rum and gets him drunk enough to agree. The town is
astonished when their new and supposedly chaste May King
gets drunker and drunker. He escapes from them and decides to
go on the rampage.

Act 3 The townsfolk search for Albert everywhere but he can't
be found; and certain clues make them suspect foul play. Just as
they are all mourning his demise, Albert turns up and apologises
for causing worry but says he is determined to run his own life
from now on.

RECORDING:

Decca SET274/6 ★●
London 1378 (3) (US)
English Chamber Orchestra
c. Benjamin Britten

Lady Billows (c)	Sylvia Fisher
Superintendent	
Budd (bs)	Owen Brannigan
Sid (t)	Joseph Ward
Nancy (s)	Catherine Wilson
Albert Herring (t)	Peter Pears

The Little Sweep

The second part, being the actual opera which the cast write, compose and
rehearse (involving the audience) in the first part of 'Let's Make an Opera'.
Text by Eric Crozier.
First performance: Aldeburgh (Jubilee Hall) April 14, 1949.

Synopsis:

Black Bob, his son Clem and their eight-year-old sweep-boy
Sam arrive at Iken Hall, Suffolk on a winter morning in 1810.
Sam gets stuck in the chimney but is rescued by the Brook
children and their visiting cousins from Woodbridge, who are
sorry for the tearful boy. They lay a false trail of soot to the open
window and the sweep and the caretaker, Mrs Baggott, and
others go off in pursuit. They decide to smuggle Sam out in a
trunk. He is given a bath and hidden in the toy-cupboard where
he is almost discovered by Mrs Baggott. Next morning he is put
in the trunk and with the help of the cousins and their nursemaid
he makes his escape.

RECORDINGS:

(*The Little Sweep* only)
Decca Eclipse ECM2166 ●
(previously LXT5163)
English Opera Group Orchestra
c. Benjamin Britten

Black Bob and		
Tom (bs)	Trevor Anthony	
Clem and Alfred (t)	Peter Pears	
Sam (boy-s)	David Hemmings	
Mrs Baggott (c)	Nancy Thomas	
Rowan (s)	Jennifer Vyvyan	
Brook children	April Cantelo,	
	Michael Ingram,	
	Marilyn Baker	
Crome children	Robin Fairhurst,	
	Gabrielle Soskin,	
	Lyn Vaughan	

HMV ASD2608 ●
Medici String Quartet
c. Philip Ledger

Black Bob and	
Tom (b)	Robert Lloyd
Clem and Alfred (t)	Robert Tear
Sam (boy-s)	Sam Monck
Mrs Baggott (c)	Heather Begg
Rowan (s)	Mary Wells
Brook children	Catherine Benson,
	Cato Fordham,
	Catherine Wearing
Crome children	David Glick,
	Colin Huehns,
	Katherine Willis

Billy Budd

Opera in 4 Acts.
Text by E. M. Forster and Eric Crozier, adapted from the story by Herman Melville.
First performance: (original version in 4 Acts) London (Covent Garden) December 1, 1951; revised in 2 Acts and heard on BBC Third Programme November 13, 1961.

Synopsis:
Scene: Aboard the battleship 'Indomitable' during the French Wars of 1797.

Act 1 In a spoken dialogue Captain Vere muses on his past life. Three sailors including Billy Budd have been captured from a passing merchantman and are immediately embroiled in the rough life and harsh discipline of the man-o'-war. Budd shows rebellious spirit and has a fight with Squeak, the spy and toady for the brutal Master-at-Arms Claggart, who now swears to get rid of him and pays a novice to help him with his evil intentions.

Act 2 He plans to involve Billy in a framed-up plot for mutiny. Billy is warned by Dansker but finds it hard to believe that anyone could be so evil.

Act 3 Claggart begins to slander Billy to the Captain, who cannot believe that such a fine fellow could be involved in such villainy. He already suspects Claggart. After a brief battle with a French ship, there is a confrontation and the Captain insists that Claggart makes the charges to Billy's face. Billy, who is afflicted with a stammer, swings his arms around and accidentally kills Claggart. The Captain is appalled but knows that he has to condemn Billy to the gallows, even though he knows of his essential goodness.

Act 4 Dansker comforts Billy while they prepare the yard-arm for his hanging. The crew start to mutiny but are quelled and the deed is done. In an epilogue Captain Vere is alone again, brooding on the impossible decision he had to make and blaming himself for his inability to solve the moral problem.

RECORDING:
Decca SET379/81 (revised version) ●
London 1390 (3) (US)
Ambrosian Chorus/London Symphony Orchestra
c. Benjamin Britten
Billy Budd (b)   Peter Glossop
Captain Vere (t)   Peter Pears
John Claggart (bs) Michael Langdon
1st Lieut.
  Redburn (b)   John Shirley-Quirk
Dansker (bs)   Owen Brannigan

Right: *Jon Vickers in the title role of* Billy Budd.

Below: *Some of the 106 characters in Britten's* Gloriana.

Gloriana

Opera in 3 Acts.
Text by William Plomer.
First performance: London (Covent Garden) June 8, 1953.

RECORDINGS:
Decca SXL6788 □
2nd Lute Song
Peter Pears (t)
Ossian Ellis (harp)

L'Oiseau-Lyre SOL60037 □
Choral Dances
London Symphony Orchestra and Chorus
c. George Malcolm

Decca Argo ZRG5424 □
Choral Dances
Elizabethan Singers

RCA ARL3 0997 □
RCA LSC-2730 (US)
Courtly Dances
Bream Consort

The Turn of the Screw

Opera in Prologue and 2 Acts
Text by Myfanwy Piper, based on the novel by Henry James.
First performance: Venice, September 14, 1954.

Synopsis:

Prologue The new governess at the country house of Bly is employed on condition that she is entirely responsible for the well-being of the children and must never trouble their guardian.
Act 1 She travels to Bly full of doubts and fears. She is warmly welcomed by Mrs Grose the housekeeper and is charmed by the house and the children; then a letter arrives dismissing Miles from his school. Neither the governess nor Mrs Grose can believe he has done wrong. While walking in the gardens the governess sees a sinister man on the tower and later the apparition stares at her through a window. Mrs Grose recognises her description of the man, and tells the governess of the dead Miss Jessel and Quint and of their excessive familiarity with the children. The Governess vows to keep Miles from any knowledge of the ghost of Quint. Miles reveals his insecurity and melancholy. At the lakeside the governess finds that the ghost of Miss Jessel is also present, and that the children are well aware of this. At night the governess and Mrs Grose discover the children communing with Quint and Miss Jessel.
Act 2 The ghosts reveal their association as lovers and their need for a soul-mate—Miles for Quint, Flora for Miss Jessel. The governess despairs of her inability to help when she is challenged by Miles to do something. She decides to leave Bly, and is confronted by Miss Jessel; the shock restores her courage. She decides that she must write to the children's guardian to ask his help. Quint persuades the boy to steal her letter. Flora slips away and is discovered by the lakeside with Miss Jessel. Flora will not admit there is a ghost. Mrs Grose believes her, and takes Flora to her guardian. The governess now battles with Quint for the boy's soul, and Miles at last admits he is pursued by 'Peter Quint, you devil' and is redeemed. But the strain has been too much for him and he dies in the governess's arms.

RECORDING:

Decca Ace of Diamonds GOM560/1 ●
English Opera Group Orchestra
c. Benjamin Britten
Quint (t)   Peter Pears
Governess (s) Jennifer Vyvyan
Miles (s)   David Hemmings
Flora (s)   Olive Dyer
Mrs Grose (s) Joan Cross
Miss Jessel (s) Arda Mandikian

A Midsummer Night's Dream

Opera in 3 Acts.
Text by Benjamin Britten and Peter Pears, based on Shakespeare's play.
First performance: Aldeburgh (re-opening of the Jubilee Hall after its rebuilding) June 11, 1960

Synopsis:

Scene: Athens and nearby.
Act 1 Enter Puck, then Oberon and Titania quarrelling. Oberon sends Puck for a magic herb. Enter Lysander and Hermia, escaping from Athens so that Hermia need not be married to Demetrius. Oberon sees Demetrius looking for Hermia and pursued by Helena and decides to resolve their problems. Puck brings the herb. The rustics come to prepare their play. Hermia and Lysander are lost and decide to sleep. Puck pours the herb into Lysander's eyes. Helena comes pursuing Demetrius and wakes Lysander who, bewitched, falls in love with her. Titania enters and falls asleep. Oberon curses and bewitches her.
Act 2 The rustics rehearse. Bottom is transformed into an ass; Titania wakes and falls in love with him. Puck reports the Titania-Bottom affair to Oberon. His mistake about the lovers is revealed when Hermia enters pursued by Demetrius. As Demetrius rests, Oberon pours the herb in his eyes. Enter Helena

pursued by Lysander. Demetrius wakes and loves her but she thinks they are all mocking her. Oberon, annoyed, sends everyone to sleep.
Act 3 Oberon orders Puck to undo the spell. Oberon and Titania make up their quarrel and plan to attend the wedding of Theseus. The lovers now wake and renew their love. Bottom wakes and the rustics gather. In Theseus's palace the play 'Pyramus and Thisbe' is at last performed. The company retire to rest and Oberon and Titania give a blessing.

RECORDING:

Decca SET338/40 ●
London 1385 (3) (US)
London Symphony Orchestra/Choirs
c. Benjamin Britten
Oberon (c-t) Alfred Deller
Titania (s)   Elizabeth Harwood
Puck (t)   Stephen Terry
Theseus (b)   John Shirley-Quirk
Hippolyta (s) Helen Watts
Lysander (t)   Peter Pears
Demetrius (b) Thomas Hemsley
Hermia (s)   Josephine Veasey
Helena (s)   Heather Harper
Bottom (bs)   Owen Brannigan

Owen Wingrave

Opera for television in 2 Acts.
Text by Myfanwy Piper, based on a short story by Henry James.
First seen on BBC-2 TV on May 16, 1971.

Synopsis:

A young man, haunted by his ancestral past, determines to take a stand against it and almost escapes from its influence. The action takes place at Paramore, the Wingrave family seat; at the Coyle's military-cramming establishment in Bayswater; at Miss Wingrave's lodgings in London; and in Hyde Park. The period is the late 19th century. A synopsis, isolated from the music, is hardly possible. The opera is devoted to philosophy and portraits of the ancestors rather than action.

RECORDING:

Decca SET501/2 ●
London 1291 (2) (US)
Wandsworth School Boys' Choir/English
Chamber Orchestra
c. Benjamin Britten
General Sir Philip
  Wingrave (t)   Peter Pears
Miss Wingrave (s) Sylvia Fisher
Owen Wingrave (b) Benjamin Luxon
Mrs Julian (s)   Jennifer Vyvyan
Kate, her
  daughter (m-s) Janet Baker
Coyle (b)   John Shirley-Quirk
Mrs Coyle (s)   Heather Harper
Lechmere (t)   Nigel Douglas
Narrator   Peter Pears

Below: *Benjamin Luxon and Janet Baker in Britten's* Owen Wingrave, *an opera especially written for television and first produced by the BBC in May, 1971.*

Above: *Peter Pears as Aschenbach and John Shirley-Quirk as the Barber in* Death in Venice.

Right: *Members of the English Opera Group in the Covent Garden production of* Death of Venice.

Death in Venice

Opera in 2 Acts.
Text by Myfanwy Piper, based on the short story by Thomas Mann.
First performance: Aldeburgh Festival, June 16, 1973. Performed at the Edinburgh Festival 1973, Venice, Brussels and Covent Garden.

Synopsis:

Act 1 Aschenbach, the famous writer, thwarted in his disciplined search for beauty, walks through the suburbs of Munich. Seeing a foreigner on the chapel steps he feels a desire to see the world. He boards ship for Venice, travelling with a party of callow youths. At Venice he is rowed to the Lido against his will. At his hotel the Manager shows him what a splendid view he has of the beach. He meets three Polish children and their governess, and falls under the spell of the Apollo-like boy Tadzio. The next day he watches the children, and particularly Tadzio at play on the beach. Ashamed, he resolves to leave the corrupting city but at the station finds an excuse to return to the Lido. In his room he realises that it is Tadzio who has drawn him back and he makes the fateful decision to dedicate his days to 'the sun, and the feasts of the sun'. The presence of Tadzio in ensuing days is symbolised in tableaux and dances, in which the boy is always the victor. Aschenbach longs to pluck up courage actually to speak to him.

Act 2 In the barber's-shop Aschenbach learns of a 'sickness' that is spreading through Venice. In the city he finds that warnings have been posted and he fears that the Polish family will leave, and compulsively begins to follow the boy everywhere. He realises that he is being corrupted by beauty, and during a visit to a barber sees that he has turned into a fop. The family are about to leave Venice. Symbolically, Tadzio walks toward the sea and Aschenbach collapses on a chair dying, as the music of his original innocence washes away the corruption that has festered in his mind.

Notes:

As with many of Britten's operas the action is tightly linked by Choral Dances, in this case where the boys on the beach take on the guise of young athletes in Greek games; they are very much a part of the visionary aspect of the opera rather than mere *divertimenti*.

RECORDING:
Decca SET381/3 ●
London 13109 (3) (US)
Members of the English Opera Group/
English Chamber Orchestra
c. Steuart Bedford
Aschenbach (t)   Peter Pears
Hotel Manager,
   Traveller etc (b)   John Shirley-Quirk
Voice of Apollo (c-t) James Bowman
Hotel Porter (t)   Kenneth Bowen

FERRUCCIO (Benvenuto) BUSONI
(b. Empoli, Italy 1.4.1886; d. Berlin 27.7.1924)

An outstanding pianist and musical theorist, Busoni was, as a composer, a formidable intellectual whose creative flow has sometimes been felt to have been impeded by the sheer complexity of his mind. Yet his music is of a nature and quality that is extraordinarily impressive; his searching mystical and metaphysical temperament gives his best music an uncompromising aura. He began his concert career as pianist at the age of seven, and studied at Graz (with Wilhelm Meyer-Remy) and at Leipzig. He held teaching posts at Helsinki (where he met Sibelius and married Gerda Sjöstrand), Moscow and America, before settling in Berlin. He is best known for his piano music, especially the huge *Fantasia contrappuntistica* and for his transcriptions of Bach. He wrote four operas, of which the last, *Doktor Faustus*, was unfinished at his death and was completed by his pupil Phillip Jarnach. *Die Brautwahl*, to his own libretto based on a story by E. T. A. Hoffman, was produced in Hamburg in 1912, and the brief *Turandot*, with spoken dialogue and based on a play by Carlo Gozzi for which he had written incidental music (on which the opera is based), appeared in 1917.

Arlecchino
Comic Opera in 1 Act.
Text by Busoni.
First performance: Zürich May 11, 1917 (double bill with 'Turandot'). London (BBC) 1939; Venice 1940; Glyndebourne 1954.

Synopsis:
The characters of the *commedia dell'arte*, Harlequin, Columbina, Doctor, Abbot and the Tailor act out a charade. Arlecchino (Harlequin) chases Annunziata (Tailor Matteo's wife) but avoids discovery by jumping out of a window. As a diversion he shouts that barbarians are invading.

Returning as a soldier, he drafts Matteo into the army. When Columbina catches him trying to chase Annunziata again, Leandro challenges him to a duel, and Arlecchino kills him with a wooden sword. The others find the body, but they are drunk and do nothing. Arlecchino returns to Annunziata and carries her off.

Notes:
The work is highly satirical and anti-war. Busoni himself said: 'The title role gives my own confessions. The Abbé expresses human forbearance and tolerance. The tailor Matteo is the duped idealist, suspicious of nothing, Columbina—the woman. After *The Magic Flute* (which I value highly) it is the most moral libretto there is.' It also parodies Wagner.

RECORDING:
HMV ALP1223 (d) ●
Glyndebourne Festival Orchestra
c. John Pritchard
Arlecchino (speaker) Kurt Gester
Matteo (b)   Ian Wallace
Abbot Cospicuo (b) Geraint Evans
Dr Bombasto (bs)   Fritz Ollendorf
Leandro (t)   Murray Dickie
Columbina (m-s)   Elaine Malbin

Doktor Faust
Opera in 2 Prologues, 1 Interlude and 3 Scenes.
Text by Busoni (not after Goethe's drama but based upon older sources and puppet plays and Christopher Marlowe's 'Dr Faustus').
First performance: Dresden May 21, 1925. London (concert version) 1937; Florence 1942.

Synopsis:
Scene: Wittenberg; Parma. Time: 15th century.
1st Prologue Three students arrive with a magic book for Faust.
2nd Prologue Faust uses the book to summon Mephistofeles, from whom he demands all knowledge and total experience. Mephistofeles agrees, but on his own terms, making Faust his servant forever. Faust, mindful of a threat to kill him by a soldier whose sister he has seduced, has to accept.

Above: *Ferruccio Busoni during his last years in Zurich.*

Interlude The soldier is praying in a cathedral, when he is surprised and killed by some other soldiers invoked by Mephistofeles.
Scene 1 The marriage of the Duke of Parma. Faust arrives and entertains the company, conjuring up a succession of visions of himself and the Duchess, to the Duke's alarm. The Duchess falls for Faust, and by morning has eloped with him.
Scene 2 At an inn in Wittenberg Faust is boasting of the beautiful Duchess he made love to on her wedding night. Mephistofeles enters to say the Duchess is dead and has left Faust the dead body of a child as a memento. But the child when burnt proves to be made of straw: in the ensuing smoke Mephistofeles conjures up Helen of Troy. Faust tries to seize the vision but it vanishes. The three original student figures return to claim the book and its key, but Faust refuses them.
Scene 3 On a winter night in Wittenberg Faust gives alms to a beggarwoman, who turns out to be the Duchess and gives him a dead child. Faust goes to the cathedral to pray but the body of the dead soldier bars his way. Entering, he is terrified to see the corpse of Helen of Troy on the crucifix. Laying the dead child on the ground he prays that his spirit can enter the child and find its atonement. Faust dies and as midnight strikes a naked youth arises from his body.

RECORDING:
DG 2709 032 ●
DG 2709 032 (d) (US)
Bavarian State Opera Chorus/Bavarian Radio Orchestra
c. Ferdinand Leitner
Faust (b)   DietrichFischer-Dieskau
Mephistofeles (t) William Cochran
Duchess (s)   Hildgard Hillebrecht
Duke (t)   Anton de Ridder
Wagner (b)   Karl Kohn

ALFREDO CATALANI
(b. Lucca 19.6.1854; d. Milan 7.8.1893)

It sometimes happens that an artist suffers the double disadvantage of shortness of years and the contemporary presence of more ear-catching, though not necessarily superior, talents. This was the case with Catalani. He was of the generation of opera composers which included Puccini », Mascagni » and Leoncavallo »: but he was under 40 when he died and his talent was more fragile. He was probably more naturally gifted than Mascagni and Leoncavallo (though not than Puccini, of course); but he did not traffic in their kind of melodramatic *verismo* which pulls the crowd. Yet he was brilliantly endowed and composed a mass which was performed when he was 14. He studied with Bazin at the Paris Conservatoire and then at the Milan Conservatory. He composed a number of operas, of which the last, *La Wally*, is the best known. *Loreley*, which was in fact a new version of his first opera, *Elda* (1880) has also survived the pressure of time.

La Wally
Opera in 4 Acts.
Text by Luigi Illica after Wilhelmine von Hillern's Die Geyer-Wally.
First performance: Milan (La Scala) January 20, 1892. New York (Metropolitan) 1909; Manchester 1919.

Synopsis:
Act 1 Wally, in love with Giuseppe Hagenbach, is urged by her father, Stromminger, to marry Vincenzo Gellner. She threatens to leave home, but doesn't admit her true love.
Act 2 After her father's death Wally finds herself rich. Gellner persists in his attentions and accuses Hagenbach of being in love with Afra, the landlady. Wally confronts Afra and Hagenbach vows vengeance. At a dance, however, Hagenbach becomes infatuated with Wally but maintains his liaison with Afra. Wally, sensing defeat, promises herself to Gellner.
Act 3 Gellner, still jealous, attempts to kill Hagenbach by pushing him over a cliff, but Hagenbach survives and Afra nurses him back to health.

Act 4 Wally, desperate and beyond hope, is about to commit suicide when Hagenbach confesses he really loves her. Hagenbach leaves; Wally rushes after him, and they both die in an avalanche.

Well-known arias:
Act 1 Ebben? . . . Ne andrò lontana (Wally)
Act 3 Nè mai dunque (Wally)

FRANCESCO CAVALLI
(b. Crema 14.2.1602; d. Venice 14.1.1676)

Cavalli, along with a number of others, among whom Pietro Antonio Cesti was prominent, kept Venetian opera's supremacy intact after the death of Monteverdi ». He took his name from his patron, a Venetian nobleman, his name at birth being Caletti-Bruni. He sang under Monteverdi at St Mark's and in 1640 became second organist at that church, rising to first organist in 1665 and *maestro di cappella* from 1668. Cavalli composed a good deal of church music, but virtually none of it has survived. His operas are a different matter: he wrote some 42 in all, of which 28 have survived in score. The most famous is *Giasone*, with *Ciro* a close second. However, neither is recorded: the two that have that distinction having been carefully (and brilliantly) edited for productions at Glyndebourne by Raymond Leppard. Cavalli's first opera, *Le Nozze di Teti e di Peleo*, was performed in 1639 at the Teatro San Cassiano, Venice, where most of his operas were produced and where he lived. In the middle of his life, Cavalli's reputation was diminished by a change in popular taste: Cesti's work made a more direct appeal to audiences desiring easier entertainment than Cavalli and his like normally provided. The consequent style depended largely on an increase in the number and quality of arias and ariettas at the expense of recitatives, and thus a diminution in dramatic tension and continuity.

L'Ormindo
Opera in 2 Acts.
Text by Giovanni Battista Faustini.
First performance: Venice (Teatro San Cassiano) 1644.

Synopsis:
The opera is set in North Africa and concerns the amatory manouevres of Ormindo, Prince of Tunis, and Amida, Prince of Tramisene, who compete for the favours of Erisbe, Queen of Morocco and Fez and wife of King Ariadeno. The plot is complicated by the passionate Sicle, Princess of Susio, who is disguised as an Arab fortune-teller and accompanied by Erice, her nurse. After many vicissitudes, Amida and Sicle are brought together.

Below: *Raymond Leppard and Jani Strasser at Glyndebourne during the* Ormindo *production.*

Above: *The libretto front of Catalani's La Wally.*

RECORDINGS:
Decca SET394/6 ●
London 1392 (3) (US)
Turin Lyric Chorus/Monte Carlo
National Orchestra
c. Fausto Cleva
Wally (s)   Renata Tebaldi
Stromminger (bs) Justino Diaz

Vincenzo
  Gellner (b)   Piero Cappuccilli
Giuseppe
  Hagenbach (t) Mario del Monaco
Afra (c)   Stefania Malagu (m-s)
Decca SET489 □
(from above)

HMV SLS869 □
Ebben? — Ne andro Lontana
Maria Callas (s)

CBS 76407 □
Ebben? — Ne andro Lontana
Renata Scotto (s)

Decca SXL6825 □
London 26497 (US)
Ebben? — Ne andro Lontana
Montserrat Caballé (s)

Decca SXL6864 □
London 26557 (US)
Ebben? — No andro Lontana
Maria Chiara (s)

Decca SXL6864 □
London 26557 (US)
Ne mai dunque
Maria Chiara (s)

Decca SDD287 □
London 25912 (US)
Ne mai dunque
Renata Tebaldi (s)

Loreley

Opera in 4 Acts.
Text by Zanardini.
First performance: Turin (Teatro Regio) February 16, 1890. London (Covent Garden) 1907; New York (Lexington Theatre) 1919.

Notes:

Like *La Wally*, this opera has strong associations with German Romanticism. Loreley, the legendary siren, is represented here a young orphan, jilted by her lover, Walter, Lord of Oberwessel. When Walter announces his intention of marrying Anna, Loreley casts her spell on him and Anna is jilted. Walter joins Loreley in a watery death and Anna dies of grief.

RECORDING:
Decca SXL6864 □
London 26557 (US)
Maria Chiara (s)

RECORDING:
Decca Argo ZNF8/10 ●
Argo ZNF8/10 (US)
London Philharmonic Orchestra/
Continuo Ensemble
c. Raymond Leppard
Ormindo (t)   John Wakefield
Amida (b)   Peter-Christoph Runge
Erisbe (m-s) Anne Howells
Sicle (s)   Hanneke van Bork
Erice (t)   Hugues Cuenod
Ariadeno (bs) Federico Davia

La Calisto

Opera in Prologue and 2 Acts.
Text by Giovanni Battista Faustini.
First performance: Venice (Teatro Sant' Apollinare) late 1651.

Synopsis:

Scene: Ancient Greece.
Prologue La Natura (Nature) and L'Eternità (Eternity) praise those who have ascended Parnassus. They object when Il Destino (Destiny) says that Jove has decreed that Calisto shall become one of the immortals.
Act 1 Jove and Mercury hope to restore nature on the wartorn earth. Jove seeks Mercury's help in winning Calisto, a nymph of Diana, who spurns his advances. At Mercury's suggestion, Jove transforms himself into the shape of the goddess Diana and lures Calisto away with him. Endimione (Endymion) laments his unrequited love for Diana, and the real goddess appears with the aged nymph Linfea. Calisto returns and, encountering the true goddess, is surprised to find her less affectionate than the imposter. Linfea broods on her virginity, but indignantly repulses the advances of a Satyr and of the god Pan.
Act 2 Diana admires the sleeping Endymion and kisses him: he awakes in her arms. The Satyr reports the affair to Pan. Juno, suspecting Jove's fidelity, comes to investigate: her suspicions are confirmed when she learns of Calisto's meeting with 'Diana' and overhears Jove making a new assignation with the nymph. Jove refuses to abandon his dalliance, abetted by Mercury, and Juno plans her revenge. Endymion meets the false 'Diana' and makes love to her: Jove is disconcerted. Endymion is taken prisoner by Pan and the Satyr, and the latter succeeds in seducing Linfea. While Calisto awaits Jove, Juno enters in a rage, accompanied by Furies, and transforms her into a small bear. Pan prepares to torture Endymion, but the real Diana comes to the rescue. Jove, now in his new shape, finds Calisto as a bear and takes her to Olympus, to shine forever in the heavens as the constellation Ursa Minor.

RECORDING:
Decca Argo ZNF11/12 ●
Argo ZNF11/12 (US)
Glyndebourne Festival Opera Chorus/
London Philharmonic Orchestra
c. Raymond Leppard
Calisto (s)   Ileana Cotrubas
Diana (m-s)   Janet Baker
Jove (b)   Ugo Trama
Linfea (t)   Hugues Cuenod
Endymion (c-t) James Bowman
Mercury (b)   Peter Gottlieb

EMMANUEL CHABRIER

(b. Ambert, Puy-de-Dôme 18.1.1841; d. Paris 13.9.1894)

Though he showed early musical gifts, which were recognised, Chabrier spent much of his life working in a Government Ministry. He took his degree in law and was for the rest of his life a musical amateur (in the best sense). But his natural gifts would not be subdued, and his compositions sparkle with Gallic exuberance and elegance. Best known for his orchestral pieces which are full of colour and vivacity, most notably the rhapsody *España*, he also wrote five operas (the last, *Briséis, ou les amants de Corinthe*, was unfinished at his death). The most famous is the brilliant comic opera *Le roi malgré lui*, although both *Gwendoline* and *Une Éducation manquée* contain excellent music, some of which is occasionally heard. Chabrier's operas have not been favoured on records, only some orchestral excerpts appearing with any regularity.

Une Éducation Manquée

Operetta in 1 Act.
Text by Eugène Leterrier and Albert Vanloo.
First performance: Paris (Théâtre des Arts) May 1, 1879. London 1961.

RECORDING:
Pathé CPTPM 130.575 (d) (Fr) ○
c. Jean-Claude Hartemann
Liliane Berton (s)
Jane Berbie (s)
Jean-Christoph Benoit (b)

Gwendoline

Opera in 2 Acts.
Text by Catulle Mendès.
First performance: Brussels (Théâtre de la Monnaie) April 10, 1886.

RECORDINGS:
HMV HQM1162 (d) □
Overture
c. Sir Thomas Beecham

Seraphim S-60108 (US) □
Overture
c. Pierre Dervaux

Mercury 75078 (US) □
Overture
c. Paul Paray

Le Roi Malgré Lui

Opera in 3 Acts.
Text by Emile de Najac and Paul Burani, based on a comedy by Francois Ancelot.
First performance: Paris (Opéra-Comique) May 18, 1887. Karlsruhe 1890. Prague 1931.

Above: Le Roi Malgré Lui *was a masterpiece, a model of good light opera, which deserves to be heard more often.*

RECORDINGS:
Decca JB10 □
London 6438 (US)
Orchestral excerpts
c. Ernest Ansermet

EMI ESD7046 □
c. Jean-Baptiste Mari
Orchestral excerpts

Mercury 75078 (US) □
Orchestral excerpts
c. Paul Paray

Below: *A scene from Chabrier's* Le Roi Malgré Lui *produced at L'Opéra-Comique in Paris, December 1959.*

GUSTAVE CHARPENTIER
(b. Dienze 25.6.1860; d. Paris 18.2.1956)

Studied at the Lille Conservatoire and then at the Paris Conservatoire in 1881. In 1885 he joined Massenet's » composition class and won the Prix de Rome in 1887 with *Didon*, a *scène lyrique*. From Rome came orchestral music—the successful *Impressions d'Italie*, and *La Vie du poète* (for soloists, chorus and orchestra)—and a fair amount of vocal music. Although he composed a great deal during a very long life, Charpentier is remembered by one work, the opera *Louise*, and for many years one aria kept his name alive, 'Depuis le jour'. He was an active worker and propagandist on behalf of the poor of Paris, especially the factory girls, and the founder of an academy for working girls, the Conservatoire Populaire de Mimi Pinson. He affected a Bohemian style of life and dress, fashionable at the time, and this was reflected in his music. *Julien*, a sequel to *Louise* which used material from the early *La Vie du poète*, was unsuccessful when it was produced at the Opéra-Comique in June, 1913.

Louise
Romance in 4 Acts.
Text by Charpentier.
First performance: Paris (Opéra-Comique) February 2, 1900. Brussels 1901; New York 1908; London (Covent Garden) 1909; New York (Metropolitan) 1921.

Synopsis:
Scene: Paris. Time: 1890s.
Act 1 Julien, a young man full of life and the artist's dreams of love and freedom, is serenading Louise. He loves her, but her mother, despising all artists, is against the match. Louise's father, however, is more reasonable; and Louise has asked Julien to write to him asking formal permission for the marriage. If he doesn't get it, she will elope with him.
Act 2 The streets of Montmartre are full of morning life and bustle. Julien tries to speak to Louise as she arrives at her work at the dressmaking factory, but she is accompanied by her mother, so Julien has to bide his time. In the second scene, Julien arrives outside the factory to serenade Louise who is being teased by her workmates. She must be in love, they giggle, seeing her silent and morose. Hearing Julien, she hurries out.
Act 3 Louise and Julien are living together in a house in Montmartre. Louise sings 'Depuis le jour' as the lights of Paris begin to shine in the dusk. Friends and locals join in celebrations. But Louise's mother comes to say that her father is dangerously ill and wants to see her; Louise goes only after her mother has promised Julien that she will return.
Act 4 Louise and her father are re-united. But the parents regard their promise that she can return to Julien as invalidated since she is living in sin. Louise sees the lights of Paris dim and hears the seductive voices of the city. Her father finally turns her out; the parents are left alone, bitter and resentful.

Well-known arias:
Act 3 Depuis le jour (Louise)

Right: *Marcel Journet was Le Père in productions of Charpentier's Louise at La Scala in 1923 and Covent Garden in 1928.*

Notes:
Louise represented what appeared at the time as a new and daring realism in musical theatre; and it is sometimes held that this realistic approach keeps the opera alive. However, it is more true to say that the 'realism' is the dated element, and it is the vein of true and passionate lyricism that still attracts. It is also claimed, with justice, that the real 'heroine' of *Louise* is the city of Paris.

RECORDINGS:
CBS 79302 (3) ●
Columbia M3-34207 (3) (US)
Ambrosian Opera Chorus/New
Philharmonia Orchestra
c. Georges Prêtre Ileana Cotrubas
Louise (s)
Julien (t)   Placido Domingo
La Mère
  (Mother) (m-s) Jane Berbié
Le Père
  (Father) (b)   Gabriel Bacquier

HMV SCLX 3846 (3) ●
Angel SX-3846 (3) (US)
Children's Choir/French National Opera
Orchestra
c. Julius Rudel
Louise (s)   Beverly Sills
Julien (t)   Nicolai Gedda
La Mère (m-s)   Mignon Dunn
Le Père (b)   José van Dam

HMV SXLP30166 and P48 □
Depuis le jour
Maria Callas (s)

Decca SET454/5 □   Decca SXL6267 □
London 1286 (2) (US)   London 25999 (US)
Depuis le jour   Depuis le jour
Joan Sutherland (s) **Pilar Lorengar** (s)

Ember CVC58 □
Depuis le jour (in Italian)
Magda Olivero (s)

MARC-ANTOINE CHARPENTIER
(b. Paris 1634; d. Paris 24.2.1704)

This French-baroque composer, who studied with Carissimi and collaborated with Molière on dramatic projects, is best remembered for his choral music, notably the sonorous *Te Deum* and the delightful *Messe de minuit* for Christmas night. He quarrelled with Lully », who largely overshadowed him during his lifetime. In 1679 he became church composer to the Dauphin and afterwards composition teacher to the Duke of Orleans. He composed many works for the theatre, of which *Médée*, called a *tragédie lyrique*, is the best known and is his one true opera.

Médée
Opera in Prologue and 4 Acts.
Text by Corneille.
First performance: Paris, December 4, 1693.

RECORDINGS:
Brunswick AXTL1049 (d) ■   L'Oiseau-Lyre SOL300 □
Vocal and Instrumental Ensemble Oiseau S300 (US)
c. Nadia Boulanger   Suite
Irma Kolassi (m-s)   English Chamber Orchestra
Paul Derenne (t)   c. Raymond Leppard
Nadine Sautereau (s)

LUIGI CHERUBINI
(b. Florence 14.9.1760; d. Paris 15.3.1842)

A most influential and serious-minded musician, Cherubini was the man Beethoven » considered (after himself) as the greatest living composer. Cherubini spent a large part of his life in Paris and is generally considered as a composer of the French school with Italian ancestry. He studied first with his father and then with Giuseppe Sarti in Venice. He spent the years 1785/6 in London in the service of George III, but two years later settled permanently in Paris, being appointed to the Royal Chapel in 1816, and becoming Director of the Paris Conservatoire in 1822. He produced some of his early works, including operas, during the period of the French Revolution. In 1805 he went to Vienna, where he met Beethoven. On his return to France, Cherubini was embittered and out of favour. He lived for ten years on the country estate of the Prince de Chimay where he composed church music, the form which occupied the latter part of his life. Still, he was a prolific composer in all forms, and wrote a great number of large scale works, including many operas. Only one, *Médée*, has retained anything like general popularity. In spite of attempts by devotees to restore the bulk of his music, Cherubini remains primarily a historical rather than a living presence.

Demofonte (Démophoon)
Opera in 3 Acts.
Text by Jean François Marmontel.
First performance: Paris (Opéra) December 5, 1788.

RECORDING:
Decca SDD206 □
Ah che forse la miei di
Teresa Berganza (s)

Médée
Opera in 3 Acts.
Text by Francois Benoit Hoffmann.
First performance: Paris (Théâtre Feydeau) March 13, 1797. Berlin (in German) 1800; London (Her Majesty's) (in Italian) 1865.

Synopsis:
Scene: Ancient Greece. Time: antiquity.
Act 1 Medea, in love with Jason, has followed him to Greece. But Jason is more interested in Glauce, daughter of Creon, King of Corinth, and Medea is banished, though her two sons are to be brought up at the Corinthian court.

Act 2 Medea later appears at the wedding of Jason and Glauce, and tries to win Jason back before it is too late, but is banished again. She plans revenge and sends Glauce a poisoned garment, leaving Jason in despair at his bride's death.

Act 3 Jason's grief simply hardens Medea's resolve for vengeance. She kills her two sons, throwing Jason deeper in despair when, surrounded by three Furies, she tells him what she has done. She sets fire to the temple, causing terror throughout the city.

Below: *A scene from Charpentier's Médée in Beckman's production at the Paris Opéra in 1961.* **Right:** *Giuditta Pasta in the title role of* Médée, *in an Italian production.*

FRANCESCO CILEA
(b. Palmi, Calabria, 26.7.1866; d. Varazza 20.11.1950)

It was due to the good offices of Verdi's » friend, librarian at the Naples Conservatoire, Francesco Florimo, that the young Cilea seriously embarked upon a musical career. He entered the Naples Conservatoire in 1881 and produced his first opera, *Gina*, in 1881 while still a student. This led to a successful career as composer and pianist. His second opera, *La Tilda*, was commissioned by the publisher Sonzogno as a result of the success of *Gina* and was produced at the Teatro Pagliano, Florence, in 1892. Cilea was appointed professor at the Reale Instituto Musicale in Florence in 1896 and remained there for eight years. Cilea's operas have always maintained popularity in Italy; but only one, *Adriana Lecouvreur*, won him real fame abroad and has remained in general circulation. He was one of several musicians to base a composition on Alphonse Daudet's play *L'Arlésienne* (in Cilea's version, an opera in 4 Acts subsequently reduced to 3, it becomes *L'Arlesiana*).

L'Arlesiana
Opera in 4 Acts.
Text by Leopold Marenco, based on the drama by Alphonse Daudet.
First performance: Milan (Teatro Lirico) November 27, 1897.

RECORDINGS:
HMV ALP1620 □
E la solita storia
Jussi Bjorling (t)

Decca GOS634/5 □
London 12101 (2) (US)
E la solita storia
Jussi Bjorling (t)

RCA LSB4106 □
E la solita storia
Jon Vickers (t)

Decca SXL6498 □
E la solita storia
Luciano Pavarotti (t)

RCA SER5613 □
RCA LSC3083 (US)
E la solita storia
Placido Domingo (t)

Decca SXL6152 □
Esser madre e un inferno
Renata Tebaldi (s)

Adriana Lecouvreur
Opera in 4 Acts.
Text by Arturi Colautti after Scribe.
First performance: Milan (Teatro Lirico) November 6, 1902. London (Covent Garden) 1904; New York (Metropolitan) 1907.

Synopsis:
Scene: Paris. Time: 19th century.
Act 1 After a busy opening scene in the Green Room of the Comédie Française the Prince de Bouillon reads a letter during the ensuing performance which hints at an assignation that night. The Prince suspects his mistress, one of the actresses. But it is really his own wife who is involved, who plans to meet Maurizio, Count of Saxony.

Act 2 When the Prince and L'Abate de Chazeuil go to the appointed place, they find no Princess, but only Maurizio. However, the Count realises neither of them know it is the Princess he is involved with, so he lets the others believe he is

Medea
1825

Notes:

Most modern performances of *Médée* use the edition made by Franz Lachner in 1855, with interpolated recitatives (originally in German). This edition is used in the recordings. The Cetra record, though 'complete' in the larger sense, contains substantial cuts.

RECORDINGS:

Cetra Opera Live LO36 (3) (m) (r. 1955) ○
Chorus and Orchestra of La Scala, Milan
c. Leonard Bernstein
Medea (Médée) (s)   Maria Callas
Jason (t)   Gino Penno
Glauce (s)   Maria Luisa Nache
Creon (bs)   Guiseppe Modesti

Columbia SAX2290/2 (d) ○
Mercury SR3-9000 (3) (d) (US)
Chorus and Orchestra of La Scala, Milan
c. Tullio Serafin
Medea (s)   Maria Callas
Jason (t)   Mario Picchi
Glauce (s)   Renata Scotto
Creon (bs)   Giuseppe Modesti

Decca SET376/8 (d) ○
London 1389 (3) (US)
Chorus and Orchestra of Academia di Santa Cecilia, Rome
c. Lamberto Gardelli
Medea (s)   Gwyneth Jones
Jason (t)   Bruno Prevedi
Glauce (s)   Pilar Lorengar
Creon (bs)   Justino Diaz

Decca SET476 □
(from above)

Hungaroton SLPX11904/6 ○★
Budapest Symphony Orchestra
c. Lamberto Gardelli
Medea (s)   Sylvia Sass
Jason (t)   Veriano Luchetti
Glauce (s)   Veronica Kincses
Creon (bs)   Kolos Kováts

Supraphon 110 0568 □
Overture
c. Jiri Ptacnik

Odyssey Y-32358 (US) □
Columbia Symphony Orchestra
Various including
Farrell, Turp

Decca SDD193 □
Ebben, tutto mi manca . . . Solo un pianto
Teresa Berganza (s)

Anacreon

Opera in 3 Acts.
Text by R. Mendouze.
First performance: Paris (Opéra) October 4, 1803.

RECORDING:

Decca SXL6320 □
London STS-15073 (US)
Overture
c. Karl Münchinger

L. Cherubini (signature)

---

meeting the Prince's mistress. Adriana Lecouvreur appears. She, too, has received an anonymous note; she discovers that Maurizio, her lover, is in fact the Count of Saxony and he has been deceiving her.

Act 3   Adriana is curious to know who the other woman is. She has her suspicions and during a ball in the Prince's house, she skilfully quizzes the Princess.

Act 4   Back at the Comédie Française it is Adriana's birthday. Among her presents is a bunch of poisoned violets. She recognises them as some she had previously given to Maurizio, from whom she demands to know the truth. But the poison is doing its work; she becomes delirious, collapses and dies in the Count's arms. To Maurizio's horror, the Prince's revenge is complete.

Well-known arias:

Act 1   Io sono l'umile ancella (Adriana)
Adriana — La dolcissima effigie (Maurizio)
Act 4   Poveri fiori (Adriana)

RECORDINGS

CBS Masterworks 79310 (3) ●
Columbia M3-34588 (3) (US)
Ambrosian Opera Chorus/Philharmonia Orchestra
c. James Levine
Adriana
  Lecouvreur (s)   Renata Scotto
Maurizio (t)   Placido Domingo
Prince (bs)   Giancarlo Luccardi
Princess (m-s)   Elena Obraztsova
Abate di
  Chazeuil (t)   Florindo Andreolli

Decca SET221/3 ○
London 13126 (US)
Chorus and Orchestra of Academia Santa Cecilia, Rome
c. Franco Capuana
Adriana
  Lecouvreur (s)   Renata Tebaldi
Maurizio (t)   Mario del Monaco
Prince (bs)   Silvio Mainico
Princess (m-s)   Giulietta Simionata

Decca SXL6017 ■
London 25715 (US)
(from above)

Decca SXL6864 □
London 26557 (US)
Io sono l'umile ancella
Sete voi non aveste—Poveri fiori
Maria Chiara (s)

Ember GVC53 □
Io sono l'umile ancella
Sete voi non aveste—Poveri fiori
Magda Olivero (s)

HMV SLS869 □
Io sono l'umile ancella
Maria Callas (s)

Decca SXLR669 □
London 26497 (US)
Io sono l'umile ancella
Montserrat Caballé (s)

Decca SDD391 □
London 25075 (US)
Adriana—La dolcissima effige
L'anima ho stanca
Carlo Bergonzi (t)

Cilea: **ADRIANA LECOUVREUR**
Renata TEBALDI
Mario del MONACO
Giulietta SIMIONATO
Giulio FIORAVANTI
FRANCO CAPUANA • Orchestra & Chorus of the Accademia di Santa Cecilia, Rome

DOMENICO CIMAROSA

(b. Aversa, Naples, 17.12.1749; d. Venice 11.1.1801)

An enormously prolific composer (his output included at least 76 operas) and hugely popular in his own time, Cimarosa is now remembered chiefly for a charming oboe concerto arranged by Arthur Benjamin, and the delicious comic opera *Il matrimonio segreto (The secret marriage)*. He studied in Naples with Sacchini » and Piccinni and immediately succeeded with his operas. In 1787 he went to St Petersburg in the service of the court of Catherine the Great, but it did not work out. On his way back from Russia he stopped off in Vienna where the Emperor Leopold II invited him to compose an opera— *Il matrimonio segreto*. The Emperor was so delighted with its first performance that he had a meal prepared for the company— and demanded the entire performance over again. Cimarosa was appointed to succeed Salieri » as Kapellmeister to the court, but the Emperor's death the same year ended Cimarosa's

tenure. He then returned to Naples and entered the King's service, but was imprisoned for his part in French revolutionary activities. On his release he headed for St Petersburg; but died at Venice on the way.

Il Fanatico per gli Antichi Romani

Opera in 2 Acts.
Text by Giovanni Palomba.
First performance: Naples (Teatro dei Fiorentini) Spring 1777.

RECORDING:
RCA Erato STU71059 □
Sinfonia
c. Armin Jordan

Below: *Cimarosa's* Il Matrimonio Segreto *so delighted Leopold II that he asked to hear the entire first performance again.*

I Due Baroni di Rocca Azura

Opera in 2 Acts.
Text by Giovanni Palomba.
First performance: Rome (Teatro Valle) February 1783.

RECORDING:
Hungaroton SLPX11585 □
c. Angelo Ephrikian
Overture

Il Matrimonio Segreto

Comic opera in 2 Acts.
Text by Giovanni Bertati after the comedy by George Colman and David Garrick.
First performance: Vienna (Burg Theatre) February 7, 1792. Prague 1792; Leipzig 1792; London 1794; New York 1834.

Synopsis:
Act 1 Geronimo, a wealthy merchant, has two daughters: the highly attractive Carolina and the plain Elisetta. He is determined to find aristocratic husbands for both; but Carolina has secretly married Geronimo's clerk, Paolino, who in an attempt to gain favour with Geronimo, introduces Count Robinson to Elisetta. But Elisetta is really in love with Paolino while Count Robinson favours Carolina.
Act 2 A further complication arises with Aunt Fidalma, who sides with Elisetta but has more than a soft spot for Paolino. With the Count intending to marry Carolina, it is time for quick thinking, especially as the other two women decide the best thing is to send Carolina to a convent. So Paolino and Carolina plan to elope but they are interrupted and have to take refuge in Carolina's room. They are discovered by Elisetta, who thinks it is the Count up to no good. When all is revealed, Geronimo has to submit and pardon the young lovers and the Count takes on Elisetta.

RECORDINGS:
DG 2709 069 (3) ○
DG 2709 069 (3) (US)
English Chamber Orchestra
c. Daniel Barenboim
Geronimo (b) Dietrich Fischer-Dieskau
Carolina (s) Arleen Augér
Elisetta (s) Julia Varady
Fidalma (m-s) Julia Hamari
Il Conte
Robinson (bs) Alberto Rinaldi
Paolino (t) Ryland Davies

DG 2537 043 ■
(from above)

RCA Erato STU71059 □
RCA Erato STU71059 (US)
Sinfonia/Aris de Geronimo/Lausanne Chamber Orchestra
c. Armin Jordan
Philippe Huttenlocher (b)

Il Maestro di Capella

Intermezzo giocoso in 1 Act.
First performance: 1790.

Notes:
A brief comedy making fun of the trials of a pompous, conceited Kapellmeister and his difficulties with his colleagues. Although not an opera, complete recordings are available and we include it as an interesting example of Cimarosa's work.

RECORDINGS:
RCA Erato STU71059 ○
RCA Erato STU71059 (US)
Lausanne Chamber Orchestra
c. Armin Jordan
Philippe Huttenlocher (b)

Decca SXL2247 (d) ●
London 33217 (US)
Covent Garden Orchestra
c. Argeo Quadri
Fernando Corena (bs)

Hungaroton SLPX11585 ○
Solisti di Milano
c. Angelo Ephrikian
Gastone Sarti (b)

AARON COPLAND
(b. Brooklyn 14.11.1900)

Sometimes known as the 'Dean of American music', Copland studied first with Rubin Goldmark then went to Paris to study with Nadia Boulanger. In 1924 he won a Guggenheim scholarship which enabled him to spend a further two years in Europe; this influence, combined with that of Stravinsky », jazz and American folk music, produced a crisp and pointful musical style. Copland has written a good deal for the theatre (though more ballet than opera) and film music. His only true opera, *The Tender Land*, is a characteristic piece in his American rustic style. *The Second Hurricane* (1937), a school opera, was first performed at the Henry Street Music School, New York, by a cast of 150 children. It concerns the efforts of a small group of children to bring relief to flood victims, to a libretto by Edwin Denby. There is also a puppet show, *From Sorcery to Science*, written in 1939. As well as composing, Copland has done much writing and campaigning on behalf of American music.

The Tender Land
Folk opera in 1 Act.
Text by Horace Everett.
First performance: New York, April 1, 1954.

Synopsis:
Two drifters, Martin and Top, reach a small farm in the American mid-west. The daughter, Laurie, falls in love with Top and they plan to elope, but Martin persuades his friend against it and the two men flee, leaving Laurie in great distress, until she begins to formulate new ideas about her life and the necessity of leaving home to find freedom.

Notes:
The Tender Land was commissioned by Richard Rodgers and Oscar Hammerstein to celebrate the 30th anniversary of the American League of Composers in 1954.

RECORDINGS:
CBS SBRG72218 (d) ○
Columbia CMS-6814 (d) (US)
Choral Art Society/New York
Philharmonic Orchestra
c. Aaron Copland
Laurie (s) Joy Clements
Martin (b) Richard Fredericks
Top (t) Richard Cassilly

RCA GL42705 □
RCA LSC-2401 (US)
Orchestral suite
c. Aaron Copland

Below: *Aaron Copland, born in 1900, is sometimes known as 'the Dean of American music', and is that country's best known composer.*

PETER CORNELIUS
(b. Mainz 24.12.1824; d. Mainz 26.10.1874)

Cornelius began his working life as an actor and started his musical career fairly late. He became interested in the New German School of opera and enthusiastically championed the ideals of Wagner » and Liszt, its chief exponents. Cornelius is mainly remembered for a few short vocal pieces, but wrote one substantial comic opera, *Der Barbier von Bagdad*, which had no success in his lifetime but became well known some 27 years later; one serious opera *Der Cid*, equally unsuccessful; and left a third, *Gunlöd*, unfinished. In 1865 he became Professor at the Royal Academy of Music in Munich, whose principal was Hans von Bülow.

Der Barbier von Bagdad
Comic Opera in 2 Acts.
Text by Peter Cornelius, based on 'The Arabian Nights'.
First performance: Weimar, December 15, 1858. Revived Hanover 1877. Karlsruhe 1884 (re-orchestrated by Mottl). New York (Metropolitan) 1890; London (Savoy) 1891. Original version revived in 1904.

Synopsis:
Act 1   Nureddin, a wealthy young man, is dying of love for Margiana, the Cadi's daughter. He recovers when Bostana, a relation of the Cadi, brings the news that Margiana will see him while her father is at prayer. To smarten himself up for the assignation, he is advised to send for Abul Hassan Ali Ebn Bekar, the best barber in Bagdad. Unfortunately the barber is so loquacious on the subject of his knowledge of the arts and sciences that Nureddin fears he may soon be too late for his appointment. He orders his servants to throw the barber out, but Abul chases them off with a knife. With tactful flattery, he at last gets the barber to work, explaining his haste to get to

Margiana. The barber is so moved by the situation that he offers to accompany Nureddin and has to be restrained by the servants.

Act 2   Margiana joyfully awaits her lover and is joined by the Cadi and Bostana. The Cadi is expecting an old rich suitor of Margiana's and has supplied a chest full of treasure. He leaves, and Nureddin and Margiana meet and join in a joyful duet, but suddenly the cries of a slave being punished are heard. Abul, watching outside the house, imagines Nureddin is being attacked and calls for help. The chest is emptied and Nureddin hidden inside just before Abul and his servants arrive. Bostana intimates that the body of Nureddin is in the chest and Abul, in sorrow, bids the servants carry the corpse away. The Cadi appears and imagines his treasure is being stolen. As he shouts 'Robbers' and Abul shouts 'Murder' confusion reigns with a battle for the chest which gives Nureddin a good shaking. The Caliph and his retinue arrive to see what is happening; calm is restored and the Cadi accuses Abul of theft. The chest is opened and Nureddin is discovered. The Cadi is persuaded that Nureddin is Margiana's only desired treasure and, with the encouragement of the Caliph, he blesses their marriage.

Notes:
Completed in 1858, the score was shown to Liszt, who produced it at Weimar. The performance was a fiasco following an organised demonstration and Liszt subsequently left Weimar. No other performance took place in the composer's lifetime. His friends believed it a worthy work and arranged a revival which was still unsuccessful; eventually Felix Mottl undertook a thorough revision and, performed at Karlsruhe, it was an enormous success at last. The opera has an excellent central character in the Barber, many fine songs including a delightful final quintet 'Salaam Aleikum', and a Mozartian overture.

RECORDING:
Columbia 33CX1400/1 (d) ●
Epic 90885/6 (d) (US)
Philharmonia Chorus and Orchestra
c. Erich Leinsdorf
Abul Hassan (bs) Oskar Czerwenka
Margiana (s)   Elisabeth Schwarzkopf
Nureddin (t)   Nicolai Gedda
The Caliph (b)   Hermann Prey
The Cadi (t)   Gerhard Unger
Bostana (c)   Grace Hoffman

Left: *Peter Cornelius, best known for Der Barbier von Bagdad.*

GORDON CROSSE
(b. Bury, Lancashire 1937)

Crosse based his earliest music on the models of Bartók » and Webern and found a strong source of inspiration in medieval music. He studied at the Accademia di Santa Cecilia in Rome for a time in 1962 and on his return undertook research in 15th century music. His association with the Workers' Educational Association from 1963 and with Benjamin Britten » through the Aldeburgh Festival led him to a special interest in writing music for children, and a succession of enjoyable choral works followed. The influence of Britten, especially of the opera *The Turn of the Screw*, is particularly clear in his first opera *Purgatory* (1966). A companion one-act opera *The Grace of Todd* followed in 1967, and *The Story of Vasco* was first performed at Sadler's Wells in 1974.

Purgatory
Opera in 1 Act.
Text based on the play by W. B. Yeats.
First performance: Cheltenham 1966.

Synopsis:
Before a ruined house, an Old Man is telling a Boy (his son) the story of the tragedies that happened in the house. He tells how his father married a well-to-do young girl and squandered all her money, eventually burning down the house when he was drunk. To avenge his mother, the son killed his father with a knife and ran away. It is the anniversary of the wedding and the ghost of the young girl, the mother, is seen at a window. The Boy now accuses his father of not giving him any of the money he took away and they struggle for the bag that contains it. The ghost of the grandfather appears at a window, drinking whisky. The Old Man, full of remorse, stabs the Boy and is left to his own purgatory.

RECORDING:
Argo ZRG810 ●
Royal Northern College of Music
Orchestra
c. Michael Lankester
The Boy (t)   Peter Bodenham
The Old Man (b)   Glenville Hargreaves

LUIGI DALLAPICCOLA
(b. Pisino, 3.2.1904; d. Florence 18.2.1975)

One of the most distinguished modern Italian composers, Luigi Dallapiccola studied at the Florence Conservatoire, where he was appointed professor in 1931. His hometown was within the boundaries of the Austro-Hungarian Empire, which meant he and his family spent the First World War at Graz. This was no great disadvantage to the young Dallapiccola as he was able to undertake a comprehensive study of German and Austrian music during this time. His own compositional style was strongly influenced by his association with Alban Berg » and, through Berg, with Schoenberg » and (especially) Webern. His own music subsequently became notable for its mixing of strict serial techniques with more traditional ones; but even his strictest music is informed with an Italian warmth, elegance and expressiveness. He became professor at Queen's College, New York, in 1956. An accomplished pianist, Dallapiccola also gave many recitals of contemporary works, often in consort with the violinist Materassi. It was these experiences which urged him towards the International Society for Contemporary Music (the ISCM). Dallapiccola wrote two operas, both original and dramatically effective. The first, *Volo di notte* (in 1 Act, based on the book by Antoine de Saint-Exupéry) was produced in Florence in May, 1940, the year of its composition. The second, *Il Prigioniero* (The Prisoner) has achieved wider circulation.

Il Prigioniero
Opera in Prologue and 1 Act.
Text by Dallapiccola after Villiers de l'Isle-Adam ('La Torture par l'espérance')
and Charles de Coster ('La Légende d'Eulenspiegel').
First performance: Florence (Teatro Communale) May 20, 1950. New York 1951.

Synopsis:
Scene: The Netherlands. Time: 16th century.
Prologue and Act 1 A Prisoner of the Spanish Inquisition is interviewed by an anonymous person and urged to tell his secrets and then escape. But is there such a thing as freedom under tyranny? The 'anonymous' person is, in fact, the Grand Inquisitor. The Prisoner escapes, but is caught and burned at the stake. Who has won?

Notes:
The resemblance of the theme to that of Goethe/Beethoven in *Egmont* is clear.

RECORDING:
Decca Headline HEAD10 ●
London 1166 (US)
University of Maryland Chorus/
National Symphony Orchestra of
Washington
c. Antal Dorati

Prisoner (bs) Maurizio Mazzieri
Madre (s) Giulia Barrera
Grand Inquisitor (t) Romano Emile

Below: *Luigi Dallapiccola, one of Italy's leading modern composers, writer of two operas.*

ALEXANDER DARGOMIZHSKY
(b. Tula 14.2.1813; d. St Petersburg 17.1.1869)

One of the lesser Russian nationalists, Dargomizhsky was a forerunner of 'The Mighty Five'. Tchaikovsky » named him a 'supreme example of the dilettante in music'; but although like several leading Russian composers he was mainly an amateur, he wrote a number of significant works and exerted an influence over the emergence of Russian national music later in the century. He wrote half a dozen operas, of which the best known is *Russalka* (or *The Water Sprite*) which is still performed in Russia. In *The Stone Guest*, orchestrated by Rimsky-Korsakov », he evolved a new kind of recitative and used Pushkin's text absolutely unchanged.

Russalka
Opera in 4 Acts.
Text by Alexander Dargomizhsky after Pushkin.
First performance: St Petersburg May 16, 1856. New York 1922; London (Covent Garden) 1931.

Notes:
Certain arias in this opera have always been great favourites with the world's leading singers. Chaliapin made a formidable impression as the Mad Miller in London in 1931; and there are others, partially represented by the following records of varying availability.

RECORDINGS:
Saga XID5050 (d) □
The young capricious wife
Olga Slobodskaya (s)
Ivor Newton (p)

HMV COLH100 (r. 1927) (d) □
Miller's Aria/Mad scene/Death of Miller
Feodor Chaliapin (b)

RCA VIC1221 □
Miller's Aria/Mad scene/Death of Miller
Alexander Kipnis (bs)

Below: *Chaliapin as the Mad Miller in Dargomizhky's Russalka, a part he played in London in 1931.*

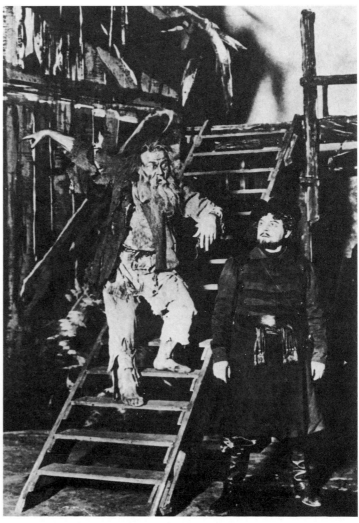

CLAUDE DEBUSSY
(b. Saint-Germain-en-Laye 22.8.1862; d. Paris 25.3.1918)

After taking lessons from one of Chopin's pupils, Mme Mauté de Fleurville, Debussy entered the Paris Conservatoire in 1873 where he studied with Lavignac, Marmontel and Durand. For two summers he was private musician to Nadezhda von Meck, the former patroness of Tchaikovsky ». In 1884 he won the Grand Prix de Rome with the cantata, or 'Scene Lyrique', *L'Enfant prodigue*. He began to find his artistic feet with the Rossetti setting (in French translation) *La Damoiselle élue* and became completely established with the orchestral *Prélude à l'après-midi d'un faune*. He was twice married, and in addition to his compositions he was a noted critic and musical journalist, being appointed music critic of *La Revue blanche* in 1901. For the last decade of his life Debussy suffered from cancer, which resulted in his death at 55 in 1918. He completed only one full opera, *Pélleas et Mélisande*, one of the supreme and most influential masterpieces of modern lyric theatre. But this is not Debussy's only dramatic work. There is the music he wrote for Gabriele d'Annunzio's *Le Martyre de saint Sébastien*; and *L'Enfant prodigue* has been presented as a one-act opera, though without marked success. Debussy continued to plan further operas until the end of his life, but none came to fruition. These include a version of the Tristan legend and one on Orpheus; a Shakespeare piece, *Comme il vous plaira* (As You Like It); and two based on stories by Edgar Allan Poe. Much of Debussy's non-stage music (the *Images*, *Nocturnes* and *La Mer* for orchestra; the *Préludes*, *Images*, *Estampes*, *Children's Corner* for piano in particular) is well known and widely popular.

Pélleas et Mélisande
Opera in 5 Acts.
Text by Maurice Maeterlinck from his play.
First performance: Paris (Opéra-Comique) April 30, 1902. Brussels 1907; New York (Metropolitan) 1908; London (Covent Garden) 1909.

Synopsis:
Scene: Kingdom of Allemonde. Time: Medieval.
Act 1 Golaud meets Mélisande while both are lost in the forest and takes her to his grandfather King Arkel's castle. They soon marry, but Mélisande then meets Golaud's younger half-brother Pelléas.
Act 2 Golaud has become suspicious that Mélisande and Pelléas are in love with each other, and after she loses her wedding ring by accident he insists that Pelléas should accompany her to look for it on the seashore.
Act 3 Becoming more suspicious, Golaud warns Pelléas to stay away from Mélisande, who is now pregnant, and interrogates his own child by a former marriage, Yniold, about their supposed relationship. Lifting Yniold on his shoulders to look into Mélisande's room, the child sees Pelléas there, and Golaud becomes inflamed with jealousy.

Act 4 Pelléas, hearing that his father is ill, begs Mélisande to come and see him before he leaves. When Goulaud hears that Pelléas is going, he confronts Mélisande and accuses her of having an affair with Pélleas, and beats her. She later goes to meet Pélleas, neither of them knowing that Golaud is hiding in the shadows, and eventually he steps out and kills Pelléas.
Act 5 Mélisande has been slightly wounded. Golaud begins to realise that his suspicions were unfounded; she confesses her love for Pelléas but insists on its innocence, and Golaud momentarily suffers a return of jealous rage, but in giving birth to a daughter Mélisande dies.

RECORDINGS:
CBS77324 (3) ●
Columbia M3-30119 (US)
Chorus and Orchestra of the Royal
Opera House, Covent Garden
c. Pierre Boulez
Pelléas (t) George Shirley
Mélisande (s) Elisabeth Söderström
Golaud (bs) Donald McIntyre
Arkel (bs) David Ward
Yniold (tr) Anthony Britten

Decca SET277/9 ●
London 1379 (3) (US)
Chorus of Grand Theatre, Geneva/
Orchestre de la Suisse Romande
c. Ernest Ansermet
Pelléas (t) Camille Maurane
Mélisande (s) Erna Spoorenberg
Golaud (b) George London
Arkel (bs) Guus Hoekman
Yniold (s) Rosine Bredy

Decca SET475 ■
(from above)

(Note: There are older, now deleted, complete recordings on Decca GOM46/48—previously LXT2711/4—with Mollet, Danco and Rehfuss, c. Ansermet; and on World Records OC210/2 with Jansen, de los Angeles and Souzay, c. Cluytens)

Below: *Elisabeth Söderström as Mélisande and David Ward as Arkel in Pélleas et Mélisande.*

Above: *Costume design for Pélleas for the Covent Garden production.*

Above: *Costume design by Charles Bianchini for Mélisande.*

LÉO DELIBES

(b. Saint-Germain-du-Val 21.2.1836; d. Paris 16.1.1891)

After studying at the Paris Conservatoire under Adolphe Adam
» Delibes held a number of appointments in the theatre and as
church organist, but in 1881 returned to the Conservatoire as
professor. Best known today as the composer of the two
popular and expert ballets, *Coppélia* and *Sylvia*, Delibes wrote
a series of lively operettas and a number of serious operas, one
of which, *Lakmé*, with its famous 'Bell Song', used to be a
favourite with coloratura sopranos and still holds its own in
France. Another Delibes opera, *Le Roi l'a dit* after Victor Hugo,
is one of these works that seems to hover on the brink of revival
without actually achieving it — at least outside France. The 5 Act
Kassya was completed by Massenet » after Delibes's death and
given at the Opéra-Comique in March, 1893.

Lakmé

Opera in 3 Acts.
Text by Edmond Gondinet and Philippe Gille after 'Le Mariage de Loti'.
First performance: Paris (Opéra-Comique) April 14, 1883. Frankfurt (in
German) 1833; London (Gaiety) 1885; New York (in English) 1886.

Left: *Some famous Lakmés — Lily*
Pons (l), Amelita Galli-Curci (r)
and Luisa Tetrazzini (c).

Synopsis:
Scene: British India. Time: 19th century.
Act 1   The British have forbidden the practice of Brahminism,
but Nilakantha, a Brahmin priest, maintains his temple with the
help of his daughter Lakmé. Two British officers, the Viceroy's
daughters and their governess, break into the temple gardens,
sightseeing, and one of the officers, Gerald, stays behind to
make sketches of some jewels. When Lakmé returns with her
companion Mallika to place flowers on the altar, Gerald
immediately falls in love with her. She implores Gerald to leave
before her father returns, as any intruder into the sacred place
must be killed.
Act 2   Nilakantha, furious at the desecration, swears vengeance.
In disguise he takes Lakmé to the bazaar in the hope of finding
his enemy. He tells Lakmé to sing, hoping that the hated one will
reveal himself. She sings the 'Bell Song' and Gerald gives himself
away. Nilakantha stabs him and, leaving him for dead, leaves,
but Lakmé finds he is not dead and has her servant take him
away to a hut in the forest.
Act 3   Gerald has recovered; he and Lakmé drink from a sacred
spring which is said to ensure eternal love. The other officer,
Frédéric, reappears to recall Gerald to his military duty; Lakmé,
realising that he will leave her, eats the flower of a poisonous
plant. Nilakantha appears and is about to kill Gerald, but
Lakmé tells him they have both drunk from the sacred spring
and if there is a sacrifice, it will be her. She dies in Gerald's arms.

Well-known arias:
Act 1   Blanche Dourga, pâle Siva (Invocation) (Lakmé)
            Dôme épais (Barcarolle) (Lakmé and Mallika)
Act 2   Où va la jeune Hindoue (Bell song) (Lakmé)

Notes:

This is a piece of much charm, but somewhat dated by its
general idiom and its 'orientalisms', of a kind much favoured in
the late 19th century. The original version was in the opéra-
comique tradition with spoken dialogue. Subsequently the
score was revised and the music made continuous; this is the
version nowadays heard, and used in recordings. The theme of
the impact of Western military personnel on the people of the
East anticipates, as do certain aspects of the music, Puccini's »
Madama Butterfly.

RECORDINGS:
Decca SET387/9 ●
London 1391 (3) (US)
Monte Carlo Opera Chorus and
Orchestra
c. Richard Bonynge
Lakmé (s)   Joan Sutherland
Gerald (t)   Alain Vanzo
Nilakantha (b) Gabriel Bacquier
Mallika (m-s) Jane Berbié
Mistress
  Benson (c)   Monica Sinclair

Decca SET488 (d) ■
London 26201 (US)
(from above)

Seraphim S-6082 (3) (US) ●
Chorus and Orchestra of the Paris
Opéra-Comique
c. Alain Lombard
Lakmé (s)   Mady Mesplé
Gérald (t)   Roger Soyer (b)
Nilakantha (b) Charles Burles (bs)

Decca LXT2738/40 (3) (d) ●
London A-4307 (3) (d) (US)
Chorus and Orchestra of the Paris
Opéra-Comique
c. Georges Sébastian
Lakmé (s)   Mado Robin
Gerald (t)   Libero de Luca
Nilakantha (b) Jean Borthayre
Mallika (m-s) Agnes Disney

(Note: The 1940 recording with Lily Pons
is also available DIS13/15)

Decca SXL2257 or SPA100 □
London 1214 (2) (US)
The Bell Song
Joan Sutherland (s)

HMV SLS5018 □
The Bell Song
Maria Callas (s)

FREDERICK DELIUS
(b. Bradford 29.1.1862; d. Grez-sur-Loing 10.6.1934)

Delius was born into a prosperous wool-trading family of German descent. It was also a musical family, though Delius was originally expected to follow a business career. When it was clear he was determined to become a musician, he was sent off to manage an orange grove in Florida, where he came under the important influence of Thomas Ward, organist at Jacksonville. Subsequently he studied at Leipzig. In 1887 he went to Norway and on his return to Leipzig met Grieg, whose advocacy was instrumental in persuading Delius's father that his son should devote his life to music. While at Leipzig Delius was deeply impressed by a great deal of music by Beethoven », Brahms, Wagner » and Tchaikovsky »—in spite of the legend that Delius despised all music but his own and that he had no time for 'academic' composers. From 1890 Delius lived in France, first in Paris and from 1897 at Grez-sur-Loing in the Seine-et-Marne district, beside the river which played so important a part in his creative work. In that year he married the painter Jelka Rosen. Delius composed six operas. Only two, *A Village Romeo and Juliet* and *Koanga*, have achieved any real popularity, though his last opera, *Fennimore and Gerda*, has been recorded and the first, *Irmelin*, was produced at Oxford under Sir Thomas Beecham, Delius's foremost interpreter and the man who did more than anyone to propagate the gospel of his art. It is worth noting that, in respect of his operas as of all his music, the long-held idea that Delius was primarily a harmonic composer somewhat deficient in melody, is way off the mark. The truth is that his melody and harmony are closely interwoven, totally interdependent, the rich harmonies a continual seedbed for long weaving strands of melody, the melody provoking richness of harmony. Only in this interaction of melody and harmony does the music of Delius ultimately fulfil itself. During the last years of his life Delius was blind and paralysed. But his mind remained active to the end and he was able to continue composing through the devoted services of Eric Fenby, who acted as his amanuensis from 1928 until Delius's death in 1934.

Irmelin
Opera in 3 Acts. (Written 1890-92.)
Text by Delius.
First performance: Oxford (New Theatre) May 4, 1953.

RECORDINGS:
HMV ASD2305 □
Angel 5-36415 (US)
Prelude
c. Sir John Barbirolli

RCA RL25079 □
Prelude
c. Norman del Mar

World Records SHB32 (m) (5) □
Seraphim S-60000 (US)
Prelude
c. Sir Thomas Beecham

Koanga
Opera in Prologue, 3 Acts and Epilogue.
Text by C. F. Keary after George Washington Cable's 'The Grandissime'.
First performance: Elberfeld (Municipal Theatre) March 30, 1904. London (Covent Garden) 1935.

Synopsis:
Scene: A plantation on the Mississippi. Time: late 18th century.
Prologue The young daughters of the planters, during a pause in celebration dancing, ask the old servant, Uncle Joe, to tell them one of his stories. An orchestral interlude paints a soundscape of Louisiana as setting for the tale.
Act 1 The mulatto girl Palmyra is singing about her life on the plantation when a cow-horn summons the slaves to another day's toil in the sugar-cane fields. The foreman, Simon Perez, starts pestering her, until the owner, Don José Martinez, enters. A new batch of slaves has arrived, and among them is Koanga, an African prince and Voodoo priest, in chains. Lamenting his fate, Koanga refuses to work; but he and Palmyra are drawn to each other, and Don José promises her to Koanga if he will work. The wedding is arranged, to the rage of Perez. There is a quintet for the principal characters. A secret about Palmyra's

Above: *One of the last pictures of Delius, taken at his French home.*

birth, known only to Don José's wife Clotilda, is not yet revealed.
Act 2 The secret is that Palmyra is the natural daughter of Clotilda's father. Clotilda tells Simon Perez and begs him to prevent the wedding. He agrees. Meanwhile the slaves prepare celebrations both for the wedding and for Don José's birthday. Dancing and singing, Palmyra and Koanga pledge their souls and Koanga renounces his past and accepts his slavery for love of her. Palmyra is temporarily separated from Koanga and is abducted by Perez and his men; Koanga demands her return, but Don José refuses. Koanga threatens to bring down the curse of Voodoo and disappears into the forest.
Act 3 A prelude invokes the swamp at dusk. The slaves, frightened, await the coming of the curse by Koanga and another Voodoo priest, Rangwan. Blood is poured on a fire as the slaves gash themselves in a frenzied dance of foreboding. Koanga imagines he hears Palmyra's lament and calls on the morning star to lead her back to him. Don José promises revenge on Koanga if the slaves will return to work. Koanga catches Perez trying to kiss Palmyra and kills him, but is caught by Don José's men and tortured. He dies beside Palmyra, who stabs herself.
Epilogue The tale told, the daughters of the plantation watch the dawn break and sunlight floods the scene.

Well-known excerpt:

Act 2 La Calinda (also heard in the early *Florida Suite*) appears at the end of the Act.

Notes:

Koanga is a legacy of Delius's years in Florida. For the HMV recording below, the text was revised by Douglas Craig and Andrew Page.

RECORDINGS:

HMV SLS974 (2) ●
Angel SX3808 (2) (US)
John Alldis Choir/London Symphony Orchestra
c. Sir Charles Groves

Koanga (b)	Eugene Holmes
Palmyra (s)	Claudia Lindsey
Don José	
Martinez (bs)	Raimund Herincx
Simon Perez (t)	Keith Erwen
Clotilda (c)	Jean Allister
Uncle Joe (bs)	Simon Estes

World Records SHB32 (5) □
Final Scene/La Calinda
London Select Choir/London Philharmonic Orchestra
c. Sir Thomas Beecham

HMV ASD2477 □
Angel S-36588 (US)
La Calinda
c. Sir John Barbirolli

Decca Argo ZRG875 □
La Calinda
c. Neville Marriner

A Village Romeo and Juliet

Lyric Drama in Six Scenes.
Text by Jelka Delius after Gottfried Keller's 'Romeo und Julia auf dem Dorfe'.
First performance: Berlin (Komische Oper) February 21, 1907. London (Covent Garden) 1910.

Synopsis:

Scene: Seldwyla, Switzerland. Time: 19th century.
Scene 1 Manz and Marti, two wealthy farmers, are ploughing their land on a fine September morning. Between them lies a strip of deserted (and disputed) land. Their children, Sali and Vrenchen, appear with their lunch. Then a man with a violin, the Dark Fiddler, appears: he is the rightful heir to the waste land, but being of doubtful parentage cannot inherit. He tells the children to play on his land and no harm will come to them until it goes under the plough. Their fathers quarrel and forbid them to play together.
Scene 2 Six years later, the family quarrels have led to mutual ruin. Sali and Vrenchen meet again at one of the derelict farms and recall their happy childhood, but realise they are no longer children.
Scene 3 The Dark Fiddler reappears and tells the young lovers how his curse has brought ruin and animosity into their lives. Sali does not believe the Fiddler means them harm, but Vrenchen is afraid. Marti has come to spy on his daughter; seeing her and Sali together, he tries to separate them by force. Sali strikes him, causing serious injury.
Scene 4 Sali and Vrenchen love each other more than ever and decide to go out into the world together. They fall asleep in each other's arms and dream that they are being married in the church of Seldwyla.
Scene 5 It is the day of the fair at Berghald. Sali and Vrenchen go there together, are recognised and become increasingly uncomfortable. Slowly they leave the fair and walk to the Paradise Garden.
Scene 6 Everything in the garden has run wild. There is an inn, a haybarge moored by the river bank, itinerant musicians and women sitting at tables. The Dark Fiddler is there, at first standing apart; when he joins the others he tells how his land was forfeited and of the hatred it led to. When Sali and Vrenchen come into view, the Fiddler and the others drink their

health. In a glow of evening light, a bargee's song is heard. Sali and Vrenchen make their choice: one moment of true happiness, and then oblivion. The Dark Fiddler plays wildly on his violin, the young lovers go to their marriage bed of hay on the barge. Sali pulls out the plug from the bottom of the barge and throws it away; the barge drifts off down the river and slowly sinks.

RECORDINGS:

HMV SLS966 (2) ●
Angel S-3784X (2) (US)
John Alldis Choir/Royal Philharmonic Orchestra
c. Meredith Davies

Manz (b)	Benjamin Luxon
Marti (b)	Noel Mangin
Sali (as child) (tr)	Corin Manley
Sali (t)	Robert Tear
Vrenchen	
(as child) (s)	Wendy Eathorne
Vrenchen (s)	Elizabeth Harwood
Dark Fiddler (b)	John Shirley-Quirk

HMV ASD2305 □
Angel S-36588 (US)
Walk to the Paradise Garden
c. Sir John Barbirolli

Decca Eclipse ECS633 □
Walk to the Paradise Garden
c. Anthony Collins

World Records SHB32 (5) □
Walk to the Paradise Garden
c. Sir Thomas Beecham

Decca Argo ZRG875 □
Walk to the Paradise Garden
c. Neville Marriner

Fennimore and Gerda

Music drama in 11 Pictures.
Text by Delius after Jens Peter Jacobsen's novel 'Niels Lyhne'.
First performance: Frankfurt, October 21, 1919.

Synopsis:

Fennimore is betrothed to Erik, a painter, whose friend Niels is also in love with her. Niels goes away for Erik's sake but the marriage of Fennimore and Erik is not a success: Erik prefers to spend time with his friends, the 'Boon companions', rather than at his easel. Fennimore, feeling neglected, asks Niels to intervene; Erik tells his friend he lacks inspiration, and Niels suggests travel as a way of broadening his senses. However, the 'Boon companions' maintain their hold on Erik and he accompanies them to a fair. Niels has sworn eternal fidelity to Fennimore and their old love reawakens, but while she is waiting for him a telegram arrives saying that Erik has been killed in a road accident. Full of guilt and anguish, Fennimore blames herself and Niels. The final picture shows Niels and Gerda, a new, pretty, teenage sweetheart, living happily on Niels's farm at harvest time.

Notes:

This opera is something of an oddity, in that the Gerda of the title does not appear until the end and plays no part in the dramatic action. The 11 'pictures' are linked by orchestral interludes which contain some of Delius's best music.

RECORDINGS:

HMV SLS991 (2) ●
Angel SX3835 (2) (US)
Danish Radio Chorus and Symphony Orchestra
c. Meredith Davies

Fennimore (s)	Elisabeth Söderström
Gerda (s)	Elisabeth Söderström
Niels Lyhne (b)	Brian Rayner Cook
Erik Refstrup (t)	Robert Tear

HMV ASD357 □
Intermezzo
c. Sir Thomas Beecham

RCA RL25079 □
Intermezzo
c. Norman del Mar

DG 25300 505 □
DG 25300 505 (US)
Intermezzo
c. Daniel Barenboim

World Records SHB32 (5) □
Intermezzo
c. Sir Thomas Beecham

Decca Argo ZRG875 □
Intermezzo
c. Neville Marriner

GAETANO DONIZETTI
(b. Bergamo 29.11.1797; d. Bergamo 8.4.1848)

This talented and industrious man was once thought to have been of Scottish descent (due partly to his predilection for Scots subjects for his operas); but this theory was disproved some time ago. Donizetti studied first at the Instituto Musicale of his native Bergamo and then at the Liceo Filharmonico in Bologna, under Mattei. He began writing operas early in his career, and after three unperformed works began his career proper with *Enrico di Borgogna* which was produced in Venice at the Teatro San Luca on November 14, 1818. Thereafter he composed operas prolifically, producing over 70 before he died, paralysed and the victim of melancholia, in the town where he was born. Donizetti, like his contemporaries Bellini » and Rossini », wrote for the great race of *bel canto* singers of that era, such as Rubini, Pasta and Grisi, and his musical style reflects those circumstances even more than Bellini's. It is sometimes facile, often superficial; yet he had a genuine dramatic gift and was a thoroughly trained musician who could handle any task to which he set his hand. Because of the decline of the type of singers and singing for which his work was designed, his operas fell into neglect for a considerable period. There were always exceptions, like *Lucia di Lammermoor* and the delectable comedies *Don Pasquale* and *L'elisir d'amore*; and the modern revival, led by the late Maria Callas, of true *bel canto* has readjusted the perspectives. But the large bulk of his operatic productions has sunk into history and will probably not surface again except in excerpt form on various recordings.

Above: *Gaetano Donizetti, composer of over 70 operas.*

Emilia di Liverpool
Opera in 2 Acts.
Text by unknown person, revised Giuseppe Checcherini, based on a melodrama by Scatizzi.
First performance: Naples (Teatro Nuovo) July 28, 1824. Revised version Naples (Teatro Nuovo) Lent 1828.

RECORDING:
Ember GVC45 □
Everest 3293 (US)
Cavatina and Rondo Finale
Joan Sutherland (s)

Anna Bolena
Opera in 2 Acts.
Text by Felice Romani.
First performance: Milan (Teatro Carcano) 26.12.1830. London 1831; New York 1843.

Act 1 Scene 1: King Henry VIII (Enrico), in love with Jane Seymour (Giovanna), plans to denounce his wife Anne Boleyn as an adultress and marry Jane instead. Scene 2: Richard, Lord Percy (Riccardo) is recalled from exile to give evidence of the Queen's infidelity, for he was once in love with her (and confesses he still is). Scene 3: Henry eventually accuses Anne of having an affair with Smeaton, a page.
Act 2 Scene 1: Anne awaits trial and Smeaton, under torture, confesses to having had an affair with her. Scene 2: Anne rejects the charges, but admits she was once in love with Percy. Scene 3: She is condemned, and loses her reason. Smeaton admits he accused Anne falsely under torture, but the execution is still to proceed. Bells and cannon acclaim the new Queen, and Anne makes a passionate denunciation.

Well-known arias:
Act 1 Guidi, ad Anna . . . Ah, segnata è la mia sorte (Anna)
Act 2 Piangete voi? . . . Al dolce guidami (Anna)

Notes:
In most modern productions the structure is altered to move Act 1, Scene 3 into Act 2. *Anna Bolena* was one of the leading vehicles for the late Maria Callas, who revived the art of *bel canto* in the 1950s. It was also the opera in which she made her triumphant return to the Italian stage after the scandal during a performance of Bellini's » *Norma* in 1957, when, ill and unable to continue, she withdrew after the first Act and was accused of insulting the President.

RECORDINGS:
Decca SET446/9 ●
London 1436 (4) (US)
Vienna State Opera Chorus and Orchestra
c. Silvio Varviso
Anna Bolena (s) Elena Suliotis
Enrico (bs) Nicolai Ghiaurov
Giovanna (m-s) Marilyn Horne
Riccardo (t) John Alexander

Decca SET522 ■
(from above)

Cetra Opera Live LO53 (3) (r. 1957) ○
Chorus and Orchestra of La Scala, Milan
c. Gianandrea Gavazzeni
Anna Bolena (s) Maria Callas
Enrico (bs) Nicola Rossi-Lemeni
Giovanna (m-s) Giulietta Simionato
Riccardo (t) Gianni Raimondi

HMV SLS878 (4) (d) ●
ABC ATS20015 (4) (US)
John Alldis Choir/London Symphony Orchestra
c. Julius Rudel
Anna Bolena (s) Beverly Sills
Enrico (bs) Paul Plishka
Giovanna (m-s) Shirley Verrett
Riccardo (t) Stuart Burrows

Decca SXL6548 □
London 26262 (US)
Piangete voi . . . A dolce guidami
Maria Chiara (s)

Ugo, Conte di Parigi
Opera in 2 Acts.
Text by Felice Romani.
First performance: Milan (La Scala) March 13, 1832.

Synopsis:
Scene: Paris. Time: 10th century.
Act 1 Folco of Anjou plans to create a rivalry between the recently crowned King Louis V (Luigi) and the famous soldier Ugo, so that the crown may be won for the house of Anjou. Ugo, however, is loyal to Louis. The King's fiancée Bianca secretly loves Ugo and despises Louis, but has a rival for Ugo's affections in her sister Adelia. Louis blesses the match between Adelia and Ugo but the jealous Bianca now declares her love for Ugo and

potions', which are no more than cheap wine, thinly disguised. Nemorino drinks some, and immediately becomes inebriated — and bolder. The army troop is ordered to move on and the Sergeant wants to marry Adina quickly; Nemorino is too drunk to do anything to prevent it.

Act 2   Nemorino enlists with the troop to obtain some money, with which he buys more 'elixir' and breaks up the wedding festivities with loud boasts. Adina secures Nemorino's discharge from the troop and faints in his arms. All ends well; Nemorino comes to his senses, Dulcamara sells out, and the Sergeant puts a brave face on his misfortune and departs for the wars.

Well-known arias:
Act 1   Quanto è bella (Nemorino)
Chiedi all'aura lusinghiera (Adina and Nemorino)
Udite, udite, o rustici (Dulcamara)
Act 2   Una furtiva lagrima (Nemorino)
Prendi, prendi, per me sei libero (Adina)

RECORDINGS:
Decca SET503/5 ★ ●
London 13101 (3) (US)
Ambrosian Singers/English Chamber
Orchestra
c. Richard Bonynge
Adina (s)   Joan Sutherland
Nemorino (t)   Luciano Pavarotti
Sergeant Belcore (b) Dominic Cossa
Dulcamara (bs)   Spiro Malas

Decca SET564 ■
London 26343 (US)
(from above)

Left: *A performance of Donizetti's best comic opera, L'Elisir d'Amore.*

Decca Ace of Diamonds GOS566/7 ●
London 63524 (3) (US)
Maggio Musicale Fiorentino
c. Francesco Molinari-Pradelli
Adina (s)   Hilde Gueden
Nemorino (t)   Giuseppe di Stefano
Sergeant Belcore (b) Renato Capecchi
Dulcamara (bs)   Fernando Corena

London 33231 (US) ■
(from above)

Supraphon 112 0621/3 ●
Czech Philharmonic Chorus/Prague
Chamber Orchestra
c. Ino Savini
Adina (s)   Fulvia Ciano
Nemorino (T)   Ferrucio Tagliavini
Sergeant Belcore (b) Giani Maffeo
Dulcamara (bs)   Giuseppe Valdengo

Decca SXL6839 □
London 26510 (US)
Quanto e bella
Una furtiva lagrima
Luciano Pavarotti (t)

HMV SAN180/1 (d) ●
Angel S-3701 (2) (US)
Chorus and Orchestra of Rome Opera
c. Francesco Molinari-Pradelli
Adina (s)   Mirella Freni
Nemorino (t)   Nicolai Gedda
Sergeant Belcore (b) Mari Sereni
Dulcamara (bs)   Renato Capecchi

RCA SER5613 □
Una furtiva lagrima
Placido Domingo (t)

RCA RK11749 □
Una furtiva lagrima
Enrico Caruso (t)

Pearl GEMM146 □
Una furtiva lagrima
Beniamino Gigli (t)

CBS 79210 (2) ●
Columbia M3-34585 (3) (US)
Chorus and Orchestra of the Royal
Opera House, Covent Garden
c. John Pritchard
Adina (s)   Ileana Cotrubas
Nemorino (t)   Placido Domingo
Sergeant Belcore (b) Ingvar Wixell
Dulcamara (bs)   Geraint Evans

demands that Ugo should become betrothed to her instead. Ugo is horrified, and Louis, believing Ugo to be disloyal, orders his arrest.

Act 2   Bianca comes to Ugo in prison to persuade him to lead a revolt against Louis. Ugo refuses, but his troops have started the revolt without him; he puts down the rebellion and again assures Louis of his loyalty and his lack of interest in Bianca. Louis gives Ugo his sword and takes him with Adelia to the chapel, where they are married. The sound of the celebrations infuriates Bianca who drinks poison and dies, bequeathing her hatred and her love to those concerned.

RECORDING:
Opera Rara OR1 (3) (US) ●
Geoffrey Mitchell Choir/New
Philharmonia Orchestra
c. Alun Francis
Luigi V (m-s)   Della Jones
Ugo (t)   Maurice Arthur
Folco di Angiò (b) Christian de Plessis
Emma (s)   Eiddwen Harrhy
Bianca (s)   Janet Price

L'Elisir d'Amore

Opera in 2 Acts.
Text by Felice Romani after Eugène Scribe's 'Le Philtre'.
First performance: Milan (Teatro della Canobbiana) May 12, 1832. London 1836; New York 1838.

Synopsis:
Scene: Italy. Time: 1800s.
Act 1   Nemorino, an honest peasant lad, is in love with the wealthy Adina, but can't bring himself to tell her. Adina relates the story of Tristan and Isolde and the love potion which brought them together, and laments that there is nothing like that now to enslave women. Then an army troop arrives in the town, headed by Sergeant Belcore; he and Adina are immediately attracted. Then comes the quack Dulcamara with his 'magic

Lucrezia Borgia

Opera in Prologue and 2 Acts.
Text by Felice Romani after Victor Hugo.
First performance: Milan (La Scala) December 26, 1833. London 1839; New York 1844.

Synopsis:
Scene: Venice. Time: 16th century.
Prologue   Gennaro, a young Venetian nobleman, is discovered asleep during a festival by Lucrezia Borgia, who is in disguise. Gennaro's friends arrive and one of them, Orsini, reveals her as the hated Borgia, a known murderess.
Act 1   Alfonso, Duke of Ferrara and Lucrezia's fourth husband, suspects that Gennaro is her lover. He has him arrested and forces Lucrezia to give Gennaro poison; but she has an antidote, and Gennaro escapes.

Act 2 At a banquet, Lucrezia plans to poison everyone in the belief that they are all her enemies. But Gennaro is among them, and Lucrezia reveals to him the secret that he is her illegitimate son. She begs him to use the antidote, but he refuses, saying he would rather die with the others, his friends.

RECORDINGS:
RCA SER5553/5 (d) ●
RCA LSC-6176 (3) (US)
RCA Italian Opera Chorus and
Orchestra
c. Jonel Perlea
Lucrezia Borgia (s) Montserrat Caballé
Gennaro (t) Alfredo Kraus
Maffio Orsini (c) Shirley Verrett
Alfonso, Duke of
Ferrara (b) Ezio Flagello

RCA SB6758 ■
(from above)

Decca D93D3 (3) ●
London Opera Voices/National
Philharmonic Orchestra
c. Richard Bonynge
Lucrezia Borgia (s) Joan Sutherland
Gennaro (t) Giacomo Aragall
Maffio Orsini (c) Marilyn Horne
Alfonso, Duke of
Ferrara (b) Ingvar Wixell

Decca SET269 □
London 1257 (d) (US)
Il segreto per essere felice
Marilyn Horne (m-s)

Rosamonda d'Inghilterra

Opera in 2 Acts.
Text by Felice Romani.
First performance: Florence (Teatro Pergola) February 27, 1834.

Notes:
Later revised as *Eleonora di Gujenna*. The libretto was not written for Donizetti, having been set by Carlo Coccia in 1829.

RECORDING:
Decca GOS663/5 □
Ancor non giunse—Perche non ho del
venuto
Joan Sutherland (s)

Maria Stuarda

Opera in 3 Acts.
Text by Giuseppe Bardari.
First performance: Naples (Teatro San Carlo) October 19, 1834 (as 'Buondel-monte'). Milan (La Scala) December 30, 1835 (as 'Maria Stuarda').

Synopsis:
Act 1 Mary Stewart is in prison. Talbot intercedes on her behalf with Queen Elizabeth I, and gives Leicester, who is in love with Mary, a letter and portrait from her. Leicester gives the letter to Elizabeth and urges a meeting between the two Queens.
Act 2 Mary and her trusted companion Anna Kennedy are walking in a park near Fotheringay, and Mary sings of her longing to return to France. She is apprehensive of her meeting with Elizabeth and Leicester tries to reassure her, but the encounter ends in rancour with Mary spitting at Elizabeth 'Vil bastarda', and Elizabeth orders Mary's seizure.
Act 3 Leicester pleads for Mary but Elizabeth is incensed, and in Fotheringay Mary awaits confirmation of her death sentence. She refuses a priest, but Talbot reveals himself disguised as a Catholic priest. Preparations for the execution proceed, Leicester's pleas for a stay of execution having no effect. Mary, accompanied by Anna and Talbot, is led to the block, and Leicester covers his eyes.

Well-known arias:
Act 1 Ah, quando all'ara scorgemi (Elisabetta)
Ah, rimiro il bel sembiante (Leicester)
Act 2 Oh nube! che lieve per l'aria ti aggiri (Maria)
Act 3 Deh! tu di un umile preghiera (Maria and Anna)

Notes:
Because of censorship difficulties, *Maria Stuarda* was originally presented as *Buondelmonte* with a text radically altered by Pietro Salatino and the action removed from Tudor England to Renaissance Italy. The story, after Schiller, is of course apocryphal; the meeting between Mary and Elizabeth never took place.

RECORDINGS:
Decca D2D3 (3) ●
London 13117 (3) (US)
Chorus and Orchestra of Teatro
Communale, Bologna
c. Richard Bonynge
Maria Stuarda (s) Joan Sutherland
Elisabetta (s) Huguette Tourangeau
Leicester (t) Luciano Pavarotti
Talbot (b) Roger Soyer

Decca SET624 ■
(from above)

HMV SLS848 (3) (d) ●
ABC ATS20010 (3) (US)
John Alldis Choir/London Philharmonic
Orchestra
c. Aldo Ceccato
Maria Stuarda (s) Beverly Sills
Elisabetta (s) Eileen Farrell
Leicester (t) Stuart Burrows
Talbot (b) Louis Quilico

(There are several different versions of this opera; the Decca uses the one with soprano and mezzo, the HMV that with high soprano and dramatic soprano)

Decca SXL6839 □
London 26510
Ah, rimiro il bel sembiante
Luciano Pavarotti (t)

Below: *Joan Sutherland, portrayer of so many Donizetti heroines, in the Covent Garden Maria Stuarda.*

Gemma di Vergy

Opera in 2 Acts.
Text by Emanuele Bidera after Alexandre Dumas's 'Charles VII chez ses grands vassaux'.
First performance: Milan (La Scala) December 26, 1834.

Synopsis:
Scene: Paris. Time: 15th century.
Act 1 Gemma learns that her husband, Count di Vergy, plans to divorce her because she is barren. Her grief turns to rage when she learns that her successor has already been chosen. Tamas, Gemma's Arab slave, confesses his love for her: he antagonises Rolando, the Count's squire, but Gemma intervenes when Rolando draws his dagger. Gemma learns she must enter a convent. She leaves, and Tamas enters with a bloody dagger, having killed Rolando. The Count feels remorse on seeing the dagger, believing that Gemma has killed herself. Tamas is put on trial and offered pardon if he will confess to an assassination plot against the Count. He attempts suicide and Gemma pleads for him. It seems that Gemma may win back the Count—until Ida, the new wife-to-be, arrives.
Act 2 The Count feels it is his duty to make the new marriage and father children. Gemma, disguised as a servant, enters Ida's chamber and threatens her. The Count intervenes but, while Gemma holds a dagger to Ida's throat, confesses his love for Ida. Gemma, about to kill Ida, is disarmed by Tamas: she accuses him of ingratitude. At the wedding, Tamas refuses to kill Gemma, as she asks, but begs her to go with him. Angrily, he leaves alone, while Gemma curses the happy couple. Tamas

Lucy and Edgar meet again before the latter leaves for France; Edgar thinks they should tell Ashton of their love but Lucy knows it is useless.

Act 2   Ashton has arranged that Lucy will marry Lord Arthur Bucklaw but she still refuses, so Ashton produces a forged letter purporting to prove Edgar unfaithful. At the signing of the marriage contract, however, Edgar reappears and there ensues the famous sextet in which the strands of the music and the plot are skilfully interwoven. Edgar leaves, cursing the Lammermoor family.

Act 3   In the midst of the continuing wedding celebrations news is brought (by Raymond) that Lucy has gone mad and killed her husband. Lucy appears and sings the great Mad Scene, in which she imagines herself marrying Edgar. Meanwhile Edgar himself, unaware of Lucy's dementia, wanders disconsolate among his family tombs. A procession approaches and he finds Lucy is dead; Edgar blames himself for the whole tragedy and plunges a dagger into his heart.

Well-known arias:

Act 1   Regnava nel silenzio (Lucia)
Quando rapita (Lucia)
Veranno a te sull'aure (Lucia and Edgardo)

Act 2   Chi mi frena (Sextet)

Act 3   Mad Scene (Lucia)
Fra poco a me ricovere (Edgardo)
Tu che a Dio (Edgardo)

Left: *Lucia di Lammermoor, with its famous sextet, is one of Donizetti's best-known works. Here the American soprano Beverly Sills takes the leading role.*

RECORDINGS:
Decca SET528/30 ★●
London 13103 (3) (US)
Chorus and Orchestra of the Royal Opera House, Covent Garden
c. Richard Bonynge
Lucia (s)   Joan Sutherland
Edgardo (t)   Luciano Pavarotti
Enrico
(Ashton) (b)   Sherrill Milnes
Raimondo (bs)   Nicolai Ghiaurov

Decca SET559 ■
London 26332 (US)
(from above)

Decca Ace of Diamonds GOS663/5 ●
(r. 1961)
London 1327 (3) (US)
Chorus and Orchestra of Academia di Santa Cecilia, Rome
c. John Pritchard
Lucia (s)   Joan Sutherland
Edgardo (t)   Renato Cioni
Enrico (b)   Robert Merrill
Raimondo (bs)   Cesare Siepi

London 25702 (US) ■
(from above)

HMV SLS5056 (3) (r. 1954) ●
Chorus and Orchestra of 1953 Maggio Musicale Fiorentino
c. Tullio Serafin
Lucia (s)   Maria Callas
Edgardo (t)   Giuseppe di Stefano
Enrico (b)   Tito Gobbi
Raimondo (bs)   Raffaele Arié

Cetra Opera Live L018 (3) (r. 1955) ●
Chorus and Orchestra of La Scala, Milan
c. Herbert von Karajan
Lucia (s)   Maria Callas
Edgardo (t)   Giuseppe di Stefano
Enrico (b)   Rolando Panerai
Raimondo (bs)   Nicola Zaccaria
(Side 6 of this recording uses excerpts from a 1956 performance of *Lucia*)

Columbia SAX2316/7 (d) ●
Angel S-3601 (2) (US)
Philharmonia Orchestra
c. Tullio Serafin
Lucia (s)   Maria Callas
Edgardo (t)   Ferrucio Tagliavini
Enrico (b)   Piero Cappuccilli
Raimondo (bs)   Bernard Ladysz

Angel S-35831 ■
(from above)

HMV SLS797 (3) (d) ●
ABC-ATS20006 (3) (US)
Ambrosian Opera Chorus/London Symphony Orchestra
c. Thomas Schippers
Lucia (s)   Beverly Sills
Edgardo (t)   Carlo Bergonzi
Enrico (b)   Piero Cappuccilli
Raimondo (bs)   Justino Diaz

ABC-ATS20012 (US) ■
(from above)

CBS 78242 (2) (d) ●
Chorus and Orchestra of Metropolitan Opera, New York
c. Fausto Cleva
Lucia (s)   Lily Pons
Edgardo (t)   Richard Tucker
Enrico (b)   Frank Guerrera
Raimondo (bs)   Thomas Hayward

Philips 6703 080 (3) ●
Philips 6703 080 (3) (US)
Ambrosian Singers/New Philharmonia Orchestra
c. Jésus López-Cobos
Lucia (s)   Montserrat Caballé
Edgardo (t)   José Carreras
Enrico (b)   Vincenzo Sardinero
Raimondo (bs)   Samuel Ramey

Decca SDD146 □
London 26436 (US)
Mad scene and arias
Joan Sutherland (s)

Decca SXL6377 and SXL6839 □
London 26807 and 26510 (US)
Fra poco a me ricovere
Luciano Pavarotti (t)

Philips 6593 533 □
Fra poco a me ricovere
Luciano Pavarotti (t)

---

stabs the Count and then kills himself. Gemma proclaims her innocence and her undying love for the Count; but now she waits only for the release of death.

RECORDING:
CBS Masterworks 79303 (3) ●
Columbia M3-34575 (3) (US)
Schola Cantorum/New York Opera Orchestra
c. Eve Queler
Gemma di Vergy (s)   Montserrat Caballé
Conte di Vergy (b)   Louis Quilico
Tamas (t)   Luis Lima
Ida (m-s)   Natalya Chudy
Guido (bs)   Paul Plishka

Lucia di Lammermoor
Opera in 3 Acts.
Text by Salvatore Cammarano after Walter Scott's 'The Bride of Lammermoor'.
First performance: Naples (Teatro San Carlo) September 26, 1835. Vienna 1835; London (Her Majesty's) 1838; New Orleans (in French) 1841.

Synopsis:
Scene: Scotland. Time: 18th century

Act 1   There is a long-standing feud between the families of Lord Henry Ashton (Enrico) of Lammermoor and Edgar (Edgardo) of Ravenswood. Ashton, who is also politically compromised, discovers that Edgar and his sister Lucy have been meeting in secret, and is determined to stop any liaison.

Il Campanello di Notte

Opera in 1 Act.
Text by Donizetti.
First performance: Naples (Teatro Nuovo) June 1, 1836.

Notes:

Based on a vaudeville by Brunswick, Trion and Lhérie, *La Sonnette de nuit*, it concerns an apothecary whose wedding night is constantly disturbed by his wife's former lover ringing on the night bell.

RECORDING:

DG SLPM139143 (d) ●
Chorus and Orchestra of Teatro La Fenice, Venice
c. Alfredo Lazzarini

Don Annibale (bs)	Alfredo Mariotti
Serafina (s)	Emma Bruno de Sanctis
Enrico (b)	Alberto Rinaldi

L'Assedio di Calais

Opera in 3 Acts.
Text by Salvatore Cammarano, after du Belloy's 'Le siège de Calais'.
First performance: Naples (Teatro San Carlo) November 19, 1836.

RECORDING:

Decca SXL6501 □
Al mio core oggetti amati
Huguette Tourangeau (s)

Roberto d'Evereux, Conte d'Essex

Opera in 3 Acts.
Text by Salvatore Cammarano after François Ancelot's 'Elisabeth d'Angleterre' (with plagiarisms from a libretto by Felice Romani).
First performance: Naples (Teatro San Carlo) October 29, 1837.

Synopsis:

Act 1 Scene 1 Queen Elizabeth is in love with Roberto, Earl of Essex, who is about to stand trial for treason. She has doubts of his fidelity, since he has let slip a hint of his feeling for Sarah, Duchess of Nottingham, who reciprocates his love; and demands that he produce a ring she had given him. **Scene 2** In Sarah's home, Essex, jealous of her husband Nottingham, throws down the Queen's ring and Sarah gives him a scarf.
Act 2 Everyone knows that Essex cannot survive without the Queen's intervention—and that is not likely since when he is arrested Sarah's scarf is found on him. It is recognised not only by Elizabeth but Nottingham as well, and the act ends with an ensemble in which nobody has a good word for the unfortunate Essex.
Act 3 Scene 1 Sarah hears that Essex has been condemned to death and decides to take the ring to the Queen and beg for his life, but Nottingham delays her by denouncing Essex while the sounds of the journey to the scaffold are heard outside. **Scene 2** Essex is confident that he will be pardoned, but instead a guard comes to take him to his execution. When Sarah eventually arrives to see the Queen, Elizabeth is already considering mercy, but the sound of the shot preceding the execution is heard—it is too late. Queen Elizabeth blames Sarah, until Nottingham arrives and reveals that it was he who prevented the earlier delivery of the ring, and the Queen loses her reason.

RECORDINGS:

HMV SLS787 (3) ●
ABC ATS-20003 (3) (US)
Ambrosian Opera Chorus/Royal Philharmonic Orchestra
c. Charles Mackerras

Elisabeth (s)	Beverly Sills
Roberto d'Evereux (t)	Robert Ilosfalvy
Sarah (m-s)	Beverly Woolf
Nottingham (b)	Peter Glossop

ABC ATS-20008 (US) ■
(from above)

Decca SXL6235 □
London 6486 (US)
Overture
c. Richard Bonynge

La Fille du Régiment

Opera in 2 Acts.
Text by Jules Henri Vernoy de Saint-Georges and Jean François Alfred Bayard.
First performance: Paris (Opéra-Comique) February 11, 1840. Milan (in Italian) 1840; New Orleans (in French) 1843; London (Her Majesty's) (in Italian) 1847; New York (Metropolitan) 1902.

Synopsis:

Act 1 In the middle of a battle, Tonio, a Tyrolean peasant, is found prowling around the grenadiers' camp. He is the lover of Marie the regiment's 'daughter'. The regiment is determined that she shall marry one of their own number, so Tonio joins up. The Marquise de Birkenfeld appears as a refugee, and it turns out she is Marie's aunt—and thus the humble Tonio is not an eligible suitor.
Act 2 The Marquise wants Marie to marry into the noble family of Krakenthorp. Tonio and Marie plan to elope, but before they depart, Marie sings a song of her childhood with the guardsmen. It reveals a few points of interest not known to the Marquise, who gives her blessing to Marie and Tonio, forgoing dreams of noble alliances, and all ends happily.

Well-known arias:

Act 1	Au bruit de la guerre (Apparvi alla luce) (Marie and Sulpice)
	Chacun le sait, chacun le dit (Ciascun lo dice) (Marie)
	Il faut partir (Convien partir!) (Marie)
Act 2	Salut à la France (Marie)

RECORDINGS:

Decca SET372/3 ●
London 1273 (2) (US)
Chorus and Orchestra of Royal Opera House, Covent Garden
c. Richard Bonynge

Marie (s)	Joan Sutherland
Tonio (t)	Luciano Pavarotti
Sergeant Sulpice (bs)	Spiro Malas
Marquise de Birkenfeld (c)	Monica Sinclair

Decca SET491 ■
London 26204 (US)
(from above)

Decca SXL6658 □
London 26373 (US)
Ah mes amis—Pour mon ame
Luciano Pavarotti (t)

Decca D65D3 □
Chacun le sait
Joan Sutherland (s)

Decca SXL6149 □
Il faut partir
Marilyn Horne (m-s)

Decca SXL6839 □
Pour me rapprocher de Marie
Luciano Pavarotti (t)

Poliuto

Opera in 3 Acts.
Text by Salvatore Cammarano. Expanded into 4 Acts (in French), text by Eugène Scribe, as Les Martyrs. Based on Corneille's 'Polyeucte'.
First performance: (as Les Martyrs) Paris (Opéra) April 10, 1840; (as Poliuto) Naples (Teatro San Carlo) November 30, 1848.

RECORDING:

Pye/Ember GVC47 □
Lasciando la terre
Giacomo Lauri Volpi (t)

La Favorite

Opera in 4 Acts
Text by Alphonse Royer and Gustave Vaëz after Baculard-Darnaud's 'Le Comte de Comminges' (plus Eugène Scribe).
First performance: Paris (Opéra) December 2, 1840. New Orleans 1843; Milan (La Scala, in Italian) 1843; London (Drury Lane, in English) 1843.

Synopsis:

Scene: Spain. Time: 14th century.
Act 1 Fernando, a monk who is being 'groomed' by his superior Balthazar as a successor, is obsessed by thoughts of a beautiful woman and renounces his vows. He is given a commission in the army. Unknown to him, the woman, Leonora, is mistress of King Alfonso XI.
Act 2 Fernando is now a military hero, and he and Leonora are secretly in love. The King's opponents organise a Papal Bull to force him to give up Leonora and reinstate his legitimate wife.

Left: La Fille du Régiment *opened the way to the new French operetta. Joan Sutherland has made the role of Marie very much her own in recent times.*

Act 3 Alfonso offers Fernando a reward for his military successes, and Fernando asks for Leonora's hand in marriage. Leonora, however, is worried about Fernando's feelings about her past life, and when he finds out he is disgusted and returns to the monastery.

Act 4 Leonora, disguised as a novice, confronts Fernando at the monastery; the sight of her rekindles his love, but it is too late and she dies in his arms.

Well-known arias:

Act 1 Una vergine, un angiol di Dio (Balthazar)
Bei raggi lucenti (Inez)

Act 2 Vien, Leonora, a'piedi tuoi (Alfonso)
Ah, paventa il furor d'un Dio vendicatore (Balthazar)

Act 3 A tanto amor (Alfonso)
O mio Fernando (Leonora)

RECORDINGS:
Decca D96D3 (3) ★●
London 13113 93) (US)
Chorus and Orchestra of Teatro
Communale, Bologna
c. Richard Bonynge
Fernando (t)   Luciano Pavarotti
Leonora (m-s) Fiorenza Cossotto
Alfonso XI (b) Gabriel Bacquier
Balthazar (bs) Nicolai Ghiaurov
Inez (s)   Ileana Cotrubas

Decca Ace of Diamonds GOS525/7
Richmond 63510 (3) (US) ●
Maggio Musical Fiorentino
c. Alberto Erede
Fernando (t)   Gianni Poggi
Leonora (m-s) Giulietta Simionata
Alfonso XI (b) Ettore Bastianni
Balthazar (bs) Jerome Hines
Inez (s)   Bice Magnani

Cetra Opera Live LO2 (3) (r. 1950) ●
Chorus and Orchestra of Palaccio de
Belles Artes
c. Renato Cellini
Fernando (t)   Giuseppe di Stefano
Leonora (m-s) Giulietta Simionata
Alfonso XI (b) E. Mascherini
Balthazar (bs) Cesare Siepi

Above right: *A Covent Garden production of* Don Pasquale *with Sir Geraint Evans and Gabriel Bacquier.*

Linda di Chamounix
Opera in 3 Acts.
Text by Gaetano Rossi.
First performance; Vienna (Kärthnerthortheater) May 19, 1842. London 1843; New York (Palmo's Opera House) 1847.

RECORDINGS:
Decca Ace of Diamonds SDD146 □
London 25111 (US)
Ah! tardai troppo . . . O luce di quest
anima
Joan Sutherland (s)

Decca SXL6828 □
Da quel di che l'incontrai
Joan Sutherland (s)
Luciano Pavarotti (t)

Don Pasquale
Opera in 3 Acts.
Text by Donizetti and Giovanni Ruffini after Angelo Anelli's 'Ser Marc' Antonio'.
First performance: Paris (Théâtre-Italien) January 3, 1843. Milan (La Scala) 1843; London (Her Majesty's Theatre) 1843; New York (in English) 1846.

Synopsis:
Scene: Rome. Time: 18th century.

Act 1 Don Pasquale, a miserly old bachelor, wants a wife but has no one particularly in mind. He objects to the love of his nephew Ernesto for the young widow Norina and threatens to disinherit him; but Dr Malatesta, Pasquale's friend and physician, wants to help the young people and teach Pasquale a lesson. He suggests that Pasquale marries his 'sister', and a 'marriage' is arranged, with Norina in disguise as the bride.

Act 2 The mock marriage goes ahead, with Norina acting the shy young maiden; but as soon as it is over, Norina turns into a harridan, making the old man's life a misery.

Act 3 Driven nearly out of his mind, Don Pasquale begs Dr Malatesta to do something, and he suggests that Ernesto should take Norina off his hands. Realising he has been made a fool of, Don Pasquale agrees, and all ends happily.

RECORDINGS: ●
Decca SET280/1
London 1260 (2) (US)
Chorus and Orchestra of Vienna State
Opera
c. Istvan Kertesz
Don Pasquale (b) Fernando Corena
Norina (s) Graziella Sciutti
Dr Malatesta (bs) Tom Krause
Ernesto (t) Juan Oncina

Decca SET337 ■
(from above)

DG Privilege 2705 039 (2) ●
DG Privilege 2705 039 (2) (US)
Maggio Musical Fiorentino
c. Ettore Gracis
Don Pasquale (b) Alfredo Mariotti
Norina (s) Anna Maccianti
Dr Malatesta (bs) Mario Basiola
Ernesto (t) Ugo Benelli

DON PASQUALE
CORENA SCIUTTI KRAUSE ONCINA
VIENNA OPERA ORCHESTRA & CHORUS
KERTESZ

Maria di Rohan (Il Conte de Chalais)

Opera in 3 Acts.
Text by Salvatore Cammarano, based on Lockroy's 'Un duel sous le cardinal de Richelieu'.
First performance: Vienna (Kärthnerthortheater) June 5, 1843.

RECORDING:
Philips 9500 203 □
Philips 9500 203 (US)
Nel fragor della festa
José Carreras (t)

Don Sébastian de Portugal

Opera in 5 Acts.
Text by Eugène Scribe, based on Barbosa Machado's 'Memoirs'.
First performance: Paris (Opéra) November 13, 1843.

Decca SXL6377 □
London 26087 (US)
Spirito gentil
Luciano Pavarotti (t)

Il Duca d'Alba

Opera in 4 Acts.
Text by Eugène Scribe and Charles Duveyrier.
First performance: Rome (Teatro Apollo) (in Italian) March 22, 1882.

Notes:

Donizetti left the opera incomplete, having worked on it in 1839. It was revised after his death: the libretto was translated into Italian by Angelo Zanardini and the score was edited by Matteo Salvi.

RECORDINGS:
Decca SXL6377 □
London 26087 (US)
Inosservato penetrava . . . Angelo casto
Luciano Pavarotti (t)

Philips 9500 203 □
Philips 9500 203 (US)
Inosservato penetrava . . . Angelo casto
José Carreras (t)

RECITALS:
Decca SXL6377 □
London 26087 (US)
Arias from *Lucia di Lammermoor/Duca d'Alba/La Favorita/Don Sébastian*
Luciano Pavarotti (t)
(Verdi: arias)

Decca SXL6850 □
London 26384 (US)
Arias from *L'elisir d'amore/La fille du régiment/Maria Stuarda*
Luciano Pavarotti (t)
(Verdi/Rossini)

HMV ASD2578 (d) □
ABC ATS-20001 (US)
Arias from *Lucia di Lammermoor/ Rosamonda d'Inghilterra/Linda di Chamounix/Roberto d'Evereux*
Beverly Sills (s)
(Bellini: arias)

RCA SER5591 (d) □
RCA LSC-3164 (d) US
Arias from *Torquato Tasso/Gemma di Vergy/Belisario/Parisina*
Montserrat Caballé (s)

(Many Donizetti arias appear in individual recitals by various singers. The above concentrates on those albums where this composer predominates)

ANTONÍN DVOŘÁK

(b. Nelahozeves 8.9.1841; d. Prague 1.5.1904)

The son of a butcher and innkeeper, Dvořák absorbed national folk and church music as a youth. When his musical gifts revealed themselves fully, he was sent to the organ school in Prague and subsequently joined the orchestra of the Czech National Theatre under the direction of Smetana ». His compositions soon began to establish his reputation at home and abroad. He composed fruitfully and at length in all forms, and wrote 10 operas, of which *Rusalka* has maintained an international foothold, and the diverting *The Devil and Kate* reveals a lively vitality. His serious, tragically inclined operas are not among his most successful compositions. Dvořák spent time in both England and America. His most famous symphony (No. 9) and some chamber music emanated from his American visits. He undertook his first visit to England in 1884 where he made a strong impression with his *Stabat Mater*, and became an Honorary Doctor of Music at Cambridge in 1891. He married in 1873 and in 1884 bought himself a country property which was his home for the rest of his life, alternating with travels abroad and periods in Prague. He was friends with many great international figures in music, including Brahms, Tchaikovsky » and Sibelius. As a man he appears to have been as amiable and well disposed as his music. His son-in-law was the celebrated Czech composer Josef Suk (1874-1935).

The Devil and Kate (Čert a Káča)

Opera in 3 Acts.
Text by Adolf Wenig.
First performance: Prague (National Theatre) November 23, 1899. Oxford 1932.

Synopsis:
Act 1 Lucifer is disturbed by tales of the oppressive rule of Kate, the Lady of the Manor, and sends Marbuel (as the Devil) to find out what is going on. Kate, at a country fair, finds herself dancing with Marbuel. She says she would like to visit Hell, so they both vanish through a hole in the ground, pursued by George the shepherd, who says he will bring Kate back.
Act 2 In Hell, which turns out to be rather more pleasant than expected, Marbuel is tired of Kate's continual carping. He wants her to go, but Lucifer has decreed that she stay in Marbuel's care. George arrives and is welcomed as a possible saviour. Marbuel offers him a reward to take Kate away. He waltzes her away before she realises what has happened.
Act 3 The Lady is distressed. George has rescued her on condition that she abolishes serfdom. Marbuel enters in splendour but departs hastily when he learns that Kate is after him. She is saved, and George is made her confidante and aide.

ANTONÍN DVOŘÁK
the Devil & Kate

RECORDINGS:
Rediffusion Heritage Collection
HCNL8030 (2) (m) (r. 1958) ●
(previously Supraphon LPV337/9)
Chorus and Orchestra of Prague National Theatre
c. Zdeněk Chalabala
Kate (c) Ludmilla Komancová
Marbuel (b) Přemysl Kočí
Lucifer (bs) Rudolf Asmus
Jirka (George) (t) Lubomir Havlák
Kate's Mother (c) Vera Krilová

Telefunken AN6.41170 □
Höllentanz: Overture Act III
c. Václav Neumann

Rusalka

Opera in 3 Acts.
Text by Josef Kvapil.
First performance: Prague (National Theatre), March 31, 1901. Vienna 1910; Stuttgart 1929; London (John Lewis Musical Society) 1950; Sadler's Wells 1959.

Synopsis:
Act 1 Rusalka, daughter of the Spirit of the Lake, arises from the water to announce that she wants to become human in order

Above: *Eduard Haken as the water gnome in Dvořák's* Rusalka.

to marry a handsome prince. She tells the moon of her longing in an extended song. Her father tells her to visit the witch, Ježibaba, who grants her human form but on condition that she will not speak, otherwise she and the Prince will be condemned to eternal damnation. The Prince enters and feels the presence of supernatural powers; Rusalka appears and he is captivated.

Act 2 The Palace is filled with guests for the wedding of the Prince and Rusalka. There is much gossip about the magic origins of the bride, whose silence is trying the patience of the Prince. He has been paying marked attention to a Foreign Princess. The grand ball is interrupted by the Spirit of the Lake who is distressed at the fate of his beloved daughter; the Prince tries to leave with the Foreign Princess, but Rusalka's father intervenes.

Act 3 Rusalka wanders by the lakeside, distraught; the Witch tells her that only human blood can redeem her. The Prince then enters from the wood, and begs Rusalka to return to him or to take his life. She explains that she is unable to give him human warmth, and says that if he were to kiss her he would die: he begs for the kiss of death and together they sink into the waters.

Well-known arias:
Act 1 O silver moon (Rusalka)
Act 3 Goddess of the Lake (Prince)

RECORDINGS:
Supraphon SUAST50440/3 ●
Chorus and Orchestra of Prague National
Theatre
c. Zdeněk Chalabala
Rusalka (s)   Milada Subrtova
Prince (t)   Ivo Žídek
Foreign Princess (s) Alena Mikova
Spirit of the
  Lake (b)   Eduard Haken
Witch (c)   Marie Ovcacikova

DG 136 011 □
O silver moon
Rita Streich (s)

Decca SXL6267 □
London 25995 (US)
O silver moon
Pilar Lorengar (s)

HMV SXLP30205 □
Goddess of the Lake
Joan Hammond (s)

Above: *Antonín Dvořák.*

WERNER EGK
(b. Auchsesheim, nr. Augsburg 17.5.1901)

German composer Egk's first opera, *Die Zaubergeige*, written in 1935, was an immediate success, with its pleasant score based on popular tunes and folksongs. *Peer Gynt* in 1938 was much admired by Hitler and further increased the composer's reputation. Perhaps most influenced by Stravinsky », Egk's flair for catchy melody and dramatic construction that has made him a popular composer in his own country, though not so well-known abroad. Other operas include: *Columbus* (written for radio in 1933, revised 1941); *Circe* (1948); *Irische Legende* (1954); *Der Revisor* (1957), and *Verlobung in San Domingo* (1963). He said of his own music: 'I have always been glad when I could hear a melody so well shaped and singable that one could whistle it when leaving the theatre. As a musician I could find enjoyment in contrapuntal complexities, but as an ordinary man I have never seen the sense of them'.

Die Zaubergeige
Opera in 3 Acts.
Text by Count Pocci, based on Hans Andersen.
First performance: Frankfurt, May 23, 1935.

RECORDINGS:
DG DGM19062 (d) ■
Decca 9825 (d) (US)
Chorus and Orchestra of the Bavarian
State Opera
c. Werner Egk

Kaspar (b)	Marcel Cordes
Gretl (s)	Erika Köth
Ninabella (s)	Elisabeth Lindermeier
Amandus (t)	Richard Holm
Guldensack (bs)	Max Proebstl
Cuperus (bs)	Gottlob Frick

FERENC ERKEL
(b. Gyula 7.11.1810; d. Budapest 15.6.1893)

The founder of Hungarian national opera, Erkel came from a family long noted as musicians. He showed early promise and at the age of ten was able to deputise for his father at the organ of the local church. He studied music from an early age, especially at Pozsony, which, being near Vienna, provided opportunities for musical experience. Erkel became music master to the family of Count Csáky at Kolozsvár in 1827 and remained in that position until 1834, when he entered the service of the Countess Stainlen-Saalfeld. In 1836 he became assistant conductor at the Municipal Theatre in Pest and then joined the newly-established National Theatre as musical director. He was already preoccupied with a Hungarian national opera and his first work in this direction was *Bátori Mária*, produced in August 1840. His second, *Hunyadi László*, became one of his and his country's most famous and successful operas. He was prominent in the formation of the Philharmonic Society in 1853 and became its President Conductor. He was also a considerable writer on and editor of Hungarian national music. Erkel was not the first to write Hungarian opera, but he was the virtual creator of the true national style. His operas, like those of composers in several other countries, were an offshoot of national liberation movements and inner national aspirations.

Hunyadi László
Opera in 4 Acts.
Text by Béni Egressy based on Lörinc Tóth.
First performance: Pest (National Theatre) January 27, 1844.

Notes:
Like most of Erkel's music, this opera strikes a strong patriotic note. One chorus was taken as a national affirmation, in much the same manner as several of Verdi's were in Italy at the time of the struggles for national independence.

RECORDING:
Qualiton HLPX1040/2 (m) (d) ●
Budapest Philharmonic Chorus and
Orchestra
c. Vilmos Komor
Láslo (t) József Simandi
King (b) Miklos Szabo
Maria (s) Julia Orosz

Bánk Bán

Opera in 3 Acts.
Text by Béni Egressy based on József Katona.
First performance: Pest (National Theatre) March 9, 1861.

Synopsis:
Scene: Hungary. Time: 13th century.
Act 1 While King Endre is at the wars, his wife Queen Gertrude oppresses the country. Her brother, Otto, tries to seduce Melinda, wife of the absent Bánk Bán. An uprising is planned and Bánk is sent for. Otto acquires a potion to put in Melinda's drink. However, when Melinda confronts the Queen, Otto seems to relent and supports her against Gertrude.
Act 2 Bánk is deeply troubled by the fate of Hungary, overrun by Queen Gertrude's people, the Meranians (Germans). An old serf appears and Bánk recognises the faithful Tiborc who once saved his life. The old man tells a sorry tale and Bánk gives him money. Melinda has been attacked by Otto while asleep and is full of shame and guilt. She says she must go away, although she still loves Bánk. Bánk tells Tiborc to take their son in to his charge and then goes to accuse the Queen, who at last loses control and tries to stab him. Bánk seizes the weapon and kills her.
Act 3 Melinda, Tiborc and the child are waiting to cross the Tisza river. Melinda has lost her reason and is singing a disjointed lullaby to the child. Tiborc urges haste, for a storm is brewing; but Melinda clutches the child and jumps into the river. Meanwhile King Endre has returned victorious, to find his queen dead. He accuses his courtiers, but Bánk steps forward and claims responsibility. The King is told of her misdeeds. He says that Bánk must be tried, but Bánk says only the people may judge. The King tells Bánk to draw his sword, but then Tiborc enters, followed by serfs carrying the bodies of Melinda and the child. Bánk, stricken with grief, tells the King he is avenged.

Notes:
This is another strongly nationalistic work, its subject the liberation of Hungary from oppressive foreign rule. *Bánk Bán* was written between 1844 and 1852, but it was not produced until 1861 because of the political situation and the setback to Hungarian national aspiration in 1849, when an uprising proved abortive. The work itself is strongly flavoured, but from an international standpoint is somewhat nebulous in style. Some of its best and most original aspects are the passages of imaginative scoring behind the voices.

Below: *A 1962 production of Erkel's Bánk Bán, with Klára Palánky as Gertrude and József Simándi in the title role.*

RECORDING:
Hungaroton SLPX11376/8 ●
Hungarian State Opera House Chorus/
Budapest Philharmonic Orchestra
c. János Ferencsik
Bánk Bán (t) József Simandi
Melinda (s) Karola Agay
Otto (t) József Réti
Petur Bán (b) András Faragó
Gertrude (c) Erzsébet Komlóssy
King Endre (b) Sándor Nagy

MANUEL DE FALLA
(b. Cadiz 23.11.1876; d. Alta Gracia, Argentina, 14.11.1946)

Spain's premier modern composer studied the piano from the age of eight, and then with the great man of the Spanish musical renaissance, Felipe Pedrell, who gave Falla the most powerful impetus towards his ultimate goal—the creation of a genuinely international style based on the various idioms of Spanish music. In 1907 Falla went to Paris, where he was encouraged by the leading French composers, including Debussy », Ravel » and Dukas, as well as his compatriot Isaac Albéniz. Falla returned to Spain in 1914 and did not leave again until he went to Argentina in 1939, where he stayed until his death. He was a withdrawn, ascetic, celibate, deeply religious, totally dedicated man and artist, who lived to become the embodiment of the historic spirit of Spain. He wrote only a little music; but four of his most important works were for the theatre—two ballets, one opera and a puppet opera. The opera, *La vida breve*, the first of his works he wished to acknowledge, won first prize in a competition organized by the Real Academia de Belles Artes in 1904, but despite the terms which stated that the winning work should be produced at the Teatro Real in Madrid, was given first at Nice in a French translation and did not reach Madrid until 1914. The puppet opera *El retablo de Maese Pedro* was commissioned by the Princesse de Polignac in 1923, for performance in her private theatre.

La Vida Breve

Opera in 2 Acts (originally 1 Act).
Text by Carlos Fernández Shaw.
First performance: Nice (Casino Municipal) April 4, 1913. Paris (Opéra-Comique) 1914 (both in French); Madrid (Teatro de la Zarzuela) 1914.

Synopsis:
Scene: Granada. Time: c. 1900.
Act 1 Scene 1 In a courtyard, the blacksmiths are heard lamenting the harshness of their lot. Salud, who lives with her grandmother in the house, is awaiting the arrival of Paco, her sweetheart. He arrives and there is a love duet, Salud suspicious, Paco protesting fidelity, but then Uncle Salvador arrives with news that Paco is to marry Carmela, a local rich girl, next day. **Scene 2** The famous Interlude as night falls.
Act 2 Scene 1 At the wedding reception of Paco and Carmela, there is a Flamenco and the famous Spanish Dance. Then Salud appears, and Paco hears her voice lamenting her fate, accompanied by Uncle Salvador and the grandmother. **Scene 2** Distraught and dishonoured, Salud denounces Paco, collapses and dies.

Below: *Conductor Garcia Navarro and singer Teresa Berganza, who collaborated in a recording of Falla's La Vida Breve.*

Notes:

Two misconceptions about *La vida breve* persist—that it is a kind of offshoot of the *zarzuela* style; and that Salud is a gypsy. The opera has nothing to do with *zarzuela*, despite the fact that its librettist was a leading writer in the *zarzuela* field. Salud is not a gypsy but a typification of the southern Spanish woman. Falla himself was insistent on this point.

RECORDINGS:

DG 2707 108 (2) ●
DG 2707 108 (2) (US)
Ambrosian Opera Chorus/London
Symphony Orchestra
c. Garcia Navarro

Salud (m-s)   Teresa Berganza
Paco (t)   José Carreras
Grandmother (m-s) Alicia Nafé
Uncle Salvador (bs-b) Juan Pons
Carmela (s)   Paloma Perez
                                    Inigo

(Side 4: *El amor brujo*)

HMV SAN157/8 (d) ●
Angel S-3672 (2) (US)
Spanish National Chorus and Orchestra
c. Rafael Frühbeck de Burgos

Salud (s)   Victoria de los
                                    Angeles
Paco (t)   Carlos Cossutta
Grandmother (m-s) Ines Rivadeneyra
Uncle Salvador (bs-b) Victor de Narke
Carmela (s)   Ana Maria
                                    Higueras

(Side 4: Granados: *Colección de tonadillas*)

Decca Ace of Diamonds SDD321 □
London 6224 (US)
Dances
c. Ernest Ansermet

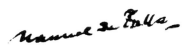

El Retablo de Maese Pedro

Puppet opera in 6 scenes.
Text by Falla after an episode in 'Don Quixote' (Cervantes).
First performance: Seville (Teatro San Fernando) March 23, 1923. Paris (house of Princesse Edmond de Polignac) 1923; Clifton, Bristol, England (Victoria Rooms) 1924; New York 1925.

Synopsis:

A puppet play within a puppet play. The Boy (or *trujamán*, meaning literally 'interpreter') narrates the story of how the fair Melisendra, daughter of the Emperor Charlemagne and wife of the Lord Gayferos, is abducted by Moors and guarded by the Moorish king Marsilius; how a Moor steals a kiss and is punished with 200 lashes; how Don Gayferos rides through the Pyrenees to rescue her; how Melisendra is rescued and the two ride off to Paris; and how they are pursued by the Moors. All this is performed with interjections from the Boy, Maese Pedro (Master Peter, the puppeteer), and Don Quixote, who has dropped in to see the show.

RECORDINGS:

RCA Erato STU70713 ●
RCA Erato STU70713 (US)
Ensemble Instrumental
c. Charles Dutoit

Boy (s)   Ana Higueras-Aragon
Maese Pedro (t)   Tomás Carrera
Don Quixote (bs) Manuel Perez
                                  Bermudez

(Harpsichord Concerto; *Psyché*)

Decca Ace of Diamonds SDD134 ●
London 15014 (US)
National Orchestra of Spain
c. Ataulfo Argenta

Boy (s)   Julita Bermajo
Maese Pedro (t)   Carlos Munguia
Don Quixote (bs) Raimunde Torres

(*El amor brujo*)

RCA Erato EFM8048 ○
Madrid Concerts Orchestra
c. Pedro de Freitas Branco

Boy (s)   Teresa Tourne
Maese Pedro (t)   Pedro Lavirgen
Don Quixote (bs) Renato Cesari

(*Three Cornered Hat* Suites)

FRIEDRICH VON FLOTOW

(b. Teutendorf 26.4.1812; d. Darmstadt 24.1.1883)

Of noble birth, Flotow was originally intended for a diplomatic career. But he went to Paris in 1827 to study under Reicha and began to compose after the revolution of 1830, presenting his stage works at private aristocratic houses. He achieved public recognition in 1839 with *Le Naufrage de la Méduse* in collaboration with Albert Grisar and Pilati. (He later rewrote this as *Die Matrosen* in 1845.) A serious opera, *Alessandro Stradella*, which he recast from some incidental music, showed that his talent was somewhat slighter than his ambition—but his lighter operas contain much charming and diverting music. His gift was clearly for the theatre; he wrote some 30 operas and operettas in various languages, plus a number of ballets and some incidental music. He also wrote an amount of instrumental music and songs. His most famous work, *Martha*, had a long run of international popularity. Between 1856 and 1863 Flotow was intendant at the theatre at Schwerin, and then returned to Paris before settling near Vienna.

Alessandro Stradella

Opera in 3 Acts.
Text by 'W. Friedrich' (Friedrich Wilhelm Riese).
First performance: Hamburg, December 30, 1844. London (Drury Lane) 1846, (Covent Garden) 1864.

RECORDING:

Supraphon 110 1637 □
Supraphon 110 1637 (US)
Overture
c. Zeljko Straka

Martha

Opera in 4 Acts.
Text by W. Friedrich after 'Lady Henriette, ou La Servante de Greenwich' by Vernoy St Georges.
First performance: Vienna (Kärntnertor Theatre) November 25, 1847. London (Drury Lane) 1849; London (Covent Garden) (in English) 1858; Paris (Théâtre-Lyrique) 1865; New York (Metropolitan) 1884.

Synopsis:

Scene: Richmond. Time: 1710.

Act 1 Scene 1 The Lady Harriet and her attendant Nancy, bored with life and love, disguise themselves as servant girls and go to Richmond Fair, Harriet as 'Martha'; Nancy as 'Julia' and Harriet's suitor (her ageing cousin Sir Tristram) as just plain 'Bob'. **Scene 2** At the Fair the Sheriff declares that all contracts of service are binding for a year. Two farmers, Lionel and Plunkett, engage the two distinguished ladies as servants. Rather than be recognised they reluctantly go to their new abode.

Act 2 In Plunkett's farmhouse the two ladies prove their lack of skill for household tasks. Plunkett pursues 'Julia' and Lionel pays court to 'Martha' who, conscious of her position, rejects him. Sir Tristram appears and the three of them make their escape.

Act 3 Plunkett and his farmer friends enjoy a drink outside an inn. A Royal hunting party is nearby, and Plunkett recognizes his 'Julia' and Lionel his 'Martha'. Lady Harriet, however, fearing to offend the Queen, has Lionel arrested as a madman. He gives Plunkett a ring from his finger and tells him to present it to the Queen.

Act 4 The ring proves Lionel to be the son of the banished Earl of Derby. He still loves Lady Harriet but doesn't trust her since the arrest. Nancy and Plunkett finally bring the couple together by arranging a copy of Richmond Fair, at which Lionel hears a familiar voice singing 'The Last Rose of Summer' (which he heard in the farmhouse). He and Lady Harriet are reunited.

Well-known arias:

Act 2 Die letzte Rose (The Last Rose of Summer) (Lady Harriet)
Act 3 Porterlied (Drinking Song) (Plunkett)
            Ach, so fromm (M'appari) (Lionel)
            Mag der Himmel euch vergeben (Lionel, Plunkett, Lady Harriet and Nancy)

Above: *Gigli as Lionel in the 1930 Covent Garden* Martha.

Notes:

The famous aria 'Ach, so fromm' or 'M'appari' was not in the original score but was interpolated for the production at the Paris Théâtre-Lyrique on December 16, 1865. The number was 'borrowed' from Flotow's opera in 2 Acts, *L'Ame en Peine* (1846). *Martha* is nowadays more a matter of extracts than a complete opera. Its rustic charms have faded somewhat, but its famous numbers remain popular; most notably 'M'appari' (since Caruso made a great hit with it) and 'The Last Rose of Summer' ('Die letzte Rose'), an old Irish tune with words by Thomas Moore which Flotow cunningly incorporated into his score. The only modern recording has not survived in the catalogue, not even the highlights from it; but both are worth looking out for.

RECORDINGS:
HMV Angel SLS944 (3) (d) ●
Angel 3753 (3) (US)
Chorus and Orchestra of Bavarian
State Opera
c. Robert Heger
Lady Harriet
  (Martha) (s) Anneliese Rothenberger
Nancy
  (Julia) (c) Brigitte Fassbaender
Lionel (t) Nicolai Gedda
Plunkett (b) Hermann Prey

HMV CSD3683 (d) ■
Angel S-36236 (US)
(from above)

Decca SXL6007 □
Die letzte Rose (The Last Rose
of Summer)
Peter Pears (t)

Decca SET247/8 □
London 1254 (2) (US)
Die letzte Rose
Joan Sutherland (s)

RCA LSB4106 □
Ach, so fromm (M'appari)
Jon Vickers (t)

RCA RL11749 □
Ach, so fromm
Enrico Caruso (t)

RCA SER5613 □
RCA LSC-3083 (US)
Ach, so fromm
Placido Domingo (t)

Decca SXL6649 □
London PAV2001/2 (US)
Ach, so fromm
Luciano Pavarotti (t)

RCA RB16129 □
Ach, so fromm
Beniamino Gigli (t)

MARCO DA GAGLIANO
(b. Gagliano, Florence, c. 1575; d. Florence 24.2.1642)

One of the leading Florentine 'reformers' who created the modern operatic style, Gagliano was a professional musician who held various official appointments at the Italian Courts. After studying at the San Lorenzo Church in Florence, he became first its instructor then *maestro di cappella*. He founded the Accademia degl'Elevati for the promotion of music and musical culture and in 1610 became *maestro di cappella* to the Duke of Tuscany, at the same time maintaining his association with the Gonzaga at Mantua. He composed many madrigals and other vocal works.

La Dafne
Opera-ballet in 2 Parts.
Text by Ottavio Rinuccini after Ovid.
First performance: Mantua 1608. Florence 1610.

Synopsis:

Prologue: sung by Ovid, whose *Metamorphoses* provide the source for the action.
Apollo pursues the Python and shoots it to death with arrows. He is then wounded by the arrows of Cupid. He pursues the nymph Dafne; but she, due to further tricks of Cupid, is changed into a laurel tree just as Apollo is on the point of catching her. She is greatly lamented by Apollo and Thyrsis.

Notes:

La Dafne was produced as the first entertainment of 1608 at Mantua, because Monteverdi » was having difficulty in finishing *L'Arianna* according to the requirement of his patron the Duke. His wife had recently died and he was in poor spirits; but he seems to have resented the production of Gagliano's piece. This was not the first Dafne opera; Jacopo Peri's » version being lost. Dafne's turning into a tree is not represented on stage but told by a narrator, the associated music rising to considerable heights in the madrigal style.

RECORDING:
DG Archive 2533 348 ●   ABC 67012 (2) (US) ●
DG Archive 2533 348 (US)   White/Vorwerk/Musica Pacifica
Hamburg Monteverdi Choir/Hamburg
Camerata Accademica
c. Jürgen Jürgens
Dafne/Venere (s) Norma Lerer
Amore/Ninfa 1 (s) Barbara Schlick
Ninfa 2 (s) Ine Kollecker
Apollo/Ovido (t) Nigel Rogers
Tirsi (t) Ian Partridge

FLORIAN GASSMANN
(b. Brüx 3.5.1729; d. Vienna 20.1.1774)

A Bohemian composer who defied his parents and left home at 13 to take up a musical career. He studied in Bologna and Venice, where he established himself as an opera composer. Later, he succeeded Gluck » as ballet composer in Vienna and directed the *opera buffa* at the Burg Theatre. He became Court conductor, a post he held until his accidental death. Gassmann also founded the Tonkünstler-Societät, Vienna's oldest music society, and was as active a teacher as composer. He wrote some 25 operas (the most successful being *L'Amore artigiano* and *La Contessina*) and a quantity of vocal, instrumental and orchestral music.

L'Amore Artigiano
Opera in 3 Acts.
Text by Carlo Goldoni.
First performance: Vienna (Burg Theatre) April 26, 1767.

RECORDING:
Decca SXL6531 □
London 6735 (US)
Overture
c. Richard Bonynge

JOHN GAY
(b. Barnstaple 16.9.1685; d. London 4.12.1732)

Gay is usually credited with the creation of one of the first and most successful ballad operas in England, *The Beggar's Opera*. In reality, his musical contribution was simply to select various popular airs to which he added the lyrics and wrote the interspersed dialogue. The actual music was already familiar, and was arranged by Johann Christoph Pepusch (1667-1752), a German composer who settled in London around 1700. It was Gay, however, who invented the story to go with it—a tale of bawdy realism, full of rogues, beggars, highwaymen and receivers. The public of the time flocked to see it and made *The Beggar's Opera* one of the most successful entertainments of the day. It had a tremendous influence, not only on further ballad-operas, including Gay's own less successful *Polly*, but on British opera as a whole. It freed opera from the dictates of the Italian and German schools and gave it its own national style. After being played countless times and becoming something of a legend, *The Beggar's Opera* was somewhat neglected until revived nearly 200 years later by Nigel Playfair, with the music skilfully revised by Frederic Austin, at the Lyric, Hammersmith in 1920. The production ran for 1,463 performances. Later revivals have always found an affectionate audience for this sturdy masterpiece, which also inspired a new copy in Kurt Weill's » *Die Dreigroschenoper*.

The Beggar's Opera
Ballad Opera in 3 Acts.
Text by John Gay.
Music collected and arranged by Pepusch.
First performance: London (Lincoln's Inn Fields) January 29, 1728. London (Covent Garden) 1732; New York 1750; Revived London (Covent Garden) (2 Acts) 1813 and 1878 (with Sims Reeves); New version (arranged Frederick Austin) London (Lyric, Hammersmith) 1920 London (Criterion) 1935 New version arranged Benjamin Britten, Cambridge 1948; Vienna 1949; Hamburg 1950.

Left: *The 1967 Aldeburgh production of* The Beggar's Opera, *with Harold Blackburn as Peachum and Bryan Drake as Lockit.*

Synopsis:
Act 1 First a brief prologue. Peachum, the notorious receiver, is going through his accounts. He and his wife discuss Captain Macheath, the highwayman; their daughter Polly has secretly married him and the scheming pair plan to turn this to their advantage by turning Macheath in to the Law, leaving Polly a well-to-do widow. Polly overhears this and later, meeting Macheath, hints at the parting to come.

Act 2 In a tavern near Newgate, Macheath and his gang plan their escapades. When they depart he muses on the ways of women. Peachum and the constables arrive and Macheath is arrested; it now transpires that Lucy, the daughter of Lockit the gaoler, partner of Peachum, has been made pregnant by Macheath and she tries to make him marry her. Peachum and Lockit are at odds over this turn of events. Macheath schemes to escape from prison with Lucy's help, but Polly returns and claims her husband. While Macheath broods on his fate, Lucy and Polly quarrel.

Act 3 Macheath has escaped from Newgate and Lockit is furious with Lucy for having helped him. Macheath is seen at a gaming house. At Peachum's house Lockit and Peachum are still trying to sort out their affairs, and swear to get Macheath in their clutches again. They plan to follow Polly to his hideout and when she comes in they attempt to bribe her to give him away. Macheath has been recaptured and condemned to be hung, he asks two of his gang to get even with Peachum and Lockit. Four more ladies appear, also claiming their rights as wives, and Macheath decides that perhaps hanging is the best way out. But he is reprieved and left to sort out his marital problems.

Well-known arias:
Act 1 Through all the employments of life (Peachum)
Pretty Polly, say (Macheath and Polly)
My heart is so free (Macheath)
Were I laid on Greenland's coast (Macheath and Polly)
Act 2 Fill every glass (Macheath and Gang)
How happy could I be with either (Macheath)
Cease your funning (Polly)
Act 3 My love is all madness and folly (Lucy)
Would I might be hanged (Macheath)

RECORDINGS:
HMV ESDW704 (2) ★●
Seraphim S-6023 (2) (US)
Pro Arte Chorus and Orchestra
c. Sir Malcolm Sargent

	speaker	singer
Polly (s)	Zena Walker	Elsie Morison
Macheath (t)	John Neville	John Cameron
Lucy (s)	Rachel Roberts	Monica Sinclair
Lockit (b)	Eric Porter	Ian Wallace
Peachum (bs)	Paul Rogers	Owen Brannigan

Argo DPA591/3 (2) ●
Argo Chamber Ensemble
c. Richard Austin

	speaker	singer
Polly (s)	Molly Lawson	Carmen Prietto
Macheath (t)	Norman Shelley	Dennis Noble
Lucy (s)	Olive Gregg	Martha Lipton
Lockit (b)	Ernest Jay	John Cameron
Peachum (bs)	Ivan Sampson	Roderick Jones

(Both the above sets use, with success, the device of having actors for the speaking parts and singers for the musical sections)

73

GEORGE GERSHWIN

(b. New York 26.9.1898; d. Hollywood 11.7.1937)

Throughout his short working life Gershwin was always torn between his natural ability to write first-rate music in a popular idiom, which made him very successful, and an ambitious streak which constantly led him to desire a reputation in the more 'respectable' fields of composition. He was also an excellent pianist and could have made a living as a performing musician. He was greatly influenced in his early days, when he worked in Tin Pan Alley, by the music of such composers as Jerome Kern and Irving Berlin. He soon built a reputation as a writer for the musical theatre; his first full-length show was *La La Lucille* in 1919 which led to such shows as *Lady Be Good* (1924) and *Funny Face* (1927), which have survived in the unforgettable hit-songs that he wrote for them. Some of his best songs were written, at the end of his career, for Hollywood films. He could easily have rested on his reputation as one of the best popular songwriters of the century; but he was persuaded by Paul Whiteman that he could and should write a larger scale work for his band to perform, and the undoubted success of *Rhapsody in Blue* in 1924 (although there were critical reservations about it) led him to write other works like *An American in Paris*, and a Piano Concerto, and to the confident belief that he could write a serious folk opera and the eventual production of *Porgy and Bess*. The acceptance of this work came gradually and Gershwin never knew its full acclaim, which came with revival performances after his sudden and tragic death of a brain tumour at the age of 38.

Porgy and Bess

Opera in 3 Acts.
Text by DuBose Heyward and Ira Gershwin, based on the play 'Porgy' by Dorothy and DuBose Heyward.
First performance: Boston (Colonial Theater) September 30, 1935. New York (Alvin Theater) October 10, 1935; Zürich 1945; London 1953.

Synopsis:
Act 1 Catfish Row, Charleston, at dawn. The cripple Porgy finds that his sweetheart Bess has been having an affair with Crown, a burly stevedore. Crown, in a drunken brawl, kills a gambler and has to make his escape. Porgy comforts Bess and takes her to live with him, while Serena Robbins, widow of the murdered man, is left to mourn.
Act 2 A picnic on Kittiwah Island. Porgy is happy and enjoys with the rest the entertainment of the swaggering Harlem Negro Sporting Life. Crown had been hiding on the island and now

Above: *The original New York production of* Porgy and Bess.

Below: *Leona Mitchell in the Decca recording of* Porgy and Bess.

VITTORIO GIANNINI

(b. Philadelphia 19.10.1903; d. New York 28.11.1966)

Brother of the soprano Dusolina Giannini, he studied music at the Milan Conservatory and at the Juilliard Graduate School. He later taught at the Juilliard and Manhattan Schools of Music in New York. He wrote a commissioned symphony for the New York World Fair of 1939 and other works include cantatas, ballets, chamber music and concertos. His operas included: *Lucidia* (Munich, 1934), *The Scarlet Letter* (Hamburg, 1938)—in which Dusolina Giannini created the part of Hester—*The Taming of the Shrew* (Cincinnati, 1953), *The Boor* (1958), *The Harvest* (Chicago, 1961), also *Flora, Beauty and the Beast* and *Blennerhasset*—the last two commissioned and produced by the Columbia Broadcasting System—and *The Servant of Two Masters* (New York City Opera, 1967). The liveliness of Giannini's operas has always been commented on; his music, fairly traditional and exuberant, is always designed to keep the plot moving swiftly along.

The Taming of the Shrew

Opera in 3 Acts.
Text by Vittorio Giannini and Dorothy Fee, based on Shakespeare.
First performance: Cincinnati, 1953. New York City Opera April 13, 1958; Kansas City 1969.

Synopsis:
Act 1 The rich young Lucentio, recently arrived in Padua, and his servant Tranio, learn that the prosperous merchant Baptista has two daughters; Katharina who has such a bad temper that no one will marry her, and Bianca, the younger, of a gentle and amiable disposition and pursued by two suitors Gremio and Hortensio. But Baptista will not allow Bianca to marry until Katharina has a husband, so someone has to be found. Lucentio also falls in love with Bianca and he plans that Tranio shall impersonate him and he will be hired as Bianca's tutor. Petruchio, a gentleman from Verona, with his servant Grumio, now arrives in Padua to find a rich wife. His friend Hortensio agrees to present Petruchio to Baptista as a suitor for Katharina, in return for which Petruchio must then present a disguised Hortensio as a music teacher for Katharina so that he can be near Bianca. All of them now go to Baptista's home, where he says that his daughters will only marry for love. Katharina exhibits her mettle by breaking a lute over Hortensio's head and pursues an argument with Petruchio, who is not deterred and says he will come back on Sunday to marry her. She says she will see him hanged first.

appears and persuades Bess to stay with him. Bess returns to Catfish Row a few days later and begs Porgy to forgive her. During a violent storm Crown reappears to take Bess back again. A boat capsizes and Crown goes to help while Bess sings 'I love you, Porgy'.

Act 3 A requiem is sung for those lost in the storm. Crown creeps back under Porgy's window to steal Bess but Porgy is ready for him. He reaches out and strangles him and is taken away by the police. The flashy Sporting Life tempts Bess to go to New York with him. Porgy returns a few days later, pardoned, bringing presents for everybody. But Bess has gone and Porgy is left to sorrow. He sets off to find her.

Well-known arias:

Act 1 Summertime (Clara)
A woman is a sometime thing (Jake)
My man's gone now (Serena)
I got plenty o' nuttin' (Porgy)
Bess you is my woman now (Porgy and Bess)

Act 2 It ain't necessarily so (Sporting Life)
I love you, Porgy (Bess)

Act 3 There's a boat dat's leavin' soon for New York (Sporting Life)
I'm on my way (Porgy)

Notes:

Gershwin first read DuBose Heyward's 'Porgy' in 1926; he immediately knew that it was the ideal subject for an opera and wrote to the author, who agreed that he should set it. But it was not until 1932 that they were able to go ahead. In the meantime the Theatre Guild had asked for permission to have it made into a musical by Jerome Kern and Oscar Hammerstein II to star Al Jolson. Heyward kept faith with Gershwin and the idea of an opera, and they set to work. It took the composer 11 months to write the piano score and nine months to orchestrate. It was enthusiastically received by the audiences at the opening performances in Boston and New York but received mixed notices, only ran for 124 performances and made a heavy loss. The real acclaim was to come with the revivals in the 1950s, when its fine songs were already accepted as classics.

RECORDINGS:

Decca SET609/11 ★●
London 13116 (3) (US)
Cleveland Chorus and Orchestra
c. Lorin Maazel
Porgy (b)   Willard White
Bess (s)   Leona Mitchell
Crown (b)   McHenry Boatwright
Serena (s)   Florence Quivar
Sporting Life (t)   Francois Clemmons

RCA RL02109 (3) ●
ARL3-2109 (3) (US)
Houston Opera Chorus and Orchestra
c. John DeMain
Porgy (b)   Donnie Ray Albert
Bess (s)   Clamma Dale
Crown (b)   Andrew Smith
Serena (s)   Wilma Shakesnider
Sporting Life (t)   Larry Marshall
(Both the above are excellent recordings, the Decca a superb studio production, the RCA having a more theatrical quality)

CBS 77319 (3) (d) ●
Columbia OSL-162 (d) (US)
Orchestra and Johnson Chorus
c. Lehmann Engel
Porgy (b)   Lawrence Winters
Bess (s)   Camilla Williams
Crown (b)   Warren Coleman
Serena (s)   Inez Matthews
Sporting Life (t)   Avon Long

CBS 61622 ■
(from above)

Coral CRL1085 □
(Original New York Cast)
c. Alexander Smallens
Decca DL-79024 (US)
Porgy (b)   Todd Duncan
Bess (s)   Anne Brown

RCA LSC-2679 (US) □
c. Skitch Henderson
Porgy (b)   William Warfield
Bess (s)   Leontyne Price

Turnabout TV37080 (3) □
Vox SVBX-5132 (US)
Porgy and Bess Suite (orchestral)
arr. George Gershwin

Act 2 Hortensio and Lucentio are wooing Bianca when Petruchio and Grumio arrive, fantastically attired and calling for Katharina who appears in a rage, boxes Grumio's ears and tears Petruchio's clothes. They answer her with a mocking serenade which contrasts with the tender wooing of Bianca by Lucentio, disguised as the tutor Cambio. They fall in love and Lucentio reveals his true identity. Katharina is finally dressed for the wedding but now Petruchio does not arrive. He sends a note to say he has been detained and will be at the church at noon precisely and will not wait. Baptista, annoyed, is inclined to call the wedding off but Lucentio, anxious to have Katharina wed, prevails upon him to relent and they all set out for the church.

Act 3 Petruchio, now wed, is mastering Katharina well, countering her violence with even more but all done with a solicitous manner. Katharina's spirit is becoming broken as she finds he is dictating what she must wear and eat and, half-starved, she has to admit that she has met her match. Bianca and Lucentio ask her help and tell her that they have been secretly married. She hides them just before Vincentio, Lucentio's father, is due to arrive. All the participants in various disguises appear,

including an actor hired to impersonate Vincentio, and there is great confusion. However, the disguises are eventually set aside, the fathers forgive and bless the marriages and even Katharina and Petruchio cease their battle and swear eternal love.

RECORDING:

Composers Recordings CRI SD-272 (2) (US) ●
Kansas City Lyric Theater Orchestra
c. Russell Patterson
Lucentio (t)   Lowell Harris
Tranio (b)   David Holloway
Baptista (bs)   J. B. Davis
Katharina (m-s)   Mary Jennings
Bianca (s)   Catherine Christensen
Gremio (s)   Robert Jones
Hortensio   Walter Hook
Petruchio   Adair McGowen

UMBERTO GIORDANO

(b. Foggia 27.8.1867; d. Milan 12.11.1948)

The son of an artisan, he was at first intended to follow in the trade, until his musical gift was recognised. He studied at Naples Conservatoire, and while still a student composed an opera, *Marina*, which attracted the attention of the publisher Sonzogno who commissioned a work from him—a piece of somewhat bloodthirsty melodrama, *Mala vita*, which was successful. From then on Giordano produced a stream of effective but often unsophisticated operas. Of these, only *Andrea Chénier* has remained popular, though one or two others are occasionally heard. He married a wealthy lady and lived comfortably; but he never repeated his early successes or really fulfilled his promise.

Andrea Chénier
Opera in 4 Acts.
Text by Luigi Illica.
First performance: Milan (La Scala) March 28, 1896. New York (Academy of Music) 1896; London (in English) 1903.

Synopsis:
Scene: Paris. Time: French Revolution.

Act 1 Andrea Chénier, a poet and dreamer, offends the guests at the Countess's ball by singing a revolutionary song when asked by the Countess's daughter Madeleine (who is in love with him) to improvise a love song. Gérard, also a revolutionary, and in pursuit of Madeleine himself, appears with beggars and ragged poor. They are driven off.

Act 2 In a café in Paris some years later, after revolution, Andrea Chénier finds himself on the wrong side of the authorities for his attitude to Robespierre. He is being watched, and Madeleine is being hunted by the same revolutionists. They plan to meet, but Gérard, who still loves Madeleine, tries to intervene, and is wounded in a fight.

Act 3 Chénier has been arrested and is up before the Tribunal, accused by Gérard. Madeleine pleads with Gérard, offering herself to him if he will spare Andrea Chénier. But it is too late: the mob is out for blood and will not relent.

Act 4 Chénier awaits execution in prison. Madeleine has bribed the jailer to let her substitute herself for a woman convict; if she cannot live with Andrea Chénier, she will die with him. She does: together they go to the guillotine.

Well-known arias:
Act 1 Un dì, all'azzuro spazio (Andrea Chénier)
Act 2 Credo a una possanza arcana (Andrea Chénier)
Act 3 Nemico della patria? (Gérard)
La mamma morta (Madeleine)
Act 4 Come un bel dì di Maggio (Andrea Chénier)
Vicino a te . . . La nostra morte (Andrea Chénier & Madeleine)

RECORDINGS:
RCA Red Seal RL02046/8 ★●
RCA ARL3-2046 (3) (US)
John Alldis Choir/National Philharmonic Orchestra
c. James Levine
Andrea Chénier (t) Placido Domingo
Madeleine
  de Coigny (s)   Renata Scotto
Countess
  de Coigny (m-s) Jean Kraft
Charles Gérard (b) Sherrill Milnes

RCA ARS1-2144 (US) ■
(from above)

RCA LSB4106 □
Un dì, all'azzuro spazio
Come un bel dì di Maggio
Jon Vickers (t)

Decca Ace of Diamonds SDD391 □
London 25075 (US)
Come un bel dì di Maggio
Carlo Bergonzi (t)

Decca Ace of Diamonds GOS600/1 ★●
London 1303 (3) (US)
Chorus and Orchestra of Accademia Santa Cecilia, Rome
c. Gianandrea Gavazzeni
Andrea Chénier (t) Mario del Monaco
Madeleine
  de Coigny (s)   Renata Tebaldi
Countess
  de Coigny (m-s) Maria Mandalari
Charles Gérard (b) Ettore Bastianini

London 25076 (US) ■
(from above)

Decca SDD390 □
London 25081 (US)
Un dì, all'azzuro spazio
Come un bel dì di Maggio
Giuseppe di Stefano (t)

Decca SXL6864 □
London 26557 (US)
La mamma morta
Maria Chiara (s)

Above: *Margaret Sheridan as Madeleine in* Andrea Chénier.

HMV SLS869 (3) □
La mamma morta
Maria Callas (s)

HMV SXLP30205 □
La mamma morta
Joan Hammond (s)

Decca SXLR825 □
La mamma morta
Montserrat Caballé (s)

Selecta/Telefunken AG6 41947 □
Telefunken AG6 41947 (US)
La mamma morta
Felicia Weathers (s)

Fedora
Opera in 3 Acts.
Text by Arturo Colautti after Sardou.
First performance: Milan (Teatro Lirico) November 17, 1898. New York (Metropolitan) 1906.

Synopsis:
Act 1 After the murder of Count Andreievich, the policeman Grech considers the suspects. He narrows them down to one—Count Loris Ipanov—but the Count has disappeared.

Act 2 Andreievich's sister, the Princess Fedora Romanov, is anxious to find the murderer. She contrives to have Ipanov attend her reception in Paris. He convinces her that it was a case of justifiable homicide, since Andreievich had betrayed Ipanov's wife and brought about her death. Fedora believes him, and they go away together.

Act 3 They live together in Switzerland while the police continue to search for the murderer. Ipanov, however, discovers that it was Fedora who first informed the police about him. He tries to kill her, and she takes poison: he relents, but it is too late and she dies.

Well-known arias:
Act 2 Amor ti vieta (Loris)
Vedi, io piango (Loris)
Act 3 Dio di giustiza (Fedora)

RECORDINGS:
Decca SET435/6 ★●
London 1283 (2) (US)
Monte Carlo Opera Chorus/Monte Carlo National Opera Orchestra
c. Lamberto Gardelli
Princess Fedora
  Romanov (s) Magda Olivero
Count Loris
  Ipanov (t)   Mario del Monaco
De Serieux (b) Tito Gobbi

Decca SET494 ■
(from above)

Decca SXL6451 □
London 26080 (US)
Amor ti vieta
Placido Domingo (t)

Decca Ace of Diamonds GOS634/5 □
London 12101 (2) (US)
Amor ti vieta
Jussi Björling (t)

MIKHAIL IVANOVICH GLINKA

(b. Novospasskoye, Smolensk 1.6.1804; d. Berlin 15.2.1857)

Glinka came from a wealthy, if not musical, family. His father intended him for government service, which he entered briefly in 1824. But the young Glinka was determined to devote his life to music. He travelled and studied abroad in his youth, but returned to Russia on the death of his father in 1834, married and settled in St Petersburg. Although he remained essentially an amateur, he made his mark and it was an important one: he is often considered the founder of Russian national music. There is some truth in this; certainly later Russians (notably Tchaikovsky ») had great admiration for and were influenced by Glinka. Of his two operas, the first, *A Life for the Tsar* was the most influential—an epoch-making work—even though it contains much pseudo-Italianism and is by no means entirely original, except in the superb choruses. His second opera *Ruslan and Ludmila* catches the true Russian national note.

A Life for the Tsar (Ivan Susanin)

Opera in 4 Acts and Epilogue.
Text by Georgy Fedorovich Rosen.
First performance: St Petersburg (Bolshoi Theatre) December 9, 1836.

Synopsis:

Scene: A village near Moscow and a Polish camp. Time: 1613.
Act 1 Ivan Susanin brings news that the Polish invaders are marching on Moscow, but his daughter's fiancé, Sobinin, declares that they have been defeated. Susanin withholds permission for his daughter Antonida to marry Sobinin until the issue is settled and a new Tsar elected, but then hears that the young Romanoff has been chosen and is reconciled.
Act 2 A great ball is in progress at the Polish headquarters. Hearing that Romanoff is to be Tsar they plan to abduct him from the monastery where he is lodging.
Act 3 Susanin and his foster-son Vanya sing of Russia's victory; but Vanya knows of the Polish plot. Preparations for the wedding of Sobinin and Antonida are interrupted by the arrival of Polish troops who try to force Susanin to lead them to the new Tsar. Susanin acquiesces, but not before he has sent Vanya ahead to warn the young Romanoff; meanwhile Sobinin organises a troop of local peasants to rescue Susanin.
Act 4 Sobinin urges his company on despite the bitter weather. Susanin meanwhile leads the Poles away from the monastery and into a forest; he confesses, and is killed.
Epilogue The crowds in Moscow rejoice in the Tsar's triumph and mourn Susanin as a hero. The Tsar enters his capital.

Notes:

The original title was *Ivan Susanin*, but when the Emperor accepted the dedication it was changed to *A Life for the Tsar*. After the 1917 revolution the original title was restored and is now used exclusively in the Soviet Union.

Well-known arias:
Act 4 They guess the truth . . . The dawn is breaking (Susanin)

RECORDINGS:
Decca Ace of Diamonds GOS646/8 ●
Richmond 63523 (3) (US)
Yugoslav Army Chorus/Orchestra of
National Opera, Belgrade
c. Oscar Danon
Ivan Susanin (bs) Milo Changalovich
Sobinin (t) Drago Startz
Antonida (s) Maria Glavachevich
Vanya (c) Militza Mladinovich

Decca Ace of Diamonds SDD282 □
Overture
c. Ernest Ansermet

Supraphon SUAST10569 □
Overture
c. Karel Sejna

Decca SXL6147 □
London 26249 (US)
They guess the truth
Nicolai Ghiaurov (bs-b)

Ruslan and Ludmila

Opera in 5 Acts.
Text by Glinka, V. F. Shirkov, N. V. Kukolnik and others, after Pushkin.
First performance: St Petersburg (Bolshoi Theatre) December 9, 1842.

RECORDINGS:
Decca Eclipse 757 □
Overture
c. Ernest Ansermet

Decca SXL6263 □
London 6785 and 6730 (US)
Overture
London Symphony Orchestra
c. Sir Georg Solti

Philips 6833 033 □
Philips 6833 033 (US)
Overture
c. Bernard Haitink

Decca SPA257 □
London 6944 (US)
Berlin Philharmonic Orchestra
Overture
c. Sir Georg Solti

Decca SXL6782 □
London 7006 (US)
Overture
c. Lorin Maazel

HMV ASD3338 □
Angel S-37409 (US)
Overture
c. André Previn

HMV ASD3421 □
Angel S-37464 (US)
Overture
c. Msitislav Rostropovitch

CBS 72628 (d) □
Columbia MS-7014/M2X-795/D3S-818/
M-31844
Overture
c. Leonard Bernstein
(A complete recording under Kondrashin on Parlophone PMA1033/6—Westminster 1401 (US)—has long been deleted)

Below right: *Petrov as* Ivan Susanin *at the Mariinsky Theatre.*

Below: *The final scene of* Ivan Susanin *at the Bolshoi Theatre, with the singers riding real horses on stage.*

CHRISTOPH WILLIBALD GLUCK

(b. Erasbach 2.7.1714; d. Vienna 15.11.1787)

After encountering the familiar parental opposition to a musical career, Gluck studied at Prague University and entered the service of Prince Melzi and studied with Sammartini in Milan. He visited London in 1745 where he met Handel ». During all this time Gluck was producing operas in the conventional Italian style, and it was not until he settled in Vienna in 1752 that he began his great work of opera reform. Previously, operas had been tailored to the traditional conceits of the period, when the drama was subservient to the vocal pyrotechnics of a tribe of virtuoso singers who thought that opera's sole purpose was to display their talents. Gluck's aim was to effect an equal marriage of music and drama; the expurgation of extraneous matter, and a more flexible and expressive style in which the music moved the drama on and added a further dimension to it. Yet for all the success of his reforming zeal, Gluck was no pedant; he could, when occasion required, return to the older tradition and make the best of it. It was this lack of rigidity that enabled him to carry out his reforms—even though his actual creative genius was not of the highest order. Gluck composed a great number of operas, but only a few have maintained their popularity. Of these, the most famous by far is *Orfeo*, which exists in both French and Italian versions.

Orfeo ed Euridice (Orphée)

Opera in 3 Acts.
Text by Raniero da Calzabigi.
First performance: Vienna (Burg Theatre) October 5, 1762. Frankfurt o/M 1764; Parma 1769; London (with additions) 1770; New York (Winter Garden Theatre) (in English) 1863.

Act 1 Orfeo (Orpheus), mourning the death of his wife Euridice, calls upon Amor (Eros), God of Love, to restore her. He is told he may go to Hades to bring her back, on one condition: that he shall not look back at her until he is once again upon the surface of the earth.
Act 2 Orfeo enters Hades, but is confronted by the Furies who at first deny him passage. He sings and they relent. He is led to the veiled figure of Euridice through the Elysian Fields.
Act 3 Obeying Amor's command, he does not look at her, but she mistakes his avoidance for indifference. Thinking she has lost his love, she begs to return to the Underworld. Orfeo, unable to stop himself, turns and embraces her. At once Euridice dies again. Orfeo sings of his loss and despair; Amor, melted by the beauty of the song, reunites the two unconditionally.

Well-known arias:

Act 1 Chiamo il mio ben (Orfeo)
Act 2 Chi mai dell'Erebo (Orfeo)
(Dance of the Furies—Orchestral)
(Dance of the Blessed Spirits—Orchestral)
E quest'asilo ameno e grato (Euridice)
Che puro ciel (Orfeo)
Act 3 Su, e con me vieni, o cara (Orfeo and Euridice)
Che fiero momento (Orfeo and Euridice)
Che farò senza Euridice (What is life?) (Orfeo)

Notes:
The part of Orfeo was originally written for male alto. When the new version was produced for Paris (*Orphée*, trans. Pierre Louis Moline; Paris [Opéra] August 2, 1774) Gluck rewrote it for tenor. It was Berlioz » who restored the original voicing, allotting the part to contralto, the version usually heard today.

RECORDINGS:

RCA SER5539/41 ●
RCA LSC-6169 (3) (US)
Polyphonic Chorus of Rome/Virtuosi di Roma/Collegium Musicum Italicum Ensemble
c. Renato Fasano
Orfeo (m-s) Shirley Verrett
Euridice (s) Anna Moffo
Amor (s) Judith Raskin

Decca SET443/4 ★●
London 1285 (2) (US)
Chorus and Orchestra of Royal Opera House, Covent Garden
c. Sir Georg Solti
Orfeo (m-s) Marilyn Horne
Euridice (s) Pilar Lorengar
Amor (s) Helen Donath

Above: *Kathleen Ferrier in her most famous role as Orfeo.*

Decca SET495 ■
London 26214 (US)
(from above)

HMV RLS725 (2) (r. 1951) ●
Chorus and Orchestra of Netherlands Opera
c. Charles Bruck
Orfeo (c) Kathleen Ferrier
Euridice (s) Greet Koeman
Amor (s) Nel Duval

DG Privilege 2726 043 (2) ●
DG 2726 043 (2) (US)
Munich Bach Choir and Orchestra
c. Karl Richter
Orfeo (b) Dietrich Fischer-Dieskau
Euridice (s) Gundula Janowitz
Amor (s) Edda Moser

RCA AT127 (d) (r. 1952) □
LVT-1041 (d) (US)
Act 2
Robert Shaw Chorale/NBC Symphony Orchestra
c. Arturo Toscanini
Orfeo (m-s) Nan Merriman
Euridice (s) Barbara Gibson

Philips 9500 023 *or* 6767 001 (4) □
Che puro ciel
Che farò senza Euridice
Janet Baker (m-s)

Decca Ace of Diamonds SDD193 □
Che puro ciel
Che farò senza Euridice
Teresa Berganza (s)

HMV ASD3375 □
Dance of the Blessed Spirits
c. Neville Marriner

RCA Gold Seal GL25160 □
Dance of the Blessed Spirits
James Galway (fl)
c. Charles Gerhardt

Decca ACL308 □
What is life
Kathleen Ferrier (c)

La Rencontre Imprévue

Opera.
Text by L. H. Dancourt.
First performance: Vienna (Burg Theatre) January 7, 1764.

RECORDING:
Philips 9500 023 *or* 6767 001 (4) □
Philips 9500 023 *or* 6767 001 (US)
Bel inconnu
Je cherche à vous faire
Janet Baker (m-s)

Alceste

Opera in 3 Acts.
Text by Raniero da Calzabigi.
First performance: Vienna (Burg Theatre) December 26, 1767. Paris (Opéra) (French) 1776.

Synopsis:

Scene: Thessaly. Time: Ancient.

Act 1 King Admetus is mortally ill, and general lamentations are led by his queen Alceste. The oracle of the gods, answering her prayers, says that the King may be saved if somebody else will die in his place. and Alceste offers herself.

Act 2 Admetus, recovered, joins in the celebrations. He learns of the condition of his recovery, but no one will tell him who is to forfeit. He sees Alceste's face, and realises the truth; he tries to withdraw from the compact; but there is no way: the gods have spoken.

Act 3 Admetus refuses to accept Alceste's sacrifice and has followed her into the Underworld. Thanatos, God of Death, tries to stop him, but Admetus defies him. Meanwhile, up on Earth, Hercules, hearing what has happened, resolves to intervene. He fights Thanatos; his courage impresses Apollo, who wrenches Alceste from the arms of death and reunites her with Admetus.

Well-known arias:

Act 1 Divinités du Styx (Alceste)
Act 2 Bannis la crainte (Admetus)
　　　　Ah, malgré moi, mon faible coeur (Alceste)

RECORDINGS:

Decca Ace of Diamonds GOS574/6 ●	HMV SXLP30166 □
Richmond 63512 (3) (US)	Divinités du Styx
Geraint Jones Singers and Orchestra	**Maria Callas** (s)
c. Geraint Jones	
Alceste (s)　Kirsten Flagstad	Decca Ace of Diamonds SDD193 *or*
Admetus (t)　Raoul Jobin	Eclipse ECS806 □
Evandro (t)　Alexander Young	Divinités du Styx
Hercules (b)　Thomas Hemsley	**Teresa Berganza** (m-s)
Cetra Opera Live L050 (2) (r. 1954) ●	Philips 9500 023 *or* 6767 001 □
Chorus and Orchestra of La Scala, Milan	Philips 9500 023 *or* 6767 001 (US)
c. Carlo Maria Giulini	Divinités du Styx
Alceste (s)　Maria Callas	**Janet Baker** (m-s)
Admetus (t)　Renato Gavarini	
Evandro (t)　Giuseppe Zampieri	
High Priest (b)　Paolo Silveri	

Paride ed Elena

Opera in 4 Acts.
Text by Raniero da Calzabigi.
First performance: Vienna (Burg Theatre) November 3, 1770.

RECORDINGS:

Philips 9500 023 *or* 6767 001 (4) □	Decca Ace of Diamonds SDD193 *or*
Philips 9500 023 *or* 6767 001 (US)	Eclipse ECS806 □
Spiagge amate	O del mio dolce ardor
O del mio dolce ardor	**Teresa Berganza** (m-s)
La bella immagini	
Di te scordarmi	Decca SXL6579 □
Janet Baker (m-s)	London 1282 (2) (US)
	O del mio dolce ardor
	Renata Tebaldi (s)

Iphigénie en Aulide

Opera in 3 Acts.
Text by François Louis and Lebland du Roullet after Racine and Euripides.
First performance: Paris (Opéra) April 19, 1774.

Synopsis:

Scene: Greece. Time: Trojan wars.

Act 1 To gain a fair wind to Troy, Agamemnon, King of Greece, must sacrifice his daughter Iphigénie. He tries to resist, but there is no contravening the will of the gods. She departs for Aulis to marry Achilles, who is unaware of the sacrifice.

Act 2 The wedding feast approaches. When Achilles learns the truth, he promises to defend Iphigénie, and Agamemnon sends Iphigénie off to Mycenae.

Act 3 There is no victory in battle for those who do not obey the gods; Agamemnon must honour the sacrifice. Once more Achilles defies the king, using an army. But the gods have taken Agamemnon's stand as evidence of good faith; they cancel the command for the sacrifice and everyone departs for the wars.

RECORDING:

RCA ARL 21104 (2) ●	(Note: Something of an
RCA ARL 21104 (2) (US)	oddity; this version is hardly
(arr. Wagner)	what Gluck wrote or
Bavarian Radio Chorus/Munich Radio	intended; but it has a kind of
Orchestra	interest in showing how
c. Kurt Eichorn	Wagner, the great music
Agamemnon (b)　Dietrich Fischer-	drama theorist, approached someone
Dieskau	else's work—someone who in a number
Iphigénie (s)　Anna Moffo	of respects anticipated Wagner's own
Achilles (t)　Ludovic Spiess	theories)
Clytemnestra (m-s)　Trudeliese Schmidt	RCA ARS1-1212 (US) ■
	(from above)

Armide

Opera in 5 Acts.
Text by Philippe Quinault after Tasso.
First performance: Paris (Opéra) September 23, 1777.

RECORDING:

Philips 9500 023 *or* 6767 001 (4) □
Philips 9500 023 *or* 6707 001 (US)
Le perfide Renaud
Janet Baker (m-s)

Iphigénie en Tauride

Opera in 4 Acts.
Text by Nicolas-Francois Giullard after Euripides.
First performance: Paris (Opéra) May 18, 1779. Vienna (in German) 1781; London (in Italian) 1796; New York (Metropolitan) (in German) 1916.

Synopsis:

Act 1 Iphigénie has become Priestess of Diana, and fears that misfortune has befallen her family; at the same time, King Thoas has forebodings of danger to himself and he demands human sacrifice. Orestes and Pylade are brought before him—they are Greek captives and will make suitable victims.

Act 2 Orestes, who has killed his own mother, is brought to the edge of madness by the Furies. Iphigénie (who, unknown to either, is Orestes' sister) discovers from him that Agamemnon has been killed by his wife Clytemnestra and that Orestes killed her in revenge. Only Electra remains.

Act 3 Iphigénie has not yet recognised her brother, but now sees a resemblance and in order to save him from Thoas plans to send him to Mycenae with a message. But Orestes will not abandon his friend Pylade. Pylade agrees to take the letter instead, hoping thereby to get help for his friend.

Act 4 The sacrifice is prepared, Iphigénie herself holding the knife. Suddenly Orestes exclaims, and Iphigénie at last recognises her brother—and her king. Thoas demands the sacrifice and Iphigénie declares she will die too. Just in time Pylade arrives with help; Thoas is killed and Diana pardons Orestes.

Well-known arias:

Act 1 O toi, qui prolongeas nos jours (Iphigénie)
　　　　De noirs pressentiments mon ame intimidée (Thoas)
Act 2 Mad Scene (Orestes)
　　　　Unis dès la plus tendre enfance (Pylade)
Act 3 O malheureuse Iphigénie (Iphigénie)
　　　　J'implore et je tremble (Iphigénie)
　　　　Chaste fille de Latone (Iphigénie)

RECORDINGS:

Cetra Opera Live L054 (2) (m) (r. 1957) ●	Decca SET520/1 □
Chorus and Orchestra of La Scala, Milan	Decca 1292 (US)
c. Nino Sonzogno	Cette nuit . . . O toi
Iphigénie (s)　Maria Callas	**Régine Crespin** (s)
Orestes (b)　Dino Dondi	
Pylade (t)　Francesco Albanese	Philips 9500 023 *or* 6767 001 (4) □
Thoas (b)　Anselmo Colzani	Philips 9500 023 *or* 6767 001 (US)
Diana (m-s)　Fiorenza Cossotto	Non cet affreux devoir
	Janet Baker (m-s)

BENJAMIN GODARD
(b. Paris 18.8.1849; d. Cannes 10.1.1895)

French violinist and composer who studied at the Paris Conservatoire in 1863. Early promise was not fulfilled and his works tended to be patchy in quality, though containing excellent pieces. He wrote six operas: *Les Bijoux de Jeanette* (1878); *Pédro de Zalaméa* (1884); *Jocelyn* (1888)—one of the least successful but immortalising the composer by virtue of its popular 'Berceuse'; *Dante* (1890); *La Vivandière*—his most successful work, performed in England by the Carl Rosa Company in 1896 and 1897; and *Les Guelfes* (1902).

Jocelyn
Opera in 4 Acts.
Text based on a poem by Lamartine.
First performance: Brussels (Théâtre de la Monnaie) February 25, 1888.

RECORDINGS:
DG 136011 □
DG 136011 (US)
Berceuse
Rita Streich (s)
(Numerous instrumental versions available)

Right: *One short orchestral snippet is all that is heard today of Benjamin Godard's once popular opera* Jocelyn.

CHARLES GOUNOD
(b. Paris 18.6.1818; d. Saint-Cloud 18.10.1893)

Gounod received his first musical education from his concert pianist mother. Later he entered the Paris Conservatoire, where he studied under Halévy », Paer and Lesueur before winning the Prix de Rome in 1839. While in Rome he was greatly influenced by Italian music (especially Palestrina), and by Italian life and art in general. Travels in Germany and Austria introduced him to German music and musicians. The theatre occupied Gounod's energies for the major part of his life. He composed 13 operas between 1850 and 1880 (including the unfinished *Maître Pierre*) and a considerable amount of incidental music. At one time Gounod appeared to be on the point of taking holy orders, and all his life he composed widely for the church; he also composed much orchestral and instrumental music and songs. As an opera composer Gounod is remembered principally by *Faust*, one of the most successful operas ever written, though its popularity has declined somewhat in our own time. His *Roméo et Juliette*, a not altogether convincing adaptation of Shakespeare (as *Faust*, for all its musical brilliance, is not a very profound adaptation of Goethe) contains a good deal of fine music but has not held its place in the repertory. Perhaps Gounod's most attractive operatic production is *Mireille*, with its warm lyricism and Provençal setting.

Sapho
Opera in 3 Acts.
Text by Emile Augier.
First performance: Paris (Opéra) April 16, 1851. Paris 1884 (revised in 4 Acts).

RECORDING:
Decca SET520/1 □   Ou suis-je? . . . O ma lyre immortelle
London 1292 (2) (US)   **Régine Crespin** (s)

Faust
Opera in 5 Acts.
Text by Jules Barbier and Michel Carré after Goethe.
First performance: Paris (Théâtre-Lyrique) March 19, 1859. Paris (Opéra) 1869 (new version with recitative and ballet); Liège 1860; London (Her Majesty's Theatre) (in Italian) 1863; New York (in Italian) 1863.

Synopsis:
Act 1 Faust, cursing life and advancing age, calls upon the Devil to aid him. Méphistophélès appears, offering wealth and power, but Faust also wants eternal youth; this he can have too, in return for his soul. Faust's hesitations are overcome by a vision of Marguerite, and the bargain is struck.
Act 2 Outside the city gates, Valentine, with his friends Wagner and Siebel, is about to depart for the wars. He prays for the safety of his sister Marguerite. Méphistophélès begins to taunt the students, especially Valentine, who points at him the hilt of a broken sword, in the form of a crucifix. After the famous Waltz, Faust enters as Marguerite passes by on her way to Mass. Siebel tries to approach her but Méphistophélès intervenes, and Faust joins her instead.
Act 3 Marguerite's garden. Siebel tries to pick flowers for Marguerite, but they wilt in his hands until he sprinkles them with holy water. Faust comes in with Méphistophélès and the devil substitutes a casket of jewels for Siebel's flowers. Marguerite, after singing the famous 'Jewel Song' is left alone with Faust. They fall in love, to sardonic laughter from Méphistophélès.
Act 4 Marguerite has been betrayed by Faust. Siebel remains faithful but to little avail. Marguerite prays, but Méphistophélès prophesies her doom. Valentine, returned from the war ('Soldiers' Chorus') realises something is wrong. He challenges Faust to a duel, but Méphistophélès intervenes and Valentine is killed, cursing Marguerite with his dying breath.
Act 5 Méphistophélès stages a Walpurgis Night ballet for Faust, who has a sudden vision of Marguerite and demands to see her. She is in prison, condemned for the murder of her child; going mad, she calls on the angels to save her. She dies and the angels take her soul.

Well-known arias:
Act 1 A moi les plaisirs (duet) (Faust and Méphistophélès)
Act 2 Avant de quitter ces lieux (Valentine)
Le veau d'or (The Golden Calf) (Méphistophélès)
Waltz (The kermesse) (Chorus)
Act 3 Faites-lui mes aveux (Siebel)
Salut! demeure chaste et pure (Faust)
Il était un roi de Thule (Marguerite)
Ah! je ris de me voir so belle (Air des bijoux—Jewel Song) (Marguerite)
Laisse-moi contempler ton visage (Faust and Marguerite)
O nuit d'amour . . . ciel radieux! (Faust and Marguerite)
Act 4 Gloire immortelle (Soldiers' Chorus)
Vous qui faites l'endormie (Faust)
Act 5 Walpurgis Night Ballet
Anges purs! Anges radieux! (Marguerite, Faust & Méphistophélès)

Right: *A production of Gounod's* Faust *at the Royal Opera House, Covent Garden.*

Above: *A lithograph by Delacroix of a scene from Goethe's Faust, the subject of Gounod's most popular opera in 1859.*

RECORDINGS:
HMV SLS816 (4) ★●
Angel S-3622 (4) (US)
Paris National Opera Chorus and
Orchestra
c. André Cluytens
Faust (t)   Nicolai Gedda
Marguerite (s)   Victoria de los
                                         Angeles
Méphistophélès (bs) Boris Christoff
Valentine (b)   Ernest Blanc

HMV ASD421 (d) ■
Angel S-35827 (US)
(from above)

Decca SET327/30 ●
London 1433 (4) (US)
Ambrosian Singers/Highgate School
Choir/London Symphony Orchestra
c. Richard Bonynge
Faust (t)   Franco Corelli
Marguerite (s)   Joan Sutherland
Méphistophélès
   (bs-b)   Nicolai Ghiaurov
Valentine (b)   Robert Massard

Decca SET431 ■
London 26139 (US)
(from above)

RCA Erato STU1031/4 ●
RCA FRL4-2493 (4) (US)
Rhine Opera Chorus/Strasbourg
Philharmonic Orchestra
c. Alain Lombard
Faust (t)   Giacomo Aragall
Marguerite (s)   Montserrat Caballé
Méphistophélès (bs) Paul Plishka
Valentine (b)   Philippe
                                         Huttenlocher

Cetra Opera Live L01 (3) (m) (r. 1949) ●
Chorus and Orchestra of Metropolitan
Opera, New York
c. Wilfrid Pelletier
Faust (t)   Giuseppe de Stefano
Marguerite (s)   Dorothy Kirsten
Méphistophélès (bs) Italo Tajo
Valentine (b)   Leonard Warren

Hungaroton SLPX11712 ■
Hungarian State Opera
c. Ervin Lukacs
Faust (t)   György Korondi
Marguerite (s)   Sylvia Sass
Méphistophélès (bs) Kolos Kováts
Valentine (b)   Lajos Miller

Decca SXL6637 □
London 26379 (US)
Le veau d'or
Joseph Rouleau (bs)

Decca SXL6147 □
London 26249 (US)
Le veau d'or
Que voulez-vous, messieurs
Nicolai Ghiaurov (bs-b)

RCA ARL1 0048 □
RCA ARL1 0048 (US)
Salut! demeure chaste et pure
Placido Domingo (t)

Decca Ace of Diamonds SDD390 □
London 25081 (US)
Salut! demeure chaste et pure
Giuseppe di Stefano (t)

Decca SXL6649 □
Salut! demeure chaste et pure
Luciano Pavarotti (t)

Mireille
Opera in 5 Acts.
Text by Michel Carré after Frédéric Mistral's 'Mirèo' (poem).
First performance: Paris (Théâtre-Lyrique) March 19, 1864. Paris 1864 (revised in 3 Acts); London (Her Majesty's Theatre) (in Italian) 1864; Chicago (in English) 1880.

Synopsis:
Act 1   Mireille, the daughter of a rich Provençal farmer, has fallen in love with Vincent, a poor young basketmaker, but her family do not approve.
Act 2   Outside the bullring at Arles, Taven, the local crone, warns the young couple that other suitors are pursuing Mireille, including the bullfighter Ourrias, who is promptly rejected while Mireille reaffirms her love for Vincent. Ourrias attacks Vincent and seriously wounds him.
Act 3   Mireille at first does not know if he is alive or dead, but he recovers and he and Mireille meet in the church of Saintes Maries de la Mer. To reach the church she has to cross the plain of Crau; she suffers sunstroke but battles on. Her father finds them, pardons their love and blesses their union.

Notes:
In other versions, Mireille dies in Vincent's arms, seeing, like the doomed Marguerite of *Faust*, a vision of heaven.

Well-known arias:
Act 1   O légère hirondelle (Mireille)
Act 2   La brise est douce (Mireille and Vincent)
              Si les filles d'Arles (Ourrias)
Act 3   Le jour se lève (Andreloux)
              Heureux petit berger (Mireille)
              Anges du Paradis (Vincent)
              Voici la vaste plaine et le désert de feu (Mireille)

RECORDINGS:
Columbia 2C 153 10613/6 (Fr) ●
(previously Columbia 33CX 1299/301)
Paris Conservatoire Orchestra
c. André Cluytens
Mireille (s)   Janette Vivalda
Vincent (t)   Nicolai Gedda
Ourrias (b)   Michel Dens
Taven (m-s)   Christianne Gayraud

Decca LXT2789 (d) ■
Paris Conservatoire Orchestra
c. Alberto Erede
Mireille (s)   Janine Micheau
Vincent (t)   Pierre Gianotti

Decca SET454/5 □
London 1286 (2) (US)
O légère hirondelle
Joan Sutherland (s)

Roméo et Juliette
Opera in 5 Acts.
Text by Barbier and Carré.
First performance: Paris (Théâtre-Lyrique) April 27, 1867. Paris (Opéra) 1888 (with ballet).

RECORDINGS:
HMV SLS943 (3) (d) ●
Angel S-3734 (3) (US)
Chorus and Orchestra of the Paris Opera
c. Alain Lombard
Juliet (s)   Mirella Freni
Romeo (t)   Franco Corelli

Angel S-36731 (US) ■
(from above)

RCA ARL1 0048 □
RCA ARL1 0048 (US)
L'amour . . . Ah, lève-toi soleil
Placido Domingo (t)

CBS 76522 □
Columbia M-34206 (US)
Depuis hier je cherche en vain
Frederica von Stade (m-s)

Le Tribut de Zamora
Opera in 5 Acts.
Text by Adolphe Philippe d'Ennery and Jules Brésil.
First performance: Paris (Opéra) April 1, 1881.

RECORDING:
Decca SET454/5 □
London 1286 (2) (US)
Ce Sarrasin disait
Joan Sutherland (s)

ENRIQUE GRANADOS
(b. Lérida 27.7.1867; d. at sea 24.3.1916)

Granados was one of several Spanish composers to study with Felipe Pedrell and to be encouraged in his ambitions towards the renaissance of Spanish music. Also, like others of his time, he went to Paris, although for only two years; ill health prevented him from making the most of it. On his return to Spain, he revealed his great talents as a concert pianist. As a composer Granados's work centred on the piano, for which he wrote many pieces, often little more than well turned genre pieces in the 19th Century Romantic style. Yet with the two books of *Goyescas*, based upon the paintings, drawings and tapestries of Francesco Goya, he found an original and genuinely Spanish idiom. These piano pieces have more than a direct bearing on the one opera out his seven to have gained international acceptance, also called *Goyescas*. The opera is unusual, because it was built out of the piano pieces, a reversal of the more familiar practice. Its launching was tragic, as Granados was drowned when the ship on which he was returning to Spain from New York after the première was torpedoed in the English Channel by a U-boat.

Goyescas
Opera in 3 Tableaux.
Text by Fernando Periquet after Goya and based on Granados's piano 'Goyescas'.
First performance: New York (Metropolitan) January 28, 1916.

Synopsis:
Scene: Madrid. Time: c. 1800.
Tableau 1   Youths and girls are tossing a *pelele* (straw man). Paquiro the bullfighter is flirting with everyone until his sweetheart Pepa arrives. Then Rosario, an aristocrat, appears looking for her lover Don Fernando, a Guards officer. Paquiro invites Rosario to a *baile de candil* (candlelight ball).
Tableau 2   At the ball, Paquiro is displeased when Rosario arrives with Fernando. Fernando's haughty attitude angers everyone, and in the end Paquiro and Fernando arrange a duel; Rosario faints. Intermezzo.
Tableau 3   Rosario, in her garden, hears a nightingale and sings her famous 'Maiden and the Nightingale'. Fernando enters and there is a long love duet, before Fernando is summoned to the duel. Rosario hears a cry; Fernando is mortally wounded and dies in her arms.

RECORDINGS:
Decca LXT5338 (d) ●
London OSA-1101 (d) (US)
Madrid Singers/National Orchestra of Spain
c. Ataulfo Argenta
Rosario (s)   Consuelo Rubio
Pepa (m-s)   Ana-Maria Iriarte
Paquiro (b)   Manuel Ausensi
Don Fernando (t)   Gines Torrano

Decca Ace of Diamonds SDD446 ▢
National Orchestra of Spain
c. Ataulfo Argenta
La maja y el ruisenor (Maiden and the nightingale)
Intermezzo
Consuelo Rubio (s)

Decca Jubilee JB50 ▢
Intermezzo
c. Rafael Frühbeck de Burgos

Above: *Enrique Granados.*

ANDRÉ ERNEST GRÉTRY
(b. Liège 11.2.1741; d. Montmorency 24.9.1813)

An enormously prolific and in his day important composer of operas, today virtually none of Grétry's operatic music survives in the record catalogues. He wrote over 70 operas and operettas and these contain much delightful, intelligent music, even if technically they tend to be somewhat plain and simplistic. We are indebted to Sir Thomas Beecham for preserving some totally charming ballet and orchestral excerpts. Grétry was a French composer of Walloon descent who played a major part in the French musical life of the late 18th and early 19th Centuries. He was an inspector of the Paris Conservatoire when it was founded in 1795, and was one of the founder members of the Institut de France, the same year. In France his operas still retain some popularity.

Zémire et Azor
Opera in 4 Acts.
Text by Jean François Marmontel.
First performance: Fontainebleau, November 9, 1771. Paris (Comédie-Italienne) December 16, 1771.

RECORDINGS:
HMV ASD1162 (d) ▢
Ballet Suite (arr. Beecham)
c. Sir Thomas Beecham

Decca L'Oiseau-Lyre SOL297 ▢
Ballet Suite
(excerpts from *L'Epreuve villageoise*—1784; *La Caravane du Caire*—1783; *Céphale et Prochis*—1773)
c. Raymond Leppard

Above: *André Gretry was an important composer of over 70 operas.*

Le Magnifique
Opera in 3 Acts.
Text by Jean-Michel Sedaine, after La Fontaine.
First performance: Paris (Comédie-Italienne) March 4, 1773.

RECORDING:
Decca SXL6531 ▢
London 6735 (US)
Overture
c. Richard Bonynge

Le Jugement de Midas
Opera in 3 Acts.
Text by Thomas d'Hele.
First performance: Paris (privately) March 28, 1778. Paris (Comédie-Italienne) June 27, 1778.

RECORDING:
Philips SAL3674 ▢
Ballet Suite (arr. Beecham)
c. Raymond Leppard

JACQUES FRANCOIS HALÉVY
(b. Paris 27.5.1799; d. Nice 17.3.1862)

The teacher of Gounod » and Bizet » (who was also his son-in-law), Halévy composed more than 40 operas and was extremely active in French musical life, both through his position as professor of harmony at the Paris Conservatoire, and later (1840) of composition, and as permanent secretary of the Académie des Beaux-Arts. He provided works for the leading opera houses and in his day gained much success. Today, his operas are rarely heard outside France; even *La Juive*, highly successful and at one time immensely popular with both singers and audiences, is virtually unrepresented.

La Juive
Opera in 5 Acts.
Text by Eugène Scribe.
First performance: Paris (Opéra) February 23, 1835.

RECORDINGS:
RCA ARL1-0447 (d) ■
RCA ARL1-0447 (US)
New Philharmonia Orchestra
c. Antonio de Almeida
Martina Arroyo (s)
Anna Moffo (s)
Richard Tucker (t)

RCA RL11749 □
Rachel, quand du Seigneur
Enrico Caruso (t)

Hungaroton SLPX11428 □
Rachel, quand du Seigneur
Josef Simandi (t)

Right: *The final scene from Halévy's* La Juive, *as it was seen at Covent Garden in July 1850, performed in Italian with Pauline Viardot, Tamberlik and Pololini.*

GEORGE FRIDERIC HANDEL
(b. Halle 23.2.1685; d. London 14.4.1759)

The operatic world of Handel's time was dominated by a race of fashionable, frequently gifted, but mostly conceited singers, for whom Handel wrote. He was obliged to use the contemporary forms and conventions in his operas and rarely rebelled, as Gluck did; although there is the story of him holding an obstreperous *prima donna* out of the window and threatening to drop her into the street if she did not mend her ways (there is an even better story that it was, in fact, two *prima donne*, one in each hand, who had persisted in quarrelling in his presence. But for the most part Handel abided by the rules of the day and composed accordingly. Of course, being a man of genius, he frequently turned it to his own advantage; his operas are full of superb arias and deep expression; and as he grew older he subtly tightened and economised the structure and form of his operas so that the worst excesses were at least tamed. But whatever else may be argued, Handel's operas are an essential part of his genius, without which no proper understanding of him is possible. Handel's early career was as a musician in the Hamburg opera house, where his first stage work, *Almira*, was produced. He then moved to Italy for five years, where he associated with Alessandro Scarlatti », founder of the Neapolitan school of opera, then settled permanently in London and became a naturalised Englishman. We need not go into the details of his career as an opera impresario and composer, except perhaps to note that his turning from opera to oratorio for the last 20 years of his life was commercially rather than artistically motivated. He finally found the embattled London operatic scene too perilous and unrewarding and decided to give the English what they wanted—large and splendid oratorios on biblical subjects.

Rodrigo
Opera in 3 Acts.
Text by: Unknown.
First performance: Florence, c. 1707.

RECORDING:
Pye GSCG14086 □
Orchestral Suite
c. Sir John Barbirolli

Agrippina
Opera in 3 Acts.
Text by Vincenzo Grimani.
First performance: Venice (Teatro San Giovanni Crisostimo) December 26, 1709.

RECORDINGS:
DG 2535 242 □   HMV ASD3182 □
DG 2535 242 (US)   Angel S-37176 (US)
Overture   Overture
c. Karl Richter   c. Neville Marriner

Rinaldo
Opera in 3 Acts.
Text by Giacomo Rossi (Italian) and Aaron Hill (English) after Tasso.
First performance: London (Queen's Theatre) February 24, 1711. Dublin 1711; Naples 1718.

Synopsis:

Act 1 Argante, King of Jerusalem, enters in a chariot, followed by Armida, whose chariot is drawn by flying dragons. The crusader Rinaldo and his love Almirena are together in a grove, then a black cloud carries off Armida and Almirena, leaving two Furies in their place, who mock Rinaldo before disappearing.
Act 2 Two Mermaids, or Sirens, tempt the innocent Rinaldo

aboard an enchanted boat with the Spirit of a beautiful woman at the helm. The boat sails away with Rinaldo and the Spirit. Armida, in the enchanted garden of her palace, transforms herself into Almirena.

Act 3 Armida's palace is a fortress on a mountain, guarded by Spirits, above the cave of a Christian magician. The Spirits repulse an attack by Goffredo, co-leader, with Eustazio, of the crusade, but a second assault, assisted by the magician, succeeds. Rinaldo and Armida, both aided by Spirits, fight each other in the enchanted garden. After an interlude for a grand military revue, Rinaldo storms and captures Jerusalem, routing and pursuing Argante.

Notes:

The plot is confusing but the action highly spectacular, as befitted Handel's first operatic success in London. Argante's first aria, accompanied by trumpets, was taken from Handel's *Aci, Galatea e Politemo* (not *Acis and Galatea*). *Rinaldo*, written in haste, contains many borrowings.

RECORDINGS:
CBS 79308 (3) ●
Columbia M3-34592 (US)
La Grande Ecurie et la Chambre du Roy
c. Jean-Claude Malgoire
Rinaldo (c) Carolyn Watkinson
Almirena (s) Ileana Cotrubas
Armida (s) Jeanette Scovotti

Decca SXL6360 □
London 6586 (US)
Overture/March and Battle
c. Richard Bonynge

Il Pastor Fido
Opera in 3 Acts.
Text by Giacomo Rossi after Battista Guarini.
First performance: London (Queen's Theatre) November 22, 1712.

RECORDING:
Decca Argo ZRG686 □
Argo 5442 (US)
Pour les chasseurs, I & II
c. Neville Marriner

Teseo
Opera in 3 Acts.
Text by Nicola Francesco Haym.
First performance: London (Queen's Theatre) January 10, 1713.

RECORDING:
Decca SXL6360 □
London 6586 (US)
Overture
c. Richard Bonynge

Radamisto
Opera in 3 Acts.
Text by Nicola Francesco Haym, from 'L'amor tiranico'.
First performance: London (King's Theatre) April 27, 1720.

RECORDINGS:
Decca SXL6496 □
London 6711 (US)
Overture
c. Richard Bonynge

DG 2535 242 □
DG 2535 242 (US)
Overture
c. Karl Richter

Ottone
Opera in 3 Acts.
Text by Nicola Francesco Haym.
First performance: London (King's Theatre) January 12, 1723.

RECORDING:
Philips 6599 053 □
Philips 6599 053 (US)
Overture
c. Raymond Leppard

Decca Argo ZRG501 □
Vieni o figlia; La speranza
Bernadette Greevy (c)

Giulio Cesare in Egitto
Opera in 3 Acts.
Text by Nicola Francesco Haym.
First performance: London (King's Theatre) February 20, 1724.

Synopsis:

Act 1 Egypt in 48 BC: Caesar has defeated Pompey. Achillas, sent by Ptolemy, enters with Pompey's head. Pompey's wife, Cornelia, mourns, and his son, Sextus, swears revenge. Cleopatra seeks Caesar's promise to dethrone Ptolemy in her favour, and plans to aid Sextus in his revenge. Sextus breaks in on Caesar and Ptolemy to challenge the latter to a duel, and he and his mother Cornelia are imprisoned.

Act 2 Cleopatra plans an entertainment for Caesar. The imprisoned Cornelia rejects Achillas's advances; she urges Sextus on to revenge. Caesar praises Cleopatra's beauty, but hears that a mob is approaching to kill him; Cleopatra begs him to escape and calls on the gods for pity.

Act 3 Defeated by Ptolemy, Cleopatra is a prisoner. Caesar escapes by swimming the Nile, but is in great danger. The dying Achillas gives Sextus a signet ring that will command his troops; Caesar takes it and, with its aid, rescues Cleopatra. Caesar and Cleopatra enter Alexandria in triumph, Cornelia and Sextus deliver the crown of Ptolemy, who has succumbed to their vengeance, and Cleopatra is proclaimed Queen of Egypt. She and Caesar declare their love.

Well-known arias:
Act 1 Presti omai l'Egizia terra (Caesar)
L'empio, sleale, indegno (Ptolemy)
Va tacito e nascosto (Caesar)
Act 2 V'adoro pupille (Cleopatra)
Deh piangete, o mesti lumi (Cornelia and Achilles)
Si spietata, il tuo rigore sveglia? (Ptolemy)
L'angue offeso mai riposa (Sextus)
Se pietà di me non senti (Cleopatra)
Act 3 Dall'ondoso periglio (Caesar)
Da tempeste il legno infranto (Cleopatra)

Right: *Huguette Tourangeau sings the role of Sextus, son of Pompey's widow Cornelia, in Handel's opera Giulio Cesare in Egitto.*

RECORDINGS:

RCA SER5561/3 (d) ●
RCA LSC-6182 (3) (US)
New York City Opera Chorus and
Orchestra
c. Julius Rudel

Guilio Cesare (bs-b)	Norman Treigle
Cleopatra (s)	Beverly Sills
Cornelia (c)	Maureen Forrester
Sextus (m-s)	Beverly Wolff
Ptolemy (bs)	Spiro Malas

Decca Ace of Diamonds SDD213 ■
London 25876 (US)
London New Symphony Orchestra
c. Richard Bonynge
Joan Sutherland (s)
Margreta Elkins (m-s)
Marilyn Horne (m-s)
Monica Sinclair (c)
Richard Conrad (t)

Decca Ace of Diamonds SDD288 □
Richmond 33200 (US)
5 Arias (in German)
Lisa della Casa (s)

Tamerlano

Opera in 3 Acts.
Text by Agostino Piovene/Nicola Francesco Haym.
First performance: London (King's Theatre) October 31, 1724.

Synopsis:

Act 1   The Tartar Tamerlano has defeated and captured Bajazet, Emperor of Turkey. Andronico, Tamerlano's Greek ally, is in love with Bajazet's daughter, Asteria, whom Tamerlano, although betrothed to the Princess Irene, also desires. Andronico, ordered to approach Asteria on Tamerlano's behalf, unwillingly obeys. To the surprise of all and the anger of her father, Asteria accepts Tamerlano.

Act 2   When Bajazet threatens suicide, Asteria throws a dagger at Tamerlano's feet and reveals that she planned to stab him during their first embrace. Tamerlano, furious, orders the execution of both father and daughter.

Act 3   There are several more murder attempts, but at last Tamerlano is conquered by the power of love between the father and daughter, relents, and finally commits suicide.

RECORDING:

Oryx 4XLC2 (4) ●
Camden 2902 (4) (US)
Copenhagen Chamber Orchestra
c. John Moriarty

Tamerlano (c)	Gwendolyn Killebrew
Bajazet (t)	Alexander Young
Asteria (s)	Carole Bogard
Princess Irene (m-s)	Joana Simon

Camden 2773 (US) ■
(from above)

Rodelinda

Opera in 3 Acts.
Text by Antonio Savi/Nicola Francesco Haym.
First performance: London (King's Theatre) February 13, 1725.

Well-known arias:

Act 1   Dove sei (Art thou troubled) (Rodelinda)

RECORDINGS:

HMV CSD3555 (3) (d) ■
Westminster 8205 (3) (US)
Vienna Radio Orchestra
c. Brian Priestman

Rodelinda (s)	Teresa Stich Randall
Bertarido (c)	Maureen Forrester
Grimoaldo (t)	Alexander Young
Eduige (c)	Hilde Rössl-Majdan
Unolfo (c)	Helen Watts

Philips 6767 001 (4) *or* 6500 523 □
Philips 6767 001 (4) *or* 6500 523 (US)
Dove sei, amato ben?
Janet Baker (m-s)

Decca SXL6349 □
London 26067 (US)
Arias
Marilyn Horne (m-s)

Scipione

Opera in 3 Acts.
Text by Paolo Antonio Rolli after Zeno's 'Scipione nelle Spagne'.
First performance: London (King's Theatre) March 12, 1726.

RECORDINGS:

Decca SXL6496 □
London 6711 (US)
Overture
c. Richard Bonynge

HMV ESD7031 □
March
c. Kenneth Montgomery

Alessandro
Opera in 3 Acts.
Text by Paolo Antonio Rolli after Mauro's 'La superbia d'Alessandro'.
First performance: London (King's Theatre) May 5, 1726.

RECORDING:
CBS 76636 □
Columbia M-34518 (US)
Lusinghe più care
Judith Blegen (s)

Admeto
Opera in 3 Acts.
Text by Nicola Francesco Haym or Paolo Antonio Rolli after 'L'Antigona delusa da Alceste'.
First performance: London (King's Theatre) January 31, 1727.

RECORDINGS:
Philips 6599 053 □   Decca Argo ZRG501 □
Philips 6599 053 (US)   Cangio d'asperto
Overture   **Bernadette Greevy** (c)
c. Raymond Leppard

Lotario
Opera in 3 Acts.
Text from Salvi's 'Adelaide'.
First performance: London (King's Theatre) December 2, 1729.

RECORDING:
Philips 6599 053 □
Philips 6599 053 (US)
Overture
c. Raymond Leppard

Partenope
Opera in 3 Acts.
Text by Silvio Stampiglia.
First performance: London (King's Theatre) February 24, 1730.

RECORDING:
Philips 6599 053 □
Philips 6599 053 (US)
Overture
c. Raymond Leppard

Left: *A production of Handel's Giulio Cesare in Egitto by the Hamburg State Opera Company.*

Poro
Opera in 3 Acts.
Text by Samuel Humphreys from Metastasio's 'Alessandro nell' Indie'.
First performance: London (King's Theatre) February 2, 1731.

RECORDING:
Philips 6599 053 □
Philips 6599 053 (US)
Overture
c. Raymond Leppard

Ezio
Opera in 3 Acts.
Text by Samuel Humphreys from Metastasio's original.
First performance: London (King's Theatre) January 15, 1732.

RECORDING:
Decca Argo ECS736 □
Argo ZRG504 (US)
Se un bell' ardire
Forbes Robertson (bs)

Sosarme
Opera in 3 Acts.
Text by Matteo Noris from his play 'Alfonso primo'; English version by Samuel Humphreys.
First performance: London (King's Theatre) February 15, 1732.

Synopsis:
In the ancient kingdom of Lidia, Haliates and his son Argones are quarrelling over the throne. Sosarme, king of Media, is betrothed to Argones's sister, Elmira, and tries without success to mediate in the dispute; and Altomarus, an insidious official, provokes the matter in the hope of securing the succession for his grandson Melus, who is also the natural son of Haliates.

Notes:
Dramatically this is one of Handel's weakest operas, but musically it is one of the finest. The plot is muddled (which is not unusual) and lacking in true drama (which is less usual), and is hardly worth detailing; what matters is the string of superb arias and concerted numbers Handel poured into it, especially in Act 2, where one marvellous number succeeds another.

RECORDINGS:
Decca L'Oiseau-Lyre ●   Decca L'Oiseau-Lyre OLS109 ■
St Anthony Singers/St Cecilia Orchestra   (from above)
c. Anthony Lewis
Sosarme (c-t)   Alfred Deller   Decca SXL6360 □
Haliates (t)   William Herbert   London 6586 (US)
Argones (t)   John Kentish   Overture
Altomarus (bs) Ian Wallace   c. Richard Bonynge
Elmira (s)   Margaret Ritchie
Melus (c)   Helen Watts
Thurston Dart (hpscd)

Orlando
Opera in 3 Acts.
Text by Grazio Bracciolo after Ariosto's 'Orlando furioso'.
First performance: London (King's Theatre) January 27, 1733.

RECORDINGS:
Philips 6599 053 □   HMV ESD7059 □
Philips 6599 053 (US)   O how dark the path we follow
Overture   **Owen Brannigan** (bs)
c. Raymond Leppard

Ariana
Opera in 3 Acts.
Text by Pietro Pariati's 'Arianna e Teseo'.
First performance: London (King's Theatre) January 26, 1734.

RECORDING:
HMV ASD3182 □
Angel S-37176 (US)
Overture
c. Neville Marriner

nor is he swayed when Bradamante reveals her true identity. Melisso and Morgana try unsuccessfully to persuade Bradamante to leave.

Act 2 Melisso tries to cure Ruggiero of his infatuation by posing as Atlante, his former tutor. She gives him a magic ring which breaks Alcina's spell, although he still suspects that Bradamante's presence is a magical trick. Alcina's plan to transmogrify 'Ricciardo', who resists her charms, is prevented by Morgana. Ruggiero untruthfully asserts that he still loves Alcina, but Oronte tells Alcina that Ruggiero plans to leave and also reveals 'Ricciardo's' deception. Bradamante and Ruggiero are reconciled, but Alcina and Morgana now plot against them.

Act 3 Morgana at last accepts Oronte. Bradamante is determined to release Alcina's bewitched lovers before she and Ruggiero leave. Oronte warns Alcina, but in spite of her wiles Bradamante and Ruggiero confront her and smash the urn containing her magical powers. Alcina and Morgana dissolve and depart, the former lovers are restored to their proper shapes, and all ends happily.

Well-known arias:

Act 1 Tornami a vagheggiar (Alcina)

Act 2 Pensa a chi geme d'amor piagata (Melisso)
Ah! mio cor! (Alcina)

RECORDINGS:
Decca Ace of Diamonds GOS509/11 ●
London 1361 (3) (US)
London Symphony Orchestra
c. Richard Bonynge
Alcina (s) Joan Sutherland
Bradamante (c) Monica Sinclair
Ruggiero (m-s) Teresa Berganza
Oronte (t) Luigi Alva
Morgana (s) Graziella Sciutti

Decca SXL6191 □
London 25941 (US)
Ah! mio cor!
Tornami a vagheggiar
Joan Sutherland (s)

Decca Argo ZRG686 □
Argo ZRG686 (US)
Overture/Ballet music/Dream music
c. Neville Marriner

Left: *Joan Sutherland in Handel's Alcina at Dallas.*

Ariodante
Opera in 3 Acts.
Text by Antonio Salvi after Ariosto's 'Orlando furioso'.
First performance: London (Covent Garden) January 8, 1735.

RECORDINGS:
Decca Argo ZRG686 □
Argo ZRG686 (US)
Overture/Sinfonia pastorale/Ballo
c. Neville Marriner

Decca SXL6360 □
London 6586 (US)
Overture
c. Richard Bonynge

HMV ESD7031 □
Dream music
c. Kenneth Montgomery

Philips 6500 523 *or* 6767 001 (4) □
Philips 6500 522 *or* 6767 001 (4) (US)
Dopo notte
Janet Baker (m-s)

Alcina
Opera in 3 Acts.
Text by Antonio Marchi after Ariosto's 'Orlando furioso'.
First performance: London (Covent Garden) April 16, 1735.

Synopsis:

Act 1 Bradamante, posing as her warrior brother Ricciardo, searches for her betrothed, Ruggiero, with her guardian Melisso. Shipwrecked on Alcina's magic island, they encounter Alcina's sister, Morgana, who falls in love with 'Ricciardo'. Alcina welcomes them to her palace, where Ruggiero is so much under her spell that he will not heed their entreaties. Oronte, Alcina's general, loves Morgana and seeks to dispose of 'Ricciardo'. He warns Ruggiero that Alcina is attracted by 'Ricciardo' and may decide to dispose of Ruggiero by enchantment into an unpleasant form—the fate of her former lovers. Ruggiero will not believe it;

Atalanta
Opera in 3 Acts.
Text by Belisario Valeriani's 'La caccia in Etolia'.
First performance: London (Covent Garden) May 12, 1736.

RECORDINGS:
Decca SET268 □
London 1257 (d) (US)
Cara selve
Joan Sutherland (s)

Decca Argo ZRG501 □
Argo ZRG501 (US)
Cara selve
Bernadette Greevy (c)

Philips 6500 523 *or* 6767 001 (4) □
Philips 6500 523 *or* 6767 001 (4) (US)
Cara selve
Janet Baker (m-s)

Decca SXL6650 □
London 26391 (US)
Cara selve
Luciano Pavarotti (t)

CBS 76636 □
Columbia M-34518 (US)
Cara selve
Judith Blegen (s)

Anchor WGS8169 □
Say to Irene
Jan Peerce (t)

Arminio

Opera in 3 Acts.
Text by Antonio Salvi.
First performance: London (Covent Garden) January 12, 1737.

RECORDING:
Decca SXL6496 ☐
London 6711 (US)
Overture
c. Richard Bonynge

Berenice

Opera in 3 Acts.
Text by Antonio Salvi.
First performance: London (Covent Garden) May 18, 1737.

RECORDINGS:

Decca ECS711 ☐	Decca SXL6360 ☐	HMV ESD7031 ☐
Argo 5442 (US)	London 6586 (US)	Overture
Overture	Overture	c. Kenneth Montgomery
c. Boyd Neel	c. Richard Bonynge	
		Decca SXL6862 ☐
Decca Argo ZK2 ☐		Overture
Overture		c. Karl Münchinger
c. Neville Marriner		

Faramondo

Opera in 3 Acts.
Text by Apostolo Zeno.
First performance: London (King's Theatre) January 3, 1738.

RECORDINGS:

HMV ESD7031 ☐	Decca SXL6496 ☐
Overture	London 6711 (US)
c. Kenneth Montgomery	Overture
	c. Richard Bonynge
Decca Argo ECS578 ☐	
Argo ZRG504	Decca SXL6262 ☐
Honour and arms (Si tra ceppi)	London 33226 (US)
Forbes Robertson (bs)	Si tra ceppi
	Geraint Evans (bs)

Serse (Xerxes)

Opera in 3 Acts.
Text by Niccolò Minato.
First performance: London (King's Theatre) May 15, 1738.

Well-known arias:
Act 1   Ombra mai fù (Handel's Largo)

Notes:

This, one of Handel's last operas before he turned to oratorio, shows his formal skill and powers of characterisation at their best. In its mixture of the serious and the comic, as well as in its range of expression, it anticipates Mozart. The opera opens with the famous Larghetto aria 'Ombra mai fù, which time has somehow transmogrified into 'Handel's Largo', with religioso connotations. The aria, far from being religious, is sung by Serse, a character so eccentric that he has fallen in love with a plane tree and thanks it in song for offering shade on a hot day. For the rest, *Serse* contains the familiar ingredients of the opera seria—love, war, intrigue and a fair degree of posturing. But the music is superb.

RECORDINGS:

Westminster 8202 (3) (US) ●
Vienna Academy Chorus/Vienna Radio Orchestra
c. Brian Priestman
Serse (c)   Maureen Forrester
Romilda (s)   Lucia Popp
Arsameme (c)   Maureen Lehane
Atalanta (s)   Marilyn Tyler
Amastre (c)   Mildred Miller
Ariodate (bs)   Thomas Hemsley
Elviro (bs)   Owen Brannigan

Philips 6500 523 *or* 6767 001 (4) ☐
Philips 6500 523 *or* 6767 001 (US)
Ombra mai fù
Janet Baker (m-s)

Hungaroton SLPX11428 ☐
Ombra mai fù
Jozsef Simandy (t)

RCA RL11749 ☐
Ombra mai fù
Enrico Caruso (t)

Deidamia

Opera in 3 Acts.
Text by Paolo A. Rolli.
First performance: London (Lincoln's Inn Fields Theatre) January 10, 1741.

RECORDINGS:

Decca SXL6496 ☐	DG 2535 242 ☐
London 6711 (US)	Overture
Overture	c. Karl Richter
c. Richard Bonynge	

ADDITIONAL RECORDINGS:
Decca Argo ZRG686 ☐
Argo ZRG686 (US)
Handel Ballet Music: Excerpts from
Alcina, Il Pastor Fido, Ariodante
Academy of St Martin in the Fields
c. Neville Marriner

Decca SXL6496 ☐
London 6711 (US)
Handel Overtures: Excerpts from
*Arminio, Giulio Cesare, Judas
Maccabaeus, Radamisto, Scipio,
Semele*
English Chamber Orchestra
c. Richard Bonynge

Decca SXL6360 ☐
London 6586
Handel Overtures and Sinfonias:
Excerpts from *Ariodante, Berenice,
Esther, Rinaldo, Solomon, Sosarme,
Teseo, Jephtha, Rinaldo, Solomon*
English Chamber Orchestra
c. Richard Bonynge

Philips Universo 6599 053 ☐
Philips Universo 6599 053
Handel Overtures: Excerpts from
*Lotario, Esther, Admeto, Alcina,
Orland, Poro, Partenope, Ottone*
English Chamber Orchestra
c. Raymond Leppard

Below: *Handel turned to oratorio later in life, after a career spent battling against operatic conventions.*

There are certain works of Handel that fall between opera and oratorio/cantata/masque. One is the masque *Acis and Galatea* (c. 1720) (which contains the robust, popular 'O Ruddier than the cherry'). This work is contained on:
Decca Argo ZRG886/6 ●
c. Neville Marriner

DG 2708 038 (2) ●
c. John Eliot Gardiner

Decca L'Oiseau-Lyre SOL60011/2 ●
c. Sir Adrian Boult

Also, *Semele*, styled a 'secular oratorio' but like *Acis* often given in operatic form, is contained on:
Decca L'Oiseau-Lyre OLS111/3 ●
c. Anthony Lewis
and
Vanguard 10127/9 (US) ●
c. Johannes Somary

JOSEPH HAYDN
(b. Rohrau, 31.3.1732; d. Vienna 31.5.1809)

Until a few years ago many music lovers would have been surprised to learn that Haydn wrote more than 20 operas—and some would have been surprised to hear that he had written any at all. However, opera was an important part of his musical duties at Esterház, the great palace of the Esterházy family; it was widely said at the time that if one wanted to hear good opera, one went to Esterház. He had first entered their service in 1761, when his previous employer, Count Morzin, had disbanded his orchestra. The following year Prince Paul Anton Esterházy died and was succeeded by his brother, Prince Nicolaus, under whom Haydn lived and worked happily until Nicolaus's own death in 1790. Thereafter there was no Esterházy

Below: Joseph Haydn, composer of more than 20 operas.

musical establishment; but Haydn continued in the family employ for the remainder of his life, his freedom to travel and accept outside engagements greatly increased. Haydn was the son of a wheelwright and suffered a good deal of poverty in his youth. As a small boy he was a chorister at St Stephen's Cathedral in Vienna, but afterwards eked out a living by freelance performing and teaching. He married in 1760; like Mozart », he courted one of two sisters but had to marry the other (in his case when his first choice entered a convent); but unlike Mozart he found no happiness in his choice. Thus he became something of a judicious philanderer. In composition he was largely self-taught; and his engagement at Esterház encouraged him to develop his talent and his originality to the full. In addition to his operas proper, Haydn wrote a number of puppet operas, a form which interested him considerably.

Acide e Galatea
Festa teatrale—opera seria.
Text by Giannambrogio Migliavacca.
First performance: Esterház, January 11, 1763.

RECORDING:
Decca Argo ZRG5498 □
Argo ZRG5498 (US)
Overture
c. Neville Marriner

L'Infedeltà Delusa
Burletta.
Text by: Unknown.
First performance: Esterház, July 26, 1773.

Synopsis:
The mercenary Filippo hopes that his daughter, Sandrina, will wed the wealthy young Nencio. But Sandrina loves the peasant Nanni, whose sister, Vespina, loves and is loved by Nencio. Nencio, for material gain and social advantage, is prepared to marry Sandrina. Vespina takes action, assuming a variety of disguises, including those of a nagging old woman, a drunken German flunkey, a notary, and a nobleman. She tells Filippo that Nencio is already married, and hints to Nencio that the greedy Filippo is seeking a richer match for Sandrina. When all seems inextricably confused, the resourceful girl transposes the names on the marriage contracts, so that the true lovers are united.

Notes:
Vespina's disguises perhaps anticipate, on a lesser scale, Mozart's Despina in *Così fan tutte*. *L'Infedeltà delusa* was produced for the visit of the Empress Maria Theresa to Esterház during September 1773.

RECORDING:
Hungaroton SLPX11832/4 ●
Ferencz Liszt Chamber Orchestra
c. Frigyes Sandor
Filippo (t)   István Rozsos
Sandrina (s)   Julia Pászthy
Vespina (s)   Magda Kalmár
Nencio (t)   Attila Fülöp
Nanni (bs)   József Gregor

Il Mondo della Luna
Dramma giocosa in 3 Acts.
Text by Carlo Goldoni.
First performance: Esterház, August 3, 1777.

Synopsis:
Act 1   The pseudo-astrologer Ecclitico tricks the wealthy merchant Buonafede into believing that all kinds of delights can be seen through a supposed telescope. Buonafede offers to pay him, but Ecclitico desires Clarice, one of the merchant's daughters. The second daughter, Flamina, is in love with Ernesto; and the valet Cecco loves Lisetta, the housekeeper. Since Buonafede obstructs these liaisons, Ecclitico provides him with a 'magic' potion which will enable him to travel through the heavens. Buonafede drinks and swoons, dreaming that he is on the way to the delights of the moon.

Act 2   Ecclitico's garden is disguised as a moon-scape to fool Buonafede. Cecco, posing as 'Emperor', and Ernesto, as 'Hesperus', lecture Buonafede on womanizing; Cecco takes Lisetta, whom Buonafede is attempting to seduce, as his 'Empress'. Buonafede offers the keys to his treasures on earth, which he no longer needs; the offer is accepted and the disguises are then thrown off, revealing his foolishness.

Act 3   Back on earth again, Buonafede at first blusters but then forgives everyone. His keys are returned and, amid lovers' uniting and general rejoicing, all agree on the delights of the 'world of the moon'.

RECORDING:
Philips 6769 003 (4) ●
Philips 6769 003 (US)
Members of Choeurs de la Radio Suisse Romande/Orchestre de Chambre de Lausanne
c. Antal Dorati
Ecclitico (t)   Luigi Alva
Buonafede (b)   Domenico Trimarchi
Lisetta (m-s)   Frederica von Stade
Clarice (s)   Edith Mathis
Flamina (s)   Arleen Augér
Ernesto (c)   Lucia Valentini Terrani
Cecco (t)   Anthony Rolfe Johnson

La Vera Costanza
Drama giocosa in 3 Acts.
Text by Francesco Puttini.
First performance: Esterház, April 2, 1779.

Synopsis:
Act 1   Baroness Irene, Marquis Ernesto, the maid Lisetta, and the fop Villotto are shipwrecked on an island, where they meet Rosina and her brother Masino. The Baroness recognises Rosina as the sweetheart of her nephew, Count Errico, and seeks to end the romance by marrying off Rosina to Villotto—not knowing that Rosina and Errico are already married and have a son. Villotto is overjoyed, until Errico threatens to shoot him. Ernesto, who cannot marry Irene until she has solved the problem of Errico, seeks Masino's aid in the matchmaking by threats. Lisetta seeks to seduce Masino. Errico decides to test Rosina's love, and is satisfied when she begs for death rather than have to marry Villotto—until the Baroness shows him a picture of the attractive bride she has chosen for him elsewhere.

Act 2   Ernesto pleads with Rosina to wed Villotto: the conversation is overheard and misinterpreted by the others. All denounce Rosina, who decides to flee. Errico, thinking her false, orders Villotto to kill her, but Lisetta tells Errico he is mistaken; repentant, he sets off after Rosina. Villotto is about to kill Masino, who tries to protect his sister, but Lisetta prevents him. Errico finds a weeping child—in fact, his son—who leads him to Rosina. He begs her forgiveness and defies the Baroness and Ernesto.

Act 3   Still attempting to separate Errico and Rosina, the Baroness sends forged letters to set them at loggerheads, but they see through her ruse. At last the Baroness capitulates, accepts Rosina as her nephew's bride, and marries Ernesto.

RECORDING:
Philips 6703 077 (3) ●
Philips 6703 077 (3) (US)
Orchestre de Chambre de Lausanne
c. Antal Dorati
Rosina (s)   Jessye Norman
Count Errico (t)   Claes H. Ahnsjö
Villotto (bs)   Wladimiro Ganzarolli
Lisetta (s)   Helen Donath
Baroness Irene (s)   Kari Lövaas
Marquis Ernesto (t)   Anthony Rolfe Johnson
Masino (b)   Domenico Trimarchi

L'Isola Disabitata

Anzione teatrale in 2 Parts.
Text by Pietro Matastasio.
First performance: Esterház, December 6, 1779.

Synopsis:

Part 1 Gernando, Costanza his wife, and her younger sister Silvia are shipwrecked on an island; Gernando and others of the party are captured by pirates. Thirteen years later, still on the island, Costanza, convinced that Gernando had deserted her, laments continually and teaches Silvia that all men are hateful. Gernando and his friend, Enrico, free at last, come, Gernando fearing that he will never find Costanza. Silvia, unseen, observes Enrico with wonder.

Part 2 Gernando finds an inscription carved by Costanza on a rock; he thinks her dead, and Enrico tries to reassure him. Silvia encounters Enrico and is perturbed by her emotions towards him; she tells him that Costanza is alive. Alone but apart, Costanza and Gernando mourn. At last they meet: Costanza reproaches Gernando and swoons, and is revived by Enrico. At last Costanza realises Gernando's fidelity and embraces him; Silvia embraces Enrico; and all ends happily.

RECORDING:
Philips 6700 119 (2) ●
Philips 6700 119 (2) (US)
Orchestre de Chambre de Lausanne
c. Antal Dorati
Costanza (m-s) Norma Lerer
Silvia (s) Linda Zoghby
Gernando (t) Luigi Alva
Enrico (b) Renato Bruson

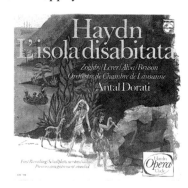

La Fedelta Premiata

Dramma giocoso in 3 Acts.
Text from Giovanni Battista Lorenzi's 'L'infedelità fedele'.
First performance: Esterház, February 25, 1781.

Synopsis:

Act 1 The nymphs and shepherds at the Temple of Diana of Cumae are troubled by a curse: a pair of faithful lovers must periodically be sacrificed to a monster until 'an heroic soul shall offer his own life'. The priest Melibeo welcomes Amaranta, who feigns love for him. Lindoro, Amaranta's brother, is accused of deserting Nerina in favour of Celia ('Fidelle'). Count Perrucchetto courts Amaranta, angering Melibeo. Fileno, lamenting his lost love, Celia, meets Nerina, who brings him to a glade where Celia sleeps, watched by Lindoro. Celia recognises Fileno, but, realising that Lindoro and Melibeo are plotting to have herself and her lover sacrificed to the monster, denies all knowledge of Fileno. Melibeo is suspicious: he warns Celia that she must accept Lindoro or face the monster.

Act 2 Melibeo tells Nerina how to win Fileno, who, believing Celia fickle, flirts with Nerina. In a hunting interlude, Perrucchetto is pursued by a bear and Fileno rescues Amaranta from a wild boar. Fileno, despairing of Celia, decides on death; he carves on a tree the inscription that he died for 'faithless Fidelle'. Celia sees it and mourns. Melibeo plans to find Celia and Perrucchetto together and take them as the monster's next victims; Amaranta is furious at Perrucchetto's supposed philandering. Fileno looks for Celia, without success. All now realise Melibeo's duplicity; he comes to sacrifice Celia and Perrucchetto.

Act 3 Celia and Fileno are reconciled, but despair of ever being united; Fileno decides to make the voluntary sacrifice that will end the curse. He is about to hurl himself into the monster's jaws when, in a transformation scene, the goddess Diana appears and declares that the curse is lifted. Diana decrees that Fileno shall be united with Celia and Perrucchetto with Amaranta. Melibeo is justly punished, and all rejoice at the judgement of Diana.

RECORDINGS:
Philips 6707 028 (4) ●
Philips 6707 028 (4) (US)
Choeurs de la Radio Suisse Romande/
Orchestre de Chambre de Lausanne
c. Antal Dorati
Celia (c) Lucia Valentini
Fileno (t) Tonny Landy
Amaranta (m-s) Frederica von Stade
Count
Perrucchetto (b) Alan Titus
Nerina (s) Ileana Cotrubas
Lindoro (t) Luigi Alva
Melibeo (b) Maurizio Mazzieri
Diana (s) Kari Lövaas

Hungaroton SLPX11854/7 ●
Chamber Chorus of the Ferencz Liszt
Academy/Ferencz Liszt Chamber
Orchestra
c. Frigyes Sándor
Celia (s) Júlia Pászthy
Fileno (t) Attila Fülöp
Amaranta (s) Veronika Kincses

Count
Perruchetto (bs) Gábor Vághelyi
Nerina (s) Mária Zempléni
Lindoro (t) István Rozsos
Melibeo (bs) József Gregor
Diana (s) Ilona Tokody

Orlando Paladino

Dramma eroicomico in 3 Acts.
Text by Nunziato Porta after Ariosto.
First performance: Esterház, December 6, 1782.

Synopsis:

Act 1 The shepherdess Eurilla is warned by her father, Licone, that warriors are approaching. Rodomonte, King of Barbary, enters and arrogantly demands to know if a French knight has passed by. He learns that Angelica, Queen of Cathay, is in the nearby castle with her lover, Medoro. Angelica fears that the mad Orlando will harm Medoro; she seeks help from the sorceress Alcina. Orlando's squire, Pasquale, encounters the blustering Rodomonte, who wishes to challenge Orlando. Medoro leaves Angelica, swearing undying love; Orlando enters, raving of Angelica and brandishing his sword.

Act 2 Rodomonte challenges Orlando, but Eurilla warns them that Angelica plans to escape with Medoro. By the sea, the frightened Medoro is joined by Eurilla and Pasquale, who flirts with Eurilla but is repulsed. Angelica, in a panic, threatens to drown herself, but is prevented by Medoro, and their escape is thwarted by Orlando. At the castle, Eurilla is beginning to be won over by Pasquale; Rodomonte arrives with the sorceress Alcina, who tells him that Angelica and Medoro are under her protection.

Act 3 By the River Lethe, Alcina claims that she has cured Orlando's madness, but warns it may return. Angelica is pursued by savages; Medoro is wounded. Angelica mourns Medoro but Alcina reassures her. Orlando and Rodomonte are at last reconciled; the spell of Charon, at Alcina's command, has cured Orlando. Angelica and Medoro, and Eurilla and Pasquale, declare their love, while Orlando departs for new adventure.

RECORDING:
Philips 6707 029 (4) ●
Philips 6707 029 (4) (US)
Orchestre de Chambre de Lausanne
c. Antal Dorati
Eurilla (s) Elly Ameling
Angelica (s) Arleen Augér
Orlando (t) George Shirely
Rodomonte (b) Benjamin Luxon
Alcina (b-s) Gwendolyn Killebrew
Medoro (t) Claes H. Ahnsjö
Pasquale (b) Domenico Trimarchi

Decca SXL6531 □
London 6735 (US)
Overture
c. Richard Bonynge

Joseph Haydn

HANS WERNER HENZE
(b. Gütersloh 1.7.1926)

Henze probably ranks with Benjamin Britten » as the most important opera composer of the post-World War II period. Many have written one or two operas: Henze and Britten have kept the stream flowing. Henze studied with Wolfgang Fortner at Heidelberg and then with René Leibowitz in Paris. He adopted a deliberately 'progressive' stand, influenced by Schoenberg » but not adhering to Schoenberg's strict principles. He worked much in ballet during the 1950s, gaining considerable theatre experience which he has put to good use in his operas. He composed six operas of admirable quality before 1970, when he announced that he considered opera 'finished' as a medium, though he admitted that there would still be music and drama. His strong Marxist sympathies have a good deal to do with his attitude and appear to have influenced his music and position in recent years, sometimes in a way that unquestionably tends to undermine his best creative abilities by leading him to put emphases in the wrong places. But he remains a potent force in contemporary music and, whatever the form his future musical dramas may take, the operas he has written are a major contribution. They have been often produced, especially in Europe, but regrettably little recorded.

Elegie fur Junge Liebende
(Elegy for Young Lovers)
Opera in 3 Acts.
Text by W. H. Auden and Chester Kallman (in English).
First performance: Schwetzingen Festival (Munich Opera) (in German), May 20, 1961. Glyndebourne (in English) July 19, 1963.

Notes:
The story concerns a group of people in an Austrian Alpine hotel: the poet Gregor Mittenhofer, his young mistress Elisabeth, his patroness and secretary Carolina, Dr Reischmann and his son Toni, and the widow Mack whose husband disappeared 40 years before when in the mountains on their honeymoon. The plot builds to the birth of a poem by Mittenhofer, which he eventually reads in public, after Elisabeth and Toni have died together in the mountains. This brief outline gives only the bare bones: the variety of meanings and the psychological insights into each character provide the highly distinctive and memorable 'flesh'.

RECORDING:
DG SLPM 138 876 (d) ■
Berlin Radio Orchestra
c. Hans Werner Henze
Mittenhofer (b)   Dietrich
                                  Fischer-Dieskau
Carolina (m-s)   Martha Mödl
Elisabeth (s)   Liane Dubin
Reischmann (bs) Thomas Hemsley
Toni (t)   Lorin Driscoll
Frau Mack (s)   Catherine Sayer

Below: *Hans Werner Henze, an important opera composer whose works have sadly been largely ignored on record.*

FERDINAND HÉROLD
(b. Paris 28.1.1791; d. Paris 19.1.1833)

After private music tuition, Hérold entered the Paris Conservatoire in 1806, studying composition under Méhul, whose work he always admired and copied. Although he wrote many attractive orchestral pieces, he is chiefly remembered as an opera composer—although none survive on the stage and only *Zampa* (1831) remains a familiar title because of the everlasting popularity of its overture. Hérold wrote 22 operas in all; most were produced at the Paris Opéra-Comique, the most highly rated in France being *Le Pré aux clercs* (1832). He produced works of a high standard in the *opéra-comique* vein, and showed a promise that was cut short by his death from consumption.

Zampa
Opera in 3 Acts.
Text by Anne Honoré Joseph Mélesville.
First performance: Paris (Opéra-Comique) May 3, 1831.

RECORDINGS:
Decca SDD192 □
London STS-15217 (US)
Overture
c. Ernest Ansermet

CBS 61748 □
Columbia MS-6988 and M-31815 (US)
Overture
c. Leonard Bernstein

Decca SXL6235 □
London 6486 (US)
Overture
c. Richard Bonynge

HMV ESD7010 □
Overture
c. Sir Charles Groves

HMV ASD3548 □
Westminster 8331 (US)
Overture
c. Gennady Rozhdestvensky

Decca ECS547 □
Overture
c. Jean Martinon

Below: *Ferdinand Hérold portrayed in 1832, the year before he died.*

BERNARD HERRMANN
(b. New York 29.6.1911; d. Hollywood 24.12.1975)

Herrmann is best known as an extremely gifted writer of film music (*Citizen Kane, The Magnificent Ambersons, Jane Eyre, Anna and the King of Siam, Snows of Kilimanjaro, North by Northwest* etc) and as an adventurous conductor who did much to propagate new music in America. He also composed a good deal of concert music, including a symphony and a cantata *Moby Dick*. His most ambitious work, on which he laboured consistently over a long period, is the opera *Wuthering Heights*, but it remains unproduced on stage.

Wuthering Heights
Opera in 3 Acts.
Text from Emily Brontë's novel.
Composed (completed) 1950; unproduced in the theatre.

Notes:
The opera does not penetrate deeply into the emotional and physical texture of the novel, but follows the story reasonably closely and makes a genuine impression.

RECORDING:
Unicorn UNB400 (4) (d) ●
Elizabethan Singers/Pro Arte Orchestra
c. Bernard Herrmann
Heathcliff (b)	Donald Bell
Nelly (m-s)	Elizabeth Bainbridge
Earnshaw (b)	John Kitchiner
Mr Lockwood	
(b)	David Kelly
Cathy (s)	Morag Beaton
Joseph (bs)	Michael Rippon
Edgar Linton (t)	John Ward
Isabella	
Linton (m-s)	Pamela Bowden

Below: *Bernard Herrmann.*

PAUL HINDEMITH

(b. Hanau 16.11.1895; d. Frankfurt 28.12.1963)

One of the most important and influential German composers of the 20th century, Hindemith studied in Frankfurt where he became leader of the orchestra in 1915 and founded a string quartet with the Turkish violinist Licco Amar. As well as making headway with his own works, he taught composition at the Berlin Hochschule until 1938, when he and his works were condemned as 'degenerate' under Nazism. During the later 1930s Hindemith was active in the administration of music in Turkey, and in 1939 emigrated to the US. After World War II he returned to Europe, where he continued to compose and played a leading part in the revival of German music after the Nazi aberration. Hindemith was the inventor of what became known as *Gebrauchsmusik*, or 'utility music', of which he wrote a number of examples. By no means all his music falls into this category or was meant to; but it did have a considerable impact on the post-1918 musical world. Hindemith composed a number of operas, of which the experimental *Cardillac* became best known on the stage. Both *Mathis der Maler* and *Die Harmonie der Welt*, although occasionally staged, have become best known through the symphonic music Hindemith extracted from them.

Cardillac

Opera in 3 Acts (originally 4).
Text by Hindemith from Ferdinand Lion after E. T. A. Hoffmann.
First performance: Dresden, November 9, 1926. Zurich (revised version) 1952.

Synopsis:
Scene: Paris. Time: late 17th century.
Cardillac, a famous jeweller and goldsmith, is so obsessed with the perfection of his work that he cannot bear to part with it; he is passionately convinced that the artist and his work should never be separated. In consequence, he murders his customers, and matters get out of hand when an opera singer becomes involved after her lover buys a belt from Cardillac and when his own daughter's lover, an army officer, is drawn into the web. In the end Cardillac goes out of his mind, confesses to the murders and is killed by the mob.

RECORDINGS:
DG 2707 042 (2) ●
DG 2707 042 (US)
Cologne Radio Chorus and Orchestra
c. Joseph Keilberth

Cardillac (b)	Dietrich Fischer-Dieskau
Cardillac's daughter (s)	Leonore Kirschstein
Officer (bs)	Donald Grobe
Prima donna (s)	Elisabeth Söderström

Mathis der Maler

Opera in 7 Scenes.
Text by Hindemith, based on the altar-piece of the 16th-century painter Matthias Grünewald.
First performance: Zurich, May 28, 1938. Stuttgart 1946.

Synopsis:
Scene: Mainz. Time: c. 1525.
During the Peasants' Revolt of the early 16th century, Mathis, a painter, wants to help the peasants. He appeals to the Cardinal, who is sympathetic but can do nothing because of the edicts of the Church. After a battle between peasants and soldiers Mathis rescues the daughter of the peasant leader, but she soon dies. Mathis feels the approach of old age, and wants only to find a quiet place to end his days.

RECORDINGS:
DG SLPM138769 (d) ■
Berlin RIAS
c. Leopold Ludwig
Mathis (b)   Dietrich Fischer-Dieskau
Ursula (s)   Pilar Lorengar
Cardinal (bs) Donald Grobe

Decca SXL6445 □
London 6665 (US)
Symphony (1934)
c. Paul Kletzki

Telefunken DS 48019 (2) □
Symphony (1934)
c. Paul Hindemith

CBS 61347 □
Columbia MS-6562 (US)
Symphony (1934)
c. Eugene Ormandy

Unicorn RHS312 □
Nonesuch 71307 (US)
Symphony (1934)
Jascha Horenstein

Die Harmonie der Welt

Opera in 5 Acts.
Text by Hindemith, based on the life and theories of the 17th-century German astronomer Johann Kepler.
First performance: Munich, August 11, 1957.

RECORDING:
Everest SDBR3226 □
Symphony
c. Paul Hindemith

Below: *Paul Hindemith, once the leader of the orchestra at the Frankfurt Opera.*

95

GUSTAV HOLST
(b. Cheltenham 21.9.1874; d. London 25.5.1934)

A leading English composer of the so-called 'renaissance', Holst (of Swedish descent) was a potent and enigmatic figure. He studied under Stanford » at the Royal Academy, where he was a close friend of Ralph Vaughan Williams », and subsequently became a trombonist with the Carl Rosa Opera Company. In 1903 he became music master at Edward Alleyn School and in 1907 musical director at Morley College, but it was his appointment in 1905 as music master at St Paul's School for Girls in Westminster that set a seal on his subsequent life. Holst was a great teacher, a man of sympathy and perception and a musician who combined a severely practical approach to the making of music with a far-ranging imagination in the composition of it. Later in life, painful neuritis resulting from an accident made the act of writing an arduous task; this has sometimes been seen as the primary reason for the increasing economy and austerity of his music, as well as for the frequent use of ostinatos; this seems a specious argument—both the economy and the ostinatos stemmed from some deeper necessity of his creative being, even if the effects of his physical infirmity may have accorded with the natural bent of his talent. Holst wrote nine operas and operettas, three of which remained unpublished. Throughout his life Holst had an abiding interest in Sanskrit: two adjacent operas in his catalogue are derived from that source, and those, separated by only two years, are remarkable for their stylistic contrast. The first, *Sita* (1906) is large and extravagant ('good old Wagnerian bawling', Holst himself said of it). *Sávitri* (1908) is so different that it is only recognisable as being by the same hand by exercising imaginative insight into the creative processes of both operas. Of Holst's other operas, the ballet music from *The Perfect Fool* has become especially popular.

Sávitri
Chamber Opera in 1 Act.
Text by Holst from the Mahabharata.
First performance: London (Wellington Hall) December 5, 1916.

Synopsis:
Sávitri hears the voice of Death. Her husband, Satyaván, is heard approaching; it is he whom Death has come for. There is a duet between Sávitri and Death; she is promised anything she desires, except Satyaván's life. He dies, although he has told Sávitri that she is under the spell of Maya (illusion). But so great is Sávitri's love that Satyaván is restored to life.

RECORDING:
Decca Argo ZNF6 ●
Argo ZNF6 (US)
Purcell Singers/English Chamber
Orchestra

c. Imogen Holst
Sávitri (m-s) Janet Baker
Satyaván (t) Robert Tear
Death (bs) Thomas Hemsley

The Perfect Fool
Opera in 1 Act.
Text by Holst.
First performance: London (Covent Garden) May 14, 1923.

RECORDINGS:
Decca Jubilee JB49 ☐
Ballet Music
c. Sir Adrian Boult

HMV ASD3097 ☐
Ballet Music
c. Andre Previn

The Tale of the Wandering Scholar
Opera in 1 Act (Op. 50)
Text by Clifford Bax.
First performance: Liverpool (private) 1934.

Synopsis:
Scene: France. Time: 13th century.
In a French farmhouse in April, Alison is preparing to receive the local priest, Father Philippe, and sends her husband Louis off to market. Father Philippe begins to eye Alison lustfully, then a Wandering Scholar, Pierre, arrives and the priest is obliged to cover his face. Hoping to avoid the return of Louis, he then tries to climb a rickety ladder to get out of sight; but when Louis does come home the usual complications ensue.

RECORDING:
HMV ASD3097 ●
Angel S-37152 (US)
English Opera Group/English Chamber
   Orchestra
c. David Bedford
Alison (s)   Norma Burrowes
Louis (bs)   Michael Rippon
Father Philippe (bs) Michael Langdon
Pierre (t)   Robert Tear

Below: *A rare performance of Holst's Savitri at the Snape, Aldeburgh, in June 1974. The singers are Philip Landridge (tenor) and Janet Baker (mezzo-soprano) in the main roles.*

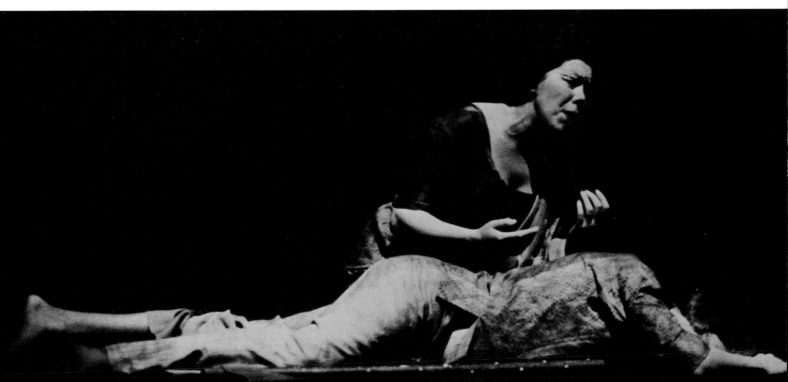

ENGELBERT HUMPERDINCK
(b. Siegburg 1.11.1854; d. Neustrelitz 27.11.1921)

Many of those who think the music dramas of Wagner » heavy, obtuse and overbearing may be surprised that the most successful (and enduringly popular) opera of Engelbert Humperdinck, one of Wagner's most devoted followers and his assistant in the production of *Parsifal* at Bayreuth, should be the entrancing fairy tale *Hänsel und Gretel*. In fact, *Hänsel und Gretel* goes back beyond the woodland scenes in Wagner's *Siegfried* to the roots of German Romantic opera in Weber », to the magic elements in *Der Freischütz* and *Oberon*. Humperdinck studied first in Cologne and then in Munich and met Wagner in 1879. Travels through Europe brought him to Barcelona, where he was professor at the Conservatoire in 1885-87. He subsequently taught at the Hoch Conservatoire in Frankfurt between 1890 and 1896, during which period he also worked as music critic for the influential *Frankfurter Zeitung*. In 1896 he was granted a professorship at the instigation of Kaiser Wilhelm II (who hated Wagner), and in 1900 became head of the Meisterschule for composition in Berlin. Humperdinck wrote seven operas, but only the first, *Hänsel und Gretel* for which his sister wrote the text, has significantly outlived him.

Hänsel und Gretel
Fairy tale opera in 3 Acts.
Text by Adelheid Wette after the Brothers Grimm.
First performance: Weimar (Court Theatre) December 23, 1893. Basle 1894;
London (Daly's Theatre) (in English) 1894; New York (in English) 1895.

Synopsis:

Act 1   The two children, Hänsel and Gretel, are supposed to be working in their impoverished cottage, but when Gertrude, the mother, comes in she finds them dancing instead, for they are hungry and have to keep their spirits up. Gertrude is angry and accidentally knocks over the jug containing the milk for supper, so she sends the children out into the woods to look for berries. She is thoroughly despondent, but when her husband, Peter, comes home he is in an excellent mood, for he has done some good business and has some provisions. When Gertrude tells him that she has sent Hänsel and Gretel into the woods, he is horrified, for he has heard of a wicked witch there who cooks and eats little children. The two parents rush off to the rescue.

Act 2   The children are in the woods, eating berries and picking flowers. They know that they must fill the basket before going home, but it is getting dark, and they begin to be afraid as mysterious forms take shape in the twilight. The Sandman appears, and after they have sung their prayers they go to sleep in peace, while angels descend from Heaven and there is a Dream Pantomime.

Act 3   Next morning the children awake, feeling hungry; they see a house made of gingerbread and begin to eat it. A voice from within angrily asks who is eating the house, and the witch emerges. She puts Hänsel in a kennel to be fattened for the pot, while Gretel is made to bring him food. The witch tells Gretel to prepare the oven for baking, but Gretel pretends not to know how. Meanwhile, Hänsel has escaped from the kennel and has overheard the witch's spell of disenchantment. When the witch goes to inspect the oven, the children push her inside, slam the door, and sing a waltz song. The oven flies open: the witch is baked into a delicious cake. All the children baked into cakes by the witch come back to life at Gretel's touch. The parents, Peter and Gertrude, reappear and the family is united again.

Well-known arias and excerpts:

Act 1   Brüderchen komm tanz mit mir (Dancing duet) (Gretel and Hänsel)

Act 2   Cuckoo duet (Gretel and Hänsel)
Sandman's Song
Evening Prayer (Gretel and Hänsel)
Dance Pantomime

Act 3   Witch's Song
Gingerbread Waltz

RECORDINGS:

Decca D131D2 (2) ★●
Vienna Boys' Choir and Vienna
Philharmonic Orchestra
c. Georg Solti
Hänsel (s)	Brigitte Fassbaender
Gretel (s)	Lucia Popp
Gertrude (m-s)	Julia Hamari
Peter (b)	Walter Berry
Witch (m-s)	Anny Schlemm

HMV SLS5145 (2) (r. 1954) ★●
Choirs of Loughton School for Girls and
Bancroft's School/Philharmonia
Orchestra
c. Herbert von Karajan
Hänsel (s)	Elisabeth Grümmer
Gretel (s)	Elisabeth Schwarzkopf
Gertrude (m-s)	Maria von Ilosvay
Peter (b)	Josef Matternich
Witch (c)	Else Schürhoff

RCA ARL20637 (2) ●
RCA ARL20637 (US)
Bavarian Radio Chorus and Orchestra
c. Kurt Eichhorn
Hänsel (s)	Anna Moffo
Gretel (s)	Helen Donath
Gertrude (m-s)	Charlotte Berthold
Peter (b)	Dietrich Fischer-Dieskau
Witch (m-s)	Christa Ludwig

RCA ARS1-0792 (US) ■
(from above)

HMV SXDW3023 (2) (in English) ●
London Boy Singers/Sadler's Wells
Chorus and Orchestra

c. Mario Bernardi
Hänsel (s)	Patricia Kern
Gretel (s)	Margaret Neville
Gertrude (m-s)	Rita Hunter
Peter (b)	Raimund Herincx
Witch (m-s)	Ann Howard

Angel S-3648 (2) (US) ●
Vienna Philharmonic Orchestra
c. Andre Cluytens
Hänsel (s)	Anneliese Rothenberger
Gretel (s)	Irmgard Seefried
Gertrude (m-s)	Grace Hoffman

Telefunken ER 6.35074 (2) (d) ●
Telefunken 2635074 (2) (US)
Dresden Choir and State Orchestra
c. Otmar Suitner
Hänsel (s)	Ingeborg Springer
Gretel (s)	Renate Holm
Gertrude (m-s)	Gisela Schröter
Peter (b)	Theo Adam
Witch (m-s)	Peter Scheier (t)

Telefunken AN6 41179 ■
(from above)

World Records ST736 (d) □
Seraphim S-60056
Orchestral selection (orch. Kempe)
c. Rudolf Kempe

Columbia SAX2417 (d) □
Angel S-36175 (US)
Orchestral selection
c. Otto Klemperer

Classics for Pleasure CFP40263 □
Overture
c. James Lockhart

HMV ASD3131 □
Overture
c. André Previn

Below: *The 1976 BBC-2 TV version of Humperdinck's* Hänsel und Gretel.

LEOŠ JANÁČEK
(b. Hukvaldy, Moravia, 3.7.1854; d. Moravia-Ostrava 12.8.1928)

Usually accounted one of the three great Czech composers (the others were Dvořák » and Smetana »), Janáček was lastingly influenced by the folk music and dialect of northern Moravia. His family was poor (his father was a local schoolteacher) but were keen musical amateurs and he learnt his first music at home. He began his serious musical studies at the Augustine monastery in Brno and then went to the Organ School in Prague. He quarrelled with his teacher, returned to Brno, after briefly visiting Vienna and Leipzig, and became conductor of the Brno Philharmonic Society. Around this time he began to compose. All his life he held teaching posts and was greatly revered by his pupils.

Janáček's musical style was formed out of the elements of national folk song and its associated rhythms, the inflexions of Moravian speech, and the sounds of nature, which he heard with the keenest of ears and reproduced in his music with an absolute accuracy which sometimes amounted to deliberate onomatopoeia. Janáček wrote 11 operas. For a long time only one or two, notably *Jenůfa*, were popular outside his homeland; but in recent years others have been recognised as masterpieces and performed throughout the world. He was a true original, in some respects the Moravian counterpart of Bartók » in Hungary and Manuel de Falla » in Spain, but basically unique: he has been seen as one of the seminal figures of modern music, outside the Schoenberg » orbit.

Jenůfa (Jeji Pastorkyňa)
Opera in 3 Acts.
Text by Janáček after Gabriela Preissová's drama of Moravian rural life.
First performance: Brno, January 21, 1904. Vienna (State Opera) (in German) 1918; New York (Metropolitan) (in German) 1924.

Synopsis:
Scene: A Moravian village. Time: 19th century.
Act 1   Jenůfa is pregnant by Steva, who has gone to the army recruiting office. No-one knows of her condition. Laca, Steva's half-brother, is bitterly jealous, being in love with Jenůfa himself. Steva returns, drunk and boastful; he has not been drafted. Kostelnicka, Jenůfa's mother, tells her that she and Steva may not marry until he has stayed sober for a year. Laca tries to kiss Jenůfa, is rebuffed, and slashes her cheek.
Act 2   Six months later, Jenůfa has given birth to a son, but the birth has been concealed. Steva refuses to marry her because her beauty has been marred; Laca offers to marry her, until he finds out about the baby. Kostelnicka assures him that the baby is dead—and then kills it. Jenůfa, dazed by drugs that Kostelnicka has given her, agrees to marry Laca.
Act 3   Three months later, preparations for the wedding are under way. Also, Steva is going to marry Karolka. As Jenůfa and Laca are leaving for the church, blessed by the Grandmother and Kostelnicka, news arrives that the baby's body has been found. Jenůfa is accused, but Kostelnicka confesses. Karolka breaks with Steva, and Laca is conscience-stricken, believing that his disfigurement of Jenůfa led to the tragedy. Kostelnicka, forgiven by Jenůfa, is led away, and Jenůfa bids farewell to Laca; but his love for her is genuine, and in it she is reborn.

RECORDINGS:
Supraphon 112 0711/2 (d) ●
Angel S-3756 (2) (US)
Chorus and Orchestra of the National
Theatre, Prague
c. Brohumil Gregor
Jenůfa (s)   Libuše Domanínska
Kostelnicka (s)   Nadézda Kniplová
Steva (t)   Ivo Zidek
Laca (t)   Vilém Pribyl
Grandmother (c) Marie Mrázová
(This recording was made in
collaboration between EMI and
Supraphon, and was first issued as
HMV SLS946 (d))

Supraphon 112 0791 ■
(from above)

Right: *Jenůfa was the only one of Janáček's operas to be known outside his homeland until the revival of interest in his work during recent years. It was first performed in Brno in January 1904.*

Mr Brouček's Excursion to the Moon
(Výlet Pana Broučka na Mešic)
Opera in 1 Act.
Text by Viktor Dyk and others after Svatopluk Čech.
First performance: Prague (National Theatre) April 23, 1920.

Mr Brouček's Excursion into the 15th Century
(Výlet Pana Broučka do XV Stol)
Opera in 1 Act.
Text by Frantisek Procházka after Svatopluk Čech.
First performance: Prague (National Theatre) April 23, 1920.

These two one-Act operas, though composed some years apart (the first was begun in 1908, but not completed until seven years later; the second dates from 1917) are linked together as one opera to provide a single evening's entertainment, known as *The Excursions of Mr Brouček*.

Synopsis:
In the first opera, Mr Brouček travels to the moon (with the assistance of a quantity of alcohol) and has a number of strange adventures. In the second, he time-travels into the Hussite world of the 15th century for more exploits.

Notes:
In both works, Janáček shows a sardonic wit and a vein of sharp-edged parody as he pillories, albeit with good humour, the foibles of mankind, including excessive patriotism and the pomposities of pretentious 'artists'.

RECORDING:
Supraphon SUAST50531/3 ●
Prague Smetana Theatre Chorus/Prague
National Theatre Orchestra
c. Václav Neumann
Mr Brouček (t)   Bohumir Vich
Mazal (t)   Ivo Zídek
Sexton (bs-b)   Premysl Koci
Málinka (s)   Libuse Domanínská
Würfl (bs)   Karel Berman
Child Prodigy (s)   Helena
                        Tattermuschová

Far left: *A scene from the English National Opera production of Janáček's* The Adventures of Mr Brouček *at the London Coliseum. This first English production was conducted by Charles Mackerras.*

Above: The first London production of Kátya Kabánova *was at Sadler's Wells in 1951.*

Kátya Kabanová

Opera in 3 Acts.
Text by Janáček after Vincenc Cervinka's translation of Ostrovsky's 'The Storm'.
First performance: Brno, November 23, 1921. Cologne (in German) 1922; London (Sadler's Wells) 1951.

Synopsis:
Scene: Kalinov, by the Volga. Time: c. 1860.

Act 1   Boris is in love with Kátya Kabanová, wife of Tichon Ivanich Kabanov. Kabanicka, Tichon's domineering mother, orders Tichon to go away; he agrees, and Varvara, a foster-child in the Kabanov family, chides him for not standing up for himself and his wife. Kátya, afraid of her own feelings, begs her husband to order her not to see another man while he is away, a request which Tichon half accedes to.

Act 2   Varvara offers to arrange a meeting between Kátya and Boris; Kátya hesitates, then agrees. In the garden, Varvara's sweetheart Kudrash sings a serenade as he waits for Varvara. Boris enters and tells Kudrash he has an assignation; Kudrash cautions him about having a relationship with a married woman. Kátya and Boris meet. She is conscience-stricken, but allows her feelings to rule her and love prevails.

Act 3   During a great storm, people shelter in an old barn. Kátya is tormented by guilt now that Tichon is back. She confesses and runs out into the storm; Tichon and the servant Glasha search for her. Varvara and Kudrash, despite the former's forebodings, go away together. Kátya, half delirious, wishes only to see Boris again; he appears and they embrace, even speaking of the future, but Kátya is overcome and throws herself into the river. Tichon tries to save her but is prevented by Kabanicka, whom he accuses of causing his wife's death.

RECORDINGS:
Supraphon SUAST50781/2 ●
Chorus and Orchestra of Prague
National Theatre
c. Jaroslav Krombholc
Kátya (s)   Drahhomira Tikalová
Boris (t)   Beno Blachut
Kabanicka (c) Ludmilla Komancová
Varvara (m-s) Ivana Mixová
Kudrash (t)   Viktor Koci

Decca D51D2 (2) ★ ●
London 12109 (2) (US)
Vienna State Opera Chorus/Vienna
Philharmonic Orchestra
c. Charles Mackerras
Kátya (s)   Elisabeth Söderström
Boris (t)   Petr Dvorský
Kabanicka (c) Nadézda Kniplová
Varvara (m-s) Libusa Márová
Kudrash (t)   Zdenék Svehla

The Cunning Little Vixen (Príhody Lišky Byštrousky)

Opera in 3 Acts.
Text by Rudolf Tesnohlidek.
First performance: Brno, November 23, 1924.

Synopsis:
Act 1   The Forester is settling down to sleep in the wood when Sharpears the vixen enters; he captures her. In his yard, she kills some fowls and the Forester's wife demands that she be shot, but she escapes.

Act 2   Sharpears is back in the wood. The Forester, the Schoolmaster and the Priest all lament over the gypsy girl Terynka, with whom they are in love. The Forester chases Sharpears and shoots at her. She is attracted to the dog-fox Goldenmane, and they are married.

Act 3   Sharpears lures the poacher Harasta away while her cubs eat his stolen chickens. Furious, he shoots at them but kills Sharpears instead. Later, after marrying Terynka, Harasta gives her a foxfur muff and the Forester laments that it came from Sharpears. The next spring, the Forester is sleeping in the wood again when a foxcub enters, the image of its mother Sharpears. Nature and the story have come full circle.

RECORDING:
Supraphon MS1181/2 ●
Chorus and Orchestra of Prague National
Theatre
c. Bohumil Gregor
Forester (b)   Zdenek Kroupa
His wife (c)   Jaroslava Procházková
Schoolmaster (t) Jan Hlavsa
Priest (bs)   Dalibor Jedlicka
Harasta (bs)   Jozef Heriban

The Makropulos Affair (Vec Makropulos)

Text by Janáček after Karel Capek.
First performance: Brno, December 18, 1926. Prague 1928; Frankfurt 1929; London (Sadler's Wells) 1964; Edinburgh 1970; New York (City Opera) 1970.

Synopsis:
Scene: Prague. Time: 1920s.

Act 1   While Vítek, clerk to lawyer Dr Kolenatý is clearing up papers concerning the long-standing Gregor v. Prus case, in which an inheritance is disputed, Albert Gregor, one of the protagonists, enters. He is followed by Vítek's daughter Kristina, a young singer who is an admirer of the famous *prima donna* Emilia Marty. Emilia then arrives with Kolenatý and shows an uncanny knowledge of the case, asserting that Baron Prus, who died allegedly childless in 1827, was in fact the father of Ferdinand MacGregor by the singer Ellian MacGregor. She claims to know of a document, in the vaults of the rival claimant, the present Baron Prus, that will settle the issue. Kolenatý doesn't believe her, but Gregor sends him to check. He returns with the evidence. Emilia Marty offers to give him written proof, but he refuses.

Act 2   In the opera house, Prus seeks Emilia. His son, Janek, arrives with Kristina; she is obsessed with Emilia and tells Janek that her career comes before love. The old Count Hauk-Sendorf comes with flowers for Emilia and recognises a startling likeness to his old mistress, the Spanish singer Eugenia Montez; astonishingly it transpires that Emilia *is* Eugenia. Left alone,

Right: *A scene from* The Makropulos Affair *at Sadler's Wells.*

Baron Prus and Emilia question each other, making much play with the initials 'E.M.', which may stand for Emilia Marty, Eugenia Montez, Ellian MacGregor, or Elina Makropulos (the surname under which the illegitimate child of Prus's ancestor was registered). There is another unexamined package in Prus's archives, but he won't part with it. Gregor returns and although he senses something unnatural about Emilia, confesses his continuing love for her. But when she demands that he retrieve the Prus document from the lawyer he threatens to kill her, whereupon she shows him a scar proving that someone has tried to do so before. Gregor departs, leaving Emilia asleep. She wakes to find Janek and asks him to steal the document for her. But Prus returns, is captivated by Emilia, and agrees to give her the unopened package in return for sleeping with her.

Act 3   Prus gives her the package the next morning. Then news is brought that Janek has committed suicide because of her. It transpires that she was born in 1549 and made to drink an elixir by her father, Hieronymus Makropulos, alchemist to the Emperor Rudolph II, which gave her 300 years of life, now up. Her identities included Ellian MacGregor, and she was also the Elina Makropulos who bore Baron Prus's son, Ferdinand. She must now renew life with the elixir, or die. She declines into extreme old age as she tells the tale. She gives the 'secret' to Kristina who burns it. Emilia at last dies and finds peace.

RECORDING:
Supraphon SUAST50811/2 ●
Chorus and Orchestra of Prague National Theatre
c. Bohumil Gregor
Emilia Marty (s)   Libuse Prylová
Albert Gregor (t)   Ivo Zídek
Kristina (m-s)   Helena Tattermuschová
Janek (t)   Viktor Koci
Vitek (t)   Rudolf Vonásek
Jaroslav Prus (bs)   Premysl Koci

From the House of the Dead (Z Mrtvého Domu)

Opera in 3 Acts.
Text by Janáček after Dostoyevsky (unfinished).
First performance: Brno, April 12, 1930. Berlin (Kroll Opera) 1931; Wiesbaden 1954; Edinburgh 1964.

Synopsis:
Scene: Siberia. Time: 19th century.
Act 1   A new prisoner, Alexandr Petrovic Gorjancikov, is brought to the Russian camp. Questioned by the Commandant, he says he is a political prisoner and is taken off to be flogged. Skuratov, the camp entertainer, sings a folk song, and Luka Kuzmic tells a story.

Act 2   On the banks of the River Irtysh the prisoners enjoy a brief holiday. Gorjancikov offers to teach the Tartar boy Alyeya to read and write. Skuratov tells of his crime; a play, based on the Don Juan theme, takes place. Gorjancikov and Alyeya are talking and drinking tea when another prisoner attacks and wounds Alyeya.

Act 3   In the prison hospital Alyeya tells how he has read the Bible and been impressed by the message that men should love their enemies. Luka is dying; Skuratov mourns for his lost love. Shishkov tells his story. Gorjancikov is taken away by the guards; the Commandant, drunk, asks Gorjancikov to forgive him for the flogging, and tells him he is to be freed. Alyeya is in despair; the other prisoners release the wounded eagle they have cared for. As Gorjancikov leaves, the order to resume work is given and prison life returns to bitter normality.

Notes:
The text, based fairly freely on Dostoyevsky's autobiographical novel *The House of the Dead*, is set to music of extraordinary originality and effectiveness; a kind of sophisticated simplicity. The all-male cast (though in the recording the part of the boy Alyeya is taken by a soprano) gives the opera a particular textural stamp—it has been seen as in some ways a forerunner of Britten's *Billy Budd*—and has not endeared it to wider audiences. Rather than deploying a conventional 'plot', it is a series of episodes in the life of the central figure, with subsidiary characters presented with penetrating insight. In some ways it anticipates the writings of Solzhenitzyn: only the political system has (nominally) altered.

RECORDING:
Supraphon SUAST50705/6 ●
Chorus and Orchestra of Prague National Theatre
c. Bohumil Gregor
Gorjancikov (b)   Václav Bednár
Alyeya (s)   Helena Tattermuschová
Filka Morosov (Luka) (t)   Beno Blachut
Commandant (bs) Jaroslav Horacek
Skuratov (t)   Ivo Zídek
Shishkov (bs)   Premysl Koci

SCOTT JOPLIN
(b. Texarkana, Texas 24.11.1868; d. New York 1.4.1917)

The black composer and pianist Scott Joplin is now acknowledged to be the leading composer of ragtime, although this was not fully appreciated until many decades after his death. The delicacy and charm of his music puts him above most other composers in the same genre, and pieces like 'Maple Leaf Rag', 'The Cascades' and 'The Entertainer' guarantee his immortality. Joplin, however, died an unfulfilled man, driven to insanity by his ambition to exploit ragtime in more substantial ways, notably in opera. An early effort in this direction, *The Guest of Honor*, was lost, but most of his last years were spent in writing *Treemonisha*. All his time, effort and money was spent in trying to get it completed and staged, without the ultimate success that he hoped for.

Treemonisha
Opera in 3 Acts.
Text by Joplin.
Trial performance in 1915, but first stage performance: Houston (Miller Theater), May 1975. New York 1975.

Synopsis:
On a plantation in Arkansas in 1866, the blacks, after their emancipation, are still ignorant and superstitious. Ned and his wife Monisha had longed for a child who could be educated to lead their people to freedom, and their prayers were answered when they found a newly-born baby girl under a tree near their cabin. So that the child would grow up believing them to be her real parents, they took her away and Monisha returned with her eight weeks later, to the surprise of the neighbours. They name the child Treemonisha. The action of the opera begins in 1884, when she is 18, starting her career as a teacher and leader. She is concerned about the ignorance of the people and their reliance on their voodoo leaders; she is abducted by the conjurors and is about to be thrown into a hornets' nest when she is rescued by her friends, who now see the evil of superstition and ask her to be their leader.

Well-known arias:
Act 1 The corn-huskers (Chorus)
　　　Goin' around (Chorus)
　　　The sacred tree (Monisha)
Act 2 Aunt Dinah has blowed de horn (Chorus)
Act 3 A real slow drag (Treemonisha and Chorus)

Notes:
As an untutored musician, with no experience of opera, Joplin produced an uneven work which is a patchwork of Victorian song and ragtime elements. Nevertheless, the opera comes startlingly to life in such moments as the rousing choruses and the 'slow drag' finale. It has been sympathetically orchestrated by Gunther Schuller.

RECORDING:
DG 2707 083 (2) ●
DG 2707 083 (2) (US)
Houston Grand Opera Chorus and Orchestra
c. Gunther Schuller
Treemonisha Carmen Balthrop
Monisha Betty Allen
Remus Curtis Rayam
Ned Willard White

Right: *Scott Joplin.*

DIMITRI KABALEVSKY
(b. St Petersburg (Leningrad) 30.12.1904)

Best known outside Russia for his suite *The Comedians* and for a number of symphonies and concertos, Kabalevsky appears to have fitted easily into official Soviet artistic requirements, composing fluently in a straightforward, melodious, non-experimental—and sometimes banal—style, especially (and inevitably) in his 'official' choral/orchestral productions. He showed early aptitude for the piano and entered the Scriabin School of Music in Moscow in 1918; then he studied piano with Catoire and composition with Miaskovsky at the Moscow Conservatoire, where he later became professor of composition. Kabalevsky was a genuinely and, at his best, distinctively gifted musician who played a leading part in Soviet musical life. Like most leading Russian composers, he was deeply influenced by folk material. He wrote three operas, of which *Colas Breugnon* is most familiar, notably from its rumbustious overture.

Colas Breugnon (The Craftsman of Clamecy)
Opera in 3 Acts.
Text by V. Bragin after Romain Rolland's novel 'Colas Breugnon'.
First performance: Leningrad, 1938. Revised 1968.

Notes:
The opera is now more generally known under the name of its eponymous hero, replacing the original title *The Craftsman of Clamecy* (or, sometimes, *The Master of Clamecy*).

RECORDINGS:
Columbia/Melodiya M3-33588 (3)(US) ●
Moscow Musical Theatre

RCA Victrola VICS1068 (d) □
Overture
c. Fritz Reiner

HMV SXLP20099 (d) □
Overture
c. Alexander Gibson

(there is also a Toscanini RCA RB6607 (d), appallingly recorded but thrillingly performed)

Right: *In the front row, three well-known Russian composers—Kabalevsky, Glière and Prokofiev.*

ZOLTÁN KODÁLY
(b. Kecskemét 16.12.1882; d. Budapest 6.3.1967)

Kodály was, with Béla Bartók », the leading Hungarian composer of the first half of the 20th century. Like Bartók, with whom he collaborated in collecting and editing Hungarian folk song, he was a dedicated folk music enthusiast. Kodály had no serious musical education until he entered the Budapest Conservatoire in 1900 (simultaneously studying science at the University of Budapest). In 1906, after writing his thesis on folk song, he became a professor at the Conservatoire and in 1919 was appointed deputy director. He was active in the Institute for the Study of Continental Music through the 1920s and 1930s, and in 1945 became president of the new Hungarian Arts Council. He became Honorary Doctor of Music at Oxford University in 1960, and was awarded the Gold Medal of the Royal Philharmonic Society in 1967, the year of his death.

Kodály wrote a great deal of music in various forms, especially choral works. He was also a notable musicologist with much published work to his credit. Kodály wrote no real opera, though two of his works for the theatre may be admitted. In both, Kodály, noting the failure of Bartók's *Bluebeard's Castle* with theatre audiences, set himself to accustom those audiences to the sound and texture of Hungarian folk song. *Háry János*, basically a play with music but also described as a comic opera, and *The Spinning Room*, a sequence of choruses, songs, ballads and dances in seven scenes and one Act, were both originally designed to bring folk material to the theatre as a preparation for 'work of a higher order'. Perhaps the exact category of each is not very important; both are delightful exercises. There is a third work which approaches operatic classification: *Czinka Panna*, with text by Béla Balázs. This was a purely occasional piece written for the celebration of the 1848 Centenary and has not been heard outside Hungary.

Háry János
Comic Opera in 3 Acts.
Text by Béla Paulini and Zsolt Harsányi, after János Garay's poem.
First performance: Budapest, October 16, 1926.

Synopsis:
The story concerns the anecdotes of an old peasant soldier, veteran of the Napoleonic Wars. In accordance with the old tradition that a speaker who begins with a sneeze is telling the truth, the work commences thus. Háry's exploits are possibly apocryphal: he defeats Napoleon single-handed; is loved by the Empress Marie-Louise but rejects her for his own sweetheart, Orzse; solves a crisis or two in Vienna; then returns home to settle into a loquacious old age with Orzse (who, however, is dead by the time of the tale-spinning and cannot contradict Háry's stories).

Notes:
Háry János (or János Háry as he would be called in Hungary) was an historical figure; the poet János Garay knew him in his old age—but the tales themselves go back to Magyar folklore.

RECORDING:
Decca SET399/400 ●
London 1278 (2) (US)
Wandsworth School Boys' Choir/
Edinburgh Festival Chorus/London
Symphony Orchestra
Narrator   Peter Ustinov
Marie-Louise (s)   Olga Szönyi
Empress (s)   Márgit László
Orzse (m-s)   Erszébet Komlössy
Hary/Napoleon (b) György Melis
Bombazine (b)   Zsolte Bende
Marczi (bs-b)   Laszló Palócz
c. István Kertész
(This recording is hardly complete—although all the music is included, not only that from the popular Suite, and the 'action' is linked by Ustinov's narration, the action is dramatically contrived and foreshortened)

Decca SXL6631 ■
London 26390 (US)
(from above)

CBS 61193 □
Columbia MS-7408 (US)
Orchestral Suite
c. George Szell

RCA GL42698 □
Seraphim S-60209 (US)
Orchestral Suite ·
c. Erich Leinsdorf

Decca SXL6713 *or* SXLM6665/7 (3) □
London 2313 (3) (US)
Orchestral Suite
c. Antal Donati

The Spinning Room (Székelyfonó)
Lyric scenes with folk songs from Transylvania.
First performance: Budapest (Royal Hungarian Opera) April 24, 1932.

Notes:
Even less a true opera than *Háry János*. The slight dramatic continuity is itself derived from folklore. The work has been called a 'dramatic rhapsody' or 'operatic folk ballad', but it really has no classification. However, it contains some excellent music, mostly choral, and effectively displays Kodály's 'Hungarian counterpoint', as he liked to call it, a notable feature being the playing of two folk tunes simultaneously (a parallel with Charles Ives); also part-writing in imitation.

RECORDING:
Supraphon SLPX11504/5 ●
Soloists/Budapest Philharmonic Chorus
and Orchestra
c. János Ferencsik

Left: *Adrienne Csengery, György Melis and Gabriella Számado in a scene from* Háry János.
Right: *György Melis as Háry János.*

ERICH WOLFGANG KORNGOLD

(b. Brno 29.5.1897; d. Hollywood 29.11.1957)

Korngold is best known for his film scores, including many for Errol Flynn epics, of which a useful compilation has been made by RCA (SER5664). But in his youth he was seen as a virtual prodigy in Vienna, where several of his 'serious' works made a great impression. He composed orchestral music, including a symphony recorded by the late Rudolf Kempe, and a violin concerto recorded by Heifetz (it was originally written for Hubermann). But his primary fame came from his operas, two of which, *Der Ring des Polycrates* and *Vera Violanta* were premiered by Bruno Walter in Munich; but the most successful, *Die tote Stadt*, was the only one to have been recorded. Korngold's operatic style is derived from a German form of *verismo* with elements of expressionism—effective, if at times somewhat diffusely focused.

Der Ring des Polykrates

Opera in 1 Act.
Text based on a comedy by Heinrich Teweles.
First performance: Munich, March 28, 1916.

RECORDING:
Rediffusion ERS6502 □
Diary Song (Korngold songs)
Polly Jo Baker (s)

Die tote Stadt

Opera in 3 Acts.
Text by Erich and Julius (father) Korngold (as 'Paul Schott') after Georges Rodenbach's play 'Bruges-la-morte'.
First performance: Hamburg and Cologne (simultaneous production) December 4, 1920. New York (Metropolitan) 1921; Prague 1922.

Synopsis:
Scene: Bruges. Time: 19th century.
Act 1   Paul's life is devoted to the memory of his dead wife, Marie. One day, however, he meets Marietta, a dancer and Marie's double; much to the disgust of his housekeeper and his friend, he invites her back to his house. When Marietta has gone, the ghost of Marie appears and encourages Paul to embrace life once again.
Act 2   Paul follows Marietta through the streets, accompanied by her vaudeville colleagues.
Act 3   Marietta again visits Paul's house, and he makes love to her. But guilt and remorse over his disloyalty to Marie overwhelm him, and he strangles Marietta with a plait of Marie's hair—then he wakes up and realises that the murder was just a nightmare; Marietta returns for her umbrella, and Paul makes up his mind to depart from the 'city of the dead'.

Well-known arias:
Act 1   Gluck das mir verblieb (Marietta)

RECORDINGS:
RCA ARL3 1199 (d) ★●
RCA ARL3 1199 (d) (US)
Tölz Boys' Choir/Bavarian Radio
Chorus/Munich Radio Orchestra
c. Erich Leinsdorf
Paul (t)   René Kollo
Marie/Marietta (s)   Carol Nesbett
Frank (b)   Benjamin Luxon
Brigitta (m-s)   Rose Wagemann

Decca SXL6265 □
London 26381 (US)
Gluck das mir verblieb
Pilar Lorengar (s)

Rediffusion ERS6502 □
Gluck das mir verblieb (Korngold songs)
Polly Jo Baker (s)
George Calusdian (pno)

Die Kathrin

Opera in 2 Acts.
Text by Korngold.
First performance: Stockholm, October 1939.

RECORDING:
Rediffusion ERS6502 □
Letter Song and Prayer
(Korngold songs)
Polly Jo Baker (s)

Above, right and below: *Korngold's Die tote stadt was first seen in December 1920. Following the recognition of Korngold, mainly as a writer of music for films, the opera has been revived in Munich and New York (the production from which these scenes are taken) and recorded in Munich.*

ERNST KŘENEK

(b. Vienna 23.8.1900)

Křenek studied at the Vienna Academy of Music and afterwards at the Berlin Musikhochschule. He spent many years in provincial German opera-houses, at the same time writing operas and orchestral and chamber works. His first opera, *Die Zwingburg*, was written when he was 22, and the future trends of his work were apparent in *Der Sprung über den Schatten* in 1924, which combined jazz and atonal idioms. *Orpheus and Eurydike* was produced while he was working at Kassel in 1926, and his best-known and most successful work, *Jonny spielt auf*, in 1927. He turned to a more romantic idiom for his grand opera *Leben des Orest*. In the late 1920s Křenek settled in Vienna, where he was much influenced by Berg » and Webern: he used the twelve-note technique in *Karl V*, a large-scale musical drama that included elements of pantomime and film. This was banned by the Nazis in 1934 and was eventually produced in Prague in 1938. Finding the oppression of the Nazis too much to cope with, the composer emigrated to America; he became well-known as a teacher, settling in California, and continued to compose. He has always striven to move with contemporary fashions and to use them to create music that has a popular appeal; a difficult task which he has pursued with success.

Jonny spielt auf

Opera in 2 parts and 11 scenes.
Text by Ernst Křenek.
First performance: Leipzig, February 10, 1927. Munich 1929. New York (Metropolitan) 1929.

Notes:

Composed during 1925-26 when Křenek was assistant to Paul Bekker at the Kassel State Theatre, *Jonny spielt auf* caused a sensation as the first opera to use the jazz idiom in a wholehearted way. Its theme—black people conquering the world with their music—was unpopular in a Germany still occupied by American troops (including blacks) and the first performance in Munich degenerated into a riot and had to be abandoned. The work eventually became accepted and has had an influential career; perhaps more often referred to than heard, but firmly making its mark in operatic history.

RECORDING:
Philips SAL3498 (d) ○
Philips 836 725 AX (d) (US)
Vienna Academy Chamber Choir/
Vienna Volksoper Orchestra
c. Heinrich Hollreiser

Max (t)   William Blankenship
Anita (s)   Evelyn Lear
Jonny (bs)   Gerd Feldhoff
Daniello (b)   Thomas Stewart
Yvonne (s)   Lucia Popp

ROBERT KURKA

(b. Cicero, Illinois 22.12.1921; d. New York 12.12.1957)

Of Czech descent, Kurka found much of his inspiration in the literature of Czechoslovakia which included that extremely funny and highly satirical masterpiece *The Good Soldier Schweik* by Jaroslav Hasek, on which Kurka based an opera that was produced by the New York City Opera in 1958. The book is very episodic in nature; Kurka's opera tended to be the same, and was criticised on these grounds. But the music, now chiefly heard in the suite that the composer compiled from the operatic material, caught the spirit of *Schweik* well. Kurka had studied with Otto Luening and Darius Milhaud » and absorbed many influences. His style was mid-European rather than American and the closeness to Kurt Weill », sharp, pithy, sardonic and jazz-influenced, has been noted in the *Schweik* music. Kurka died of leukemia when he was only thirty-five thus leaving much promise unfulfilled.

The Good Soldier Schweik

Opera in 2 Acts.
Text by Lewis Allen, based on the book by Jaroslav Hasek.
First performance: New York (City Opera) April 23, 1958.

RECORDINGS:
Candide CE31089 (US) □
Orchestral suite
c. Siegfried Landau

Louisville S-656 (US) □
Orchestral suite
c. Whitney

ÉDOUARD LALO

(b. Lille 27.1.1823; d. Paris 22.4.1892)

Of Spanish descent, Lalo studied violin and cello at the Lille Conservatory and then in Paris. He studied composition privately and played the viola in the Armingaud-Jacquard Quartet. He started to compose seriously around 1865, the year he married the singer Mlle Bernier de Maligny, who frequently performed his songs. He is now best remembered for his *Symphonie espagnole*, written in 1873, and his Cello Concerto of 1883, but he became quite a prolific composer of all forms of music. Of his three attempts at opera, the first, *Fiesque* (1866), was never produced; and the third, *La Jacquerie*, was left unfinished and given a posthumous production in 1895. The second, *Le Roi d'Ys* (1888), became well known and is still performed in France. Its *Aubade* was made famous by Melba, and the Overture is a popular concert item.

Le Roi d'Ys

Opera in 3 Acts.
Text by Edouard Blau.
First performance: Paris (Opéra-Comique) May 7, 1888. New Orleans 1890; London (Covent Garden) 1901.

RECORDINGS:
Decca SDD192 □
London STS-15217 (US)
Overture
c. Ernest Ansermet

Philips 6500 927 (US) □
Overture (Symphony, etc)
c. Antonio de Almeida

HMV SLS5105 (3) □
(previously Columbia SAX2481)
Angel S-3736 (3) (US)
Vainement ma bien-aimée
Nicolai Gedda (t)

Delta TQD3005 (d) □
Aubade
Nellie Melba (s)

Left: *A production of* Le Roi d'Ys *at the Paris Opéra.*

Right: *A poster for* Le Roi d'Ys *by A. F. Gorguet, 1888.*

LE ROI D'YS

POËME DE EDOUARD BLAU

MVSIQVE DE: E. LALO

PARIS, G. HARTMANN ET Cie

RUGGIERO LEONCAVALLO
(b. Naples 8.3.1858; d. Florence 9.8.1919)

Some opera composers write their own libretti, and some are quite good at it; Leoncavallo was one of these. He was well trained for the task. After studying music at the Naples Conservatoire, he went to Bologna to attend the literary classes held there by the Italian poet and writer Giosué Carducci. He then embarked, with varying success, on a career of opera composing, being one of those who made a huge impact with an early work and spent the rest of his life trying to repeat it. Not that *I Pagliacci* is necessarily his best opera, though it is no doubt his most theatrically effective. He also wrote a *La Bohème* which had a modest success—but Puccini's » version was produced at precisely the same time. Of Leoncavallo's other operas little is now heard outside Italy, where Italian opera houses do him occasional honour by production. His ambitious trilogy dealing with the Italian Renaissance under the overall title 'Crepusculum' never came to final fruition, though the first piece, *I Medici*, was produced (but failed to impress). Production was achieved with *Zazà* and with *Der Roland*, an opera commissioned by Kaiser Wilhelm II, based on Willibald Alexis's romance *Der Roland von Berlin*. Leoncavallo's later works, some pretty slight, never repeated the success of *I Pagliacci*.

I Pagliacci

Opera in Prologue and 2 Acts.
Text by Leoncavallo.
First performance: Milan (Teatro del Verme) May 21, 1892. Vienna 1892; London (Covent Garden) 1893; New York (Metropolitan) 1893.

Synopsis:
Scene: Calabria. Time: 19th century.
Prologue   The piece is a 'play within a play'. Tonio, in clown's costume, invites the villagers to watch the entertainment.
Act 1   The strolling players prepare to perform in the village square. Tonio and the leading player, Canio, are rivals: Tonio desires Canio's wife, Nedda, who rejects him but plans to elope with a villager, Silvio. Tonio, seeking revenge, tells Canio, but Silvio escapes and Nedda refuses to name her lover.
Act 2   Before the play starts, Nedda, on the pretext of collecting money from the audience, manages to warn Silvio that Canio is seeking revenge. The play's traditional story is that of Harlequin and Columbina, who plan to elope, leaving Columbina's husband Pagliacco. Harlequin sings to Columbina, and Pagliacco hears the closing words; they are the same as those Canio heard Nedda say to Silvio. Forgetting that he is performing in a play, Canio challenges Nedda once more, threatening her with a knife. The villagers and Nedda realise that the play has turned to horrifying reality; Nedda, terrified, calls out to Silvio for help, but too late. Canio stabs and kills both her and Silvio.

Well-known arias:
Prologue   Si può? Signore, Signori (Toni)
Act 1   Qual fiamma . . . Oh! che volo d'augelli (Nedda)
Vesti la giubba (On with the motley) (Canio)
Act 2   O Colombina, il tenero fido Arlecchin (Arlecchino/Beppe)
No! Pagliaccio non son (Canio)
Suvvia, così terribile (Nedda)

Notes:
I Pagliacci, robust and somewhat coarse like its creator, was an example of unabashed *verismo* of considerable crudity (only in part alleviated even in the hands of so sophisticated and fastidious a conductor as Herbert von Karajan), but its impact has made it a lasting favourite.

Above: *Ruggiero Leoncavallo.*

RECORDINGS:
DG 2709 020 (3) ★●
DG 2709 020 (3) (US)
Chorus and Orchestra of La Scala, Milan
c. Herbert von Karajan
Tonio (b) Giuseppe Taddei
Canio (t) Carlo Bergonzi
Nedda (s) Joan Carlyle
Silvio (b) Rolando Panerai

DG Privilege 2535 199 ■
DG 136281 (US)
(from above)

RCA SER5635/6 ●
RCA LSC-7090 (US)
John Alldis Choir/London Symphony Orchestra
c. Nello Santi
Tonio (b) Sherrill Milnes
Canio (t) Placido Domingo
Nedda (s) Montserrat Caballé
Silvio (b) Barry McDaniel

Below: *Lorna Haywood as Nedda in the English National Opera production of* I Pagliacci.

HMV SLS819 (3) ●
Chorus and Orchestra of La Scala, Milan
c. Tullio Serafin
Tonio (b) Tito Gobbi
Canio (t) Giuseppe di Stefano
Nedda (s) Maria Callas
Silvio (b) Rolando Panerai

Decca D83D3 (3) ●
London OSAD13102 (3) (US)
London Voices/Finchley Children's
Music Group/National Philharmonic
Orchestra
c. Giuseppe Patané
Nedda (s) Mirella Freni
Canio (t) Luciano Pavarotti
Tonio (b) Ingvar Wixell
Silvio (b) Lorenzo Saccomani
(As often on stage, this short opera is
paired with Mascagni's *Cavalleria
Rusticana* on the Decca, Deutsche
Grammophon and HMV recordings
above)

Decca Ace of Diamonds GOS658/9 ●
London 1212 (2) (US)
Chorus and Orchestra of Academia di
Santa Cecilia, Rome
c. Francesco Molinari-Pradelli
Tonio (b) Cornell MacNeil
Canio (t) Mario del Monaco
Nedda (s) Gabriella Tucci
Silvio (b) Renato Capecchi

Decca Ace of Diamonds SDD418 ■
London 25334 (US)
(from above)

Decca SET403/4 ●
London 1280 (2) (US)
Chorus and Orchestra of Academia di
Santa Cecilia, Rome
c. Lamberto Gardelli
Tonio (b) Robert Merrill
Canio (t) James McCracken
Nedda (s) Pilar Lorengar
Silvio (b) Tom Krause

Decca SET490 ■
London 26203 (US)
(from above)

(Von Karajan extracts most musical meat
from Leoncavallo's meagre talent. Mario
del Monaco sings with maximum
emotion; dramatically, Callas/Gobbi
are, as always, pre-eminent. The RCA is
excellent middle-course and of lasting
value; the latest Decca is best engineered)

Decca SXL6262 □
Prologue
Geraint Evans (b)

DG Privilege 135008 □
Prologue
Dietrich Fischer-Dieskau (b)

Decca SXL6083 □
London 25833 (US)
Prologue
Robert Merrill (b)

Decca SXL6864 □
London 26262 (US)
Qual fiamma avea nel guardo
Maria Chiara (s)

Decca SET247/8 □
London 1254 (2) (US)
Qual fiamma avea nel guardo
Joan Sutherland (s)

HMV SLS5104 (2) □
Qual fiamma avea nel guardo
Maria Callas (s)
(Memorial album)

RCA RL11749 □
Recitar—Vesti la giubba
Enrico Caruso (t)

HMV ALP1620 □
Recitar—Vesti la giubba
Jussi Björling (t)

Decca SXL6451 or RCA SER613 □
London 26080 or RCA LSC-3251 (US)
Recitar—Vesti la giubba
Placido Domingo (t)

Decca SXL6649 □
London PAV2001/2 (US)
Recitar—Vesti la giubba
Luciano Pavarotti (t)
(most tenors have addressed themselves
to this famous piece, and many have
recorded it. Caruso's version was
particularly popular)

Chatterton

Opera in 4 Acts.
Text by Leoncavallo (written 1876).
First performance: Rome (Teatro Nationale) March 10, 1896.

RECORDING:
RCA SER5635/6 □
Montserrat Caballé (s)
Placido Domingo (t)
Sherrill Milnes (b)

La Bohème

Opera in 4 Acts.
Text by Leoncavallo after Murger.
First performance:
Venice, May 6, 1897. Paris 1899.

RECORDING:
RCA SER5635/6 □
Montserrat Caballé (s)
Placido Domingo (t)
Sherrill Milnes (b)

RCA SER5613 □
Testa adorata
Placido Domingo (t)

Zazà

Opera in 4 Acts.
Text by Leoncavallo.
First performance:
Milan, November 10, 1900.

RECORDING:
RCA SER5635/6 □
Montserrat Caballé (s)
Placido Domingo (t)
Sherrill Milnes (b)

Below: *Melba as Nedda, De Lucia as Canio, in* I Pagliacci *(1893).*

FRANCO LEONI
(b. Milan 24.10. 1864; d. London 8.2.1949)

Leoni, a younger contemporary of Puccini » and like him a pupil of Ponchielli », settled in England in 1896 and produced operas during the first decades of the century. Although he lived and died so recently, he seems a mysterious figure: there is disagreement about the date of his death and he does not appear in leading books of reference (including *Grove*, 1954). Even the date of the premiere of his most famous opera is variously given as 1905 and 1907, though the former is favoured. Leoni belongs to the Puccini school: his music is sometimes said to be little more than imitation Puccini, but it has a pleasant lyric quality and is theatrically effective.

L'Oracolo
Opera in 1 Act.
Text by Camillo Zanoni after a play by C. B. Fernald.
First performance: London (Covent Garden) June 28, 1905. New York (Metropolitan) 1915.

Synopsis:
Scene: San Francisco (Chinatown). Time: 19th century.
The opium-seller Cim-Fen murders Uin-San-Lui, lover of Ah-Joe, and kidnaps the child of Ah-Joe's uncle, the merchant Hu-Tsin. Ah-Joe becomes insane, and Cim-Fen is strangled with his own pigtail by the wise Uin-Sci, father of Uin-San-Lui.

Notes:
The complex plot is reasonably clearly deployed, with pleasing musical highlights and good opportunities for the singers. There are well-turned set pieces and ensembles. The part of Cim-Fen was created by the great baritone Antonio Scotti, who sang it first at Covent Garden, later at the Metropolitan, and subsequently throughout America for the rest of his career. It was the part in which he gave his farewell performance in 1933.

RECORDING:
Decca D34D2 (2) ●
London 12107 (2) (US)
John Alldis Choir/Finchley Children's
Music Group/National Philharmonic
Orchestra
c. Richard Bonynge
Cim-Fen (b)   Tito Gobbi
Ah-Joe (s)   Joan Sutherland
Uin-San-Lui (t) Ryland Davies
Uin-Sci (bs)   Richard Van Allan
Hu-Tsin (bs)   Clifford Grant
(side 4 contains Leoni's incidental music
to J. B. Fagan's play *The Prayer of the Sword*)

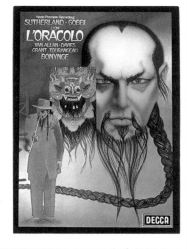

Below: *Richard Van Allan during the Decca recording of Leoni's L'Oracolo.*

ALBERT LORTZING
(b. Berlin 23.10.1801; d. Berlin 21.1.1851)

Although he received some music lessons as a boy, Lortzing's main experience came from travelling with his parents, who were keen amateur singers. Their leather business failed in 1812, so they turned professional, performing in Breslau, where young Lortzing was able to listen to opera rehearsals and performances and to continue his private studies. The family wandered all over Germany for various engagements, with Lortzing taking juvenile roles and composing instrumental music and songs. In 1823 he married an actress and pursued a similar existence. His first attempt at opera was a serious subject, but he had a natural bent for comedy and most of his future works were in the lighter Rossini »/Donizetti » vein, with a strong Germanic flavour. His first work of this kind, *Die beiden Schützen* (1837) was produced in Leipzig and was immediately taken up by opera houses in Berlin, Munich and Prague; but his real success came with *Zar und Zimmermann* (also 1837). This opera became popular after a Berlin performance in 1839, played in no less than 18 German opera houses the following year, and has remained one of the most frequently performed light operas in the repertoire. After three more modest successes, Lortzing wrote what is usually considered his best work, *Die Wildschütz* (1842), a well-constructed piece with a strong sense of parody, Mendelssohn and Handel » being among the models used. In a more romantic vein, with echoes of Weber », was *Undine* (1845), which was followed by a return to the comic vein in *Der Waffenschmied* in 1846. Lortzing wrote 14 operas; he deserves his fame for producing a distinct type of German comic opera that brackets him with Nicolai ».

Zar und Zimmermann
Comic opera in 3 Acts.
Text by Lortzing, based on the play 'Le Bourgmestre de Sardam' by Mélesville, Merle and Boirie.
First performance: Leipzig (Municipal Theatre) December 22, 1837. Berlin 1839; London (Gaiety) (in English) 1871.

RECORDINGS:
Seraphim S-6020 (3) (US)●
Opera Orchestra
c. Robert Heger
Peter I,
  Tsar of Russia (b) Hermann Prey
Peter Ivanov (t)   Peter Schreier
Van Bett (bs)   Gottlob Frick
Marie (s)   Erika Koth
Widow Browe (m-s)   Annelies Burmeister
Marquis de
  Chateauneuf (t)   Nicolai Gedda

HMV HQS1059 (d) ■
(from above)

Decca SXL6039 (d) □
Seven arias
Vienna State Opera Chorus/Vienna
Volksoper Orchestra
c. Peter Ronnefeld
Hilde Gueden (s)
Eberhard Waechter (b)
Oskar Czerwenka (bs)
Waldemar Kmentt (t)

Telefunken AJ6 42232 (r. 1937) □
Lebe wohl
Peter Anders (t)

Undine
Opera in 3 Acts.
Text by Lortzing, based on a story by Friedrich de la Motte and his libretto written for E. T. A. Hoffmann.
First performance: Magdeburg, April 21, 1845.

RECORDING:
Telefunken AJ6 42232 (r. 1937) □
Vater, Mutter
Peter Anders (t)

Der Waffenschmied
Comic opera in 3 Acts.
Text by Lortzing, based on the comedy 'Liebhaber und Nebenbuhler in einer Person' by Friedrich Wilhelm von Ziegler.
First performance: Vienna (Theater an der Wien) May 31, 1846.

RECORDING:
Decca SXL6039 (d) □
Five arias
Vienna State Opera Chorus/Vienna
Volksoper Orchestra
c. Peter Ronnefeld

Oskar Czerwenka (bs)
Hilde Gueden (s)
Waldemar Kmentt (t)

JEAN-BAPTISTE LULLY

(b. Florence 28.11.1632; d. Paris 22..3.1687)

Born Giovanni Battista Lulli, he Gallicised his name and became a naturalised Frenchman. From poor beginnings, Lully rose to a pre-eminent position in French music and became a favourite of Louis XIV. While serving in the kitchens of the king's cousin, Mlle de Montpensier, he was discovered to be a musician and from that time rose rapidly. He became a member of the famous Vingt-Quatre Violons du Roi (the '24 violins') and eventually led the group, adding wind and other instruments and achieving standards that led to the greatly enhanced independence of his own orchestral writing. Lully even formed a special band for his favourite musicians, Les Petits Violons, outshining the original '24'. He was greatly given to intrigue and high living and was frequently involved in scandal; but he was also dedicated to his art and took immense pains over the production as well as the composition of his operas. He virtually founded the French operatic style, Italian-based but with unmistakable French characteristics. Lully's long association with the poet Philippe Quinault, a follower of Corneille, ensured him a steady stream of excellent libretti; and between 1662 and 1671 he collaborated with Molière in a series of comédie-ballets of outstanding quality. He created the form of sinfonia or *ouverture* (or 'French overture') in the form 'slow-quick-slow', the slow sections majestic, the middle allegro in fugal form, which became known as the 'Lully overture' and was used by most of the later Baroque composers, including Bach and Handel ». He was also a prolific and successful composer of church music; and it was one of these works that indirectly brought about his death. He was an exponent of the then embryonic art of the conductor, beating time by banging the end of a staff on the floor. While thus directing a performance of a *Te Deum* he crushed his toe; gangrene set in and he eventually died.

Lully wrote many operas. Much of their music is conventional, stylised and lacking in true variety, but he was genuinely gifted, highly intelligent—and always had an eye to the main chance. Thus, he succeeded where others might have failed. The king's patronage was invaluable, not only for Lully himself but for the whole of French opera of the time, for Louis ordained that all operas produced at the Académie Royale de Musique should be printed at public expense and so preserved. Lully's importance in the evolution of Baroque music, especially French music, was immense. But his influence was as much political as musical, and it is, perhaps, for this reason that his music has survived less well than his reputation.

Alceste, ou le Triomphe d'Alcide

Opera in Prologue and 5 Acts.
Text by Philippe Quinault after Euripides.
First performance: Paris (Opéra) January 19, 1674.

Notes:

The subject is the same as that of Handel's » *Admeto* and Gluck's » *Alceste* (q.v. for synopsis). There are variations, of course, in the development, including a kind of sub-plot with 'mirror characters', leading to some by-play, and a good deal of reference to affairs of the day with some unsubtle flattery of King Louis.

RECORDINGS:
CBS 79301 (3) ●
Columbia M3-34580 (3) (US)
Maitrise Nationale d'Enfants/Raphaël
Passaquet Vocal Ensemble/La Grande
Ecurie et la Chambre du Roy
c. Jean-Claude Malgoire
Alceste (s)   Felicity Palmer
Admète (t)   Bruce Brewer
Alcide/Eole (bs) Max van Egmond
Diane/others (s) Renée Auphan

CBS 76551 ■
(from above)

Isis

Opera in Prologue and 5 Acts.
Text by Philippe Quinault.
First performance: Saint-Germain, January 5, 1677. Paris 1677.

RECORDING:
Erato STU70313 □
Caillard Vocal Ensemble/Paillard
Chamber Orchestra
c. Jean-François Paillard

Nadine Sautereau (s)
Jocelyn Chamonin (s)
André Mallabrera (c-t)
Roger Soyer (b)

Armide et Renaud

Opera in Prologue and 5 Acts.
Text by Quinault after Tasso.
First performance: Paris (Opéra) February 15, 1686.

RECORDING:
Erato STU70313 □
Caillard Vocal Ensemble/Paillard
Chamber Orchestra
c. Jean-François Paillard

Nadine Sautereau (s)
Jocelyn Chamonin (s)
André Mallabrera (c-t)
Roger Soyer (b)

OTHER RECORDINGS:
Decca L'Oiseau-Lyre SOL301 □
Oiseau-Lyre SOL301 (US)
Pièces de symphonie: suites from *Acis et Galathée* (Anet/Paris, 1686); *Amadis* (Paris, 1684); *Atys* (Saint-Germain/Paris 1676); *Béllérophon* (Paris 1679); *Persée* (Paris, 1682); *Phaeton* (Versailles/Paris, 1683; *Thésé* (Saint-Germain/Paris 1675)
English Chamber Orchestra
c. Raymond Leppard

Among the Lully/Molière comédie-ballets, Le Bourgeois gentilhomme has always been the most popular (the play also attracted Richard Strauss, who wrote

some splendid incidental music for it).

Lully's music is on:
Harmonia Mundi HM20320/1 ●
(formerly BASF BAC3078/9)
Members of Tölz Boys' Choir/La Petite Band
c. Gustav Leonhardt

(In the 1950s there was a complete recording on Decca, LXT5211/3 (d), of the play and its music in French, including the 'Ballet des nations'. The work is not an opera and was never intended to be; but there is a good deal of music, much of it vocal.)

Below: *A design for the scenery for Lully's Armide in 1686—after Jean Berain.*

AIMÉ MAILLART
(b. Montpellier 24.3.1817; d. Moulins 26.5.1871)

Maillart studied music at Montpellier, at the Paris Conservatoire, in Rome and Germany. He returned to Paris and had the honour of seeing his first opera *Gastibelza* open the new National Opera, founded by Adolphe Adam », on November 15, 1847. Later known as the Théâtre Lyrique, it was also there that Maillart's most successful opera *Les Dragons de Villars* (known in Germany as *Das Glöckchen des Eremiten*) had its first performance in 1856, and was highly acclaimed. He was a pleasure-loving character and would only write when inclined, devoting most of his last years to idle pursuits. He managed to write six operas but none of them equalled the charming *Dragons de Villars* which ought to be heard more fully and more often.

Les Dragons de Villars
Opera in 3 Acts.
Text by Joseph Philippe Lockroy and Eugène Cormon.
First performance: Paris (Théâtre Lyrique) September 19, 1856.

RECORDING:
Decca SXL6235 □
London 6486 (US)
Overture
c. Richard Bonynge

FRANK MARTIN
(b. Geneva 15.9.1890; d. Geneva 20.11.1974)

The most originally gifted and influential Swiss composer, apart from Honegger, Frank Martin studied in Geneva with Joseph Lauber and then went to Zürich, Rome and Paris before settling in his native Geneva. He was an adherent and teacher of the theories of Jacques-Dalcroze, especially in the operation of rhythm which these proposed. Extremely prolific in nearly all forms of music, he achieved international fame with several compositions, most notably the superlative *Petite Symphonie concertante* for harp, piano, harpsichord and double string orchestra, and the secular oratorio on the Tristan theme, *Le Vin herbé*, for 12 solo voices and seven string instruments. The latter has been given in stage productions; but it rightly belongs to oratorio and not to opera. Martin's most ambitious opera is *Der Sturm*, although the scenic oratorio *La Mystère de la Nativité* is also sometimes claimed for the stage; the other opera is *Monsieur Pourceaugnac*.

Der Sturm (The Tempest)
Opera in 5 Acts.
Text from Shakespeare's 'The Tempest', translated by Schlegel.
First performance: Vienna (State Opera) June 17, 1956.

Notes:
Der Sturm is a setting of Shakespeare's play virtually complete. The score is highly expert and varied, using jazz idioms to stylise some of the courtly scenes.

RECORDING:
DG SLPM 138 871 (d) □
DG SLPM 138 871 (d) (US)
Berlin Philharmonic Orchestra
c. Frank Martin
Dietrich Fischer-Dieskau (b)

Right: *Frank Martin, the influential and prolific Swiss composer.*

BOHUSLAV MARTINŮ
(b. Polička 8.12.1890; d. Liestal, Switzerland 29.8.1959)

A leading Czech composer of the first half of the 20th century, Martinů, after revealing a precocious talent for music, entered the Prague Conservatoire in 1906 but was twice expelled because other interests prevented him from meeting the official requirements. He became a member of the Czech Philharmonic Orchestra in 1913, continuing his studies. During World War I he returned to Polička, and afterwards came back to Prague to study with Josef Suk. By this time he had written his first published works. In 1923 he went to Paris, where he became a pupil of Albert Roussel. He found Paris stimulating but encountered difficulties. He married in 1931 and lived in penury for some time, being saved only when, faced with heavy bills for his wife's hospitalisation, he won the $1000 Coolidge Prize with his String Sextet (1932). Martinů remained in Paris, making slow headway, until the Hitler war drove him and his wife to America, where Koussevitsky performed his *Concerto grosso* in Boston and commissioned a symphony. After the war he went briefly to Prague but returned to America in 1948 to continue teaching. For the last two years of his life he lived in Switzerland. Martinů composed operas throughout his career: the first, *The Soldier and the Dancer*, appeared in 1928; the last, *The Marriage* (after Gogol) was presented by NBC television in 1953. *Juliette*, probably his most significant opera and the only one recorded, is generally regarded as an important landmark.

Juliette (or The Key to Dreams)
Opera in 3 Acts.
Text by Georges Neveux after his play 'Juliette ou la Clef des Songes'.
First performance: Prague, 1938.

Notes:
Georges Neveux was much influenced by Surrealism. *Juliette*, like his other well-known work, *Le Voyage de Thésée*, has no plot that one can define and analyse; it is more nearly a sequence of poetic and symbolic evocations, shifting between dream and reality. To try to impose a 'story line' on it is to obscure rather than illuminate its imaginative provenance. Author and composer are at one in avoiding any form of literalism, let alone dramatic realism.

RECORDING:
Supraphon SUAST50611/3 ●
Chorus and Orchestra of Prague National Theatre
c. Jaroslav Krombholc
Juliette (s)   Maria Tauberová
Michel (t)   Ivo Žídek
Police Officer/
   Postman (t)   Antonin Zlesak
Grandpa/Youth (bs) Jaroslav Horacek

Right: *Bohuslav Martinů*

PIETRO MASCAGNI
(b. Leghorn 7.12.1863; d. Rome 2.8.1945)

Like Leoncavallo », with whom he is indissolubly linked by fate and convenience, Mascagni wrote one opera which achieved huge and instant success and thereafter failed to repeat it. But that does not mean that he spent the rest of his life doing inferior work; some of his later pieces, notably the charming and disarming *L'Amico Fritz*, though not so blatantly effective as *Cavalleria Rusticana*, must be accounted in every other way superior. He was yet another of those who took to music against parental wishes: intended by his father for a career in law, he went in some secrecy to the Instituto Cherubini, which led to a short-lived family row. A nobleman then sponsored him at the Milan Conservatoire, where he studied under Ponchielli » and others. Mascagni was not a good student, and soon left to join a travelling opera company, finally marrying and settling down to earn a living by teaching. He won an important competition with *Cavalleria Rusticana* in 1889 and established himself as a success with its production in Rome the following year. His later operas, though not challenging its success, brought fame enough to make him prosperous, content and complacent. He was also a successful conductor.

Cavalleria Rusticana
Opera in 1 Act.
Text by Guido Menasci and Giovanni Targioni-Tozzetti after Giovanni Verga.
First performance: Rome (Teatro Costanzi) May 17, 1890. Stockholm 1890; Philadelphia 1891; London (Shaftesbury Theatre) 1891.

Synopsis:
Set in a Sicilian village at Easter, 1890, this is, like *Pagliacci*, an example of Italian operatic *verismo* at its most crude and blatant. Turiddu serenades his former sweetheart Lola, now the wife of the teamster Alfio. Santuzza, Turiddu's wife, begs him to be faithful. Church bells ring for Easter. Lucia, Turiddu's mother, tells Santuzza and Alfio that he is visiting the nearby village; they do not believe her. Turiddu enters, ignores Santuzza, and follows Lola into church. Santuzza tells Alfio of the affair, and when Turiddu leaves the church Alfio challenges him to a knife fight (after the well-known Intermezzo). Turiddu sings a drinking song and offers Alfio a glass: Alfio knocks the glass away, a deliberate insult, and Turiddu bites Alfio's ear, the Sicilian acceptance of the challenge. The villagers are frightened, knowing the two will fight to the death. Turiddu leaves, bidding farewell to his mother and telling her to take care of Santuzza if he should lose. A cry is heard off stage and Santuzza collapses as news comes that Turiddu is dead.

Well-known arias:
O Lola, ch'ai di latti (Turiddu)
Il cavallo scalpita (Alfio)
Easter Hymn (Santuzza and Chorus)
Voi lo sapete (Santuzza)
Fior di giaggiolo (Lola)
No, no Turiddu, rimani, rimani ancora (Santuzza and Turiddu)
Intermezzo (Orchestra)
Viva il vino spumeggiante (Turiddu)

RECORDINGS:

DG 2709 020 (3) ★●	Decca SET343/4 ●
DG 2709 020 (3) (US)	London 1266 (US)
Chorus and Orchestra of La Scala, Milan	Chorus and Orchestra of Rome Opera
c. Herbert von Karajan	c. Silvio Varviso
Santuzza (s) Fiorenza Cossotto	**Santuzza** (s) Elena Suliotis
Turiddu (t) Carlo Bergonzi	**Turiddu** (t) Mario del Monaco
Lola (m-s) Adriane Martino	**Lola** (m-s) Stefania Malagu
Alfio (b) Giangiacomo Guelfi	**Alfio** (b) Tito Gobbi
Mamma	**Mamma**
Lucia (s) Marie Allegri	**Lucia** (m-s) Anna di Stasio

DG Privilege 2535 199 ■	Decca SET490 ■
DG 136281 (US)	London 26203 (US)
(from above)	(from above)

HMV SLS819 (3) ●	Decca D83D3 (3) ●
Chorus and Orchestra of La Scala, Milan	London OSAD13102 (US)
c. Tullio Serafin	London Voices/National Philharmonic
Santuzza (s) Maria Callas	Orchestra
Turiddu (t) Giuseppe di Stefano	c. Gianandrea Gavazzeni
Lola (m-s) Anna-Maria Canalli	**Santuzza** (s) Julia Varady
Alfio (b) Rolando Panerai	**Turiddu** (t) Luciano Pavarotti
Mamma	**Lola** (m-s) Carmen Gonzales
Lucia (m-s) Ebe Ticozzi	**Alfio** (b) Piero Cappuccilli
	Mamma Lucia (m-s) Ida Bormida

Below: *A scene from Mascagni's* Cavalleria Rusticana, *the work by which its composer is best remembered.*

Decca Ace of Diamonds GOS588/90 ●
London 1330 (3) (US)
Chorus and Orchestra of Accademia di
Santa Cecilia, Rome
c. Tullio Serafin
Santuzza (s) Giulietta Simionato
Turiddu (t) Mario del Monaco
Lola (c) Anna Raquel-Satre
Alfio (b) Cornell MacNeill
Mamma
  Lucia (m-s) Anna di Stasio

Decca Ace of Diamonds SDD418 ■
London 25334 (US)
(from above)

Decca Ace of Diamonds GOS634/5 ●
London 12101 (US)
Chorus and Orchestra of Maggio
Musicale Fiorentino
c. Alberto Erede
Santuzza (s) Renata Tebaldi
Turiddu (t) Jussi Björling
Lola (m-s) Lucia Danieli
Alfio (b) Ettore Bastianini
Mamma
  Lucia (m-s) Rina Corsi

CBS 61640 ●
Chorus and Orchestra of Metropolitan
Opera, New York
c. Fausto Cleva
Santuzza (s) Margaret Harshaw
Turiddu (t) Richard Tucker
Lola (m-s) Mildred Miller
Alfio (b) Frank Guarerra
Mamma
  Lucia (m-s) Thelma Votipka
(Note: The opera is paired with
Leoncavallo's *Pagliacci* on DG 2709 020,
HMV SLS819, Decca D83D3 and Decca
Ace of Diamonds GOS588/90)

HMV SLS856 or P48 □
Voi lo sapete
Maria Callas (s)

Decca SXL6152 □   HMV ASD2591 □
·London 25912 (US)   Voi lo sapete
Voi lo sapete   **Grace Bumbry** (c)
Renata Tebaldi (s)

Decca Ace of Diamonds SDD313 □
Voi lo sapete
Régine Crespin (s)

HMV ASD3459 □
Angel S-37501 (US)
Voi lo sapete
Elena Obratzova (m-s)

Decca SXLR6825 □
London 26497 (US)
Voi lo sapete
Montserrat Caballé (s)

RCA ARL10048 or Decca SXL6451 □
RCA LSC-3083 or London 26080 (US)
Vivo il vino spumeggiante
Placido Domingo (t)

Decca SET403/4 □
London 1280 (2) (US)
Vivo il vino spumeggiante
James McCracken (t)

Above: *Piero Cappuccilli
recording* Cavalleria Rusticana.

L'Amico Fritz

Opera in 3 Acts.
*Text by P. Suardon (N. Daspuro and others) after the novel by Emile Erckmann
and Alexandre Chatrian.*
*First performance: Rome (Teatro Costanzi) October 31, 1891. London (Covent
Garden) 1892; New York (Metropolitan) 1894.*

Synopsis:
Scene: Mésanges, France. Time: 19th century.
Act 1 Fritz Kobus, a wealthy young landowner, has sworn
never to marry but his friend Rabbi David bets him that he will.
It is Fritz's birthday, and he is greatly taken with Suzel, daughter
of his steward, who hands him a bunch of flowers. Beppe the
gypsy thanks Fritz for his bounty to the poor. David tells Fritz
that he should marry Suzel, but Fritz, amused, wagers his
orchard that he won't.
Act 2 In the courtyard of Fritz's farm, Suzel and the peasant
girls sing of springtime and love. Fritz appears, attracted by
Suzel's song, and she offers him cherries. Beppe and David
arrive from the town; David secretly tells Suzel that the scene
reminds him of the biblical tale of Rebekah and Isaac, and asks if
she will give the same answer as Rebekah. Davis is sure Suzel is
in love with Fritz, and Fritz, to his dismay, is beginning to feel
the first stirrings himself. He departs to the town, leaving Suzel
in tears.
Act 3 A village wedding is preparing. Fritz cannot get Suzel
out of his mind; Beppe guesses the truth and confesses his own
unrequited love for the girl. Fritz is furious when David says he
has made arrangements for Suzel's marriage to a local youth.
But eventually he and Suzel are united, David wins the wager
and gives the orchard to Suzel as a wedding present.

Well-known arias:
Act 1 Son pocchi fiori (Caterina)
Act 2 Suzel, buon di . . . (Fritz and Suzel)
Act 3 O amore, o bella luce del core (Fritz)
    Non mi resta che il pianto (Suzel)

RECORDING:
HMV SLS5107 (2) ●
Angel S-3737 (2) (US)
Chorus and Orchestra of Royal Opera
House, Covent Garden
c. Gianandrea Gavazzeni
Fritz (t) Luciano Pavarotti
Suzel (s) Mirella Freni
Rabbi David (b) Vincenzo Sardinero
Beppe (m-s) Laura Didier
    Gambaradella

Iris

Opera in 3 Acts.
Text by Luigi Illica.
*First performance: Rome (Teatro Costanzi) November 22, 1898. Milan (La Scala)
(revised) 1899; New York (Metropolitan) 1908.*

Synopsis:
Scene: Japan. Time: 19th century.
Act 1 Iris awakes at dawn. She has dreamed of monsters, but
the image dissolves as the sun rises. Osaka, a wealthy young
man who desires Iris, brings a marionette show to her dwelling.
He has Iris abducted during the performance, but leaves money
so as to make it legal. Her father, Il Cieco, thinks she has gone
voluntarily, and sets out angrily to bring her back.
Act 2 Osaka tries to make love to Iris, but she does not
respond, believing that pleasure and death are the same thing.
Osaka gives up, but Kyoto has Iris dressed in transparent robes,
astonishing the people by her beauty. Iris hears her father's
voice and greets him, but still believing her to have left at her
own will he flings mud at her and she throws herself into a
sewer.
Act 3 Beggars and street people, dredging the sewers at
daybreak, find Iris's body and begin to strip off her jewels and
garments. But slowly she recovers consciousness, while the light
reflected from Mount Fujiyama spreads and spirit voices speak
to her. Her strength returns and she acclaims the sun, then slips
symbolically into a field of blossoms that surround her.

RECORDINGS:
Cetra Opera Live LP15 (4) (r. 1956) ●
Chorus and Orchestra of Teatro dell'
Opera
c. Gianandrea Gavazzeni
Iris (s) Clara Petrella
Osaka (t) Giuseppe di Stefano
Il Cieco (bs) Boris Christoff

CBS 76407 □
Columbia M-33435 (US)
Un di ero piccina al tempio
Renata Scotto (s)

Decca SXL6864 □
London 26557 (US)
Un di ero piccina al tempio
Ho farto un tristo sogno
Maria Chiara (s)

Lodoletta

Opera in 3 Acts.
Text by Gioacchino Forzano.
First performance: Rome, April 30, 1917. New York (Metropolitan) 1918.

RECORDINGS:
CBS 76407 □
Ah, il suo nome—Flammen, perdonami
Renata Scotto (s)

Decca SXL6548 □
London 26557 (US)
Ah, il suo nome—Flammen, perdonami
Maria Chiara (s)

Decca Ace of Diamonds SDD287 □
Ah, il suo nome—Flammen, perdonami
Renata Tebaldi (s)

JULES MASSENET

(b. Montaud, nr. Saint-Etienne 12.5.1842; d. Paris 13.8.1912)

Massenet entered the Paris Conservatoire at the age of 11, studied composition with Ambroise Thomas ≫ and won the Prix de Rome in 1863. After a period in Rome he returned to Paris, married in 1866, and had his first opera, *La Grand'-tante* produced at the Opéra-Comique in 1867. He had his first real success with *Hérodiade* in 1881, and his greatest triumph with *Manon* at the Opéra-Comique in 1884. From 1878 to 1896 he was Professor of Composition at the Paris Conservatoire. Compared to such composers as Berlioz ≫, Debussy ≫ and Ravel ≫, Massenet was a rather conventional writer, but he was a leader of French opera in the traditional vein, producing a mixture of lyrical sweetness and dramatic fervour that makes his works peculiarly French and, in their period, eminently stageable. He increasingly came under Wagnerian influence. A fluent and prolific writer, he has suffered a critical reaction; but currently fresh interest is being shown in his works and recordings are gradually becoming available.

Don César de Bazan
Opera in 2 Acts.
Text by Adolphe Philippe d'Ennery and Jules Chantepie.
First performance: Paris (Opéra-Comique) November 30, 1872.

RECORDING:
Decca SXL6541 □
London 6744 (US)
Entr'acte to Act 3
c. Richard Bonynge

Le Roi de Lahore
Opera in 2 Acts.
Text by Louis Gallet.
First performance: Paris (Opéra) April 27, 1877.

RECORDING:
Decca SXL6541 □
London 6744 (US)
Prelude to Act 5 and Waltz
c. Richard Bonynge

Hérodiade
Tragic Opera in 4 Acts.
Text by Paul Milliet and Henri Grémont (Georges Hartmann), based on a story by Flaubert.
First performance: Brussels (Théâtre de la Monnaie) December 19, 1881.

RECORDINGS:
Decca SXL6501 □
C'est sa tête que je réclame
Huguette Tourangeau (m-s)

Decca SXL6637 □
London 26379 (US)
Dors, o cité perverse
Joseph Rouleau (bs)

Above: *Geoffrey Chard (centre) as Lescaut in the English National Opera production of Massenet's Manon.*

Manon
Tragic Opera in 5 Acts.
Text by Henri Meilhac and Philippe Gille, based on Prévost's novel 'Manon Lescaut'.
First performance: Paris (Opéra-Comique) January 19, 1884. Liverpool 1885; New York 1885.

Synopsis:
Act 1 The Chevalier des Grieux and Manon fall in love at first sight. Taking a carriage reserved for the old *roué* Guillot de Morfontaine, they abscond to Paris.

Act 2 They are discovered living together in Paris, still unmarried, by Manon's cousin Lescaut and the nobleman de Brétigny. These two arrange to have des Grieux abducted so that Manon will form an alliance with de Brétigny.

Act 3 Manon, living a life of idle luxury with de Brétigny, hears that des Grieux has decided to enter a monastery and goes to him. Still in love with her, he falters in his resolution to become a monk.

Act 4 Reunited, the lovers gamble at the casino, where des Grieux wins a small fortune. Guillot denounces him and calls the police to arrest des Grieux as a cheat and Manon as a prostitute.

Act 5 Des Grieux is released but Manon is sentenced to deportation to America. As she is being taken to the ship, des Grieux bribes the guards to let her go. But she is so weakened by her treatment that she dies in his arms with visions of glittering gems before her.

Well-known arias:
Act 2 Adieu, notre petite table (Manon)
En fermant les yeux (des Grieux)
Act 3 Obéissons quand leur voix appelle (Manon)
Epouse que brave fille (Lescaut)
Ah! fuyez douce image (des Grieux)

RECORDINGS:
HMV SLS5119 (3) ●
Chorus and Orchestra of l'Opéra-Comique
c. Pierre Monteux
Manon Lescaut (s) Victoria de los Angeles
Chevalier des Grieux (t) Henri Legay
Lescaut (b) Michael Dens
Guillot de Morfontaine (t) Réné Herent
De Brétigny (b) Jean Vieuille

HMV SLS800 (4) (d) ●
ABC ATS-20007 (4)
Ambrosian Opera Chorus/New Philharmonia Orchestra
c. Julius Rudel
Manon Lescaut (s) Beverly Sills
Chevalier des Grieux (t) Nicolai Gedda
Lescaut (b) Gérard Souzay
Guillot de Morfontaine (t) Nico Castel
De Brétigny (b) Michel Trempont

ABC ATS-20013 (US) ■
(from above)

Decca SET439/40 □
London 1282 (US)
Adieu, notre petite table
Renata Tebaldi (s)

HMV SXLP30166 □
Angel S-35882
Adieu, notre petite table
Maria Callas (s)

HMV SLS5105 □
En fermant les yeux (and others)
Nicolai Gedda (t)

Decca SDD390 □
London 25081 (US)
En fermant les yeux (and others)
Giuseppe di Stefano (t)

Decca SXL6267 □
London 25995 (US)
Obéissons quand leur voix appelle
Pilar Lorengar (s)

Decca SXL6147 □
London 25911 (US)
Epouse que brave fille
Nicolai Ghiaurov (b)

Philips 6580 174 □
Epouse que brave fille
Gérard Souzay (b)

RCA SER5613 □
RCA LSC-3083 (US)
Ah! fuyez douce image
Placido Domingo (t)

Le Cid
Opera in 4 Acts.
Text by Adolphe d'Ennery, Louis Gallet and Edouard Blau.
First performance: Paris (Opéra) November 30, 1885.

Synopsis:
Act 1 Le Comte de Gormas believes that he is to be appointed guardian of the King's son. His daughter, Chimène, reveals her love for the soldier Rodrigo and receives her father's blessing.

Decca ECS705 ☐
Ballet music
c. Robert Irving

Decca SDD139 ☐
London STS-15051 (US)
Ballet music
c. Jean Martinon

HMV ESD7040 ☐
Klavier 522 (US)
Ballet music
c. Louis Fremaux

Decca PFS4322 ☐
London 21133 (US)
Ballet music
c. Stanley Black

Decca SXL6812 ☐
London 7032 (US)
Ballet music
c. Richard Bonynge

Columbia MS-7673 (US) ☐
Ballet music
c. Eugene Ormandy

RCA SER5613 ☐
RCA LSC-3083 (US)
O Souveraign
Placido Domingo (t)

Decca SET247/8 ☐
London 1254 (US)
Pleurez, o mes yeux
Joan Sutherland (s)

HMV P48 ☐
Pleurez, o mes yeux
Maria Callas (s)

Left: *Placido Domingo in the
title role in* Le Cid.

Rodrigo's bravery is praised at court and he is knighted. Le Comte, enraged when the King appoints Don Diego, Rodrigo's father, to the guardianship, challenges the older man to a duel and easily defeats him. In revenge, Don Diego orders Rodrigo to kill Le Comte.

Act 2 Rodrigo and Le Comte fight, and the latter is fatally wounded. Chimène is horrified to learn that Rodrigo is responsible. The Court is in festive mood, not having heard of the tragedy, but Chimène shatters the celebrations by demanding that Rodrigo be executed. Some support him, and when an envoy of the Moors arrives to declare war Rodrigo is allowed to lead the army into battle, promising to accept his punishment when he returns.

Act 3 Rodrigo bids farewell to Chimène; she confesses that she still loves him but duty bids her demand his punishment. She promises to ask for his pardon if he saves Spain, but feels guilty at her disloyalty to her father. The army seems near defeat, but Rodrigo has a vision of St James, who tells him he will be victorious.

Act 4 At the palace, Don Diego is told that Rodrigo is dead. He is shocked, but proud of his son's bravery. It is announced that Rodrigo is triumphant and alive and, true to his word, returns for his punishment: the King allows Chimène to decide how he shall die. She says he cannot be forgiven yet feels it is wrong to punish a great soldier. Rodrigo says he will not live with her scorn and is about to stab himself when Chimène weakens and says he must live. The lovers are reunited and there is great rejoicing.

Well-known arias:

Act 3 O Souveraign (Rodrigo)
Pleurez, o mes yeux (Chimène)

Notes:

The opera was enthusiastically received and was performed 53 times in little more than one year. It was regularly heard in France until World War I. America first heard it in New Orleans in 1890 and it was seen at the Metropolitan, New York, in 1897, with three members of the original cast: Jean and Edouard de Reszke and Pol Plancon.

RECORDINGS:
CBS 79300 (3) ●
Columbia M3-34211 (3) (US)
Byrne Camp Chorale/New York Opera
Orchestra
c. Eve Queler
Chimène (c)   Grace Bumbry
Rodrigo (t)   Placido Domingo
Le Comte (b)   Arnold Voketaitis
Don Diego (b)   Paul Plishka

HMV ASD3548 ☐
Westminster 8329 (US)
Overture and Ballet music
c. Boris Khaikin

Esclarmonde
Romantic Opera in Prologue, 4 Acts and Epilogue.
Text by Alfred Blau and Louis de Gramont.
First performance: Paris (Opéra-Comique) May 14, 1889.

Synopsis:

Act 1 The enchantress Esclarmonde loves the French knight Roland but fears that her father, Emperor Phorcas, a wizard, will oppose the match; her sister, Parséis, suggests she win Roland by magic. Hearing that Roland is to marry the daughter of King Cléomer of France, Esclarmonde invokes spirits to carry Roland to an enchanted island.

Act 2 On the island, Roland and Esclarmonde are joined 'in mystical union', which Roland swears to keep secret. When he is called to battle against the Saracens, Esclarmonde promises that she will join him every night.

Act 3 The city of Blois is devastated by war; Cléomer awaits the Saracen envoy, who will exact tribute of 100 virgins. Roland defeats the envoy in single combat, but surprisingly refuses the hand of Cléomer's daughter. The Bishop decides to solve the mystery: he finds Roland awaiting Esclarmonde and demands the truth, which Roland at last tells. When Esclarmonde materialises, the Bishop exorcises her; Roland is heartbroken as she disappears with the help of fiery spirits, cursing him for his faithlessness.

Act 4 At a tournament in the Ardennes, the victor will receive Esclarmonde's hand. Parséis tells Phorcas of Esclarmonde's love for Roland; the wizard says she must renounce him. Esclarmonde, who has lost her magic powers, vows to love Roland no more, and she and Phorcas disappear in a magic cloud, leaving Roland wishing for death.

Epilogue In Byzantium, Phorcas is to award Esclarmonde to the winner of the tournament. A knight in black armour, calling himself Despair, refuses her hand and says he has fought only to seek death. Esclarmonde recognises him as Roland and unveils; recognition is mutual. They are reunited, and all join in singing their praises.

Notes:

In this intensely romantic work, Massenet broke new ground in descriptive orchestral writing. His admiration for Wagner ≫ is reflected in his use of important leitmotifs throughout the work, representing Magic, the Tournament, Esclarmonde, Roland, Possession, and so on. It is a richly inspired score with fine opportunities for the singers, and only difficulties in staging due to its ambitious nature have kept it out of the opera houses.

RECORDING:
Decca SET612/4 ●
London 13118 (3) (US)
John Alldis Choir/Finchley Children's
Music Group/National Philharmonic
Orchestra
c. Richard Bonynge
Esclarmonde (s) Joan Sutherland

Parséis (m-s) Huguette Tourangeau
Roland (t)   Giacomo Aragall
Emperor
Phorcas (bs) Clifford Grant
Bishop of
Blois (b)   Louis Quilico

Werther

Lyric Drama in 4 Acts.
Text by Edouard Blau, Paul Milliet and Georges Hartmann, based on the novel by Goethe.
First performance: Vienna (Imperial Opera) February 16, 1892. Paris (Opéra) 1893; New York (Metropolitan) 1894; London (Covent Garden) 1894.

Synopsis:

Act 1 Charlotte, daughter of the Bailiff, is in love with the poet Werther; they wish to be married. Father intends her to marry Albert.

Act 2 Charlotte is now married to Albert, but the unhappy Werther cannot keep away from her.

Act 3 Charlotte and Werther continue to see each other regularly. Werther realises that the situation is hopeless and decides he must end the affair. He sends a message to Albert asking to borrow pistols.

Act 4 Charlotte finds the message and rushes to Werther's room, to find him dying. He will not let her send for help but dies happy to know that she still loves him.

Well-known arias:

Act 1 O Nature, pleine de grace (Werther)
Act 3 Va! laisse les couleurs (Charlotte)
Pourquoi ne reveiller? (Werther)

RECORDINGS:
HMV SLS5105 (3) ●
Angel S-3736 (3) (US)
L'Orchestre de Paris
c. Georges Prêtre
Charlotte (s)   Victoria de los Angeles
Werther (t)   Nicolai Gedda
The Bailiff (b)   Jean-Christophe Benoit
Albert (b)   Roger Soyer
(Side 6 contains operatic excerpts by Gedda)

Decca SET520/1 □
London 26348 (2) (US)
Va! laisse les couleurs
Régine Crespin (s)

CBS 76522 □
Columbia M-34206 (US)
Va! laisse les couleurs
Frederica von Stade (c)

HMV P48 □
Air des lettres
Maria Callas (s)

Thaïs

Opera in 3 Acts.
Text by Louis Gallet, based on the novel by Anatole France.
First performance: Paris (Opéra) March 16, 1894. New York 1907; London (Covent Garden) 1911; New York (Metropolitan) 1917; Milan (La Scala) 1942.

Below: *Janet Baker as Charlotte in* Werther *at the London Coliseum.*

Synopsis:

Scene: A Theban plain on the banks of the Nile. Time: end of 4th century AD.

Act 1 Thaïs, the dancer and actress, is a shameless courtesan but her beauty haunts all men. She has been loved by the monk Athanaël, who confides to his friend Niceas that he intends to convert her to a righteous life. He attends a banquet in her honour, where she mocks him and invites him to her house to attempt her conversion.

Act 2 Athanaël is so persuasive that Thaïs almost yields to his oratory, but returns to her pleasures. Athanaël is not discouraged and waits until she comes in penitential rags and begs him to lead her to a convent. But Athanaël is aware that it is not the love of God that has inspired him, but a jealous love of Thaïs.

Act 3 Athanaël dreams that Thaïs is dying in the convent; he hastens there and finds that it is true. She is sanctified by her conversion and looks to heaven. She dies, and he falls stricken beside her.

Notes:

The opera is known to most through its lovely symphonic intermezzo, the Méditation, which is simply a superb violin solo with harps, its melody later taken up by an invisible chorus.

RECORDINGS:
Decca GOSR639/41 (r. 1961) (3) (d) ●
Westminster 8203 (3) (US)
Chorus and Orchestra
c. Jules Etcheverry
Thaïs (s)   Renée Doria
Niceas (t)   Michel Sénéchal
Athanaël (b)   Robert Massard

HMV SLS993 (3) ●
Angel SX-3832 (3)
Alldis Choir/New Philharmonia Orchestra
c. Lorin Maazel
Thaïs (s)   Beverly Sills
Niceas (t)   Nicolai Gedda
Athanaël (b)   Sherrill Milnes

RCA ARL3-0842 (3) (d) ●
RCA ARL3-0842 (3) (US)
Ambrosian Opera Chorus/New Philharmonia Orchestra
c. Julius Rudel
Thaïs (s)   Anna Moffo
Niceas (t)   Jose Carreras
Athanaël (b)   Gabriel Bacquier

RCA ARS1-0843 (US) ■
(from above)

Philips 6580 174 □
Voilà donc la terrible cité
Gérard Souzay (b)

Pickwick PDA 036 (2) □
Méditation
c. Vilem Tausky
John Georgiadis (vln)

Decca SET523 □
Méditation
c. Richard Bonynge
John Georgiadis (vln)

La Navarraise

Lyric episode in 2 Acts.
Text by Jules Clarétie and Henri Cain.
First performance: London (Covent Garden) June 20, 1894. Paris (Opéra-Comique) 1875; New York (Metropolitan) 1921.

Synopsis:

Act 1 In a war-torn village near Bilbao, Anita, an orphan, and Araquil, a sergeant, are in love, but his father, Remigio, is against the marriage, demanding a dowry of 2,000 duros from his son's bride. The penniless Anita hears that General Garrido is offering a fortune to anyone who will kill the rebel Zuccarega. She decides to do the deed and claim the reward.

Act 2 Anita's departure and crossing of the enemy lines is reported to Araquil, who follows her to find out if she is, as some suspect, a spy. She returns with blood-stained hands and Garrido gives her a reward of 2,000 duros. Araquil has been mortally wounded. He accuses her of selling herself to Garrido but, before he dies, realises that she has acted for his sake. Anita, overcome by insanity, thinks that the distant bells she hears are tolling for her wedding and falls on the corpse of her lover.

Notes:

This rather gruesome little piece is said to be Massenet's reaction to the *verismo* school of Italian opera and, specifically, to the success of Mascagni's » then sensational *Cavalleria Rusticana*. Massenet's two short scenes, divided by an intermezzo, are full of rapid action and musical power; the work is considered effective, if not one of the composer's masterpieces.

RECORDINGS:

CBS 76403 ●	**Anita** (s)	Marilyn Horne (m-s)
Columbia M-33506 (US)	**Araquil** (t)	Placido Domingo
Ambrosian Opera Chorus/London	**Remigio** (bs)	Nicola Zaccaria
Symphony Orchestra	**Garrido** (b)	Sherrill Milnes
c. Antonio de Almeida		
Anita (s)	Lucia Popp	Decca SXL6541 □
Araquil (t)	Alain Venzo	London 6744 (US)
Remigio (bs)	Gérard Souzay (b)	Nocturne
Garrido (b)	Vincente Sardinero	c. Richard Bonynge

RCA ARL1-1114 (d) ●
RCA ARL1-1114 (US)
Ambrosian Opera Chorus/London
Symphony Orchestra
c. Henry Lewis

Right: *A Covent Garden production of* La Navarraise, *one of the composer's most effective works.*

Cendrillon

Opera in 4 Acts.
Text by Henri Cain, based on Perrault's story.
First performance: Paris (Opéra-Comique) May 24, 1899.

RECORDINGS:

Decca SET454/5 □	Decca SXL6827 □
London 1286 (2) (US)	Marche des princesses
Ah, que mes soeurs sont heureuses	c. Richard Bonynge
Joan Sutherland (s)	

CBS 76522 □
Columbia M-34206 (US)
Enfin, je suis ici
Frederica von Stade (m-s)

(A new complete recording has been issued, too late for full details to be included, on CBS 79323 (3) ●)

Le Jongleur de Notre Dame

Opera in 3 Acts.
Text by Maurice Lena.
First performance: Monte Carlo, February 18, 1902. Paris (Opéra-Comique) 1904.

RECORDING:
Decca SXL6637 □
La Vierge entend fort bien
Joseph Rouleau (t)

Chérubin

Opera in 3 Acts.
Text by Francis de Croisset and Henri Cain.
First performance: Monte Carlo, February 14, 1905. Paris (Opéra-Comique) 1905.

RECORDINGS:

Decca SET350 □	Decca SXL6541 □
Air de Nina	London 6744 (US)
Joan Sutherland (s)	Entr'acte to Act 3
	c. Richard Bonynge

Ariane

Opera in 2 Acts.
Text by Catulle Mendès.
First performance: Paris (Opéra) October 31, 1906.

RECORDING:
Decca SXL6812 □
Lamento d'Ariane
c. Richard Bonynge

Thérèse

Opera in 2 Acts.
Text by Jules Clarétie.
First performance: Monte Carlo, February 7, 1907. Paris (Opéra-Comique) 1911; London (Covent Garden) 1919.

Synopsis:

Scene: A château near Versailles. Time: 1792.

Act 1 The aristocratic soldier Armand de Clerval longs for home and remembers his old love Thérèse. Thérèse is now married to André Thorel, who bought the château when the Marquis de Clerval fled the Revolution. André, son of the former concierge, was brought up with Armand and hopes one day to return the house to him. He does not know that Thérèse was once Armand's lover and that she still prefers him to her adoring husband. Armand appears; Thérèse is shocked to see him. He tries to persuade her to go with him, but she refuses for her husband's sake. André joins them and, unaware of the situation, thinks only of hiding Armand from the revolutionaries.

Act 2 In June the next year, in the midst of the Revolution, André and Thérèse are in a house in Paris. Thérèse is terrified of the mob and begs her husband to help Armand. As the crowds press closer, André decides that Armand must escape and gives

THÉÂTRE NATIONAL DE L'OPÉRA-COMIQUE

CENDRILLON
CONTE de FÉES (d'après PERRAULT)
PAR HENRI CAIN
MUSIQUE DE J. MASSENET

Above: Cendrillon *was first performed at L'Opéra-Comique in 1899.*

RECORDING:
Decca SET572 ●
London 1165 (US)
The Linden Singers/New Philharmonia
Orchestra
c. Richard Bonynge

Thérèse (m-s)	Huguette Tourangeau
Armand (t)	Ryland Davies
André (t)	Louis Quilico
Morel (b)	Neilson Taylor

Don Quichotte
Opera in 5 Acts.
Text by Henri Cain based on Cervantes' novel.
First performance: Monte Carlo, February 19, 1910.

Synopsis:

Act 1 In the square before Dulcinée's house, her beauty is serenaded by her admirers and the crowd. The knight Don Quichotte and Sancho arrive, to the amusement of the crowd. The Knight serenades Dulcinée but is challenged to a duel by the jealous Juan. Dulcinée intercedes, telling Quichotte that she will be his Lady if he will restore to her a priceless necklace stolen by bandits.

Act 2 Sancho mocks Quichotte for his sentimental gallantry and recalls the ridiculous episodes with the herd of pigs and the windmill.

Act 3 They meet the brigands. Sancho flees but Quichotte defies them and is taken prisoner. He awaits death with Dulcinée's name on his lips. The bandits, impressed by his courage and his nobility, restore the necklace to him and beg his forgiveness.

Act 4 At a gathering, Dulcinée tires of her suitors. Quichotte and Sancho enter. She is astonished to find he has regained the necklace and embraces him. The gallant Knight asks her to marry him, but she laughs and he is once more depressed. She confesses that she is not pure and asks him to remain with her. He thanks her for her truthfulness and declares his undying love.

Act 5 While Sancho tells of his master's goodness, the old Knight lies dying in a forest glade. He grants Sancho a beautiful island for his old age: the 'island of dreams'.

RECORDING:
Everest/Cetra S-440/2 (US) ●
Chorus and Orchestra of the Belgrade
Opera House
c. Oscar Danon

Don Quichotte (bs)	Miro Changalovich
Dulcinée (m-s)	Breda Kalef
Sancho Panza (bs)	Ladko Koröshetz

him his own papers. André goes to join his fellow citizens, leaving Armand and Thérèse alone. He persuades her to join him that evening, then Morel enters to say that André has been arrested. Thérèse lets Armand go, promising to meet him later. From the window, she sees her husband in the tumbril on the way to the guillotine. He calls to her and she realises where her duty lies. *'Vive le roi'*, she cries, and joins her husband on the way to execution.

JOHANN SIMON MAYR
(b. Mendorf, Bavaria 14.6.1763; d. Bergamo 2.12.1845).

Mayr, an Italian composer of German extraction, was an important figure in the field of opera, and not only because he was the teacher of Donizetti » when he was professor of composition at the Institute Musicale at Bergamo. He began by composing oratorios; but when the death of his patron Count Pesenti left him in difficult circumstances he took the advice of Piccini and tried his hand in the theatre. His first opera *Saffo, ossia I tri d'Apollo Leucadio*, was produced at Venice (Teatro La Fenice) in 1794, and was a great success. As a consequence Mayr found himself the recipient of many commissions for operas and by 1824 had composed at least 60. He carried on the reforms of Gluck » in Italy where he exerted a considerable influence on the evolution of opera. He is credited with the inauguration of the orchestral crescendo which Rossini » used to such effect, and with the ensemble writing which gave Donizetti many invaluable clues. He also played an important part in giving independence to the orchestra. Not much of his work has survived; that which has shows him to have been a careful and diligent worker whose best inventions just miss that total memorability by which immortality is won.

Medea in Corinto
Opera in 2 Acts.
Text by Felice Romani.
First performance: Naples (Teatro San Carlo), November 28, 1813.

Notes:
The story of Medea taking a savage revenge on Jason and his bride-to-be Creusa (Glauce) is familiar in legend and from Euripides's tragedy. It was used by Marc-Antoine Charpentier » and by Cherubini » for operas. Romani's text for Mayr is a good one, and the opera is effective both musically and dramatically.

RECORDING:
Vanguard VCS10087/9 (d) ●
Vanguard VCS 10087/9 (US)
Clarion Concerts Chorus and Orchestra
c. Newell Jenkins

Medea (s)	Marisa Galvany
Creusa (s)	Joan Patenaude
Ismene (s)	Molly Stark
Jason (t)	Allen Cathcart
Aegeus (t)	Robert White
Creonte (b)	Thomas Palmer

GIAN CARLO MENOTTI
(b. Cadegliano 7.7.1911)

During the 1940s and 1950s, the operas of Menotti achieved near-sensational worldwide acclaim. This was due to two factors: one political, the other artistic. The political motif was introduced in Menotti's first full-length opera, *The Consul*, which eloquently and poignantly expressed the human condition when confronted with the indifference, insensitivity and outright brutality of political systems and bureaucracies. Artistically, attention was focused on an approach to opera that blended *Puccini* »-like emotionalism with a kind of naturalism (sometimes naïve, but theatrically effective) that, if not anti-opera, was at any rate anti-Grand Opera. Italian by birth—he emigrated to America early in his life, before he had made an impact in music—Menotti has the characteristic Italian warmth of expression. On the other hand, his best work is overtly, sometimes even self-consciously, contemporary in its stripping away of old traditions. The result caused considerable furore. His later work has not extended the elements that gave him his original success. Much of his appeal is sentimental (but so is part of Puccini's) and a good deal of it lies in the way in which it presents characters with whom ordinary people can immediately identify, unencumbered by too many 'operatic' distractions. That is perhaps an over-simplification, but it contains a kernel of truth. Musically, Menotti's operas are not distinguished; but they are unfailingly effective, and the music fits the drama.

Apart from *The Consul*, Menotti's best known stage works are *Amelia at the Ball*, *The Medium*, *The Telephone*, *Amahl and the Night Visitors*, *The Saint of Bleecker Street* and *Maria Golovin*. He has been closely associated with the international music festival at Spoleto.

The Medium
Opera in 2 Acts.
Text by Menotti.
First performance: Columbia University (Brander Matthews Theatre) May 8, 1946. New York 1947; London (Aldwych) 1948; Paris 1968.

Synopsis:
Scene: USA. Time: the present
Act 1 Madame Flora (Baba), her daughter Monica, and Toby, a mute, prepare for a séance. The clients arrive and the séance begins. It is fraudulent, but suddenly Baba cries out: someone, or something, has touched her, and she is terrified. The clients are dismissed and they leave, asking who is afraid of their dead, while Baba tries to find out who played the trick on her.
Act 2 Some days later the clients return and Baba tries to tell them that she is a fraud. She has tried to make Toby admit that he touched her; but without success, despite a whipping. The clients will not believe they have been cheated, but they are sent away; so is Toby. Baba gets drunk and falls asleep, while Toby returns and hides behind the curtain of the puppet theatre. Baba wakes in panic, seizes a revolver and fires. A spot of blood appears on the curtain: 'I've killed the ghost,' cries Baba. Toby falls forward, dead, dragging the curtain with him.

Notes:
Menotti has written that in spite of its subject and somewhat strange action, this is an opera of ideas, contrasting the world of reality, which Baba cannot understand, and a supernatural one in which she cannot believe. Menotti wrote the libretto as he always does (he also wrote that for Samuel Barber's *Vanessa*) and, as always, text and music are convincingly fused. The subject was suggested to him by a séance which he attended in Salzburg in 1936. For the first New York production of *The Medium*, Menotti wrote a short, comic, curtain-raiser, *The Telephone*, which is often given as a kind of prelude. It has been recorded thus in America, but has never appeared in the English catalogue.

RECORDINGS:

CBS 73204 (d) ●			Philips ABL3387 (d) ●	
Columbia MS-7387 (US)			Symphony Orchestra	
Washington Opera Society Orchestra			c. Emanuel Balaban	
c. Jorge Mester			Madame Flora	
Madame Flora			(Baba) (c)	Marie Powers
(Baba) (c)	Regina Resnik		Monica (s)	Evelyn Keller
Monica (s)	Judith Blegen		Madame	
Madame			Gobineau (s)	Beverly Dame
Gobineau (s)	Emily Derr		Monsieur	
Monsieur			Gobineau (b)	Frank Rogier
Gobineau (b)	Julian Patrick		Madame	
Madame			Nolan (m-s)	Catherine Mastice
Nolan (m-s)	Claudine Carlson			

Amahl and the Night Visitors
Opera in 1 Act (originally for television).
Text by Menotti
First performance (television): New York (NBC), December 24, 1951. Florence 1953; BBC Television 1967; Hamburg (State Opera) 1968.

Synopsis:
The crippled boy Amahl sits outside his mother's house playing a pipe. She calls him, but he will not come, saying there is a brilliant new star in the sky. In the distance are heard the voices of the Three Kings, who are following the star. They stop at the house; Amahl questions them. Amahl goes to fetch other shepherds. The Kings tell of the Child they are seeking and the rich presents they have for Him. Amahl's mother, driven by poverty, tries to steal some of the jewels; King Melchior says she

Below left: *Amahl and the Three Kings in Menotti's opera.*

Below: *From a BBC-2 TV production of* Amahl and the Night Visitors.

may keep what she has taken, for the Child will have no need of treasure. While his mother is gripped by the story of the Child and wants to return the jewels, Amahl wants to give his homemade crutch as his offering. He throws it down and begins to walk without it, then begs to be allowed to accompany the Kings and is finally allowed to, no longer in need of any support.

Notes:

Menotti has told how, in Italy, it was not Santa Claus but the Three Kings who brought presents to children at Christmas. Later, in America, when he was asked for a Christmas television opera by NBC, he was at first at a loss for a subject: then he remembered his childhood with his brother and how they would wait for the Kings. Also he does not mention, but it is recorded elsewhere, that he himself had an infirm leg that was cured after a visit to a shrine. Thus *Amahl*, like *The Medium*, had its origins in a personal experience.

RECORDINGS:
RCA LSB4075 ●
Victor LSC-2762 (US)
Chorus and Orchestra
c. Herbert Grossman
Amahl (tr)   Kurt Yaghjian
Mother (s)   Martha King
King Melchior (b) Richard Cross
King Kaspar (t)   John McCollum
King Balthazar (bs) Willis Patterson
Page (b)   Julian Patrick

RCA RB16083 (m) (d) ●
(previously HMV ALP1196)
Victor LM1701 (m) (US)
c. Thomas Schippers
Original NBC cast including
Chet Allen (tr)
Rosemary Kuhlmann (s)

Amelia al Ballo

Opera in 1 Act.
Text by Menotti (originally in Italian).
First performance: Philadelphia (in English—tr. G. Meade) April 1, 1937. New York (Metropolitan) (in English) 1938; San Remo (in Italian) 1938; Berlin 1947.

RECORDING:
Columbia 33CX1166 (d) ●
Chorus and Orchestra of La Scala, Milan
c. Nino Sanzogno
Margherita Carosio (s)
Rolando Panerai (b)
(recorded in Italy during the 1950s)

The Consul

Opera in 3 Acts.
Text by Menotti.
First performance: Philadelphia, March 1, 1950.

RECORDING:
Brunswick LAT8012/3 (d) ●
c. Lehman Engel
Patricia Neway (s)
Leon Lishner (bs)
Marie Powers (c)
Cornel MacNiel (b)

Below: *A scene from the English National Opera production of Menotti's The Consul.*

GIACOMO MEYERBEER
(b. Berlin 5.9.1791; d. Paris 2.5.1864)

Meyerbeer (born Jakob Liebmann Beer), is characterised as a 'controversial figure'. His reputation, exaggeratedly inflated during his lifetime, was savagely deflated as fashion changed and old jealousies combined with sudden 'discoveries' of the emptiness of his music to reduce him to something like a caricature. He was a Jew, rich, and successful, all ingredients likely to invite hostility. Meyerbeer composed the grandest of Grand Opera in Paris at a time when that form of entertainment was inordinately popular. His operas are full of brilliant spectacle, extravagant setting, and set pieces rewarding for the top international singers of the day. He showed his musical gifts early; his family (unusually) encouraged them from the outset. His father was a banker and the son inherited a fortune from a relative named Meyer, on that account changing his original name to Meyerbeer. In spite of precocious talent, he did not achieve early success, being thoroughly conscientious and taking time to acquire experience and technique. He was a student in Germany with Weber », and after hearing Hummel play in Vienna retired for further piano study before resuming his public career. He studied vocal composition in Italy for a while and produced operas both there and in Germany, though without making a mark. In 1824 he went to Paris for a performance of one of his operas and made the French capital his headquarters for the rest of his life. After his first huge success in Paris with *Robert le Diable* in 1831, he was set for fashionable success and fortune. His frequent librettist was Eugène Scribe, himself a significant figure in the French theatre. He became known and accepted as a French composer, though in 1842 he became General Music Director of Berlin at the instigation of the King of Prussia and represented German music at the International Exhibition in London in 1862. Meyerbeer's operas no doubt contain elements of empty rhetoric, of a too facile eclecticism, of wilful extravagance and sundry other faults and failings. But there remains much in them of true quality, giving lasting pleasure.

Robert le Diable

Opera in 5 Acts.
Text by Eugène Scribe.
First performance: Paris (Opéra) November 21, 1831.

RECORDING:
Decca SET454/5 □
London 1286 (US)
En vain l'espère—Idole de ma vie
Joan Sutherland (s)

Les Huguenots

Opera in 5 Acts.
Text by Eugène Scribe and Emile Deschamps.
First performance: Paris (Opéra) February 29, 1836. Cologne (I.F. Castelli) 1837; New Orleans 1839; London (Covent Garden) (in German) 1842.

Synopsis:
Scene: Touraine and Paris. Time: 1592.
Act 1 Among the guests at a banquet given by the Catholic Count de Nevers are the Huguenot soldiers Raoul de Nangis and his friend Marcel. Called to sing in praise of his lady love, Raoul sings of an unknown lady he rescued from rowdy students; Marcel sings a Lutheran song and a Huguenot battle song. The assembly is amused rather than annoyed. A lady arrives to see Nevers; Raoul recognises his unknown love.
Act 2 Queen Marguerite de Valois knows of Raoul's love for the lady—Valentine, daughter of the Catholic Count de St Bris —and hopes to reconcile the rival religious factions by their marriage. Valentine ends her betrothal to Nevers at the Queen's command, but Raoul, believing she is Nevers's mistress, refuses her hand.
Act 3 In Paris, preparations are made for the wedding of Nevers and Valentine, but feelings between Catholics and Huguenots run high over Raoul's behaviour. He challenges St Bris. Valentine warns Raoul of a plot to ambush and kill him: Raoul learns that she truly loves him.

Above: *The Florence Opera production of Giacomo Meyerbeer's posthumously performed opera* L'Africaine.

Act 4   Raoul visits Valentine, now married to Nevers, and narrowly escaped being caught with her. He overhears a plot to massacre the Huguenots on St Bartholomew's Night. Nevers refuses to participate and is imprisoned. In spite of Valentine's fears for him, Raoul is determined to warn the Huguenot leaders.

Act 5   Raoul reaches the Huguenots, but the massacre has begun. He shelters with Marcel in a churchyard. Valentine enters: Nevers is dead and she is free to marry Raoul, but he refuses on religious grounds. Valentine says she will die with him, as a Huguenot. Raoul is wounded; St Bris and his men close in, firing. Too late, St Bris realises that one of the Huguenots he has killed is his own daughter.

Well-known arias:

Act 1   Plus blanche que la blanche hermine (Raoul)
        Piff, paff, piff (Huguenot battle song) (Marcel)
        Une dame noble et sage (Urbain)
Act 2   O beau pays de la Touraine (Marguerite)
Act 3   Rataplan (Soldiers)
        En mon bon droit j'ai confiance (Septet)
Act 4   Parmi les pleurs (Valentine)
        Oh, ciel! Où courez-vous? . . . (Raoul and Valentine)

RECORDINGS:
Decca SET460/3 ●
London 1437 (4) (US)
Ambrosian Opera Chorus/New
Philharmonic Orchestra
c. Richard Bonynge
Raoul de Nangis (t) Anastasios Vrenios
Valentine (s)   Martina Arroyo
Queen
  Marguerite (s)   Joan Sutherland
Count de Nevers (b) Dominic Cossa
Count de St Bris (b) Gabriel Ghiuselev
Urbain (m-s)   Huguette
                         Tourangeau

Decca SET513 ■
London 26239 (US)
(from above)

Decca SXL6147 □
London 25911 (US)
Piff, paff, piff
Nicolai Ghiaurov (bs-b)

Decca SXL6637 □
London 26379 (US)
Piff, paff, piff
Joseph Rouleau (bs)

Decca SXL6149 □
London 26064 (US)
Nobles seigneurs—Une dame noble et
sage
Marilyn Horne (m-s)

Decca SXL2257 □
London 1214 (2) (US)
O beau pays de la Touraine
A ce mot seul s'anime
Joan Sutherland (s)

DG 2530 073 □
O beau pays de la Touraine
A ce mot seul s'anime
Montserrat Caballé (s)

Le Prophète
Opera in 5 Acts.
Text by Eugène Scribe.
First performance: Paris (Opéra) April 16, 1849. London (Covent Garden) 1849;
New Orleans 1850.

Synopsis:
Scene: The Low Countries. Time: 1534-35.

Act 1   Fides, mother of John of Leyden, and Bertha, John's betrothed, seek permission for the marriage from Count Oberthal. Recognising them as Anabaptists, the Count has them beaten and abducts Bertha.

Act 2   John plans to exploit his likeness to a picture of King David in Münster Cathedral. The Count pursues Bertha, who has escaped, and captures Fides, threatening to execute her if Bertha is not returned to him. John is forced to agree.

Act 3   John, proclaimed a Prophet of divine birth, leads the Anabaptists against Münster. Count Oberthal is captured: John says Bertha shall decide his fate. An attack by the Anabaptists fails in John's absence, but he rallies his forces and leads them to victory.

Act 4   John is to be crowned Emperor in captured Münster. Fides, believing her son dead, comes there to beg. At the coronation she recognises her son, but John, fearing that the fiction of his divine birth will be exposed, orders his soldiers to run him through if the woman repeats her claim to be his mother. To save him, Fides remains silent.

Act 5   The Anabaptists have turned against their Prophet, John. He is reconciled with his mother, but Bertha, believing the Prophet has killed John, plans to blow up the castle containing the Prophet and his followers. Recognising John, too late to reverse her plan, she kills herself. John decides to accept the death Bertha has planned and arranges for all his enemies to be present when the explosion occurs. Fides stands beside her son as the magazines explode.

Well-known arias:

Act 1   Mon coeur s'élance (Bertha)
Act 2   Sous les vastes arceaux d'un temple magnifique (John)
        Ah, mon fils (Fides)
Act 3   Skaters' Ballet (Les Patineurs)
Act 4   Coronation March
Act 5   O Prêtres de Baal (Fides)

RECORDINGS:
CBS 79400 (4) ●
Columbia M434340 (US)
Boys' Choir of Haberdashers' Aske
School/Ambrosian Opera Chorus/
Royal Philharmonic Orchestra
c. Henry Lewis
John of Leyden (t) James McCracken
Bertha (s)   Renata Scotto
Fides (m-s)   Marilyn Horne
Count Oberthal (b) Jules Bastin

Dinorah (Le Pardon de Ploërmel)

Opera in 3 Acts.
Text by Jules Barbier and Michael Carré.
First performance: Paris (Opéra-Comique) April 4, 1859.

RECORDINGS:
Decca SET454/5 ☐
London 1286 (US)
Dors petite
Joan Sutherland (s)

Decca SET247/8 ☐
London 1254 (2) (US)
Ombre legère
Joan Sutherland (s)

HMV SLS5018 (2) ☐
Angel S-3696 (2) (US)
Ombre legère
Maria Callas (s)

DG 136011 *or* 135020 ☐
Ombre legère
Rita Streich (s)

L'Africaine

Opera in 5 Acts.
Text by Eugène Scribe.
First performance: Paris (Opéra) April 28, 1865 (posthumous).

RECORDINGS:
RCA SER5613 ☐
RCA LSC-3083 (US)
O Paradis
Placido Domingo (t)

RCA RL11749 ☐
O Paradis
Enrico Caruso (t)

Decca Ace of Diamonds SDD391 ☐
O Paradis
Carlo Bergonzi (t)

DARIUS MILHAUD

(b. Aix-en-Provence 4.9.1892; d. Geneva 22.6.1974)

An immensely prolific and ingenious composer in all forms, Milhaud studied at the Paris Conservatoire, his teachers including Vincent d'Indy and Paul Dukas. Between 1917 and 1918 he was attached to the French Legation in Rio de Janeiro: this had a considerable influence on many of his compositions, where a Brazilian background is prominent. During the 1920s he was a member of the celebrated French group of composers known as 'Les Six'. In 1940 he went to the United States and stayed there throughout the war years, returning to France in 1947 and becoming professor at the Paris Conservatoire. Among Milhaud's numerous works are several operas, some on a large scale and others what he called 'minute-operas'. The range as well as the quantity of his music is enormous and his fertile mind led him to experimental work and the search for new forms. He wrote a great deal of incidental music for the theatre, including some for Paul Claudel's *Christophe Colomb*, as well as the large-scale and originally-structured opera of the same name in 2 Acts and 27 scenes. The two are connected musically only by one small pendant.

Les Choëphores

Opera in 1 Act.
Text by Paul Claudel, translated from Aeschylus.
First performance: Paris (concert) June 15, 1919; Brussels (stage) March 27, 1935.

Notes:

This is the second of three pieces based on *The Oresteia* of Aeschylus, entitled *Orestie*. The other two are *Agamemnon* (first) and *Eumenides* (third). *Choëphores* deals with the relationship between Elektra and Orestes, the brother and sister who murdered their mother, Clytemnestra, in revenge for her and her lover's killing of their father, Agamemnon. The work falls between the poles of opera proper and incidental music, though it is usually classified as opera.

RECORDING:
Columbia AMS-6396 (US) ●
Schola Cantorum/New York
Philharmonic Orchestra
c. Leonard Bernstein

Elektra (s)　Irene Jordan
Orestes (b)　McHenry Boatwright
Clytemnestra (s)　Virgina Bobikian
Narrator　Vera Zorina

ITALO MONTEMEZZI

(b. Vigasio 4.8.1875; d. Verona 15.5.1952)

Originally trained as an engineer in Milan, Montemezzi took up music after some initial setbacks and obtained his diploma at the Milan Conservatoire in 1900. He produced his first opera, *Giovanni Gallurese*, at Turin in January 1905; its success was such that he could look forward to a prosperous future. His second opera, *Hellera*, also produced in Turin, was not so successful, but his third, *L'Amore dei tre re*, opened at La Scala, Milan, in April, 1913, and established his reputation. It has become his most enduring composition. Montemezzi spent ten years from 1939 in America, continuing to compose and conduct, returning to Italy in 1949. As a composer he was attracted neither to the learned nor the *verismo* schools: he wished, he declared, only to create an atmosphere in which his characters could work out their dramatic personalities.

L'Amore dei tre re

Opera in 3 Acts.
Text by Sem Benelli after his own tragic poem.
First performance: Milan (La Scala) April 10, 1913. London (Covent Garden) 1914; New York (Metropolitan) 1914.

Synopsis:

Scene: A castle in Italy. Time: 10th century.
Act 1　In a darkened hall, the blind old King Archibaldo is present, but barely visible. It is hinted that Archibaldo's daughter-in-law Fiora, wife of his son Manfredo by a political marriage, is involved with Avito, her former lover. Flaminio, the castle guard, watches on the old king's behalf. They suspect that Avito is in the castle, but Manfredo returns from the wars and diverts attention.
Act 2　Manfredo again goes to war, after trying to convince Fiora of his love for her. But when he has gone Fiora returns to

Avito. Archibaldo almost catches them together, but Flaminio intervenes. Archibaldo accuses Fiora of infidelity, but she will not reveal the name of her lover. Enraged, he strangles her.
Act 3　Fiora lies on a bier in the castle crypt. Archibaldo has spread poison on her lips, knowing that her secret lover will come to bestow a last kiss before the burial. Avito enters and kisses Fiora. Then Manfredo appears, sees Avito and realises the truth; he challenges his rival, but Avito dies from the poison, telling Manfredo of his great love for Fiora. Manfredo too kisses the corpse and dies. Archibaldo then enters and touches the corpse beside the bier, believing justice to have been done—only to find that it is the body of his son.

Notes:

Symbolic meanings have been read into the opera: Fiora represents Italy; Archibaldo the hated invader; Manfredo the heir whose hand was used in bribery; and Avito the true prince.

RECORDINGS:
RCA Red Seal RL01945 (2) ●
RCA ARL2-1945 (2) (US)
Ambrosian Opera Chorus/London
Symphony Orchestra
c. Nello Santi
Archibaldo (bs)　Cesare Siepi
Fiora (s)　Anna Moffo
Avito (t)　Placido Domingo
Manfredo (bs)　Pablo Elvira
Flaminio (t)　Ryland Davies

Cetra OLPC1212 (m) (d) (r. 1955) ●
Chorus and Orchestra of Radiotelevisione, Milan
c. Arturo Basile
Sesto Bruscantini (bs)
Clara Petrella (s)
Aldo Bertocci (t)

CLAUDIO MONTEVERDI

(b. Cremona ?.5.1567; d. Venice 29.11.1643)

Monteverdi was one of the most important figures in the history of opera and in the overall evolution of Western music. Much of his output, especially his operatic work, has been lost, but the more one knows of his music the more certain one is of his position. Monteverdi was the son of a physician. He was a choirboy at Cremona Cathedral, where he was a pupil of Marc' Antonio Ingegneri, and during this period published his first compositions. He served the ducal court at Mantua and in 1594/5 married Claudia Cataneo; she died in 1607 leaving him with two young children. In 1613 he went to Venice, where he was elected *maestro di cappella* at St Mark's. He took holy orders in 1630.

Monteverdi composed much church music and his many madrigals are among the finest ever written. But only three complete operas have survived, plus one or two works which are not true operas. To call him the last madrigal composer and the first opera composer says something important about him, although neither is historically correct. The composers of the Florentine school, including Caccini, Cavalli » and Peri » (whose *Euridice*, which Monteverdi probably heard, is sometimes referred to as the first true opera) called themselves the Camerata. They wished to return dramatic music to the old Greek principles, with declamation for a single voice in what they called *stile recitative*. This was altogether too rigid and formal, though important as an evolutionary movement. It fell to Monteverdi to breathe the spirit of genius into the emergent ideals, to make the idiom flexible, genuinely creative and truly expressive. This he did in a series of masterpieces; we can only lament that so little has survived. In addition to true operas, Monteverdi wrote pioneering works classified as 'opera-ballet', which inhabit a kind of hinterland between true opera and the dance drama.

Below: *The English National Opera production of Monteverdi's Orfeo.*

La Favola d'Orfeo

Opera in Prologue and 5 Acts.
Text by Alessandro Striggio.
First performance: Mantua, February 24 (?) 1607.

Synopsis:
Prologue An orchestral toccata is followed by a monologue by La Musica, declaiming her power.
Act 1 Nymphs and shepherds celebrate the wedding of Orfeo and Euridice with song and dance.
Act 2 Orfeo sings for the shepherds, but is interrupted by a Messenger with news of Euridice's death. The shepherds are horrified; the news is a crushing blow to Orfeo.
Act 3 Orfeo determines to descend into Hades to rescue Euridice; he gains admission by the power and beauty of his song.
Act 4 Proserpine and the captive spirits prevail on Pluto to release Euridice, on condition that Orfeo does not look at her until they have reached the upper world. Orfeo, triumphant, looks back to see if Euridice is following, whereupon she has to return to the underworld.

Act 5 Orfeo, mad with grief, wanders in despair. He calls on Nature to mourn with him. His father, Apollo, comes to tell him that he is to live in immortality among the stars, where he will see Euridice. Both ascend to heaven, to the chorus's farewell.

Notes:
Modern revivals of *Orfeo* began with the version prepared by Vincent d'Indy in 1905. Other important productions were those by the late Sir Jack Westrup at Oxford in 1925 (London 1929); Respighi's of 1934; and Hans Redlich's in 1936 in Zurich. More recently there have been Raymond Leppard's production at Sadler's Wells in 1965 and the recent presentations by Kent Opera. *Orfeo* was revived in New York in 1960, Leopold Stokowski conducting.

RECORDINGS:

DG 2723 018 (3) ●	World Records SOC237/9 (Erato) ●
DG 2710 015 (3) (US)	**Orfeo** (t) Eric Tappy
Hamburg Monteverdi Choir/Instrumental	**Euridice** (m-s) Magali Schwartz
Ensemble	**La Musica** (s) Wally Staempfli
c. Jürgen Jürgens	**Nymph** (s) Yvonne Perrin
Orfeo (t) Nigel Rogers	**Prosperine** (s) Juliette Bise
Euridice/	**Pluto** (bs) Jakob Staempfli
La Musica (s) Emilia Petrescu	**Apollo** (t) Theo Attmeyer
Nymph/	
Proserpine (m-s) Anna Reynolds	Telefunken AW6.41930 □
Pluto (bs) Stafford Dean	Mira, deh, mira Orfeo
	Cathy Berberian (s)

Telefunken FK6.35020 (3) ●
Telefunken 3635020 (3) (US)
Concentus Musicus
c. Nikolaus Harnoncourt
Orfeo (t)   Lajos Kozma
Euridice/
La Musica (s) Rotraud Hansmann
Nymph/
Proserpine (s) Elko Katanosaka
Hope/
Messenger (m-s) Cathy Berberian
Pluto (bs) Jacques Villisech

Telefunken DN6.41175 ■
(from above)

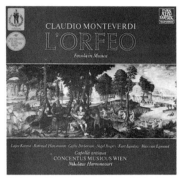

L'Ariana

Opera in Prologue and 8 Scenes.
Text by Ottavio Rinuccini.
First performance: Mantua, May 28, 1608.

Notes:
All that has survived of this opera is the great 'Lament', which became enormously popular throughout Italy as soon as it appeared.

RECORDING:

Telefunken AW6.41930 □	Erato STU 70848 □
Lasciatemi morire	Lasciatemi morire
Cathy Berberian (s)	Lausanne Baroque Ensemble and
	Chamber Orchestra
Telefunken AW6.41257 □	c. Michel Corboz
Lasciatemi morire	
Karla Schean (s)	

DG 2533 146 □
Lasciatemi morire
Hamburg Monteverdi Choir

Il Ballo delle Ingrate

Opera-ballet.
Text by Ottavio Rinuccini.
First performance: Mantua, June 4, 1608.

Notes:
This is not really an opera, though it might be called an opera in embryo. It is an entertainment of a kind suitable for the wedding celebrations that took place in the Mantuan ducal family, Gonzaga, in 1608. The poet Ottavio Rinuccini was the librettist of the earliest known operas, Peri's *Dafne* (which has not survived) and *Euridice*. *Il Ballo* includes the mythological figures Venus, Cupid and Pluto: the central episode is a dance

sequence. Hans Redlich regards this as an 'unmistakable descendant of the French *ballet de coeur*' and an ancestor of the modern opera-ballet such as Stravinsky's » *Pulcinella* from Pergolesi.

RECORDING:
Philips 6500 457 ●
Philips 6500 457 (US)
Ambrosian Singers/English Chamber Orchestra
c. Raymond Leppard

Heather Harper (s)
Lillian Watson (s)
Anne Howells (s)
Luigi Alva (t)
John Wakefield (t)
Stafford Dean (bs)

Il Combattimento di Tancredi e Clorinda
Dramatic cantata.
Text by Tasso.
First performance: Venice 1624.

Notes:
Like *Il Ballo*, this is not an opera, though it has enough operatic elements to justify its inclusion. It concerns the Christian knight Tancredi and the Saracen maid Clorinda, a female warrior of courage and resource. Challenged by Tancredi (she is dressed as a man, in armour), she is mortally wounded in the course of the fight but forgives him and asks for Christian baptism, which he gives her. In the Preface to this piece Monteverdi outlined some of his theories, most notably those which led to his great innovations of *pizzicato* and *tremolo* to heighten emotion, altering the entire instrumental spectrum. Both this work and *Il Ballo* appeared in Monteverdi's *Eighth Book of Madrigals*.

RECORDING:
Philips 6500 457 ●
Philips 6500 457 (US)
Ambrosian Singers/English Chamber Orchestra
c. Raymond Leppard
Heather Harper (s)
Lillian Watson (s)
Anne Howells (s)
Luigi Alva (t)
John Wakefield (t)
Stafford Dean (bs)

Telefunken A56 41132 ●
Telefunken 641132 (US)
c. Gustav Leonhardt

Vox TV340185 ●
Vox VSPS-18 (5) (US)
c. Gunter Kehr

Nonesuch 71090 (US) ●
c. Loehrer

Il Ritorno d'Ulisse in Patria
Opera in Prologue and 5 Acts.
Text by Giacomo Badoaro.
First performance: Venice (Teatro San Cassiano) February 1641.

Synopsis:
Prologue This features allegorical figures of Human Frailty, Time, Love and Fortune. It is usually omitted.
Act 1 Penelope laments the continued absence at the wars of her husband Ulysses (Ulisse), who has been away for 20 years. In the second scene Jove and Neptune discuss the frailties of men. Ulysses is cast up on a beach where Minerva, disguised, finds him, and tells him to hurry home to reclaim his palace and throne.
Act 2 Eumete, an old herdsman, ponders the contrasting lots of ordinary men and princes, to the disadvantage of the latter. Ulysses arrives, in disguise. Minerva appears on Telemaco's (Penelope and Ulysses' son) ship, and then again on land, when Telemaco, Eumete and Ulysses (still unrecognised) meet. Telemaco sends Eumete to tell Penelope that he has returned; Ulysses reveals himself to Telemaco, to the joy of both. In the meantime, Penelope resists her unwanted suitors and hopes for Ulysses' return.
Act 3 Ulysses comes to the palace disguised as a beggar. Penelope, despairing of his return, has set a trial for her suitors:

he who can draw Ulysses' bow shall win her. No one can. To everyone's surprise the 'old beggar' draws it, though he disclaims the prize, then he kills the suitors. Penelope suspects a trick — until Ulysses' old nurse, Ericlea, identifies him by a scar.

Notes:
The original version of the opera was not published until 1923, when it appeared in Vienna. Doubts were voiced about its authenticity; but is now generally accepted as the work of Monteverdi, from both internal and external evidence. The score is now usually presented in the 1942 edition of Luigi Dallapiccola », in which the Prologue is omitted and the original five Acts reduced to three. There was an earlier (concert) edition by Vincent d'Indy. Many subsequent revivals have taken place, including Erich Kraack's adaptation at Wupperthal in 1959. Raymond Leppard's version at Glyndebourne in 1972 was also notable. (Recorded in 1979.)

RECORDINGS:
Turnabout TV37016/8S ●
Vox SVBX5211 (3) (US)
Santini Chamber Orchestra
c. Rudolf Ewerhart

Penelope (m-s)	Maureen Lehane
Ulisse (Ulysses) (t)	Gerland English
Telemaco (t)	William Whitesides
Giove (Jove) (t)	Bernhard Michaelis
Minerva (s)	Antonia Fahberg
Ericlea (c)	Margarethe Bence
Eumete (t)	Helmut Kretschmar

Telefunken GK6.35024 (4) ●
Telefunken 46 35024 (4) (US)
Vienna Concentus Musicus
c. Nikolaus Harnoncourt

Penelope (m-s)	Norma Lerer
Ulisse (t)	Sven Ellasson
Telemaco (t)	Karl Hansen
Giove (t)	Ladislaus Anderko
Minerva (s)	Rotraud Hansmann
Ericlea (c)	Anne-Marie Muhle
Eumete (b)	Max von Egmond

Below: *The effective staging of Monteverdi's Il Ritorno d'Ulisse in Peter Hall's production at Glyndebourne, first seen in 1972 and revived in 1979.*

L'Incoronazione di Poppea
Opera in Prologue and 3 Acts.
Text by Giovanni Busenello.
First performance: Venice (Teatro SS. Giovanni e Paolo), late 1642.

Synopsis:
Scene: Rome. Time: *c.* AD 55.
Prologue (Sometimes omitted.) A quarrel between goddesses: Fortune and Virtue argue their respective merits until Love enters and sends them packing.

Act 1 Ottone, lover of Poppea, returns from war to find he has been displaced by the Emperor Nero. Nero hesitantly promises to abandon the Empress Octavia and marry Poppea, who, exultant, brushes aside warnings that the Empress may seek revenge. Octavia is full of self-pity, which Seneca tells her is unbefitting for an Empress. Seneca is warned by Pallas, Goddess of Wisdom, that to interfere is to invite his own death: as a Stoic, he welcomes the prospect. Nero announces his intention to marry Poppea and Seneca is enraged; Nero orders Seneca's death. Ottone, meanwhile, tries to reconcile his love for Poppea with the necessity of killing her.

Act 2 Seneca dies and Nero, delighted, celebrates. Octavia presses Ottone to murder Poppea. Disguised in the clothes of his new love Drusilla, Ottone goes to Poppea's garden, but she is guarded by the Goddess of Love.

Act 3 Drusilla is accused of the attempted murder of Poppea, but Ottone confesses. Nero sentences Ottone to banishment; Drusilla says she will go with him. Nero believes that Octavia encouraged the murder plot and must be exiled. Untruthfully protesting her innocence she prepares to leave Rome. Nero and Poppea are united.

Notes:

Monteverdi was 75 when he wrote this opera, a feat compared to Verdi's » with *Falstaff*. It is generally recognised as his supreme masterpiece. There have been many modern productions, including one by Raymond Leppard. Roger Norrington's Kent Opera production in 1974 is generally recognised as being as near as possible to Monteverdi's original.

RECORDINGS:
Telefunken AW6.35247 (5) ●
Telefunken 635247 (5) (US)
Vienna Concentus Musicus
c. Nikolaus Harnoncourt
Poppea (s) Helen Donath
Nerone (Nero) (s) Elisabeth Söderström
Ottavia (m-s) Cathy Berberian
Ottone (c-t) Paul Esswood
Seneca (bs) Ciancarlo Luccardi
Drusilla (s) Rotraud Hansmann

Telefunken 641974 (US) □
(from above)

Telefunken AW6.41930 □
Disprezzata Regina
Tu che diagli avi miei
Addio Roma
Cathy Berberian (m-s)
Paul Esswood (c-t)
(The Harnoncourt versions of *Orfeo*,
Il Ritorno d'Ulisse in patria,
L'incoronazione di Poppea and *Il
combattimento di Tancredi e Clorinda*
are collected and issued together on 12
Telefunken discs as JY6.35376)

HMV SLS908 (2) (d) ○
Seraphim S-6073 (2) (US)
Glyndebourne Festival Chorus/Royal
Philharmonic Orchestra
c. John Pritchard
Poppea (s) Magda Laszlo
Nerone (t) Richard Lewis
Octavia (s) Francis Bible
Seneca (bs) Carlo Cava

Below: *Delia Wallis as Poppea and Robert Ferguson as Nero in the Sadler's Wells production of* The Coronation of Poppea.

DOUGLAS MOORE

(b. Cutchogue, N.Y. 10.8.1893; d. Greenport, Long Island 25.7.1969)

The American composer Douglas Moore was educated at Yale, served in the US Navy during World War I, and then went to Europe to study with Vincent d'Indy, Ernest Bloch and Nadia Boulanger. Returning to America, he held a succession of musical appointments and in 1934 won a Guggenheim Fellowship. During all this time he composed and made considerable progress, evolving a personal idiom that was tuneful and basically romantic, with a strong foundation of American folk music. Moore wrote in all forms. His best-known operas are *The Ballad of Baby Doe* and *The Devil and Daniel Webster*, which appears to have had a wider appeal than the Pulitzer Prize-winning *Giants in the Earth* (1950). He also wrote the operettas *The Headless Horseman* and *The Emperor's New Clothes*, and the chamber opera *White Wings*.

The Devil and Daniel Webster

Folk Opera in 1 Act.
Text by Stephen Vincent Benét.
First performance: New York (Martin Beck Theater) May 18, 1939.

Synopsis:

Scene: New Hampshire. Time: 1840s.

The citizens of Cross Corners celebrate the marriage of Jabez and Mary Stone. Jabez, once poor, is now rich and a State Senator. Daniel Webster, the great New England political hero, is a guest; so is Mr Scratch, a Boston lawyer who proves to be the Devil in disguise, with a black box full of lost souls. The neighbours realise that Jabez has sold his soul to the Devil, denounce him, and flee. Jabez tells Mary how he came to make his dreadful bargain. Daniel Webster promises to help Jabez: when he demands a jury for his client, Scratch summons from the pit a jury of infamous American traitors and criminals and a hanging-judge from witch-trial days. Daniel Webster's powers of oratory defeat Scratch and rescue Jabez. The neighbours rush in to drive the Devil out of New England, and the festivities continue.

Notes:

This is often considered to be Moore's most successful opera. The text is based on Stephen Vincent Benét's famous short story that appeared in *The Saturday Evening Post* in 1936. Author and composer collaborated in 1937-38 to produce this musical version. Using everyday speech, it is a folk opera by virtue of its simple musical expression, which captures the spirit of the square-dance, early New England music-making and the brave spirit of pioneering America. It is totally American in outlook and style, owing nothing to European models, and is frequently performed. Alfred Frankenstein called it 'as artful, eloquent and effective a statement of the principles of American democracy as has ever been written'.

RECORDING:
Desto DST-6450 (US) ●
Westminster WST14050 (d) (US)
Festival Choir and Orchestra
c. Armando Aliberti
Daniel Webster (b) Lawrence Winters
Jabez Stone (bs) Joe Blankenship
Mary Stone (s) Doris Young
Mr Scratch (t) Frederick Weidner

The Ballad of Baby Doe

Opera in 2 Acts.
Text by John Latouche.
First performance: Central City, Co., July 7, 1956. New York 1958.

Notes:

The story is taken from a true incident in Leadville, Colorado, dating from the 1880s to the 1930s. Horace Tabor, the richest

man in Colorado in the 1880s, whose fortune was founded on silver, took as his second wife Elizabeth Baby Doe. She had left her husband and he had divorced his wife, Augusta, a situation fraught with social peril in those days. Horace lost his fortune in the silver 'collapse' of the 1890s, dying three years later. On his deathbed he urged his wife never to leave the Matchless Mine on which his fortune had been founded—and with dog-like fidelity she lived beside it in a wooden hut until she froze to death in 1935. The opera is a direct representation of these events. The recording, originally made in 1958 under the auspices of the Koussevitzky Music Foundation, was restored in 1976 for the American Bicentennial and the concurrent centenary of the State of Colorado.

RECORDING:
DG 2709 061 (3) ●
DG 2709 061 (3) (US)
New York City Opera Chorus and Orchestra
c. Emerson Buckley
Horace Tabor (b) Walter Cassel
Elizabeth Baby Doe (s) Beverly Sills
Augusta (m-s) Frances Bible

Carry Nation

Opera in 2 Acts.
Text by William North Jayme.
First performance: Lawrence (University of Kansas) 1966. New York City Opera 1968.

Synopsis:

Act 1 Carry's frustrated Mother takes in Charles as a boarder because he is a physician, but he proves to be an alcoholic. Although Carry's Father shames him into joining evening prayers, Charles does not reform. In springtime, he declares his love for Carry in Shakespearian words and, when Father objects, brandishes a flask of liquor. At a hoedown in summer, Carry agrees to marry Charles in spite of her parents' opposition.

Act 2 Carry, now pregnant, hears that Charles is often too drunk to attend to his patients, but he is enraged when she begs him to reform. She writes to her parents for money, and her Father sees a chance to win back his daughter. Charles and his friends drunkenly revive Civil War memories in a tavern, and Carry cannot persuade him to leave. Father persuades her to abandon Charles. In the final scene, Carry, whose Mother is now insane, reads a letter from Charles and tells her baby that he is much better and will soon return. When Father brings news of Charles's death, Carry blames herself and asks God for a reason to go on living. Thus, the opera sets the scene for Carry's prohibition crusade.

Notes:

The opera is based on the story of Carry Nation (1846-1911) who, at the age of 53, began to campaign against drinking and gambling establishments in Kansas and later led a 'saloon-smashing' campaign throughout America, also visiting England. She became disliked as a 'self-righteous meddler', but died confident that she had done all she could for the cause of prohibition.

RECORDING:
Desto DC6463/65 (3) (US) ●
New York City Opera Chorus and Orchestra
c. Samuel Krachmalnick
Carry Nation (m-s) Beverly Wolff
Father (bs b) Arnold Voketaitis
Mother (s) Ellen Faull
Charles (b) Julian Patrick

Below: *Douglas Moore's The Ballad of Baby Doe was given its New York première by the City Center Opera in 1956.*

WOLFGANG AMADEUS MOZART

(b. Salzburg 27.1.1756; d. Vienna 5.12.1791)

This is no place to enlarge further upon the unique and incomparable genius of Mozart, nor upon the details of his short unhappy life; except perhaps to say that he was probably the nearest we have come to the ideal of a perfect artist. His creative force was supremely unified: virtually everything he wrote, in whatever form and on whatever scale, is unmistakably by the same hand. Mozart wrote a great deal of bread-and-butter music; by no means all of his output consists of immortal masterpieces. But even his lesser work is nearly always impeccably written and contains at times flashes of inspiration only possible to the highest order of talent.

Mozart lived for only 36 years, but crowded into them an immense amount of creative activity. His was not a happy life—he never had a truly satisfying relationship, having married his wife Constanze Weber only after unsuccessfully courting her sister Aloysia, a singer—and during his childhood was not always wisely exploited by his father; this no doubt contributed to his later difficulties. He appears to have been a somewhat feckless and unreliable man; one reason why he found it hard, throughout his life, to obtain regular employment in official positions, for which he regularly applied. However, what may appear as personal faults were closely bound up with that sense of the unrealisable ideal of which his music eloquently speaks.

Mozart possessed a potent dramatic sense which gives his operas and other works a particular stamp. He wrote some 22 operas, as well as a number of other dramatic works for voices, and at least six of them are among the supreme masterpieces of the musical theatre. In his other music, notably the concertos, the operatic style can be seen to be operative, showing once again the total unity and integration of his genius. All the major operas and some of the lesser ones and fragments are now well represented on record.

Bastien und Bastienne
Songspiel in 1 Act.
Text by Friedrich Wilhelm Weiskern (from the French) with additions by J. H. F. Müller.
First performance: Vienna, October 1768.

Synopsis:
Bastienne, forsaken by Bastien, is advised by Colas to feign indifference. He tells Bastien that she now has a rich suitor; Bastien, upset, tells Bastienne that he was bewitched by the Lady of the Manor, who desires him, and in the end they are reconciled.

RECORDINGS:
DG 2537 038 ●
DG 2537 038 (US)
Salzburg Mozarteum Orchestra
c. Leopold Hager
Bastien (t)   Claes H. Ahnjö
Bastienne (s) Edith Mathis
Colas (bs)   Walter Berry

Philips Mozart Edition 6747
(Volume 14) (8) ●
originally ABL3010 (m) (d) (r. 1954)
Vienna Symphony Orchestra
c. John Pritchard
Bastien (t)   Waldemar Kmennt
Bastienne (s) Ilse Hollweg
Colas (bs)   Walter Berry

Turnabout TV346285 □
Vox TV346285 (US)
Overture
c. Joerg Faerber

La Finta Semplice
Opera buffa in 3 Acts.
Text by Marco Coltellini after Carlo Goldoni.
First performance: Salzburg, May 1, 1769.

RECORDING:
HMV SXLP30213 □
Angel S-36869 (US)
Overture
c. Neville Marriner

(an unsatisfactory complete recording under Bernhard Paumgartner, dating from 1956, is included in Volume 15 of the Philips Mozart Edition 6747 388, originally ABL3106/7 (m) (d))

Mitridate, ré di Ponto
Opera seria in 3 Acts.
Text by Vittorio Amadeo Cigna-Santi.
First performance: Milan (Teatro Regio Ducal) December 26, 1770.

Synopsis:
Act 1 Sifare and Farnace, sons of King Mitridate, contend for the love of Aspasia, who favours Sifare, and Farnace is betrothed anyway to Ismene, a Parthian princess. Mitridate is reported killed in battle; Farnace seeks the throne. In the temple, Farnace ignores Aspasia's refusal to marry him and drags her to the altar. Sifare intervenes, but fraternal strife is interrupted by the return of Mitridate

Act 2 Ismene and Farnace quarrel. Mitridate suspects Farnace of treachery and threatens him with death, suggesting that Ismene marry Sifare instead, but she refuses. Aspasia is now to marry Mitridate, but he suspects her of infidelity. Mitridate, preparing for war against Rome, appoints Farnace and Ismene to rule in Asia. Farnace seeks peace with Rome. A messenger comes to offer terms and Farnace is imprisoned as a traitor. Sifare listens as Mitridate suggests to Aspasia that she marry Sifare instead of himself; when she protests her fidelity, he accuses her of intrigue with Farnace and she admits her love for Sifare. Mitridate declared that he has been betrayed and swears vengeance.

Act 3 Mitridate says that both his disloyal sons must die. Aspasia tries to commit suicide, and Mitridate offers to spare Sifare if she yields to him. She refuses, and Mitridate sends her poison. Sifare strikes the cup from her hand, declaring that the conflict between love and duty is such that he prefers death. Farnace is released by the Romans, who offer him the throne, but he now has doubts. Mitridate is victorious against the Romans but stabs himself. He realises Sifare is brave and loyal and gives Aspasia to him. Ismene tells Mitridate that Farnace, too, is loyal: he has burned the Roman fleet. Mitridate dies happy.

Notes:
Mozart was only 14 when he addressed himself to this formidable subject, based on Racine.

RECORDINGS:
DG 2440 180 (4) ●
DG 2440 180 (4) (US)
Camerata Academica of Salzburg Mozarteum
c. Leopold Hager
Mitridate (t) Werner Hollweg
Aspasia (s) Arleen Auger
Sifare (s)   Edith Gruberova
Farnace (c) Agnes Baltsa
Ismene (c) Ileana Cotrubas
Arbate (s)   Christine Weidinger

Turnabout TV34628S □
Vox TV34628S (US)
Overture
c. Joerg Faerber

Ascanio in Alba
Opera in 2 Acts.
Text by Abbate Giuseppe Parini.
First performance: Milan (Teatro Regio) October 17, 1771.

RECORDING:
Turnabout TV34628S □
Vox TV34628S (US)
Overture
c. Joerg Faerber

Il Sogno di Scipione
Dramatic Serenade.
Text by Pietro Metastasio.
First performance: Salzburg, April 29, 1772.

RECORDING:
Turnabout TV 34628S □
Vox TV 34628S (US)
Overture
c. Joerg Faerber

Lucio Silla

Opera seria in 3 Acts.
Text by Giovanni da Gamerra.
First performance: Milan (Teatro Regio Ducal) December 26, 1772.

RECORDINGS:

Turnabout TV34628S □
Vox TV34628S (US)
Overture
c. Joerg Faerber

Decca Eclipse ECS740 □
London STS-10588 (US)
Overture
c. Peter Maag

HMV SXLP30213 □
Angel S-36869 (US)
Overture
c. Neville Marriner

La Finta Giardiniera

Opera buffa in 3 Acts.
Text by (probably) Ranieri de Calzabigi, revised Marco Coltellini.
First performance: Munich (Court Theatre) January 13, 1775.

Synopsis:

Act 1 Ramiro, guest of Don Anchises, Podestá (Mayor) of Lagonera, loves his host's niece, Arminda, who is to marry Count Belfiore. Anchises confesses his love for Sandrina, but the jealous Serpetta interrupts. Sandrina, who is posing as a gardener, reveals that she has a lover she longs to see again, and repulses Anchises's advances. Nardo, her brother, pursues Serpetta but encounters difficulties. Belfiore arrives to marry Arminda; he proves to be Sandrina's missing lover.

Act 2 Refused by Arminda, Ramiro swears revenge on Belfiore, who is at cross purposes with Arminda because of Sandrina's presence. Nardo continues his difficult wooing of Serpetta, and Sandrina decides to try to delay Belfiore's wedding.

Act 3 Belfiore and Sandrina abscond and are brought back. Anchises believes, wrongly, that his cunning has solved all the problems. At last, after many complications, the pairing of the lovers is resolved.

RECORDINGS:

Philips 6703 039 (3) ●
or 6747 388 (8)
Mozart Edition (Volume 15)
as above (US)
North German Radio Chorus and Orchestra
c. Hans Schmidt-Isserstedt
Don Anchises
  (Podestá) (t)   Gerhard Unger
Sandrina (s)   Helen Donath
Count Belfiore (t)   Werner Hollweg
Arminda (s)   Jessye Norman
Ramiro (m-s)   Tatiana Troyanos
Serpetta (s)   Ileana Cotrubas
Nardo (bs)   Hermann Prey

Everest/Cetra S-444/3 (US) ●
Orchestra and Chorus of Stuttgart
c. Rolf Reinhardt
Don Anchises
  (Podestá) (t)   Werner Hohmann
Sandrina (s)   Margot Guillaume
Count Belfiore (t)   Gustav Neidlinger
Arminda (s)   Hetty Plumacher
Ramiro (m-s)   Elinor Junker-Giesen
Serpetta (s)   Gertrud Jenne
Nardo (bs)   Alfred Pfeifle

Il Ré Pastore

Drama with music in 2 Acts.
Text by Metastasio after Tasso, revised Giambattista Varesco.
First performance: Salzburg, April 23, 1775.

Synopsis:

The royal family of Sidon have been liberated by Alexander the Great from the tyrant Strato, and now live as shepherds and shepherdesses. Strato's daughter and her lover Agenore, a friend of Alexander, arrive in the country, and a familiar pattern of conflict between love and duty ensues.

Notes:

The pastoral setting is charming, and a string of arias do not significantly advance the 'action' but make a thoroughly diverting impression.

Well-known arias:

Act 2 L'amerò, sarò constante (Aminta)

RECORDINGS:

BASF BAC3072/4 (Ger) ●
Mozarteum Orchestra, Salzburg
c. Leopold Hager
Aminta (s)   Edith Mathis

Elisa (s)   Arleen Auger
Agenore (t)   Werner Krenn
Alessandro (t)   Peter Schreier
Tamiri (s)   Sona Ghazarian

Everest/Cetra S-449/2 (US) ●
Tonstudio Orchestra, Stuttgart
c. Gustav Lund
Aminta (s)   Agnes Giebel
Elisa (s)   Käthe Nentwig
Agenore (t)   Werner Hohmann
Alessandro (t)   Albert Weikenmeier
Tamiri (s)   Hetty Plümacher

RCA PVL2 9086 (SER5567/8) (d) ●
Orchestra of Naples
c. Denis Vaughan
Aminta (s)   Reri Grist
Elisa (s)   Lucia Popp
Agenore (t)   Nicola Monti
Alessandro (t)   Luigi Alva
Tamiri (s)   Arlene Saunders

HMV SXLP30213 □
Angel S-36869 (US)
Overture
c. Neville Marriner

Turnabout TV34628S □
Turnabout TV34628S (US)
Overture
c. Joerg Faerber

Decca SDD335 □
L'amerò sarò constante
Erna Spoorenberg (s)

Decca ECS557 □
L'amerò sarò constante
Hilde Gueden (s)

RCA SER5675 □
RCA AGL1-2124 (US)
L'amerò sarò constante
Margaret Price (s)

Pye TPLS13064 □
L'amerò sarò constante
Rita Streich (s)

Philips 6500 042 □
Se vincendo
Werner Hollweg (t)

Decca SET268 □
Voi che fausti
Richard Conrad (t)

Zaïde

German Singspiel (unfinished).
Text by Johann Andreas Schachtner.
First performance: c. 1780.

Synopsis:

Act 1 Sultan Soliman's slaves, Gomatz among them, sing as they work at their task of stonebreaking. Gomatz delivers a 'melodrama' (speech with musical accompaniment) and then falls asleep. Zaïde, the Sultan's favourite, admires him and leaves money, a portrait and a letter of assignation. Gomatz wakes, finds the gifts, and swears fidelity to her. Allazim, the overseer, helps the two to abscond.

Act 2 The Sultan is angry; Osmin, Captain of the Guard, blames Allazim for the escape. The fugitives are captured and Zaïde defies the Sultan. Allazim, who once saved the Sultan's life, offers his own life for those of the lovers but Soliman refuses. Zaïde accepts all the blame.

Notes:

There are alternative endings: in one, the lovers are found to be brother and sister; in the other, used for the recording, Allazim softens the Sultan's heart and remains as his adviser while the lovers depart in peace. The work clearly anticipates the setting of *Die Entführung aus dem Serail*. No overture or finale exists: Symphony No 32 in G (K.318) is used for the former (some authorities think it was intended as such by Mozart); the March (K.335, No 1) for the latter. The gaps in the libretto are filled by adapted dialogue.

RECORDINGS:

Philips 6700 097 (2) ●
Philips 6700 097 (2) (US)
(also in Volume 14 of the Mozart Edition)
Berlin State Orchestra
c. Bernhard Klee
Zaïde (s)   Edith Mathis
Gomatz (t)   Peter Schreier
Allazim (bs)   Ingvar Wixell
Sultan Soliman (t)   Werner Hollweg
Osmin (bs)   Reiner Süss

Decca SET548/9 □
Ruhe sanft
Lucia Popp (s)

Idomeneo, rè di Creta

Opera seria in 3 Acts.
Text by Giambattista Varesco after Antoine Danchet.
First performance: Munich (Court Theatre) January 29, 1781. Vienna 1786; Rotterdam 1880; Glasgow (in English) 1934; Tanglewood, Mass. 1947.

Synopsis:

Act 1 Ilia, a Trojan princess captured by the hated Greeks,

loves Idamante, son of their king Idomeneo. Idamante orders the release of the prisoners to celebrate his father's return, but Arbace brings news of his shipwreck. The jealous Electra sings of her love for Idamante. Idomeneo survives the shipwreck, and as a tribute to Neptune promises to sacrifice the first person to welcome him when he returns home. Idamante is that person.

Act 2 Arbace advises Idomeneo to send Idamante and Electra to Argos. Idomeneo, knowing his son's love for Ilia, is sad, but Electra rejoices. After a peaceful embarkation the angry Neptune sends a storm and a fearsome sea monster.

Act 3 Idamante prepares to fight the monster. Idomeneo, worried at breaking his promise to Neptune, exiles Idamante, and then, because of the havoc caused by the monster, agrees to sacrifice him. News comes that Idamante has slain the monster, and he agrees to be sacrificed, but Ilia offers to die in his place. Neptune, relenting, agrees that Idomeneo shall abdicate in favour of Idamante and Ilia. All are happy except Electra, who departs angrily.

Well-known arias:
Act 1 Padre, germani, addio (Ilia)
Act 2 Non temer, amato bene (Idamante)
Se il padre perdei (Ilia)
Fuor del mar ho un mar in seno (Idomeneo)
Act 3 Zeffiretti lusinghieri (Ilia)
Torna la pace al core (Idomeneo)

RECORDINGS:
Philips 6703 024 (3) ●
Philips 839 758/60 (US)
(Also in Volume 15 of Mozart Edition—6747 836)
BBC Chorus and Symphony Orchestra
c. Colin Davis
Idomeneo (t) George Shirley
Idamante (t) Ryland Davies
Ilia (s) Margheretta Rinaldi
Electra (s) Pauline Tinsley
Arbace (t) Robert Tear

DG 2740 195 (4) ●
DG 2740 195 (4) (US)
Leipzig Radio Choir/Dresden State Orchestra
c. Karl Böhm
Idomeneo (t) Wieslaw Ochman
Idamante (t) Peter Schreier
Ilia (s) Edith Mathis
Electra (s) Julia Varaday
Arbace (t) Hermann Winkler

HMV SLS965 (3) (d) ●
Leipzig Radio Chorus/Dresden State Orchestra
c. Hans Schmidt-Isserstedt
Idomeneo (t) Nicolai Gedda
Idamante (t) Adolf Dallapozza
Ilia (s) Anneliese Rothenberger
Electra (s) Edda Moser

HMV ALP515/7 (d) ●
Seraphim S-6070 (3) (US)
Glyndebourne Chorus and Orchestra
c. John Pritchard
Idomeneo (t) Richard Lewis
Idamante (t) Leopold Simoneau
Ilia (s) Sena Jurinac
Electra (s) Lucille Udovic

Decca SET548/9 □
Overture
c. Istvan Kertesz

Turnabout TV34628S □
Vox TV34628S (US)
Overture
c. Joerg Faerber

Philips 6768 050 □
Overture
c. Neville Marriner

Seraphim S-60037 (US) □
Overture
c. Colin Davis

RCA LRL1 5077 □
RCA AGL1-1532
Non piu . . . Non temer, amato bene
Margaret Price (s)

Decca ECS557 □
Non temer, amato bene
Se il padre
Hilde Gueden (s)
(the aria 'Non temer, amato bene' (K.490) was added by Mozart to the fourth performance of *Idomeneo*, a concert performance in Vienna, with the text possibly provided by Da Ponte. It was a text Mozart obviously admired for he set it again as a concert aria, K.505, soon after)

Die Entführung aus dem Serail
Comic Singspiel in 3 Acts.
Text by Christoph Friedrich Bretzner revised by Gottlieb Stephanie, Jr.
First performance: Vienna (Burg Theatre) July 16, 1782. London (Covent Garden) (as The Seraglio—W. Dimond) November 24, 1827; New York 1860.

Synopsis:
Scene: Turkey. Time: 16th century.
Act 1 Belmonte seeks to rescue Constanze, her English maid

Above: *The English Opera Group production of Mozart's* Idomeneo.

Blonde, and his own servant Pedrillo, who have been captured and are now in the palace of the Pasha. Osmin, overseer of the harem, comes out to pick figs; Belmonte accosts him, in the hope of making contact with Pedrillo, now a gardener, who is hated by Osmin for his womanising. Pedrillo plans to smuggle Belmonte into the palace as an architect. The Pasha desires Constanze, who declares that she loves another.

Act 2 Osmin, jealous of Pedrillo, pursues Blonde. Constanze still resists the Pasha. Pedrillo tells Blonde of the planned rescue, then goes to divert Osmin by making him drunk. Belmonte and Constanze are reunited. Belmonte and Pedrillo question their ladies' fidelity, but apologise when Constanze weeps and Blonde scolds.

Act 3 The rescue ship arrives and the captain and Pedrillo rig up ladders. A deaf-mute guard alerts the tipsy Osmin, who sings of revenge while the lovers are recaptured. Brought before the Pasha, while Osmin makes accusations, Constanze pleads love as her excuse and Belmonte promises a ransom from his father. Unfortunately, Belmonte's father is the Pasha's enemy, and the Pasha utters dire threats. Belmonte and Constanze agree to die together, but the Pasha decides to show his magnanimity by releasing his captives.

Well-known arias:
Act 1 Wer ein Liebchen hat gefunden (Osmin)
Solche hergelauf 'ne Laffen
O wie ängstlich, o wie feurig (Belmonte)
Ach, ich liebte, war so glücklich (Constanze)
Marsch, marsch, marsch (Belmonte, Constanze and Pedrillo)
Act 2 Durch Zärtlichkeit und Schmeichen (Blonde)
Traurigkeit ward mir zum Loose (Constanze and Blonde)
Marten aller Arten (Constanze)
Welche Wonne, welche Lust (Blonde)
Vivat Bacchus (Osmin and Pedrillo)
Act 3 Im Mohrenland gefangen war (Pedrillo)
Welch' ein Geschick (Belmonte and Constanze)

RECORDINGS:
DG 2740 102 (3) ●
DG 2709 051 (3) (US)
Leipzig Radio Choir/Dresden State Orchestra
c. Karl Böhm
Belmonte (t) Peter Schreier
Constanze (s) Arleen Auger
Osmin (bs) Kurt Moll
Blonde (s) Reri Grist
Pedrillo (t) Harald Neukirch
(the third record contains *Der Schauspieldirektor*)

DG 2726 051 (2) ●
Bavarian State Opera Chorus and Orchestra
c. Eugen Jochum
Belmonte (t) Fritz Wunderlich
Constanze (s) Erika Köth

Osmin (bs) Kurt Böhme
Blonde (s) Lotte Schadle
Pedrillo (t) Friedrich Lenz

Decca Eclipse ECM730/1 (m) (r. 1950) ●
Vienna Opera Chorus/Vienna Philharmonic Orchestra
c. Josef Krips
Belmonte (t) Walter Ludwig
Constanze (s) Wilma Lipp
Osmin (bs) Endre Koreth
Blonde (s) Emmy Loose
Pedrillo (t) Peter Klein

World Records SOC235/6 ★●
Seraphim S-6025 (2) (US)
Vienna State Opera Chorus/Vienna Philharmonic Orchestra
c. Josef Krips

Belmonte (t) Nicolai Gedda
Constanze (s) Anneliese Rothenberger
Osmin (bs) Gottlob Frick
Blonde (s) Lucia Popp
Pedrillo (t) Gerhard Unger

HMV SLS5153 (2) ●
Angel SBL3555 (US)
Beecham Choral Society/Royal
Philharmonic Orchestra
c. Sir Thomas Beecham
Belmonte
　(t/spkr) Léopold Simoneau/
　　　　　Manfred Schmidt

HMV SLS773 (2) (d) ●
(previously Columbia 33CX1462/3 (d)
and HMV HQS1050/1 (d)
Angel S-3555 (2) (US)
Beecham Choral Society/Royal
Philharmonic Orchestra
c. Sir Thomas Beecham
Belmonte (t) Leopold Simoneau
Constanze (s) Lois Marshall
Osmin (bs) Gottlob Frick
Blonde (s) Ilse Hollweg
Pedrillo (t) Gerhard Unger

L'Oca del Cairo
Opera buffa (unfinished).
Text by Giovanni Battista Varesco.
First performance: 1783.

RECORDING:
Decca SXL6262 □
Ogni momento
Geraint Evans (bs)

Lo Sposa Deluso (ossia la Rivalità di tre Donne per un Solo Amante)
Opera buffa (unfinished).
Text by (possibly) Da Ponte.
First performance: 1783.

Synopsis:
In Leghorn, Bocconio, a rich old bachelor, awaits his bride Eugenia, a noble Roman lady. His niece Bettina and her lover Asdrubale chide him, and Pulcherio, his misogynist friend, is scornful. Eugenia arrives, is not greeted with the formal dignity she thinks is her due, and threatens to leave. Pulcherio attemps to reconcile her and Bocconio, but Eugenia suddenly recognises Asdrubale as a former lover whom she believed dead, and swoons. Bocconio, puzzled, hurries off in search of medicine while Asdrubale berates Eugenia for unfaithfulness; Bocconio returns, and a memorable trio ensues.

RECORDING:
Philips 9500 011 ●
(also in Mozart Edition Volume 15)
Philips 9500 011 (US)
London Symphony Orchestra
c. Colin Davis
Bocconio (bs) Clifford Grant

Eugenia (s) Felicity Palmer
Asdrubale (t) Anthony Rolfe Johnson
Pulcherio (t) Robert Tear
(this record also contains *Der Schauspieldirektor*)

Der Schauspieldirektor
Comedy in 1 Act.
Text by Gottlieb Stephanie Jr.
First performance: Vienna, February 7, 1786.

Above: Der Schauspieldirektor, *again by the English Opera Group.*

Synopsis:
Herr Frank, the impresario, is trying to form a theatrical company. Two actresses vie with each other, then two singers each perform an aria and sing in a trio with the tenor, Herr Vogelsang. Vogelsang then expounds on the nobility of art and artists while the two ladies complacently agree, except when they forget themselves and squabble. There is a final Vaudeville in which pious sentiments are expressed, confirmed by the simple-minded Herr Buff.

RECORDINGS:
Philips 9500 011 ●
(also in Mozart Edition Volume 15)
Philips 9500 011 (US)
London Symphony Orchestra
c. Colin Davis
Madame Herz (s) Ruth Welting
Mademoiselle
　Silberklang (s) Ileana Cotrubas
Vogelsang (t) Anthony Rolfe
　　　　　　　Johnson
Herr Buff (b) Clifford Grant

DG 2740 (3) ●
DG2709 051 (3) (US)
Dresden State Opera Orchestra
c. Karl Böhm
Madame Herz (s) Reri Grist
Mademoiselle
　Silberklang (s) Arleen Auger
Vogelsang (t) Peter Schreier
Herr Buff (b) Kurt Moll
(this record also contains *Die Entführung*)

Le Nozze di Figaro
Commedia per musica (opera buffa) in 4 Acts.
Text by Lorenzo da Ponte after Beaumarchais.
First performance: Vienna (Burg Theatre) May 1, 1786. Prague 1786; London (Haymarket) 1812; New York (in English) 1824.

Synopsis:
Act 1 At the castle of Aguafrescas, near Seville, Figaro and Susanna are to marry and are measuring the room they will occupy. It is situated between those of the Count, who has designs on Susanna and threatens to revive the *droit de seigneur*, and the Countess. Marcellina hopes that Susanna's resistance will so enrage the Count that he will order Figaro to marry her instead; Bartolo, jealous of Figaro, plots with Marcellina. Cherubino has incurred the Count's wrath by his pursuit of Barbarina: he asks Susanna to intercede, then hides in a chair, covered by a gown, when the Count enters. The Count woos Susanna, then hides behind the same chair when the music master, Basilio, comes in. Basilio discusses the various love affairs; the angry Count emerges and sends him off to deal with Cherubino, who is thereupon discovered. The Count realises he has spoken too freely. Peasants march in at Figaro's direction and praise the Count, who agrees to overlook Cherubino's behaviour on condition that the youth accepts a commission in the Count's old regiment.

Act 2 The Countess laments the Count's neglect, but Figaro schemes to mend matters. He informs the Countess that the Count has an evening assignation, planning that Cherubino will replace Susanna at the meeting. Cherubino hides in the Countess's bedroom when the Count enters. Told that it is Susanna in the locked room, the suspicious Count orders the door to be forced. Cherubino escapes, and when the door is opened Susanna emerges. The Count apologises, but his suspicions of Figaro revive when the gardener, Antonio, claims he saw Cherubino jump from the window. Figaro averts this danger, but now Marcellina enters, with Basilio and Bartolo, claiming that Figaro has promised to marry her. The Count promises to judge the matter.

Act 3 Susanna agrees to a rendezvous with the Count and then lets him overhear her telling Figaro that the Count has judged in their favour. Annoyed, the Count orders Figaro to marry Marcellina or compensate her. But it emerges that Figaro is the illegitimate son of Marcellina and Bartolo. The Countess reaffirms her love for the Count; she dictates a note to Susanna, making an assignation with him. Wedding preparations begin; Cherubino confides to Figaro that he wants to marry Barbarina. Amid the celebrations, Susanna delivers the note to the Count.

Act 4 Because of confusion over the assignation note, Figaro suspects Susanna's fidelity. Susanna and the Countess exchange

identities. Cherubino, seeking Barbarina, mistakes the Countess for Susanna and tries to kiss her; the Count intervenes. Figaro pretends to be taken in by the disguises and flirts with the 'Countess': Susanna slaps him. The Count is deceived into thinking the Countess unfaithful, but at last his various errors are brought home to him. All the misunderstandings are resolved and the lovers paired off; the action ends in general rejoicing.

Well-known arias:

Act 1   Se a caso Madama (Figaro)
        Se vuol ballare (Figaro)
        La vendetta (Bartolo)
        Non so più cosa son, cosa faccio (Cherubino)
        Non più andrai (Figaro)
Act 2   Porgi Amor (Countess)
        Voi che sapete (Cherubino)
        Cognoscete, signor Figaro (Count)
Act 3   Crudel, perchè finora (Count and Susanna)
        Vedrò mentr'io sospiro (Count)
        Dove sono? (Countess)
        Che soave zeffiretto (Countess and Susanna)
Act 4   Aprite un po' quegli occhi (Figaro)
        Deh vieni non tardar (Susanna)

RECORDINGS:
HMV SLS5125 (3) ●
Angel S-3608 (4) (US)
Philharmonia Chorus and Orchestra
c. Carlo Maria Giulini
Count
  Almaviva (b)   Eberhard Wächter
Countess
  Almaviva (s)   Elisabeth Schwarzkopf
Figaro (b)   Giuseppe Taddei
Susanna (s)   Anna Moffo
Cherubino (m-s) Fiorenza Cossotto
Bartolo (bs)   Ivo Vinco
Basilio (t)   Renato Ercolani
Barbarina (s)   Elisabetta Fusco

Angel S-35640 (US) ■
(from above)

Philips 6707 014 (4) ★●
Philips 6707 014 (4) (US)
BBC Chorus and Symphony Orchestra
c. Colin Davis
Count
  Almaviva (b)   Ingvar Wixell
Countess
  Almaviva (s)   Jessye Norman
Figaro (bs)   Wladimiro Ganzarolli
Susanna (s)   Mirella Freni
Cherubino (s)   Yvonne Minton
Bartolo (bs)   Clifford Grant
Basilio (t)   Robert Tear
Barbarina (s)   Lillian Watson

Philips 6500 434 ■
Philips 6500 434 (US)
(from above)

DG 2740 139 (4) ●
DG 2711 007 (4) (US)
German Opera Chorus and Orchestra
c. Karl Böhm
Count   Dietrich
  Almaviva (b)   Fischer-Dieskau
Countess
  Almaviva (c)   Gundula Janowitz
Figaro (bs)   Hermann Prey
Susanna (s)   Edith Mathis
Cherubino (m-s) Tatiana Troyanos
Bartolo (bs)   Peter Lagger
Basilio (t)   Martim Vantim
Barbarina (s)   Barbara Vogel

Decca Ace of Diamonds GOS585/7 ●
London 1402 (4) (US)
Vienna State Opera Chorus/Vienna
Philharmonic Orchestra
c. Erich Kleiber
Count
  Almaviva (b)   Alfred Poell

Countess
  Almaviva (s)   Lisa della Casa
Figaro (bs)   Cesare Siepi
Susanna (s)   Hilde Gueden

Decca SDD237 ■
London 25045 (US)
(from above)

HMV SLS995 (4) ●
John Alldis Choir/English Chamber
Orchestra
c. Daniel Barenboim
Count   Dietrich
  Almaviva (b)   Fischer-Dieskau
Countess
  Almaviva (s)   Heather Harper
Figaro (bs)   Geraint Evans
Susanna (s)   Judith Blegen
Cherubino (m-s) Teresa Berganza

HMV SLS955 (4) (d) ●
John Alldis Choir/National Philharmonic
Orchestra
c. Otto Klemperer
Count
  Almaviva (b)   Gabriel Bacquier
Countess
  Almaviva (s)   Elisabeth Söderström
Figaro (bs)   Geraint Evans
Susanna (s)   Reri Grist
Cherubino (m-s) Teresa Berganza

Decca Eclipse ECS743/5 ●
Vienna State Opera Chorus/Vienna
Philharmonic Orchestra
c. Erich Leinsdorf
Count
  Almaviva (b)   George London
Countess
  Almaviva (s)   Lisa della Casa
Figaro (bs)   Giorgio Tozzi
Susanna (s)   Roberta Peters
Cherubino (m-s) Rosalind Elias

Decca SPA514 ■
(from above)

DG 2728 004 (3) ●
Berlin RIAS Chamber Choir/Berlin
Radio Symphony Orchestra
c. Ferenc Fricsay
Count   Dietrich
  Almaviva (b)   Fischer-Dieskau
Countess
  Almaviva (s)   Maria Stader
Figaro (bs)   Renato Capecchi
Susanna (s)   Irmgard Seefried
Cherubino (m-s) Hertha Töpper

Seraphim S-6002 (3) (US) ●
Dresden State Opera Chorus and
Orchestra
c. Otmar Suitner
Count
  Almaviva (b)   Hermann Prey
Countess
  Almaviva (s)   Hilde Gueden
Figaro (bs)   Walter Berry
Susanna (s)   Anneliese Rothenberger

Note the following historical complete
recordings:
Everest/Cetra S-424/3 (3) ●
RAI Chorus and Orchestra
c. Fernando Previtali
Dora Gatta (s)/**Italo Tajo** (bs)/**Fernando
Corena** (bs)

Cetra Opera Live L08 (3) ●
Vienna State Opera Chorus/Vienna
Philharmonic Orchestra
c. Wilhelm Furtwängler
Paul Schoeffler (bs)/**Elisabeth
Schwarzkopf** (s)/**Erich Kunz** (b)/**Irmgard
Seefried** (s)/**Peter Klein** (t)
(r. Salzburg 1953 in German)

Cetra Opera Live L070 (3) (r. 1954) ●
Chorus and Orchestra of La Scala, Milan
c. Herbert von Karajan
Mario Petri (t)/**Elisabeth Schwarzkopf**
(s)/**Roland Panerai** (b)/**Irmgard
Seefried** (s)/**Sena Jurinac** (s)

Decca Ace of Diamonds SDD280 ●
c. Jack Brymer
'Figaro' arr. for Wind Ensemble by
Johann Wendt

Decca SET548/9 □
c. Istvan Kertesz
Overture and 5 items

Below: The Marriage of Figaro *remains one of the most perfect operas, both musically and dramatically.*

Don Giovanni
Drama giocoso (opera buffa) in 2 Acts.
Text by Lorenzo da Ponte.
First performance: Prague (Opéra) October 29, 1787. Vienna (Burg Theatre) 1788; London (Haymarket) 1817; New York (Park Theatre) 1826.

Synopsis:
Scene: Seville. Time: 17th century.
Act 1   Don Giovanni (Don Juan) struggles with Donna Anna, observed by his somewhat discontented servant, Leporello. The Commendatore, Donna Anna's father, challenges Don Giovanni and is mortally wounded; Donna Anna, bringing Don Ottavio to the rescue, finds her father dead and vows vengeance. Don Giovanni's former love, Donna Elvira, bewails her lot and is told by Leporello that she is only one of many. At a rustic wedding, Giovanni is attracted by the bride, Zerlina, and summons the wedding party to his castle; to the suspicion of the bridegroom, Masetto. The Don expresses love for Zerlina but she is warned against him by Elvira, as is Donna Anna, who, learning that Giovanni is her father's killer, prevails upon Don Ottavio to undertake revenge. Giovanni orders general celebrations and Leporello plies the villagers with wine; Anna, Elvira and Ottavio join the party, masked. Masetto sees Giovanni lead Zerlina to another room. When Zerlina screams Giovanni accuses Leporello of molesting her, but Masetto and the three masked guests burst in and call the Don to account. He draws his sword and fights his way out.
Act 2   Don Giovanni mollifies Leporello with money and

praise and changes identities with him. Leporello diverts Donna Elvira, who has again accepted the Don as her lover, while Giovanni pursues her maid. Masetto and the villagers find 'Leporello', who sends them after 'Don Giovanni'; Masetto remains and 'Leporello' beats him. 'Don Giovanni' and Elvira encounter the real Don's accusers, whereupon Leporello hides in a churchyard, where the Statue of the Commendatore utters words of warning. The Don jestingly invites the Statue to supper and later, while he makes merry at home, the Statue appears and demands admittance. It orders that the Don repent of his ways, but he refuses and devils come to drag him to damnation. Leporello tells those the Don has wronged what has happened; all are well satisfied. Donna Anna agrees to marry Don Ottavio, Donna Elvira decides to enter a convent, Masetto and Zerlina are reunited and Leporello goes in search of a better master.

Well-known arias:

Act 1   Notte e giorno faticar (Leporello)
Madamina (Catalogue song) (Leporello)
Ho capito, Signor, si (Masetto)
Là ci darem la mano (duet) (Giovanni and Zerlina)
Ah, fuggi il traditor (Donna Elvira)
Or sai chi l'onore (Donna Anna)
Dalla sua pace (Ottavio)
Fin ch' han dal vino (Giovanni)
Batti, batti, o bel Masetto (Zerlina)
Protegga il giusto cielo (trio) (Elvira, Giovanni and Leporello)

Act 2   Deh, vieni alla finestra (Giovanni)
Vedrai, carino (Zerlina)
Il mio tesoro intanto (Don Ottavio)
Mi tradi qual alma ingrata (Elvira)
O statua gentillissima (duet) (Leporello and Giovanni)
Non mi dir (Donna Anna)

RECORDINGS:

HMV SLS5038 (4) ●
Angel S-3605 (4) (US)
Philharmonia Chorus and Orchestra
c. Carlo Maria Giulini
Don Giovanni (b)   Eberhard Waechter
Leporello (bs)   Giuseppe Taddei
Donna Anna (s)   Joan Sutherland
Donna Elvira (s)   Elisabeth Schwarzkopf
Don Ottavio (t)   Luigi Alva
Commendatore (bs)   Gottlob Frick
Zerlina (s)   Graziella Sciutti
Masetto (b)   Piero Cappuccilli

Angel S-35642 (US) ■
(from above)

DG 2740 194 (3) ●
Vienna State Opera Chorus/Vienna
Philharmonic Orchestra
c. Karl Böhm
Don Giovanni (b)   Sherrill Milnes
Leporello (bs)   Walter Berry
Donna Anna (s)   Anna Tomova-Sintov
Donna Elvira (s)   Teresa Zylis-Gara
Don Ottavio (t)   Peter Schreier
Commendatore (bs)   John Macurdy
Zerlina (s)   Edith Mathis
Masetto (b)   Dale Düsing

Philips 6707 022 (4) ●
Philips 6707 022 (4) (US)
(also in Mozart Edition 6747 385)
Chorus and Orchestra of Royal Opera House, Covent Garden
c. Colin Davis
Don Giovanni (b)   Ingvar Wixell
Leporello (bs)   Wladimiro Ganzarolli
Donna Anna (s)   Martina Arroyo
Donna Elvira (s)   Kiri Te Kanawa
Don Ottavio (t)   Stuart Burrows
Commendatore (bs)   Luigi Roni

Zerlina (s)   Mirella Freni
Masetto (b)   Richard Van Allan

HMV SLS923 (4) (d) ●
Angel S-3700 (US)
New Philharmonia Chorus and Orchestra
c. Otto Klemperer
Don Giovanni (b)   Nicolai Ghiaurov
Leporello (bs)   Walter Berry
Donna Anna (s)   Claire Watson
Donna Elvira (s)   Christa Ludwig
Don Ottavio (t)   Nicolai Gedda

Decca Ace of Diamonds GOS604/6 ●
London 1401 (4) (US)
Vienna State Opera Chorus/Vienna
Philharmonic Orchestra
c. Josef Krips
Don Giovanni (b)   Cesare Siepi
Leporello (bs)   Fernando Corena
Donna Anna (s)   Suzanne Danco
Donna Elvira (s)   Lisa della Casa
Don Ottavio (t)   Anton Dermota

Decca Ace of Diamonds SDD382 ■
London 25115 (US)
(from above)

Decca SET412/5 ●
London 1434 (4) (US)
Ambrosian Singers/English Chamber Orchestra
c. Richard Bonynge
Don Giovanni (b)   Gabriel Bacquier
Leporello (bs)   Donald Gramm
Donna Anna (s)   Joan Sutherland
Donna Elvira (s)   Pilar Lorengar
Don Ottavio (t)   Werner Krenn

Decca SET496 ■
London 26215 (US)
(from above)

DG Privilege 2728 003 (3) ●
Berlin RIAS Chamber Choir/Berlin Radio Orchestra
c. Ferenc Fricsay

DG 2711 006 (4) or 2740 108 ●
DG 2711 006 (4) (US)
Czech Choir, Prague/Prague National Theatre Orchestra
c. Karl Böhm
Don Giovanni (b)   Dietrich Fischer-Dieskau
Leporello (bs)   Ezio Flagello
Donna Anna (s)   Birgit Nilsson
Donna Elvira (s)   Martina Arroyo
Don Ottavio (t)   Peter Schreier
Commendatore (bs)   Martti Talvela
Zerlina (s)   Reri Grist
Masetto (b)   Alfredo Mariotti

Classics for Pleasure CFP40246 ■
Scottish Chamber Choir and Orchestra
c. Sir Alexander Gibson
John Shirley-Quirk (b)
Sheila Armstrong (s)
Rachel Mathest (s)
Ann Murray (s)
Robert Tear (t)
Stafford Dean (b)

Note the following historical recordings:
Cetra Opera Live L27 (3) (r. 1942) ●
Metropolitan Opera Chorus and Orchestra
c. Bruno Walter
Ezio Pinza (bs)/**Rose Bampton** (m-s)/
Jarmila Novotná (s)/**Charles Kullman** (t)/**Alexander Kipnis** (bs)/**Bidu Sayao** (s)

Vienna State Opera Chorus/Vienna Philharmonic Orchestra
c. Wilhelm Furtwängler
Cesare Siepi (bs)/**Elisabeth Schwarzkopf** (s)/**Elisabeth Grummer** (s)/**Otto Edelmann** (bs)/**Anton Dermota** (t)/**Erna Berger** (s)/**Walter Berry** (bs)

Philips 6500 783 □
Philips 6500 783 (US)
arr. for wind ensemble by Johann Georg Triebensee
Netherlands Wind Ensemble

Cetra Opera Live L7 (4) (r. Salzburg 1954) ●

Below: *Mozart's Don Giovanni, with Sir Geraint Evans in the title role.*

Così fan tutte (ossia la Scuola Degli Amanti)

Opera buffa.
Text by Lorenzo da Ponte.
First performance: Vienna (Burg Theatre) January 26, 1790. Prague 1791; Frankfurt (in German) 1791; London (Haymarket) 1811; New York (Metropolitan) 1922.

Synopsis:
Scene: Naples. Time: late 18th century.

Act 1   The officers Ferrando and Guglielmo end an argument by wagering Don Alfonso that their sweethearts, the sisters Fiordiligi and Dorabella, will remain faithful to them. Don Alfonso, refusing to belief any women capable of such fidelity tells the ladies that their lovers must leave for the wars and is much amused by the touching farewells that ensue. The maid, Despina, suggests that the sisters enjoy a flirtation while their lovers are away and, bribed by Don Alfonso, admits two suitors: Ferrando and Guglielmo, disguised as Albanians. Each woos the other's love, but the ladies affirm their constancy to their absent lovers. The rejected 'Albanians' pretend to take

poison and seem about to die until Despina, masquerading as a doctor skilled in Mesmerism, revives them. Recovering, the 'Albanians' affect the belief that they are in Paradise.

Act 2 Persuaded by Despina that it will do no harm, the sisters soften towards the 'Albanians': Fiordiligi pairs with Ferrando and Dorabella with Guglielmo. Don Alfonso leads them into the garden. Dorabella accepts a medallion from Guglielmo and gives him Ferrando's miniature, which she had sworn to cherish. Fiordiligi, more resistant, tells Dorabella that they really should follow their true loves to the wars—but she succumbs to Ferrando when he threatens suicide. Despina says she will fetch a notary to draw up the marriage contracts, but during the wedding celebrations martial music is heard and Don Alfonso announces that the officers are returning. To the confusion of the sisters, Ferrando and Guglielmo appear without disguise, and Guglielmo unmasks the 'notary' as Despina. Both men go in search of the 'Albanians'. When they return in part-disguise the plot is exposed: Don Alfonso wins his bet and the ladies beg forgiveness. All ends happily, but . . . *Così fan tutte*: thus do all women.

Well-known arias:

Act 1 Come scoglio (Fiordiglio)
Un' aura amorosa (Ferrando)
Act 2 Per pietà, ben mio, perdona (Fiordiglio)

RECORDINGS:

HMV SLS5028 (3) ●
Angel S-3631 (4) (US)
Philharmonia Chorus and Orchestra
c. Karl Böhm
Fiordiligi (s)   Elisabeth Schwarzkopf
Dorabella (s)   Christa Ludwig
Ferrando (t)   Alfredo Kraus
Guglielmo (b)   Giuseppe Taddei
Don Alfonso (b)   Walter Berry
Despina (s)   Hanny Steffek

Angel S-36167 (US) ■
(from above)

Philips 6707 025 (4) ●
(also in Mozart Edition 6747 280 (12 discs))
Philips 6707 025 (4) (US)
Chorus and Orchestra of Royal Opera House, Covent Garden
c. Colin Davis
Fiordiligi (s)   Montserrat Caballé
Dorabella (s)   Janet Baker (m-s)
Ferrando (t)   Nicolai Gedda
Guglielmo (b)   Wladimiro Ganzarolli
Don Alfonso (b)   Richard Van Allan
Despina (s)   Ileana Cotrubas

DG 2709 059 (3) ●
DG 2709 059 (3) (US)
Vienna State Opera Chorus/Vienna Philharmonic Orchestra
c. Karl Böhm
Fiordiligi (s)   Gundula Janowitz
Dorabella (s)   Brigitte Fassbaender
Ferrando (t)   Peter Scheier
Guglielmo (b)   Hermann Prey
Don Alfonso (b)   Rolando Panerai
Despina (s)   Reri Grist

DG 2537 037 ■
(from above)

Decca Ace of Diamonds GOS543/5 ●
Richmond 63508 (3) (US)
Vienna State Opera Chorus/Vienna Philharmonic Orchestra
c. Karl Böhm
Fiordiligi (s)   Lisa della Casa
Dorabella (s)   Christa Ludwig
Ferrando (t)   Anton Dermota
Guglielmo (b)   Erich Kunz
Don Alfonso (b)   Paul Schoeffler
Despina (s)   Emmy Loose

Decca Ace of Diamonds SDD208 ■
(from above)

HMV SLS961 (4) ●
John Alldis Choir/New Philharmonic Orchestra
c. Otto Klemperer
Fiordiligi (s)   Margaret Price
Dorabella (s)   Yvonne Minton (m-s)
Ferrando (t)   Luigi Alva
Guglielmo (b)   Geraint Evans
Don Alfonso (b)   Hans Sotin (bs)
Despina (s)   Lucia Popp

Decca D10D4 (4) ●
London 1442 (4) (US)
Chorus and Orchestra of Royal Opera House, Covent Garden
c. Georg Solti
Fiordiligi (s)   Pilar Lorengar
Dorabella (s)   Teresa Berganza (m-s)
Ferrando (t)   Ryland Davies
Guglielmo (b)   Tom Krause
Don Alfonso (b)   Gabriel Bacquier
Despina (s)   Jane Berbié

Decca SET595 ■
(from above)

World Records SOC195/7 (m) ●
Philharmonia Chorus and Orchestra
c. Herbert von Karajan
Fiordiligi (s)   Elisabeth Schwarzkopf
Dorabella (s)   Nan Merriman (m-s)
Ferrando (t)   Léopold Simoneau
Guglielmo (b)   Rolando Panerai
Don Alfonso (b)   Sesto Bruscantini
Despina (s)   Lisa Otto

Cetra Opera Live L013 (3) (m) (r. 1956) ●
Chorus and Orchestra of La Scala, Milan
c. Guido Cantelli
Fiordiligi (s)   Elisabeth Schwarzkopf
Dorabella (s)   Nan Merriman
Ferrando (t)   Luigi Alva
Guglielmo (b)   Rolando Panerai
Don Alfonso (b)   Franco Calabrese
Despina (s)   Graziella Sciutti

RCA Erato STU7110 (3) ●
RCA Erato FRL3-2629 (3) (US)
Chorus of Opera du Rhin/Strasbourg Philharmonic Orchestra
c. Alain Lombard
Fiordiligi (s)   Kiri Te Kanawa
Dorabella (s)   Teresa Stratas
Ferrando (t)   David Rendall
Guglielmo (b)   Philippe Huttenlocher
Don Alfonso (b)   Jules Bastin
Despina (s)   Frederica von Stade (m-s)

RCA SER575/8 (d) ●
RCA LSC-6416 (4) (US)
Chorus and New Philharmonia Orchestra
c. Erich Leinsdorf
Fiordiligi (s)   Leontyne Price
Dorabella (s)   Tatiana Troyanos
Ferrando (t)   George Shirley
Guglielmo (b)   Sherrill Milnes
Don Alfonso (b)   Ezio Flagello
Despina (s)   Judith Raskin

Below: Die Zauberflöte, *in a production at the Royal Opera House, Covent Garden.*

Die Zauberflöte (The Magic Flute)
German Opera in 2 Acts.
Text by Emanuel Schikaneder (and possibly C. L. Giesecke).
First performance: Vienna (Theater auf der Wieden) September 30, 1791. Prague 1792; London (Haymarket) (in Italian) 1811; New York (in English) 1833.

Synopsis:

Act 1 The Egyptian prince Tamino is being chased among rocks and crags by a serpent. He calls for aid and then swoons. Three Ladies, attendants of the Queen of the Night, slay the serpent and, struck by the young man's good looks, report his presence to the Queen. Tamino, reviving, encounters the bird-catcher Papageno, who claims to have killed the serpent. The Ladies return and padlock Papageno's mouth, and give Tamino a portrait of the Queen's daughter, Pamina, who is the captive of the evil magician, Sarastro. Tamino is enraptured. The Queen appears; Papageno's mouth is unlocked and he is given a set of magic chimes, while Tamino receives a magic flute. In Sarastro's palace, the Moor Monostatos is molesting Pamina when Pagapeno enters and frightens Monostatos; he then tells Pamina that help is at hand. The Three Young Men conduct Tamino through three temples: in the Temple of Nature, he learns that Sarastro is not an evil magician but a high priest of Isis and Osiris. Monostatos tries to capture Tamino, Pagageno and Pamina, but Sarastro intervenes, explaining that he has taken Pamina to protect her from her mother, the Queen of the Night. Monostatos is punished and Tamino and Pamina are prepared for initiation into the mysteries.

Act 2 Tamino and the frightened Papageno are told they must undergo ordeals, but Papageno is pleased to be told that he will be given a woman. Monostatos recaptures Pamina, protesting love for her, but she is rescued by the Queen of the Night, who gives her a dagger to kill Sarastro. Sarastro appears and tells them that vengeance has no place in his temple. Papageno has great difficulty in his ordeal of silence, as he is being pestered by an old woman. Tamino's ordeal is that he must not speak to Pamina, but she misunderstands and mourns her loss. Papageno's old woman changes into a young girl, Papagena, when he swears fidelity, although he fails his ordeal by speaking thus. Three Genii, moved by Pamina's plight, resolve to aid her.

During the Trial by Fire and Water, Tamino is confronted by two Men at Arms. Pamina advises him to use the magic flute: with its aid they pass through fire and water and are welcomed into the temple. Papageno, separated from Papagena, seeks death, but the Young Men tell him to sound his chimes—and Papagena returns. A last effort by the Queen of the Night, her Three Ladies and Monostatos is repulsed. The powers of light triumph and Sarastro blesses the love of Tamino and Pamina.

Well-known arias:

Act 1 Der Vogelfänger bin ich ja (Papageno)
Dies Bildnis ist bezaubernd schön (Tamino)
O zittre nicht, mein lieber Sohn (Queen of the Night)
Wie stark is nicht dein Zauberton (Tamino)

Act 2 O Isis und Osiris (Sarastro)
Alles fühlt der Liebe (Monostatos)
Der Hölle Rache (Queen of the Night)
In diesen heil'gen Hallen (Sarastro)
Ach, ich fühl's, es ist verschwunden (Pamina)
Ein Mädchen oder Weibchen wünscht Papageno sich (Papageno)

Notes:

Both Mozart and the librettist Schikaneder were Freemasons and members of the same Lodge. Masonry was at that time outlawed under the Empress Maria Theresa, so Schikaneder, with Mozart's active support, used his text to promote the Masonic cause by representing the rites and beliefs on stage in the guise of a species of pantomime. It has often been argued, probably with justification, that the characters referred to various leading personages and affairs of the day, most notably an identification of the Queen of the Night with Maria Theresa. Whether this is true or not, the genius of Mozart remains supreme: into the apparent hocus-pocus of much of the libretto, he poured an incomparable flow of great music. *The Magic Flute* stands, and will always stand, as a monument to the human spirit and to human aspiration.

RECORDINGS:

HMV SLS912 (30 ●
Angel S-3651 (3) (US)
Philharmonia Chorus and Orchestra
c. Otto Klemperer
Tamino (t)   Nicolai Gedda
Pamina (s)   Gundula Janowitz
Papageno (b) Walter Berry
Sarastro (bs) Gottlob Frick
Queen of
  the Night (s) Lucia Popp
Monostatos (t) Gerhard Unger
Papagena (s) Ruth Margret Putz

HMV ASD2314 (d) ■
Angel S-36315 (US)
(from above)

HMV SLS5052 (3) ●
Vienna Singverein/Vienna Philharmonic Orchestra
c. Herbert von Karajan
Tamino (t)   Anton Dermota
Pamina (s)   Irmgard Seefried
Papageno (b) Erich Kunz
Sarastro (bs) Ludwig Weber
Queen of
  the Night (s) Wilma Lipp

Monostatos (t) Peter Klein
Papagena (s) Emmy Loose

DG 2709 017 (3) ●
DG 2709 017 (3) (US)
Berlin RIAS Chamber Choir/Berlin Philharmonic Orchestra
c. Karl Böhm
Tamino (t)   Fritz Wunderlich
Pamina (s)   Evelyn Lear
Papageno (b) Dietrich Fischer-Dieskau
Sarastro (bs) Franz Crass
Queen of
  the Night (s) Roberta Peters
Monostatos (t) Friedrich Lenz

DG 136 440 ■
DG 136 440 (US)
(from above)

Decca SET479/81 ●
London 1397 (3) (US)
Vienna State Opera Chorus/Vienna Philharmonic Orchestra
c. Georg Solti
Tamino (t)   Stuart Burrows
Pamina (s)   Pilar Lorengar
Papageno (b) Hermann Prey
Sarastro (bs) Martti Talvela
Queen of
  the Night (s) Cristina Deutekom

Decca SET527 ■
London 26257 (US)
(from above)

World Records SH158/60 (m) (r. 1938) ●
Favres Solosten Vereinigung/Berlin Philharmonic Orchestra
c. Sir Thomas Beecham
Tamino (s)   Helge Roswaenge
Pamina (s)   Tiana Lemnitz
Papageno (b) Gerhard Husch

Sarastro (bs) Wilhelm Streinz
Queen of
  the Night (s) Erna Berger

Decca Ace of Diamonds GOS501/3 ●
Richmond 63507 (3) (US)
Vienna State Opera Chorus/Vienna Philharmonic Orchestra
c. Karl Böhm
Tamino (t)   Léopold Simoneau
Pamina (s)   Hilde Gueden
Papageno (b) Walter Berry
Sarastro (bs) Kurt Boehme
Queen of
  the Night (s) Wilma Lipp

Decca Ace of Diamonds SDD218 ■
(from above)

DG 2701 015 (m) ●
(previously DGM18267/9) (3)
RIAS Chamber Chorus/RIAS Symphony Orchestra
c. Ferenc Fricsay
Tamino (t)   Ernst Haefliger
Pamina (s)   Maria Stader
Papageno (b) Dietrich Fischer-Dieskau
Sarastro (bs) Josef Greindl
Queen of
  the Night (s) Rita Streich
(this recording includes the spoken dialogue, delivered by a separate cast of actors and actresses paralleling the singers)

DG Heliodor 89653 (d) ■
(from above)

Angel S-3807 (3) (US) ●
Bavarian State Opera Chorus and Orchestra
c. Wolfgang Sawallisch
Tamino (t)   Peter Schreier
Pamina (s)   Anneliese Rothenberger
Papageno (b) Hermann Prey
Sarastro (bs) Walter Berry
Queen of
  the Night (s) Wilma Lipp

Cetra Opera Live L044 (3) (m) ●
(r. Salzburg 1937)
Vienna State Opera Chorus/Vienna Philharmonic Orchestra
c. Arturo Toscanini
Tamino (t)   Helge Roswaenge
Pamina (s)   Jarmila Novotna
Papageno (b) Willi Dorngraf-Fassbaender
Sarastro (bs) Alexander Kipnis
Queen of
  the Night (s) Julie Osvath

Cetra Opera Live L09 (3) (m) ●
(r. Salzburg 1951)
Vienna State Opera Chorus/Vienna Philharmonic Orchestra
c. Wilhelm Furtwängler
Tamino (t)   Anton Dermota
Pamina (s)   Irmgard Seefried
Papageno (b) Erich Kunz
Sarastro (bs) Josef Greindl
Queen of
  the Night (s) Wilma Lipp

La Clemenza di Tito

Opera seria in 2 Acts.
Text by Caterino Mazzolà after Metastasio.
First performance: Prague (National Theatre) August 6, 1791. London (King's Theatre) 1806.

Synopsis:

Scene: Rome. Time: about AD 80.

Act 1 Vitellia is determined to prevent the Emperor Titus from marrying her rival Berenice, and conspires with Sextus, who is in love with her, to kill Titus. However, Titus changes his mind and decides to marry Sextus's sister, Servilia, instead; Annius, in love with Servilia, asks Sextus to intercede on his behalf. Titus now realises that he can make everyone happy by marrying Vitellia—luckily for her, the plan for Titus's murder misfires and someone else dies instead.

Act 2 Titus knows that Sextus had planned to betray him. Annius tells Sextus to beg for mercy, but Vitellia, fearing that her part will come to light, urges him to flee, but Sextus is arrested and condemned to death by the Senate. Titus signs the death warrant, but tears it up afterwards, while Vitellia, guilt-stricken, confesses her part in the plot and is also forgiven by the merciful Titus.

Well-known arias:

Act 1 Parto, parto (Sextus)
Act 2 Non più di fiori (Vitellia)

RECORDINGS:

Philips 6703 079 (3) ●
(also in Volume 13, with *Idomeneo*, of the Mozart Edition 6747 386 (6))
Philips 6703 079 (3) ●
Chorus and Orchestra of Royal Opera House, Covent Garden
c. Colin Davis
Emperor Titus
  (Tito) (t)   Stuart Burrows
Vitellia (m-s) Janet Baker
Sextus (m-s)   Yvonne Minton
Servilia (s)   Lucia Popp
Annius (m-s)   Frederica von Stade

Decca SET357/9 ●
London 1387 (3) (US)
Vienna State Opera Chorus/Vienna

Philharmonic Orchestra
c. István Kertesz
Titus (t)   Werner Krenn
Vitellia (s)   Maria Casula
Sextus (m-s)   Teresa Berganza
Servilia (s)   Lucia Popp
Annius (m-s)   Brigitte Fassbaender

Decca SET432 ●
(from above)

Philips 6500 660 □
Philips 6500 660 (US)
Arias
Janet Baker (m-s)

MODEST MUSSORGSKY
(b. Karevo, Pskov, 21.3.1839; d. St Petersburg 28.3.1881)

The most profoundly Russian and powerfully gifted of all Russian composers (apart from Tchaikovsky ≫), Mussorgsky did not find his way in music (or even into it at all) until he became associated with Dargomizhsky ≫ and the ubiquitous Balakirev in the late 1850s. He came of a wealthy landowning family and served in the Imperial Army, sending in his papers in 1858 in order to concentrate on music. He developed more according to his own natural genius than to any systematic tuition. After the decline of his family fortunes following the freeing of the serfs in 1861, he subsisted on a modest salary from government employment, but dissipation gradually undermined his health and damaged his talent and he died in poverty. His achievements were great (though only partially recognised during his lifetime), and might have been greater but for drink and loose living. He was never robust in health and of a highly nervous disposition; thus his life pattern was to some degree predestined. Mussorgsky always had great sympathy with the common people and sought in his music accurately to reproduce the inflexions and accentuations of their speech. In this he anticipated, and to a fair extent inspired, similar efforts by such later composers as Falla ≫ in Spain and Janáček ≫ in Moravia. Mussorgsky achieved this both in solo songs and in opera. The sympathy and the gift were partly inherited, partly acquired: although he came of a prosperous family, his maternal grandmother had been a serf.

Boris Godunov

Opera in Prologue and 4 Acts.
Text by Mussorgsky after Pushkin's drama and the 'History of the Russian Empire' by Nikolai Mikhailovich Karamazin.
First performance: St Petersburg (Imperial Opera), February 8, 1874. St Petersburg (Imperial Opera) (R-K version), 1896. Paris (Opéra) (R-K) 1908; New York (Metropolitan) (R-K in Italian) 1913; London (Drury Lane), (R-K) 1913; Leningrad (original version) 1928; London (Sadler's Wells) (original version, in English) 1935.

Synopsis:
Scene: Russia and Poland. Time: 1598-1605.
Prologue   At a monastery near Moscow, the people beg Boris to take the vacant throne of the Tsar. At first he refuses, then accepts, the people hail him at his coronation in the Kremlin. He sings a prayer for success, full of foreboding.
Act 1   The old monk Pimen tells the young monk Grigori that Boris murdered the Tsarevich Dimitri to gain the throne: if Dimitri had survived, he would now be the same age as Grigori. The renegade monks Varlaam and Missail arrive at a frontier inn with Grigori, who wishes to escape to Poland to foment rebellion by impersonating Dimitri. The police arrive seeking a fugitive; Grigori, made to read their warrant aloud, tries to throw suspicion on Varlaam, who retaliates by reading it correctly and thus incriminating Grigori, who flees.
Act 2   Boris's daughter, Xenia, laments the death of her betrothed and is comforted by the nurse, with whom Tsarevich Feodor quarrels. Boris enters and dismisses the women; he is pleased by Feodor's grasp of affairs. Prince Shuisky, a dubious counsellor, tells Boris of the Polish plot and the supposed Dimitri. After Shuisky graphically recalls Dimitri's murder, Boris, alone, is conscience-stricken, and prays for forgiveness.
Act 3   Grigori, having proclaimed himself Dimitri, raises support at the court of the Polish Princess Marina Mnishek, who wishes to marry him and thus become Tsarina. She is encouraged by the Catholic Bishop Rangoni, who hopes that the Church of Rome will prevail over the Orthodox Church in Russia. Grigori agrees to Rangoni's demands as the price of Marina, but is put out by Marina's obvious ambition and her lack of interest in him as a man. Nevertheless, the couple declare their love.
Act 4   In Moscow, a crowd gathers at a church where a Requiem has been said for the dead Dimitri. Grigori, the 'false Dimitri', has been excommunicated, but many believe in his

cause. The people beg Boris for bread; a holy simpleton complains that urchins have robbed him and asks Boris to kill them as he killed Dimitri. Shuisky wants to arrest the simpleton, but Boris asks instead for his prayers: the simpleton says he cannot pray for Boris and sings instead of the sadness of Russia. The Boyars (noblemen) discuss the 'false Dimitri'; Shuisky tells of Boris's troubled mind. Boris addresses his counsellors and Shuisky brings in Pimen to tell of a miracle at the murdered Dimitri's tomb. Boris, knowing death is near, instructs Feodor in the duties of a Tsar; after the chanting of monks and the tolling of bells, he dies. In the final scene, the trouble-makers Varlaam and Missail dispute with two Jesuits. The false Dimitri sets off for Moscow with his forces. Tyranny will be replaced by tyranny: in the falling snow, the simpleton laments the sorrows of Holy Russia.

Well-known scenes and arias:
Prologue	Coronation Scene (Boris and People)
Act 1	Still one more page (Pimen)
	In the town of Kazan (Varlaam)
Act 2	I have attained the highest power (Boris)
Act 3	Ah, poor Marina (Marina)
	Polonaise
Act 4	Cathedral Scene (People)
	One evening when I was alone (Pimen)
	I am dying (Boris)
	Tears and sorrow always, Russian people (Simpleton)

Notes:
Mussorgsky was, as Professor Gerald Abraham has observed, 'completely a dramatic composer'. In his greatest opera *Boris Godunov* (one of the greatest ever written), the dramatic and lyric elements in his genius meet in magnificent confrontation, superbly balanced in opposition.

RECORDINGS:

HMV Angel SLS1000 (4) (orig. ver.) ●
Angel SX-3844 (4) (US)
Polish Radio Chorus of Cracow/Cracow
Philharmonic Boys' Chorus/Polish
National Radio Symphony Orchestra
c. Jerzy Semkow
Boris Godunov (bs) Martti Talvela
Dimitri (Grigori) (t) Nicolai Gedda
Pimen (bs) Leonard Mróz
Marina (m-s) Bożena Kinasz
Varlaam (bs) Aage Haugland
Missail (t) Kazimierez Pustelak
Shuisky (t) Bogdan Paprocki
Feodor (m-s) Wiera Baniewicz
Simpleton (t) Paulos Raptis

Decca SET514/7 ●
London 1439 (4) (US)
Vienna Boys' Choir and Sofia Radio
Chorus/Vienna State Opera Chorus/
Vienna Philharmonic Orchestra
c. Herbert von Karajan
Boris
  Godunov (bs-b) Nicolai Ghiaurov
Dimitri (Grigori) (t) Ludovico Spiess
Pimen (bs) Martti Talvela
Marina (s) Galina
    Vishnevskaya
Varlaam (bs) Anton Diakov
Missail (t) Milen Paunov
Shuisky (t) Aleksei
    Maslennikov
Feodor (s) Najejda
    Dobrianowa
Simpleton (t) Aleksei
    Maslennikov

Decca SET 557 ■
London 26300 (US)
(from above)

Left: *Boris Christoff in the
role of Boris Godunov.*

CBS 77396 (3) ●
Columbia D4S-696 (4) (US)
Bolshoi Theatre Chorus and Orchestra
c. Alexander Melik-Pashaev
Boris
  Godunov (bs-b) George London
Dimitri (Grigori) (t) Vladimir Ivanovsky
Pimen (bs) Mark Reshetin
Marina (s) Irina Arkhipova
Varlaam (bs) Alexei Gueleva
Missail (t) Nicolai Zahjarov
Shuisky (t) Gyorgy Shulpin
Feodor (m-s) Maria Mitukova
Simpleton (t) Anton Grigoryev

HMV SLS5072 (4) ●
Choeurs Russe de Paris/Orchestre
National de Radiodiffusion Francais
c. Issay Dobrowen
Boris Godunov (bs) Boris Christoff
Dimitri (Grigori) (t) Nicolai Gedda
Pimen (bs) Boris Christoff
Missail (t) André Bielecki
Marina (m-s) Eugenia Zareska
Varlaam (b) Boris Christoff
Shuisky (t) André Bielecki
Feodor (m-s) Eugenia Zareska
Simpleton (t) Wassili Pasternak
(Note: The version edited and arranged
by Dimitri Shostakovich has been
recorded in East Germany (in German)
with Theo Adam as Boris, the Leipzig
Radio Chorus and Dresden State
Orchestra, c. Herbert Kegel—Telefunken
AS6.41290.)

Saga SAGA5174 □
CMS/Summit 1020 (US)
Nicolai Rossi-Lemini (bs)

Decca SXL6038 □
Pimen's Monologue
Nicolai Ghiaurov (bs-b)

Decca SXL6262 □
Pimen's Monologue
Geraint Evans (b)

Khovanshchina

Opera in 5 Acts.
Text by Mussorgsky and Vladimir Stassov.
*First performance: St Petersburg (Kononov Hall), February 21, 1886. Paris
(Théâtre des Champs-Élysées) (ed. Stravinsky and Ravel), 1913; London (Drury
Lane) 1913; New York (Metropolitan) 1931.*

Synopsis:

Scene: Moscow and a country estate. Time: late 17th century.
Act 1 The Boyar Shaklovity warns the Tsar that Prince Ivan
Khovansky plots to gain the throne for his son, Prince Andrey,
with the support of the Old Believers. Executions and punishments
have led to civil unrest. Prince Ivan enters with Prince Andrey,
who is courting Emma. Princess Marfa, Andrey's former lover,
taunts him and he attacks her. Ivan, also desiring Emma, orders
Andrey to bring her to him: Andrey threatens to stab her
instead. Ivan appoints Andrey a Colonel and orders a march on
the Kremlin.
Act 2 Prince Golitsyn hears from the Regent Sophia, who
loves him, and wonders if he can trust her. Marfa predicts that
Golitsyn will be banished; angered, he orders her thrown into
the marshes. Golitsyn and Ivan quarrel over Golitsyn's lapse
from support of the Old Believers; Dosifey, leader of the Old
Believers, tries to reconcile them. An envoy tells of the Regent's
proclamation denouncing the Khovanskys; Ivan says that Tsar
Peter the Great knows of the Khovansky plot (Khovanshchina).
Act 3 Marfa, who has escaped Golitsyn's wrath, laments her
rejection by Andrey; Dosifey urges her to forget him and work
for the cause. The Tsar's guards run amok and the people are
ready to revolt, but Ivan advises patience.
Act 4 Ivan is entertained by his retinue and ignores the
warning of an assassination plot brought by Varsonofiev,
Golitsyn's servant. Boyar Shaklovity, arriving with news that
the Regent has convened a Grand Council, stabs Ivan to death.

The Old Believers' cause is lost. Golitsyn is exiled. Marfa warns
Dosifey that the Tsar's army is approaching the Old Believers'
forest hideout; she is sent to fetch Andrey to face a martyr's
death. Andrey, seeking Emma, insults Marfa, but she tells him
of his father's death and offers to save him. As Khovansky's men
are led to execution, the Tsar grants pardon.
Act 5 Marfa and Andrey are with the Old Believers, under
official persecution. Dosifey says a last prayer; Andrey and
Marfa reaffirm their love; then Dosifey leads them all to death
by fire. The onlookers are deeply moved as Andrey and Marfa
pray for the salvation of Russia.

Well-known arias:
Act 5 Dosifey's Prayer

Notes:

The later and unfinished *Khovanshchina* represents a supreme
fusion of drama and lyricism little less than that of *Boris
Godunov*. The 'editing' of the latter and completion of the
former by Rimsky-Korsakov, in each case leading to an alien
sophistication and 'civilising' process, has tended to blur the
harsh outlines and ethnic truth of Mussorgsky's art and vision.
On the other hand, it is easy to be too hard on Rimsky: whatever
else he did, it was probably because of him that Mussorgsky's
masterpieces obtained a firm foothold: 'undiluted' Mussorgsky
was too much for contemporary audiences; the grind of his
exposed harmonies and the often brutal truth of his declamation
is decidedly uncomfortable. Rimsky made it palatable.

RECORDINGS:

HMV Melodiya SLS5023 (3) ●
Angel S4125 (3) (US)
Bolshoi Theatre Chorus and Orchestra
c. Boris Khaikin
Ivan
  Khovansky (bs) Alexei Krivchenya
Prince Andrey (t) Vladislav Pyavko
Prince Golitsyn (t) Alexei Maslennikov
Boyar
  Shaklovity (b) Viktor Nechipailo
Dosifey (bs) Alexander Ognivtsev
Marfa (m-s) Irina Arkhipova
Emma (s) Tamara Sorokina
Varsonofiev (bs) Yuri Korolev

Decca Ace of Diamonds GOS619/21 ●
Richmond 64504 (3) (d) (US)
Belgrade National Opera Chorus and
Orchestra
c. Kreshimir Baranovich
Ivan
  Khovansky (bs) Nicholas Tzveych
Prince Andrey (t) Alexander
    Marinkovich
Prince Golitsyn (t) Drago Startz
Boyar
  Shaklovity (b) Dushan Popovich
Dosifey (bs) Miro Changalovich
Marfa (m-s) Melanie
    Bugarinovich
Emma (s) Sofia Janovich

CRD 'Harmonia Mundi' HMB4-124
(4) ●
Monitor 90104/7 (US)
Svetoslav Obretenov Chorus/Sofia
National Radio Orchestra
c. Athanas Margaritov
Ivan
  Khovansky (bs) Dimiter Petkov
Prince Andrey (t) Lyubomir Bodurov
Prince Golitsyn (t) Lyuben Mikhailov
Boyar
  Shaklovity (b) Stoyan Popov
Dosifey (bs) Nikola Gyuselev
Marfa (b-s) Alexandrina
    Milcheva-Nonova
Emma (s) Maria Dimchevska
Varsonofiev (bs) Dimiter Dimitrov
(Note: These recordings use the edition
prepared by Rimsky-Korsakov after
Mussorgsky's death. The opera was left
unfinished and much work remained to
be done. But Rimsky's version was later
seen (as was his version of *Boris*) as too
smooth and conventional in
orchestration, so other 'completions'
were undertaken. Paul Lamon and B. V.
Assafiev undertook to put together and
publish everything Mussorgsky left, in
the late 1920s; Stravinsky and Ravel
made an edition for Paris in 1913 but
that seems to have foundered;
Shostakovich made his version, which
was used in Moscow and London
during the 1960s, in 1959.)

Sorochintsy Fair

Unfinished Opera.
*Text based on Gogol. Various versions by Sakhnovsky (1913), Cesar Cui (1917),
Tcherepnin (1923), Shebalin (1931).*
*First performance: St Petersburg (Comedia Theatre) (original form), December
30, 1911.*

Notes:

The opera is set in Sorochinsk, Ukraine, in the 19th century. The
score is full of evocative Russian folk songs and dances. In
certain respects, *Sorochintsy Fair* looks forward to *Petrouchka*.

RECORDING:
HMV Melodiya ASD3101 □
Introduction/Gopak
c. Yevgeny Svetlanov

OTTO NICOLAI

(b. Königsberg 9.6.1810; d. Berlin 11.5.1849)

Nicolai's active and successful career was brought to an abrupt end when he died from a stroke at the early age of 39. He had a very unhappy childhood but was helped by various patrons who took charge of him. One of them sent him to Rome as organist to the Prussian Embassy, which allowed him to continue his studies. He was appointed to the Court in Vienna in 1841 and the following year founded the Philharmonic concerts. In Berlin he became director of the Cathedral choir in 1847 and officiated at the Court Opera. As a composer Nicolai was prolific and competent; but nothing he wrote came near to the lasting success of his opera *The Merry Wives of Windsor*. It is a sparkling piece, not least its ebullient overture, which has long delighted many who do not know the pleasures of the opera itself.

RECORDINGS:
DG 2740 159 (3) ●
DG 2709 065 (3) (US)
Chorus of German State Opera/Berlin
Staatskapelle
c. Bernhard Klee
Sir John Falstaff (bs) Kurt Moll
Herr Fluth (Ford) (b) Bernd Weikl
Herr Reich
  (Page) (bs)   Siegfried Vogel
Frau Fluth
  (Mistress Ford) (s) Edith Mathis
Frau Reich
  (Mistress Page) (s) Hanna Schwarz
Anne Reich (Page) (s) Helen Donath

DG 2537 039 ■
(from above)

Decca D86D3 (3) ●
London OSA13127 (3) (US)
Bavarian Radio Symphony Orchestra
and Chorus
c. Rafael Kubelik
Sir John Falstaff (bs) Karl Ridderbusch
Herr Fluth (Ford) (b) Wolfgang Brendel
Herr Reich
  (Page) (bs)   Alexander Malta
Frau Fluth
  (Mistress Ford) (s) Helen Donath
Frau Reich
  (Mistress Page) (m-s) Trudeliese Schmidt
Anne Reich (s)   Lilian Sukis

HMV SXLP30210 □
Overture
c. Herbert von Karajan

Die Lustigen Weiber von Windsor (The Merry Wives of Windsor)

Opera in 3 Acts.
Text by Hermann von Mosenthal, after Shakespeare.
First performance: Berlin (Hofoper) March 9, 1849; London (Her Majesty's) (in Italian) 1864; New York (Metropolitan) 1900.

Synopsis:

Scene: Windsor. Time: 14th-15th Century.
Act 1 Frau Fluth (Mistress Ford) and Frau Reich (Mistress Page) in the garden. They compare amorous letters each has received from Sir John Falstaff. Herr Reich (Page) wishes his daughter Anne to marry Junker Spärlich (Slender) and tells Fenton that neither he nor Dr Caius is acceptable. Mistress Ford decides to teach Falstaff a lesson, and when he arrives she pretends to give in to him. Ford bursts in, saying he has caught his wife deceiving him, and starts a search. Falstaff is hidden in a laundry basket which is to be dumped in the river.
Act 2 Ford, disguised, finds Falstaff carousing in the Garter Inn. He interrogates the jovial knight, but without much success. In the garden, Anne's three suitors serenade her; Fenton romantically, the other two somewhat ridiculously. Ford returns and institutes another search for his wife's supposed lover. Falstaff is smuggled out, this time disguised as a deaf old woman.
Act 3 In Mistress Page's house, she sings a ballad. In Windsor Forest, Falstaff is bemused by various figures, including Anne and Fenton in the guise of Titania and Oberon. Falstaff makes passes at Mistresses Ford and Page, but ends up discomforted, just as the ladies had planned. All ends happily, without malice and with much rejoicing.

Well-known arias:

Act 1 Nun eilt herbei (Mistress Ford)
Act 2 Als Büblein klein (Falstaff)
        Wie Freu' ich mich (Falstaff and Ford)
        Horch, die Lerche singt im Hain (Fenton)

Above left: *Decca recording of The Merry Wives of Windsor.*

CFP40263 □
Overture
c. James Lockhart

Supraphon 110 1637 □
Overture
c. Zeljko Straka

Decca SXL6383 *or* Jubilee JB47 □
London 6605 (US)
Overture
c. Willi Boskovsky

Columbia MS-7085 (US) □
Overture
c. Leonard Bernstein

London STS-15021 *or* STS-15233 (US) □
Overture
c. Albert Wolff

Telefunken AJ6 42232 (r. 1937) □
Horch, die Lerche singt im Hain
Peter Anders (t)

Above: *Ahnsjö and Sukis in the Bavarian TV production.*

DG 135 020 □
Nun eilt herbei
Rita Streich (s)

Below: *Helen Donath and Trudeliese Schmidt as Fraus Fluth and Reich.*

138

CARL NIELSEN
(b. Nørre-Lyndelse 9.6.1865; d. Copenhagen 3.10.1931)

During the 1950s Nielsen was set up as a kind of Scandinavian rival to Sibelius, especially by those who thought him undervalued and Sibelius grossly overrated, and the real nature of his music was for a time obscured. Like Sibelius, he was primarily a symphonist; but there the resemblance ends. There is none of the sense of natural hostility and severity of resistance to it of Sibelius in the music of Carl Nielsen, where an unforced warmth and easy humanity combine with occasional outbreaks of sardonic humour and satirical harshness. Nielsen entered the Copenhagen Conservatoire as a pupil of Niels Gade at the age of 18 and later became conductor of the Royal Danish Theatre Orchestra, as well as conductor of the Music Society and Director of the Conservatoire. Until about 1950 his music was little known and appreciated outside Scandinavia; since then, his popularity has been strong and assured. Nielsen wrote two operas, of widely differing character, both of which are available on records.

Saul og David
Opera in 4 Acts.
Text by Einar Christiansen.
First performance: Copenhagen (Royal Theatre), November 29, 1902. Göteborg 1928; Stockholm 1930.

Synopsis:
Act 1 Israel in Biblical times: King Saul, his son Jonathan, and the priests and people await the prophet Samuel, who alone can make the sacrifice for victory over the Philistines. Saul, losing patience, performs the sacrifice himself; Samuel pronounces him dethroned and outcast. After trying without success to comfort his father, Jonathan brings in the shepherd boy David, who loves Saul's daughter, Michal, to comfort the King.

Act 2 While David sings to Saul, Abner brings news of the Philistines' approach. Their champion, the gigantic Goliath, has challenged any Israelite to single combat. Saul is worried, but David says he will fell Goliath with his sling. Michal and the other women express their emotions concerning the fight; all rejoice following David's victory, and Saul gives Michal's hand to David. But Saul grows jealous of David, hurls a javelin at him, and banishes him.

Act 3 Jonathan and Michal lament David's absence. David enters the camp, stands over the sleeping Saul, then awakens the guard. Saul can no longer doubt his loyalty. But Samuel, before dying, tells David to proclaim himself king and anoints him. Saul fails to reassert his authority: his orders to arrest David and Michal are not obeyed.

Act 4 Saul and Abner consult the Witch of Endor: Samuel's spirit predicts that Saul and Jonathan will die in battle against the Philistines. Jonathan and Saul are wounded in the battle: Jonathan, seeing David, declares him to be the Lord's anointed and then dies; Saul, fearful of capture, falls on his sword. The survivors hail King David.

RECORDING:
Unicorn RHS 343/5 (in English) ●
John Alldis Choir/Danish Radio Chorus
and Symphony Orchestra
c. Jascha Horenstein
(retakes c. Joel Lazar)
Saul (bs)	Boris Christoff
Jonathan (t)	Willy Hartmann
David (t)	Alexander Young
Michal (s)	Elisabeth Söderström
Samuel (bs)	Michael Langdon
Abner (bs)	Kim Borg
Witch of	
Endor (m-s)	Sylvia Fisher

Maskarade
Comic Opera in 3 Acts.
Text by Vilhelm Andersen after Ludwig Holberg.
First performance: Copenhagen, November 11, 1906.

Synopsis:
Scene: Copenhagen. Time: 1732

Act 1 Leander, son of Jeronimus, and his valet, Henrik, have hangovers after a masquerade (a masked ball). Leander dreams of finding again a beautiful girl he met there, although he is engaged to marry the daughter of his father's friend, Mr Leonard. Henrik warns his master of the danger of a breach of promise action. Magdelone, Jeronimus's wife, enacts the delights of the masquerade; Jeronimus orders her to her room. He laments Leander's lack of respect for parental authority; Mr Leonard tells him that his daughter, too, is rebellious and refuses to marry Leander. Suspecting illicit affairs, Jeronimus orders his oafish servant, Arv, to keep watch. Jeronimus lectures Leander, but Henrik relieves the tension with a song of comical effrontery. Leander must apologise to Mr Leonard, although he still refuses to marry his daughter.

Act 2 Arv is continually tricked by Henrik. At the masquerade, Leander meets the girl he desires, not realising that she is really Mr Leonard's wilful daughter, Leonora, accompanied by her maid, Pernille. Jeronimus discovers that Leander and Henrik have slipped away and, deciding to go himself to the masquerade, sends Arv to buy disguises. Mr Leonard and Magdelone, failing to recognise each other in disguise, go together to the masquerade; Jeronimus and Arv arrive as Bacchus and Cupid.

Act 3 All make merry at the masquerade until the moment for unmasking comes. Leander and Leonora, having been interrupted by Jeronimus, who does not recognise them in disguise, at last discover their mutual love. Only Jeronimus, tipsy and made to look a complete fool, does not realise the true state of affairs.

RECORDING:
Unicorn RHS 350/2 ●
Danish Radio Symphony Chorus and
Orchestra
c. John Frandsen
Jeronimus (bs-b)	Ib Hansen
Leander (t)	Tonny Landy
Henrik (b)	Mogens Schmidt-Johansen
Magdelone (c)	Gurli Plesner
Leonora (s)	Edith Brodersen
Arv (t)	Christian Sørensen

Below: *Willy Hartmann as Leander and Ellen Winther as Leonora in Nielsen's opera* Maskarade, *recently recorded.*

JACQUES OFFENBACH
(b. Cologne 20.6.1819; d. Paris 5.10.1880)

After studying at the Paris Conservatoire, without much enthusiasm, and pursuing an early career as an orchestral musician, conductor and cello virtuoso, Offenbach tried to establish himself as a composer of operetta. Finding it difficult to get his works staged, he established his own theatre, Les Bouffes-Parisiens, in 1855. He gradually established a reputation both in France and abroad (his works appeared regularly in London and were a considerable inspiration to composers like Sullivan »; and in Vienna, where they influenced Suppé and Strauss ») and had his first great success with the satirical *Orphée aux Enfers* (*Orpheus in the Underworld*). Although he wrote around 100 operettas, many starring Hortense Schneider, including such lasting classics as *La Belle Hélène, Geneviève de Brabant, La Grande Duchesse de Gérolstein, La Vie Parisienne* and *La Périchole*, his ultimate ambition was to produce a grand opera. His final days were spent in writing *Les Contes d'Hoffmann*, but he died before he could hear the first performance. The music of all Offenbach's operettas is a blend of frivolous gaiety (the famous Can-Can from *Orpheus* is an obvious example) and tender lyricism—as in the Letter Song from *La Périchole*. Much of his work, some of it hastily written but nearly always containing some excellence, remains neglected: we tend to hear the same handful of popular pieces performed in London and elsewhere in the kind of pantomimic productions that Offenbach himself frequently sanctioned in his lifetime. There is a great need to hear the principal works in their original Bouffes-Parisiens styling, and for a further exploration of the less frequently heard works like *Les Brigands* and *Geneviève de Brabant*. This is most likely to come about through authentic recordings. The ballet *Gaité Parisienne*, arranged by Rosenthal in 1938, offers a good chance to capture the flavour of Offenbach's music. His one full-length ballet, *Le Papillon* (with its once popular Valse de Rayons, frequently used as an Apache Dance), has also been recorded.

Le Mariage aux Lanternes
Opérette in 1 Act.
Text by Jules Dubois (Marcel Carré and Léon Battu) (revised version of 'Le Trésor à Mathurin').
First performance: Paris (Bouffes-Parisiens) October 10, 1857. Vienna (Carl) 1858; London (Lyceum) 1860; London (Gaiety) 1871; Vienna (Theater an der Wien), 1889.

RECORDING:
Decca ECS547 □
Overture
c. Jean Martinon

Orphée aux Enfers
Opéra-bouffon in 2 Acts.
Text by Hector Crémieux and Ludovic Halévy.
First performance: Paris (Bouffes-Parisiens) October 21, 1858. Berlin 1860; Vienna 1861; London (Haymarket) (in English) 1865. Revised version in 4 Acts, Paris (Gaité) 1874; London (Royalty) 1876; Vienna (Carl) 1892.

Synopsis:
Orpheus's wife Eurydice has grown tired of his incessant violin playing and is having an affair with Pluto (known in earthly guise as Aristée), god of the Underworld. She informs Orpheus of her voluntary demise and goes to Hades with Pluto. Orpheus is privately delighted but is told by L'Opinion Publique that he should rescue her. With Jupiter's permission, he sets off for the Underworld with a party of gods and goddesses. Jupiter finds Eurydice, turns himself into a fly, and flirts with her. The gods express their admiration for Eurydice in a lively Can-Can. Jupiter says that Orpheus may lead Eurydice from Hades but will lose her if he looks back to see if she is following. The dull fellow obeys, much to the annoyance of Jupiter, who hurls a thunderbolt. Orpheus turns and sees his wife who joyfully returns to her admirers. The gods even steal Orpheus's magical song.

Above: *The English National Opera production of* Orpheus.

Well-known arias:
Act 1 Ah! Seigneur, ah! quel supplice (Orphée and Eurydice)
Invocation a Mort: La mort m'apparait (Eurydice)
Act 3 Quand j'étais roi de Béotie (John Styx)
Belle insecte à l'aile adorée (Jupiter and Eurydice)
Act 4 Can-Can (Ensemble)

RECORDINGS:
Musidisc 261 (2) or CV944/5 (Fr) ●
Everest/Cetra S-438 (2) (US)
(original 2 Act version)
Paris Philharmonic Chorus and Orchestra
c. René Leibowitz
Eurydice (s) Claudine Collart
Orpheus (t) Jean Mollien
Aristée (t) André Dran
Jupiter (b) Bernard Demigny
John Styx (b) Jean Hoffmann

HMV CSD1316 ○
(abridged in English)
Sadler's Wells Chorus and Orchestra
c. Alexander Faris
Eurydice (s) June Bronhill
Orpheus (t) Kevin Miller
Aristée (t) Jon Weaving
Jupiter (b) Eric Shilling
John Styx (b) Alan Crofoot

Fr. Voix de son Maitre CO51-12.108 □
c. Jules Gressier

Decca SDD192 □
London STS-15217 (US)
Overture
c. Ernest Ansermet

Decca ECS547 □
Overture
c. Jean Martinon

HMV ESD7034 □
Klavier 517 (US)
Overture
c. Louis Frémaux

Columbia MS-7085 (US) □
Overture
c. Leonard Bernstein

La Belle Hélène
Opéra-bouffe in 3 Acts.
Text by Henri Meilhac and Ludovic Halévy.
First performance: Paris (Variétés) December 17, 1864. Vienna 1865; London 1866; London (Gaiety) 1871.

Synopsis:
Helen, Queen of Sparta, and her ladies pray to Venus to send them lovers. Venus sends Paris to win Helen, who, bored with her husband and charmed by Paris, tries to resist on rational grounds while yielding emotionally. Orestes is delighted because her example makes all the wives of the land unfaithful to their husbands. Paris returns, disguised as a High Priest, and chides them all for their bad behaviour. Helen yields to Paris and is carried off to Troy.

Well-known arias:
Act 1 Amours divins (Helen)
Au Mont Ida trois déesses (Paris)
Act 2 Dis moi, Vénus (Helen)
Oui, c'est un rêve (Helen and Paris)
Act 3 Un mari sage (Orestes)

RECORDINGS:
Everest S-458 (2) ●
Everest S-458 (2) (US)
Musidisc CV940/1 (Fr)
Paris Philharmonic Chorus and Orchestra
c. René Leibowitz
Helen (s)   Janine Linda
Paris (t)   André Dran
Menelaus (t)   Roger Giraud
Agamemnon (b)   Jacques Linsolas
Achilles (b)   Jean Mollien
Orestes (s)   Loly Vadarnini

Decca SDD192 □
London STS-15217 (US)
Overture
c. Ernest Ansermet

Decca ECS547 □
Overture
c. Jean Martinon

HMV ESD7034 □
Klavier 517 (US)
Overture
c. Louis Frémaux

Decca SET520/1 □
London 26248 (2) (US)
Dis-moi, Venus
Regine Crespin (s)

Barbe-Bleu
Opera-bouffe in 3 Acts.
Text by Henri Meilhac and Ludovic Halévy.
First performance: Paris (Variétés) February 5, 1866. London 1866; Vienna (Theater an der Wien) 1866; New York 1870.

RECORDINGS:
Decca ECS547 □
Overture
c. Jean Martinon

HMV ESD7034 □
Klavier 517 (US)
Overture
c. Louis Frémaux

La Vie Parisienne
Opéra-bouffe in 4 Acts.
Text by Henri Meilhac and Ludovic Halévy.
First performance: Paris (Palais-Royal) October 31, 1866. Vienna 1867; London 1872.

Synopsis:
Scene: Paris. Time: 1867.

Act 1 Gardefeu and Bobinet meet the *demi-mondaine* Métella, whom both love, at the station, but she is with another man and ignores them. They swear to ignore Paris's loose women in future. Gardefeu persuades the guide Joseph, who is meeting a wealthy Swedish Baron and his wife, to change identities with him. A Brazilian millionaire arrives on the spree.

Act 2 At Gardefeu's house, which he pretends is a hotel, the Swedes are given separate rooms. The Baron is pursuing Métella, who comes for a reconciliation with Gardefeu. Encountering the Baroness, she leaves angrily. Gardefeu intends

Below: La Vie Parisienne, *successfully revived in London.*

to divert the Baron so he may seduce the Baroness; he enlists the aid of Gabrielle the glover and Frick the bootmaker, disguised as a widow and an army officer.

Act 3 Bobinet, masquerading as an admiral, with the chambermaid Pauline as his wife, plays host at a party. Pauline concentrates on the Baron; everyone drinks heartily.

Act 4 Confusion reigns at the Brazilian millionaire's masked ball. Métella and the Baroness, respectively chasing Gardefeu and the Baron, join forces. A fight between Gardefeu and the Baron is narrowly averted. The millionaire falls in love with Gabrielle and, at last, all ends happily.

Well-known arias:
Act 1 Je suis Bresilién (Brazilian)
Act 2 Je suis veuve (Gabrielle)
Act 3 Tout tourné, tourné, tourné (Ensemble)
Act 4 A minuit sonnant (Metella)

RECORDINGS:
HMV SLS5076 (2) ●
Angel SX-3839 (2) (US)
Voix de son Maitre C165-14 123/4 (Fr)
Orchestra and Chorus of the Capitole, Toulouse
c. Michel Plasson
Bobinet (b)   Michel Trempont
Gardefeu (t)   Michel Sénéchal
Métella (s)   Régine Crespin
**Baron de
 Gondremarck** (b) Luis Masson
**Baroness de
 Gondremarck** (s) Christine Chateau
**The Brazilian   Jean-Christophe
 and Frick** (b)   Benoit
Gabrielle (s)   Mady Mesplé

Decca 125.011/2 (Fr) ●
Chorus and Orchestra
c. Francois Rauber
Bobinet (b)   Henri Gui
Gardefeu (t)   Michel Caron
Métella (s)   Danièle Millet
**Baron de
 Gondremarck** (b) Jacques Mareuil
**Baroness de
 Gondremarck** (s) Christiane Harbell
**The Brazilian
 and Frick** (b)   Luc Barney
Gabrielle (s)   Nicole Broissin

Decca 117.011 (Fr) ■
(from above)

HMV ESD7034 □
Klavier 517 (US)
Overture
c. Louis Frémaux

La Grande-Duchesse de Gérolstein
Opéra-bouffe in 3 Acts.
Text by Henri Meilhac and Ludovic Halévy.
First performance: Paris (Variétés) April 12, 1867. Vienna 1867; London 1867.

Synopsis:
Act 1 Soldiers and their sweethearts drink before battle; Wanda bids farewell to Fritz. The gallant and amorous General Boum desires Wanda. As part of Baron Puck's scheme, Baron Grog is sent to Gérolstein to persuade the Grand Duchess to marry Prince Paul, but the Grand Duchess desires Fritz. She promotes him Commander-in-Chief; Paul, Puck and Boum are furious.

Act 2 After the bloodless battle, the Duchess hints to Fritz of her love. She lodges him in the Red Chamber, scene of a famous murder—which Paul, Boum and Puck plan to repeat. The Duchess, enraged because Fritz still loves Wanda, joins their conspiracy.

Act 3 The conspirators are joined by Baron Grog, who so bewitches the Duchess that she abandons the plot and decides to marry Paul. But she permits a trick to embarrass Fritz: as he serenades his newly-wed bride, Wanda, a crowd bursts in and calls upon him to prepare for battle at once.

Act 4 In camp, the company toasts the newly-married Duchess and Paul. Fritz enters, dishevelled; he has been tricked into a duel. The Duchess strips him of command. Her flirtation with Grog is fruitless. Puck is promoted, Boum is reinstated, and the Duchess is left with Paul—but she sees another handsome young man during the finale.

Well-known arias:
Act 1 Et pif paf pouf (Boum)
         Ah! que j'aime les militaires (Grande-Duchesse)
         Voici le sabre de mon père (Grande-Duchesse)
Act 2 Dites-lui qu'on remarqué (Grand-Duchesse)

RECORDINGS:

CBS 79207 (2) ●
Columbia M2-34576 (2) (US)
Orchestra and Chorus of Capitole de
Toulouse
c. Michel Plasson
La Grande
   Duchesse (s)   Régine Crespin
Fritz (t)   Alain Vanzo
Prince Paul (bs)   Charles Burles
Baron Puck (b)   Claude Méloni
Général Boum (b)   Robert Massard
Wanda (s)   Mady Mesplé

Saga 5446 □
Overture and vocal items
c. René Leibowitz

Decca ECS547 □
Overture
c. Jean Martinon

HMV ESD7034 □
Klavier 517 (US)
Overture
c. Louis Frémaux

Decca SET454/5 □
London 1286 (2) (US)
Dites-lui qu'on remarqué
Joan Sutherland (s)

CBS 76522 □
Columbia M-34206 (US)
Dites-lui qu'on remarqué
Frederica von Stade (m-s)

Decca SET454/5 □
London 1286 (2) (US)
Ah! que j'aime les militaires
Joan Sutherland (s)

Decca SET520/1 □
London 26248 (2) (US)
Ah! que j'aime les militaires
Régine Crespin (s)

RECORDINGS:

World Records OC147/8 (2) (d) ●
from Columbia FCX786/7 (Fr)
Now Pathé CO53-10.669/70 (Fr)
René Duclos Choir and Orchestra of
Concerts Lamoureux
c. Igor Markevitch
La Périchole (s)   Suzanne Lafaye
Piquillo (t)   Raymond Amade
Viceroy (b)   Louis Noguera

Pathé CO51-10.352 (Fr) ■
(from above)

RCA FRL2-5994 (2) (US) ●
Erato STU70.994/5 (Fr)
Chorus and Strasbourg Philharmonic
Orchestra
c. Alain Lombard
La Périchole (s)   Régine Crespin
Piquillo (t)   Alain Vanzo
Viceroy (b)   Jules Bastin

Decca SET520/1 □
London 26248 (2) (US)
Tu n'est pas beau—Je t'adore; O mon
cher amant; Ah, quel dîner
Régine Crespin

CBS 76522 □
Columbia M-34206 (US)
Ah, quel dîner
Frederica von Stade (s)

Barclay 920.029 (Fr) □
O mon cher amant; Que les hommes sont
bêtes; Je t'adore brigand
Suzy Delair (s)

RCA SER5589 (d) □
Tu n'est pas beau
Leontyne Price

Robinson Crusoë

Opéra-comique in 3 Acts.
Text by Eugène Cormon and Hector Crémieux, based on Defoe.
First performance: Paris (Opéra-Comique) November 23, 1867. London (Camden Festival) 1973; London (Sadler's Wells) 1976.

RECORDING:

Decca SET454/5 □
London 1286 (2) (US)
Conduissez-moi vers celui que j'adore
Joan Sutherland (s)

La Périchole

Opéra-bouffe in 3 Acts.
Text by Henri Meilhac and Ludovic Halévy, based on Prosper Mérimée's 'La Carosse du Saint Sacrement'.
First performance: Paris (Variétés) October 6, 1868. Vienna (Theater an der Wien) 1869; London (Princess') 1870. Expanded to 3 Acts in 1874.

Synopsis:

Act 1   The Governor's birthday is celebrated at 'The Three Cousins' inn in Lima, Peru. Don Andrès de Ribeira, the Viceroy, is present incognito. The singers Piquillo and Périchole try without success to raise money for their marriage. Périchole catches the Viceroy's eye. Inviting her to dinner, he reveals his identity and offers her a place at court; she reluctantly accepts and writes a farewell letter to Piquillo. No unmarried lady may reside at court—but the husband chosen at random for Périchole is Piquillo. Plied with drink, Piquillo fails to recognise his token bride as Périchole.

Act 2   Next morning Piquillo demands the reward for agreeing to a token marriage, intending to search for Périchole. Ordered to present his 'wife' to the Viceroy, he discovers it is Périchole and is angry and jealous. He denounces her as false; angry, the Viceroy has him imprisoned.

Act 3   Piquillo, in prison, is reconciled with Périchole. They try to bribe the gaoler—but he is the Viceroy in disguise. He orders them chained up in the same cell, where their fetters are secretly removed by an old prisoner, the Marquis de Santarem. The three overpower the Viceroy and escape, taking refuge at 'The Three Cousins'. The Viceroy threatens to flog the inn's proprietors for aiding the fugitives, who emerge and solicit pardon. Touched by their love, the Viceroy releases them with a gift of jewellery.

Well-known arias:

Act 1   Le Conquerant et la jeune Indienne (Périchole and Piquillo)
       O mon cher amant (Périchole)
Act 2   Mon Dieu, que les hommes sont bêtes (Périchole)
Act 3   Tu n'est pas beau (Piquillo)

Right: *Joan Sutherland sang the triple lead to Placido Domingo's Hoffmann in Decca's The Tales of Hoffmann.*

La Fille du Tambour-Major

Opéra-comique in 3 Acts.
Text by Henri Charles Chivot and Alfred Duru.
First performance: Paris (Folies-Dramatiques) December 13, 1879. Vienna (Theater an der Wien) 1880; London (Alhambra) 1880.

RECORDINGS:

Decca SXL6235 □
Overture
c. Richard Bonynge

HMV ASD 3311 (*Gaité Parisienne*) □
Angel S-37209 (US)
Overture
c. Manuel Rosenthal

Pathé CO51-12192 (Fr) □
(available on Fr. Decca 115.184/5)
Michel Dens (b), **Liliane Chatel** (s),
Nadine Sautereau (s), **Suzanne Lafaye**
(m-s), **Dominique Tirmont** (b)
Chorus and Orchestra de la Société des
Concerts du Conservatoire
c. Félix Nuvolone

Les Contes d'Hoffmann (The Tales of Hoffman)

Opéra in a Prologue, 3 Acts and an Epilogue.
Text by Jules Barbier and Michel Carré, based on stories by Ernst Theodor Amadeus Hoffmann (1776-1822).
First performance: Paris (Opéra-Comique) February 10, 1881. Vienna (Ringtheater) 1881; New York 1882; Vienna (Theater an der Wien) 1883; Berlin 1905; London (Adelphi) 1907; London (Covent Garden) 1910.

Synopsis:

Prologue   At Luther's Tavern in Nuremburg, Lindorf and his friends have been discussing the romance between Hoffmann and Stella, an opera singer. The poet enters the tavern and is requested to tell the story of his three great loves.

Act 1   Hoffmann loves the inventor Spalanzani's daughter, Olympia. At a party she literally dances him off his feet until her

father hurries her away. Olympia proves to be a mechanical doll and is smashed by Coppélius, her co-inventor, whom Spalanzani has deceived.

Act 2 A palace overlooking the Grand Canal in Venice (see notes below). Hoffmann is determined not to fall in love again, but the sorcerer Dapertutto gives Giulietta, a courtesan, a magic diamond with which to ensnare him. She steals his shadow with a magic mirror and leaves him to fight with Schlemil, her bewitched lover. Hoffmann wins, but Giulietta has gone.

Act 3 A room in Crespel's house in Munich. Hoffmann now loves Crespel's daughter, the consumptive Antonia, a young singer. He discovers that the sinister Dr Miracle has advised her to sing to cure her illness. This kills her; Hoffmann sends for a doctor—but it is Dr Miracle who comes.

Epilogue At the tavern, Hoffmann finishes his story and falls dead drunk. Stella comes in and, finding him insensible and not knowing how much he loves her, tosses a flower at him and leaves with Lindorf.

Well-known arias:

Prologue Il était un fois à la cour d'Eisenach (Legend of Kleinzack) (Hoffmann and Students)

Act 1 Ah, vivre deux (Hoffmann)
Les oiseaux dans la charmille (Doll's song) (Olympia)

Act 2 Belle nuit, o nuit d'amour (Barcarolle) (Nicklausse and Giulietta)

Act 3 Scintille diamant (Dapertutto)

Notes:

It was Offenbach's ambition to write a grand opera, but he died in 1880 with only a piano score completed and the first act scored for orchestra. The first auditions had been held at his house in 1879, and he had heard some of the music rehearsed; he wrote to the Director of L'Opéra-Comique: "Hurry up and stage my opera, I haven't much time left and my only wish is to attend the opening night". There were many delays and his last wish was unfulfilled. He died with the score in his hands. The orchestration was completed by Ernest Guiraud. Because of the opera's length, the Venetian scene was omitted for the première and the famous Barcarolle was added to Act 3. The opera was tampered with in subsequent performances, recitatives were added and the order of events frequently changed, and only in fairly recent times have attempts been made to return to Offenbach's original conception.

RECORDINGS:
Decca SET545/7 (3) (original) ●
London 13106 (3) (US)
Choruses of Radio Suisse Romande and
Pro Arte of Lausanne and Du Brassus/
L'Orchestre de la Suisse Romande
c. Richard Bonynge
Hoffmann (t) Placido Domingo
His Muse/
  Nicklausse (m-s) Tourangeau
Olympia/Giulietta/
  Antonia/
  Stella (s) Joan Sutherland
Lindorf/Coppélius/
  Dapertutto/
  Dr Miracle (bs) Gabriel Bacquier

Decca SET569 ■
London 26369 (US)
(from above)

HMV SLS858 (3) (d) ●
ABC 3 ATS-20014 (3) (US)
John Alldis Chorus and London
Symphony Orchestra
c. Julius Rudel
Hoffmann (t) Stuart Burrows
His Muse/
  Nicklausse (m-s) Susanne Marsee
Olympia/Giulietta/
  Antonia/
  Stella (s) Beverly Sills
Lindorf/Coppélius/
  Dapertutto/
  Dr Miracle (bs) Norman Treigle

HMV SLS918 (3) (d) ●
Angel S-3667 (3) (US)
Choeurs René Duclos/Orchestre de la
Société des Concerts du Conservatoire
c. André Cluytens
Hoffmann (t) Nicolai Gedda
His Muse/
  Stella (m-s) Renée Faure
Olympia (s) Gianna d'Angelo
Giulietta (s) Elisabeth
   Schwarzkopf
Antonia (s) Victoria de los
   Angeles
Lindorf (bs) Nikola Guiselev
Coppélius/
  Dr Miracle (bs) George London
Dapertutto (bs) Ernest Blanc

Angel S-36413 (US) ■
(from above)

Decca D65D3 and SET 454/5 □
London 1286 (2) (US)
Les oiseaux dans la charmille
Joan Sutherland (s)

DG 135074 □
Les oiseaux dans la charmille
Rita Streich (s)

Decca SPA347 □
Barcarolle
c. Sir Georg Solti

CARL ORFF
(b. Munich 10.7.1895)

Orff's entire musical life has been centred on Munich, where he was born, and where he founded the Günter Schule in 1925. It is difficult to define the ingredients that make up his music: his style remains obstinately individual, distinctive, and, in its way, original. He has had substantial influence on aspects of contemporary musical life. Briefly, his aim was to by-pass the Romantic Age, and its obsession with harmony, and return music to its very roots. It is hard to put his works into any specific category: most have a theatrical background, yet only two or three of them could be called operas. His most famous work *Carmina Burana* is not strictly an opera, being written as a scenic cantata, but it was often staged. We include here only those compositions that may properly be called operas.

Der Mond
Fairy-tale opera in five scenes.
Text by Orff after the Brothers Grimm.
First performance: Munich, February 5, 1939. New York 1956.

Synopsis:
The stage is divided between Earth and the Underworld. In between sits the Narrator, who tells of a place where the moon does not shine. Four boys from that place see what they think is the Moon and steal it. When they return to their own land they are welcomed. But now they have grown old and demand a quarter of the moon each to be buried with them in their graves. The wish is granted, and the world grows dark. But in the Underworld the quarters are pieced together again and the ensuing light awakens the dead. Up in Heaven, Petrus (Peter) wonders what it is all about and goes down to find out. Saying the natural order must not be disturbed, he takes the moon and hangs it on a star so that its light shines on all the world, and tells the dead to go back to sleep.

RECORDINGS:
Philips 6700 083 (2) ●
Philips 6700 083 (2) (US)
Leipzig Radio Chorus and Symphony
Orchestra
c. Herbert Kegel
Narrator (t) Eberhard Büchner
Boys 1. (b) Fred Teschler
    2. (bs) Horst Lunlow
    3. (t) Helmut Klotz
    4. (bs) Armin Terzibaschian
Peter (b) Reiner Süss

Columbia 33CX1534/5 (m) (d) ●
Philharmonia Orchestra
c. Wolfgang Sawallisch
Narrator (t) R. Christ
Boys 1. (bs) K. Schmidt-Walter
    2. (bs) H. Garmi
    3. (t) P. Kuen
    4. (bs) A. Peter
Peter (bs-b) H. Hotter

Below: *The German composer Orff, best known for* Carmina Burana.

Die Klüge

Opera in 6 scenes.
Text by Orff after the Brothers Grimm.
First performance: Frankfurt, February 20, 1943. London 1959.

Synopsis:

The Peasant is in prison, accused of stealing a gold pestle, part of a gold mortar he has found and taken to the King. His lamentations are heard by the King who sends for the Peasant's daughter and makes her his wife. A Muleteer and Donkey Man comes to the King for judgement over the ownership of a foal. The King decides in favour of the Muleteer, but the Queen is found, next day, drawing a fishing net across the grass, and tells the King that if a mule can bear a foal, he can catch fish on grass. He sends her packing, saying she may take one chest with her, containing what she most values. He finds himself in the chest, drugged. The King takes her in his arms, and the Peasant hints that she has found the pestle after all.

Notes:

Die Klüge, otherwise known as *The King and the Wise Woman* has often been produced with puppets. Orff himself insists that the costumes and masks must be fanciful.

RECORDING:
Columbia SAX2257/8 (d) ●
Philharmonia Orchestra
c. Wolfgang Sawallisch
King (b)   Marcel Cordes
Peasant (bs)   Gottlob Frick
Wise Woman (s)   Elisabeth Schwarzkopf
Donkey Man (t)   Rudolf Christ
Muleteer (bs)   Benno Kusche

Antigonae

Tragedy in 1 Act.
Text by Friedrich Hölderlin after Sophocles.
First performance: Salzburg, August 9, 1949.

Synopsis:

The brothers Eteocles and Polynices have both been killed, fighting on opposite sides in the siege of Troy. Creon the King orders that Polynices's body shall not be buried because he has been on the wrong side. Antigone defies the order and buries her brother's body, but is condemned to death. Haemon, Antigone's betrothed, argues for her but Creon is adamant. A warning comes from old Tiresias, the blind soothsayer; but it is too late. Antigone and Haemon commit suicide, as does Creon's wife, Eurydice. The obstinate king is left alone to mourn.

Notes:

In this work Orff has made a successful attempt to recreate the drama of ancient Greece with its fusion of music, drama and dance, in modern terms. The textures are spare, the instrumentation (six pianos, four harps, nine double basses, six flutes, six oboes, six (muted) trumpets, and a battery of kettledrums and other percussion) skilfully used and highly effective. It is a large work, its single act lasting over three hours; and that, coupled with the extravagant instrumentation, has not helped make it popular. But it more than worth extended exploration, and it is a pity that there is no recording currently in the British catalogues.

RECORDINGS:
DG SLPM138 717/8 (d) ●
Bavarian Radio Chorus and Orchestra
c. Rafael Kubelik
Antigonae (s)   Inge Borkh
King Kreon
  (Creon) (b)   Charles Alexander
Haemon (t)   Fritz Uhl
Tiresias (t)   Ernst Haefliger
Eurydice (c)   Hetty Plumacher

Philips ABL 3116 □
Scenes 4 and 5
Vienna Symphony Orchestra/Members
of the Vienna State Opera Chorus

c. Heinrich Hollreiser
Antigonae (s)   Christl Goltz
Creon (b)   Hermann Uhde
Messenger (bs)   Josef Greindl
Eurydice (c)   Hilde Rössl-Majdan
(Note: This recording was made under the personal supervision of the composer.)

FERNANDO PAER

(b. Parma 1.6.1771; d. Paris 3.5.1839)

A composer of Italian birth who became French by adoption, Paer studied music in Parma and by the age of 20 was established as a conductor in Venice. He married the singer Riccardi and in 1798 was invited to Vienna, where she was singing at the Court Opera, and produced his opera *Camilla* there. He was an opera conductor in Dresden from 1803 to 1806, where he produced his *Sargino* (1803)—a work full of charming melodic invention—and *Leonora*—an Italian version of Gaveaux's opera on which Beethoven's » *Fidelio* was also based. Beethoven was an admirer of Paer's music, and his own score shows some sign of Paer's influence. In 1806 Paer accompanied Napoleon to Warsaw and Posen and settled in Paris in 1807 as his court composer. In this position he began to make a substantial fortune, continuing under Louis Philippe and as singing teacher to the Empress Marie Louise. He succeeded Spontini » as musical director of the Theatre Italien in 1812, his considerable influence waning somewhat with the arrival of Rossini » on the scene. In his heyday he composed some fifty works for the theatre. His Italian operas were fluent and attractive; his operas to German and French librettos sometimes more ambitious but generally less successful, although his most popular work was *Le Maître de Chapelle* produced in 1821. Other operas bore titles which clearly reflect his adherence to literary fashions of his time—*Il nuovo Figaro* (after Beaumarchais), *Idomeneo* and *La sonnambula*.

Sargino

Opera in 3 Acts.
Text by
First performance: Dresden, May 26, 1803.

RECORDING:
Decca SXL6531 □
London 6735 (US)
Overture
c. Richard Bonynge

Le Maître de Chapelle

Opera in 2 Acts.
Text by Sophie Gay, based on Duval's comedy 'Le Souper Imprevu'.
First performance: Paris, March 29, 1821. London (Covent Garden) 1845; New York 1852.

Synopsis:

The story concerns a fashionable opera composer of the day and his attempts to be 'with-it'.

Notes:

The opera appears to be a send-up of Paer's growing rival Rossini, then so much in vogue, and the overture is reminiscent of *The Thieving Magpie*. The opera remained popular at the Opéra-Comique in Paris into the 20th century and was still being heard in London to the end of the 19th.

RECORDING:
Inedits 995 004 (Fr) ●
Stéphane Caillat Chorus/ORTF Chamber Orchestra
c. Jean Paul Kreder
Célénie (s)   Mady Mesplé
Gertrude (s)   Isabelle Garcisanz
Benetto (t)   Michel Sénéchal
Firmin (t)   Pierre Pégaud
Barnabé (b)   Jean-Christophe Benoit
Sans Quartier (b)   Yves Bisson

Leonora

Opera in 2 Acts.
Text by Jean Nicolas Bouilly.
First performance: Dresden, October 1804.

RECORDING:
Decca D130D3 (3) ●
Bavarian Symphony Orchestra
c. Peter Maag
Leonora (s)   Ursula Koszut
Florestano (t)   Siegfried Jerusalem
Don Pizzaro (t)   Norbert Orth
Rocco (bs)   Giorgio Tadeo
Giacchino (b)   Wolfgang Brendel
Marcellino (s)   Edita Gruberova

(The Leonora libretto was first set in French by Gaveaux, then by Paer, Mayr (1805) and Beethoven (1805). This recording is an interesting link in this creative chain.)

GIOVANNI PAISIELLO

(b. Taranto 8.5.1740; d. Naples 5.6.1816)

A talented, industrious producer of *opera buffa*, Paisiello won and deserved considerable contemporary fame. He is reputed to have written over 100 operas, including *Il Barbiere di Siviglia*; ousted eventually by Rossini's version », written to the same text. After studying at the Conservatorio Sant' Onofrio, Paisiello began to compose choral music. He set out on his true path with *Il ciarlone* (1764) and over the years produced comic operas at Bologna, Modena and Parma, before settling in Naples. In 1776 he was offered, and accepted, a lucrative post at St Petersburg by the Empress Catherine. After eight years he began to make his way back to Italy where he became *maestro di cappella* to Ferdinand IV, and continued to produce operas, both *buffa* and *seria*. His official position was threatened with the temporary overthrow of the Royal State in 1799, but he soon regained it when the Royal House was restored.

Il Barbiere di Siviglia
Opera in 2 Acts.
Text by Giuseppe Petrosellini after Beaumarchais's 'Le Barbier de Séville'.
First performance: St Petersburg, October 26, 1782. Subsequently many performances throughout Europe.

Notes:
The libretto is substantially the same as that used by Rossini for his *Barbieri*. At that time Paisiello's piece was still immensely popular and Rossini encountered opposition for having been so presumptuous as to set the text of an old favourite. He made a gesture by asking the ageing Paisiello for permission, but it still took a little time for the Rossini version to win the greater lasting popularity.

RECORDING:
Delysé DS6079/80 (d) ●
Everest/Cetra S 443/2 (2) (US)
Piccolo Teatro Musicale del Collegium Italicum; I Virtuosi di Roma
c. Renato Fasano
Almaviva (t)   Nicola Monti
Rosina (s)   Graziella Sciutti
Don Basilio (bs)   Mario Petri
Dr Bartolo (bs)   Renato Capecchi
Figaro (b)   Rolando Panerai

Below: A scene from Paisiello's *Il Barbiere di Siviglia* at Salzburg.

Nina, ossia La pazza per amore (Nina, or the Lunatic from Love)
Comic Opera in 3 Acts.
Text by Giuseppe Carpani and G. B. Lorenzi after Marsollier.
First performance: Naples (Caserta Palace) June 25, 1789 (private). Florence (Teatro Fiorentino) 1790.

RECORDING:
Decca Ace of Diamonds SDD193 ☐
Il mio ben quando verra
Teresa Berganza (m-s)

GIOVANNI BATTISTA PERGOLESI

(b. Jesi 4.1.1710; d. Pozzuoli 16.3.1736)

Pergolesi was one of those fragile geniuses who reveals a rare talent, but dies before it has time to mature. He was little appreciated in his own lifetime (he is said to have been once hit on the head by an orange hurled by a member of an irate audience during the first performance of his *opera seria*, *L'Olimpiade* in January, 1735). Yet he shot to fame almost immediately after his death at the age of 26. Suddenly his works were performed everywhere, but little consolation for Pergolesi who was buried in a pauper's grave. There is some mystery about his early life; even more about his compositions. Many works have been attributed to him without convincing evidence, mostly in the instrumental and choral fields. But enough is established as authentic to secure him his place. In the opera field, Pergolesi's lasting memorial is the delightful comedy *La serva padrona*. However, the work upon which Pergolesi's fame chiefly rests is his *Stabat Mater*, which he composed in the Capuchin monastery at Pozzuoli, where he went at the end of 1735, poor of health, knowing he had not long to survive.

La serva padrona
Intemezzo in two parts.
Text by Gennaro Antonio Federico.
First performance: Naples (Teatro San Bartolommeo) August 28, 1733.

Synopsis:
Part 1 Uberto is completely under the thumb of his maid Serpina who keeps him waiting three hours for his chocolate. He sends for another servant, Vespone (a 'mute' part) to help him out. Uberto thinks the best idea is for him to marry and Vespone must find him a wife. Not necessary, says Serpina; she will marry him!
Part 2 Serpina sets a trap for Uberto by pretending she has found a lover, the fierce Captain Tempest (Vespone in disguise). Uberto thinks that perhaps he does love her after all, but as soon as Serpina spots this, she reverts to her former viperish ways. She tells Uberto the Captain will not marry her without a large dowry and that he will force Uberto to marry her instead. He agrees, the Captain arrives, the betrothal is fixed. The disguise is revealed, but Uberto has fallen into the trap.

Notes:
The delightful, sparkling overture is very familiar. The little opera became, later in the century, a piece in the '*Guerre des Buffons*' in Paris, where the Franco/Italian operatic war was raging. *La serva* achieved a great number of acclaimed performances, first at the Opéra and then at the Comédie-Française.

RECORDINGS:
Pye Ensayo NEL2014 ●
English Chamber Orchestra
c. Antonio Ros-Marbá
Uberto (bs)   Renato Capecchi
Serpina (s)   Carmen Bustamente

Saga SAGA5360 (d) ●
Members of Hamburg Radio Symphony
c. George Singer
Uberto (bs)   Nicola Rossi-Lemeni
Serpina (s)   Virginia Zeani

Nonesuch H-71043 (d) ●
Nonesuch H-71043 (US)
Pomeriggi Musicali del Teatro Nuovo di Milano
c. Ettore Gracis
Uberto (bs)   Leonardo Monreale
Serpina (s)   Mariella Adani

Telefunken 641034 (Ger.) ●
Telefunken 641034 (US)
Berlin State Opera Orchestra
c. Helmut Köch
Uberto (bs)   Rainer Süss
Serpina (s)   Olivera Miljakovic (m-s)

BASF 'Harmonia Mundi' 2521022-7.UK (Ger.) (d) ●
Collegium Aureum

Uberto (bs)   Siegmund Nimsgern (bs-b)
Serpina (s)   Maddalena Bonifaccio

Everest/Cetra S-445/1 (US) ●
I Virtuosi di Roma
c. Renato Fasano
Uberto (bs)   Sesto Bruscantini
Serpina (s)   Renata Scotto

Decca Ace of Diamonds SDD193 ☐
Stizzoso mio stizzoso
Teresa Berganza (m-s)

JACOPO PERI
(b. Rome 20.8.1561; d. Florence 12.8.1633)

Peri is credited with having written the first opera, in the modern sense, to have survived. His *Euridice* appeared in 1600 (published 1601), just before a setting of the same subject by Giulio Caccini. Both were written for the marriage of Henry IV of France and Marie de Médicis in 1600. Caccini's opera was not given complete until 1602 and Peri's *Dafne*, which would otherwise have been the first opera, has not survived. Peri was a pupil at the church of San Lorenzo, Florence, and later became *maestro di cappella* to the Médici family. He was a singer and lutanist as well as a composer. He belonged to that group of musicians and poets known as the Camerata who, in the belief that they were restoring the Greek principles of music and drama, produced the earliest forms of opera, virtually by accident. Like Peri, most were little more than amateurs, but their work, although soon superseded, was important in that it paved the way for future developments. They aimed to present dramatic action in a naturalistic way, the musical settings designed to adhere as closely as possible to speech. Their monodic style (the *stile rappresentativo*) had serious limitations; but it sowed seeds that were to grow into formidable trees.

Euridice
Opera in Prologue and 5 Scenes.
Text by Ottavio Rinuccini.
First performance: Florence (Pitti Palace) October 6, 1600 (with some items by Caccini).

Synopsis:
The Prologue announces the theme and the story then follows the classical outlines. Nymphs and shepherds celebrate the wedding of Orpheus and Eurydice, Orpheus sings of his happiness and offers a prayer to Venus, then the messenger Dafne announces Eurydice's death. Orpheus wants to kill himself but Venus tries to console him and urges him to demand Eurydice back from Pluto in Hades. Orpheus by his song and prayer obtains her release; nymphs and shepherds bewail the fate of the pair, and a message comes that Orpheus and Eurydice have returned reunited.

Notes:
The action is carried forward by solo voices in the new *stile rappresentativo*. Rinuccini omits the condition that Orpheus must not look at Eurydice or she must return to Hades: Orpheus's song alone secures the release and return. At the first performance Peri himself sang the name part.

RECORDINGS:
Harmonia Mundi HM2.478 (2) ●
Telefunken 2635014 (2) (US)
Coro Polifonico di Milano/Solisti di Milano
c. Angelo Ephrikian
La Tragedia/Venus/
  Persephone (c)   Adele Bonay
Euridice (s)   Nerina Santini
Orfeo (t)   Rodolfo Farolfi
Arcetro (b)   Gastone Sarti
Dafne (m-s)   Elene Barcis

DG Archiv 2533 305 □
O durezza di ferro; Tra le donne;
Bellissima regina
Nigel Rogers (t)

AMILCARE PONCHIELLI
(b. Paderno Fasolaro, Cremona 31.8.1834; d. Milan 16.1.1886)

Hardly a major composer, even where opera is concerned, Ponchielli was nevertheless a skilful and industrious one. He studied at the Milan Conservatoire from 1843 until 1854 and two years later produced his first opera *I promessi sposi*, which he then revised and re-presented. In 1881 he was appointed *maestro di cappella* at Bergamo and composed a famous hymn to the memory of Garibaldi. The only opera of Ponchielli's that is still widely remembered is *La Gioconda*, and largely because of the orchestral excerpt 'Dance of the Hours', and the tenor aria 'Cielo e mar!'

La Gioconda
Opera in 4 Acts.
Text by Arrigo Boito (under the anagrammatic pseudonym Tobia Gorrio) after Victor Hugo's 'Angelo'.
First performance: Milan (La Scala) April 8, 1876. London (Covent Garden) 1883; New York (Metropolitan) 1883.

Synopsis:
Scene: Venice. Time: 17th Century.
Act 1 'The Lion's Mouth'. Outside the Ducal palace. Barnaba, an Inquisition spy, is in love with La Gioconda, but she, in turn, loves the noble Enzo Grimaldo, a Genoese outlaw disguised as a sea captain. Barnaba insinuates that La Gioconda's mother, La Cieca, is a witch. She has to be rescued from the mob by Enzo's crew. The inquisitor Alvise enters with his wife Laura and pardons La Cieca. Barnaba then contrives that Alvise apprehends Enzo eloping with Laura, to whom he was once engaged. La Gioconda overhears, but misunderstands.
Act 2 'The Rosary'. Barnaba and Isepo, the public scribe, bring Laura to Enzo's ship. The two greet each other passionately. La Gioconda arrives and sees the inquisitor approaching with his guards. Laura reveals a rosary and La Gioconda realises she was the masked lady who interceded for her mother in the witch hunt. Laura escapes, and Enzo sets fire to his boat.
Act 3 'The House of Gold'. In Alvise's house, the inquisitor plans vengeance on Laura: he leaves her with orders to poison herself. La Gioconda gives Laura a drug that will allow her to feign death. Believing Laura dead, Alvise entertains his guests ('The Dance of the Hours'). Barnaba discovers La Cieca hiding in the house and she says she has been praying for the dead Laura. Alvise displays Laura's supposed corpse and Enzo attempts to stab him but is apprehended by guards.
Act 4 'The Orfano Canal'. La Gioconda promises to give herself to Barnaba if he arranges Enzo's escape. Laura realises she loves Enzo and they both escape on a waiting boat, arranged by La Gioconda. Barnaba comes to claim his reward but La Gioconda stabs herself.

Notes:

La Gioconda is a large-scale Grand Opera; somewhat crude but full of dramatic spirit. It is similar to Meyerbeer » in its coloured spectacle and spates of concerted song and dance. Each Act has its separate title.

Well-known arias:

Act 1 Feste e pane! (People)
　　　 Voce di donna, o d'angelo (Blind Woman, etc.)
　　　 O monumento! Regia e bolgia dogale! (Barnaba)
Act 2 Ah! Pescator affonda l'esca (Barnaba, etc.)
　　　 Cielo e mar! (Enzo)
　　　 L'amo come il fulgor del creato (Gioconda and Laura)
Act 3 Dance of the Hours (orchestral)
Act 4 Suicidio! . . . in questi fieri momenti . . . (Gioconda)

RECORDINGS:
Ember GVC34/6 (m) ●
Turin Radio Chorus and Orchestra
c. Antonio Votto
La Gioconda (s)　Maria Callas
Laura (m-s)　　 Fedora Barbieri
Enzo Grimaldo (t) Gianni Poggi
Alvise (bs)　　　Guilo Neri
La Cieca (c)　　 Maria Amadini
Barnaba (b)　　 Paolo Silveri

Decca SET364/6 ●
London 1388 (3) (US)
Chorus and Orchestra of Accademia di
Santa Cecilia di Roma
c. Lamberto Gardelli
La Gioconda (s)　Renata Tebaldi
Laura (m-s)　　 Marilyn Horne
Enzo Grimaldo (t) Carlo Bergonzi
Alvise (bs)　　　Nicolai Ghiaurov
La Cieca (c)　　 Oralia Dominguez
Barnaba (b)　　 Robert Merrill

Decca SET450 ■
London 26162 (US)
(from above)

Decca Ace of Diamonds GOS609/11 ●
Richmond 63518 (3) (US)

Chorus and Orchestra of Maggio
Musicale Fiorentino
c. Gianandrea Gavazzeni
La Gioconda (s)　Anita Cerqueti
Laura (m-s)　　 Giulietta Simionato
Enzo Grimaldo (t) Mario del Monaco
Alvise (bs)　　　Cesare Siepi
La Cieca (c)　　 Franca Sacchi
Barnaba (b)　　 Ettore Bastianini

Decca D63D3 (3) ●
London 13123 (3) (US)
Chorus and Orchestra of Accademia di
Santa Cecilia di Roma
c. Fernando Previtali
La Gioconda (s)　Zinka Milanov
Laura (m-s)　　 Rosalind Elias
Enzo Grimaldo (t) Giuseppe di Stefano
Barnaba (b)　　 Leonard Warren

Columbia SAX2359/61 (d) ●
Seraphim S-6031 (3) (US)
Chorus and Orchestra of La Scala, Milan
c. Antonio Votto
La Gioconda (s)　Maria Callas
Laura (m-s)　　 Fiorenza Cossotto
Enzo Grimaldo (t) Pier Miranda
　　　　　　　　　　Ferraro
Barnaba (b)　　 Piero Cappuccilli

Il Figliuol Prodigo

Opera in 3 Acts.
Text by Angelo Zanardini.
First performance: Milan (La Scala) December 26, 1880.

RECORDING:
Philips 9500 203 □
Philips 9500 203 (US)
Il Padre
José Carreras (t)

Below: *A production at Verona of Ponchielli's melodramatic opera* La Gioconda.

FRANCIS POULENC

(b. Paris 7.1.1899; d. Paris 30.1.1963)

Poulenc received a classical education but his interest in music led to piano lessons with Ricardo Viñes. He acquired a theoretical knowledge of music from various sources. By the time he joined the Army in 1918, he had written one or two compositions inspired by Erik Satie. After the War, continuing to idolise Satie, he became one of the group of French composers known as 'Les Six'—the others being Auric, Durey, Honegger, Milhaud » and Tailleferre—which also led to his meeting and being influenced by Jean Cocteau. Poulenc's musical activity was largely outside the theatre, and all his music retained a very individual style and an unschooled freshness of outlook, veering between the light, frivolous, satirical vein that he inherited from Satie and the deep seriousness of his religious works. His few operas reveal the different sides of his nature. A comédie-bouffe *Le Gendarme Incompris* was written in 1920; then no further opera until the brilliantly satirical *Les Mamelles de Tirésias* in 1947, a piece frequently produced and recently heard in London. *Les Dialogues des Carmélites* (Milan 1957) was a complete contrast, a profound and serious work. An interesting 'operatic monologue' *La Voix Humaine*, text by Cocteau, is a 45-minute soprano solo at one end of a telephone.

Les Mamelles de Tirésias

Opéra-bouffe in 2 Acts.
Text by Guillaume Apollinaire.
First performance: Paris (Opéra-Comique) June 3, 1947. New York 1953; Aldeburgh 1958.

Notes:

The surrealistic plot concerns a husband and wife who change sex. He produces 40,000 children before he reverts to manhood —and advises the audience to follow his example.

RECORDING:
Voix de son Maître CO61-12.510 (Fr) ●　**Thérèse** (s)　　Denise Duval
Columbia 33CX1218 (d) (UK)　　　　　 **Le Mari** (t)　　 Jean Giraudeau
Chorus and Orchestra of l'Opéra-Comique　**Le Gendarme** (b) Émile Rousseau
c. André Cluytens

Les Dialogues des Carmélites

Opera in 3 Acts.
Text by Georges Bernanos, based on Gertrude von le Fort's novel 'Die letzte am Schafott' (1931) and a film scenario.
First performance: Milan (La Scala) January 26, 1957. San Francisco 1957; London (Covent Garden) 1958.

Notes:

The opera tells of the Carmelite nuns of Compiègne who defied the revolutionary tribune of 1794 and went to the guillotine.

RECORDING:
Voix de son Maître C153-12.801 (3)
(Fr) ●
HMV FALP523/5 (d) (UK)
Chorus and Orchestra of Théâtre National
de l'Opéra
c. Pierre Dervaux
Blanche de la Force (s) Denise Duval
La Prière (m-s)　　　Denise Scharley
La nouvelle Prière (s)　Régine Crespin
Mère Marie (m-s)　　 Rita Gorr
Soeur Constance (s)　 Lilian Berton
Le Chevalier da la
　　Force (t)　　　　Pierre Finel
Le Marquis de la
　　Force (b)　　　　Xavier Depraz

Above: *Francis Poulenc.*

La Voix Humaine

Tragédie lyrique in 1 Act.
Text by Jean Cocteau.
First performance: Paris (Opéra-Comique) February 6, 1959. New York (Carnegie Hall) 1960; Edinburgh Festival 1960.

Notes:

The piece dramatises a telephone conversation between a jilted young woman and her lover.

RECORDING:
Voix de son Maître C065-12.052 (Fr) ○　Orchestra of L'Opéra-Comique
Vox OPL160 (d) (US)　　　　　　　　　c. Georges Prêtre
　　　　　　　　　　　　　　　　　　La Voix (s) Denise Duval

SERGEI PROKOFIEV
(b. Sontsovka 23.4.1891; d. Moscow 5.3.1953)

A remarkable child prodigy, Prokofiev studied composition at the St Petersburg Conservatoire under Rimsky-Korsakov » and Liadov (as did Stravinsky »). After the Russian Revolution he travelled abroad and in 1922 settled in Paris, which remained his home base until 1933 when he returned to Russia as a permanent citizen: being obliged by the authorities to make a firm decision as to where he wanted to settle. His music has a spiky brittleness but with a particular kind of lyricism that keeps trying to escape. During his Russian years, Prokofiev tried, but did not always succeed, to obey the official directive of simple, direct music for the people. But he was too much of an artist and creator to be bound by this and inevitably he fell foul of the party line. Prokofiev's dramatic gift was always strong and he composed a number of operas and ballets of the highest quality. The range of his operas is wide (from the fantastic *Love of Three Oranges* to the epic *War and Peace*). At his best, Prokofiev remains one of the foremost figures of 20th-century music.

Above: *Examples of Soviet theatrical art: Rabinovich's designs for* The Love of Three Oranges *by Sergei Prokofiev, first produced in Chicago in 1921.*

The Love of Three Oranges
Opera in Prologue and 4 Acts.
Text by Prokofiev after Carlo Gozzi.
First performance: Chicago, December 30, 1921. New York, 1922; Milan (La Scala) 1917; Edinburgh 1962.

Synopsis:
Prologue The Trumpeter announces the Herald who tells of the hypochondriac Prince, son of the King of Clubs.
Act 1 The King, learning that his son's condition is incurable, worries about who will succeed him, and swears that his niece Clarissa shall never do so. The King and Pantalon decide the Prince can be cured by making him laugh; but Leandro, who wants to marry the willing Clarissa, plans to bore the Prince into total decline. Fata Morgana, the witch and Leandro's protector, takes a hand.
Act 2 Truffaldino, the royal jester, tries fruitlessly to cheer up the morose Prince. Fata Morgana intervenes but falls into a tussle with Truffaldino. The Prince bursts into laughter and the witch curses him, saying that he shall fall in love with three oranges and follow them to the ends of the earth.
Act 3 The Prince and Truffaldino are told where to find the oranges and that they must be opened near water. They find the oranges, and Truffaldino, being thirsty and not near water, cuts one open. Out steps a princess and dies from dehydration; the same happens with the second orange. The Prince, who has been sleeping, wakens and orders the burial of the two girls. He then cuts open the third orange and out steps the Princess Ninetta who is saved from death by a bucket of water produced by the Ten Reasonable Spectators. Then Ninetta is turned into a rat by Fata's maid, Smeraldina, who takes the princess's place.
Act 4 The King's magician Tchelio argues with Fata and is then left alone. Leandro finds a large rat in the throne room, which is soon transformed into Ninetta by Tchelio. Leandro, Clarissa and Smeraldina are condemned but are rescued by Fata Morgana.

Notes:
The whole opera is a play, not so much on words, as on the traditions of the *commedia dell'arte*, as in Gozzi's original. The best known music is undoubtedly the Orchestral Suite Prokofiev made from it.

RECORDINGS:
HMV SLS813 (2) (d) ●
Angel S-4109 (2) (US)
Chorus and Orchestra of Moscow Radio
c. Dzhamal Dalgat
King of Clubs (bs) Victor Ribinsky
Prince (t) Vladimir Makhov
Leandro (b) Boris Dobrin
Princess
  Ninetta (m-s) Lyutsia Rashkovets
Truffaldino (t) Yuri Yelnikov

Classics for Pleasure CFP40262 □
Symphonic Suite
c. Constantin Silvestri

Philips 6582 011 □
Mercury 73030 (US)
Symphonic Suite
c. Antal Dorati

Columbia MS-0545 *or* M-31812 □
Symphonic Suite
c. Eugene Ormandy

L'Ange de Feu (The Flaming Angel)
Opera in 5 Acts.
Text by Prokofiev after Valery Bruisoff's novel.
First performance: (concert) Paris (Théâtre des Champs-Elysées) November 25, 1954. (Stage) Venice, September 14, 1955; London (Sadler's Wells), 1965.

Synopsis:
Scene: Germany. Time: 17th century.
Act 1 Ruprecht, at an inn, meets the distraught Renata who tells him about an angel (Madiel) who, surrounded by fire, appeared to her when she was a child and predicted she would be a saint. Her later desire for a lover drove the angel away, but he said he would return in human form. When Renata met Count Heinrich she swore he was an angel, which he denied. She lived with him for a year, then he left her and she has been pursued by a fiend ever since. The innkeeper enters, saying Renata is bewitched. Ruprecht, after unsuccessfully trying to seduce her, becomes involved in the strange business.
Act 2 Cologne. Renata and Ruprecht have been searching fruitlessly for Heinrich. With the aid of Jacob Glock they buy more magic books, but to no avail. Glock takes Ruprecht to the philosopher Agrippa von Nettelsheim, who turns out to be a master of the black arts, but he will not help.
Act 3 Renata has found Heinrich's whereabouts and is convinced he is an impostor. She tells Ruprecht she is his, if only he will kill Heinrich. He enters Heinrich's house and Renata, seeing him, realises he is, in fact, Madiel, and tells Ruprecht to allow himself to be killed; he is wounded and tended by Renata who swears, if he dies, to go into a convent.
Act 4 Renata tells the still weak Ruprecht that she will enter a convent. He says he loves her and she tries to kill herself. Faust and Mephistofeles are watching and they ask Ruprecht to show them the town.
Act 5 Renata is in the convent. The Mother Superior wants to know why the convent is under apparent attack by devils. The Inquisitor arrives; most of the nuns oppose Renata. Mephistofeles and Ruprecht appear, and the Inquisitor sentences Renata to death as a heretic.

Notes:
The opera had a chequered career. Prokoviev hoped that Mary Garden would produce it in Chicago after *The Love of Three Oranges*; but she resigned as director before anything could come of it. Bruno Walter showed some interest in Berlin in 1926; but to no avail. Koussevitzky gave some parts in Paris, but after that the score was lost and surfaced in Paris during the 1950s, after Prokofiev's death.

RECORDING:
Decca Ace of Diamonds GOSR652/4 ●
ORTF Choir/Paris Opera Orchestra
c. Charles Bruck
Renata (s) Jane Rhodes
Ruprecht (b) Xavier Depraz (bs)

Agrippa (t) Paul Finel
Mephistofeles (t) Jean Giraudeau
Faust/
Inquisitor (bs) Anuré Vessiers

War and Peace (Viona y Mir)

Opera in 13 Scenes.
Text by Prokofiev and Mira Mendelson after Tolstoy.
First performance: (orig. version, cut) Moscow, June 7, 1945. ('Final version')
Leningrad, April 1, 1955; Florence, 1953; New York (NBC TV) 1957; London
(Sadler's Wells) 1972; Australia (Sydney Opera) 1973.

Synopsis:

Scene: Various parts of Russia. Time: 1806-12.
Part 1 (Peace) After the Epigraph, a massive chorus that introduces the theme of the Russian national character in the face of war and invasion, seven scenes take us through the meeting of Prince Andrei and Natasha at the New Year's Eve Ball; their parting; the intrigues of the good Pierre Bezukhov's flighty wife Hélène and her amorous brother Anatol; Natasha's abortive elopement plans with Anatol; Pierre's confession of love for Natasha; the outbreak of war.
Part 2 (War) Six scenes that depict the impact of invasion on a country and its people: Andrei, embittered by Natasha, is at Borodino, serving under Russia's Commander-in-Chief Field-Marshal Kutuzov; Andrei and Pierre embrace for the last time; Napoleon is worried about taking Moscow; Kutuzov is worried about retreating or defending Moscow; the fire of Moscow deprives Napoleon of victory; the death of Andrei in Natasha's arms; the French winter retreat; Pierre's liberation; Kutuzov and the Russian spirit triumphant.

Notes:

The opera went through several stages of evolution. At first it was mostly concerned with personal matters; but the Hitler war was raging and Russia was again under the invader. So Prokofiev was urged to insert more martial and patriotic material. The result is a mixture of two opposing elements. In the first part (Peace) we have a picture of a slightly decadent, aristocratic Russian society warmed by personal involvements. The second part (War) shows that society's break-up under invasion. Some see the patriotic music in Part 2 as simply a response to the needs of the moment which are no longer valid. But that response is a universal feeling, especially in Russia. To make an opera out of Tolstoy's huge novel was a near impossible task yet Prokofiev and his collaborator achieved it. *War and Peace* is as richly generated an opera as any to come out of Russia since *Boris Godunov.*

RECORDING:
HMV Melodiya SLS837 (4) ●
Columbia/Melodiya M4-33111 (4) (US)
Chorus and Orchestra of Bolshoi
Theatre, Moscow
c. Alexander Melik-Pashayev

Prince Andrei	
Bolkonsky (b)	Yevgeny Kibalko
Countess Natasha	
Rostova (s)	Galina Vishnevskaya
Count Ilya	
Rostov (bs)	Nikolai Shchegolkov
Countess Hélène	
Bezuhova (m-s)	Irina Arkhipova
Count Pierre	
Bezuhov (t)	Vladimir Petrov
Prince Anatol	
Kuragin (t)	Alexei Maslennikov
Denisov (b)	Boris Shapenko
Field Marshal	
Kutuzov (bs)	Alexei Krivchenya
Napoleon (b)	Pavel Lisitsian

(Note: The cast is enormous; only the principals can be listed, even though others are important in the action. The Russian recording is somewhat less complete than the version by Sadler's Wells Opera in 1972, but gives a more than adequate representation of the score.)

Betrothal in a Monastery (The Duenna)

Opera in 4 Acts.
Text by Prokofiev and Mira Mendelson based on Sheridan's 'The Duenna'.
First performance: Leningrad, November 3, 1946.

Synopsis:

Don Jerome, from Seville, wants his pretty daughter Luisa to marry the ageing fish merchant Don Mendoza. Luisa is in love with Antonio and defies her father. Her companion, the Duenna, plays tricks which result in her own marriage to Don Mendoza while Luisa and Antonio trick Don Jerome and are married. A secondary plot concerns the uniting of Luisa's brother, Fernando, and his sweetheart Clara. The monastery of the title occupies the penultimate scene, where there is an orgy of tipsy monks and Prokofiev permits himself some barbs of anti-clericism.

Notes:

The idea for this sparkling *opera buffa* was suggested by Mira Mendelson in 1940. She was then a student and had collaborated in a production of Sheridan's play. (She was later to become Prokofiev's wife and collaborated with him on several projects. She wrote some verses for this opera.) Prokofiev wrote the libretto himself, staying close to Sheridan's text, which had in any case been intended for operatic production and included popular 18th-century airs. In general the composer bends the emphasis towards the two pairs of lovers and slightly away from the more obvious satire and humour. The score is full of colourful music, with many dances and festivities in the Spanish manner. The opera went into rehearsal at the Stanislavsky Music Theatre in 1941; but the German invasion of Russia prevented public production, which had to wait until 1946.

RECORDING:
Everest/Cetra S-465 (3) (US) ●
Chorus and Orchestra of the
Stanislavsky Musical Theatre, Moscow
c. K. Abdullayev

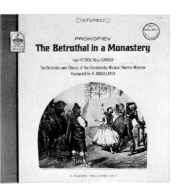

Don Jerome (t)	N. Korshunov
Luisa (s)	V. Kaevchenko
Isaac Mendoza (bs)	E. Bulavin
Antonio (t)	A. Mistchevsky
Duenna (c)	T. Yanko
Fernando (b)	J. Krutov
Fr Augustine (bs)	I. Petrov

The Story of a Real Man

Opera in 4 Acts.
Text by Prokofiev and Mira Mendelson after Boris Polevoi's novel.
First performance: (private) Leningrad (Kirov Theatre) December 3, 1948.

Notes:

This opera has had little success and has not been published. Prokofiev wrote it at a time when he was under censure from official critics, and hoped it would restore his fortunes. He filled it with 'clear, melodic episodes' and 'interesting authentic folk songs of the Russian north' (Nestyev). The style was popular and simplified; the result (predictably) was unimpressive. The story from an 'inspiring' novel of the time dealing with the war, was a little too self-consciously 'heroic'. It concerns the exploits of a valiant Soviet flyer in the war who is shot down behind enemy lines, crawls back, though seriously wounded, has his leg amputated, loses the will to carry on and is revived by the example of an old Bolshevik Commissar. At the same time it deals with the life of the Russian people under war conditions, but does not do this with any great conviction—hence the opera's hostile reception. As well as folk material, two numbers from the arrangements Prokofiev issued as Op. 104, the score includes some items from his music for the film *Ivan the Terrible*. A sick, disillusioned man at the time of its composition, Prokofiev seems to have approached it as therapeutic . . . maybe identifying himself subconsciously with the 'hero', the 'real man'.

RECORDING:
ABC Melodiya WGS08317/2 ●
Westminster 8317 (2) (US)
USSR Bolshoi Theatre Chorus and
Orchestra
c. Mark Ermler

Alexei (b)	Yevgeny Kibkalo
Olga (s)	Glafira Deomidova
Commissar (bs)	Artur Eizen
Andrei (bs)	Georgi Pankov
Kukushkin (t)	Alexei Maslennikov
Vasili	
Vasilevich (bs)	Mark Reshetin
Petrovna (s)	Antonia Ivanova
Varilissa (c)	Vera Smirnova

GIACOMO PUCCINI
(b. Lucca 22.12.1858; d. Brussels 29.11.1924)

Puccini's father died while he was still a child, but his mother arranged a special Royal grant to help with her son's musical education and in 1880 he entered the Milan Conservatoire where he studied under Bazzini and Ponchielli ». The latter encouraged Puccini to enter his first opera (*Le Villi*) into a competition: even though it was beaten by Mascagni's » entry (*Cavalleria Rusticana*), Puccini's effort was eventually produced, in 1884, and led to a commission to write another opera from the publisher Ricordi—the unsuccessful *Edgar*. In 1893, however, Puccini scored his first major success at Turin with *Manon Lescaut*, and from then established himself as the most prominent and popular opera composer of his time. He might not have possessed the depth and range of Verdi », but he did have a sure touch for the theatre and an unfailing ability to match dramatic situations with appropriate music and memorable melody. His style is frankly emotional, often sentimental, sometimes melodramatic, seldom fastidious; yet he found a distinctive idiom within a conventional framework. Even if his music sometimes sounds old-fashioned and his later experiments, designed to catch up with modern ideas, are not always viable, his operas remain supremely convincing and obstinately indestructible. In short: it is easy to criticise Puccini, but impossible not to enjoy him.

Le Villi
Opera in 1 Act (new version in 2 Acts).
Text by Ferdinando Fontana.
First performance: Milan (Teatro dal Verme) May 31, 1884. Turin (Teatro Reggio) (2 Acts) December 26, 1884; New York (Metropolitan) 1908.

Synopsis:
Act 1 After Robert and Anna's betrothal feast Robert departs on a voyage swearing eternal love to Anna.
Act 2 Robert forgets his vow, however, and is having a fine time in Mayence, paying expensive court to a lady of more than dubious character. He returns home dispirited. The Villi (Witches) dance around mocking him. Then funeral music is heard from the house of Wulf the mountaineer, Anna's father. Anna's ghost becomes one of the dancing witches. Robert begs forgiveness, but falls dead as the chorus sings a chiding Hosanna round his body.

Notes:
The story is the same as that used by Adam for the ballet *Giselle* and James Loder's play with music *The Night Dancers*. This, Puccini's first opera, was a modest success on its original production (especially in the 2 Act revision); but it is not much heard outside Italy.

Well-known arias:
Act 1 Se come voi piccina

RECORDINGS:
RCA DPS 2052 (2) (d) ●
RCA LSC7096 (2) (US)
Vienna Academy Chamber Chorus/
Vienna Volksoper Orchestra
c. Anton Guadagno
Roberto (t) Barry Morell
Anna (s) Adriana Maliponte
Wulf (b) Matteo Manuguerra
Narrator G. de Monaco
(coupled with Edgar, Act 2)

CBS 76407 □
Columbia M-33435 (US)
Se come voi piccina
Renata Scotto (s)

HMV ASD2632 □
Se come voi piccina
Montserrat Caballé (s)

RCA SER5674 □
RCA LSC-3337 (US)
Se come voi piccina
Leontyne Price (s)

Above: *Giacomo Puccini.*

Edgar
Opera in 4 Acts (new version in 3 Acts).
Text by Ferdinando Fontana after Alfred de Musset's 'La coupe et les lèvres'.
First performance: Milan (La Scala) April 21, 1889. Ferrara (3 Acts) February 28, 1892.

Synopsis:
Act 1 Fidelia loves Edgar, who repulses the advances of his former love, the gypsy girl Tigrana, foster-sister of Fidelia and Frank. Spurning Frank's declaration of love, Tigrana mocks the villagers at prayer. They drive her from the village, but Edgar declares he will go with her, setting fire to his house as an act of defiance. Frank challenges him to a duel: they fight, and Frank is wounded. Edgar and Tigrana flee together.
Act 2 Weary of a life of debauchery, Edgar longs for Fidelia. In spite of Tigrana's entreaties, he decides to join a troop of soldiers. Their captain is Frank; but the two men are reconciled and Edgar goes with the soldiers, leaving Tigrana, who swears to be revenged.
Act 3 Edgar has been killed in battle. Soldiers bear in a body in full armour. Edgar's gallantry is praised, but a Monk who claims to have heard his dying confession says that he was a profligate and a criminal. All now curse Edgar: only Fidelia proclaims his innocence. Frank and the Monk bribe Tigrana to denounce Edgar as a traitor to his country. The angry soldiers rush to remove the body from its place of honour—but the suit of armour is empty. The Monk now reveals himself as Edgar and embraces the faithful Fidelia. Tigrana stealthily approaches Fidelia and stabs her. She is arrested by the soldiers as Edgar falls weeping by Fidelia's body.

Notes:
Edgar has never made much headway. Puccini himself appeared to think little of it, judging by various tart remarks he made. There are hints in the score of the Puccini to come, but the libretto has been universally condemned as preposterous rubbish, even by operatic standards.

RECORDINGS:
CBS Masterworks 79213 (2) ●
Columbia M2-34584 (2) (US)
New York Schola Cantorum/Opera
Orchestra of New York
c. Eve Queler
Edgar (t) Carlo Bergonzi
Fidelia (s) Renata Scotto
Tigrana (m-s) Gwendolyn Killebrew
Gualtiero (bs) Mark Munkittrick
Frank (b) Vincente Sardinero

RCA DPS2052 □
RCA LSC-7096 (US)
Vienna Academy Chamber Choir/
Vienna Volksoper Orchestra
c. Anton Guadagno
(coupled with La Villi)
Act 2
Barry Morell (t), **Nancy Stokes** (s),
Walker Wyatt (b)

Manon Lescaut
Opera in 4 Acts.
Text by Marco Praga, Domenico Oliva and Luigi Illica after Abbé Prévost's novel.
First performance: Turin (Teatro Regio) February 1, 1893. London (Covent Garden) 1894; New York (Metropolitan) 1907.

Synopsis:
Scene: France. Time: 18th century.
Act 1 A busy scene in Amiens; Edmondo, mooning about love, is taunted by the crowd. A carriage arrives with the rich Geronte, Lescaut, and his sister Manon, who is en route to a convent. The Chevalier des Grieux is captivated by her and makes an assignation. But Geronte plans to elope with Manon himself. Edmondo overhears Geronte's plot and tells des Grieux, who in turn elopes with Manon—in the coach Geronte paid for. Lescaut tells the incensed Geronte that the couple will soon run out of money.
Act 2 Manon, true to her brother's prophecy, has left des Grieux and returned to live in luxury with Geronte. She still loves des Grieux, who, Lescaut tells her, has made a fortune at the gambling tables. He enters and they fall into each other's arms. Geronte catches them and rushes off to the police. Manon

wastes too much time gathering her jewellery and is arrested on an immorality charge.

Act 3   Manon is condemned to deportation to the French colony of Louisiana. Des Grieux and Lescaut fail at an escape plan, and des Grieux begs the ship's captain to take him as well.

Act 4   Manon and des Grieux have left New Orleans and are on a huge, desolate plain. She is in a state of collapse and begs des Grieux to let her die alone. He goes for help but when he returns, Manon dies in his arms.

Notes:

Manon Lescaut was Puccini's first success and soon achieved worldwide acclaim. Early commentators remarked on the opera's 'symphonic structure'. Although this was misunderstood at the time, it was to become characteristic of Puccini's operas.

Well-known arias:

Act 1   Donna non vidi mai simile a questa (Des Grieux)
Act 2   In quelle trine morbide (Manon)
      Ah, Manon mi tradisce il tuo folle pensier (Des Grieux)
Act 3   Intermezzo (orchestral)
Act 4   Sola, perduta, abbandonata (Manon)

RECORDINGS:
HMV SLS962 (2) ★●
Angel S-3782 (2) (US)
Ambrosian Opera Chorus/New
Philharmonia Orchestra
c. Bruno Bartoletti
Manon Lescaut (s) Montserrat Caballé
Chevalier
  des Grieux (t)   Placido Domingo
Geronte
  di Ravoir (bs)   Noel Mangin
Lescaut (b)   Vincente Sardinero
Edmondo (t)   Robert Tear
Ship's Captain (bs) Gwynne Howell

Decca Ace of Diamonds GOS607/8 ●
London 1317 (3) (US)
Chorus and Orchestra of Accademia di
Santa Cecilia di Roma
c. Francesco Molinari-Pradelli
Manon Lescaut (s) Renata Tebaldi
Chevalier
  des Grieux (t)   Mario del Monaco
Geronte
  di Ravoir (bs)   Fernando Corena
Lescaut (b)   Mario Borello
Edmondo (t)   Piero de Palma
Ship's Captain (b) Antonio Sacchetti

Decca SXL6011 ■
London 25713 (US)
(from above)

HMV SLS5051 (2) □
Angel S-36934 (US)
Donna non vidi mai; In quelle trine
morbide, Oh, saro lapiu bella
Montserrat Caballé (s)
Placido Domingo (t)

Above: *Beverly Sills as Manon in Puccini's version of Prévost's* Manon Lescaut.

La Bohème

Opera in 4 Acts.
Text by Giuseppe Giacosa and Luigi Illica, after Henri Murger's novel.
First performance: Turin (Teatro Reggio) February 1, 1896. Manchester 1897; London (Covent Garden) 1897; New York 1898; New York (Metropolitan) 1900.

Synopsis:

Scene: Paris. Time: *c.* 1830.

Act 1   The poet Rodolfo, the painter Marcello, the philosopher Colline and the musician Schaunard all live in poverty in a garret. It is Christmas Eve, the stove has gone out, there is no food or wine. Rodolfo sacrifices his latest masterpiece to light the fire just as Schaunard arrives with supplies. The landlord Benoit and his rent demand are fobbed off, and all, except Rodolfo, depart for the Café Momus. There is a knock at the door; it is Mimi the seamstress whose candle has gone out. She collapses in a coughing fit and loses her key. As they look for it Rodolfo touches her tiny, frozen hand and sings his famous aria. The two sing an impassioned love duet and join the others who are calling from the street.

Act 2   The Café Momus. Among the revellers is Musetta, an old flame of Marcello. She promptly drops her current beau, the ageing Alcindoro, and there is a good deal of by-play and jollity. The act ends with the hapless Alcindoro being left to pick up all the bills.

Act 3   It is February and Mimi, whose health is worse than ever, is about to part from the insanely jealous Rodolfo. Marcello, now a sign-painter, is quarrelling with Musetta, but they are still together.

Act 4   In the garret both Rodolfo and Marcello are regretting hasty actions and lost loves. No one has heard from Mimi, and Musetta has a new, rich protector. Musetta enters, saying that Mimi is mortally ill and wants to die where she and Rodolfo first met. Colline goes off to sell his coat to provide fuel and food. With deep feeling Rodolfo and Mimi recall their earlier days together, their love slowly rekindling. As Musetta and the others return, Mimi dies.

Notes:

La Bohème is unquestionably a masterpiece, but is also different from Puccini's other operas in the way it combines a taut, economical conversational style with Puccini's natural lyricism and emotional ripeness. This combination not only sets *La Bohème* firmly among the modern operas but also among the Romantic ones. Like Puccini's earlier works it is built on symphonic principles, but significantly advancing them. Each Act is in fact a 'Movement', worked out and developed with consummate skill. A significant achievement.

Well-known arias:

Act 1   Che gelida manina (Your tiny hand is frozen) (Rodolfo)
      Mi chiamano Mimi (Mimi)
      O soave fanciulla (Rodolfo and Mimi)
Act 2   Quando me'n vo', soletta per la via (Musetta's Waltz Song)
Act 3   Donde lieta usci (Mimi)
      Addio, dolce svegliare (Rodolfo, Mimi, Marcello and Musetta)
Act 4   Ah, Mimi tu più non torni (Rodolfo)
      Te lo rammenti (Mimi)

RECORDINGS:
RCA AT203 (2) (r. 1952) ●
Chorus/NBC Symphony Orchestra
c. Arturo Toscanini
Rodolfo (t)   Jan Peerce
Mimi (s)   Licia Albanese
Marcello (b)   Fernando Valentini
Musetta (s)   Anne McKnight
Colline (bs)   Nicola Moscona
Schaunard (b) George Cehanovsky

HMV SLS896 (2) ●
Seraphim S-6099 (2) (US)
RCA Victor Chorus and Orchestra
c. Sir Thomas Beecham
Rodolfo (t)   Jussi Björling
Mimi (s)   Victoria de los Angeles
Marcello (b)   Robert Merrill
Musetta (s)   Lucine Amara
Colline (bs)   Giorgio Tozzi
Schaunard (b) John Reardon

Above: *The Bohemian Parisian setting of Puccini's* La Bohème.

Decca SET565/6 ●
London 1299 (2) (US)
German Opera Chorus/Berlin
Philharmonic Orchestra
c. Herbert von Karajan.
Rodolfo (t)   Luciano Pavarotti
Mimi (s)   Mirella Freni
Marcello (b)   Rolando Panerai
Musetta (s)   Elizabeth Harwood
Colline (bs)   Nicolai Ghiaurov
Schaunard (b)   Gianni Maffeo

Decca SET5791 ■
London 26399 (US)
(from above)

HMV SLS5059 (2) ●
Chorus and Orchestra of La Scala, Milan
c. Antonio Votto
Rodolfo (t)   Giuseppe di Stefano
Mimi (s)   Maria Callas
Marcello (b)   Rolando Panerai
Musetta (s)   Anna Moffo
Colline (bs)   Nicola Zaccaria
Schaunard (b)   Mario Spatafora

Decca 5D2 (2) ●
London 1208 (2) (US)
Chorus and Orchestra of Accademia di
Santa Cecilia di Roma
c. Tullio Serafin
Rodolfo (t)   Carlo Bergonzi
Mimi (s)   Renata Tebaldi
Marcello (b)   Ettore Bastianini
Musetta (s)   Gianna d'Angelo
Colline (bs)   Cesare Siepi
Schaunard (b)   Renato Cesare

Decca Jubilee JB11 ■
London 25201 (US)
(from above)

HMV SLS907 (2) ●
Angel S-3643 (2) (US)
Chorus and Orchestra of Rome Opera
c. Thomas Schippers
Rodolfo (t)   Nicolai Gedda
Mimi (s)   Mirella Freni
Marcello (b)   Mario Sereni
Musetta (s)   Mariella Adani
Colline (bs)   Feruccio Mazzoli
Schaunard (b)   Mario Basiola

Angel S-36199 (US) ■
(from above)

RCA ARL2 0371 ●
RCA ARL2 0371 (2) (US)
John Alldis Choir/Wandsworth School
Boys' Choir/London Philharmonic
Orchestra
c. Sir Georg Solti
Rodolfo (t)   Placido Domingo
Mimi (s)   Montserrat Caballé
Marcello (b)   Sherrill Milnes
Musetta (s)   Judith Blegen
Colline (bs)   Ruggero Raimondi
Schaunard (b)   Vincenzo Sardinero

RCA LSC-6095 (2) (US) ●
Rome Opera Chorus and Orchestra
c. Erich Leinsdorf
Rodolfo (t)   Richard Tucker
Mimi (s)   Anna Moffo
Marcello (b)   Robert Merrill
Musetta (s)   Janet Costa
Schaunard (b)   Philip Maero

RCA LSC-2655 and VCS-7093 ■
(from above)

Tosca

Opera in 3 Acts.
Text by Giuseppi Giacosa and Luigi Illica, after Sardou's play.
First performance: Rome (Teatro Costanzi) January 14, 1900. New York (Metropolitan) 1901.

Synopsis:
Scene: Rome. Time: 1800.
Act 1   Cesare Angelotti, an escaped political prisoner, enters the church of Sant' Andrea della Valle and hides in the private chapel. Cavaradossi enters and uncovers his painting of a beautiful woman often seen praying in the church. He sings of his real love, the singer Floria Tosca. Angelotti comes out of hiding and recognises his friend Cavaradossi who, hearing Tosca's voice outside, hurriedly gives him a basket of food. Tosca is suspicious and jealous but she and Cavaradossi make an assignation for that night. When she has gone Cavaradossi gives Angelotti the key to his villa. They leave. Baron Scarpia and his men arrive, hot on Angelotti's trail, and clues suggest a connection between the escapee and Cavaradossi. Tosca comes back and Scarpia, who desires her, sows the seeds of doubt and jealousy.
Act 2   Scarpia's apartments. He broods over Angelotti's recapture and the prospect of seeing Tosca, to whom he has sent a message. Cavaradossi has been arrested and led to the torture chamber. Scarpia's men find Angelotti, but he has committed suicide. Tosca begs for her lover's life. Scarpia says there is a price: her surrender to him. She agrees and Scarpia writes a safe-conduct pass but says there must be a mock execution. She sees a knife and stabs him; then arranges candles round the body, takes the pass and leaves.
Act 3   The Castle Sant' Angelo. Cavaradossi learns of his execution and sings of his beloved Tosca. She arrives and tells him the plan: when he is 'shot' he must feign death, then they can escape. The ritual takes place and Cavaradossi falls to the ground—and is, to Tosca's horror, genuinely dead. Scarpia's body has been discovered and as the guards come after Tosca she jumps to her death from the battlements.

Notes:
With *Tosca* Puccini approached more deliberately the *verismo* style much in favour at the time. There is great care for natural detail. The opera is certainly melodramatic, with passions being more insistent than the characters as individuals. The sexual confrontations are crude but, on the other hand, there is much lyric surge and melodic power; plus several instances of genuine dramatic interplay. It may not possess the subtlety and ease of *La Bohème* but, nonetheless, *Tosca* remains true Puccini.

Well-known arias:
Act 1   Recondita armonia (Cavaradossi)
Non la sospiri la nostra casetta (Cavaradossi and Tosca)
Te Deum (Tosca, Chorus)
Act 2   Già mi dicon venal (Scarpia)
Vissi d'arte, vissi d'amore (Tosca)
Act 3   È lucevan le stelle (Cavaradossi)
O dolce mani mansuete e pure (Cavaradossi)

RECORDINGS:

HMV SLS825 (2) (p.s) (r.1952) ●
Chorus and Orchestra of La Scala, Milan
c. Victor de Sabata
Tosca (s)   Maria Callas
Cavaradossi (t)   Giuseppe di Stefano
Baron Scarpia (b)   Tito Gobbi
Angelotti (bs)   Franco Calabrese

Decca 5BB 123/4 ●
London 1284 (US)
Vienna State Opera Chorus/Vienna
Philharmonic Orchestra
c. Herbert von Karajan
Tosca (s)   Leontyne Price
Cavaradossi (t)   Giuseppe di Stefano
Baron Scarpia (b)   Giuseppe Taddei
Angelotti (bs)   Carlo Cava

Philips 6700 108 (2) ●
Philips 6700 108 (2) (US)
Chorus and Orchestra of Royal Opera
House, Covent Garden
c. Colin Davis
Tosca (s)   Montserrat Caballé
Cavaradossi (t)   José Carreras
Baron Scarpia (b)   Ingvar Wixell
Angelotti (bs)   Samuel Ramey

RCA ARL2 0105 (2) ●
RCA ARL2 0105 (2) (US)
John Alldis Choir/Wandsworth School
Boys' Choir/New Philharmonic
Orchestra
c. Zubin Mehta
Tosca (s)   Leontyne Price
Cavaradossi (t)   Placido Domingo
Baron Scarpia (b)   Sherrill Milnes
Angelotti (bs)   Clifford Grant

RCA ARL1-0567 ■
(from above)

DG 2707 087 (2) ●
DG 2707 087 (US)
French Radio Chorus/National Orchestra
of France
c. Msitislav Rostropovich
Tosca (s)   Galina Vishnevskaya
Cavaradossi (t)   Franco Bonelli
Baron Scarpia (b)   Matteo Manuguerra
Angelotti (bs)   Antonio Zerbini

HMV Angel SLS917 (2) ●
Angel S-3655 (2) (US)
Paris Opera Chorus/Paris Conservatoire
Orchestra
c. Georges Prêtre
Tosca (s)   Maria Callas
Cavaradossi (t)   Carlo Bergonzi
Baron Scarpia (b)   Tito Gobbi
Angelotti (bs)   Leonardo Monreale

HMV ASD2300 ■
Angel S-36236 (US)
(from above)

Decca Ace of Diamonds GOS612/3 ●
London 1210 (2) (US)
Chorus and Orchestra of Accademia di
Santa Cecilia di Roma
c. Francesco Molinari-Pradelli
Tosca (s)   Renata Tebaldi
Cavaradossi (t)   Mario del Monaco
Baron Scarpia (b)   George London
Angelotti (bs)   Silvio Maionica

Decca Ace of Diamonds SDD334 ●
London 25218 (US)
(from above)

Cetra Opera Live L041 (2) (m)
(r. Mexico City, 1952) ●
Chorus and Orchestra of Palacio de
Bellas Artes, Mexico City
c. Guido Picco
Tosca (s)   Maria Callas
Cavaradossi (t)   Giuseppe di Stefano
Baron Scarpia (b)   Piero Campolonghi

Decca SET341/2 ●
London 1267 (2) (US)
Chorus and Orchestra of Accademia di
Santa Cecilia di Roma
c. Lorin Maazel
Tosca (s)   Birgit Nilsson
Cavaradossi (t)   Franco Corelli
Baron Scarpia (b)   Dietrich
Fischer-Dieskau

Madama Butterfly

Opera in 3 Acts.
Text by Giacosa and Illica after David Belasco's play on John Luther's story.
First performance: Milan (La Scala) February 17, 1904. London (Covent Garden) 1905; New York (Metropolitan) 1907.

Synopsis:
Scene: Nagasaki, Japan. Time: Early 20th century.
Act 1   Lieutenant B. F. Pinkerton of the US Navy is to contract a marriage with a local girl Cio-Cio-San, known as 'Butterfly'. For him it is purely a pastime; but, as the American

Left: *A Covent Garden production of the ever-popular* Madama Butterfly, *first performed there in 1905 with Emmy Destinn in the leading role.*

RECORDINGS:
HMV SLS927 (3) ●
Angel S-3702 (3) (US)
Chorus and Orchestra of Rome Opera
c. Sir John Barbirolli
Cio-Cio San
  (Butterfly) (s) Renata Scotto
Lt Pinkerton (t) Carlo Bergonzi
Suzuki (m-s) Anna di Stasio
Sharpless (b) Rolando Panerai

HMV ASD2453 ■
Angel S-36567 (US)

Decca SET584/6 ●
London 13110 (3) (US)
Vienna State Opera Chorus/Vienna
Philharmonic Orchestra
c. Herbert von Karajan
Cio-Cio-San (s) Mirella Freni
Lt Pinkerton (t) Luciano Pavarotti
Suzuki (m-s) Christa Ludwig
Sharpless (b) Robert Kerns

Decca SET605 ■
London 26455 (US)
(from above)

HMV SLS5015 ●
Chorus and Orchestra of La Scala, Milan
c. Herbert von Karajan
Cio-Cio-San (s) Maria Callas
Lt Pinkerton (t) Nicolai Gedda
Suzuki (m-s) Lucia Danieli
Sharpless (b) Mario Boriello

HMV SLS5128 (3) ●
Angel S-3604 (3) (US)
Chorus and Orchestra of Rome Opera
c. Gabriele Santini
Cio-Cio-San (s) Victoria de los Angeles
Lt Pinkerton (t) Jussi Björling
Suzuki (m-s) Miriam Pirazzini
Sharpless (b) Mario Sereni

Angel S-35821 (US) ■
(from above)

CBS Masterworks 79313 (3) ●
Ambrosian Opera Chorus/Philharmonia
Orchestra
c. Lorin Maazel
Cio-Cio-San (s) Renata Scotto
Lt Pinkerton (t) Placido Domingo
Suzuki (m-s) Gillian Knight
Sharpless (b) Ingvar Wixell

Decca D68DR3 (3) ●
London OSA13121 (3) (US)
Chorus of Gran Teatro del Liceo/
Barcelona Symphony Orchestra
c. Armando Gatto
Cio-Cio-San (s) Montserrat Caballé
Lt Pinkerton (t) Barnabé Marti
Suzuki (m-s) Silvana Mazzieri
Sharpless (b) Franco Bordoni

Decca D4D3 (3) ●
London 1314 (3) (US)
Chorus and Orchestra of Accademia di
Santa Cecilia di Roma
c. Tullio Serafin
Cio-Cio-San (s) Renata Tebaldi
Lt Pinkerton (t) Carlo Bergonzi
Suzuki (m-s) Fiorenza Cossotto
Sharpless (b) Enzo Sordello

Decca Jubilee JB22 ■
London 25084 (US)
(from above)

HMV Greensleeves ESD7030 ■
(in English)
Sadler's Wells Chorus and Orchestra
c. Bryan Balkwill
Cio-Cio-San (s) Marie Collier
Lt Pinkerton (t) Charles Craig
Suzuki (m-s) Ann Robson
Sharpless (b) Gwyn Griffiths

Consul Sharpless warns, for her it is something different. As it turns out Butterfly has renounced her religion which brings down the wrath of her uncle, the Bonze or High Priest. After the marriage Butterfly and Pinkerton are left alone and they sing an impassioned duet.

Act 2 Three years have passed since Pinkerton was called away from Japan on duty. Butterfly, who has a young son by him, faithfully assures her doubting maid, Suzuki, that 'one fine day' he will return. Sharpless arrives, the bearer of bad news: Pinkerton has married an American and is coming back with his bride. Sharpless cannot bring himself to tell Butterfly, who is urged unsuccessfully by Goro the marriage broker to marry the wealthy Yamadori. She reflects on ending her life when a gun salute is heard from the harbour: Pinkterton's ship. Butterfly, her son, and Suzuki keep a vigil by the window.

Act 3 Next morning. Suzuki has persuaded Butterfly to get some sleep. Soon, Pinkerton and Sharpless enter. Suzuki realises the bitter truth and Pinkerton, full of remorse, leaves the house in a daze. Butterfly appears and is met by Sharpless and Pinkerton's wife, Kate. Quietly she asks them to take a message to Pinkerton: to come for his son in half an hour. She ceremoniously stabs herself as Pinkerton arrives.

Notes:
The first performance of *Madama Butterfly* was a famous fiasco; but Puccini revised it within ten months and it reopened at Brescia conducted by Toscanini. It was a total success, and has remained so. Puccini's use of Japanese tunes to create atmosphere was once regarded as a talking point; today it is seen as a not entirely successful device, the opera's other qualities being more interesting and memorable. *Madama Butterfly* was originally a 2-Act opera, but Act 2 was divided into two parts, making it in effect a 3-Act opera.

Well-known arias:
Act 1 Vieni la sera (Pinkerton and Butterfly)
Act 2 Un bel dì vedremo (One fine day) (Butterfly)
Scuoti quella fronda di ciliegio (Butterfly and Suzuki)
Sai cos' ebbe cuore (Butterfly)
Act 3 Io so che alle sue pene (Pinkerton, Sharpless and Suzuki)

La Fanciulla del West

Opera in 3 Acts.
Text by Guelfo Civinini and Carlo Zangarini after David Belasco's play 'The Girl of the Golden West'.
First performance: New York (Metropolitan) December 10, 1910. London (Covent Garden) 1911; Milan (La Scala) 1912.

Synopsis:
Scene: USA mining camp. Time: c. 1850.

Act 1 In the Polka saloon, run by Minnie, there is the usual card playing and drinking. Jack Rance, the Sheriff, is in love with Minnie, and on the track of the outlaw Ramerrez. Dick Johnson appears and, much to Rance's anger, seems to know Minnie. The miners and Rance go off to search for Ramerrez, who has been seen near the camp, leaving Johnson and Minnie alone. They agree to meet later that night.

Act 2 In Minnie's hut, she and Johnson are having supper and, owing to heavy snow, he is to spend the night. He hides as Rance and some of the others appear. The Sheriff has a photo of Ramerrez, whom Minnie recognises as Johnson. When they leave, Minnie turns to Johnson who admits his real identity, goes out and is wounded by a shot from Rance. He staggers back and Minnie, who admits she loves him, hides him in the loft. Rance returns and finds his quarry only when a drop of blood falls on his hand. Minnie challenges Rance to three hands of

poker: if she wins, Johnson goes free. Each wins a hand and Minnie, using substitute cards, wins the third, aces high.

Act 3 A hunt is going on for Ramerrez/Johnson and he is eventually caught and handed over to Rance, who swears to hang him. The outlaw asks that Minnie be told he has escaped and will not return, but just then she enters and pleads with the men she has looked after for years to do one thing for her. One by one they agree and she and Johnson go off together to start a new life.

Notes:

A highly successful opera, in which Puccini made some experiments with more modernistic technique. Certainly, *La Fanciulla* contains less 'hit numbers' than many other Puccini operas, but he had an alert mind that picked up much going on around in the musical world and the technique to make profitable use of it.

Well-known arias:

Act 3 Ch'ella mi creda libero e lontano (Johnson)

RECORDINGS:
DG 2709 078 (3) ●
DG 2709 078 (3) (US)
Chorus and Orchestra of Royal Opera House, Covent Garden
c. Zubin Mehta
Minnie (s) Carol Neblett
Jack Rance (b) Sherrill Milnes
Dick Johnson (t) Placido Domingo

Decca Ace of Diamonds GOS594/6 ●
London 1306 (3) (US)
Chorus and Orchestra of Accademia di Santa Cecilia di Roma
c. Franco Capuana
Minnie (s) Renata Tebaldi
Jack Rance (b) Cornell MacNeil
Dick Johnson (t) Mario del Monaco

Decca Ace of Diamonds SDD333 ■
London 25196 (US)
(from above)

HMV SLS5079 (3) ●
Seraphim S-6074 (3) (US)
Chorus and Orchestra of La Scala, Milan
c. Lovro von Matačić
Minnie (s) Birgit Nilsson
Jack Rance (b) Andrea Mongelli
Dick Johnson (t) Joao Gibin

Cetra Opera Live L064 (3) (r. 1954) ●
Chorus and Orchestra of Teatro Communale di Firenze
c. Dimitri Mitropolous

Above: *Carol Neblett in the title role of Puccini's* La Fanciulla del West.

La Rondine

Opera in 3 Acts.
Text by Giuseppe Adami from the German of Alfred Maria Willner and Heinrich Reichert.
First performance: Monte Carlo, March 27, 1917. Bologna 1917; Rome 1918; New York (Metropolitan) 1928; England (Opera Viva) 1966.

Synopsis:

Scene: Paris. Time: Second Empire.

Act 1 Rambaldo and his mistress Magda are throwing a party. He gives her a necklace and she reminisces about her youth when she used to flirt and dance at Bullier's café on the Left Bank. Ruggero enters and people begin to leave for Bullier's. Lisette, the maid, dressed in some of Magda's clothes, embraces the poet Prunier. Magda reappears, dressed as a young girl.

Act 2 At Bullier's, Ruggero dances with Magda and she tells him of an incident in the old days when she fell in love at the café with an unknown young man. Rambaldo enters and Lisette, who has entered with Prunier, is hurried out of sight with Ruggero. Magda tells Rambaldo she is in love and will not return to him, and goes off with Ruggero.

Act 3 Magda realises she will have to tell Ruggero's family of her past life. Lisette, who has failed as an actress, wants her old job back. Prunier tells Magda that Rambaldo will have her back at any time. Magda tells Ruggero the truth: she is a courtesan and cannot meet his family as if she were a blushing bride. Sadly, she leaves with Lisette and returns to her protector.

Notes:

La Rondine was commissioned as an operetta by a Viennese publisher in 1912, but was not completed until the end of World War I. It contains a good deal of light music and some waltzes, but could scarcely be called an operetta. It was also a total failure, perhaps because it was outside Puccini's normal and natural style. Although he could handle comedy his natural bent was for emotionally dark-hued lyricism.

Well-known arias:

Act 1 Chi il bel sogno di Doretta (Magda)
Ore dolci e divine (Magda)

RECORDING:
RCA DPS2055 (2)
RCA LSC-7048 (2) (US)
RCA Italiana Chorus and Orchestra
c. Francesco Molinari-Pradelli

Magda (s) Anna Moffo
Ruggero (t) Daniele Barioni
Rambaldo (b) Mario Sereni
Lisette (s) Graziella Sciutti
Prunier (t) Piero de Palma

Il Trittico

Three 1 Act Operas.
Texts: Il tabarro: Giuseppe Adami after Didier Gold; Suor Angelica and Gianni Schicchi: Giovacchino Forzano.
First performance: New York (Metropolitan) December 14, 1918.

Synopses:

Il tabarro

Scene: Paris. Time: early 20th century.

On Michele's barge on the Seine, work is finishing for the day. Giorgetta, Michele's wife, offers the workmen a drink while Michele goes on shore in a sour temper. Giorgetta and the stevedore Luigi are in love, but Michele suspects the truth. They make an assignation for later that night, and will use their familiar signal of a lighted match to indicate that it is all clear. Michele asks Giorgetta why she never comes to be warmed under his cloak now, since the death of their child, and she replies that it is because they are getting older. He goes up on deck and lights his pipe. Luigi takes the match as the signal and appears. Michele throttles him, and hides the body under his cloak. Giorgetta comes up and asks him to warm her under the cloak; he pulls it back and reveals the truth.

Suor Angelica

Scene: A convent. Time: 17th century.

Sister Angelica, daughter of a noble family, is spending a life of atonement in a convent for a sin: she has an illegitimate child. Her aunt, the Princess, visits her. When Angelica asks about the child she is told that it died two years ago. Desperate, she prepares a poison, drinks it, and prays to the Virgin Mary that she may not die in sin. A vision of the Virgin and a child appears as she dies.

Gianni Schicchi

Scene: Florence. Time: 1299.

Buoso Donati has died: his family gather round to offer prayers and condolences, but are thinking more of their possible inheritances. There is a rumour that the old man has left his money to the monks, and after the will is discovered this is found to be true. They turn to the sharp-witted Gianni Schicchi for help. He gets into bed and when the doctor calls imitates Buoso's voice and says he is much better. The doctor goes and a lawyer is sent for. Schicchi continues the impersonation and has a new will drawn up, leaving to each relative a small portion; but the biggest share for himself. No one can complain for all are implicated in the fraud. When it is done, and he owns the house,

Above: Gianni Schicchi *in a Royal Opera House production.*

he gets rid of all the relatives and arranges for his daughter, Lauretta, to marry Rinuccio, a nephew of Zita, Buoso's cousin.

Notes:

Puccini always wanted the three 1 Act operas that make up *Il Trittico* to be given together as a single evening's entertainment. They are well contrasted: *Il tabarro* is a piece of Grand Guignol in the *verismo* style; *Suor Angelica* is supposed to be mystical but hardly goes better than the sentimental; *Gianni Schicchi* is a piece of comedy that some regard as Puccini's masterpiece. In fact it has long been popular on its own. *Il tabarro* has also made a favourable independent impression. Only *Angelica* has made no headway.

Well-known arias:

Suor Angelica
   Senza Mamma (Angelica)
Gianni Schicchi
   O mio babbino caro (Lauretta)

RECORDINGS:

HMV SLS 5066 (3) ●
Il tabarro
Chorus and Orchestra of Rome Opera House
c. Vincenzo Bellezza
Michele (b)   Tito Gobbi
Luigi (t)   Giacinto Prandelli
Giorgetta (s)   Margaret Mas
Suor Angelica
Chorus and Orchestra of Rome Opera House
c. Tullio Serafin
Suor Angelica (s)   Victoria de los
                         Angeles
La Zia
   (Princess) (m-s) Fedora Barbieri
La Badessa
   (Abbess) (m-s)   Mina Doro
Gianni Schicchi
Chorus and Orchestra of Rome Opera House
c. Gabriele Santini
Gianni Schicchi (b) Tito Gobbi
Lauretta (s)   Victoria de los
                         Angeles
Rinuccio (t)   Carlo del Monte
Zita (m-s)   Anna Maria Canali
(Note: The above, not separately available in the UK, are in processed stereo except for *Gianni Schicchi*, which is available in America as Angel S-35473.)

CBS Masterworks 79312 (3) ●
Columbia M-34570, M-34505 and M-34534 (US)
Ambrosian Opera Chorus/New Philharmonia Orchestra
c. Lorin Maazel
Il tabarro
Michele (b)   Ingvar Wixell
Luigi (t)   Placido Domingo
Giorgetta (s)   Renata Scotto
Suor Angelica
Desborough School Choir/Ambrosian Opera Chorus/New Philharmonia Orchestra
c. Lorin Maazel
Suor Angelica (s)   Renata Scotto
Princess (m-s)   Marilyn Horne
Abbess (m-s)   Patricia Payne
Gianni Schicchi
London Symphony Orchestra
c. Lorin Maazel
Gianni Schicchi (b) Tito Gobbi
Lauretta (s)   Ileana Cotrubas
Rinuccio (t)   Placido Domingo
Zita (m-s)   Anna di Stasio
(Note: The above were formerly available in the UK as independent issues on CBS 76641, 76570 and 76563.)

Decca SET236/8 ●
London 1364 (3) (US)
Il tabarro
Chorus and Orchestra of Maggio Musicale Fiorentino
c. Lamberto Gardelli
Michele (b)   Robert Merrill
Luigi (t)   Mario del Monaco
Giorgetta (s)   Renata Tebaldi
Suor Angelica
Chorus and Orchestra of Maggio Musicale Fiorentino
c. Lamberto Gardelli
Suor Angelica (s)   Renata Tebaldi
Princess (m-s)   Giulietta Simionato
Abbess (m-s)   Lucia Danieli
Gianni Schicchi
Chorus and Orchestra of Maggio Musicale Fiorentino
c. Lamberto Gardelli
Gianni Schicchi (b) Fernando Corena
Lauretta (s)   Renata Tebaldi
Rinuccio (t)   Agostino Lazzari
Zita (m-s)   Lucia Danieli
(Note: The above are also available separately as SXL6122 (US London 1151), SXL6123 (US London 1152) and SXL6124 (US London 1153).)

Suor Angelica (independent version)
RCA SER5673
RCA ARL1-2712 (US)
Chorus and Orchestra of Accademia di Santa Cecilia di Roma
c. Bruno Bartoletti
Suor Angelica (s)   Katia Ricciarelli
Princess (m-s)   Fiorenza Cossotto
Abbess (m-s)   Maria Grazia Allegri
Gianni Schicchi (independent version)
Cetra Opera Live L065 (r. 1949) ●
Metropolitan Opera House Chorus and Orchestra
c. Giuseppe Antonicelli
Gianni Schicchi (b) Italo Tajo
Lauretta (s)   Licia Albanese
Rinuccio (t)   Giuseppe di Stefano
Zita (m-s)   Cloe Elmo
Il tabarro (independent version)
RCA LSC-3220 (US)
New Philharmonia Orchestra
c. Erich Leinsdorf
Michele (b)   Sherrill Milnes
Luigi (t)   Placido Domingo
Giorgetta (s) Leontyne Price

Turandot

Opera in 3 Acts (unfinished by Puccini).
Text by Giuseppe Adami and Renato Simoni after Gozzi.
First performance: Milan (La Scala) April 25, 1926. Buenos Aires 1926; New York (Metropolitan) 1926; London (Covent Garden) 1927.

Synopsis:

Scene: Peking. Time: Ancient.

Act 1 The Prince of Persia has failed to answer the three riddles set by the Princess Turandot in return for her hand, and must now die. In the crowd is Timur, the blind King of Tartary, and his faithful slave girl, Liù. He is overjoyed to meet his son Calaf, whom he thought dead, but tells him to keep his identity secret. The Prince of Persia's execution procession enters and Turandot herself appears to give the signal for sentence to be carried out. Calaf falls under her spell and is determined to win her at any cost.

Act 2 The dignitaries Ping, Pang and Pong lament the state of China as drum rolls announce the impending trial of Calaf. He answers Turandot's three riddles correctly but the princess says she will not be given to a foreign prince like a slave. Calaf says he will forfeit his life if she discovers his identity.

Act 3 Ping, Pang and Pong offer Calaf anything he wants if he will just reveal his name; but he remains indifferent. Turandot's guards have captured Timur and Liù, who says only she knows the secret. Under torture she refuses to tell and when asked what gives her such fortitude she replies 'it is love'. She stabs herself. Calaf admonishes Turandot for her cruelty and then kisses her. Powerless, Turandot begs Calaf to go and take his secret with

him; but he reveals his name and dedicates his life to Turandot. She announces that she has discovered the stranger's name: it is Love.

Notes:

Puccini died before he had completed the score of *Turandot*. It was finished by Franco Alfano, using sketches left by Puccini for a great love duet. Toscanini once again conducted the first performance, and at the point where Alfano took over, stopped the performance, turned to the audience, and announced: 'Here the Master's work ends'. The oriental atmosphere is less obviously evoked than in *Madama Butterfly* and the melodic sweep and harmonic structure are as far 'advanced' as Puccini ever went.

Well-known arias:

Act 1 Non piangere, Liù (Calaf)
Act 2 In questa reggia (Turandot)
Act 3 Nessun dorma (Calaf)
       Tu, che di gel sei cinta (Liù)

RECORDINGS:
Decca SET561/3 ●
London 13108 (3) (US)
John Alldis Choir/Wandsworth School
Boys' Choir/London Philharmonic
Orchestra
c. Zubin Mehta
Turandot (s) Joan Sutherland
Calaf (t) Luciano Pavarotti
Liù (s) Montserrat Caballé
Timur (bs) Nicolai Ghiaurov
Emperor (t) Peter Pears

Decca SET573 ■
London 26377 (US)
(from above)

HMV SLS5135 (3) ●
Angel SCLX3857 (3) (US)
Cathedral School Choir/Rhine Opera
Chorus/Strasbourg Philharmonic
Orchestra
c. Alain Lombard
Turandot (s) Montserrat Caballé
Calaf (t) José Carreras
Liù (s) Mirella Freni
Timur (bs) Paul Plishka
Emperor (t) Michel Sénéchal

HMV SLS921 (3) ●
Angel S-3671 (3) (US)
Chorus and Orchestra of Rome Opera
House
c. Francesco Molinari-Pradelli
Turandot (s) Birgit Nilsson
Calaf (t) Franco Corelli
Liù (s) Renata Scotto
Timur (bs) Bonaldo Giaiotti
Emperor (t) Angelo Mercuriali

RCA SER564/5 ●
RCA LSC6149 (3) (US)
Chorus and Orchestra of Rome Opera
House
c. Erich Leinsdorf
Turandot (s) Birgit Nilsson
Calaf (t) Jussi Björling
Liù (s) Renata Tebaldi
Timur (bs) Giorgio Tozzi
Emperor (t) Alessio de Paolis

Decca Ace of Diamonds GOS622/4 ■
RCA LSC-2539 (US)
(from above)

London 1308 (3) ●
London 1308 (3) (US)
Chorus and Orchestra of Accademia di
Santa Cecilia di Roma
c. Alberto Erede
Turandot (s) Inge Borkh
Calaf (t) Mario del Monaco
Liù (s) Renata Tebaldi
Timur (bs) Nicola Zaccaria
Emperor (t) Gaetano Fanelli

Above: *Birgit Nilsson in the leading role in Puccini's opera Turandot.*

PUCCINI COLLECTIONS
RCA SER5674
RCA LSC3337 (US)
'Puccini Heroines': arias from *La Bohème;
Edgar; La Fanciulla del West; Madama
Butterfly; Manon Lescaut; La Rondine;
Tosca; Le Villi*
Leontyne Price (s)

HMV ASD2632
Angel 36711 (US)
Puccini Arias from: *La Bohème; Gianni
Schicchi, Madama Butterfly; Manon
Lescaut; La Rondine; Tosca; Turandot;
Le Villi*
Montserrat Caballé (s)

Decca SPA365
'The World of Puccini' excerpts from: *La
Bohème; Tosca; Madama Butterfly;
Turandot*
Renata Tebaldi (s)
Carlo Bergonzi (t)
Ettore Bastianini (b)
George London (b)
Mario del Monaco (t)
Giuseppe di Stefano (t)

Decca 533/4
'Favourite Composer'—a two-disc
selection from earlier Decca Puccini
opera sets

HENRY PURCELL
(b. London 1659; d. London 21.11.1695)

Purcell was England's greatest composer between the death of William Byrd and the rise of Edward Elgar. Had he not died at the age of 36 and had he lived in a more ordered and sophisticated musical environment he would certainly have achieved much more—especially where opera was concerned. In vocal music Purcell was caught between the French and Italian influences in an age of transition, by the requirements of a thoroughly secularised Church. Also he was hampered by poor libretti and enfeebled stage convention. In his instrumental music, however, he could break free and establish his own style. Purcell held a number of official positions after the Restoration and in 1967 succeeded his master John Blow » as organist of Westminster Abbey. He soon became a noted and successful composer for church and theatre, and wrote much ceremonial music for Royal and State occasions.

Dido and Aeneas
Opera in Prologue and 3 Acts.
Text by Nahum Tate after Virgil.
First performance: London (Mr Josias Priest's Boarding School for Girls, Chelsea) December 1689.

Synopsis:
Prologue In spite of a Prologue appearing in the libretto, the music has never turned up. Either Purcell failed to set the music or it has been lost.
Act 1 Dido, Queen of Carthage, is consoled and encouraged by her lady-in-waiting, Belinda, to marry Aeneas; but she is uncertain. Aeneas arrives and after a cold reception is accepted. A Sorceress plots the downfall of Dido and Carthage.
Act 2 All are sheltering in a grove during the course of a hunt. A storm approaches and everyone makes for cover except Aeneas, who meets a figure of Mercury (one of the Sorceress's cronies in disguise) who tells him to leave Carthage and found the new Troy. With doubts about leaving Dido, he agrees.
Act 3 The Trojan fleet prepares to leave, much to the delight of the gloating Sorceress. Aeneas, torn between love and duty, says he will stay with Dido and defy the gods; but she remains unimpressed and he leaves. Dido, realising that death must

RECORDINGS:
L'Oiseau-Lyre SOL60047 ●
L'Oiseau SOL 60047 (US)
St Anthony Singers/English Chamber
Orchestra
c. Anthony Lewis
Dido (m-s) Janet Baker
Aeneas (b) Raimund Herincx
Belinda (s) Patricia Clark
Sorceress (m-s) Monica Sinclair

Philips 6500 131 ●
Philips 6500 131 (US)
John Alldis Choir/Academy of St-Martin-
in-the-Fields
c. Colin Davis
Dido (s) Josephine Veasey
Aeneas (b) John Shirley-Quirk
Belinda (s) Helen Donath
Sorceress (m-s) Elizabeth Bainbridge

HMV SXLP30275 ●
Angel S-36359 (US)
Ambrosian Singers/English Chamber
Orchestra
c. Sir John Barbirolli
Dido (s) Victoria de los Angeles
Aeneas (b) Peter Glossop
Belinda (s) Heather Harper
Sorceress (m-s) Patricia Johnson

DG Archiv 198 424 ●
DG Archiv 198 424 (US)
Hamburg Monteverdi Choir/NDR
Chamber Orchestra
c. Charles Mackerras
Dido (s) Tatiana Troyanos
Aeneas (b) Barry McDaniel
Belinda (s) Sheila Armstrong
Sorceress (m-s) Patricia Johnson

RCA Erato STU71091 ●
English Chamber Choir and Orchestra
c. Raymond Leppard
Dido (s) Tatiana Troyanos
Aeneas (b) Richard Sitwell
Belinda (s) Felicity Palmer
Sorceress (m-s) Patricia Kern

Vanguard HM46 ●
Vanguard HM46 (US)
Oriana Concert Choir and Orchestra
c. Alfred Deller
Dido (s) Mary Thomas
Aeneas (b) Maurice Bevan
Belinda (s) Honor Sheppard
Sorceress (c) Helen Watts

World Records SH117 ●
Mermaid Theatre Singers and Orchestra
c. Geraint Jones
Dido (s) Kirsten Flagstad
Aeneas (b) Thomas Hemsley
Belinda (s) Elisabeth Schwarzkopf
Sorceress (m-s) Arda Mandikian

Decca SET615 ●
London 1170 (US)
London Opera Chorus/Aldeburgh
Festival Strings
c. Steuart Bedford
Dido (m-s) Janet Baker
Aeneas (t) Peter Pears
Belinda (s) Norma Burrowes
Sorceress (m-s) Anna Reynolds
(Note: This recording uses the new edition
of the score made by Benjamin Britten
and Imogen Holst. It contains a number
of variants and emendations in an effort
to get as near as possible to the original,
or its nearest modern equivalent.)

come, sings her great air 'When I am laid in earth', and bids farewell to Aeneas and to life.

Notes:

Purcell's only true opera, *Dido and Aeneas* remains a landmark. The overture (lacking the Prologue music) is in the French (Lully) style and sets the true tones of the tragedy.

Well-known arias:

Act 1   Ah, Belinda, I am prest with torment (Dido)

Act 3   When I am laid to earth (Dido)

King Arthur, or the British Worthy

Drama with music in Prologue, 5 Acts and Epilogue.
Text by John Dryden.
First performance: London (Dorset Gardens Theatre) summer 1691. New York 1808; Cambridge 1928.

Notes:

This is one of the most elaborate of Purcell's 'non-operas' or, at best, 'semi-operas'. It is more in the line of a stage play with extended musical numbers. The original score was lost after the first performance, but reconstructions have been made for subsequent performance. There is some superb music embedded in this, as in other works of a similar kind, notably *The Fairy Queen* (see below). Dryden was of course a major poet and dramatist; but the conventions of the Restoration theatre prevented the emergence of a fully realised work.

RECORDING:
L'Oiseau-Lyre SOL60008/9 ○
St Anthony Singers/Philomusica of London
c. Anthony Lewis
Elsie Morison (s)
Heather Harper (s)
Mary Thomas (s)
John Whitworth (c-t)
Wilfred Brown (t)
David Galliver (t)
John Cameron (b)
Trevor Anthony (bs)
Hervey Alan (bs)

Below: *An English Opera Group production of Purcell's* King Arthur.

The Fairy Queen

Drama with music in Prologue and 5 Acts.
Text by (probably) Elkanah Settle from Shakespeare's 'A Midsummer Night's Dream'.
First performance: London (Dorset Gardens Theatre) May 1692. Cambridge 1920.

Notes:

Much the same may be said of this as of *King Arthur* (above). The music consists mostly of songs and masque-like pieces at the ends of the acts. Nothing of Shakespeare's original text was retained, not even the words of his songs. The result is a hotch-potch; but with some marvellous music. The score of this also was lost but was later recovered, following a once famous advertisement. The Cambridge production of 1920 was the first since its original première.

RECORDINGS:
Decca SET499/50 ○
London 1290 (2) (US)
Ambrosian Opera Chorus/English Chamber Orchestra
c. Benjamin Britten
Jennifer Vyvyan (s)
James Bowman (c-t)
Peter Pears (t)
Mary Wells (s)
Ian Partridge (t)
Norma Burrowes (c)
John Shirley-Quirk (b)
Owen Brannigan (bs)

Decca SET560 ■
(from above)

L'Oiseau-Lyre OLS121/3 (p.s) ○
St Anthony Singers/Boyd Neel Orchestra
c. Anthony Lewis
Elsie Morison (s)
Jennifer Vyvyan (s)
Peter Pears (t)
John Whitworth (c-t)
Thomas Hemsley (b)
Trevor Anthony (bs)
(Note: The above recordings are given as 'abridged'. This means, of course, that the music is complete but the rest—the drama, that is, and internal references—is omitted.)

Below: *A scene from* The Fairy Queen, *based on Shakespeare's Midsummer Night's Dream.*

The Indian Queen

Play with music.
Text by John Dryden and Robert Howard.
First performance: London (Drury Lane) 1695.

Notes:

This is, like *The Tempest* (see below), even more nebulously referred to as an 'opera'. It is mostly a matter of incidental music integrated into the drama, though much of it is excellent.

RECORDINGS:
L'Oiseau-Lyre SOL294 ○
L'Oiseau-Lyre S294 (US)
St Anthony Singers/English Chamber Orchestra
c. Charles Mackerras
April Cantelo (s)
Wilfred Brown (t)
Robert Tear (t)
Christopher Keyte (bs)
Raymond Leppard (hpd)

Vanguard HM234 ○
Vanguard HM234 (2) (US)
Deller Singers/King's Music
c. Alfred Deller
Alfred Deller (c-t)
Jean Knibbs (s)
Paul Elliot (t)
Maurice Bevan (b)
Honor Sheppard (s)
(coupled with music for *Timon of Athens*)

Classics for Pleasure CFP40208 □
Vanguard HM31SD (US)
Trumpet Overture
Virtuosi di Zagreb/Virtuosi of England
c. Arthur Davidson

The Tempest

Play with music.
Text by (?) Shadwell after Shakespeare.
First performance: London (Dorset Gardens) 1695.

RECORDING:
L'Oiseau-Lyre SOL60002 □
Philomusica of London
c. Anthony Lewis
Jennifer Vyvyan (s)
Herbert Alan (bs)

SERGEI RACHMANINOV

(b. Oneg, Novgorod 1.4.1873; d. Beverly Hills, California, 28.3.1943)

Known mainly for his Second Symphony and Second Piano Concerto, Rachmaninov's vocal and operatic music is much less appreciated; yet his music for voices contains some of his best, most authentic work. He studied at the Moscow Conservatoire with Nikolai Sverev, and continued his studies with Tanayev and Arensky. In 1892 he won the Gold Medal for composition and soon became in demand all over the world as a conductor and particularly as a pianist. He visited the US for the first time in 1909, but returned to Moscow the following year and stayed there until 1917, when the Revolution drove him away for ever. He settled in America but returned to Europe for frequent visits. Rachmaninov completed three operas (the first, *Aleko* written while he was still a student). All three have been recorded but not all remain available.

Aleko

Opera in 1 Act.
Text by V. I. Nemirovich-Danchenko after Pushkin's 'The Gypsies'.
First performance: Moscow, May 9, 1893.

Synopsis:

Zemfira, daughter of the chief of the gypsies, has taken up with Aleko, a stranger from the city. He is jealous of Zemfira and when he finds her with her young gypsy lover he stabs and kills them both. The old chief rebukes Aleko for bringing trouble and disharmony to his people and leaves him to face the world alone, keeping the secret of his guilt as best he may.

Notes:

The opera, though admired by Tchaikovsky ≫, did not make much headway after its early performances and was in fact disliked by Rachmaninov himself later in his life. The big *scena* for Aleko was one of the triumphs of Chaliapin; otherwise revivals have been few and mostly amateur.

RECORDINGS:
Balkanton BOA1530 (2) ●
Monitor 90102/3 (US)
Vocal Ensemble of Bulgarian Radio and
Television/Plovdiv Symphony Orchestra
c. Ruslan Raychev
Aleko (bs)   Nikola Gyuzelev
Gypsy Chief (bs) Dimiter Petkov
Zemfira (s)   Blagovesta
                       Karnobatlova-
                       Dobreva
Young gypsy (t)   Pavel Kurshumov
(Note: These records are imported by
The Gramophone Exchange, 80-82
Wardour Street, London W1, England.)

HMV ASD3369 □
Angel S-37260 (US)
Intermezzo and Women's Dance
c. André Previn

Columbia SAX5278 □
Romance of the Young Gypsy
Nicolai Gedda (t)

Decca SXL6038 □
London 25769 (US)
Cavatina
Nicolai Ghiaurov (bs-b)

Right: *The Russian pianist and composer Sergei Rachmaninov.*

JEAN-PHILIPPE RAMEAU

(b. Dijon 25.9.1683; d. Paris 12.9.1764)

The son of a church organist at Dijon, Rameau received his first musical training at home. He was intended for the law and attended a Jesuit college, but as soon as his true gifts were recognised he studied music seriously and was sent to travel in Italy in the best musical circles. He soon returned to France, where he was was appointed organist first at Avignon and then at Clermont-Ferrand before going to Paris in 1705. Finding little success in Paris, he returned to Dijon and took over his father's post as organist. He subsequently worked at Lyons before returning to Clermont-Ferrand. In 1722 he again left for Paris, where his theoretical *Traité de l'harmonie* was published. This gained him some notoriety and brought his name to the attention of musical circles. He now began to make his mark in the theatre and came to occupy a two-fold position: first with Couperin, as one of the great French clavecinistes who were greatly to influence the later French composers; second, as a major figure in French baroque opera who, before Gluck ≫, laid the foundations of true music drama. In the latter he was handicapped by poor libretti and by the stultifying conventions of the time. Although he was an admirer of Lully ≫, especially in the matter of recitative, he offended the contemporary 'Lullistes' by introducing elements of French naturalism into the predominantly severe Italian style of Lully. Rameau increased the range and scope of the orchestra in opera and he also wrote, in the custom still prevailing, the hybrid form of opera-ballet as well as true opera. The former works do not really come within our scope; but we include brief references for guidance, and as they contain fine examples of Rameau's expressive style.

Hippolyte et Aricie

Tragédie in Prologue and 5 Acts.
Text by Abbé Simon Joseph de Pellegrin.
First performance: Paris (Opéra) October 1, 1733.

Synopsis:

The opera deals with the classic story from Ancient Greece, treated in drama by Euripides and Racine (*Phèdre*), in which Hippolyte (Hypolitos), the illegitimate son of Thésée (Theseus) and the Amazon Hippolyta, is made by Aphrodite to attract the violent passion of his step-mother, Phèdre, and is in turn cursed by Thésée and, before he is killed by Neptune, involved with Aricie, a princess of Athens. The opera hinges upon the latter part of the action and legend. It was revised in 1742.

Notes:

Hippolyte et Aricie was Rameau's first attempt at serious opera. It had been preceded by the *opéras-comique* and the lyric tragedy *Samson*, which were unsuccessful. *Hippolyte* aroused the opposition of the 'Lullistes' (Rameau was to suffer a similar experience in reverse when Pergolesi's ≫ *La Serva Padrona* was given in Paris and the notorious *'guerre des bouffons'* broke out between the supporters of the new light Italian style and the French classicists, represented by Rameau). After his death, Rameau's art was vindicated; but the confrontation had disturbed him. *Hippolyte et Aricie* thus became something of a spearhead, although the actual 'war' came a little later.

Below: *Rameau's first opera was* Hippolyte et Aricie *in 1733.*

The Miserly Knight

Opera in 1 Act.
Text after Pushkin.
First performance: Moscow, January 24, 1906.

Notes:

This effective 1 Act piece about a miserly knight strongly tested and provoked by a greedy and unscrupulous son and an equally unprepossessing and totally dishonest usurer, was originally intended for Chaliapin, though apparently he never actually sang it. The story is again by Pushkin and has a sharp edge of satire and irony finely matched by Rachmaninov's setting, which is taut, economical and perfectly structured. The only recording, from Russia, has not survived in the catalogue.

RECORDING:
HMV ASD2890 (d) ●
Angel S-4121 (2) (Us) (*Isle of the Dead*)
Moscow Radio Symphony Orchestra
c. Gennady Rozhdestvensky

Lev Kuznetsov (t)
Alexei Usmanov (t)
Ivan Budrin (b)
Sergei Yakovenko (b)

Francesca da Rimini

Opera with Prologue, 2 Scenes and Epilogue.
Text by Modest Tchaikovsky after Dante and Pushkin.
First performance: Moscow, January 24, 1906.

Synopsis:

Prologue   The poet Dante and the Ghost of Virgil descend into the Inferno. The Ghost tells Dante that the wretched creatures within are the souls of those who have ruined their lives with too much sexual indulgence—among them are the lovers Paolo and Francesca of Rimini.

Scene 1   Malatesta is off to war. He suspects his wife Francesca of being in love with his younger brother Paolo, who conducted Malatesta's courtship by proxy, leading Francesca to believe she was to marry him instead. Francesca tells Malatesta she wishes to enter a convent while he is away but he says he has appointed Paolo to look after her.
Scene 2   Francesca tries to resist Paolo's passionate urgings, but at last capitulates. Malatesta returns and kills them both.
Epilogue   Paolo and Francesca have told their story and departed. Dante is overcome with emotion amid sounds of the souls of the damned, lamenting happy days that are no more.

Notes:

This opera's lack of success is blamed on the libretto by Tchaikovsky's brother. The music, however, contains some of the composer's best writing.

RECORDING:
HMV Melodiya ASD3490 ●
Columbia Melodiya M2-34577 (2) (US)
Bolshoi Theatre Chorus and Orchestra
c. Mark Ermler
Dante (t)   Alexander Laptyev
Ghost of Virgil (b) Michael Maslov
Francesca (s)   Makvala Kasrashvili
Paolo (t)   Vladimir Atlantov
Lancetto (bs)   Yevgeny Nestorenko

RECORDINGS:
L'Oiseau-Lyre SOL286/8 ●
L'Oiseau-Lyre S286/8 (US)
St Anthony Singers/English Chamber Orchestra
c. Anthony Lewis
Hippolyte (t) Robert Tear
Aricie (s)   Angela Hickey
Phèdre (m-s)   Janet Baker
Thésée (b)   John Shirley-Quirk

CBS 79314 (3) ●
English Bach Festival Chorus/La Grande Ecurie et la Chambre du Roy
c. Jean-Claude Malgoire
Hippolyte (t) Ian Caley
Aricie (s)   Arleen Augér
Phèdre (m-s)   Carolyn Watkinson
Thésée (bs)   Ulrik Cold

Les Indes Galantes

Ballet héroique in 3 Acts.
Text by Louis Fuzelier.
First performance: Paris (Opéra) August 23, 1735.

RECORDING:
Erato STU70850/3 ●
Chorus/Orchestra Paillard
c. Jean-Francois Paillard
Hébé (s)   Gerda Hartman
Osman (b) Philippe Huttenlocher

CBS 77365 (3) (d) ●
Columbia M3-32973 (3) (US)
La Grande Ecurie et la Chambre du Roy
c. Jean-Claude Malgoire
Hébé (s)   Anne-Marie Rodde
Osman (b) Christian Tréguier

Castor et Pollux

Tragédie in 5 Acts.
Text by Pierre Joseph Justin Bernard.
First performance: Paris (Opéra) October 24, 1737.

Synopsis:

Act 1   Castor and Pollux, the Heavenly Twins, are both in love with Thélaïre. Castor is killed in a fight and the sorrowing Thélaïre implores Pollux to ask Jupiter to restore Castor to life.
Act 2   In spite of his own love for Thélaïre, Pollux agrees. He prays to Jupiter, who says that Castor may be restored to life if Pollux renounces immortality and if Thélaïre and Pollux take Castor's place.
Act 3   Pollux agrees, but Castor refuses, although agreeing to return for one day.
Act 4   In spite of the pleas of Thélaïre, Castor insists upon returning to the underworld.
Act 5   Jupiter relents in the face of such fraternal loyalty. He restores Pollux and grants both brothers immortality.

Notes:

Castor and Pollux was highly successful. It contains a good deal of Rameau's finest and most 'experimental' music. It achieved more than 250 performances in Paris in less than 50 years and was frequently given at the Paris Opéra up to World War II.

RECORDING:
Telefunken HF6 35048 (4) ●
Telefunken 4635048 (4) (US)
Stockholm Chamber Choir/Vienna
Concentus Musicus
c. Nikolaus Harnoncourt
Castor (t)   Zeger Vandersteene
Pollux (b)   Gérard Souzay
Minerve (s) Jeanette Scovotti
Venus (s)   Marta Schèle
Phebe (m-s) Norma Lerer
Jupiter (bs) Jacques Villisech

Les Fêtes d'Hébé

Ballet in 3 Acts.
Text by Antoine Gautier de Montdorge.
First performance: Paris (Opéra) May 21, 1739.

RECORDING:
RCA Erato STU71089 □
Monteverdi Choir and Orchestra
c. John Eliot Gardner

Act 3—La danse
Jill Gomez (s)
Anne-Marie Rodde (s)
Jean-Claude Orliac (t)

Le Temple de la Gloire

Fête in 5 Acts.
Text by Voltaire.
First performance: Versailles November 27, 1745.

RECORDING:
L'Oiseau-Lyre SOL297 □
L'Oiseau-Lyre S297 (US)
Suite No. 1
English Chamber Orchestra
c. Raymond Leppard
(this recording also contains a Grétry ballet suite)

L'Oiseau-Lyre SOL302 □
L'Oiseau-Lyre S302 (US)
Suite No. 2
English Chamber Orchestra
c. Raymond Leppard
(this recording also contains *L'Europe galante* by Campa)

Zoroastre

Tragédie in 5 Acts.
Text by Louis de Cahusac.
First performance: Paris (Opéra) December 5, 1749.

RECORDINGS:
Turnabout TV34435S □
Turnabout TV34435S (US)
Hamburg Chamber Orchestra
c. Richard Kapp
Lou Ann Wyckoff (s)
Bruce Brewer (t)

DG Archiv 2533 303 □
Seven Dances
Melkus Ensemble

MAURICE RAVEL
(b. Ciboure 7.3.1875; d. Paris 28.12.1937)

Sometimes loosely paired with Debussy », Ravel was different in almost every respect. In some ways he is closest in creative evolution to the poet W. B. Yeats; both began in the style of the late Romantic era, and each developed in the post-1918 years a more 'modernist' technique. There the parallel ends, but it is worth noting if only because it tends to highlight a direction taken by thought and feeling, and therefore art, following World War I. It had begun before that, of course: Schoenberg », Stravinsky » and Richard Strauss » had each in his way set the death seal on the Romantic movement (although Strauss was to return to something like it). After 1920 Ravel's music became more economical, more concise, more intellectual; but it still remained the production of the same creative faculty that had produced the romantically inclined, more indulgent and luxurious earlier works. Ravel's early life and training produced no conflicts. His family moved to Paris immediately after his birth; he had piano lessons as a child and went eventually to the Paris Conservatoire in 1889. Always a fastidious composer, Ravel wrote comparatively little, but through his transcriptions from one medium to another he made many of his works go a long way. If we disregard a very early operatic project on *Shéhérazade*, a subject which always fascinated him and on which he later wrote a fine song cycle, Ravel composed two small operas, *L'Heure espagnole* and *L'Enfant et les sortilèges*. Considering their suitability for recording, it is surprising that only early versions survive in the catalogue.

L'Heure Espagnole
Opera in 1 Act.
Text by Franc-Nohain (Maurice Legrand).
First performance: Paris (Opéra-Comique) May 19, 1911. London (Covent Garden) 1919; Chicago 1920; New York 1920; Milan (La Scala) 1929 (with Conchita Supervia).

Synopsis:
Scene: Toledo. Time: 18th century.
Torquemada, a staid and forgetful clockmaker, is off on his rounds. It is also the day his wife, Concepción, enjoys a little dalliance and she is rather put out when the muleteer Ramiro arrives to have his watch looked at and is told by Torquemada to wait until he returns. But he is strong and carries a heavy case clock upstairs for Concepción. Her lover Gonzalve arrives and hides in another case clock, which the dutiful Ramiro also carts upstairs. Then another of Concepción's admirers arrives: the banker Don Inigo Gomez. He is hidden in another case clock and is also carried upstairs by the eager Ramiro. He is so strong and willing that Concepción falls for him and takes him upstairs. Torquemada returns to find two dejected gentlemen hiding in his clocks—but is somewhat mollified when he sells each of them a large timepiece. Concepción and Ramiro come down and Torquemada joins in the final quintet.

Notes:
Although it is about Spain and uses Spanish idioms, *L'Heure Espagnole*, like Bizet's » *Carmen*, is not Spanish music but French music set in Spain. It is full of sophisticated wit and subtlety. A musical comedy, Ravel called it, and so it is: superior comedy and superior music.

RECORDING:
Decca Eclipse ECS786 ●
Orchestre de la Suisse Romande
c. Ernest Ansermet
Concepción (s) Suzanna Danco
Torquemada (t) Michel Hamel
Gonzalve (t) Paul Derene
Ramiro (b) Heinz Rehfuss
Don Inigo Gomez (bs) Andre Vessieres

Above: *Ravel's* L'Heure Espagnole *at the Royal Opera House.*

L'Enfant et les Sortilèges
Opera in 2 Parts.
Text by Colette.
First performance: Monte Carlo, March 21, 1925. Paris (Opéra-Comique) 1926; San Francisco 1930.

Synopsis:
Part 1 The Child is supposed to be doing his lessons. His mother sees he has done nothing except make blots on the table and he is condemned to stay alone in his room until supper. He smashes up the furniture and toy animals and starts to sulk. To his alarm the objects he has taken for inanimate come to life and turn on him. This 'war' continues until the Child takes pity on the Squirrel, whose paw has been broken. Two cats sing a love duet.
Part 2 In the garden the Child is accused of cruelty by the trees and other vegetation he has mutilated. Soon, the Child realises the error of his ways and binds the Squirrel's broken paw. Suddenly all returns to normal. The Child calls out 'Mama' and all problems are resolved.

Notes:
This opera is difficult to present. It requires a large cast for such a short work, and is so virtually untranslatable that much would be lost in the process. Colette's scenario began as a theme for a ballet submitted to the Paris Opéra. It was then sent to Ravel, who was serving at the time at the Front in World War I. He turned it into an opera and completed it in 1924.

RECORDINGS:
Decca Ace of Diamonds SDD168 ●
Richmond 33086 (US)
Geneva Motet Choir/Orchestre de la Suisse Romande
c. Ernest Ansermet
The Child (m-s) Flore Wend (s)
Mama etc (c) Marie Lise de Montmollin
Tom Cat etc (bs) Pierre Mollet
Princess/
Squirrel (s) Suzanne Danco
Frog etc (t) Hugues Cuénod

DG 138 675 (US) ●
Paris National Orchestra
c. Lorin Maazel
The Child (m-s) Françoise Ogeas (s)
Mama etc (c) Claudine Collard
Tom Cat etc (bs) Camille Mauraine (b)
Princess/
Squirrel (s) Sylvaine Gilma
Frog etc Michel Sénéchal

Below: *1939 costume design by Paul Colin for* L'Enfant et les Sortilèges.

EMIL NIKOLAUS VON REZNIČEK

(b. Vienna 4.5.1860; d. Berlin 2.8.1945)

Rezniček, like many embryo composers, originally studied law. When already a married man, he went to the Leipzig Conservatory to study music under Reinecke and Jadassohn. He gained experience as a theatre conductor and conducted a military band in Prague. From 1896 to 1899 he was court conductor at Weimar and Mannheim. In 1906 he was appointed Professor of Music in Berlin and taught at the Hochschule für Musik from 1920 to 1926. He conducted the Warsaw Opera from 1907 to 1908 and the Komische Oper in Berlin from 1908 to 1911. Rezniček wrote a number of operas, beginning with *Die Jungfrau von Orléans* in 1886, *Satanella* in 1887 and *Emerich Fortunat* in 1888, but his first and most lasting success was with *Donna Diana* in 1894. Little is now heard of his work beyond the sparkling overture to this opera, which holds promise of much pleasant music to be rediscovered.

Donna Diana
Opera in 3 Acts.
Text by Rezniček based on a comedy by Moreto.
First performance: Prague (Deutsch Theater) December 16, 1894.

RECORDINGS:
HMV ESD7010 □
Overture
c. Sir Charles Groves

Columbia MS-7085 (US) □
Overture
c. Leonard Bernstein

Decca JB47 □
London 6605 (US)
Overture
c. Willi Boskovsky

London STS-15021 and STS-15223
(US) □
Overture
c. Albert Wolff

NIKOLAI RIMSKY-KORSAKOV

(b. Tikhvin, Novgorod, 18.3.1844; d. St Petersburg 21.6.1908)

Rimsky-Korsakov began his professional life as an officer in the Russian Imperial Navy and remained so until he was 30. All the time, however, he studied music and began composing. His first symphony, written mostly while he was away on service duty, was a considerable success when Balakirev conducted it in the St Petersburg Music School in December 1865. Rimsky-Korsakov resigned from the navy in 1873, though he had been appointed professor of composition at the St Petersburg Conservatoire two years earlier. He lived to be a powerful and lasting influence on Russian musical life. He was a great master of orchestration and also had a reputation for editing and 'completing' other composers' operas, notably those of Mussorgsky » and Borodin ». Rimsky-Korsakov himself composed 17 operas, mostly on Russian historical or legendary themes. Many brought out the fantastic, often humorous side of the Russian character, but they have not been all that widely appreciated outside Russia.

The Maid of Pskov (Pskovityanka)
Opera in 4 Acts.
Text by Rimsky-Korsakov after Lev Alexandrovich Mey's play.
First performance: St Petersburg (Maryinsky Theatre) January 13, 1873. 2nd revision, St Petersburg (Panayevsky Theatre) April 18, 1895. Paris, 1909; London (Drury Lane), 1913.

RECORDINGS:
HMV SLS881 (7) □
Overture
c. Yevgeny Svetlanov

CBS 73589 □
Columbia M-34543 (US)
Prelude Act 3 *(arr. Stokowski)*
c. Leopold Stokowski

Mlada
Opera-Ballet by Rimsky-Korsakov, Borodin, Cui, Mussorgsky, Minkus (unfinished).
Text by V. A. Krilov.
First performance: None recorded (compl. 1872).

RECORDINGS:
Turnabout TV34689S □
Turnabout TV34689S (US)
Suite
c. Richard Kapp

HMV ASD3093 □
Angel S-372277 (US)
Procession of the Nobles
c. Sir Adrian Boult

HMV SXLP30101 □
Angel S-37227 (US)
Procession of the Nobles
c. Anatole Fistoulari

HMV ASD3549 □
Procession of the Nobles
c. Mark Ermler

A May Night (Msiskaya Noch)
Opera in 3 Acts.
Text by Rimsky-Korsakov after Gogol.
First performance: St Petersburg (Maryinsky Theatre) January 21, 1880. London (Drury Lane) 1914; Oxford (in English) 1931.

Synopsis:
Scene: A Russian village. Time: 19th century.
Act 1 Levko serenades his love, Hanna. She is worried that Levko's father, the Mayor, will not accept their marriage. He

Above: *Nikolai Rimsky-Korsakov.*

tells her of the legend surrounding an old castle on the far side of the lake. As the crowds return Levko hears someone singing beneath his window: his own father. Levko and his friends decide to teach the foolish old man a lesson by singing a rude song outside his house.
Act 2 The Mayor and his spinster sister-in-law are entertaining a rich man who plans to open a distillery on the site of the castle. They are interrupted by Levko and his cronies singing their song. In the ensuring mêlée the Mayor's sister-in-law is locked up by mistake and is then accused by the crowd of being a witch. The Mayor orders the streets to be cleared.
Act 3 In the ruined castle Levko sings a love song in praise of Hanna's beauty. He identifies a water nymph as being Rusalka, step-daughter of Pannochka, who drowned herself in the lake when she discovered Rusalka was a witch. In gratitude, the ghost of Pannochka gives Levko a document that will remove his father's objection to his marriage; it is in fact an indictment of the Mayor's ineptitude and an instruction for the wedding to proceed. General rejoicing follows.

Notes:
This was Rimsky-Korsakov's second opera. He wrote operas in three categories, the 'Peasant', the 'Heroic' and the 'Fantastic', this one falling into the first. The role of the Mayor was originally created by Stravinsky's father.

Well-known arias:
Act 1 Song about the Village Mayor (chorus)
Act 3 How calm, how still the night (Levko)

RECORDINGS:
DG 2709 063 (3) ●
DG 2709 063 (3) (US)
Moscow Radio Chorus and Symphony
Orchestra
c. Vladimir Fedoseyev
Mayor (bs)   Alexei Krivchenya
Levko (t)   Konstantin Lisovsky
Sister-in-Law (m-s) Anna Matyushina
Hanna (m-s)   Lyudmilla Sapegina
Clerk (bs)   Gennady Troitsky
Distiller (t)   Yuri Yelnikov

HMV ASD3200 □
Song about the Village Mayor
Soviet Army Ensemble

Decca SDD281 □
London 6012 (US)
Overture
c. Ernest Ansermet

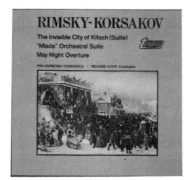

The Snow Maiden (Snegurochka)

Opera in Prologue and 4 Acts.
Text by Rimsky-Korsakov after N. Ostrovsky's play.
First performance: St Petersburg (Maryinsky Theatre) February 10, 1882. New York (Metropolitan) 1922; London (Sadler's Wells) 1933.

Synopsis:
Prologue Fairy Spring and Winter have a daughter of 16—Snegurochka, the Snow Maiden. She must be hidden from the touch of the sun god, Yarilo, or she will melt away and die. She is taken North and given into the care of the Spirit of the Wood, and is adopted by Bobil and Bobilicka, who are captivated by her beauty.
Act 1 Snegurochka falls in love with Lehl, the shepherd, but he is not interested. Mizgir, a wealthy young man who has come to marry Koupava, falls instead for Snegurochka and jilts Koupava, who in despair would take her own life but for the intervention of the cheerful Lehl.
Act 2 Koupava appeals to the Tsar for recompense. Mizgir, meanwhile, has been rejected by Snegurochka. The Tsar is so struck by Snegurochka's beauty that he declares that it is a sin against Yarilo that she has no lover, and commands that she find one.
Act 3 Festivities in the Holy Wood. Lehl sings a song which so pleases the Tsar that he is granted a free kiss from any girl he chooses. He picks out Koupava—much to Snegurochka's shame. When Mizgir pursues her, the Spirit of the Wood intervenes.
Act 4 Snegurochka appeals to her mother, who grants her wish that she be loved. But the awakening of love for her is fatal, for it means a ray from the sun god has touched her, and she must die. As she melts away Mizgir drowns himself in the lake.

Below: *The Tale of Tsar Saltan at the Bolshoi Theatre, with Petrov.*

Notes:
This is one of Rimsky-Korsakov's 'fantastic' operas and is perhaps the most lyrical and varied. As well as writing often in a broadly folk style, Rimsky-Korsakov also introduces some genuine Russian folk tunes. He was enchanted by Ostrovsky's fairy-tale of the coming of spring, and wrote the score in an unusually short time.

RECORDINGS:
HMV Melodiya SLS5102 (4) ●
Columbia Melodiya M4-34599 (4) (US)
Moscow Radio Symphony Chorus and
Orchestra
c. Vladimir Fedoseyev
Spring/Lehl (s)   Irina Arkhipova
Snegurochka
  (Snow Maiden) (s) Valentina Sokolik
Mizgir (b)   Alexander
                       Moksyakov
Koupava (s)   Lidiya
                       Zakharenko
Tsar Berendey (t) Anton Grigoriev

Decca Ace of Diamonds GOS642/5 ●
Chorus and Orchestra of Belgrade
National Opera
c. Kreshimir Baranovich
Snegurochka
  (Snow Maiden) (s) Sofyia Jankovich
Mizgir (b)   Dushan Popovich
Koupava (s)   Valeria Heybalova
Lehl (m-s)   Militza
                       Miladinovich

Tsar Berendey (t) Stepan
                       Andrashevich

Decca SDD282 □
Suite
c. Ernest Ansermet

Mlada

Opera (see Mlada above).
Text adapted from Krilov's for ballet-opera (1872).
First performance: St Petersburg (Maryinsky Theatre) November 1, 1892.

Notes:
Mlada began as a composite opera-ballet by Rimsky-Korsakov, Cui, Mussorgsky », Borodin » and Minkus, but it never made much headway. In 1892 Rimsky-Korsakov recast the libretto and set it himself.

Christmas Eve (Notch Pered Rozhdestvom)

Opera in 4 Acts.
Text by Rimsky-Korsakov after Gogol.
First performance: St Petersburg (Maryinsky Theatre) December 10, 1895.

RECORDING:
Decca Ace of Diamonds SDD281 □   Suite
London 6036 (US)   c. Ernest Ansermet

Sadko

Opera in 4 Acts.
Text by Rimsky-Korsakov and V. I. Belsky.
First performance: Moscow (Solodovnikov Theatre) January 7, 1898.

RECORDINGS:
HMV ASD3436 □   Decca Ace of Diamonds SDD281 □
Lullaby of the Sea Princess London 6036 (US)
Galina Vishnevskaya (s) Suite
                             c. Ernest Ansermet

Decca SXL6038 □
London 25769 (US)
Song of the Viking Guest
Nicolai Ghiaurov (bs-b)

The Tale of Tsar Saltan (Skazka o Tsarie Saltanie)

Opera in 4 Acts.
Text by V. I. Belsky after Pushkin.
First performance: Moscow (Solodovnikov Theatre) November 3, 1900. London 1933; New York 1937.

RECORDINGS:
HMV SXLP30190 □   HMV ASD3549 □
May you grow like a mighty oak   Angel S-40259 (US)
Bolshoi Theatre   Suite
c. Mark Ermler   c. Konstantin Ivanov

Decca Ace of Diamonds SDD282 □   Decca Ace of Diamonds SDD281 □
London 6012 (US)   London 6036 (US)
Suite   Flight of the Bumblebee
c. Ernest Ansermet   c. Ernest Ansermet

The Tsar's Bride (Tsarskays Nevesta)

Opera in 4 Acts.
Text by I. F. Tumenev after L. A. Alexandrovich.
First performance: Moscow (Solodovnikov Theatre) November 3, 1899.

Notes:

This tale of a luckless girl whose love is overwhelmed by the courtship of Tsar Ivan the Terrible is full of typically Russian inconsistencies and incomprehensibilities, but it is a vital and stimulating piece. The Tsar's theme which acts as a kind of *leitmotif* is an authentic Russian folk theme.

RECORDINGS:
HMV Melodiya SLS885 (3) (d) ●
Angel Melodiya S-4122 (US)
Bolshoi Theatre Chorus and Orchestra
c. Fuat Mansurov
Galina Vishnevskaya (s)
Irina Arkhipova (m-s)

HMV Melodiya SLS881 (7) □
Overture
c. Yevgeny Svetlanov

Pan Voyevoda

Opera in 4 Acts.
Text by I. M. Tumenev.
First performance: St Petersburg (Conservatoire) October 16, 1904.

RECORDING:
HMV ASD3549 □
Suite
c. Mark Ermler

The Legend of the Invisible City of Kitezh and the Maiden Fevronia (Skazhanie o nevidimom gradie Kitezh i dieve Fevronie)

Opera in 4 Acts.
Text by V. I. Belsky after Pushkin.
First performance: St Petersburg (Maryinsky Theatre) February 20, 1907.

RECORDINGS:
Turnabout TV34689S □
Turnabout TV34689S (US)
Suite
c. Richard Kapp

Supraphon SUAST50099 □
Suite
c. Vaclav Smetacek

Above: *Stage design for* The Golden Cockerel *at the Zimin Theatre.*

The Golden Cockerel (Zolotoy Petushok) (Coq d'Or)

Opera in 3 Acts.
Text by V. I. Belsky.
First performance: Moscow (Solodovnikov Theatre) October 20, 1909.

Notes:

For some peculiar reason the censors refused to sanction the first performance of this, Rimsky-Korsakov's last opera, and it was not given until after the composer's death. Its magnificent coloured spectacle and dramatic point have long made it a popular international success. The Orchestral Suite is also a popular favourite.

RECORDINGS:
Philips 6582 012 □
Mercury 75016 (US)
Suite
c. Antal Dorati

Supraphon SUAST50099 □
Suite
c. Vaclav Smetacek

Decca Eclipse ECS543 □
Suite
c. Ernest Ansermet

HMV ASD3141 □
Suite
c. Paavo Berglund

DG 2548 247 □
Suite
c. Igor Markevitch

Angel S-40259 (US) □
Suite
c. Konstantin Ivanov

RCA AGL1-1528 (US) □
Suite
c. Erich Leinsdorf

Turnabout 34668 (US) □
Suite
c. Charles Munch

Columbia MS-6092 (US) □
Suite
c. Eugene Ormandy

RINALDO DI CAPUA

(b. Capua or Naples c. 1710; d. Rome after 1770)

Reported to be the illegitimate son of a nobleman, little else is known of the life of this prolific Italian composer. He wrote some *opera seria* but is known mostly for his *opera buffa*, which occupied the latter part of his life. His comic operas are in the line of Pergolesi » and Cimarosa ». Rinaldo did not, as was once claimed, invent the accompanied recitative, but he was the first composer to introduce instrumental passages into the recitatives at points of strong passion or distress. Towards the end of his life he suffered a misfortune when his son sold off his carefully collected works as waste paper. The redoubtable Dr Burney, who saw Rinaldo in Rome in 1770, described him as an elderly and impoverished man. That is the last that is known about him.

La Zingara

Intermezzo in 1 Act.
Early performances: Paris (Opéra) 1753. Pesaro 1775.

Synopsis:

This simple plot revolves around the gypsy girl Nisa (La Zingara) and her plans to cajole a rich old miser for purposes other than pure love. To this end several twists occur, and, at one stage, Nisa's brother appears disguised as a bear: a turn of events that caused great astonishment at the time.

RECORDING:
Turnabout TV34033S ●
Turnabout TV34033S (US)
Mainz Chamber Orchestra
c. Gunther Kehr

Nisa (s) Anneliese Monkewitz
Tagliaborsa (t) Rodolfo Malacarne
Calcante (bs) Laerte Malaguti

GIOACCHINO ROSSINI

(b. Pesaro 29.2.1792; d. Passy (Paris) 13.11.1868)

Rossini, like Bellini » and Donizetti », was one of the three big names in Italian opera in the early part of the 19th century. He joined a theatre as accompanist and singer at the age of 13. At 15 he had already started to compose and went to the Liceo Musicale in Bologna, where he studied counterpoint with Padre Mattei and cello with Cavedagni. In 1808 his cantata *Il painto d'armonia sulla morte d'Orfeo* won first prize there, and two years later his first comic opera *La cambiale di matrimonio* was produced at the Teatro San Moisè in Venice. From then Rossini went from success to success; his progress was triumphant as opera after opera spread his fame throughout Europe . . . and filled his purse. He was best known for his *buffa*, or comic, operas; but he also had successes in the field of Italian *opera seria* and in the loose tradition of French grand historical opera. A tendency to work too hastily and leave things to the last moment, so that he had to pillage his own works for inspiration, hardly dented his reputation. Then, at the age of 37, Rossini virtually retired from composing and spent the rest of his days enjoying himself. He lived in Bologna and Paris, had a mistress (Olympe Pellissier), and entertained his friends lavishly. Although he composed no more operas, Rossini still wrote a few more works, including his *Stabat Mater* and the *Petite Messe solennelle*. Also, he was active in the encouragement of singing and took seriously his duties as Director of the Bologna Liceo, until 1847 when he was forced to leave due to political upheaval. He left Bologna, lived for a time in Florence, but returned to Paris in 1855 and spent the rest of his life there.

Above: *Gioacchino Rossini (1792-1868)—an early portrait.*

La Cambiale di matrimonio (The Marriage Market)

Comic Opera in 1 Act.
Text by Gaetano Rossi.
First performance: Venice (Teatro San Moisè) November 3, 1810.

Notes:

Rossini's first comic opera, composed when he was 18, already sets his typical tone and style. The story, wildly unbelievable,

concerns Slook, a Canadian tycoon, who is in England looking for a bride. He makes a marriage contract with Fanny, but she is in love with Eduardo, so Slook magnanimously releases her. The piece is a rarity nowadays, and the only complete recording, commissioned by the publishing firm of Ricordi, has long been unobtainable.

RECORDINGS:
Delysé DS6082/3 (d) ●
Piccolo Teatro del Collegium Musicum/
Virtuosi di Roma
c. Renato Fasano
Slook (b)   Renato Capecchi
Fanny (s)   Renata Scotti
Eduardo (t) Nicola Monti
Tobia (b)   Rolando Panerai

Decca SET247/8 □
London 1254 (2) (US)
Vorrei spiegarvi
Joan Sutherland (s)

Philips 6500 878 □
Philips 6500 878 (US)
Overture
c. Neville Marriner

L'Inganno Felice (The Happy Deceit)

Comic Opera in 1 Act.
Text by Giuseppe Foppa.
First performance: Venice (Teatro San Moisè) January 8, 1812.

RECORDING:
Philips 6500 878 □
Philips 6500 878 (US)
Overture
c. Neville Marriner

La Scala di seta (The Silken Ladder)

Comic Opera in 1 Act.
Text by Gaetano Rossi after Planard's 'L'Echelle de soie'.
First performance: Venice (Teatro San Moisè) May 9, 1812.

Notes:

This little piece has a famous overture which is generally thought to include the first appearance of the 'Rossini crescendo'.

RECORDINGS:
Philips 6500 878 □
Philips 6500 878 (US)
Overture
c. Neville Marriner

World Records SH313 □
Overture
c. Sir Thomas Beecham

DG 2530 144 □
DG 2530 144 (US)
Overture
c. Herbert von Karajan

Decca Jubilee JB 33 □
London 6204 (US)
Overture
c. Pierino Gamba

DG Heliodor 2548 171 □
Overture
c. Tullio Serafin
(Complete recording previously available
on RCA SER5502/3 (d); and Nixa
PLP591 (d) ●)

Il Signor Bruschino

Comic Opera in 1 Act.
Text by Giuseppe Foppa.
First performance: Venice (Teatro San Moisè) January 1813.

Notes:

A typically involved plot of mistaken identities and frustrated love affairs—a true operatic farce made digestible by some delightful music in Rossini's most jovial vein, as typified by the popular overture.

RECORDINGS:
Turnabout TV34158 ●
Turnabout TV34158 (US) (d)
Milan Philharmonic Orchestra
c. Ennio Gerelli
Gaudenzio (b)   Renato Capecchi
Sofia (s)   Elda Ribetti
Bruschino Sr (b) Carmelo Maugeri
Bruschino Jr (t) Carlo Rossi
Florville (t)   Luigi Pontiggia

Philips 6500 878 □
Philips 6500 878 (US)
Overture
c. Neville Marriner

DG 2530 559 □
DG 2530 559 (US)
Overture
c. Claudio Abbado

Tancredi

Opera Seria in 3 Acts.
Text by Gaetano Rossi after Tasso and Voltaire.
First performance: Venice (Teatro La Fenice) February 6, 1813.

RECORDINGS:
Philips 6500 878 □
Philips 6500 878 (US)
Overture
c. Neville Marriner

HMV SXLP30143 □
Seraphim S60058 (US)
Overture
c. Carlo Maria Giulini

Decca Eclipse ECS 531 □
Overture
c. Pierino Gamba
(This overture was purloined by Rossini
from his earlier opera *La pietra del
paragone* (1812), which has a complete
recording in the US on Vanguard71183/4)

L'Italiana in Algeri (The Italian girl in Algiers)
Comic Opera in 2 Acts.
Text by Angelo Anelli.
First performance: Venice (Teatro San Benedetto) May 22, 1813.

Synopsis:
Act 1   Mustafa, Bey of Algiers, is tired of his complaining wife
Elvira, and tries to marry her off to his Italian slave Lindoro,
who says he will marry only if he is in love. Isabella, searching
the world for her lost lover (Lindoro) is shipwrecked and
brought to the palace as a prisoner. Mustafa, who wants an
Italian wife, thinks his problems are answered.

Act 2   Isabella and Lindoro plan to escape, taking the other
Italian prisoners with them. Isabella, brought to Mustafa, puts
him to the test: he must close his eyes to all infidelitiès and sleep
soundly. He fails the first time, but tries again and falls into deep
slumber. Isabella, Lindoro and the prisoners sail away,
triumphant, and Mustafa, upon awakening, realises his mistake
and returns to Elvira.

Notes:
Rossini wrote this work at top speed, completing the score in
less than a month. Its style and structure are based on the
commedia dell'arte instead of formal operatic practice. It was an
immediate success and reveals Rossini's genius in full flood.

Well-known arias:
Act 1   Gia d'insolito ardore (Mustafa)
Act 2   Per liu, che adoro (Isabella)
Le femmine d'Italia (Haly)
Amici in ogni evento . . . Pensa alla patria (Isabella)

RECORDINGS:
Decca SET262/4 ●
London 1375 (3) (US)
Chorus and Orchestra of Maggio
Musicale, Florence
c. Silvio Varviso
Isabella (m-s) Teresa Berganza
Lindoro (t) Luigi Alva
Mustafa (bs) Fernando Corena
Elvira (s) Giuliana Tavolaccini
Haly (b) Paolo Montarsolo

Decca SXL6210 ■
(from above)

Il Turco in Italia (The Turk in Italy)
Comic Opera in 2 Acts.
Text by Felice Romani.
*First performance: Milan (La Scala) August 14, 1814. London (King's Theatre)
1821; New York 1826.*

Synopsis:
Scene: Naples. Time: 18th century.
Act 1   Prosdocimo, the poet, has been told to write a new
comedy, but thinks that yet another joke about a young wife
and old husband is too much. Just then Don Geronio, an old
man, enters with his young wife, Fiorilla, to have his fortune
told. She has a young lover, Narciso, and a new admirer: the
Turk Selim. Fiorilla thus reflects on the complexities of life, and
Prosdocimo sees his comedy emerging. In her house, Fiorilla is
entertaining Selim. Geronio enters and sets on the Turk, but the
situation is saved by Fiorilla who arranges to see Selim that
night.

Act 2   Geronio, not content with his lot, is told by the poet to
be firm. Down in the gypsy quarter Selim is looking for omens,
and sees his old love Zaida. Prosdocimo is upset at this turn in
his comedy's events; but just then Narciso enters and Fiorilla
arrives pursued by her irate husband. She and Zaida quarrel
and the poet is satisfied once more with the turn of events.

Act 3   Prosdocimo, still intent on his comedy, dispatches
Geronio to apprehend his wife and Selim. The Turk decides to
buy Fiorilla from her husband. After various confrontations
between lovers, wronged women and husband, the poet plans a
complex of disguises and mixed identities at a ball to be held that
evening. Ultimately, Fiorilla confesses her sins, Selim returns to
Turkey with Zaida, and Prosdocimo finally has the ending for
his play.

Notes:
The opera is these days given in 3 Acts instead of the original 2.
There is no other change in the structure or story.

RECORDINGS:
HMV SLS5148 (2) ●
Chorus and Orchestra of La Scala, Milan
c. Gianandrea Gavazzeni
Fiorilla (s) Maria Callas
Prosdocimo (b) Mariano Stabile
Zaida (m-s) Jolanda Gardino
Geronio (bs) Franco Calabrese
Don Narciso (t) Nicolai Gedda
Selim (bs) Nicola Rossi-Lemini

Philips 6500 878 □
Philips 6500 878 (US)
Overture
c. Neville Marriner

RCA RL31379 □
Overture
c. Claudio Abbado

Elisabetta, Regina d'Inghilterra
Opera Seria in 2 Acts.
Text by Giovanni Schmidt.
*First performance: Naples (Teatro San Carlo) October 4, 1815. London 1818;
Paris 1822.*

Synopsis:
Scene: London. Time: 16th century.
Act 1   Leicester returns from military victory in Scotland,
bringing with him sons of the Scottish nobility. Among them is
his wife Matilda, whom he has married in secret. He tells her she
is foolish to come; being a relative of Mary, Queen of Scots, she
is in great danger. Matilda knows of Elizabeth's love for
Leicester, and Norfolk, finding out about the marriage, tells the
Queen. She confronts Leicester and offers to make him her
Consort. He refuses, and the Queen has them both arrested.

Act 2   Elizabeth demands that Matilda renounce Leicester in
return for the freedom of herself and her brother Henry.
Leicester defies the Queen and tears up the document. Meanwhile,
Elizabeth sees through Norfolk's treachery and has him banished.
She goes to the Tower to visit Leicester before his execution and
Norfolk attempts to kill her; she denounces him and sentences
him to death. Leicester and Matilda are pardoned, to the acclaim
of the people.

Notes:
In this opera, Rossini made two innovations: he supported the
recitatives with orchestral accompaniment, and wrote out the
vocal ornaments. For the overture, he 'borrowed' his own
overture from the opera *Aureliano in Palmira* (1813). Indeed,

two years after writing *Elisabetta* he purloined the same overture for his *Il Barbiere di Siviglia*. Also, one of Elisabetta's arias has a striking similarity to one in *Il Barbiere*.

RECORDINGS:
Philips 6703 067 (3) ●
Philips 6703 067 (3) (US)
Ambrosian Singers/New Philharmonia
Orchestra
c. Gianfranco Masini
Elisabetta (s)   Montserrat Caballé
Leicester (t)   José Carreras
Matilde (s)   Valerie Masterton
Norfolk (t)   Ugo Benelli
Enrico (Henry) (m-s) Rosanne Creffield

Philips 6598 533 ☐
Philips 6598 533 (US)
Della cieca fortuna
José Carreras (t)

RCA RL31379 ☐
Overture
c. Claudio Abbado

Torvaldo e Dorliska

Comic Opera in 2 Acts.
Text by Cesare Sterbini.
First performance: Rome (Teatro Valle) December 26, 1815.

RECORDING:
Decca SXL6235 ☐
London 6486 (US)
Overture
c. Richard Bonynge

Il Barbiere di Siviglia (The Barber of Seville)

Comic Opera in 2 Acts.
Text by Cesare Sterbini after Beaumarchais.
First performance: Rome (Teatro Argentina) February 20, 1816. London (Haymarket) 1818; New York (in English) 1819.

Synopsis:

Scene: Seville. Time: 18th century.
Act 1   Count Almaviva is in love with Rosina, ward of old Dr Bartolo, and serenades her. Figaro plans a meeting between them. Bartolo is suspicious: he hopes to marry Rosina himself, assisted by the music master Don Basilio. The Count sings to Rosina that his name is Lindoro. Inside Bartolo's house Basilio plots. Figaro tells Rosina that Lindoro is his cousin and in love with her. Almaviva, disguised as a tipsy soldier, gains entrance to the house, but is recognised and arrested. He is released when it is discovered he is a Grandee of Spain.
Act 2   Almaviva again gets into the house, this time disguised as a music teacher, supposedly representing a sick Basilio. All goes well until Basilio arrives, but he is convinced he really is

unwell, and departs. Bartolo confronts the lovers. He arouses Rosina's jealousy and she tells of the escape she and the Count propose to make. While Bartolo fetches the police, Figaro saves the situation, producing a lawyer so that the two young lovers are safely married by the time Bartolo returns.

Notes:

The first performance of *The Barber* was a failure, partly because of the popularity of Paisiello's » opera on the same subject. But other reasons contributed to its failure: the bad production, and many signs of carelessness in the score. By the next night all the problems had been ironed out, and *The Barber* was launched upon its happy way.

Well-known arias:

Act 1   Ecco ridente in cielo (Almaviva)
         Largo al factotum (Figaro)
         Se il mio nome saper (Almaviva)
         Una voce poco fa (Rosina)
         La calumnia (Basilio)
         Dunque io son (Rosina and Figaro)
Act 2   Buona sera, mio Signore (quintet)
         Zitti, zitti, piano, piano (Rosina, Figaro and Almaviva)

RECORDINGS:
HMV SLS853 (3) ★ ●
Angel S-3559 (3) (US)
Philharmonia Chorus and Orchestra
c. Alceo Galliera
Rosina (s)   Maria Callas
Count Almaviva (t) Luigi Alva
Figaro (b)   Tito Gobbi
Bartolo (bs)   Fritz Ollendorf
Basilio (bs)   Nicola Zaccaria

Angel S-35936 (US) ■
(from above)

DG 2709 041 (3) ●
DG 2709 041 (3) (US)
Ambrosian Chorus/London Symphony
Orchestra
c. Claudio Abbado
Rosina (m-s)   Teresa Berganza
Count Almaviva (t) Luigi Alva
Figaro (b)   Hermann Prey
Bartolo (bs)   Enzo Dara
Basilio (b)   Paolo Montarsolo

DG 2538 324 ■
(from above)

Decca SET285/7 ●
London 1381 (3) (US)
Rossini Chorus and Orchestra of Naples
c. Silvio Varviso
Rosina (m-s)   Teresa Berganza
Count Almaviva (t) Ugo Benelli
Figaro (b)   Manuel Ausensi
Bartolo (bs)   Fernando Corena
Basilio (bs-b)   Nicolai Ghiaurov

Decca SXL6271 ■
London 26007 (US)
(from above)

DG Privilege 2728 005 (3) ●
Bavarian Radio Chorus and Orchestra
c. Bruno Bartoletti
Rosina (s)   Gianna d'Angelo
Count Almaviva (t) Nicola Monti
Figaro (b)   Renato Capecchi
Bartolo (bs)   Giorgio Tadeo
Basilio (bs)   Carlo Cava

Decca D38D3 (3) ●
Chorus and Orchestra of Maggio
Musicale Fiorentino
c. Alberto Erede
Rosina (m-s)   Giulietta Simionato
Count Almaviva (t) Alvinio Misciano
Figaro (b)   Ettore Bastianini
Bartolo (bs)   Fernando Corena
Basilio (bs)   Cesare Siepi

Cetra Opera Live L034 (3) (r. 1956) ●
Chorus and Orchestra of La Scala, Milan
c. Carlo Maria Giulini
Rosina (s)   Maria Callas
Count Almaviva (t) Luigi Alva
Figaro (b)   Tito Gobbi
Bartolo (bs)   Melchiorre Luise
Basilio (bs)   Nicola Rossi-Lemeni

HMV SLS985 (3) (d) ●
Angel SX-3761 (3) (US)
John Alldis Choir/London Symphony
Orchestra
c. James Levine
Rosina (s)   Beverly Sills
Count Almaviva (t) Nicolai Gedda
Figaro (b)   Sherrill Milnes
Bartolo (bs)   Renato Capecchi
Basilio (bs)   Ruggero Raimondi

Angel S-37237 (US) ■
(from above)

Cetra Opera Live L03 (3) (r. 1950) ●
Metropolitan Opera Chorus and
Orchestra
c. Alberto Erede
Rosina (s)   Lily Pons
Count Almaviva (t) Giuseppe di Stefano
Figaro (b)   Giuseppe Valdengo
Bartolo (bs)   Salvatore Baccaloni
Basilio (bs)   Jerome Hines

RCA Victrola VICS6102 (4) (d) ●
RCA LSC-6143 (4) (US)
Metropolitan Opera Chorus and
Orchestra
c. Erich Leinsdorf
Rosina (s)   Roberta Peters
Count Almaviva (t) Cesare Valletti
Figaro (b)   Robert Merrill
(One of the merits of this is that it

Left: *Henriette Sontag was a famous Rosina, in London 1828.*

represents a complete and uncut rendering of Rossini's score)

HMV SLS5156 (3) ●
Angel S-3638 (3) (US)
Glyndebourne Chorus/Royal
Philharmonic Orchestra
c. Vittorio Gui
Rosina (s)   Victoria de los
                                 Angeles
Count Almaviva (t) Luigi Alva
Figaro (b)   Sesto Bruscantini

Angel S-36207 (US) ■
(from above)

Chorus and Orchestra of Maggio
Musicale Fiorentino
c. Olivero de Fabritiis
Angelina/
   Cenerentola (m-s) Giulietta Simionato
Baron Magnifico (b) Paolo Montarsolo
Prince Ramiro (t)   Ugo Benelli
Dandini (b)   Sesto Bruscantini

Decca SET345 ■
(from above)

HMV SXLP30143 □
Seraphim S-60058 (US)
Overture
c. Carlo Maria Giulini

Otello, ossia il Moro di Venezia
Opera in 3 Acts.
Text by Marchese Francesco Berio di Salsa after Shakespeare.
First performance: Naples (Teatro del Fondo) December 12, 1816. London 1822; New York 1826.

RECORDING:
Philips 9500 098 □
Assisa a' pie d'un salice
Frederica von Stade (m-s)

La Cenerentola, ossia La Bontà in Trionfo
Comic Opera in 2 Acts.
Text by Jacopo Ferretti after Etienne's French libretto.
First performance: Rome (Teatro Valle) January 25, 1817. London (Haymarket) 1820; New York 1826.

Synopsis:
Act 1 Alidoro, philosopher and tutor to Prince Ramiro, enters the house of Don Magnifico, Baron of Mountflagon, disguised as a beggar. He finds Angelina, otherwise known as Cenerentola (or Cinderella), doing the housework. She shows him kindness while her two step-sisters (Clorinda and Thisbe) rebuff him. The Baron tells the sisters he dreamt that one of them will marry the Prince. The Prince arrives disguised as his own valet, Dandini; and immediately he and Angelina fall in love. Then Dandini arrives posing as the Prince. The sisters are invited to the ball at which the Prince will choose a bride. Angelina is told to stay home. At the ball Angelina appears as an unknown lady of quality, much to the discomfort of her two step-sisters.
Act 2 Dandini, still posing as the Prince, is rejected by Angelina, who says she is in love with his 'valet'. She tells the Prince she will marry him but he must first find out her real identity. She gives him a bracelet, keeping its pair herself. Back home, the sisters are still suspicious of the strange lady who looks so like their maid. Alidoro arranges a violent storm, and the Prince and Dandini arrive seeking shelter. Angelina tries to hide her face but the Prince sees the bracelet and all is revealed. At the palace, the wedding is prepared. Angelina obtains a pardon for the Baron and the sisters.

Notes:
La Cenerentola is full of rich Rossini humour and brilliant vocal writing, with sparkling ensembles. The name part is written for a *coloratura* contralto, a rare specimen. As with Rosina in *The Barber*, originally for mezzo, the part has often been appropriated by sopranos; but today the tendency is to return to Rossini's original conception.

Well-known arias:
Act 1 Una volta c'era un rè (Cenerentola)
Act 2 Nacqui all'affano, al pianto (Cenerentola)

RECORDINGS:
DG 2709 039 (3) ●
DG 2709 039 (US)
Scottish Opera Chorus/London
Symphony Orchestra
c. Claudio Abbado
Angelina/
   Cenerentola (m-s) Teresa Berganza
Baron Magnifico (b) Paolo Montarsolo

Prince Ramiro (t)   Luigi Alva
Dandini (b)   Renato Capecchi

DG Privilege 2538 324 (*Il Barbiere*) ■
(from above)

Decca Ace of Diamonds GOS631/3 ●
London 1376 (3) (US)

La Gazza Ladra (The Thieving Magpie)
Opera in 3 Acts.
Text by Giovanni Gherardini after d'Aubigny and Caigniez' French melodrama 'La Pie Voleuse'.
First performance: Milan (La Scala) May 31, 1817. London (King's Theatre) 1821; New York (in French) 1831.

RECORDINGS:
HMV SXLP30158 □
Seraphim S-1034 (US)
Overture
c. Sir Thomas Beecham

DG 35 2530 □
DG 35 2530 (US)
Overture
c. Claudio Abbado

HMV SXLP30143 □
Seraphim S-60058 (US)
Overture
c. Carlo Maria Giulini

Classics for Pleasure CFP 40077 □
Seraphim S-60282 (US)
Overture
c. Colin Davis

Decca Jubilee 33 □
London 6204 (US)
Overture
c. Pierino Gamba
(This is one of Rossini's most famous and popular overtures with the opening side-drum rattle and bouncy main theme. Recordings are too numerous to list individually.)

Mosè in Egitto (Moses in Egypt)
Opera in 4 Acts.
Text by Andrea Leone Tottola.
First performance: Naples (Teatro San Carlo) March 5, 1818. Revised version in French with text by G. L. Balochi and V. J. E. de Jouy, as Moïse et Pharon, Paris (Opéra) March 26, 1827.

Notes:
Rossini substantially revised and re-wrote the opera for Paris, and it is the later version which is usually heard, though to an Italian text. The famous prayer, 'Dal tuo stellato soglio' did not appear in the first performance but was added for the Naples revival a year later.

RECORDING:
Columbia TWO390 □
Dal tuo stellato soglio
Orchestra of Royal Opera House, Covent Garden and soloists
c. Lamberto Gardelli

La Donna del Lago (The Lady of the Lake)
Opera in 2 Acts.
Text by A. L. Tottola after Sir Walter Scott.
First performance: Naples (Teatro San Carlo) September 24, 1819. London (King's Theatre) 1823; New York (in French) 1829.

RECORDING:
Decca SXL6584 □
London 25910 (US)
Mura felici
Tanti affetti in tal momento
Marilyn Horne (m-s)

Semiramide
Opera seria in 2 Acts.
Text by Gaetano Rossi after Voltaire.
First performance: Venice (Teatro La Fenice) February 3, 1823. London (Haymarket) 1824; New York (Metropolitan) 1893.

Synopsis:
Act 1 Semiramide, Queen of Babylon, has murdered her husband, Nino, with the help of Assur and is in love with Arsace, the army commander who is, unknown to her, her own son. Arsace loves the Princess Azema. At the temple the ghost of Nino proclaims Arsace his successor and tells him the truth of

Arsace's relationship to Semiramide.

Act 2 Assur is furious at the news of Arsace's succession, and he goes to the temple to kill him. Semiramide, who now knows Arsace is her son, goes to warn him. As Arsace and Assur fight Semiramide intervenes and is mortally struck. Arsace becomes King of Babylon and is hailed as the avenger of his father's murder.

Notes:

Wagner's jibe about *Semiramide* exhibiting the worst traits of Italian opera was no doubt a piece of special pleading. It might not be a masterpiece; but it does contain a marvellous chance for soprano-contralto combination. Melba and Sofia Scalchi sang it at the Metropolitan in 1893, and Sutherland and Simionato in 1962. Rossini, never a slouch, wrote the opera in three weeks.

RECORDINGS:
Decca SET317/9 ●
London 1383 (3) (US)
Ambrosian Opera Chorus/London
Symphony Orchestra
c. Richard Bonynge
Semiramide (s) Joan Sutherland
Arsace (m-s) Marilyn Horne
Assur (b) Joseph Rouleau

Decca SET391 ■
London 26086 (US)
Also Decca SET456 ■
London 26169 (US)
(from above)

Le Siège de Corinthe (The Siege of Corinth)
Opera in 3 Acts.
Text by Alexandre Soumet and Luigi Balocchi.
First performance: Paris (Opéra) October 9, 1826.

Notes:

The Siege of Corinth is a French revision of an Italian *opera seria*, *Maometto II*, produced in Naples in 1820. The story concerns the siege of Greeks by the Turks in 1459.

RECORDINGS:
Decca SXL6584 □
London 25910 (US)
Arias from Act 3
Marilyn Horne (m-s)

Decca Eclipse ECS 531 □
Overture
c. Pierino Gamba

DG 2530 559 □
DG 2530 559 (US)
Overture
c. Claudio Abbado

Le Comte Ory
Opera in 2 Acts.
Text by Eugène Scribe and Charles Gaspard Delestre-Poirson.
First performance: Paris (Opéra) August 20, 1827. London (King's Theatre) 1828.

Synopsis:

The story concerns the exploits of the raffish young count in pursuit of Adèle, sister of the Comte de Formoutiers who has gone off on the crusades and left her unguarded in the castle. Despite a number of ingenious ploys the Comte Ory fails to win the lady and when the crusading warriors return the Count is unmasked.

Notes:

With the exception of *Guillaume Tell* (produced the following year) this is Rossini's only truly French opera—the others being adaptations of earlier Italian works. It has been a great favourite in France but neglected elsewhere until the Glyndebourne revival under Vittorio Gui in 1954.

RECORDING:
HMV HQM1073/4 (m) (d) ●
Glyndebourne Opera Chorus and
Orchestra
c. Vittorio Gui

Comte Ory (t) Juan Oncina
Raimbaud (b) Michel Roux
Adèle (s) Sari Barabas

Guillaume Tell (William Tell)
Opera seria in 3 Acts.
Text by Victor Joseph Étienne de Jouy and Hippolyte Louis Florent Bis, after Schiller.
First performance: Paris (Opéra) August 3, 1829. London (Drury Lane) 1830. New York (in English) 1831.

Synopsis:
Scene: Switzerland. Time: 13th century.

Act 1 At the Shepherd Festival by the Lake of Lucerne, Melchthal blesses the young couples. His son Arnold loves Mathilde but does not seek a blessing. Gessler, the tyrannical governor, arrives with his guards. Leuthold the shepherd has killed one of Gessler's men to protect his daughter, and is helped to escape by Guillaume Tell. In revenge Gessler has Melchthal arrested.

Act 2 Arnold and Mathilde meet in a valley. Arnold is told that his father, Melchthal, has been killed by Gessler. They swear to avenge him.

Act 3 In celebration of the centenary of Austrian rule in Switzerland, Gessler has his hat placed on a pole in the market place of Altdorf and requires that all bow to it. Tell refuses to bow, and is recognised as the man who helped Leuthold escape. Gessler orders Tell to show what a man he is by shooting an apple off his son Jemmy's head. Tell's arrow flies true and splits the apple. He tells Gessler that the second arrow was intended for him, if the first had failed. Gessler orders Tell's arrest; but the Swiss revolt, and Tell's second arrow fells Gessler. The tyrant's rule is broken.

Notes:

The overture is an eternal favourite and a fine piece. The opera itself is perhaps too long, but being Rossini's last opera, he probably intended it to be his masterpiece, however long.

RECORDINGS:
HMV SLS970 (5) ●
Angel S-3793 (5) (US)
Ambrosian Opera Chorus/Royal
Philharmonic Orchestra
c. Lamberto Gardelli

Guillaume Tell (b) Gabriel Bacquier
Mathilde (s) Montserrat Caballé
Arnold (t) Nicolai Gedda
Melcthal (b) Gwynne Howell
Gessler (bs) Louis Hendriks

OVERTURES

There are countless collections of Rossini overtures, and many more that have been deleted. Those from which individual items have been listed under the various operas are all recommended. Here is a collective list for convenience:

Philips 6500 878
Philips 6500 878 (US)
Academy of St-Martins-in-the-Fields
c. Neville Marriner

CBS 30108
New York Philharmonic Orchestra
c. Leonard Bernstein

Philips 9500 349
Philips 9500 349 (US)
Academy of St Martins-in-the-Fields
c. Neville Marriner

Classics for Pleasure CFP40077
Seraphim S-60282 (US)
Royal Philharmonic Orchestra
c. Colin Davis

DG 2530 144
DG 2530 144 (US)
Berlin Philharmonic Orchestra
c. Herbert von Karajan

DG 2530 559
DG 2530 559 (US)
London Symphony Orchestra
c. Claudio Abbado

RCA RL31379
London Symphony Orchestra
c. Claudio Abbado

RCA Camden CCV5020
RCA LSC2318 (US)
Chicago Symphony Orchestra
c. Fritz Reiner

Decca Jubilee JB33 *or* Eclipse ECS531
(older)
London 6204 (US)
London Symphony Orchestra
c. Pierino Gamba

DG Heliodor 2548171
Rome Opera House Orchestra
c. Tullio Serafin

HMV SXLP 30143
Seraphim S-60058 (US)
Philharmonia Orchestra
c. Carlo Maria Giulini

Other recordings of overtures not generally listed above:
HMV SXLP30203
Angel S-35890 (US)
Philharmonia Orchestra
c. Herbert von Karajan

RCA AT108
NBC Symphony Orchestra
c. Arturo Toscanini

Pye Ensato LGD023
English Chamber Orchestra
c. Enrique Garcia Asensio

Decca Phase 4 PFS4386
London 21164 (US)
Royal Philharmonic Orchestra
c. Carlos Paita

NINO ROTA
(b. Milan 3.12.1911)

Born into a family of musicians, Rota studied music in Milan with Orefice and Pizzetti and in Rome with Casella, graduating from the Conservatory of Santa Cecilia in 1929. From 1930 to 1932 he lived in America with a grant from the Curtis Institute, studying composition with Rossario Scalero and conducting with Fritz Reiner. After studying literature at Milan University, he began a teaching career in 1937. In 1950, Rota became director of the Conservatory of Bari. His earliest works were an oratorio written in 1923 and a musical play *The Swineherd Prince (Il principe porcaro)*, based on Hans Andersen, in 1926. His later operas include *Ariodante* (after Ariosto), produced in Parma in 1942; *Il Cappello di paglia di Firenze* (The Florentine Straw Hat) (Palermo, 1955); *La notte di un nevrastenico* (The Night of a Neurasthenic) (1959, and at La Scala, Milan, in 1960); and *La visita meravigliosa* (The Marvellous Visit) (Palermo, 1970). He is best known outside Italy as the composer of the music for all of Fellini's films and also for Zeffirelli's *Romeo and Juliet*, Visconti's *Rocco and his Brothers*, Coppola's *The Godfather*, and many other important Italian films. His music, as heard in *Il Cappello di paglia di Firenze*, is partly in a traditional vein, with hints of Mozart » and Donizetti », and partly in the manner of Satie or Weill », with hints of popular song and music hall. In a modern world of unappealing music it comes across with remarkable freshness and vitality.

Il Cappello di paglia di Firenze
Musical farce in 4 Acts.
Text by Ernesta and Nino Rota, based on the comedy 'The Italian Straw Hat' by Eugene Labiche and Marc-Michel.
First performance: Palermo (Teatro Massimo) April 1955. Milan (La Scala) 1958.

Synopsis:
Act 1 It is the wedding day of the wealthy Fadinard and Elena, daughter of the bumpkin Nonancourt. Fadinard's horse has eaten the expensive Florentine straw hat belonging to Anaide, who pursues him with her lover, Emilio. Elena's uncle, Vezinet, brings a present in a box. While Fadinard awaits his bride, Anaide and Emilio arrive and demand an identical replacement hat. Elena arrives with Nonancourt, who is furious because his shoes are too tight. After confessing that the hat was given her by her jealous and brutal husband, Anaide swoons; Emilio threatens a duel, and the butler, Felice, is sent to look for a new hat.

Act 2 Fadinard himself tries to buy an identical hat and learns that the only one was sold to the Baroness di Champigny. He arrives at her villa as she is preparing to entertain the famous violinist Minardi and, mistaken for the violinist, pretends to be the Baroness's suitor, asking for her hat as a keepsake. The wedding party arrives, assuming this to be the reception. The

Baroness explains that the hat has been given to her god-daughter, Madame Beaupertuis. The tipsy wedding guests burst in; Fadinard leads them away, leaving the Baroness prostrated.

Act 3 Fadinard disrupts the Beaupertuis household while seeking the hat, in spite of the opposition of Signor Beaupertuis, who proves to be Anaide's jealous husband. Again the wedding party arrives; Nonancourt changes his tight shoes for a pair of Beaupertuis's. Elena is sent to a bedroom to prepare for the wedding; Beaupertuis, believing his wife is entertaining her lover, storms in and disturbs the half-clad ladies. Nonancourt realises he is in the wrong house. Fadinard departs to try to save Anaide from her husband; Beaupertuis, limping in Nonancourt's shoes, follows with a gun.

Act 4 At home, Fadinard orders the presents returned and the wedding cancelled. Elena is determined it shall take place, despite her father's fury. When Uncle Vezinet's box proves to contain a Florentine straw hat, Fadinard hastens to fetch Anaide. The guests, leaving with their returned presents, are arrested for theft and imprisoned. Fadinard returns with Anaide to find Nonancourt has taken the hat. Emilio attempts to retrieve it from the police-post while Fadinard hides Anaide from her husband. Emilio throws the hat from a window and it lodges on an electric wire. He cuts the wire; in the resulting darkness, Anaide retrieves the hat and puts it on. She scolds her husband for his negligence. Nonancourt recognises Fadinard's good intentions and announces that the wedding will take place after all; the guests are released and celebrate. Beaupertuis forgives Anaide. Everyone goes home, leaving Fadinard and Elena exhausted, but at last united.

RECORDING:
RCA RL31153 (3) (d) ●
RCA RL31153 (3) (US)
Orchestra Sinfonica e Coro di Roma
c. Nino Rota

Fadinard (t)	Ugo Benelli
Nonancourt (bs)	Alfredo Mariotti
La Baronessa di Champigny (m-s)	Viorica Cortez
Elena (s)	Daniela Mazzuccato Meneghini
Beaupertuis (b)	Mario Basiola
Anaide (s)	Edith Martelli
Emilio (b)	Giorgio Zancanaro

Right: *Nino Rota, Milanese composer of several operas, and well known for his music for many successful films.*

JEAN-JACQUES ROUSSEAU
(b. Geneva 28.6.1712; d. Ermenonville 2.7.1778)

Famed more as a philosopher and author, Rousseau nonetheless possessed a strong and individual musical nature. He had no particular musical training apart from being a chorister until about 1730, when he was 18; but his influence on music was considerable. He is chiefly remembered for his opera *Le Devin du village* in which he sought to take the formal rhetoric out of opera and return it to nature. He wrote a great deal on music; his *Lettre sur la musique française* summing up his thoughts on the matter—that single-line melody was the only natural music and that all else, including harmony and instrumental writing, must be subservient to it.

Le Devin du Village (The Village Soothsayer)
Opera in 1 Act with spoken dialogue.
Text by Rousseau.
First performance: Fontainebleu October 18, 1752 (with overture and recitatives by Pierre de Jelyotte and Francoeur). Paris (Opéra) March 1, 1753 (Rousseau's total work); London 1776; New York 1790.

Notes:
This is one of the first operas to use spoken dialogue as an integral part of the structure. The plot is the same as for Mozart's » *Bastien and Bastienne* except for different names and the intervention of a chorus near the end. The impact of the piece came from its 'naturalism', even so, the language is more courtly than colloquial; opera still had some way to go before it could convincingly portray the common people in their own idioms.

RECORDING:
CRD/Arion ARN38157 ●
Chamber Orchestra
c. Roger Cotte

Colette (s)	Ana Maria Miranda
Colin (t)	Serge Wilfart
Le Devin (bs)	Bernard Cottret

ANTON RUBINSTEIN
(b. Vekhvotinets, Volhynia 28.11.1829; d. Peterhof 20.11.1894)

A world famous pianist and composer, Rubinstein, although of Russian nationality, was of German-Polish descent. He first appeared in public at the age of nine, later studied for a time with Liszt and was active in teaching in Germany and Russia. He was attached to the household of the Grand Duchess Helena Pavlovna for some years and continued to travel after 1854, founding the St Petersburg Conservatoire in 1862. He was a prolific composer in nearly all forms, although not a great deal of his music is regularly heard today. Of his many operas only *The Demon* has managed a tentative survival.

The Demon
Opera in Prologue and 3 Acts.
Text by Pavel Alexandrovich Viskovatov after Lermontov.
First performance: St Petersburg January 25, 1875. London (Covent Garden) 1881.

RECORDING:
Decca SXL6147 □
London 25911 (US)
I am he
Nicolai Ghiaurov (b)

ANTONIO SACCHINI
(b. Florence 14.6.1730; d. Paris 6.10.1786)

The son of a poor fisherman, he was heard singing by the composer Durante, who sent him to the Naples Conservatory and taught him composition. While there, Sacchini himself taught, and his intermezzo *Fra Donato* was produced. After his first successful opera *Andromaca*, 1761, he gave up teaching to concentrate on composition. He went to London in 1772, where he produced 17 popular operas. In 1782 he went to Paris; his masterpiece *Oedipe à Colone* (1785) was suppressed through political intrigue and the frustration was said to have hastened his death. Although he wrote some 60 operas, his work has not survived.

La Contadina in Corte
Opera in 2 Acts.
Text by Sacchini.
First performance: Rome 1765. Vienna 1782.

RECORDING:
Decca SXL6531 □
London 6735 (US)
Overture
c. Richard Bonynge

CAMILLE SAINT-SAËNS
(b. Paris 9.10.1835; d. Algiers 16.12.1921)

A child prodigy, Saint-Saëns began serious musical study at seven and in 1848 went to the Paris Conservatoire as an organ scholar, and studied under Benoist and Halévy ». In 1853 he was appointed organist at the Saint-Merry church, Paris; in 1857 he was appointed to the Madeleine. He was a prolific composer who, although largely traditional and conservative in his own work, was a champion of new French music. He travelled widely and was immensely successful, a fact which led to some jealousy. An impeccable craftsman with a near infallible sense of form and apt orchestration, Saint-Saëns composed 12 operas, of which only *Samson et Dalila* has survived with any degree of international recognition.

Samson et Dalila
Opera in 3 Acts.
Text by Ferdinand Lemaire.
First performance: Weimar (Court Theatre) (in German) December 2, 1877. Paris 1890.

Synopsis:
Scene: Gaza. Time: BC.
Act 1 The Philistines are oppressing the Israelites. Samson successfully rouses the Jews from their lethargic despair, and the mocking Philistine Abimelech is killed by Samson, with his own sword. The Hebrews, led by Samson, revolt and win victory. Dalila comes with other Philistines to honour the conqueror and he falls again for her seductive beauty.
Act 2 Dalila is determined to discover the secret of Samson's huge strength. He arrives, but only to say goodbye. She seductively wins him back, but still Samson will not reveal the secret of his strength. Finally, though, he yields—his strength is his hair. Dalila, triumphant, summons the Philistines.
Act 3 Samson has had his eyes put out and is in prison. He is led to witness the celebrations of the again victorious Philistines. In Dagon's temple he is mocked and jeered at, not least by Dalila herself. He prays for one last return of his strength, and exerts all his power against two pillars, bringing the entire temple down upon the unsuspecting Philistines.

Notes:
Because of its biblical subject, the opera was banned by the French authorities and was first produced in Germany. It was finally presented in France in 1890. It was for long a popular favourite in the world's opera houses, attracting many of the leading singers of the day: Kirkby Lunn appeared in the 1909 Covent Garden revival; Caruso at the Metropolitan in 1915.

Above: Samson et Dalila *produced at the Paris Opéra in 1976.*

Well-known arias:
Act 1 Je viens célébrer la victoire (Dalila)
Act 2 Amour, viens aider ma faiblesse (Dalila)
Mon coeur s'ouvre à ta voix (Dalila)
Act 3 Bacchanale

RECORDINGS:
HMV SLS905 (3) (d)●
Angel S-3639 (3) (US)
René Duclos Choir, French Opera Orchestra
c. Georges Prêtre
Dalila (s) Rita Gorr
Samson (t) Jon Vickers
High Priest (b) Ernest Blanc

Angel S-36210 (US) ■
(from above)

RCA ARL3-0662 (d) (3) ●
RCA ARL3-0662 (3) (US)
Bavarian Radio Chorus and Orchestra
c. Giuseppe Patané
Dalila (s) Christa Ludwig
Samson (t) James King
High Priest (b) Bernd Weikl

HMV SXLP30166 or HMV SLS5104 (2) □
Angel S-31147 or Camden P 48 (2) (US)
Printemps qui commence
Maria Callas (s)

HMV ASD3459 □
Angel S-37501 (US)
Samson recherchant ma presence
Mon coeur s'ouvre à ta voix
Elena Obraztsova (s)

Decca SET439/40 □
London 1282 (US)
Samson recherchant ma presence
Amour, viens aider ma faiblesse
Mon coeur s'ouvre à ta voix
Renata Tebaldi (s)
(in Italian)

Decca Eclipse ECS 808 or Ace of Diamonds SDD222 □
London 26248 (US)
Mon coeur s'ouvre à ta voix
Regine Crespin (s)

Decca Eclipse ECS 808 □
Bacchanale
c. Anatole Fistoulari

Ascanio
Opera in 5 Acts.
Text by Louis Gallet after Dumas and Paul Meurice's 'Benvenuto Cellini'.
First performance: Paris (Opéra) March 21, 1890.

RECORDING:
Decca SET520/1 □
London 1292 (2) (US)
Chanson de Scozzone
Régine Crespin (s)

ANTONIO SALIERI
(b. Legnano 18.8.1750; d. Vienna 7.5.1825)

Salieri's principal claim to fame is the saga of his intrigues against Mozart ». It was once said he poisoned him, but that theory has long been discredited. Salieri was, in many ways, a generous and helpful man, and after Mozart's death helped his son. Yet he deliberately undermined Mozart's chances and reputation. He composed much in the style of the day, with skill but no marked originality. His many operas were quite successful but are now forgotten. Beethoven » dedicated his Op.12 violin sonatas to Salieri and also consulted him on small matters of music, even calling himself at one time 'Salieri's pupil'.

La Fiera di Venezia
Opera in 3 Acts.
Text by Gaston Boccherini.
First performance:
Vienna (Hoftheater) 1772.

RECORDING:
Decca SXL6531 □
London 6735 (US)
Sinfonia
c. Richard Bonynge

Right: *Antonio Salieri (1750-1825) was a dominant figure in the Italian opera of his time, a rival of Mozart's. Title page of* Tarara, *Paris 1787.*

ALESSANDRO SCARLATTI
(b. Palermo 2.5.1660; d. Naples 24.10.1725)

One of the most important figures in the evolution of opera, Alessandro Scarlatti may, with justice, be called the founder not only of the Neapolitan school of opera but of the entire classical style in concerted music as brought to perfection by Haydn », Mozart » and ultimately Beethoven ». He began his professional life in Rome, where his family moved when he was 12. Restrictions of the church hampered his operatic composing, but he continued to write operas for patrons in other cities. In all he composed some 115 operas, most of which contain music of great beauty but not all of which survive. In addition he wrote important chamber cantatas. Scarlatti's operatic innovations came through his ensemble of perplexity'—a device whereby several people sing at the same time about the same thing. Ultimately, this led to the quartets, quintets and sextets of later composers such as Donizetti », Bellini » and Rossini », and Verdi » and Wagner » in their turn. Scarlatti's son, Domenico, is famed for his rich series of harpsichord sonatas but he does not figure in operatic history.

Above: *Alessandro Scarlatti, who lived and worked mainly in Naples.*

L'Honestà ne gli Amori
Opera in 3 Acts.
Text by Felice Parnasso.
First performance: Rome (Palazzo Bernini) February 6, 1680.

RECORDING:
Hungaroton SLPX1289 □
Alexander Sved (b)

Il Pompeo
Opera seria in 3 Acts.
Text by Niccolo Minato.
First performance: Rome (Teatro Colonna) January 25, 1683.

RECORDINGS:
Hungaroton SXLP1289 □
Gia il sole dal Gange
Alexander Sved (b)

Pavilion SHE511 □
Gia il sole dal Gange
Eduard Hain de Larz (b)

Decca SXL6650 □
London 26391 (US)
Gia il sole dal Gange
Luciano Pavarotti (t)

Decca SXL6579 □
London 26303 (US)
O cessate di piargami
Renata Tebaldi (s)

Gli equivoci in Amore, overa la Rosaura
Opera in 3 Acts.
Text by Giovanni Battista Lucini.
First performance: Rome (French Embassy, Palazzo della Cancelleria) December, 1690.

RECORDING:
Decca Ace of Diamonds SDD206 □
Un cor da voi ferito
Elitropio d'amore

Teresa Berganza (m-s)
Felix Lavilla (p)

Pirro e Demetrio
Opera in 3 Acts.
Text by Adriano Morselli.
First performance: Naples (Teatro San Bartolomeo) January 28, 1694.

RECORDING:
L'Oiseau-Lyre SOL323 □
Rugiadose, odorose, violette graziaso
Stuart Burrows (t)

Flavio Cuniberto
Opera in 3 Acts.
Text by Matteo Noris.
First performance: Rome (Teatro Capranica) 1696.

RECORDING:
Decca Ace of Diamonds SDD206 □
Chi vuolo innamorarsi
Teresa Berganza (m-s)
Felix Lavilla (p)

La Donna Ancora e Fedele
Opera in 3 Acts.
Text by Domenico Filippo Contini.
First performance: Naples (Teatro San Bartolomeo) 1698.

RECORDING:
L'Oiseau-Lyre SOL323 □
Son tutto duolo
Stuart Burrows (t)
John Constable (p)

OTHMAR SCHOECK
(b. Brunnen 1.9.1886; d. Zürich 8.3.1957)

One of the most important and prolific of Swiss composers, Schoeck studied at the Zürich Conservatoire and later in Leipzig under Max Reger. He spent most of his life in Zürich, teaching and composing. He was a particularly fine song writer, an aptitude that passed into his operas. He worked also in hybrid forms and in incidental music of varying integration. But his true operas are genuinely dramatic and full of powerful music.

Penthesilea
Opera in 2 Acts.
Text by Schoeck based on Heinrich von Kleist's drama.
First performance: Dresden (State Opera) January 8, 1927.

Notes:
In classical mythology Penthesilea was queen of the Amazons and was slain by Achilles when she came to help the Trojans after Achilles had killed Hector. In Kleist's version both Penthesilea and Achilles are killed, thus turning the drama more in the direction of romantic passion than of classical restraint. Schoeck's music matches Kleist's conception supremely well. He uses a mixture of rhythmical speech somewhat after the manner of Carl Orff » and soaring melodic paragraphs which intensify the action with great force, notably at the magnificent climax.

RECORDING:
Harmonia Mundi 49 22485/6 ○
Hamburg Radio Choir/Cologne Radio Choir and Symphony Orchestra
c. Zdenek Macal
Penthesilea (m-s) Carol Smith

Achilles (bs) Roland Herman
Prothoe (s) Hana Janku
Diomedes (t) William Blankenship
High Priestess (c) Raili Kostia

ARNOLD SCHOENBERG
(b. Vienna 13.9.1874; d. Los Angeles 13.7.1951)

It is impossible to exaggerate the importance of Schoenberg and his work. He showed early musical ability and studied for a while with Alexander von Zemlinsky (whose sister he married), but was otherwise self-taught. He worked for a time in cabaret and operetta while advancing his own compositions, and held several teaching posts in Germany and Austria until Nazi policies forced him to leave for America, where he spent the rest of his life, teaching and composing. Schoenberg was an inspiring teacher, and among his famous pupils were Alban Berg » and Anton Webern. Schoenberg began composing in a post-Wagnerian manner, pushing chromaticism to its limits, in works such as *Verklärte Nacht*, *Gurrelieder* and the symphonic poem *Pelléas und Mélisande*. His first Chamber Symphony (1906) was a key work, creating a considerable furore when it appeared. He finally rejected tonality with his Three Pieces for piano, Op.11 (1908), and confirmed this with the Three Orchestral Pieces, Op.16. He then moved over to serialism. Although he did not invent it, he made it his own, and the leading force in modern music. He wrote a large amount of music in various forms, including two operas, the comedy *Von Heute auf Morgen* and the powerful *Moses und Aron*; he completed the text shortly before his death. There is also *Erwartung*, styled a 'monodrama' for single voice and orchestra which is sometimes described as an opera, and *Die glückliche Hand*—a 'drama mit Musik' (1910-13).

Below: *Schoenberg's* Moses und Aron *at Covent Garden in 1965.*

Von Heute auf Morgen (From One Day to Tomorrow)
Opera in 1 Act.
Text by 'Max Blonda' (Gertrud Kolisch, Schoenberg's second wife).
First performance: Frankfurt February 1, 1930. Naples 1953; Holland Festival 1958.

Synopsis:
A married couple return from a party. They quarrel. The gasman arrives demanding payment, but the wife says she has spent all the money on clothes. A singer who had taken her fancy at the party telephones, saying he has wagered that the light in the window is the light from her eyes. She says that it is an electric bulb. Whoever wins the wager must get the couple to meet them at a café. The wife dresses up, and the husband is furious with jealousy. In the end both find they really love each other and resume their natural ways.

Notes:
Although written in the 12-tone style and often complex, the work is expressive and enjoyable, with some highly effective scoring.

RECORDING:
CBS 77223 (2) (d) (US) ●
Columbia Symphony Orchestra
c. Robert Craft
Wife (s) Erika Schmidt
Husband (bs-b) Derrik Olsen
Wife's Friend (s) Heather Harper
Tenor (t) Herbert Schachtschneider

Moses und Aron
Opera in 3 Acts.
Text by Schoenberg.
First performance: Hamburg Nordwestdeutsche Rundfunk (broadcast) March 12, 1954.

Synopsis:
Act 1 Moses is summoned to lead the Israelites out of bondage. He is old and does not feel equal to the task; but is told that his brother Aron will speak for him. Both meet in the wasteland, but have different ideas about how the task should be done. They bring God's message to the Israelites, who remain perplexed and demand a God they can understand. Moses realises he has failed to deliver his message. Aron, however, rouses the people with his fervour, and celebrates his triumph as the Israelites set out on the journey through the desert.
Act 2 The Israelites are camped below Mount Sinai while Aron and the Elders complain of Moses' continued absence. Aron tries to explain that it is the result of Moses' closeness to God, and saves the situation by promising to give tangible evidence of God's form; he sends for gold. The people then rejoice in a great orgy at the Dance before the Golden Calf. It

fades away and Moses appears bearing the tablets. Aron tells him that what he has done derived from Moses' own conceptions which he was called upon to interpret. Moses smashes the tablets, and the Israelites prepare to resume their journey.

Act 3 (This part was never composed.) The libretto has a long dialogue between Moses and Aron. Aron is now a prisoner; Moses insists upon the ideal nature of his conception of God and on Aron's misrepresentation of it. Aron tries to defend himself. He is released, but falls dead. (When used, this Act is spoken.)

Notes:
Schoenberg began work on his opera in 1931 and finished Act 2 in 1932. He did not return to it for nearly 20 years. The text to Act 3 was finished but was never set to music.

RECORDINGS:
CBS 79201 (2) ●
Columbia M2-33594 (2) (US)
BBC Singers/Orpheus Boys' Choir/
BBC Symphony Orchestra
c. Pierre Boulez
Moses (speaker) Günter Reich
Aron (t) Richard Cassilly
Young girl (s) Felicity Palmer
Invalid (c) Gillian Knight
Young man (t) John Winfield
Priest (bs) Richard Angas

Young Girl (s) Eva Csapo
Invalid (c) Elfride Obrowsky
Young man (t) Roger Lucas
Priest (bs) Werner Mann
(Note: Both recordings present only the first two Acts.)

Philips 6700 084 (2) (d) ●
Philips 6700 084 (2) (US)
Chorus and Orchestra of Austrian Radio
c. Michael Gielen
Moses (speaker) Günter Reich
Aron (t) Louis Devos

FRANZ SCHUBERT
(b. Vienna 31.1.1797; d. Vienna 19.11.1828)

As one of the greatest songwriters of all time, it might be expected that Schubert would turn his hand to writing opera; indeed, he did, but success in the theatre constantly eluded him. Although some of his narrative songs contradict the contention, it has often been said that Schubert lacked dramatic sense and, whether by mischance or misjudgment, he never found a libretto that give him the proper inspiration or produced an effective work for the stage. As the theatre was the one medium that could bring real wealth and fame to a composer in Schubert's time, his failure in this realm was of real concern. Between 1814 and 1827 he produced a number of dramatic scores, fragments and sketches, never losing the hope of operatic success. He composed or began 17 stage works in all, but the only opera to be properly staged in his lifetime was the singspiel *Die Zwillingsbrüder*, commissioned by the Kärntnerthor Theater, which managed seven performances. Others have since been given isolated performances, but with the exception of one or two pleasant overtures, and the incidental music to *Rosamunde*, Schubert's stage works are still neglected. They may never find a place in the theatre, unless substantially edited and rewritten, but they contain delightful music which is well worth hearing.

Das Teufels Lustschloss
Opera in 3 Acts.
Text by Auguste von Kotzebue.
No known performances.

RECORDING:
Decca SXL6090 □
Overture
c. Istvan Kertesz

Der Vierjährige Posten
Singspiel in 1 Act.
Text by Theodor Körner.
First performance: Dresden, September 23, 1896.

RECORDING:
Philips 9500 170 □
Overture
c. Edo de Waart

Claudine von Villa Bella
Singspiel in 3 Acts.
Text by Goethe.
First performance (Act 1): Vienna (Gemeindehaus Wieden) April 26, 1913 (Acts 2 and 3 were lost in a fire).

RECORDINGS:
HMV HQS1261 □
Liebe schwärmt auf ellen Wegen
Elly Ameling (s)

HMV COLH131 (d) □
Hin und wieder fliegen die Pfeile
Elisabeth Schumann (s)

Philips 9500 170 □
Hin und wieder fleigen die Pfeile; Liebe schwärmt auf allen Wegen
Elly Ameling (s)

Above: *Franz Schubert had little success with his 15 stage works.*

Die Freunde von Salamanka
Singspiel in 2 Acts.
Text by Johann Mayrhofer.
First performance (extracts): Vienna (Musikvereinssaal) December 19, 1875. Halle, May 6, 1928.

Notes:
The Act 2 duet (No. 12) 'Gelagert unter'm hellen Dach' is immediately familiar as the melody upon which Schubert based the delightful variations of the 4th movement of his Octet, written some nine years later.

RECORDING:
Philips 9500 170 □
Gelagert unter'm hellen Dach
Elly Ameling (s)
Claes-H. Ahnsjö (t)

Die Bürgschaft
Opera in 3 Acts.
Text by unknown.
First performance: Vienna (Wiener Schubertbund) March 7, 1908.

RECORDING:
Philips 9500 170 □
Die Mutter sucht ihr liebes Kind; Welche Nacht hab'ich erlebt; Horch die Seufzer
uns'rer Mutter
Elly Ameling (s)
and others

Die Zwillingsbrüder
Singspiel in 1 Act.
Text by Georg von Hofmann, based on 'Les Deux Valentins'.
First performance: Vienna (Kärntnerthor Theater) June 14, 1820.

Synopsis:
Anton awakens Lieschen on her 18th birthday, the day of their betrothal, and gives her flowers. Lieschen's father had promised her to Franz Spiess, if he returned from the Foreign Legion within 18 years; at the last moment he appears and claims her hand, in spite of her father's entreaties. Franz, an unpleasant character, is angry at this reluctance, and rushes to the magistrate to collect a dowry of 1,000 thalers. Franz's twin brother, Friedrich, long believed dead, appears. Lieschen and

her father, believing him to be Franz, are astonished when they find him happy to bless the marriage with Anton. Friedrich is surprised to receive 1,200 thalers (the dowry plus interest). The happy couple meet the real Franz, who tries to separate them by force. They conclude that he is schizophrenic; he is arrested and taken to court. Friedrich appears and the puzzle is solved. Franz and Friedrich are delighted to be reunited; so are Lieschen and Anton.

RECORDINGS:
HMV ASD3300 (d) ●
Chorus and Orchestra of the Bavarian State Opera
c. Wolfgang Sawallisch
The Mayor/
 The Father (bs) Kurt Moll
Lieschen (s)   Helen Donath
Anton (t)   Nicolai Gedda
Franz and
 Friedrich Spiess (b) Dietrich
         Fischer-Dieskau

HMV ASD2495 (d) □
Angel S-36609 (US)
Overture
c. Yehudi Menuhin

Philips 9500 170 □
Der Vater mag wohl immer Kind mich nennen
Elly Ameling (s)

Alfonso und Estrella

Opera in 3 Acts.
Text by Franz von Schober.
First performance (abridged): Weimar, June 24, 1854 (conducted by Franz Liszt).

Notes:

Schubert thought the overture unsuitable for the work and,

intending to write another, used the original for the first performance of *Rosamunde* in 1823.

RECORDINGS:
HMV ASD2495 (d) □
Angel S-36609 (US)
Overture
c. Yehudi Menuhin

Philips 9500 170 □
Von Fels und Wald umrungen; Wer bist du, holdes Wesen; Freundlich bist du mir

erschienen; Könnt' ich ewig hier verweilen; Lass dir als Erinnerungszeichen
Elly Ameling (s)
Claes-H. Ahnsjö (t)

Philips 9500 307 *and* 6767 001 □
Könnt' ich ewig hier verweilen
Janet Baker (m-s)

Die Verschworenen

Singspiel in 1 Act.
Text by I. F. Castelli, based on Aristophanes' comedies 'Ecclesiazusae' and 'Lysistrata'.
First performance: (concert) Vienna (Musikvereinsaal) March 1, 1861; (stage) Frankfurt am Main, August 29, 1861.

Note:

The name of the opera was later changed, by order of the censor, to *Der Häusliche Krieg.*

RECORDINGS:
Philips 9500 170 □
Ich schleiche bang und still herum
Elly Ameling (s)

CBS 76476 □
Ja, wir schworen
Judith Blegen (s)

Fierrabas

Opera in 3 Acts.
Text by Josef Kupelwieser, based on the old French romance 'Fierrabas' and the legend 'Eginhard und Emma'.
First performance: (abridged concert performance) Vienna (Theater in der Josefstadt) May 7, 1835; (stage) Vienna (Redoutensaal) February 9, 1858.

RECORDING:
Decca SXL6090 □
Overture
c. Istvan Kertesz

ROBERT SCHUMANN
(b. Zwickau, Saxony 8.6.1810; d. Endenich 29.7.1856)

Unquestionably, Schumann is one of the great composers of song (*lieder*), instrumental music and even symphony (and one unchallenged concerto); but not of opera, though on one occasion he devoted time and attention to that subject. It is, therefore, hardly relevant here to examine his influence, or that of his wife, Clara, on the young Brahms and others. His single opera, though it has been occasionally revived and (quite recently) broadcast, has bequeathed an overture to the general currency; his incidental music to Byron's *Manfred* produced another. (There was an early operatic effort, *Der Corsair*, also after Byron; but only a few fragments were written.)

Genoveva

Opera in 3 Acts.
Text by Robert Reinick, adapted by Schumann, after Ludwig Tieck and Friedrich Hebbel.
First performance: Leipzig (Municipal Theatre) June 25, 1858.

RECORDINGS:
Decca SXL6320 □
Overture
c. Karl Münchinger

Columbia MS-6581 (US) □
Overture
c. Leonard Bernstein

Angel S-36606 (US) □
Overture
c. Otto Klemperer

DG 2535 805 □
DG 138955 (US)
Overture
c. Rafael Kubelik

WILLIAM SHIELD
(b. Swalwell, Co. Durham 5.3.1748; d. Brightling, Sussex 25.1.1829)

Orphaned at the age of nine, Shield was apprenticed to a shipbuilder but studied music with Charles Avison in Newcastle. He appeared as an amateur violinist and led subscription concerts at Newcastle from 1763. In 1772 he went to London to become second violinist with the Opera orchestra, and became principal viola the following year. His first opera, *The Flitch of Bacon* in 1778, was a great success and he was composer to Covent Garden from 1778 to 1791 and from 1792 to 1807. In 1791 he met Haydn » in London and visited France and Italy. He wrote treatises on harmony and thorough-bass which were published in 1800 and 1817, and in 1817 was appointed Master of the King's Music. Shield was writing at a time when Covent Garden, Drury Lane and other theatres that staged opera were regularly giving works by English composers like himself and Charles Dibdin. He produced more than 50 stage works. These were light and mainly in the prevalent Italian style but contained much pleasant music that deserves revival.

Rosina

Opera in 2 Acts.
Text by Frances Brooke.
First performance: London (Covent Garden) December 31, 1782.

RECORDINGS:
Decca SXL6254 (d) ●
The Ambrosian Singers/London Symphony Orchestra
c. Richard Bonynge
Rosina (s)   Margreta Elkins
Phoebe (s)   Elizabeth Harwood
William   Monica Sinclair (c)
Mr Belville (t) Robert Tear
Captain Belville (b) Kenneth Macdonald

Decca SET268 *and* SDD317 □
Light as thistledown; When William at Eve
Joan Sutherland (s)

Right: *William Shield.*

DMITRI SHOSTAKOVICH
(b. St Petersburg 25.9.1906; d. Moscow 9.8.1975)

Shostakovich is the most important Soviet composer after Prokofiev »; but whereas half Prokofiev's creative life was spent in the West, Shostakovich was at all times intimately involved with Soviet musical activities. He entered the St Petersburg Conservatoire in 1919, studying with Steinberg, Nikolaiev and Glazunov ». By 1925, when he left the Conservatoire, he had already shown his hand as a prolific and original composer. He made an immediate impression with his brilliant and witty First Symphony and continued to develop at a great pace. Throughout his life, Shostakovich tended to conflict with the official 'line', especially during the years of Stalin's dictatorship; despite the familiar acts of obeisance and apparent penance, there was always, as in the famous case of the Fifth Symphony and its "reply to just criticism", a certain sense of irony and irreverence concealed behind the formal gesture. He is best known for his series of symphonies—15 in all—and for an even longer series of string quartets, the medium to which he became most closely attached in his later years. He wrote, like his Soviet contemporaries, a number of 'official' works which, though entirely sincere, are no better and no worse than anyone else's. Shostakovich wrote two operas, both of which got him into trouble with the authorities, totally contrasted though they are. He left an unfinished project for an opera on Gogol's *The Gamblers*; since this was undertaken in 1942, its abandonment had nothing to do with failing health or approaching death: the increasing grind and tension of the war years, no doubt, had something to do with it. Although the two operas he completed show great merits, along with some less convincing features, it seems likely that symphony and string quartet rather than opera suited Shostakovich's creative gifts best.

Below: *Shostakovich's* The Nose *at the English National Opera.*

The Nose
Opera in 3 Acts.
Text by Y. Preis after Gogol.
First performance: Leningrad, January 18, 1930.

Synopsis:
Act 1   In Tsarist Russia, the shape of a man's nose is important, particularly among Civil Servants. The arrogant Adjutant Major Kovalev has a high opinion of himself, and is greatly shaken when his nose forsakes him, first reappearing in his barber's breakfast roll.
Act 2   Pursuing an independent existence, the Nose poses as a City Councillor, among other escapades, and treats Kovalev with contempt. He advertises for news of its whereabouts; in a passage in eight-part fugue, newspaper advertisers read out their copy.
Act 3   Arrested by the police when boarding a coach, the Nose is returned to Kovalev—but it will not fit him. A doctor, who considers purchasing it, advises pickling in vodka and vinegar. At last, Kovalev's nose is restored to its proper shape and function.

Notes:
This brilliant and brittle satire was produced successfully when 'advanced' music was not banned in the Soviet Union. Later critics decided it was a bad joke, inaugurating a period of increasingly abrasive relationships between Soviet composers and critics. The opera dropped out of circulation and, although subsequently revived, has not become fully established, although there was a 1979 production at the English National Opera.

RECORDING:
HMV Melodiya SLS5088 (2) ●
Soloists, Chorus and Instrumental
Ensemble of Moscow Musical Theatre
c. Gennady Rozhdestvensky

Plato Kouzmitch
   Kovalev (b) Edward Akhimov
The Nose   A. Lomonossov

Katerina Ismailova (Lady Macbeth of Mtsensk)
Opera in 4 Acts.
Text by Shostakovich and Y. Preis after Nikolai Leskov.
First performance: Leningrad, January 22, 1934. Moscow 1934; Cleveland 1935; Dusseldorf 1959.

Synopsis:
Scene: Russia. Time: mid-19th century.
Act 1   Katerina, married to the weak and ineffectual Zinovy Borisovich, is bored and angry, but dare not offend her wealthy father-in-law, Boris Timofeevich Ismailov. Her husband leaves on business and she begins a passionate affair with Sergei, an employee of Ismailov.
Act 2   Boris catches Sergei climbing from Katerina's window and has him bound and beaten. In revenge, Katerina kills Boris with poisoned mushrooms, but is haunted by the dead man. Zinovy questions her and begins to beat her; Katerina and Sergei strangle Zinovy and hide his body in the cellar.
Act 3   At their marriage, Katerina and Sergei are tormented by thoughts of Zinovy's body. A drunken guest goes to the cellar for replenishment and complains of a fearful smell; the rotting corpse is discovered. Katerina and Sergei try to flee but are arrested.
Act 4   The guilty couple are condemned to Siberia. At a transit camp, Sergei takes up with Sonyetka, who promises to yield to him in exchange for Katerina's warm stockings. Sergei persuades Katerina to give him the stockings, but when she realises his purpose she attacks Sonyetka; both plunge over a bridge and are drowned. The column of convicts sets off for Siberia.

Notes:
The opera caused a famous furore. In 1934 it was warmly praised, but by 1936 the changing political climate led to Shostakovich being denounced as, among other things, bourgeois, formalist, muddled, discordant, incomprehensible and (oddly) 'leftist'. At this time, rehearsals for the Fourth Symphony—with its honourable relationships to both Mahler (Sixth Symphony) and Stravinsky (*Rite of Spring*)—were in progress. Shostakovich immediately withdrew it, replacing it a year later with the more conventional Fifth Symphony. For some years there were rumours of a revised version of the opera, but it eventually appeared with only minor musical and textual changes. Shostakovich's first title was that of Leskov's story, *Lady Macbeth of the District of Mtsensk*; this title continued in use abroad, although *Katerina Ismailova* was the title given when the composer re-edited the work in 1956.

RECORDINGS:
HMV SLS5157 (3) (original) ●
Ambrosian Opera Chorus/London
Philharmonic Orchestra
c. Msitislav Rostropovich
Katerina (s)   Galina Vishnevskaya
Boris Ismailov (bs) Dimiter Petkov
Sergei (t)   Nicolai Gedda
Zinovy Ismailov (t) Werner Krenn
Priest (bs)   Leonard Mróz
Shabby Peasant (t) Robert Tear

Melodiya/Angel S-40022 (US) ■
(from above)

BEDŘICH SMETANA
(b. Litomyšl 2.3.1824; d. Prague 12.5.1884)

Smetana was a musical prodigy, giving his first public piano recital at the age of eight, although at first his parents opposed any idea of a musical career, only yielding when his determination became clear. He went to Prague to study, on a pittance, but after initial hardships was fortunate in securing a post as music master to the family of Count Leopold Thun, on the recommendation of the director of the Conservatoire, J. B. Kittl, in 1844. He was involved in the abortive Czech uprising against Austrian rule in 1848, married his childhood sweetheart, the pianist Kateřina Kolařová, and founded a music school with the financial help of Liszt », who greatly influenced his development. In 1856 Smetana went to Sweden, where he taught at Göteborg and became conductor of the Philharmonic Society. When his wife's health failed, he decided to return to Prague: she died at Dresden on the way home, in 1859, and he returned to Sweden for a short time, after marrying Bettina Ferdinandova in 1860. After touring for a year or two, he settled finally in Prague in 1863, founding another school for national music. In 1864 the Czech National Theatre was established and he began to write for it the series of operas on which his principal fame rests, beginning with *The Brandenburgers in Bohemia*. All Smetana's operas are on Czech national subjects. For this reason, and also because they depend for their full meaning on the original language, they found difficulty in crossing national frontiers, though they had great success at home. But one, *The Bartered Bride*, became an international success, and others, notably *Dalibor*, slowly gained a wider hearing as musical horizons expanded. Smetana's orchestral music, especially the cycle of symphonic poems *Má Vlast*, is widely popular, and his piano music, owing a good deal to Liszt, has also made some headway. He became deaf in 1874, a shattering experience which found musical expression in the string quartet *From My Life*, but continued to compose until he lost his reason, spending the last year of his life in an asylum.

Above: *Smetana led the way in creating Czechoslovakian opera.*

The Brandenburgers in Bohemia (Braniboři v Čechách)

Opera in 3 Acts.
Text by Karel Sabina.
First performance: Prague (Czech Theatre) January 5, 1866.

Notes:
This, Smetana's first patriotic opera, has been likened to *Boris Godunov* in subject matter, though the libretto is flawed and Smetana had not yet found his mature voice.

RECORDING:
HMV SLS777 (3) (d) ●	**Olbramovic** (bs)	Karel Kalaš
Supraphon SUAST50541/3	**Oldrich** (b)	Jiri Joran
Chorus and Orchestra of Prague National	**Junos** (t)	Ivo Žídek
Theatre	**Ludise** (s)	Milada Subrtová
c. Jan Tichy	**Jrir** (t)	Bohumir Vich

The Bartered Bride (Prodaná nevěsta)

Opera in 3 Acts.
Text by Karel Sabina.
First performance: Prague (Czech Theatre) May 30, 1866. Revised final version 1869. Chicago 1893; London (Drury Lane) 1895 (in German).

Synopsis:
Scene: A Bohemian village. Time: mid-19th century.
Act 1 Mařenka loves Jeník, although she knows that her parents plan a more advantageous match for her. Jeník tells her that he is of good family but has been driven out by a jealous step-mother. Advised by the marriage-broker, Kečal, Mařenka's parents want her to marry Vašek, son of the landowner, Micha, by his second marriage; Micha's first son has disappeared.
Act 2 As Jeník drinks at the inn, Kečal offers him money to foresake Mařenka, but is refused. Vašek, sent by his mother to woo his bride, does not realise that Mařenka is the chosen girl; she tells him that another village girl loves him and Vašek tries to find her. Kečal, fearing for his commission, again offers Jeník money. Jeník now agrees—on condition that Mařenka marries

Micha's first son; he signs an agreement and is denounced for bartering away his beloved.
Act 3 A circus comes to the village. Vašek falls in love with Esmeralda, the tightrope walker. When a clown announces that the man who masquerades as a 'real live American bear' is drunk, Esmeralda suggests that Vašek takes his place. Vašek's parents demand that he court the bride they have chosen. Mařenka is furious because Jeník has 'sold' her, and Vašek begins to consider marrying her. Jeník treats the whole affair as a joke and tells the furious Mařenka to sign the contract so that Kečal will give him the money. The village gathers to celebrate the betrothal of Mařenka to 'the son of Tobias Micha'. Jeník is recognised by Micha and his wife as the son of Micha's first marriage; Mařenka, asked to choose between her two suitors, immediately chooses Jeník. The frustrated Kečal becomes a laughing stock. A bear enters; panic threatens until a voice from within the skin assures everyone that it is only poor Vašek.

Notes:
The Bartered Bride is a 'folk opera' of the best kind, full of delightful tunes and national dances, with the famous overture setting the mood. But at first it was regarded in Prague as too 'Wagnerian' and not truly nationalistic in spirit.

RECORDINGS:
Angel S-3642 (3) (US) ●		HMV SXLP30199 □
RIAS Chamber Choir and Bamberg		Overture and Dances
Symphony Orchestra		c. Sir Adrian Boult
c. Rudolf Kempe		
Mařenka (s) Pilar Lorengar		Decca SPA202 □
Jeník (t) Fritz Wunderlich		Overture and Dances
Vašek (t) Marcel Cordes		c. Istvan Kertesz
Kečal (bs) Gottlob Frick		
(in German)		Seraphim S-60098 □
		Overture and Dances
Supraphon SUAST50397/9 ●		c. Rudolf Kempe
Artia S-82 (3) (US)		
Chorus and Orchestra of Prague National		Classics for Pleasure CFP40290 □
Theatre		Overture and Dances
c. Zdenek Chalabala		c. James Loughran
Mařenka (s) Drahomira Tikalová		
Jeník (t) Ivo Žídek		Columbia MS-6879 (US) □
Vašek (t) Oldrich Kovář		Overture and Dances
Kečal (bs) Eduard Haken		c. Leonard Bernstein
Rediffusion Heritage HCNL8009/10		DG 2530 244 □
(m) ●		DG 2530 244 (US) □
(previously Supraphon LVP91/3 —1954)		Dances
Smetana Theatre Chorus/Prague		c. Herbert von Karajan
National Theatre Orchestra		
c. Jaroslav Vogel		Decca PFS4144 □
Marenka (s) Milada Musilová		London 21028 (US)
Jeník (t) Ivo Žídek		Overture
Kečal (bs) Karel Kalaš		c. Stanley Black
Vašek (t) Oldrich Kovář		

Dalibor

Opera in 3 Acts.
Text by Joseph Wenzig (in German —trans. Ervín Špindler).
First performance: Prague (National Theatre) May 16, 1868. Vienna (in German) 1892; Chicago 1924.

Synopsis:

Scene: Prague. Time: 15th century.

Act 1 The knight Dalibor, having avenged the execution of his friend, Zdeněk, by laying waste Ploškovice and killing the Burgrave, faces trial before the King. The people regard Dalibor as their champion. The King calls Milada, sister of the dead Burgrave, to testify. Dalibor, claiming that his action was justified by the killing of Zdeněk (a violinist, whose solo instrument is heard throughout), defies the King. Even Milada is impressed by his steadfastness and, when he is condemned to life imprisonment, pleads for him in vain. She confesses to Jitka, an orphan befriended by Dalibor, that she loves the knight; Jitka urges her to help free him.

Act 2 Outside the castle where Dalibor is imprisoned, Jitka reveals to Vítek, Dalibor's page, that Milada has entered the prison disguised as a boy. Inside, she has become the assistant of the gaoler, Beneš, who receives warning of a popular uprising. Beneš is sympathetic when the prisoner asks for a violin and tells Milada to take it to him. Before Milada arrives, Dalibor has a vision of Zdeněk. Milada reveals her identity to him and confesses her love.

Act 3 Beneš warns the King of the danger of an uprising; he tells him of the disappearance of his young assistant and of the discovery of preparations for Dalibor's escape, which Beneš has prevented. The King condemns Dalibor, who had thought escape assured, to death. Milada, Jitka, Vítek and their followers await Dalibor's signal to attack the castle, but hear instead the tolling of the death bell. They attack; at last, Dalibor emerges with the mortally wounded Milada in his arms. As troops arrive, Dalibor stabs himself and dies with her.

Notes:

The parallel with *Fidelio* is almost too obvious to remark. 'Rescue' operas were popular everywhere, especially in an atmosphere of oppression and foreign dominance. An alternative ending has Dalibor executed before the attack, in which Milada is killed.

RECORDINGS:

Supraphon SUAST50971/3 ●
Genesis 1040/2 (US)
Chorus and Orchestra of Prague National Theatre
c. Jaroslav Krombholc
Dalibor (t) Vilém Přibyl
King Vladislav (b) Jindrich Jinrák
Milada (s) Naděžda Kniplova
Beneš (bs) Jaroslav Horácek

Supraphon LPV98/100 (d) (m) (1954) ●
Chorus and Orchestra of Prague National Theatre
c. Jaroslav Krombholc
Dalibor (t) Beno Blachut
King Vladislav (b) Václav Bednář
Milada (s) Marie Podalová
Beneš (bs) Karel Kalaš

Libuše

Opera in 3 Acts.
Text by Joseph Wenzig (in German —trans. Ervín Špindler).
First performance: Prague (Czech National Theatre) June 11, 1881. Vienna 1924.

Synopsis:

Act 1 Libuše, the pagan ruler of Bohemia, is to judge a law suit between two brothers concerning their father's estate. She prays for guidance in judging the case. One brother, Chrudoš, claims that the elder should inherit all; the other, Šťáhlav, says he will accept Libuše's judgment. She decides that the brothers must either manage the estate jointly or divide it between them. Chrudoš objects and, when the Council upholds Libuše's decision, storms out, denouncing her as a weak woman. Libuše decides to renounce power in favour of a husband, and says that she will marry her childhood sweetheart, Přemysl of Stadice.

Act 2 Lutobor, uncle of the two brothers, is distressed by the involvement in the quarrel of his daughter, Krasava, who confesses that she loves Chrudoš but rejected him to provoke him to action. Šťáhlav and his sister, Radmila, join the discussion. Lutobor orders Krasava to persuade Chrudoš to accept Libuše's judgment. Chrudoš is disabused of the suspicion that Krasava loves Šťáhlav, and the brothers are reconciled. While harvesters work near Přemysl's farmhouse, he sings of Libuše and of the peace of the countryside. News arrives that Libuše has chosen him as her husband.

Act 3 Awaiting Přemysl, Libuše confirms the brothers' reconciliation and the betrothal of Chrudoš and Krasava. She prays to the spirit of her father, Krok, before joining the bridal procession. While awaiting the arrival of Libuše and Přemysl, Šťáhlav and Krasava persuade Chrudoš to moderate his arrogant behaviour. Přemysl swears to serve the people 'and, with Libuše, asks the blessing of the gods. He orders Chrudoš to kneel before Libuše as penance for insulting her and, when Chrudoš obeys, honours him as a man of spirit and courage. Libuše, inspired, prophesies the heroic future of the Czech people in six 'pictures' of Czech history.

Notes:

Libuše was written for the opening of the Czech National Theatre in 1881. Smetana regarded it as a 'festive tableau' rather than an opera, and wanted it to be given only on those occasions for which, because of its close connection with Czech history and national aspirations, it was particularly fitted.

RECORDING:

Supraphon SUAST50701/4 (4) ●
Chorus and Orchestra of Prague National Theatre
c. Jaroslav Krombholc
Libuše (s) Naděžda Kniplová
Přemysl (b) Václav Bednár
Chrudoš (bs) Zdeněk Kroupa
Šťáhlav (t) Ivo Žídek
Krasava (s) Milada Subrtová
Lutobor (bs) Karel Berman

HMV SLS5157 (3) (original) ●
Ambrosian Opera Chorus/London Philharmonic Orchestra
c. Msitislav Rostropovich
Katerina (s) Galina Vishnevskaya
Boris Ismailov (bs) Dimiter Petkov
Zinovy Ismailov (t) Werner Krenn
Sergei (t) Nicolai Gedda

The Two Widows (Dvě vdovy)

Opera in 2 Acts.
Text by Emanuel Züngel after P. J. F. Malefille.
First performance: Prague (Czech National Theatre) March 27, 1874. New version with recitatives, Prague 1878; Hamburg 1881.

Synopsis:

Act 1 Karolina Záleska, lady of the manor, is invited to the village harvest festival. She advises her widowed cousin, Anežka, to take this opportunity to find a new husband. Mumlal, the gamekeeper, complains of an inept poacher in the woods; Karolina sends Mumlal to catch the malefactor. Ladislav, the poacher, wants nothing better than to be caught and taken to the manor, so he may be near Anežka. Karolina's order for the trial of Ladislav causes general excitement; Mumlal is asked by the young people, including Toník and Lidka, if Ladislav's arrest has anything to do with love, and they deride him when he answers brusquely.

Act 2 Ladislav sings of spring while Karolina and Anežka vie for his favours. He woos Anežka, who pretends to reject him. Karolina takes Ladislav with her to the festival, leaving Anežka disconsolate. Mumlal complains of Karolina's flirtatious behaviour at the festival, and gets a box on the ear in a comic scene with Toník and Lidka. Ladislav confesses to Karolina that love brought him to the manor; Anežka, seeing them together, draws the wrong conclusion. Alone with Karolina, Anežka

confesses her love for Ladislav, who happily overhears. All ends happily at a banquet; only Mumlal is left complaining.

Notes:
The opera is a lively comedy in what Smetana himself called 'a distinguished salon style'. It has a number of Mozartean affinities, although its early hearers again complained of Wagnerisms.

RECORDING:
Supraphon 112 2041/3 ●
Chorus and Orchestra of Prague National
Theatre
c. Frantisek Jílek
Karolina (s) Nada Sormová

Anezka (s) Marcela Machotková
Ladislav (t) Jirí Zahradnícek
Mumlal (bs) Jaroslav Horácek
Toník (t) Zdenek Svehla
Lidka (s) Daniela Sounová

The Kiss (Hubička)
Opera in 2 Acts.
Text by Eliška Krásnohorská after Karolina Světlá.
First performance: Prague (Czech National Theatre) November 7, 1876.

Synopsis:
Act 1 Lukáš is in love with Vendulka; he has married another to please his parents, but his wife is now dead. Vendulka's old aunt, Martinka, favours the match, but Paloucký, Vendulka's father, gives consent grudgingly, thinking the two are both too self-willed to get on. Vendulka refuses to let Lukáš kiss her before the wedding, causing their first quarrel. They make it up,

and then Lukáš's child is brought in. Again Lukáš tries to kiss Vendulka, and again they quarrel; Lukáš departs in a rage. Vendulka rocks the child to sleep, and falls asleep herself. Awaking to see Lukáš kissing another girl outside her window, to get his revenge, she decides she must leave this place of humiliation.
Act 2 In a wood frequented by smugglers, Lukáš seeks Vendulka and is in turn sought by his brother-in-law, Tomeš, who tells Lukáš that if he apologises Vendulka will forgive him. Vendulka arrives with Martinka, a friend of the chief smuggler, and sings of her grief, not knowing that Lukáš is nearby. Martinka tries to persuade her to return home. When Paloucký, chief smuggler, Lukáš and Tomeš arrive at Martinka's cottage, explanations are made and all is forgiven: Lukáš apologises to Vendulka and gets the kiss he desires.

RECORDING:
Rediffusion Heritage HCNL 8006/7 (m)
previously Supraphon LPV142/4 (m) (d)
(r. 1958) ●
Chorus and Orchestra of Prague National
Theatre
c. Zdenek Chalabala
Vendulka (s) Ludmilla Cervinková
Lukás (t) Ben Blachut
Paloucký (bs) Karel Kalas
Tomes (b) Premsyl Koci

(Dame) ETHEL SMYTH
(b. London 23.4.1858; d. Woking 9.5.1944)

A formidable musician and feminist, Ethel Smyth devoted a great deal of her apparently inexhaustible energy to opera. She composed six herself, had them all produced, mostly in Germany, and generally made a large impression at a time when English music, let alone English opera, was hardly regarded as indispensable. She studied at the Conservatoire at Leipzig, and spent a good deal of her early life abroad. She was a passionate suffragette, but although sent to prison for the cause in 1911 she was obviously forgiven by 1922, when she was created Dame of the British Empire. It has been said that her devotion to the cause of women, plus a series of demanding personal relationships, helped diminish her artistic stature and limit her output. Yet the list of her compositions is as long as many from composers without exterior distractions, and there is no reason to suppose that the quality would have been higher had her life been other than it was. She did not compose much in her last years, partly because she seems to have become convinced that it was her sex that stood in the way of wider recognition, and partly (during her last ten years) because of a distortion in her hearing. She was

also a fluent prose writer and her autobiographical writings, in particular, have lasting value. Little of Ethel Smyth's music is, or has been, recorded. A good case could be made for her most successful opera, *The Wreckers*, which Bruno Walter warmly recommended to Gustav Mahler just before he resigned as director of the Vienna Opera; and, perhaps, another for *The Boatswain's Mate*, a jolly piece based on a story by W. W. Jacobs. The overture to the former was a favourite of Sir Thomas Beecham, on whom Ethel Smyth wrote a memorable monograph in 1935.

The Wreckers
Opera in 3 Acts.
Text by Henry Brewster in French from his drama 'Les Baufrageurs'.
First performance: Leipzig, November 11, 1906. London 1909.

RECORDING:
HMV ASD2400 □
Overture
c. Sir Alexander Gibson

LOUIS SPOHR
(b. Brunswick 5.4.1784; d. Kassel 22.10.1859)

A prolific, successful and highly popular composer and violinist of the first part of the nineteenth century, Spohr's reputation virtually died with him. He was certainly a great executant, and his compositions are unfailingly melodious, well-made—and conventional. He was a figure of significance in the musical world of his day, the associate of such as Wagner » and Mendelssohn. But, like all who remain firmly fixed within the conventions of their day, he did not outlast it and was at the mercy of changing fashion. Some of his music has been revived and gives simple pleasure, but further rehabilitation is unlikely. Spohr composed ten operas, of which only an excerpt or two is to be heard today.

Zemire und Azor
Opera in 2 Acts.
Text by Johann Jakob Ihlee, after Marmontel's French libretto.
First performance: Frankfurt, April 4, 1819. Vienna 1821.

RECORDING:
Rubini GVC45 □
Everest 3293 (US)
Rose softly blooming
Joan Sutherland (s)

Right: *Louis Spohr, whose* Faust *in 1816 is usually credited with being one of the first true romantic operas.*

GASPARO SPONTINI

(b. Maiolati 14.11.1774; d. Maiolati 24.1.1851)

Spontini was the son of poor peasants and was initially intended for the priesthood, but an uncle's help enabled him to study music. In 1791 he went to the Conservatoire de' Turchini at Naples. He produced his first opera, *I puntigli delle donne*, in Rome in 1796, and thereafter produced a series of operas, mostly in Naples and Paris. He held a number of official appointments, including court composer to the Empress Joséphine in Paris, where he first went in 1803. He was Napoleon's favourite composer, and in 1807 his opera *La Vestale* scored a triumphant success in Paris: it has remained his one lasting work. He was called to the court of Friedrich Wilhelm III in Berlin in 1820; but after that monarch's death his position became impossible, partly because of Spontini's quarrelsome and litigious behaviour. He returned to Paris in 1842, after being threatened with imprisonment in Berlin, visited various continental centres, and returned to his home town where he died three years after becoming deaf. He composed many operas; but only *La Vestale* has maintained a tenuous hold.

Above: *Spontini believed his masterpiece was* Olympia (1819).

Notes:

The libretto was originally written for Boïeldieu » and later rejected by Méhul. The score contains some famous numbers and brought Spontini instant fame. In the following 50 years it was given at the Paris Opéra 213 times and was produced in most of the world's major opera houses. It was a vehicle for the art of the late Maria Callas, who sang it at La Scala in 1955. Spontini himself claimed that he should be regarded as the successor to Gluck » rather than as the rival of Cherubini ». The subject also recalls Bellini », as does the emotional tone of several of the set pieces.

Above: *Poster for* La Vestale, *the opera that established Spontini.*

La Vestale

Opera in 3 Acts.
Text by Etienne de Jouy.
First performance: Paris (Opéra) December 16, 1807. Milan (La Scala) 1824;
London (King's Theatre) 1926; New York (Metropolitan) 1925.

Synopsis:
Scene: Ancient Rome.
Act 1 While his triumph is prepared, the victorious Licinio confesses to his friend Cinna that he still loves Giulia, who was betrothed to him before becoming a Vestal priestess. Giulia asks the Chief Priestess to excuse her from greeting the victor in the temple, but is reminded of her solemn duty. After plotting with Cinna to abduct Giulia, Licinio is crowned in triumph.
Act 2 In the temple, the Chief Priestess warns Giulia that the sacred flame must not be allowed to go out. Giulia prays that her love for Licinio may end, but when he enters she lets the sacred flame die while they declare their mutual affection. The Pontifex Maximus sentences Giulia to be buried alive for her negligence; she prays only that Licinio should not be blamed.
Act 3 Licinio rages against the sentence and Cinna fears he will resort to violence. The Pontifex Maximus refuses to show mercy, so Licinio tries to take the blame. Giulia's black veil is placed on the altar: only if it burns can she be forgiven. Ordered to descend into her tomb, she bids farewell and, to protect her lover, pretends not to know him. But a flash of lightning sets the veil alight and Giulia is forgiven by the goddess Vesta.

Well-known arias:
Act 1 E l'amore un mostro (Licinio)
Act 2 Tu che invoco . . . Su questo sacro altare (Giulia)
O nume tutelar (Giulia)
Act 3 Caro oggetto (Giulia)

RECORDINGS:

Cetra Opera Live L033 (3) (m) ●
Chorus and Orchestra of La Scala, Milan
c. Antonio Votto
Giulia (s)   Maria Callas
Licinio (t)   Franco Corelli
Chief Priestess (m-s) Ebe Stignani
Cinna (b)   Enzo Sordello
Pontifex   Nicola
Maximus (bs)   Rossi-Lemeni

HMV SLS5057 (4) □
Tu che invoco
Maria Callas (s)

Agnes von Hohenstaufen

Opera in 3 Acts.
Text by Ernst Raupach.
First performance: Berlin (Court Opera) June 12, 1829. (Act 1 alone, May 28, 1827).

Notes:

This was Spontini's last completed opera. A re-write of his earlier opera on an English subject, *Milton*, did not materialise except in fragments. Ernst Raupach was official librettist to the Berlin Opera, and together he and Spontini set to work on an operatic work based on German medieval history. True to his reputation for thoroughness, Spontini embarked upon an intensive study of the period. The subject was a new departure for him, but he was not deterred. The long Act 1 was given by itself before the opera was completed. The complete opera was produced to coincide with the wedding celebrations of Prince Wilhelm, who later became Emperor Wilhelm I of the newly-united Germany. Spontini was not satisfied with its original form: accordingly, the Baron von Lichtenstein and others reworked the libretto and Spontini himself revised the musical score. The new version was given on December 6, 1837.

RECORDING:

Cetra Opera Live L025 (3) (m) (r. 1954) ●
Orchestra and Chorus of Teatro
Communale di Firenze
c. Vittorio Gui
Francesco Albanese (s)
Franco Corelli (t)
Enzo Mascherini
Dorothy Dow
Anselmo Colzan
(In its Italian version the opera is entitled
Agnese di Hohenstaufen.)

(Sir) CHARLES VILLIERS STANFORD

(b. Dublin 30.9.1852; d. London 29.3.1924)

Although probably best remembered now as a teacher, administrator and encourager of young musicians at the beginning of the English musical renaissance, Stanford was a prolific composer. His songs and church music are still heard, but little of his orchestral and instrumental music survives in current performance. With typical Irish doggedness, he composed operas at a time when there was not much hope of production, and virtually none of securing a permanent foothold. Of his 11 operas (or rather ten operas and one Act), two were unpublished and one not produced. Of the rest, two were first produced in Germany, where he had studied as a young man. An overture and an aria or two get an occasional airing, otherwise little survives from Stanford's theatrical industry.

Shamus O'Brien

Opera in 2 Acts.
Text by George H. Jessop after Sheridan Le Fanu.
First performance: London (Opéra-Comique) March 2, 1896.

RECORDING:
Pearl GEM123 □
Overture
c. Sir Charles Stanford

Right: *Charles Stanford.*
Below: Shamus O'Brien *performed by the John Lewis Partnership Music Society.*

JOHANN STRAUSS

(b. Vienna 25.10.1825; d. Vienna 3.6.1899)

The son of a famous composer and orchestra leader, also named Johann Strauss, who tried at first to dissuade his son from following in his footsteps. Music was too much in the family blood, however, and soon young Strauss was running an orchestra in partnership with Josef Lanner. After a quarrel he formed his own and eventually, when his father died, took over his orchestra. He became renowned as a composer of music for the ballroom, especially for his fine concert waltzes which were admired by composers such as Brahms and Wagner » and made him an international figure. Initially, Strauss was not very interested in the theatre, and it was his wife who persuaded him to try his hand. His first attempt, *Die Lustigen Weiber von Wien* written in 1869, came to nothing because Strauss could not get the actress he wanted for the leading part. *Indigo* in 1871 was a moderate success, and *Karneval in Rom* in 1873 was a failure. Then, a year later, a splendid libretto inspired him to write *Die Fledermaus*—possibly the greatest Viennese operetta of all time. In spite of many other attempts, Strauss did not achieve this quality again until *Der Zigeunerbaron*. Again Strauss hit a rich vein with, in some ways, an even more substantial score than *Die Fledermaus*. His final success was *Wiener Blut* but by then he was old, and left the completion of the score to other hands and did not live to see the first performance.

Below: *Johann Strauss, whose* Die Fledermaus *is the apex of Viennese operetta.*

Indigo und die Vierzig Räuber

Operetta in 3 Acts.
Text by Maximilian Steiner.
First performance: Vienna (Theater an der Wien) February 10, 1871.

RECORDING:
Decca SXL6495 □
London 6707 (US)
Overture
c. Willi Boskovsky

Karneval in Rom (Der Carneval in Rom)

Operetta in 3 Acts.
Text by Josef Braun.
First performance: Vienna (Theater an der Wien) March 1, 1873.

RECORDING:
Decca SXL6692 □
Overture
c. Willi Boskovsky

Die Fledermaus

Operetta in 3 Acts.
Text by Carl Haffner and Richard Genée, based on the comedy 'Le Reveillon' by Henri Meilhac and Ludovic Halévy.
First performance: Vienna (Theater an der Wien) April 5, 1874. Berlin 1874; Paris 1875; London 1876; New York 1879; Vienna (Opera) 1894.

Synopsis:

Act 1 Gabriel von Eisenstein's house in Vienna. Outside, we hear Alfred, tenor, serenading Eistenstein's wife Rosalinde. Her maid, Adele, hopes to go to a ball that evening at Prince Orlofsky's, but Rosalinde refuses her leave, saying Eisenstein has to spend five days in prison. Alfred enters and tells Rosalinde he will be back later, when her husband is safely away. Eisenstein arrives with his incompetent lawyer Dr Blind, and Rosalinde puts on a great show of concern. Dr Falke enters. He has come to seek revenge on his old friend Eisenstein who, at a previous dance, had left him drunkenly, to find his way home in daylight dressed as a bat. Falke secretly persuades Eisenstein to come to Orlofsky's party before going off to jail in the morning. He agrees—and goes off to change, reappearing, to Rosalinde's surprise, in evening dress. After a song of mock farewell, Alfred arrives, in merry mood. Then Herr Frank, the prison governor, arrives to collect Eisenstein, and takes off the hapless Alfred instead.

Act 2 At Orlofsky's party. The Prince tells everyone they may do as they like as long as they stay masked. Eisenstein appears disguised as a Marquis Renard and is surprised to meet a masked lady who looks remarkably like Adele, but she convinces him otherwise. He fails, however, to recognise Rosalinde, heavily disguised as a Hungarian Countess, and flirts with her. She manages to take his chiming watch to keep as evidence, and sings a Csardas to prove her nationality. All join in a drinking song and in the end Eisenstein and Frank, now uproariously drunk, both help each other off to the prison.

Act 3 At the prison Alfred will not stop singing, to the annoyance of Frosch the drunken jailer. Adele arrives, convinced that Herr Frank can give her a stage career. Eisenstein arrives and he and Frank try to unravel the mystery of the singing prisoner. Rosalinde arrives to rescue Alfred and they are both cross-examined by Eisenstein, disguised as a lawyer. He finally reveals his identity as Falke arrives and confesses the trick he has played on them all. Everything is forgiven, and all declare that the real culprit is the demon champagne!

Well-known arias:

Act 1 So muss allein ich bleiben (Rosalinde, Eisenstein and Adele)
Trinke, Liebchen, trinke schnell (Alfred)
Act 2 Chacun à son goût (Orlofsky)
Mein Herr Marquis (Adele)
Dieser Anstand, so manierlich (Rosalinde and Eisenstein)
Klänge der Heimat (Rosalinde)
Act 3 Champagner hat's verschuldet (Rosalinde and All)

RECORDINGS:
HMV SLS964 (2) ●
Angel S-3790 (2) (US)
Vienna State Opera Chorus/Vienna
Symphony Orchestra
c. Willi Boskovsky

Eisenstein (t)	Nicolai Gedda
Rosalinde (s)	Anneliese Rothenberger
Adele (s)	Renate Holm
Prince Orlofsky	Brigitte Fassbaender (c)
Alfred (t)	Adolf Dallapozza
Dr Falke (b)	Dietrich Fischer-Dieskau

HMV ASD2891 ■
(from above)

DG 2707 088 (2) ★●
DG 2707 088 (2) (US)
Bavarian State Opera Chorus/Bavarian
State Orchestra
c. Carlos Kleiber

Eisenstein (t)	Hermann Prey
Rosalinde (s)	Julia Varady
Adele (s)	Lucia Popp
Prince Orlofsky	Iwan Rebroff (bs)
Alfred (t)	René Kollo
Dr Falke (b)	Bernd Weikl

DG 2740 176 ■
(from above)

Decca SXL6015/6 ●
London 1249 (2) (US); also 1319 (3)
(with Gala sequence)
Vienna State Opera Chorus/Vienna
Philharmonic Orchestra
c. Herbert von Karajan

Eisenstein (t)	Waldemar Kmentt
Rosalinde (s)	Hilde Gueden
Adele (s)	Erika Koth
Prince Orlofsky	Regina Resnik (c)
Alfred (t)	Giuseppe Zampieri
Dr Falke (b)	Walter Berry

Above: Die Fledermaus *at the Royal Opera House.*

Decca SXL6155 ■
London 25923 (US)
(from above)

Decca SET540/1 ●
London 1296 (2) (US)
Vienna State Opera Chorus/Vienna
Philharmonic Orchestra
c. Karl Böhm

Eisenstein (t)	Eberhard Wächter
Rosalinde (s)	Gundula Janowitz
Adele (s)	Renate Holm
Prince Orlofsky	Wolfgang Windgassen (t)
Alfred (t)	Waldemar Kmentt
Dr Falke (b)	Heinz Holecek

Decca SET600 ■
(from above)

Decca DPA585/6 (1951) ○
Vienna State Opera Chorus/Vienna
Philharmonic Orchestra
c. Clemens Krauss

Eisenstein (t)	Julius Patzak
Rosalinde (s)	Hilde Gueden
Adele (s)	Wilma Lipp
Prince Orlofsky	Sieglinde Wagner (c)
Alfred (t)	Anton Dermota
Dr Falke (b)	Alfred Poell

HMV RLS728 (2) (r. 1955) ●
Philharmonia Chorus and Orchestra
c. Herbert von Karajan

Eisenstein (t)	Nicolai Gedda
Rosalinde (s)	Elisabeth Schwarzkopf
Adele (s)	Rita Streich
Prince Orlofsky	Rudolph Christ (t)
Alfred (t)	Helmut Krebs
Dr Falke (b)	Erich Kunz

CBS 78245 (2) (in English) (r. 1950) ●
Odyssey Y2 32666 (2) (US)

New York Metropolitan Opera Chorus
and Orchestra
c. Eugene Ormandy

Eisenstein (t)	Charles Kullman
Rosalinde (s)	Ljuba Welitsch
Adele (s)	Lily Pons
Prince Orlofsky	Martha Lipton (c)
Alfred (t)	Richard Tucker
Dr Falke (b)	John Brownlee

HMV CSD1266 (in English) ■
Sadler's Wells Chorus and Orchestra
c. Wilem Tausky

Eisenstein (s)	Alexander Young
Rosalinde (s)	Victoria Elliot
Adele (s)	Marion Studholme

Classics for Pleasure CFP40251 □
(with *Der Zigeunerbaron*)
Vienna Philharmonic Orchestra
c. Heinrich Hollreiser

Eisenstein (t)	Kurt Equiluz
Rosalinde (s)	Hilde Gueden
Adele (s)	Anneliese Rothenberger

(Numerous recordings of the Overture)

Cagliostro in Wien

Operetta in 3 Acts.
Text by F. Zell and Richard Genée.
First performance: Vienna (Theater an der Wien) February 27, 1875.

RECORDING:
Decca SXL6332 □
Overture
c. Willi Boskovsky

Blinde Kuh

Operetta in 3 Acts.
Text by Rudolf Kneisel.
First performance: Vienna (Theater an der Wien) December 18, 1878.

RECORDING:
HMV SLS5017 (4) □
Angel S-37099 (US)
Overture
c. Willi Boskovsky

Prinz Methusalem

Operetta in 3 Acts.
Text by Carl Treumann.
First performance:
Vienna (Carltheater) January 3, 1877.

RECORDING:
Decca SXL6383 (d) *or* JB47 □
Overture
c. Willi Boskovsky

Der Spitzentuch der Königin

Operetta in 3 Acts.
Text by Heinrich Bohrmann-Riegen and Richard Genée.
First performance: Vienna (Theater an der Wien) October 1, 1880.

RECORDING:
Decca SXL6332 □
Overture
c. Willi Boskovsky

JOHANN STRAUSS

Eine Nacht in Venedig
Operetta in 3 Acts.
Text by F. Zell and Richard Genée.
First performance: Berlin (Friedrich-Wilhelm Städtisches Theater) October 3, 1883. Vienna (Theater an der Wien) 1883. New version by Hubert Marischka and Erich Korngold, Vienna (State Opera) 1923. London 1944.

Synopsis:
Scene: A small square in Venice. Time: 18th century.

Act 1 Carnival time, and Guido, the amorous Duke of Urbino, is arranging a lavish reception for the senators and their wives. The ageing Senator Delacqua, who has a young and very beautiful wife, Barbara, is worried about the Duke's intentions. So he sends her off to visit her aunt at Murano, and plans to take his cook, Ciboletta, along in her place. His plan is overheard by Caramello, the Duke's confidante and barber. He takes the place of the gondolier and intends to convey Barbara to the Duke's reception. Barbara, however, has other ideas—to see her lover, the handsome naval officer Enrico, a nephew of her husband, at the masked carnival. So she arranges for her friend, Annina, to take her place in the gondola.

Act 2 The Duke, in his palace, awaits Barbara's arrival. Caramello enters with his masked passenger and discovers he has brought his own sweetheart along for the Duke's pleasure, and tries to drag Annina away. He reveals to the Duke that Delacqua's 'wife' is really his cook, and he keeps up the pretence. Caramello and his friend Pappacoda—Ciboletta's fiancé—(now acting as waiters) uneasily watch their respective sweethearts being ogled by the Duke, but they manage to prolong the meal, knowing that the Duke must traditionally attend the midnight carnival in St Mark's Square.

Act 3 A carnival in the Cathedral Square. The Duke is getting along excellently with Annina. Ciboletta manages to console Pappacoda, while Caramello bemoans the treachery of women. Delacqua finds his wife with Enrico, but she says she was kidnapped by an unknown gondolier and rescued by Enrico. The Duke, now in benovolent mood, restores Annina to the distraught Caramello, but makes him promise to marry her and become his steward. Everyone indulges in the carnival mood.

Well-known arias:
Act 1 Komm' in die Gondel (Caramello)
Act 2 Treu sein, das liegt mir nicht (Duke of Urbino)
Act 3 Ach! wie so herrlich zu schau'n (Lagunen Walzer) (Caramello)

RECORDINGS:
HMV 'Concert Classics'
SXDWS3043 (2) ●
Philharmonia Chorus and Orchestra
c. Otto Ackermann
Duke of Urbino (t) Nicolai Gedda
Caramello (t) Erich Kunz
Delacqua (b) Karl Dönch
Pappacoda (t) Peter Klein
Annina (s) Elisabeth Schwarzkopf
Ciboletta (s) Emmy Loose

Philips 'Fontana' 6530 047 ■
Radio Chorus, Leipzig/Dresden
Philharmonic Orchestra
c. Heinz Rögner

Duke of Urbino (t) Martin Ritzmann
Caramello (t) Harald Neukirch
Annina (s) Elisabeth Ebert

HMV SLS5017 (4) or ESD7061 □
Angel S-37099 (US)
Overture
c. Willi Boskovsky

Der Zigeunerbaron
Operetta in 3 Acts.
Text by Ignaz Schnitzer, based on the novel 'Saffi' by Maurus Jókai.
First performance: Vienna (Theater an der Wien) October 24, 1885.

Synopsis:
Scene: Near the Hungarian village of Banat. Time: mid-18th century.

Act 1 In the distance lies a derelict castle, in the foreground a deserted village with one respectable house left. In a disreputable hut Czipra, an old gypsy woman, watches Ottokar (son of Mirabella, who is governess to Arsena, daughter of the miserly pig-breeding farmer Zsupán) dig each day for a treasure which will enable him to marry Arsena. Sándor Barinkay, heir to the castle, arrives by boat with Carnero, the Commissioner for Oaths, and recounts his family history while Carnero sends for Zsupán and tells Barinkay of the fair Arsena. Czipra tells their fortunes: Barinkay will marry a wife who will discover the treasure for him, and Carnero is told he will find a treasure he has lost. Zsupán arrives and agrees to witness Barinkay's claims to the castle, and it is suggested that Barinkay might marry Arsena. Mirabella arrives, and turns out to be Carnero's long-lost wife; she had thought him lost in battle, but Carnero shows little joy at the restoration of this particular treasure. Arsena arrives but is not very co-operative as she wants to marry Ottokar, and also claims aristocratic descent which means she can only marry nobility. Barinkay, left brooding, hears a gypsy girl singing—Czipra's foster-daughter Saffi. When Saffi enters he is immediately attracted, and agrees to dine with the girl and

Below: Eine Nacht in Venedig; an English National Opera production.

her mother. Barinkay is introduced to the gypsies as the new squire, and they accept him as their baron and swear allegiance. Barinkay introduces Saffi as his wife, but Carnero is not everyone except Zsupán.

Act 2 Saffi dreams of the whereabouts of the treasure; she and Barinkay search and find it. Zsupán finds his cart stuck in the mud and orders the gypsies to help him, but instead they rob him and his cries for help bring everyone to the scene. Barkinkay introduces Saffi as his wife, but Carnero is not satisfied with the legal aspects. At this point Ottokar finds a few of the coins which Saffi and Barinkay have dropped, and is disappointed to learn that the treasure is already found. An army recruiting party arrives under the command of Homonay, a friend of Barinkay's who supports the legality of Barinkay's marriage and meanwhile pressgangs Zsupán and Ottokar into the army to fight the Spaniards. Czipra reveals that Saffi is really the daughter of the last Pasha of Hungary, and is therefore a princess; Barinkay sadly realises that he cannot marry anyone so exalted, and decides to join the army too.

Act 3 All of them are now in Vienna celebrating a victorious battle. Even Zsupán has a story to tell. The soldiers return and it is revealed that Homonay, Barinkay and Ottokar are heroes and have been given the rank of noblemen. There is now no obstacle to the marriage of Saffi and Barinkay, Ottokar and Arsena, and all rejoice.

Well-known arias:

Act 1 Als flotter Geist (Barinkay)
Ein Falter schwirrt ums Licht (Arsena)
So elend und so treu (Saffi)

Act 2 Mein Aug' bewacht (Czipra, Saffi and Barinkay)
Schatzwalzer (Czipra, Saffi)

Act 3 Wer uns getraut (Barinkay, Saffi)

RECORDINGS:

HMV 'Concert Classics' SXDW3046 (2)●
Philharmonia Chorus and Orchestra
c. Otto Ackermann
Graf Peter
  Homonay (b) Hermann Prey
Sándor Barinkay (t) Nicolai Gedda
Kálmán Zsupán (b) Erich Kunz
Arsena (s) Erika Koth
Czipra (m-s) Gertrud Burgsthaler-
      Schuster
Saffi (s) Elisabeth
      Schwarzkopf

Angel S-3612 (2) (US) ●
Singverein der Gesellschaft der Musikfreunde in Wien/Vienna Philharmonic Orchestra
c. Heinrich Hollreiser

Graf Peter
  Homonay (b) Walter Berry
Sándor Barinkay (t) Karl Terkal
Kálmán Zsupán (b) Erich Kunz
Arsena (s) Anneliese
      Rothenberger
Czipra (m-s) Hilde Rössl-Majdan
Saffi (s) Hilde Gueden

Classics for Pleasure CFP40251 □
(with *Die Fledermaus*)
(from above)

Decca SXL6256 □
Overture and Entrance March
c. Willi Boskovsky

(Many recordings of the Overture)

Ritter Pasman

Operetta in 3 Acts.
Text by Lajos Dóczy.
First performance: Vienna (Hofoperntheater) January 1, 1892.

RECORDING:
Decca SXL6332 or SXL6740 □
London 6641 (US)
Csárdás
c. Willi Boskovsky

Wiener Blut

Operetta in 3 Acts.
Text by Victor Léon and Leo Stein. Score completed by Adolf Müller, Jr.
First performance: Vienna (Carltheater) October 25, 1899.

Synopsis:

Act 1 It is 1815, the year of the Vienna Congress, and the heads of state spend their evenings in romantic intrigue, especially Graf Zedlau, an ambassador who is having affairs with two ladies: the ballerina Franzi, his permanent mistress whom he has installed in a villa, and Pepi, an attractive model who is the fiancée of his valet Josef. Zedlau's wife Gabriele, who thinks him a dull dog, has returned to her father's house. Josef comes to look for his master at the villa but finds only a suspicious Franzi, who wants to know where he is. So does her father, Herr Kagler, who wants to meet him. Zedlau arrives and manages to convince Franzi of his fidelity, but when she departs dictates a letter to Pepi. Josef, taking it down, admires the winning phrases, not realising they are intended for his own girlfriend. As Zedlau leaves Pepi arrives with a dress for Franzi, and she and Josef look forward to an evening out. The dress does not fit Franzi, who asks Pepi to take her place as principal dancer that evening. The old Prime Minister, Prince Ypsheim-Gindelbach, arrives and, believing Franzi to be Gabriele, tells her that Zedlau is having an affair with a dancer. This is overheard by Herr Kagler. Total confusion arises when Gabriele arrives and the Prime Minister assumes her to be Franzi. To avoid scandal Zedlau asks the Prime Minister to present Gabriele as his wife.

Act 2 At a diplomat's ball, Gabriele is very suspicious of the goings-on but is secretly pleased that Zedlau is not as dull as she supposed. Franzi is annoyed with Zedlau because she thinks he and Gabriele are still intimate. Zedlau is pleased to find Pepi present; she has quarrelled with Josef and agrees to see Zedlau later. When Pepi leads the ballet, Gabriele is convinced she is Franzi. Zedlau, committed to a date with Pepi, refuses to take out either Franzi or Gabriele that evening so Gabriele arranges to meet the Prime Minister, who still thinks she is Franzi, and introduces her to Franzi whom he assumes to be Gabriele.

Act 3 In a Hietzing casino to a background of schrammel music, the three couples look for quiet spots in which to flirt; the Prime Minister with Gabriele, who is hoping to surprise Zedlau; Josef with Franzi, bent on the same end; and Zedlau with Pepi. Josef loyally goes to warn Zedlau of his wife's presence and is furious to find his fiancée with him. Gabriele and Franzi join in denouncing Pepi. Fortunately the happy music puts them all in good humour and they see the funny side of the affair. Zedlau decides that he is still attracted by Gabriele, and Josef forgives Pepi, while the old Prime Minister is as confused as ever. They put it all down to the effects of Wiener Blut.

Notes:

Strauss was asked in 1899 to write this opera, but was unwell and no longer had strength for the effort. But he helped to select the music from his once popular but now neglected pieces; the waltz 'Wiener Blut', written in 1873, was used as the main theme. The task of putting the score together was left to Adolf Müller, Jr (a composer himself, and musical director at the Theater an der Wien) who worked well with librettists Léon and Stein. Opening four months after Strauss's death, it was a total failure. Staged again in 1901 it was a popular success and has remained a close rival to the composer's best operettas.

Well-known arias:
Act 1 Drausst in Hietzing (Pepi and Josef)
Act 2 Das Wiener Blut (Waltz) (Gabriele)

Der Waldmeister

Operetta in 2 Acts.
Text by Gustav Davis.
First performance: Vienna (Theater an der Wien) December 4, 1895.

RECORDING:
Decca SXL6419 or SXL6740 □
London 6641 (US)
Overture
c. Willi Boskovsky

RECORDINGS:

HMV 'Concert Classics' SXDW3042 (2)●
Angel S-35156 (2) (d) (US)
Philharmonia Chorus and Orchestra
c. Otto Ackermann
Prime Minister (b) Karl Dönch
Graf Zedlau (t) Nicolai Gedda
Gabriele (s) Elisabeth
      Schwarzkopf
Franzi (s) Erika Köth
Josef (b) Erich Kunz
Pepi (s) Emmy Loose

HMV SLS5074 (2) ●
Angel SX-3831 (2) (US)
Cologne Opera Chorus/Philharmonia Hungarica
c. Willi Boskovsky
Prime Minister (b) Klaus Hirte

Graf Zedlau (t) Nicolai Gedda
Gabriele (s) Anneliese
      Rothenberger
Franzi (s) Renate Holm
Josef (t) Heinz Zednik
Pepi (s) Gabriele Fuchs

Everest S-172 (2) (US) ●
Vienna State Opera Chorus/Vienna Symphony Orchestra
c. Robert Stolz
Prime Minister (b) Benno Kusche
Graf Zedlau (t) Rudolf Schock
Gabriele (s) Hilde Gueden
Franzi (s) Margit Schramm
Josef (t) Ferry Gruber
Pepi (s) Wilma Lipp

RICHARD STRAUSS
(b. Munich 11.6.1864; d. Garmisch-Partenkirchen 8.9.1949)

One of the last major composers to reach the hearts and minds of the larger public—and certainly one of the last German composers to do so—Strauss was also among the last prolific composers of opera. He has been called a man who began as a 'progressive' and ended as a 'conservative'; but the fact that those words need placing in quotes shows that they are not essentially relevant. Richard Strauss had a long life and was active to its end: he survived long enough to see the collapse and destruction of the Germany he knew and loved. He was a musician through and through; the son of a horn player and a prodigy who had published compositions to his credit from the age of ten. His earliest influences stemmed from both Brahms and Wagner » —and also from Mozart ». He held many conducting and directing appointments in Germany, becoming conductor of the Berlin Philharmonic Orchestra in 1894, and was always a prolific composer in all forms, including opera. His career was interrupted but not seriously affected by two World Wars. He married Pauline de Ahna, the singer who had taken the lead in his first opera, *Guntram*, in 1894, and they remained together until Strauss's death in 1949; Frau Strauss died in 1950. Strauss's operas are rich and varied. The most significant single fact in the series is his close collaboration with his librettist, the poet Hugo von Hofmannsthal, who wrote all Strauss's texts from *Elektra* (1906) to *Arabella* (1930). Hofmannsthal's death in 1929 was a severe blow, but it did not prevent Strauss from continuing to write opera: Stefan Zweig, and then Josef Gregor, became his collaborators. A valuable insight into the collaboration between Strauss and Hofmannsthal comes from their letters, issued in English as *The Correspondence between Richard Strauss and Hugo von Hofmannsthal*, translated by Hanns Hammelemann and Ewald Osers (Collins, London, 1961). Even if Strauss frequently seemed to share the German failing of being unable to distinguish between a commonplace idea and a genuinely powerful one, he knew a good libretto when he saw it: the quality of Hofmannsthal's text is an integral part of the quality of Strauss's operas.

Guntram
Opera in 3 Acts.
Text by Strauss.
First performance: Weimar (Court Opera) May 10, 1894. Revised 1940.

RECORDING:
RCA ARL1 0333 □
RCA ARL1 0333 (US)
Fass' ich sei bang
Leontyne Price (s)

Below: *Richard Strauss in a 1898 portrait when he was aged 34.*

Salome
Opera in 1 Act.
Text from Oscar Wilde's play, translated into German by Hedwig Lachmann.
First performance: Dresden (Court Opera) December 9, 1905. Manhattan Opera (in French) 1909; London (Covent Garden) 1910.

Synopsis:
Scene: Galilee. Time: *c.* AD 30.
Salome, daughter of Herodias (who has slain her husband, Salome's father, so that she might marry Herod), hears the voice of Jokanaan (John the Baptist) from his dungeon, and wishes to see him. Narraboth, Captain of the Guard, desires Salome; he agrees to escort her, but kills himself after seeing her attempt to seduce Jokanaan and be rejected. Herod's lust for Salome incurs Herodias's scorn. Talk of the Messiah increases Herod's fear of Jokanaan's prophecies. Salome, asked to dance as a diversion, performs the Dance of the Seven Veils, and Herod promises her anything she desires. Still enraged by Jokanaan's rebuff, she demands his head. Reluctantly, Herod agrees, but when Jokanaan's head is brought in and Salome kisses the lips that would not meet hers in life, he is horrified and orders the soldiers to crush her to death.

Notes:
The subject and its treatment not unnaturally caused trouble in the early days: the opera was banned in England at one time and was withdrawn after one performance at the Metropolitan, New York. The Dance of the Seven Veils in particular gave offence, and the whole opera was regarded as degraded and obscene. However, it soon surmounted these difficulties, the vividness and dramatic point of the music overriding puritanical objections.

RECORDINGS:

Decca SET228/9 ●
London 1218 (2) (US)
Vienna Philharmonic Orchestra
c. Sir Georg Solti
Salome (s)　　　Birgit Nilsson
Herod (t)　　　　Gerhard Stolze
Herodias (m-s)　Grace Hoffmann
Jokanaan (b)　　Eberhard Waechter
Narraboth (t)　　Waldemar Kmentt

DG 2707 052 (2) ●
DG 2707 052 (2) (US)
Hamburg Opera Orchestra
c. Karl Böhm
Salome (s)　　　Gwyneth Jones
Herod (t)　　　　Richard Cassilly
Herodias (m-s)　Mignon Dunn
Jokanaan (b)　　Dietrich Fischer-Dieskau
Narraboth (t)　　Wieslaw Ochman

Decca SET457 (d) ■
London 26169 *or* 25991 (US)
(from above)

HMV SLS5139 (2) ★●
Angel SBLX-3848 (2) (US)
Vienna Philharmonic Orchestra
c. Herbert von Karajan
Salome (s)　　　Hildegard Behrens

Herod (t)　　　　Karl-Walter Böhm
Herodias (m-s)　Agnes Baltsa
Jokanaan (b)　　José van Dam
Narraboth (t)　　Wieslaw Ochman

DG 2530 963 □
DG 2530 963 (US)
Dance; Final scene
French National Orchestra
c. Leonard Bernstein
Montserrat Caballé (s)

Decca SXL6657 (final scene) □
London 26397 (US)
Vienna Philharmonic Orchestra
c. Christoph von Dohnányi
Anja Silja (s)

DG 2530 349 □
DG 2530 349 (US)
Dance of the Seven Veils
Berlin Philharmonic Orchestra
c. Herbert von Karajan

HMV ESD7026 □
Seraphim S-60297 (US)
Dance of the Seven Veils
Dresden State Orchestra
c. Rudolf Kempe

Elektra
Opera in 1 Act.
Text by Hugo von Hofmannsthal after Sophocles.
First performance: Dresden (Court Opera) January 25, 1909. New York (Manhattan Opera) (in French) 1910; London (Covent Garden) 1910.

Synopsis:
Scene: Ancient Mycenae.
Elektra has been condemned by her mother, Klytemnestra, and step-father Aegisthus, to live like an animal. The only servant who shows her affection is beaten. Elektra is determined to be revenged on Klytemnestra and Aegisthus, who murdered her father, Agamemnon, and hopes for the aid of her brother, Orestes. Her sister, Chrysothemis, fears the worst. Klytemnestra, now ugly and dissolute, asks the advice of Elektra, who speaks

darkly of a woman who must be a blood sacrifice. News comes of Orestes' death; Elektra now demands the aid of Chrysothemis. A stranger who comes ostensibly with news of Orestes' death reveals himself to Elektra as Orestes. He enters the palace, and a cry from Klytemnestra tells Elektra that part of her vengeance is accomplished. Aegisthus wonders at Elektra's behaviour, enters the palace, and reappears screaming. He, too, is killed. Elektra dances in a frenzy and at last falls dead, as Chrysothemis hammers on the door of the palace.

Notes:

The harsh dissonances and 'cruelty' of *Elektra* have long since been accepted. Many have seen in this opera and in *Salome* an accurate representation of the disintegration that was overtaking Europe at the time, reaching its apotheosis in 1914.

Well-known arias:

Allein! Weh, ganz allein! (Elektra)

RECORDINGS:
Decca SET354/5 ●
London 1269 (2) (US)
Vienna State Opera Chorus/Vienna
Philharmonic Orchestra
c. Sir Georg Solti

Elektra (s)	Birgit Nilsson
Klytemnestra (m-s)	Regina Resnik
Orestes (b)	Tom Krause
Chrysothemis (s)	Marie Collier
Aegisthus (t)	Gerhard Stolze

DG 2707 011 (2) ●
DG 2707 011 (2) (US)
Dresden State Opera Chorus and
Orchestra
c. Karl Böhm

Elektra (s)	Inge Borkh
Klytemnestra (m-s)	Jean Madiera
Orestes (b)	Dietrich Fischer-Dieskau
Chrysothemis (s)	Marianne Schech
Aegisthus (t)	Fritz Uhl

RCA RL42821 (m) □
Final scene
c. Sir Thomas Beecham

Der Rosenkavalier (The Knight of the Rose)

Opera in 3 Acts.
Text by Hugo von Hofmannsthal.
First performance: Dresden (Court Opera) January 26, 1911. London (Covent Garden) 1913; New York (Metropolitan) 1913.

Synopsis:

Scene: Vienna. Time: 18th century.

Act 1 After a prelude on the act of lovemaking, Octavian is revealed, kneeling at the bedside of Princess von Werdenberg (the Feldmarschallin, called the Marschallin). Baron Ochs, an oafish relative from the country, demands to see the Marschallin, at the same time making advances to her maid. Ochs asks the Marschallin if she has appointed a Knight of the Rose, to take the symbolic offering of a silver rose to Sophie, daughter of the rich and recently ennobled Faninal, whom Ochs has decided to wed. Ochs also wishes the Marschallin to recommend an attorney, but the business is put off until the morning levée. After the levée, the Marschallin reflects that her youthful lover Octavian will soon seek a younger woman; she sends a servant after him with the silver rose.

Act 2 The *parvenu* Faninal is honoured by the attention of Baron Ochs. Sophie and her duenna, Marianne, await the suitor, but when Octavian arrives with the silver rose, he and Sophie immediately fall in love. Sophie detests Ochs on sight. Alone, Sophie and Octavian declare their love, but they are surprised by the scandalmongers Valzacchi and Annina. Ochs returns and Octavian forthrightly informs him of the situation: they fight and Ochs, slightly wounded, complains bitterly. When Sophie refuses to marry Ochs, Faninal orders her to a convent. Octavian has noticed that Valzacchi and Annina are put out by Ochs's failure to reward them. While Ochs lies on a couch, humming his favourite waltz, he is delighted to receive a

note suggesting an assignation with the Marschallin's maid.
Act 3 Valzacchi and Annina are now in Octavian's pay. Octavian has taken a room at an inn and has disguised himself as a girl. Ochs arrives and makes advances, but Octavian holds him off. Ochs is subjected to various tricks: Annina appears as a woman in mourning, claiming to be Ochs's deserted wife. The Baron calls the police but, realising that he will be made to look foolish, proceeds to deny all knowledge of the affair, even claiming not to know the angry Faninal. The Marschallin, called by Ochs's servant, passes the matter off as a joke. Sophie is despondent, but the Marschallin contrives to send Ochs packing and brings the young couple together. She is sad to lose Octavian to Sophie, but she has always known that she must eventually relinquish him to a younger woman. After a great trio for the Marschallin, Octavian and Sophie, the remaining strands of the action are brought together.

Notes:

The most popular and frequently performed German opera written this century, *Der Rosenkavalier*'s enduring appeal rests on three principal factors: a profusion of memorable melody, including the famous waltz sequences; an unmistakable style and elegance; and the marvellously drawn figure of the Marschallin, so full of emotional grace and generous humanity. It also has that aura of nostalgia which, especially nowadays, has an irresistible appeal. Nor should one forget the genuine comic elements.

Well-known arias:

Act 1 Di rigori armato il seno (Italian aria) (Singer)
Die Zeit im Grunde (Marschallin)
Act 2 Mir ist die Ehre Widerfahren (Presentation of the Rose) (Sophie)
Waltzes (Orchestral)
Act 3 Hab' mir's gelobt, ihn lieb zu haben (Trio) (Marschallin, Sophie, Octavian)

RECORDING:
HMV SLS810 (4) ★●
Angel S-3563 (4) (US)
Philharmonia Chorus and Orchestra
c. Herbert von Karajan

Marschallin (s)	Elisabeth Schwarzkopf
Octavian (m-s)	Christa Ludwig
Baron Ochs (bs)	Otto Edelman
Sophie (s)	Teresa Stich-Randall
Faninal (b)	Eberhard Waechter
Italian Singer (t)	Nicolai Gedda

Angel S-35645 (US) ■
(from above)

Decca SET418/21 ●
London 1435 (US)
Vienna State Opera Chorus/Vienna
Philharmonic Orchestra
c. Sir Georg Solti

Marschallin (s)	Régine Crespin
Octavian (m-s)	Yvonne Minton
Baron Ochs (bs)	Manfred Jungwirth
Sophie (s)	Helen Donath
Faninal (b)	Otto Weiner
Italian Singer (t)	Luciano Pavarotti

Decca SET487 ■
London 26200 (US)
(from above)

Decca 4BB115-8 (4) ●
Vienna State Opera Chorus/Vienna
Philharmonic Orchestra
c. Erich Kleiber

Marschallin (s)	Maria Reining
Octavian (m-s)	Sena Jurinac
Baron Ochs (bs)	Ludwig Weber
Sophie (s)	Hilde Gueden
Faninal (b)	Alfred Poell

Philips 6707 030 (4) ●
Philips 6707 030 (4) (US)
Helmond Concert Choir/Netherlands

Opera Chorus/Rotterdam Philharmonic
Orchestra
c. Edo de Waart

Marschallin (s)	Evelyn Lear
Octavian (m-s)	Frederica von Stade
Baron Ochs (bs)	Jules Bastin
Sophie (s)	Ruth Welting
Faninal (b)	Derek Hammond Stroud
Italian Singer (t)	José Carreras

CBS 77416 (4) (d) ●
Columbia D4M-30652 (4) (US)
Vienna State Opera Chorus/Vienna
Philharmonic Orchestra
c. Leonard Bernstein

Marschallin (s)	Christa Ludwig
Octavian (s)	Gwyneth Jones
Baron Ochs (bs)	Walter Berry
Sophie (s)	Lucia Popp
Faninal (bs)	Ernst Gutstein
Italian Singer (t)	Placido Domingo

DG 2721 162 (4) ●
DG 2721 162 (4) (US)
Chorus and Orchestra of Dresden State
Opera
c. Karl Böhm

Marschallin (s)	Marianne Schech
Octavian (s)	Irmgard Seefried
Baron Ochs (bs)	Kurt Böhme
Sophie (s)	Rita Streich
Italian Singer (t)	Rudolf Franci

World Records SH181/2 (m) (r. 1933) ○
Vienna Philharmonic Orchestra
c. Robert Heger

Marschallin (s)	Lotte Lehmann
Octavian (m-s)	Maria Olszewska
Baron Ochs (bs)	Richard Mayr
Sophie (s)	Elisabeth Schumann

(The EMI with von Karajan and the incomparable Marschallin of Elisabeth

Schwarzkopf is something special: although by no means modern, the sound has been most skilfully made to sound so. The Decca/Solti has all the brilliance and vigour associated with that combination, but also a becoming grace and elegance. The CBS/Bernstein, commemorating a memorable occasion in Vienna when Leonard Bernstein took the town by storm, is currently withdrawn from the UK lists, but may well return. There are a few touches of *schmaltz*, not entirely out of place, and the horns bray a little; but it is a winning set, far outlasting its defects. The old Kleiber/Decca is most notable for the conductor's skill with the orchestral contribution. The newer Philips has much in its favour though may not immediately seem to equal the others. The DG/Böhm is showing its age. The 1933 recording, now on World Records, preserves the fabulous Vienna cast of the period before World War II.

It, too, is something special; unique and irreplaceable. Both Deccas and the DG give the complete score; HMV and CBS have small cuts.)

Classics for Pleasure CFP40217 ■
Scottish National Orchestra
c. Sir Alexander Gibson
Marschallin (s)   Helga Dernesch
Octavian (m-s)   Teresa Cahill
Baron Ochs (bs)   Michael Langdon
Sophie (s)   Anne Howells

Camden Classics CCV5051 □
RCA VICS-1561 (US)
Waltzes
Chicago Symphony Orchestra
c. Fritz Reiner

HMV ASD 3074 □
Waltzes
Dresden State Orchestra
c. Rudolf Kempe

Below: Ariadne auf Naxos *was first staged at Covent Garden in 1924.*

Ariadne auf Naxos

Opera in Prologue and 1 Act.
Text by Hugo von Hofmannsthal.
First performance: Vienna (State Opera) October 4, 1916. London (Covent Garden) 1924; New York 1934.

Synopsis:

Prologue   In the house of a *nouveau riche* Viennese, an operatic entertainment is about to take place. But before the opera he has commissioned can begin, he directs that it shall be 'brightened up' with an intermezzo on the Harlequinade pattern. The young Composer protests, and is hardly consoled when he learns that the 'entertainment' is to be an integral part of his opera. He is in despair, but Zerbinetta, the pretty *soubrette* who is to feature in the Intermezzo, persuades him that if a few cuts are made in the opera and a few in the play all will be well. The Composer falls in with the plan; then, too late, realises what he has done. The story of the opera is outlined and discussed.

The Opera   Ariadne is desolate on the island of Naxos. She has lost Theseus and wishes to die. She lies outside her cave, watched over by three nymphs. Enter the Harlequinade and Zerbinetta; they try without success to cheer her. Even Zerbinetta's coruscant colatura aria is to no avail. The nymphs announce that the young god Bacchus is nearby. Ariadne hears his voice calling for Circe and mistakes him for the welcome messenger of death. She falls into his arms—but the expected embrace of death becomes the embrace of love and passion. Zerbinetta is pleased, but not surprised.

Notes:

This is the second, restructured version. Originally the opera section was designed to go with a shortened performance of Molière's *Le Bourgeois Gentilhomme*, for which Strauss had written some splendid incidental music. However, the idea proved impractical: the mixing of a play and an opera put an unacceptable strain on theatre resources and audience endurance alike. The original was given in Stuttgart on October 25, 1912, and at once the impracticalities were apparent. It was played quite widely in that form, and has been occasionally revived. There are some who think it the better of the two; among them Sir Thomas Beecham, who conducted the first London performance at His Majesty's in 1913. But the second version was generally accepted, if not as definitive. Recordings are always of the second version. The orchestra is reduced, from the inflation of much of Strauss, to a mere 39 players.

RECORDINGS:

Decca D103D3 (3) ●
London Philharmonic Orchestra
c. Sir Georg Solti
Composer (s)   Tatiana Troyanos
Dancing Master (t) Heinz Zednik
Harlequin (b)   Barry McDaniel
Zerbinetta (s)   Edita Gruberova
Ariadne (s)   Leontyne Price
Bacchus (t)   René Kollo

HMV SLS936 (3) ●
Dresden State Opera Orchestra
c. Rudolf Kempe
Composer (s)   Teresa Zylis-Gara
Dancing Master (t) Peter Schreier
Harlequin (b)   Hermann Prey
Zerbinetta (s)   Sylvia Geszty
Ariadne (s)   Gundula Janowitz
Bacchus (t)   James King

Decca 2BB112/4 ●
London 13100 (3) (US)
Vienna Philharmonic Orchestra
c. Erich Leinsdorf
Composer (s)   Sena Jurinac
Dancing Master (t) Murray Dickie
Harlequin (b)   Walter Berry
Zerbinetta (s)   Roberta Peters
Ariadne (s)   Leonie Rysanek
Bacchus (t)   Jan Peerce

RCA RL42821 (m) □
Overture; Final scene
c. Sir Thomas Beecham

Die Frau ohne Schatten (The Woman Without a Shadow)

Opera in 3 Acts.
Text by Hugo von Hofmannsthal.
First performance: Vienna (State Opera) October 10, 1919. Salzburg 1932; San Francisco 1959; London 1966.

Synopsis:

Act 1   The Emperor and Empress love each other deeply, but the Empress is of supernatural origin: being barren, she casts no shadow. A messenger announces that unless the Empress can acquire a shadow, and thus conceive, she must return in three days to her father, Keikobad. The Emperor will be turned to stone. With her Nurse, the Empress goes to the dwelling of Barak the dyer. The Nurse tries to persuade Barak's Wife to part with her shadow; although Barak desires children, his Wife is tempted.

Act 2   Although she is becoming desperate, the Empress pities the Wife's distress. The Wife tells Barak that she has sold her shadow, and with it her unborn children. Furious, Barak tries to kill her. The Empress says she will not take the shadow, and Barak's Wife confesses she has not really sold her shadow— although she wishes to. The earth opens and swallows up Barak's dwelling.

Act 3   In a subterranean vault, Barak and his Wife seek each other. The Empress is summoned to the Emperor's trial at Keikobad's court. Even when the Emperor is petrified, with only his eyes left alive to plead with her, the Empress refuses to accept Barak's Wife's shadow. Her steadfastness is rewarded: she is bathed in light and it is seen that she now casts a shadow. The restored Emperor joins her and the voices of their unborn children are heard. Barak and his Wife, too, are reunited.

Notes:

Die Frau ohne Schatten is the most complex and 'difficult' of the Strauss/Hofmannsthal operas. The text, taken from Hofmannsthal's own play, is full of symbolism. Central to the theme is the purification of the two couples: the excessively proud and

remote on one side; the too earthy and acquisitive on the other. But it goes much deeper than that. Strauss's music, too, is complex and ambitious.

RECORDINGS:
Decca GOS534/7 ●
Richmond 64503 (4) (US)
Vienna State Opera Chorus/Vienna Philharmonic Orchestra
c. Karl Böhm

Empress (s)	Leonie Rysanek
Emperor (t)	Hans Hopf
Nurse (m-s)	Elisabeth Höngen
Barak (b)	Paul Schoeffler
Barak's Wife (s)	Christel Goltz
Spirit (bs)	Kurt Böhme

Barak (b)	Dietrich Fischer-Dieskau
Barak's Wife (s)	Inge Borkh
Spirit (bs)	Hans Hotter

DG 2721 161 (4) ●
previously SLPM138 911/4
DG 2721 161 (4) (US)
Bavarian State Opera Chorus and Orchestra
c. Joseph Keilberth

Empress (s)	Ingrid Bjoner
Emperor (t)	Jess Thomas
Nurse (s)	Martha Mödl

Intermezzo
Opera in 2 Acts.
Text by Richard Strauss.
First performance: Dresden (State Opera) November 4, 1924. New York 1963; Edinburgh Festival 1965.

RECORDING:
DG 2740 160 (5) □
Symphonic interludes
c. Richard Strauss (1927)

Die Ägyptische Helena (The Egyptian Helen)
Opera in 2 Acts.
Text by Hugo von Hofmannsthal.
First performance: Dresden (State Opera) June 6, 1928. New York 1967.

RECORDING:
RCA LSB4083 □
Victor LSC2849 (US)
Awakening Scene (Act 2)

Leontyne Price (s)
(This recording also contains excerpts from *Salome*)

Arabella
Opera in 3 Acts.
Text by Hugo von Hofmannsthal.
First performance: Dresden (State Opera) July 1, 1933. London (Covent Garden) 1934; New York (Metropolitan) 1955.

Synopsis:
Scene: Vienna. Time: 1860.
Act 1 To retrieve the fortune he has gambled away, Graf Waldner must marry his daughter, Arabella, to a wealthy man. His younger daughter, Zdenka, loves Matteo; but Matteo desires Arabella, who ignores him. Arabella is fascinated by a stranger, Mandryka, heir to a fortune, who sees her portrait and falls in love.
Act 2 Arabella is introduced to Mandryka at a ball and they realise that their love is mutual. She asks for one hour to say goodbye to her girlhood. The sprightly Fiakermilli gives Arabella a bouquet and sings a polka. Zdenka gives Matteo a letter, supposedly from Arabella, making an assignation in an hotel room. Mandryka, overhearing this, is astonished: believing Arabella fickle, he flirts with Fiakermilli. At last, Mandryka and Arabella's parents go in search of her.
Act 3 Matteo and Arabella meet, to her surprise, on the hotel staircase. Mandryka enters with Arabella's parents, and it seems that he and Matteo will fight a duel. Zdenka confesses that it is she, not Arabella, who has been in the darkened hotel room with Matteo. She threatens suicide. Arabella forgives Zdenka, who is bestowed upon Matteo by Graf Waldner, but is cool towards Mandryka: she asks for a glass of water and goes upstairs. Reappearing, she descends the staircase and hands the glass to Mandryka. He drinks and then dashes the glass to the floor: all is forgiven.

Notes:
Arabella does not quite repeat the success of *Der Rosenkavalier*. It has many of the same ingredients, including waltzes, but lacks, in its more frivolous tone, the overall charm and depth of its famous predecessor. There are some fine character sketches and some lovely musical passages. *Arabella* was the last of the Strauss/Hofmannsthal collaborations. In July 1929, Hofmannsthal's son, Franz, committed suicide, and Hofmannsthal himself died of a stroke on the day of the funeral.

RECORDINGS:
Decca GOS571/3 ●
Richmond S63522 (3) (US)
Vienna State Opera Chorus/Vienna Philharmonic Orchestra
c. Sir Georg Solti

Arabella (s)	Lisa della Casa
Zdenka (s)	Hilde Gueden
Mandryka (b)	George London
Matteo (t)	Anton Dermota
Graf Waldner (bs)	Otto Edelmann
Fiakermilli (s)	Mimi Coertse

Matteo (t)	Georg Paskuda
Graf Waldner (bs)	Karl-Christian Kohn
Fiakermilli (s)	Eva Maria Rogner

DG 2721 163 (3) ●
previously SLMP138883/5
DG 2721 163 (3) (US)
Bavarian State Opera Chorus and Orchestra
c. Joseph Keilberth

Arabella (s)	Lisa della Casa
Zdenka (s)	Anneliese Rothenberger
Mandryka (b)	Dietrich Fischer-Dieskau

Daphne
Opera in 1 Act.
Text by Josef Gregor.
First performance: Dresden (State Opera) October 15, 1938. New York 1960.

Synopsis:
Scene: Ancient Greece.
Daphne, daughter of the fisherman Peneios, feels at one with nature; she ignores the shepherd Leukippos, who loves her. Peneios believes that the gods will walk the earth again, but Daphne refuses to join the fertility festival in honour of Dionysus. When the god Apollo appears as a herdsman, Daphne feels a mystic affinity for him, but repulses his advances. The festivities approach a climax: Leukippos, in female attire, asks Daphne to dance. The indignant Apollo raises a storm, and the shepherds, fearing for their flocks, depart: Leukippos suggests that Apollo should depart also. Apollo draws his bow and, when Daphne refuses to go with him, fells Leukippos. Daphne is desolated, blaming herself for her lover's fate. The remorseful Apollo begs the pardon of Dionysus and Zeus: he asks Zeus to bestow the chaste Daphne upon him in the form of a tree. Daphne is slowly transformed into a laurel, thus becoming truly at one with nature.

Notes:
Strauss, like Nietzsche, was devoted to the ideal of Greek classical mythology. This late opera was one result of that devotion. It is a splendid, somewhat neglected, piece.

RECORDING:
DG 2721 190 (2) ●
DG 2721 190 (2) (US)
Vienna State Opera Chorus/Vienna Symphony Orchestra
c. Karl Böhm

Daphne (s)	Hilde Gueden
Leukippos (t)	Fritz Wunderlich
Apollo (t)	James King
Peneios (bs)	Paul Schoeffler

Die Liebe der Danae (The Love of Danae)
Opera in 3 Acts.
Text by Josef Gregor.
First performance: Salzburg August 14, 1952. London (Covent Garden) 1953.

Synopsis:
Act 1 King Pollux, besieged by creditors, is not believed when he announces that his daughter, Danae, will wed Midas, who turns all he touches to gold. Danae dreams of showers of gold,

and refuses an insufficiently wealthy suitor. She is impressed by an emissary from Midas (who is, in fact, Midas himself). When the god Jupiter arrives posing as Midas, Danae swoons.

Act 2   Jupiter comes to Danae's bedchamber. The four queens, Pollux's nieces, recognise the god, who has been their lover. Midas wishes to reveal the imposture, but Jupiter, who is posing as Midas to avert the jealousy of Juno, threatens to withdraw his gift of the golden touch. Midas comes to Danae in his true identity: she embraces him and is herself turned to gold. Jupiter and Midas vie for her favours: she chooses Midas.

Act 3   On the open road, Danae is happy when she realises that Midas has renounced his golden gift out of love for her, and is now a humble drover. The gods make merry over the affair. Jupiter manages to escape the attentions of the four queens and, advised by Mercury, showers gold on Pollux, who is still vexed by his creditors. Jupiter tries once more to win Danae but, finding her happy with Midas, departs.

Notes:

The opera was written in 1938-40 and planned for production in 1944. But after the plot on Hitler's life, all German theatres were closed: although there was a dress rehearsal before an audience, it was eight years before it was produced, at Salzburg. The recording is of that performance.

RECORDING:
Discocorp RR464 (m) ●
Vienna State Opera Chorus/Vienna Philharmonic Orchestra
c. Clemens Krauss
Danae (s)   Annelies Kupper

Pollux (t)   László Szemere
Midas (t)   Josef Gostic
Jupiter (bs)   Paul Schoeffler
Mercury (t)   Josef Traxel

Capriccio
Opera in 1 Act.
Text by Clemens Krauss.
First performance: Munich (State Opera) October 28, 1942. New York (Juilliard School) 1954; London (Covent Garden) 1953; Glyndebourne 1963.

Synopsis:
Scene: near Paris. Time: *c.* 1775.
It is the time of the operatic 'war' concerning Gluck's » reforms. A party gathers at a chateau near Paris for the birthday of the young Countess Madeleine, recently widowed. The musician Flamand has written a string sextet and the theatre director La Roche falls asleep while it is played. The Count, Madeleine's brother, is taken with the famous actress Clarion, who is expected to take part in a play written by the poet Olivier. The Count favours poetry; his sister, music. Flamand and Olivier compete for the Countess's hand. Their argument becomes both heated and sophisticated and almost gets out of hand. Countess Madeleine cannot choose between them: she is saved from the necessity of doing so by the announcement that supper is served.

Notes:
Capriccio was Strauss's last opera, though it was produced before *Die Liebe der Danae*. Although it is in one Act, *Capriccio* lasts for more than two hours without a break. It is concerned principally with arguments over the relative importance of words and music in opera, cunningly linked to human entanglements.

RECORDINGS:
DG 2709 038 (3) ●
DG 2709 038 (3) (US)
Bavarian Radio Symphony Orchestra
c. Karl Böhm
Countess (s)   Gundula Janowitz
Count (b)   Dietrich
        Fischer-Dieskau
Flamand (t)   Peter Schreier
Olivier (b)   Hermann Prey
La Roche (bs)   Karl Ridderbusch
Clarion (m-s)   Tatiana Troyanos

World Records OC230/2 (m) ●
Philharmonia Orchestra
c. Wolfgang Sawallisch
Countess (s)   Elisabeth Schwarzkopf
Count (b)   Eberhard Waechter
Flamand (t)   Nicolai Gedda
Olivier (b)   Dietrich
        Fischer-Dieskau
La Roche (bs)   Hans Hotter
Clarion (m-s)   Christa Ludwig

IGOR STRAVINSKY
(b. Oranienbaum, St Petersburg 17.6.1882; d. New York 6.4.1971)

The agile and active mind of Stravinsky acted as something of a catalyst in modern music. No man, with the possible exception of Wagner », exercised a greater influence over his age; no musical faculty was more receptive to what was going on around it and what had preceded it. Stravinsky's neo-classicism not only embraced a contemporary style of great vigour and clarity, but also entailed a delving into the past and a creative transmutation of what he found there. The son of a bass singer at the Imperial Russian Opera, Stravinsky became a pupil of Rimsky-Korsakov » in 1907, when he already had a number of compositions to his credit. But there is no doubt that his developing style was greatly influenced by that master's teaching and example, most notably in the ballet *The Firebird*, with which Stravinsky began his long association with Diaghilev and the Ballets Russes. The famous furore in Paris over *The Rite of Spring* occurred in 1913, and between the wars came the period of neo-classicism—sometimes dubbed 'Back to Bach'—with Stravinsky in the van. His constantly questing musical intelligence did not remain for long in one creative groove; yet through all the apparent changes of direction, he remained totally and unmistakably himself. His music is as immediately recognisable as any ever written. He long represented the

Above: *Igor Stravinsky, a truly international composer.*

opposite pole to Schoenberg » in modern music, as an opponent of serialism, but in the latter part of his career he again changed direction and embraced with total conviction a form of serialism nearer to Webern than that of Schoenberg himself. Intensely Russian by temperament and sympathies, Stravinsky was for the first part of his life a deep-dyed nationalist in the line of Mussorgsky », Glinka » and Tchaikovsky »; yet he was at the same time music's great cosmopolitan, whose magpie mind ranged over the entire spectrum of the art in search of material. Although essentially a man of the theatre, Stravinsky's major contribution was to the ballet rather than opera. He wrote one full-scale opera, *The Rake's Progress*, and one opera-buffa, *Mavra*. To these may be added *Le Rossignol*, an early work later made into a ballet, and the 'opera-oratorio' *Oedipus Rex*; as well as the television opera *The Flood*. Other works for the theatre, apart from the ballets proper, like *L'Histoire du Soldat*, *Renard* and *Perséphone*, fall into no clearly defined category. They can hardly be classed as opera, though they are often characterised as such for want of any better description; if only because with the exception of *L'Histoire du Soldat*, they contain singing parts. Stravinsky's fertile imagination often produced works which do not come within any traditional definition.

Le Rossignol (The Nightingale)

Opera in 3 Acts.
Text by Stravinsky and Stepan Nikolayevich Mitusov after Hans Andersen.
First performance: Paris (Opéra) May 26, 1914. London (Drury Lane) 1914; New York (Metropolitan) 1926.

Synopsis:

Act 1   The Nightingale who diverts the Fisherman from his work is invited to sing before the Emperor. She says that her voice sounds much sweeter in the forest than in the palace, but since it is the Emperor's command she will come.

Act 2   The Nightingale so enchants the Emperor that he offers her a decoration, but she says she is happy just to have charmed a great ruler. When Japanese envoys arrive with a mechanical songbird, the Nightingale flies off, to the rage of the Emperor who pronounces banishment.

Act 3   The Emperor is mortally ill: death sits at the foot of his bed. Ghosts of the Emperor's deeds, good and bad, confront him. The Nightingale comes to banish the ghosts and charms even death away; when the courtiers arrive, expecting to find the Emperor dead, the room is full of light and the Emperor has recovered. The Fisherman says they must all acknowledge the Nightingale as the voice of heaven.

RECORDING:

CBS SBRG72041 ●	c. Igor Stravinsky
Columbia KS-6327 (US)	**Nightingale** (s) Reri Grist
Chorus and Orchestra of the Opera	**Emperor** (b) Donald Gramm
Society of Washington, DC	**Fisherman** (t) Loren Driscoll

Mavra

Opera buffa in 1 Act.
Text by Boris Kochno after Pushkin.
First performance: Paris (Opéra) June 3, 1922. Berlin 1928; London (BBC) 1934.

Synopsis:

Set in Russia in the time of Charles X. Parasha is in love with a Hussar and, ordered by Mother to engage a new servant, introduces him into the house as the girl 'Mavra'. Mother and the Neighbour are deceived and the lovers are happy. Mother takes Parasha for a walk, but returns early to check on 'Mavra'. Finding 'Mavra' shaving, while singing of his love, Mother faints. The Neighbour hurries in and the Hussar jumps out of the window and makes off, leaving Parasha lamenting.

Notes:

This preposterous tale, based on Pushkin's *The House at Kolomna*, appealed to Stravinsky as a vehicle for an operatic skit. He was much attracted to the traditional Russo-Italian style of opera and, further, wished to demonstrate the falsity of certain 'picturesque' ideas about Russia, particularly to those of his French friends who were taken in by the 'tourist-office orientalism' of certain influential Russians. *Mavra* is dedicated 'to the memory of Tchaikovsky, Glinka, and Pushkin'. The music is deliberately *demodé*.

RECORDINGS:

CBS 72609 (with *Les Noces*) (d) ●	c. Gennady Rozhdestvensky
Columbia MS-6691 (d) (US)	**Parasha** (s) Ludmilla Belobragina
CBC Symphony Orchestra	**Hussar** (t) Nicolai Gutorovich
c. Igor Stravinsky	**Mother** (c) Nina Postavnicheva
Parasha (s) Susan Belinck	**Neighbour** (m-s) Anna Matyushina
Hussar (t) Stanley Kolk	
Mother (c) Patricia Rideout	
Neighbour (m-s) Mary Simmons	

Decca SDD241 (in English) ●
London STS-15102 (US)
Orchestre de la Suisse Romande
c. Ernest Ansermet
Parasha (s)   Joan Carlyle
Hussar (t)   Kenneth MacDonald
Mother (c)   Helen Watts
Neighbour (m-s) Monica Sinclair
(this recordings also contains *Renard*)

HMV ASD3104 (d) ●
Moscow Radio Symphony Orchestra

Renard

Burlesque for the stage.
Text by Stravinsky; French version by C. F. Ramuz.
First performance: Paris (Opéra) June 3, 1922 (double bill with Mavra*). New York (concert) 1923; London (BBC) 1935.*

Synopsis:

The Cock, the Goat and the Cat rail against their enemy the Fox. The Fox enters, disguised as a nun, and tries to coax the Cock from his perch. The Cock recognises the Fox, but when the Fox taunts him he jumps down and is immediately pounced on. The Fox is driven off and the Cock, back on his perch, continues complaining. The Fox returns and again tries to lure the Cock down. Again the Cock resists for a while but then jumps down. The Fox sets on him and pulls out his feathers; the Cock thinks he is done for. The Goat and the Cat distract the Fox by intimating that his wife is cuckolding him. Seizing their chance, they strangle the Fox.

Notes:

Renard, based on Russian folk tales, was intended for the Princess de Polignac's private theatre, along with Falla's » *El retablo de Maese Pedro* and Erik Satie's *Socrate*; but only Falla's work was actually given there. The score contains a part for the cembalon; Stravinsky had heard this instrument in a café in Geneva and was much taken with its sound.

RECORDINGS:

CBS 72071 (d) (with *Les Noces* etc) ●	Decca SDD241 ●
Columbia M-31124 (US)	London STS15102 (US)
Columbia Chamber Ensemble	Orchestre de la Suisse Romande
c. Igor Stravinsky	c. Ernest Ansermet
Cock (t) Loren Driscoll	**Cock** (t) Gerald English
Fox (t) George Shirley	**Fox** (t) John Mitchinson
Goat (bs) Donald Gramm	**Goat** (bs) Peter Glossop
Cat (b) William Murphy	**Cat** (bs) Joseph Rouleau
	(this recording also contains *Mavra*)

Oedipus Rex

Opera-oratorio in 2 Acts.
Text by Jean Cocteau after Sophocles, translated into Latin by J. Danielou.
First performance: (as oratorio) Paris (Théâtre Sarah Bernhardt) May 30, 1927. (Stage production) Vienna 1928; New York 1931; London (Queen's Hall) 1936.

Synopsis:

Act 1   After the Narrator has set the scene, the men of Thebes lament the plague that is raging in town and beg King Oedipus to help them. Creon returns from Delphos with the news that the murderer of Laius still lives in Thebes and must be found and punished; Oedipus says he will do it. Oedipus has sent for the blind Tiresias, the 'fountain of truth', but at first he will not answer Oedipus's questions. Provoked, Tiresias reveals that the murderer is himself a king. Oedipus accuses Creon and Tiresias of plotting against him. The chorus greets Queen Jocasta.

Act 2   Jocasta asks how her husband and her brother can argue in a stricken city. She claims that oracles invariably mislead anyone who consults them: her former husband, Laius, was to be killed by her son, according to the oracles, but he had in fact been murdered by robbers at a crossroads. Oedipus is horrified: he himself had killed a stranger at those same crossroads. The Messenger says that King Polybus is dead, and that Oedipus is his adopted son only: as a baby he had been abandoned, found by a shepherd, and given to King Polybus. Jocasta is horrified and departs. Oedipus assumes she is upset by the news of his humble origins, but then realises the truth—that he has committed patricide and incest. The Narrator tells how Jocasta has hanged herself and Oedipus has pierced his eyes with her golden pin. The chorus and the Messenger lament the Queen's suicide, and Oedipus appears, broken and blinded.

Notes:

Oedipus Rex is not an opera in any accepted sense of the term; but it is a powerful piece of drama. If it is highly stylised, it is also highly effective. In some ways it harks back to the style and

forms of Monteverdi ». It can be staged or given in concert: this makes little difference, there is virtually no 'action'. The text is in Latin and the Narrator is instructed to speak in the language of the audience.

RECORDINGS:

Decca SET616 ●
London 1168 (US)
John Alldis Choir/London Philharmonic
Orchestra
c. Sir Georg Solti
Oedipus Rex (t) Peter Pears
Jocasta (c) Kerstin Meyer
Creon (b) Donald McIntyre
Narrator Alec McCowen

Supraphon SUAST50678 ●
Turnabout 34179 (US)
Czech Philharmonic Chorus and
Orchestra
c. Karel Ančerl
Oedipus Rex (t) Ive Žídek
Jocasta (c) Vera Soukupová

Creon (b) Karel Bermann
Narrator Jean Desailly

CBS 76380 (d) ●
Columbia M33999 (US)
Harvard Glee Club/Boston Symphony
Orchestra
c. Leonard Bernstein
Oedipus Rex (t) René Kollo
Jocasta (c) Tatiana Troyanos
Creon (b) Tom Krause
Narrator Michael Wagner

CBS SBRG72131 (d) ●
Columbia M-31129 (US)
Washington Opera Society
c. Igor Stravinsky

The Rake's Progress
Opera in 3 Acts and Epilogue.
Text by W. H. Auden and Chester Kallman after Hogarth.
First performance: Venice (Teatro La Fenice) September 11, 1951.

Synopsis:
Scene: England. Time: 18th century.
Act 1 Tom and Anne are happy together in springtime, in the garden of her father, Trulove's, country house, but Trulove has doubts about Tom's stability. Tom is told by Nick Shadow that he has inherited a fortune and must travel to London. In the city, Tom leads a wild life, frequenting Mother Goose's brothel. Anne decides to go in search of him.
Act 2 Tom is unhappy; Nick advises him to marry Baba the Turk, a circus bearded lady. Anne finds Tom but he says she must forget him: he has married Baba. They part with regret. Baba tries to console Tom but, when he fails to respond, is convinced that he loves Anne and smashes the furniture in rage.

Nick persuades Tom that he can restore his fortunes with a machine that will make bread from stones.
Act 3 Tom's possessions are to be auctioned; potential customers remark on the excesses that lead to ruin. Anne seeks Tom. Sellem, the auctioneer, begins the proceedings, which culminate in the sale of Baba herself. Tom and Nick (the significance of his name now apparent) play cards in a churchyard: the stake is Tom's soul. Although Tom wins, Nick condemns him to insanity and he is taken to Bedlam, where he believes he is Adonis awaiting the coming of Venus. Anne, having witnessed his madness, is led away by Trulove; Tom raves about Venus, and dies.

Notes:
The Rake's Progress was Stravinsky's first and only full-scale opera. *Le Rossignol*, though in 3 Acts, is short and comparatively undeveloped. Also, *The Rake* is the first English text set by Stravinsky. At the Venice première in 1951, Elisabeth Schwarzkopf sang Anne Trulove and Jennie Tourel was Baba the Turk. Fritz Reiner was the conductor of the New York (Metropolitan) première on May 14, 1953, with a cast that later made the first recording, issued in the UK by Philips (ABL3055/7) and conducted by the composer.

RECORDING:
CBS 77304 (3) ●
Columbia M3S-710 (3) (US)
Sadler's Wells Chorus/Royal
Philharmonic Orchestra
c. Igor Stravinsky

Tom Rakewell (t) Alexander Young
Anne Trulove (s) Judith Raskin
Baba the Turk (m-s) Regina Sarfaty
Nick Shadow (b) John Reardon

(Sir) ARTHUR SULLIVAN
(b. London 13.5.1842; d. London 22.11.1900)

Arthur Sullivan was the second son of Thomas Sullivan, clarinettist and bandmaster of the Royal Military College, Sandhurst. Showing an early inclination for music, Arthur was entered as a chorister of the Chapel Royal. He sold his first composition at the age of 11 and won a scholarship to the Royal Academy of Music. While there, he composed incidental music for *The Tempest* and quickly earned recognition as a new hope for English music. Throughout his career he was to be torn between the expectation that he would become a respectable, 'serious' composer and the commercial success of his comic operas. Sullivan's first venture in this field was in collaboration with F. C. Burnand, on *Cox and Box*. The famous collaboration with W. S. Gilbert started with *Thespis* in 1871 and really got under way with *Trial by Jury* in 1875. A regular succession of comic operas followed, the finest and most sparkling to come from an English composer; 'serious' composition tended to take a back seat. After the highly successful *The Mikado* in 1885, there were various quarrels between the collaborators and the partnership often seemed likely to break up, but they continued to work together until *Utopia Limited* in 1892. In the meantime, Sullivan satisfied his higher aspirations with the oratorio *The Golden Legend* and the unsuccessful grand opera *Ivanhoe* in 1890. Both Sullivan and Gilbert tried to work with other collaborators, but without much success. The Savoy operas have never lost their appeal and have rarely been surpassed. Their popularity has overshadowed the other excellent music, now being rediscovered, that Sullivan wrote.

Right: *Arthur Sullivan, best known for his comic operas with Gilbert.*

Cox and Box
Triumviretta in 1 Act.
Text by F. C. Burnand.
First (private) performance: November 1866. Manchester (Prince's) December 17, 1866; London (private) April 27, 1867; London (St George's Hall) 1869.

Synopsis:
Bouncer lets his bed-sitter by day to Box, a printer on nightshift, and by night to Cox, a hatter. It works for a while, but eventually they meet and demand that Bouncer (who tries to avoid the issue by singing about his military career) give them separate rooms. This is promised; while they wait, they discover that they are in love with the same young lady. A duel seems the only answer, but Bouncer is unable to find the pistols, returning instead with a letter which tells them that the lady has married a Mr Knox. They not only swear eternal friendship, but discover that they are long-lost brothers.

Well-known arias:
Rataplan (Bouncer)
The buttercup (re-written as a duet 'The dicky bird and the owl') (Box and Cox)

RECORDINGS:
Decca TXS128 ★●
Royal Philharmonic Orchestra
c. Royston Nash
Cox (t)	Gareth Jones	
Box (t)	Geoffrey Shovelton	
Bouncer (b)	Michael Rayner	
(this recording also contains *The Zoo*)

Decca SKL4138/40 ●
London 1323 (3) (US)
New Symphony Orchestra of London
c. Isidore Godfrey

Cox (t)	Alan Styler
Box (t)	Joseph Riordan
Bouncer (b)	Donald Adams
(this recording also contains *The Gondoliers*)

Pye NSPH15 ●
Piano accompaniment, dir. Peter Murray
Cox (t)	Thomas Round
Box (t)	Lawrence Richard
Bouncer (b)	Donald Adams
(this recording also contains *Trial by Jury*)

Thespis
Extravaganza in 2 Acts.
Text by W. S. Gilbert.
First performance: London (Gaiety) December 26, 1871.

Well-known arias:
Act 1   Climbing over Rocky Mountains (Thespians)
Act 2   Little maid of Arcadee (Sparkeion)

Notes:
This was the first collaboration between Gilbert and Sullivan, commissioned by John Hollingshead of the Gaiety Theatre. Often labelled a failure, it did in fact achieve 63 performances. The libretto has survived, though apparently lacking some dialogue and lyrics as compared to the stage performance, and was reprinted in 1911, though Gilbert died that year without being able to check the proofs. The score was lost, the only surviving elements being 'Little Maid of Arcadee', which was published in 1872 as a drawing-room ballad, and 'Climbing over rocky mountains', which Sullivan re-used in *The Pirates of Penzance*. It is possible that other items were utilised elsewhere. The recording is of a reconstructed version, using music from Sullivan's less-known operas and some unpublished music.

RECORDING:
Rare Recorded Editions SRRE132/3 ●
The Light Opera Orchestra/Members of
the Fulham Light Operatic Society
c. Roderick Spencer

Trial by Jury
Dramatic Cantata in 1 Act.
Text by W. S. Gilbert.
First performance: London (Royalty) March 25, 1875.

Synopsis:
A breach of promise case begins. The Jury is admonished to show no bias in the case—but to favour the attractive plaintiff, Angelina. The male jurymen show no sympathy toward the caddish Edwin. The Learned Judge (who recounts his own history), the Foreman and the Jury are all quite plainly biased, and Counsel for the Plaintiff has no difficulty in putting his case. The Defendant offers to marry both his new sweetheart and Angelina. The Judge is not against the idea, but Counsel for the Plaintiff asks for a severe judgment, while Counsel for the Defendant claims her loss is negligible, as the Defendant has been proved worthless. The Judge solves matters by deciding to marry her himself.

Well-known arias:
When first my old, old love I knew (Edwin)
When I, good friends, was called to the bar (Judge)
Oh, gentlemen, listen I pray (Edwin)
I love him, I love him (Angelina)

RECORDINGS:
HMV SXDW3034 (2) ★●
Angel S-3589 (2) (US)
Glyndebourne Festival Chorus/Pro Arte Orchestra
c. Sir Malcolm Sargent
The Learned Judge (b)	George Baker
The Plaintiff (s)	Elsie Morison
The Defendant (t)	Richard Lewis
Counsel for the Plaintiff (b)	John Cameron
Usher (bs)	Owen Brannigan
(this recording also contains *HMS Pinafore*)

Decca SKL4579 ●
D'Oyly Carte Opera Chorus/Orchestra of the Royal Opera House, Covent Garden
c. Isidore Godfrey
The Learned Judge (b)	John Reed
The Plaintiff (s)	Ann Hood
The Defendant (t)	Thomas Round
Counsel for the Plaintiff (b)	Kenneth Sandford
Usher (bs)	Donald Adams
(this recording also contains excerpts from *Utopia Limited*)

Decca TXS113 ●
London 1167 (US)
D'Oyly Carte Opera Chorus/Royal Philharmonic Orchestra
c. Royston Nash
The Learned Judge (b)	John Reed
The Plaintiff (s)	Julia Goss
The Defendant (t)	Colin Wright
Counsel for the Plaintiff (b)	Michael Rayner
Usher (bs)	Kenneth Sandford
(this recording also contains orchestral items)

Pearl GEMM148/9 (1928 recording) ●
D'Oyly Carte Chorus and Orchestra
c. uncredited
The Learned Judge (b)	Leo Sheffield
The Plaintiff (s)	Winifred Lawson
The Defendant (t)	Derek Oldham
Counsel for the Plaintiff (b)	Arthur Hosking
Usher (bs)	George Baker

Pye NSPH15 ●
Gilbert and Sullivan Festival Chorus and Orchestra
c. Peter Murray
The Learned Judge (b)	Lawrence Richard
The Plaintiff (s)	Gillian Humphreys
The Defendant (t)	Thomas Round
Counsel for the Plaintiff (b)	Michael Wakeham
Usher (bs)	Donald Adams
(this recording also contains *Cox and Box*)

The Zoo
Musical Folly in 1 Act.
Text by Bolton Rowe.
First performance: London (St James's Theatre) June 5, 1875.

Synopsis:
Aesculapius Carboy, an apothecary, has been prevented from marrying his sweetheart Letitia by her father, and is about to hang himself near the refreshment stall at the Zoo. He is prevented from doing so by the stallholder, Eliza. Her admirer Thomas is taken ill after consuming too many refreshments, but Aesculapius sends Eliza for a prescription. It is then discovered that Thomas is an aristocrat. Letitia's father arrives and wrests her from Aesculapius, who attempts to climb into the (empty) bear pit but is again thwarted, and heads for the lion's den. Thomas returns in his ducal robes and announces he is the Duke of Islington; he persuades Letitia's father to relent, and both couples are united.

RECORDINGS:
Decca TXS128 ●
D'Oyly Carte Opera Company/Royal Philharmonic Orchestra
c. Royston Nash
Aesculapius (b)	Meston Reid
Thomas Brown (t)	Kenneth Sandford
Laetitia (s)	Julia Goss
Eliza (s)	Jane Metcalfe
Laetitia's Father (b)	John Ayldon
(this recording also contains *Cox and Box*)

Rare Recorded Editions SRRE134 ●
Fulham Light Operatic Society/Light Opera Orchestra
c. Roderick Spencer
(this recordings also contains Sullivan songs)

The Sorcerer

Comic Opera in 2 Acts.
Text by W. S. Gilbert.
First performance: London (Opéra-Comique Theatre) November 17, 1877. New York 1879.

Synopsis:

Act 1 At a garden party at Sir Marmaduke's mansion, the village of Ploverleigh celebrates the betrothal of his son, Alexis, to Lady Sangazure's daughter, Aline. All are happy except Constance, daughter of Mrs Partlett, who has an unrequited love for Dr Daly, the vicar. Sir Marmaduke was once in love with Lady Sangazure, and their love blossoms again in the happy atmosphere. Alexis is so euphoric that, after lecturing the company on true love, he reveals that he has engaged a sorcerer, Mr J. Wellington Wells, to administer to the whole village a love-potion which causes people to fall in love with the first person they see. This done, the whole company falls asleep.

Act 2 Later that evening, the villagers awake and all fall in love with the nearest person. Some unfortunate liaisons have been effected; Constance is attracted by a very ancient gentleman, Sir Marmaduke cavorts with Mrs Partlett, and the first person Lady Sangazure sees is J. Wellington Wells, who is somewhat put out because he is already engaged to a South Sea maiden. Aline falls in love with the Vicar. The sorcerer says the potion can be nullified only if someone sacrifices himself to the Devil—and he himself is deemed to be the only dispensable person. As he disappears, the rightful lovers are reunited.

Well-known arias:

Act 1 Time was when love and I were well acquainted (Dr Daly)
My name is John Wellington Wells (Wells)

RECORDING:

Decca SKL4825/6 ●
London 1264 (2) (US)
D'Oyly Carte Opera Company/Royal
Philharmonic Orchestra
c. Isidore Godfrey

Sir Marmaduke (b)	Donald Adams
Alexis (t)	David Palmer
Dr Daly (b)	Alan Styler
John Wellington Wells (b)	John Reed
Aline (s)	Valerie Masterton
Constance (s)	Ann Hood

H.M.S. Pinafore

Comic Opera in 2 Acts.
Text by W. S. Gilbert.
First performance: London (Opéra-Comique Theatre) May 25, 1878. New York 1878.

Synopsis:

Act 1 Aboard HMS Pinafore, Captain Corcoran is worried because his daughter Josephine refuses to marry Sir Joseph Porter, First Lord of the Admiralty, saying she is in love with a sailor—Ralph Rackstraw, who loves her also but is of too lowly station to reveal it. Sir Joseph comes aboard with his cousin Hebe and tells his life story; emboldened by his advocacy of democracy, Ralph declares his love for Josephine, who spurns him until the villain Dick Deadeye tries to encourage him to shoot himself.

Act 2 Captain Corcoran reveals that he might love Buttercup, a sweets-and-tobacco vendor, if he were not her social superior, and tells Sir Joseph that Josephine's reluctance is prompted by awe of his rank; Sir Joseph says love can overcome such things. Josephine and Ralph plan to elope, but Dick Deadeye thwarts their scheme. Buttercup reveals that long ago, as a nurse with Ralph and Corcoran in her care, she inadvertently switched their identities; Sir Joseph is no longer interested in a lowly tar's daughter, Josephine and Ralph are united, and the Captain is free to pursue Buttercup.

Well-known arias:

Act 1 We sail the ocean blue (Chorus)
I'm called little Buttercup (Buttercup)
I am the Captain of the Pinafore (Corcoran)
Sorry her lot who loves too well (Josephine)
I am the monarch of the sea (Sir Joseph)
When I was a lad I served a term (Sir Joseph)
A British tar is a soaring soul (Quartet)

Act 2 Never mind the why and wherefore (Trio)
He is an Englishman (Ralph and Chorus)
Many years ago (Buttercup)

RECORDINGS:

HMV SXDW3034 (2) ●
Angel S-3589 (2) (US)
Glyndebourne Festival Chorus/Pro
Arte Orchestra
c. Sir Malcolm Sargent

Sir Joseph Porter (b)	George Baker
Captain Corcoran (b)	John Cameron
Ralph Rackstraw (t)	Richard Lewis
Dick Deadeye (bs)	Owen Brannigan
Josephine (s)	Elsie Morison
Little Buttercup (c)	Monica Sinclair

(this recording also contains *Trial by Jury*)

Classics for Pleasure CFP40238 ■
(from above)

Decca SKL4081/2 ●
London 1207 (2) (US)
D'Oyly Carte Opera Company/New
Symphony Orchestra
c. Isidore Godfrey

Sir Joseph Porter (b)	John Reed
Captain Corcoran (b)	Jeffrey Skitch
Ralph Rackstraw (t)	Thomas Round
Dick Deadeye (bs)	Donald Adams
Josephine (s)	Jean Hindmarsh
Little Buttercup (c)	Gillian Knight

Decca SPA28 and STBB4/6 ■
London 25904 (US)
(from above)

Decca OPFS1/2 ●
London 12001 (2) (US)

D'Oyly Carte Opera Company/Royal
Philharmonic Orchestra
c. James Walker

Sir Joseph Porter (b)	John Reed
Captain Corcoran (b)	Thomas Lawlor
Ralph Rackstraw (t)	Ralph Mason
Dick Deadeye (bs)	John Ayldon
Josephine (s)	Valerie Masterton
Little Buttercup (c)	Christene Palmer

Pearl GEMM148/9 (recorded 1923) ●
D'Oyly Carte Opera Chorus and
Orchestra
c. uncredited

Sir Joseph Porter (b)	Frederic Ranalow
Captain Corcoran (b)	Sydney Granville
Ralph Rackstraw (t)	James Hay/ Walter Glynne
Dick Deadeye (bs)	Darrell Fancourt/ Frederick Hobbs
Josephine (s)	Violet Essex/ Bessie Jones
Little Buttercup (c)	Bertha Lewis/ Nellie Walker

Pye NSPH9 ○
Gilbert and Sullivan Festival Chorus and
Orchestra
c. Peter Murray

Sir Joseph Porter (b)	John Cartier
Captain Corcoran (b)	Michael Wakeham
Ralph Rackstraw (t)	Thomas Round
Dick Deadeye (bs)	Donald Adams
Josephine (s)	Valerie Masterton
Little Buttercup (c)	Helen Landis

The Pirates of Penzance

Comic Opera in 2 Acts.
Text by W. S. Gilbert.
First performance: Paignton (Royal Bijou Theatre) December 30, 1879. New York (Fifth Avenue Theater) December 31, 1879; London (Opéra-Comique Theatre) April 3, 1880.

Synopsis:

Act 1 The pirates celebrate on a Cornish beach. Young Frederic has completed his pirate apprenticeship and decides to leave the profession: his nursemaid, Ruth, apprenticed him by mistake to a 'pirate' instead of a 'pilot'. He falls in love at first sight with Mabel, daughter of Major-General Stanley. In spite of Frederic's warning, Mabel and her sisters are captured by the pirates. When the General untruthfully claims to be an orphan, the pirates release his daughters.

Act 2 The General puts Frederic in command of an expedition against the pirates, aided by a band of faint-hearted policemen under a Sergeant. But the Pirate King and Ruth tell Frederic that since he was born on 29 February, in leap year, he is now only five years old and is bound to remain a pirate until he is 21: Frederic implores Mabel to wait for him until 1940. The unhappy policemen, bereft of Frederic's leadership, set an ambush for the pirates, but encounter the General in his nightshirt. Battle is joined when the pirates attempt to seize the General; although victorious, the pirates submit when called upon in Queen Victoria's name, confessing that they are all really noblemen. The General bids them marry his daughters, and Frederic and Mabel are happily united.

Well-known arias:

Act 1 Pour, o pour the pirate sherry (Pirates)
Climbing over rocky mountains (Daughters)
Oh is there not one maiden breast (Frederic)
Poor wandering one (Mabel)
I am the very model of a modern major-general (Major-General)

Act 2 When the foeman bares his steel (Police)
When a felon's not engaged in his employment (Sergeant)
With cat-like tread (Police)

RECORDINGS:
HMV SXDW3041 (2) ●
Seraphim S-6102 (2) (US)
Glyndebourne Festival Chorus/Pro Arte
Orchestra
c. Sir Malcolm Sargent
Major-General
Stanley (b)   George Baker
The Pirate King (bs-b) James Milligan
Frederic (t)   Richard Lewis
Sergeant of Police (bs) Owen Brannigan
Mabel (s)   Elsie Morison
Ruth (c)   Monica Sinclair

Music for Pleasure CFP40238 ■
(from above)

Decca SKL4925/6 ●
London 1277 (2) (US)
D'Oyly Carte Opera Company/Royal
Philharmonic Orchestra
c. Isidore Godfrey
Major-General
Stanley (b)   John Reed
The Pirate King (bs-b) Donald Adams
Frederic (t)   Philip Potter
Sergeant of Police (bs) Owen Brannigan
Mabel (s)   Valerie Masterton
Ruth (c)   Christene Palmer

Decca SPA29 and STBB4/6 ■
London 25902 (US)
(from above)

Decca SKL4038/9 (d) ●
Richmond S-62517 (2) (US)
D'Oyly Carte Opera Company/New
Symphony Orchestra
c. Isidore Godfrey
Major-General
Stanley (b)   Peter Pratt
The Pirate King (bs-b) Donald Adams
Frederic (t)   Thomas Round
Sergeant of Police (bs) Kenneth Sandford
Mabel (s)   Jean Hindmarsh
Ruth (c)   Ann Drummond-
                            Grant

Pye NSPH14 ○
Gilbert and Sullivan Festival Chorus and
Orchestra
c. Peter Murray

Major-General
Stanley (b)   John Cartier
The Pirate King (bs-b) Donald Adams
Frederic (t)   Thomas Round
Sergeant of Police (bs) Lawrence Richard
Mabel (s)   Valerie Masterton
Ruth (c)   Helen Landis

World Record Club ST125 (d) ■
CMS/Summit 1025 (US)
The Linden Singers/Westminster
Symphony Orchestra
c. Alexander Faris
Major-General
Stanley (b)   Patrick Halstead
The Pirate King (bs-b) William Dickie
Frederic (t)   Edward Darling
Sergeant of Police (bs) John Gower
Mabel (s)   Elizabeth
                            Harwood
Ruth (c)   Noreen Willett

Music for Pleasure MFP2143 (d) ■
c. Sir Malcolm Sargent
George Baker (b)
Darrell Fancourt (bs)
Derek Oldham (t)
Sydney Granville (b)
Muriel Dickson (s)
Bertha Lewis (c)
(this recording consists of highlights from
the 1931 performance)

Patience

Comic opera in 2 Acts.
Text by W. S. Gilbert.
First performance: London (Opéra-Comique Theatre) April 23, 1881; (Savoy)
October 10, 1881; New York 1881.

Synopsis:

Act 1 Twenty maidens pine for the affection of the 'fleshly
poet' Reginald Bunthorne. So does Lady Jane, who knows he is
in love, unrequited, with Patience, a dairymaid. The 35th
Dragoon Guards arrive in the village and are indignant to find
their former sweethearts mooning over a long-haired aesthete
but, alone, Bunthorne reveals that his aesthetic pose is a sham.
Patience tells Angela that she once loved a boy—when she was
four years old. The poet Grosvenor proposes to Patience and is
refused; she recognises her childhood sweetheart and feels that
to love him now would be presumptuous. Bunthorne reveals his
misery to the Dragoons; he decides to raffle his hand in marriage
and Lady Jane and the maidens buy tickets. Patience agrees to
marry Bunthorne as an unselfish gesture, and the angry maidens
transfer their affections to the Dragoons—until Grosvenor
enters the marriage stakes.
Act 2 The maidens declare their love for Grosvenor, while
Lady Jane determines to capture Bunthorne, who desperately
evades her. Grosvenor reveals that he loves only Patience, who
confesses that she is unhappy with Bunthorne. The Dragoons
become aesthetes in the hope of capturing the maidens.

Bunthorne persuades Grosvenor to abandon their rivalry, but
he loses Patience, who decides it would be selfish to love him.
Grosvenor and the maidens drop their aesthetic poses and
Patience, assured of Grosvenor's ordinariness, declares she can
now love him. Bunthorne returns to Lady Jane, but she is
snapped up by a noble Lieutenant. The Dragoons choose their
brides, while Bunthorne must content himself with the aesthetic
pleasures of a tulip or a lily.

Well-known arias:
Act 1 Twenty lovesick maidens we (Maidens)
When I first put this uniform on (Colonel)
If you're anxious for to shine (Bunthorne)
Prithee pretty maiden (Patience and Grosvenor)
Act 2 Silvered is the raven hair (Lady Jane)
A magnet hung in a hardware shop (Grosvenor)
So go to him and say to him (Jane and Bunthorne)
A most intense young man (Bunthorne and Grosvenor)

RECORDINGS:
HMV SXDW3031 (2) ●
Glyndebourne Festival Chorus/Pro Arte
Orchestra
c. Sir Malcolm Sargent
Bunthorne (b) George Baker
Grosvenor (b) John Cameron
Patience (s)   Elsie Morison
Lady Jane (c) Monica Sinclair

Classics for Pleasure CFP40260 ■
(from above)

Decca SKL4146/7 ●
London 1217 (2) (US)
D'Oyly Carte Opera Company/New
Symphony Orchestra of London
c. Isidore Godfrey
Bunthorne (b) John Reed
Grosvenor (b) Kenneth Sandford
Patience (s)   Mary Sansom
Lady Jane (c) Gillian Knight

Decca SPA28, SPA147 and STBB4/6 ■
(from above)

Iolanthe

Comic Opera in 2 Acts.
Text by W. S. Gilbert.
First performance: London (Savoy) November 25, 1882. New York 1882.

Synopsis:
Act 1 Iolanthe has been condemned to death by the Fairy
Queen for marrying a mortal, but is forgiven on condition that
she never sees her husband again. Her son Strephon is in love
with Phyllis, a ward of Chancery, but the match is opposed by
the Lord Chancellor, who would like to marry her himself—
as would many peers. Strephon discusses his troubles with
Iolanthe and Phyllis is outraged to discover them together; she
does not believe Iolanthe is his mother, for, being immortal, she
looks no more than 17. Phyllis says she will marry a Peer and
Strephon asks the Fairies for help. Snubbed by the Lord
Chancellor, the Fairy Queen decides to send Strephon to the
House of Lords to reform Parliament. Phyllis begs Strephon's
forgiveness and swoons when he refuses.
Act 2 At Westminster, Private Willis, the sentry, meditates on
politics. The Fairies are much attracted by the Peers, and the
Queen, despite reminding them of the penalty for marrying
mortals, has her eye on Willis. When the Lord Chancellor
refuses Iolanthe's plea on behalf of Strephon and Phyllis, she
reveals that he is her long-lost husband, Strephon's father. The
Queen declares that Iolanthe's death sentence must now take
effect, but the Fairies reveal that they have all married Peers.
The Lord Chancellor suggests a change in the law: that Fairies
who do *not* marry mortals should die. The Queen agrees and
marries Willis; he sprouts wings and they fly off to Fairyland.

Well-known arias:
Act 1 Tripping hither, tripping thither (Fairies)
Welcome to our hearts again (Fairies)
None shall part us from each other (Phyllis and
Strephon)
The Law is the true embodiment (Chancellor)
When I went to the Bar (Chancellor)
Act 2 When all night long a chap remains (Willis)
When Britain really ruled the waves (Mountararat and
Chorus)

Oh, foolish fay (Fairy Queen)
When you're lying awake with a dismal headache
(Chancellor)

RECORDINGS:
HMV SXDW3047 (2) ●
Glyndebourne Festival Chorus/Pro Arte
Orchestra
c. Sir Malcolm Sargent
Lord Chancellor (b) George Baker
Earl of
  Mountararat (b) Ian Wallace
Earl Tolloller (t) Alexander Young
Private Willis (b) Owen Brannigan
Strephon (b) John Cameron
Queen of the
  Fairies (c) Monica Sinclair
Iolanthe (m-s) Marjorie Thomas
Phyllis (s) Elsie Morison

Classics for Pleasure CFP40238 and
CFP40260 ■
(from above)

Decca SKL4119/20 (2) ●
London 1215 (2) (US)
D'Oyly Carte Opera Chorus/New
Symphony Orchestra
c. Isidore Godfrey
Lord Chancellor (b) John Reed
Earl of
  Mountararat (b) Donald Adams
Earl Tolloller (t) Thomas Round
Private Willis (b) Kenneth Sandford
Strephon (b) Alan Styler
Queen of the
  Fairies (c) Gillian Knight
Iolanthe (m-s) Yvonne Newman
Phyllis (s) Mary Sansom

Decca SPA147 and SPA29 ■
(from above)

Decca SKL5188/9 (2) ●
London 12104 (2) (US)
D'Oyly Carte Opera Chorus/Royal
Philharmonic Orchestra
c. Royston Nash
Lord Chancellor (b) John Reed
Earl of
  Mountararat (b) John Ayldon

Earl Tolloller (t) Malcolm Williams
Private Willis (b) Kenneth Sandford
Strephon (b) Michael Rayner
Queen of the
  Fairies (c) Lyndsie Holland
Iolanthe (m-s) Judi Merri
Phyllis (s) Pamela Field

Decca STBB4/6 ■
(from above)

Pye NSPH11 ○
Gilbert and Sullivan Festival Chorus and
Orchestra
c. Peter Murray
Lord Chancellor (b) John Carter
Earl of
  Mountararat (b) Donald Adams
Earl Tolloller (t) Thomas Round
Private Willis (b) Lawrence Richard
Strephon (b) Michael Wakeman
Queen of the
  Fairies (c) Helen Landis
Iolanthe (m-s) Ann Hood
Phyllis (s) Gillian Humphreys

Princess Ida

Comic Opera in 3 Acts.
Text by W. S. Gilbert.
First performance: London (Savoy) January 5, 1884. New York 1884; London (Savoy) 1922.

Synopsis:
Act 1 King Hildebrand's court awaits the arrival of his son Hilarion's betrothed, Ida, and her father King Gama. Gama, however, arrives with his sons and says that Ida has forsworn men and opened a women's university. They are arrested, and Hilarion and his friends Florian and Cyril set out to seek Ida.
Act 2 At Castle Adamant, Ida's university, the three disguise themselves as women and are accepted as students. Ida is unmoved by Hilarion's descriptions of the suffering of Hildebrand's jilted son; Cyril gets tipsy and reveals the imposture. Confused, Ida falls into a stream; Hilarion rescues her, but she has them arrested. Hildebrand's army arrives and Ida decides to fight.
Act 3 Ida's girls are poor soldiers. Gama tells her that the outcome must be decided by combat between his sons and Hilarion; Hilarion and his friends are victorious. Hilarion then convinces Ida that they must marry in order to ensure the existence of a posterity to acclaim Ida for her work on behalf of women, and she yields to him.

Well-known arias:
Act 1 Ida was a twelvemonth old (Hilarion)
       If you give me your attention (Gama)
Act 2 Would you know the kind of maid (Cyril)
Act 3 Whene'er I poke sarcastic joke (Gama)
       This helmet I suppose (Arac, Guran and Synthius)

RECORDINGS:
Decca SKL2708/9 ●
London 1262 (2) (US)
D'Oyly Carte Opera Chorus/Royal
Philharmonic Orchestra
c. Sir Malcolm Sargent
King
  Hildebrand (bs-b) Kenneth Sandford
Hilarion (t) Philip Potter
Cyril (t) David Palmer
Florian (b) Geoffrey Skitch
King Gama (bs-b) John Reed
Princess Ida (s) Elizabeth Harwood
Melissa (m-s) Valerie Masterton

Decca SPA28 ■
(from above)

Pearl GEM129/30 (recorded 1925) ●
D'Oyly Carte Opera Chorus and
Orchestra
c. Harry Norris and George W. Byng
King
  Hildebrand (bs-b) Leo Sheffield
Hilarion (t) Derek Oldham
Cyril (t) Leo Darnton
Florian (b) Sidney Granville
King Gama (bs-b) Henry Lytton
Princess Ida (s) Winifred Lawson
Melissa (m-s) Eileen Sharp (s)

The Mikado

Comic Opera in 2 Acts.
Text by W. S. Gilbert.
First performance: London (Savoy) March 14, 1885. New York 1885.

Synopsis:
Act 1 The Mikado has made flirting a crime punishable by death. His son, Nanki-Poo, has fled the court in the guise of a wandering minstrel to escape the attentions of the elderly, ugly Katisha. Nanki-Poo loves Yum-Yum, but has abandoned his courtship on learning of her engagement to the tailor Ko-Ko. Now that Ko-Ko has been condemned for flirting, Nanki-Poo seeks Yum-Yum again, only to find that Ko-Ko has been released to become Lord High Executioner. Pooh-Bah, Lord High everything else, reveals that Ko-Ko is to marry Yum-Yum immediately. Yum-Yum and her friends, Peep-Bo and Pitti-Sing, are attracted to Nanki-Poo; he reveals his true identity to Yum-Yum, but they can find no way out of the predicament. Ko-Ko, warned that an execution is expected from him, says he will let Yum-Yum marry Nanki-Poo if he will agree to be executed in one month. Nanki-Poo agrees, but the celebrations are interrupted by Katisha, who unsuccessfully attempts to reveal his true identity.
Act 2 Yum-Yum is worried about Nanki-Poo's prospects, and matters are made worse when Ko-Ko discovers a law saying that the wife of an executed man must be buried alive. The Mikado arrives to check on the execution. Kindhearted Ko-Ko bribes Pooh-Bah to produce an affidavit of Nanki-Poo's death and sends the young couple away to marry. The Mikado enjoys a vivid description of the imaginary execution, but then discovers that the victim was his son. Aided by Katisha, he plans unpleasant punishments for all. The only chance of escape is for Ko-Ko to marry Katisha; unwillingly, he courts her and is accepted. All implore the Mikado to show mercy and, when Yum-Yum and the still-living Nanki-Poo appear, he agrees, amid general rejoicing.

Well-known arias:
Act 1 A wandering minstrel I (Nanki-Poo)
       Behold the Lord High Executioner (Chorus)
       As some day it must happen that a victim must be found (Ko-Ko)
       Three little maids from school (Yum-Yum, Peep-Bo and Pitti-Sing)
       Were you not to Ko-Ko plighted (Yum-Yum and Nanki-Poo)
Act 2 Braid the raven hair (Pitti-Sing and Girls)
       The sun whose rays (Yum-Yum)
       Brightly dawns our wedding day (Yum-Yum, Pitti-Sing, Nanki-Poo and Pish-Tush)
       Here's a how-de-do (Yum-Yum, Nanki-Poo and Ko-Ko)
       A more humane Mikado (Mikado)
       The flowers that bloom in the Spring (Ko-Ko, etc)
       On a tree by a river a little tom-tit (Ko-Ko)
       For he's gone and married Yum-Yum (All)

RECORDINGS:

HMV Concert Classics SXDW3019 (2) ●
Angel S-3573 (2) (US)
Glyndebourne Festival Chorus/Pro Arte
Orchestra
c. Sir Malcolm Sargent

The Mikado (bs)	Owen Brannigan
Nanki-Poo (t)	Richard Lewis
Ko-Ko (b)	Geraint Evans
Pooh-Bah (b)	Ian Wallace
Pish-Tush (b)	John Cameron
Yum-Yum (s)	Elsie Morison
Pitti-Sing (c)	Marjorie Thomas
Peep-Bo (s)	Jeanette Sinclair
Katisha (c)	Monica Sinclair

Classics for Pleasure CFP40238 and
CFP40260 ■
(from above)

Decca SKL4006/7 ●
London 1201 (2) (US)
D'Oyly Carte Opera Chorus/New
Symphony Orchestra
c. Isidore Godfrey

The Mikado (bs)	Donald Adams
Nanki-Poo (t)	Thomas Round
Ko-Ko (b)	Peter Pratt
Pooh-Bah (b)	Kenneth Sandford
Pish-Tush (b)	Alan Styler
Yum-Yum (s)	Jean Hindmarsh
Pitti-Sing (c)	Beryl Dixon
Peep-Bo (s)	Jennifer Toye
Katisha (c)	Ann Drummond-Grant

Decca SPA28 ■
London 25903 (US)
(from above)

World Records SOC244/5 ●
Stanyan 9009 (2) (US)
Sadler's Wells Chorus and Orchestra
c. Alexander Faris

The Mikado (bs)	John Holmes
Nanki-Poo (t)	John Wakefield
Ko-Ko (b)	Clive Revill
Pooh-Bah (b)	Dennis Dowling
Pish-Tush (b)	John Heddle Nash
Yum-Yum (s)	Marion Studholme
Pitti-Sing (c)	Patricia Kern
Peep-Bo (s)	Dorothy Nash
Katisha (c)	Jean Allister

Decca SKL5158/9 ●
London 12103 (2) (US)
D'Oyly Carte Opera Chorus/Royal
Philharmonic Orchestra
c. Royston Nash

The Mikado (bs)	John Ayldon
Nanki-Poo (t)	Colin Wright
Ko-Ko (b)	John Reed
Pooh-Bah (b)	Kenneth Sandford
Pish-Tush (b)	Michael Rayner
Yum-Yum (s)	Valerie Masterton
Pitti-Sing (c)	Peggy Ann Jones (m-s)
Peep-Bo (s)	Pauline Wales
Katisha (c)	Lyndsie Holland

Pearl GEM137/8 (1927 recording) ●
D'Oyly Carte Chorus and Orchestra
c. uncredited

The Mikado (bs)	Darrell Fancourt
Nanki-Poo (t)	Derek Oldham
Ko-Ko (b)	Henry Lytton
Pooh-Bah (b)	Leo Sheffield
Pish-Tush (b)	George Baker
Yum-Yum (s)	Elsie Griffin
Pitti-Sing (c)	Aileen Davies
Peep-Bo (s)	Beatrice Elburn
Katisha (c)	Bertha Lewis

Pye NSPH13 □
c. Peter Murray
Donald Adams (bs)
Thomas Round (t)
John Cartier (b)
Lawrence Richard (bs)
Michael Wakeham (b)
Valerie Masterton (s)
Anna Cooper
Vera Ryan
Helen Landis (c)

World Records ST119 (d) ■
CMS/Summit 1046 (US)
Linden Singers/Westminster Symphony
Orchestra
c. Alexander Faris
William Dickie (b)
Edward Darling (t)
David Croft (b)
John Gower
Ian Humphris
Elizabeth Harwood (s)
Pauline Stephens
Barbara Elsy
Noreen Willett

Ruddigore

Comic Opera in 2 Acts.
Text by W. S. Gilbert.
First performance: London (Savoy) January 22, 1887. New York 1887.

Synopsis:

Act 1 In the Cornish fishing village of Rederring, professional bridesmaids complain because the beautiful Rose Maybud will not marry and thus give them employment. They suggest that Dame Hannah, Rose's aunt, should marry, but she explains that she is sworn to maidenhood since breaking off her engagement to Sir Roderic Murgatroyd, the wicked baronet of Ruddigore. A curse on Ruddigore obliges the holder of the title to commit a daily crime or perish. Rose admits that she loves Robin Oakapple, a shy young farmer. Robin is, in fact, Sir Ruthven Murgatroyd; he has given over title and curse to his younger brother, Despard, who believes him dead. Only his servant, Adam, knows of this. The sailor Richard Dauntless, Robin's foster-brother, agrees to woo Rose on Robin's behalf, but falls in love with her himself. Mad Margaret, who loves Sir Despard, has been driven insane by his evil ways. When Despard arrives, Richard tells him that Sir Ruthven (Robin) lives, and when the villagers gather for the wedding of Rose and Robin, Despard denounces Robin as the baronet of Ruddigore. Rose returns to Richard, and Despard, free of the curse, takes back Margaret.

Act 2 In the gallery of Ruddigore Castle, lined with ancestral portraits, Robin and Adam discuss the daily crime. Rose and Richard arrive and are given permission to marry. When Robin is alone, his ancestors step from their frames and the 21st

baronet, Sir Roderic, declares that they are dissatisfied with Robin's trivial crimes: he must abduct a lady immediately. Adam is sent to capture a lady. Despard and Margaret, now respectable schoolteachers, beg Robin to abandon crime, even if it means death. He agrees, but Adam returns with Hannah as captive. She is so aggressive that Robin calls for Sir Roderic's protection: his ancestor and Hannah recognise each other as their long-lost lovers. Robin reasons that if he incurs death by neglecting his daily crime, this will be suicide, itself a crime. Therefore he should not die at all—and neither should Sir Roderic, who now admits to being still alive. Sir Roderic is united with Hannah; Robin marries Rose; Richard has to console himself with a bridesmaid.

Well-known arias:

Act 1 I know a youth who loves a little maid (Robin and Rose)
I shipped, d'ye see, in a Revenue sloop (Richard)
My boy, you may take it from me (Robin)

Act 2 When the night wind howls (Sir Roderic)
There grew a little flower (Hannah and Roderic)

RECORDINGS:

HMV Concert Classics SXDW3029 ●
Glyndebourne Festival Chorus/Pro Arte
Orchestra
c. Sir Malcolm Sargent

Sir Ruthven Murgatroyd (Robin Oakapple) (b)	George Baker
Richard Dauntless (t)	Richard Lewis
Sir Despard Murgatroyd (bs-b)	Owen Brannigan
Adam Goodheart (b)	Harold Blackburn
Rose Maybud (s)	Elsie Morison
Mad Margaret (m-s)	Pamela Bowden
Dame Hannah (c)	Marjorie Sinclair
Zorah (s)	Elizabeth Harwood
Sir Roderic Murgatroyd (bs-b)	Joseph Rouleau

Decca SKL4504/5 ●
London 1248 (2) (US)
D'Oyly Carte Opera Chorus/Royal
Opera House, Covent Garden Orchestra
c. Isidore Godfrey

Sir Ruthven Robin (b)	John Reed
Richard Dauntless (t)	Thomas Round
Sir Despard (bs-b)	Kenneth Sandford
Adam Goodheart (b)	Stanley Riley
Rose Maybud (s)	Jean Hindmarsh
Mad Margaret (m-s)	Jean Allister
Dame Hannah (c)	Gillian Knight
Zorah (s)	Mary Sansom
Sir Roderic (bs-b)	Donald Adams

Decca SPA29 and SPA147 □
(from above)

Pearl GEM133/4 (1924 recording) ●
D'Oyly Carte Chorus and Orchestra
c. uncredited

Sir Ruthven (Robin) (b)	George Baker
Richard Dauntless (t)	Derek Oldham
Sir Despard (bs-b)	Leo Sheffield
Adam Goodheart (b)	Edward Halland
Rose Maybud (s)	Elsie Griffin
Mad Margaret (m-s)	Eileen Sharp
Dame Hannah (c)	Bertha Lewis
Sir Roderic (bs-b)	Darrell Fancourt

Pye NSPH12 ■
Gilbert and Sullivan Festival Chorus and
Orchestra
c. Peter Murray
John Cartier (b)
Thomas Round (t)
Lawrence Richard (bs)
Gillian Humphreys (m-s)
Ann Hood (s)
Helen Landis (c)
Joy Roberts (s)
Donald Adams (bs)

The Yeomen of the Guard

Comic Opera in 2 Acts.
Text by W. S. Gilbert.
First performance: London (Savoy) October 3, 1888. New York 1888.

Synopsis:

Scene: The Tower of London. Time: 16th century.

Act 1 Colonel Fairfax is detained in the Tower under sentence of death for sorcery. Phoebe, who loves him, and her father, the Tower's Sergeant, Meryll, decide to risk their own lives in saving Fairfax. They plan for the Colonel to assume the role of a Yeoman by pretending to be Phoebe's brother Leonard. Jack Point, the jester, and Elsie Maynard his partner, appear to entertain the waiting crowd. Fairfax, meanwhile, wishes to marry the first girl who is willing to become his wife for the half-an-hour that is left to him, in order to have a next-of-kin to inherit his estate instead of his grasping relatives. The Lieutenant of the Tower asks for Elsie's help. Tempted, she agrees and is led blindfolded to the ceremony. Unfortunately the plot to let Fairfax escape is successful and Elsie finds herself married to a man she doesn't know. Shadbolt, the lovesick head jailer, and

Point both say they shot Fairfax during his escape.

Act 2 Fairfax is free but still a prisoner of love. He competes with Point in trying to win Elsie's affections in the role of Leonard Meryll. Elsie is won over but hears that her husband Fairfax was not killed, has been pardoned, and is on his way to claim his bride. She discovers that the man she married and the man she loves are one and the same person. Phoebe and her father marry Shadbolt and Dame Carruthers, the housekeeper of the Tower, because these two know of their part in the Fairfax plot. But poor old Jack Point loses everything; he tells the unsympathetic crowd of his lost love and dies, heartbroken.

Well-known arias:
Act 1 When maiden loves (Phoebe)
Tower warders, under orders (Meryll and Chorus)
Is life a boon? (Fairfax)
I've jibe and joke (Jack Point)
Were I thy bride (Phoebe)
Act 2 Oh! a private buffoon (Jack Point)
A man who would woo a fair maid (Fairfax, Phoebe and Elsie)
I have a song to sing-o (Jack Point)

RECORDINGS:
HMV SXDW3033 (2) ●
Glyndebourne Festival Chorus/Pro Arte Orchestra
c. Sir Malcolm Sargent

Colonel Fairfax (t)	Richard Lewis
Sergeant Meryll (b)	John Carol-Case
Jack Point (b)	Sir Geraint Evans
Wilfred Shadbolt (bs)	Owen Brannigan
Elsie Maynard (s)	Elsie Morison
Phoebe Meryll (c)	Monica Sinclair

Decca SKL4624/5 ●
London 1258 (2) (US)
D'Oyly Carte Opera Chorus/Royal Philharmonic Orchestra
c. Sir Malcolm Sargent

Colonel Fairfax (t)	Philip Potter
Sergeant Meryll (b)	Donald Adams
Jack Point (b)	John Reed

Wilfred Shadbolt (bs)	Kenneth Sandford
Elsie Maynard (s)	Elizabeth Harwood
Phoebe Meryll (c)	Ann Hood

Decca SPA15 and SPA29 ■
London 26028 (US)
(from above)

Pye NSPH10 ■
Gilbert and Sullivan Festival Chorus and Orchestra
c. Peter Murray

Colonel Fairfax (t)	Thomas Round
Sergeant Meryll (b)	Donald Adams
Jack Point (b)	John Cartier
Wilfred Shadbolt (bs)	Lawrence Richard
Elsie Maynard (s)	Valerie Masterton
Phoebe Meryll (c)	Sylvia Eaves

The Gondoliers
Comic Opera in 2 Acts.
Text by W. S. Gilbert.
First performance: London (Savoy) December 7, 1889. New York 1890.

Synopsis:
Scene: The Piazzetta, Venice. Time: About 1750.
Act 1 Two eligible gondoliers, brothers Marco and Giuseppe, are rapturously greeted by the girls, and in a blindfold game catch the two maidens they most desire—Gianetta and Tessa. The Duke and Duchess of Plaza-Toro arrive from Spain by gondola with their daughter Casilda and attendant Luiz, who are in love. The Duke explains that his daughter was married by proxy, at the age of six months, to the heir of the wealthy King of Barataria, who abdicated to become a Methodist preacher, while the Prince was stolen and taken to Venice. The King was later killed. The Duke and Duchess come to find the Prince and establish their daughter as the Queen of Barataria. Don Alhambra, the Grand Inquisitor, tells the Plaza-Toros that the Prince is now a gondolier, and assures them that the nurse, to whom the royal child was entrusted, has joined a band of brigands; but she will be found and the Prince duly identified. As the girls and gondoliers are enjoying themselves, Don Alhambra announces that either Marco or Giuseppe is the King of Barataria. Unable to decide, he says that they will both have to return to Barataria and reign jointly, and they depart.
Act 2 The Palace of Barataria, three months later. Marco and Giuseppe are reigning jointly on their two thrones. Eventually their wives arrive and all celebrate with a dance. The disapproving Don Alhambra tells the two kings about Casilda, and Gianetta and Tessa are perturbed to find that one of them is illegally married. They wait anxiously for the nurse to arrive,

while the Duke offers lessons in deportment. The nurse reveals that the real Prince is Luiz, whom she deftly substituted for her own son. All the couples are joyfully reconciled.

Notes:
This was the last real success of the Gilbert and Sullivan partnership. Both men were in ill health, and quarrelling over finances; their next two operas failed to achieve the old sparkle.

Well-known arias:
Act 1 We're called gondolieri (Marco, Giuseppe)
From the sunny Spanish shore (Duke, Duchess, Casilda, Luiz)
In enterprise of martial kind (Duke)
I stole the Prince and brought him here (Don Alhambra)
When a merry maiden marries (Tessa)
Then one of us will be a Queen (Gianetta, Tessa)
Act 2 Rising early in the morning (Marco, Giuseppe)
Take a pair of sparkling eyes (Marco)
Dance a cachucha (Chorus)
There lived a King (Don Alhambra, Marco, Giuseppe)
In a contemplative fashion (Marco, Giuseppe, Gianetta, Tessa)
Small titles and orders (Duke, Duchess)
I am a courtier grave and serious (Duke, etc)

RECORDINGS:
HMV SXDW3027 (2) ●
Seraphim S-6103 (2) (US)
Glyndebourne Festival Chorus/Pro Arte Orchestra
c. Sir Malcolm Sargent

The Duke of	
Plaza-Toro (b)	Sir Geraint Evans
Luiz (t)	Alexander Young
Don Alhambra (bs)	Owen Brannigan
Giuseppe (b)	John Cameron
Marco (t)	Richard Lewis
The Duchess (c)	Monica Sinclair
Casilda (s)	Edna Graham
Gianetta (s)	Elsie Morison
Tessa (s)	Marjorie Thomas

Classics for Pleasure CFP40260 and CFP40238 ■
(from above)

Decca SKL4138/40 (with *Cox and Box*) ●
London 1323 (3) (US)
D'Oyly Carte Opera Chorus/New Symphony Orchestra of London
c. Isidore Godfrey

The Duke of	
Plaza-Toro (b)	John Reed
Luiz (t)	Jeffrey Skitch
Don Alhambra (bs)	Kenneth Sandford
Giuseppe (b)	Alan Styler
Marco (t)	Thomas Round
The Duchess (c)	Gillian Knight
Casilda (c)	Jennifer Toye
Gianetta (s)	Mary Sansom
Tessa (c)	Joyce Wright

Decca SPA147 and SPA28 ■
(from above)

Decca SKL5277/8 (with *Marmion*) ●
London 12110 (2) (US)
D'Oyly Carte Opera Chorus/Royal Philharmonic Orchestra
c. Royston Nash

The Duke of	
Plaza-Toro (b)	John Reed
Luiz (t)	Geoffrey Shovelton
Don Alhambra (bs)	Kenneth Sandford
Giuseppe (b)	Michael Rayner
Marco (t)	Meston Reid
The Duchess (c)	Lyndsie Holland
Casilda (s)	Julia Goss
Gianetta (s)	Barbara Lilley
Tessa (c)	Jane Metcalfe

Pearl GEM141/2 (r. 1927) ○
D'Oyly Carte Chorus and Orchestra

The Duke of	
Plaza-Toro (b)	Henry Lytton
Luiz (t)	Arthur Hosking
Don Alhambra (bs)	Leo Sheffield
Giuseppe (b)	George Baker
Marco (t)	Derek Oldham
The Duchess (c)	Bertha Lewis
Gianetta (s)	Winifred Lawson

Pye NSPH8 ■
Gilbert and Sullivan Festival Chorus and Orchestra
c. Peter Murray

The Duke of	
Plaza-Toro (b)	John Cartier
Luiz (t)	Glyn Adams
Don Alhambra (bs)	Donald Adams
Giuseppe (b)	Michael Wakeham
Marco (t)	Thomas Round
The Duchess (c)	Helen Landis
Gianetta (s)	Gillian Humphreys
Tessa (c)	Ann Hood

Ivanhoe
Opera in 5 Acts.
Text by Julian Sturgis, based on Sir Walter Scott.
First performance: London (Royal English Opera House) January 31, 1891.

Well-known arias:
Act 2 Ho! jolly Jenkins (Friar Tuck)

RECORDING:
Pearl SHE509 □
O awful depth: Forgive thy son
Sylvia Eaves (s)
Thomas Round (t)

Utopia Limited

Comic Opera in 2 Acts.
Text by W. S. Gilbert.
First performance: London (Savoy) October 7, 1893. New York 1894.

Synopsis:

Act 1 In a Utopian market place, King Paramount finds little opportunity to be a despot, as he is constantly watched by two Wise Men, Scaphio and Phantis, who report his least default to Tarara, the Public Exploder. The King's eldest daughter Princess Zara comes home from Girton with a degree and the 'Flowers of Progress', various examples of the British ruling class who can help the King to model his kingdom on British constitutional lines. This upsets the Wise Men and Lady Sophy, governess to the younger daughters, who plans to marry the King.

Act 2 The British visitors suggest that a soirée should take place. In the meantime Captain FitzBattleaxe has fallen in love with Zara. The Wise Men plan an uprising against British domination. Also, it is disclosed, to Sophy's horror, that the scandal sheet 'The Palace Peeper' is written by the King. The new constitution has worked so well that lawyers, doctors, and the army are all out of work. Rebellion is about to break out when Zara suggests the introduction of party politics, which will restore the normal measures of crime and corruption, fill the jails and restore Utopia to normality.

RECORDINGS:

Decca SKL5225/6 ●
London 12105 (2) (US)
D'Oyly Carte Opera Chorus/Royal
Philharmonic Orchestra
c. Royston Nash

King Paramount (bs)	Kenneth Sandford
Scaphio (b)	John Reed
Phantis (b)	John Ayldon
Captain FitzBattleaxe (t)	Meston Reid
Princess Zara (s)	Pamela Field
Lady Sophy (c)	Lyndsie Holland

Decca SKL4579 (with *Trial by Jury*) ■
London 1155 (US)
D'Oyly Carte Opera Chorus/Royal
Opera House Orchestra
c. Isidore Godfrey

King Paramount (bs)	Donald Adams
Scaphio (b)	John Reed
Phantis (b)	John Sandford
Captain FitzBattleaxe (t)	Thomas Round
Princess Zara (s)	Ann Hood
Lady Sophy (c)	Jean Allister

Decca SPA515 ■
(from above)

The Grand Duke

Comic Opera in 2 Acts.
Text by W. S. Gilbert.
First performance: London (Savoy) March 7, 1896.

Synopsis:

Act 1 In the market square of the Grand Duchy the forthcoming marriage of Lisa and Ludwig, both of a theatrical company, is being celebrated. As the company is due to perform it is decided to have the wedding breakfast before the wedding. Ludwig reveals to the company's manager, Ernest Dummkopf, who plans to overthrow the Duke, that the plot has been discovered. The Notary, Dr Tannhäuser, suggests that Ludwig and Ernest should invoke an old law and fight a duel with cards, so the winner, whoever draws the higher card, can tell the Duke the loser was the instigator of the plot. The card-duel law is to be abolished the next day, so the 'dead' man will be able to come to life again with reputation unblemished. Ludwig draws the higher card and is deemed the winner. The Grand Duke appears, a miserly, beggarly man, looking forward to marrying the wealthy, but equally mean, Baroness von Krankenfeldt. She has heard that the Duke was betrothed in his youth to the Princess of Monte Carlo but hears that the contract is void if the Princess is not married before she comes of age — also the next day. The Duke now hears of the plot to depose him and, in a gloomy state, is receptive to the plan that Ludwig becomes Grand Duke so he can be deposed instead. So they repeat the card-duel and Ludwig also wins that. Ernest's leading lady, Julia, declares he must now marry her, much to Lisa's sorrow.

Act 2 Next morning the company wait to herald Ludwig and Julia. Ludwig announces his intention of reintroducing the habits and customs of ancient Greece, and revokes the law about the statutory duel. The Baroness now claims that, as he is the Grand Duke, he must marry her. Then the Prince of Monte Carlo arrives with his daughter to claim her right to marry the real Grand Duke. Dr Tannhäuser now discovers that a mistake has been made with the duel, and Ludwig has not earned the Dukedom and cannot revive the law. So all is resolved, and the Baroness flirts with the Prince of Monte Carlo.

RECORDING:

Decca SKL5239/40 ●
London 12106 (2) (US)
D'Oyly Carte Opera Chorus/Royal
Philharmonic Orchestra
c. Royston Nash

Duke Rudolph (b)	John Reed
Ernest Dummkopf (t)	Meston Reid
Ludwig (b)	Kenneth Sandford
Dr Tannhäuser (b)	Michael Rayner
Baroness von Krankenfeldt (c)	Lyndsie Holland
Julia Jellicoe (m-s)	Julia Goss
Lisa (s)	Jane Metcalfe

The Rose of Persia

Comic Opera in 2 Acts.
Text by Basil Hood.
First performance: London (Savoy) November 29, 1899. New York 1900.

Synopsis:

Act 1 Abu el Hassan, a rich merchant, likes to entertain the beggars and outcasts of the city. The Sultana has been visiting the house disguised as a dancing girl accompanied by three of the Sultan's slaves, and is detected when her husband sends a priest and the police to bring some of the guests to the palace for his inspection.

Act 2 The Sultan orders all those concerned to be put to death, but is dissuaded by a favourite slave. Instead, Abu is ordered to tell a story by instalments with the penalty of death if the ending is unhappy; he persuades the Sultan that the ending cannot be happy if he is executed, and his life is spared.

RECORDING:

Rare Recorded Editions SRRE152/3 ●
Orphean Singers, Soloists and Orchestra
c. James Walker

Left: *Kenneth Sandford as King Paramount, the would-be despot of* Utopia Limited.

KAROL SZYMANOWSKI
(b. Timashkovka 6.10.1882; d. Lausanne 29.3.1937)

The first Polish composer after Chopin to make a major international reputation (the only possible exception was Moniuszko), Szymanowski was born into a cultured and wealthy landowning Polish family in the Ukraine. He showed early musical gifts which were encouraged, especially because he suffered an accident in childhood which did permanent damage to one of his legs and prevented him from carrying on a normal, active life. He entered the Warsaw Conservatoire in 1903 and lived for a time in Berlin. His family was ruined by the Russian Revolution of 1917 and thereafter he suffered much poverty, in spite of a growing reputation as a pianist and composer, until he was appointed professor of composition and later director of the Warsaw State Conservatoire. His health, never robust, finally broke down in 1936; despite treatment in France and Switzerland he died of tuberculosis in the Lausanne clinic where he had been obliged to spend his last days. Szymanowski's music is unique in various respects. His travels, especially to Africa, widened his musical horizons and influenced his development. Chopin and Scriabin, and later Richard Strauss », contributed to the original synthesis he gradually developed; but Wagner » was from the beginning a major source of inspiration. A combination of individual vision and folk cultures lies at the heart of Szymanowski's creative force. What he achieved lies outside any of the familiar schools or movements in 20th century music; this is particularly evident in his well-known first violin concerto and also in his opera *King Roger*. This, apart from the single Act *Hagith*, constitutes his only venture into operatic composition (there is also an operetta, but it was not finished and never performed).

King Roger (Król Roger)
Opera in 3 Acts.
Text by Szymanowski and Jaroslav Iwaszkiewicz.
First performance: Warsaw, June 19, 1926. London (New Opera Company) 1975.

Synopsis:
Scene: Sicily. Time: 12th century.
Act 1 In the Byzantine cathedral, the Archbishop asks King Roger to protect the Church against the doctrines of the young Shepherd. At the urgings of his wife, Roxana, Roger hears the Shepherd: Roxana is impressed but Roger is disturbed, and considers ordering the Shepherd's death. He orders the Shepherd to come to the palace.
Act 2 Roger awaits the Shepherd, uneasy at the growing affinity between the young man and Roxana, who celebrates the

PYOTR ILYICH TCHAIKOVSKY
(b. Kamsko-Votinsk 7.5.1840; d. St Petersburg 6.11.1893)

Like several other Russian composers and writers, Tchaikovsky began as an amateur, while working in a government department. He learnt music as a child: he could play the piano competently by the age of six, and later studied with Zaremba. The turning point came in 1862, when he entered the newly-founded Conservatoire at St Petersburg, and then, three years later, went as professor of composition to the Moscow Conservatoire, itself newly-founded by Nicolas Rubinstein. Tchaikovsky became familiar with the nationalist school, 'The Five', but although he sympathised with some of their objectives, he was never one of them. His sympathies led him to the theatre, though he was not a natural dramatist in the mould of Verdi » or Wagner ». His tendency to compose episodically (as in his famous recognition of his weaknesses as a symphonist) is strongly in evidence in his theatre music, opera and ballet. Structurally, his operas may be faulted; but they are, at their best, tremendously effective, full of superb music and, as always with Tchaikovsky, unforgettable melody. A strain of genuine pathos informs many of the scenes. They are hugely popular in Russia, and at least two have gained, and retained, an international foothold. Of the others, scenes and excerpts add to the general delight given by the music of this most popular of composers. It was once the fashion to sneer at Tchaikovsky, largely because he wrote good tunes, but this is no longer the case. He stands in the world's eye as in Stravinsky's » estimation: 'the largest talent in Russia, and, with the exception of Mussorgsky's », the truest'. He wrote ten operas in all: indeed, his first recognition came from opera and he persevered with the form to the end of his life. He was not always lucky, either in his subject or its handling—and still less its reception, especially early in his career; but he persevered, despite subjective doubts. He said it took heroism to refrain from writing operas, and confessed frankly that 'I don't possess this heroism'.

Below: *Tchaikovsky was unable to resist the call of opera.*

The Voyevode (A Dream on the Volga)
Opera in 3 Acts.
Text by Tchaikovsky and A. N. Ostrovsky, after the latter's play.
First performance: Moscow (Bolshoi Theatre) February 11, 1869.

RECORDING:
Turnabout TV34548S □
Turnabout TV34548S (US)
Overture; Entr'acte; Dance of the Maids
Bamberg Symphony Orchestra
c. Janos Furst
(Oprichnik)

The Oprichnik
Opera in 2 Acts.
Text by Tchaikovsky, based on the play by Ivan Ivanovich Lazhechnikov.
First performance: St Petersburg (Maryinsky Theatre) April 24, 1874.

RECORDING:
Turnabout TV34548S □
Turnabout TV34548S (US)
Overture and Dance
Bamberg Symphony Orchestra
c. Janos Furst
(Tchaikovsky concert—see above)

Yevgeny Onyegin (Eugene Onegin)
Opera in 3 Acts.
Text by Tchaikovsky and Konstantin S. Shilovsky after Pushkin.
First performance: Moscow (Maly Theatre) March 29, 1879.

Synopsis:
Scene: A country estate and St Petersburg. Time: 18th century.

approach of the Shepherd and his followers with an evocative song. The Shepherd announces that he has been sent by God from Benares on the Ganges, in the name of everlasting love. Roger is shocked by the blasphemy, but Roxana sings again and then joins in an Arabian dance. Roger orders the Shepherd to be chained, but the Shepherd bursts his bonds and casts them at the King's feet. The Shepherd calls on Roxana and the others to follow him; Roger, left alone, casts off his crown and announces that he, too, will become a pilgrim.

Act 3 In a ruined Greek temple, Roger's faithful servant, Edrisi, urges the despairing King to call aloud; an echo answers, first in Roxana's voice, then in the Shepherd's, urging Roger to have no fear. Roxana tells Roger of the Shepherd's all-pervading presence and together they throw flowers on the altar fire. The Shepherd and his followers now have the form of the Greek god Dionysus (Bacchus) and his train. After a wild dance, Roger and Edrisi are again left alone. The King, having gained wisdom from his trials, joyfully greets the rising sun.

Notes:
The central theme of the opera, the dichotomy of Christianity and paganism, is represented both by the setting, Sicily, and the opening scene in the Byzantine cathedral, with its complementary aspects of East and West. The libretto is something of a jumble; but the music is original and frequently of surpassing beauty. Szymanowski's mysticism is a permeating force, but the intellectual side of the story, and of the eponymous central character, is somewhat played down. Thus, the pantheism of the Shepherd's philosophy has a stronger impact than the Christian ideal. One suspects that the composer—not only here, but throughout his work—was more on the side of pantheism than of theism.

RECORDING:
Aurora AUR5061/2 ●
previously Muza XL0250/2 (m)
Chorus and Orchestra of Warsaw State Opera
c. Mieczyslaw Mierzejewski
King Roger II (b) Andrzej Hioski
Roxana (s) Hanna Rumowska
Edrisi (t) Zdzislaw Nikodem
Shepherd (t) Kazimierz Pustelak

Right: *Karol Szymanowski (1882-1937), the gifted Polish modern romantic composer.*

Above: *Curtain for* Eugene Onegin, *Kirov Theatre, Leningrad 1926.*

Act 1 At a country house, Madame Larina and the nurse Filipievna make jam, while Tatiana and Olga practise a duet. The young poet Lensky, Olga's betrothed, arrives with his friend Eugene Onegin. Tatiana and Onegin are mutually attracted; in the famous Letter Scene, Tatiana expresses her love. Onegin is deeply touched by Tatiana's declaration, but cannot respond in kind: his love for her is no more than brotherly.

Act 2 A grand birthday ball is given for Tatiana. Her dance with Onegin stimulates gossip among the older folk, who know of Onegin's dubious reputation. Onegin deliberately provokes Lensky by dancing with Olga, and is challenged to a duel. Arriving for the combat, Lensky sings his great farewell to the joys of life: they fight, and Lensky is killed.

Act 3 Some years later, Onegin attends a ball in St Petersburg. Tatiana arrives with Prince Gremin, who sings of her beauty, and Onegin is surprised to learn that they are married. He conceals his feelings until Tatiana leaves, then pours out his love. At Gremin's house, Tatiana receives a love-letter from Onegin. Together, they muse on what might have been: she refuses to go with Onegin, leaving him alone and desolate.

Notes:
This is Tchaikovsky's most popular opera; he called it 'Lyric Scenes', indicating its episodic structure. But he found exactly the right music for Pushkin's verse-novel. He appears to have begun from the famous Letter Scene and worked both ways from that.

Well-known excerpts:
Act 1 Tatiana's Letter Scene
Act 2 Lensky's aria
Acts 2/3 Waltz and Polonaise (orchestra)
Act 3 Prince Gremin's aria
Onegin's final aria

RECORDINGS:
Decca SET596/8 ●
London 13112 (3) (US)
John Alldis Choir/Orchestra of Royal Opera House, Covent Garden
c. Sir Georg Solti
Tatiana (s) Teresa Kubiak
Onegin (b) Bernd Weikl
Lensky (t) Stuart Burrows
Olga (m-s) Julia Hamari
Gremin (bs) Nicolai Ghiaurov

Decca SET599 ■
(from above)

HMV SLS951 (3) ●
Angel S-4115 (3) (US)
Chorus and Orchestra of Bolshoi Theatre, Moscow
c. Mstislav Rostropovich

Tatiana (s) Galina Vishnevskaya
Onegin (b) Yuri Mazurok
Lensky (t) Vladimir Atlantov
Olga (c) Tamara Sinyavskaya
Gremin (bs) Alexander Ognivtsev

HMV ASD2771 ■
(from above)

Decca GOS551/3 ○
Richmond 63509 (3) (US)
Chorus and Orchestra of Belgrade National Opera
c. Oscar Danon
Tatiana (s) Valeria Heybalova
Onegin (b) Dushan Popovich
Lensky (t) Drago Startz
Olga (m-s) Biserka Tzveych
Gremin (bs) Miro Changalovich

The Maid of Orleans

Opera in 4 Acts.
Text by Tchaikovsky based on Vassily Andreyevich Zhukovsky's Russian version of Schiller's play.
First performance: St Petersburg (Maryinsky Theatre) February 25, 1887.

Synopsis:
Scene: France. Time: 1430-31.

Act 1 Joan and the village girls decorate the Druid's oak. Joan's father, Thibaut, arrives with her suitor, Raimond, but Joan says that marriage is not her destiny. Distant fires are seen and refugees fleeing from the invading English arrive: Joan foresees the defeat and expulsion of the invaders. She realises

that her time has come and, not without hesitation, accepts her destiny.

Act 2 The King, with Agnes Sorel, his mistress, and the soldier Dunois, is entertained at Chinon castle. Dunois fails to persuade the King to take action. News of another defeat arrives; then news of victory through the intervention of an unknown girl. Joan enters, singles out the King and tells him of his secret prayers, and speaks of her own life.

Act 3 Joan vanquishes Lionel, a Burgundian allied with the English, but spares his life. They fall in love and Lionel joins the French King's forces. At his coronation at Rheims, King Charles VII hails Joan as the saviour of France; but Thibaut denounces his daughter as an agent of the devil. Joan hesitates to defend herself because of guilt over her love for Lionel. Dunois challenges anyone to come to Joan's defence: Lionel steps forward—but sudden thunderclaps convince everyone of Joan's guilt. She is banished and reproaches Lionel, who offers protection, as the cause of her downfall.

Act 4 In a wood, Joan ponders her love for Lionel, who joins her. Their love duet is interrupted by heavenly voices telling Joan that she must atone for her sin by suffering and death. English soldiers kill Lionel and capture Joan. She is condemned to death: in Rouen, she is tied to the stake and the fire is lit.

Notes:

The story is implausible and totally unhistorical. Schiller's drama was even worse: it ended with Joan's escape, her rescue of the French King and her death in battle. The whole Joan/Lionel entanglement is apochryphal. Tchaikovsky made a few alterations from his source material, notably in the last Act, from Jules Barbier's *Jeanne d'Arc*. The opera has taken more hard knocks from critics than it deserves. It has not, to be sure, the charm and conviction of *Eugene Onegin* or of the later *Pikovaya Dama*. Nor does the characteristic episodic treatment suit a historical drama. But the central figure of Joan appealed to Tchaikovsky and aroused his sympathy. For that alone, the opera is worth attention.

RECORDINGS:
HMV SLS852 (4) (d) ●
Columbia/Melodiya M4-33210 (4) (US)
Chorus and Orchestra of Moscow Radio
c. Gennady Rozhdesvensky
Joan (m-s) Irina Arkhipova
Thibaut (bs) Yevgeny Vladimirov
King Charles VII (t) Vladimir Makhov
Lionel (b) Sergei Yavkovenko

Decca SDD222 □
Farewell, forests
Regina Resnik (m-s)

Mazeppa
Opera in 3 Acts.
Text by Tchaikovsky and Victor Petrovich Burenin after Pushkin.
First performance: Moscow (Bolshoi Theatre) February 15, 1884. Liverpool 1888; New York 1933.

Synopsis:
Scene: Little Russia. Time: early 18th century.

Act 1 Mariya, daughter of Kochubey, loves the Cossack Hetman Mazeppa. Andrei, a young Cossack, is hopelessly in love with Mariya. Kochubey refuses Mazeppa's request for Mariya's hand, saying that he is too old. Mazeppa has the willing Mariya carried off; the women of Kochubey's household weep for her. Kochubey, resolving to be revenged by revealing Mazeppa's intrigues with the Swedes to the Tsar, sends Andrei with the message.

Act 2 The Tsar, who trusts Mazeppa, has Kochubey handed over to him. Orlik, Mazeppa's servant, summons the torturer in an unavailing attempt to make Kochubey reveal the whereabouts of his treasure. Mariya, not knowing of her father's fate, asks Mazeppa why he seems cold towards her. Mazeppa tells her of his plan to establish and rule an independent Ukrainian state. Mariya's mother tells her of Kochubey's plight and asks her to beg Mazeppa for mercy. Kochubey and Iskra, Governor of

Poltava, arrive at the place of execution. Kochubey prays and the axe falls: too late, Mariya and her mother rush in.

Act 3 After a battle piece, Kochubey's garden is seen, neglected and derelict. Andrei, pursuing Swedish fugitives, laments his inability to settle accounts with Mazeppa, who now enters with Orlik. Mazeppa fights with Andrei, who is mortally wounded. Mariya appears, almost insane with guilt over her father's death. Orlik tells Mazeppa to ignore the crazed woman, and drags him away. Alone, Mariya takes Andrei's head in her hands as he dies.

RECORDING:
Cetra Opera Live L043 (3) (m) ●
Chorus and Orchestra of Teatro
Communale di Firenze
c. Jonel Perlea
Mazeppa (b) Ettore Bastianini
Mariya (s) Magda Olivero
Kochubey (bs) Boris Christoff

Pikovaya Dama (The Queen of Spades/ Pique Dame)
Opera in 3 Acts.
Text by Tchaikovsky and Modest Tchaikovsky after Pushkin.
First performance: St Petersburg (Maryinsky Theatre) December 19, 1890.

Synopsis:
Scene: St Petersburg. Time: late 18th century.

Act 1 A public garden in St Petersburg: Sourin and Tchekalinsky enter, followed by Hermann and Count Tomsky. Hermann tells how he loves an unknown beauty. Prince Yeletsky joins them, elated because he has just become engaged to Lisa, whom Hermann recognises as his beloved. Lisa is the grand-daughter of the mysterious Countess: the old woman is reputed to have been a great gambler, possessing the magical secret of the 'three cards'. Hearing this story from Tomsky, Hermann is greatly disturbed. Alone in her room, Lisa can think only of Hermann, who looks like a 'fallen angel'. Hermann appears and declares his love, but when the Countess arrives he hides, brooding over the 'three cards'. The Countess departs: Hermann and Lisa embrace.

Act 2 At a masked ball, Yeletsky is troubled by Lisa's despondency. Sourin and Tchekalinksy plan to trick Hermann, who is obsessed by the 'three cards'. Lisa sends Hermann a key so that he may visit her. On his way to Lisa, Hermann hears voices and hides in the Countess's bedroom. The Countess enters, dismisses her attendants, and sings to herself of the past. Seeing Hermann, she is frightened: he reassures her and asks for the secret of the 'three cards'. Refused, he draws a pistol—and the Countess dies of fright. Hermann cries out in despair, then finds Lisa in the room. She realises that he desires only the secret of the cards.

Act 3 Hermann has attended the Countess's funeral and is conscience-stricken. A letter from Lisa makes an assignation by a canal. The door flies open and the ghost of the Countess enters to offer Hermann the secret of the cards—if he promises to marry Lisa. The three cards are: Three, Seven, Ace! Lisa meets Hermann, but he rejects her, thinking only of the cards, and she throws herself into the canal. In the gambling house, Hermann plays the first two cards and wins. Playing against Yeletsky, he stakes everything on the third card—and loses, with the Queen of Spades. The ghost of the Countess appears, and the crazed Hermann stabs himself.

Notes:

This opera is more dramatically structured than *Eugene Onegin* or *The Maid*. Pushkin's poem needed a good deal of modification for stage purposes; but this was skilfully accomplished. The scene by the canal in Act 3 was inserted by Tchaikovsky against his brother Modest's advice. Apparently Tchaikovsky felt that a woman was needed to fill out the Act, and the audience would want to know what became of Lisa. The emotional temper of

the opera is parallel to that of the last two symphonies, which it bisects chronologically.

Well-known arias:
Act 1 Lisa's *scena* and aria
Act 2 The Countess's soliloquy
Act 3 Lisa's aria ('Twill soon be midnight)

RECORDINGS:
DG 2740 176 (4) ●
DG 2711 019 (4) (US)
Tchaikovsky Choir/French Radio
Children's Chorus/French National
Orchestra
c. Mstislav Rostropovich

Hermann (t)	Peter Gougaloff
Lisa (s)	Galina Vishnevskaya
Countess (c)	Regina Resnik
Prince Yeletsky (b)	Bernd Weikl
Count Tomsky (b)	Dan Iordàchescu

DG 2537 042 ■
(from above)

Decca GOS568/70 ●
Richmond 63516 (US)
Yugoslav Army Chorus/Radio Belgrade
Children's Chorus/Belgrade National
Radio Orchestra
c. Kreshimir Baranovich

Hermann (t)	Alexander Marinkovich
Lisa (s)	Valeria Heybalova
Countess (m-s)	Melanie Bugarinovich
Prince Yeletsky (b)	Dushan Popovich
Count Tomsky (b)	Jovan Gligor

Yolanta (Iolanthe)
Opera in 1 Act.
Text by Modest Tchaikovsky based on Henrik Hertz's play.
First performance: St Petersburg (Maryinsky Theatre) December 18, 1892.
London (Camden Festival) 1968.

Synopsis:
Scene: Provence. Time: 15th century.
Yolanta, the blind daughter of King René of Provence, is kept in total seclusion so that she will not know that she differs from other people. King René brings a Moorish doctor, who says that a cure is possible only if Yolanta is told the truth and develops the will to see. Her father refuses. Robert, Duke of Burgundy, who is betrothed to Yolanta but has never seen her and knows nothing of her blindness, arrives with Count Vaudémont. Robert loves another and wishes to break off the engagement. When Robert and Vaudémont happen upon the sleeping Yolanta, Vaudémont is enchanted by her, soon learning of her blindness. The King is angry and threatens Vaudémont with death unless he can teach Yolanta to see. Robert departs to fetch his followers to Vaudémont's aid, but the King tells Vaudémont that his threat was meant only as a spur to Yolanta, who has fallen in love with the young man's voice. The Doctor leads in Yolanta, blindfolded. The blindfold is removed: she can now see. All ends happily.

Notes:
Yolanta was originally designed as a single Act complement to *The Nutcracker*, the two to be given on the same evening. The libretto, by Modest Tchaikovsky, was based on Zvantsev's translation of Hertz's play *Kong Renés Datter*, itself derived from Hans Andersen.

RECORDING:
HMV SLS5123 (2) (d) ●
Columbia/Melodiya M2-34595 (2) (US)
Chorus and Orchestra of Bolshoi
Theatre, Moscow
c. Mark Ermler

Yolanta (s)	Tamara Sorokina
King René of Provence (bs)	Yevgeny Nesterenko
Count Vaudémont (t)	Vladimir Atlantov
Robert, Duke of Burgundy (b)	Yuri Mazurok
Doctor (b)	Vladimir Valaitis

GEORG PHILIPP TELEMANN
(b. Magdeburg 14.3.1681; d. Hamburg 25.6.1767)

Long-lived and enormously prolific, Telemann was largely self-taught: he studied the scores of his great contemporaries and predecessors, including Lully ». He studied languages and science at the University of Leipzig, where he went in 1700, and four years later was appointed organist of the New Church. He also founded a 'Collegium musicum' among the students. The same year he briefly served one prince and then entered the service of another at Einstadt. Tours through Europe helped give his style a marked eclecticism with a total mastery of all forms of music. He was not an original musical thinker, but he was a thoroughly learned one. His principal fame, until the Baroque revival of the post-1945 years, centred on his association with J. S. Bach, who was appointed Cantor at Leipzig after Telemann, the first choice, had declined the offer. The two had already encountered each other during Bach's time at Weimar. Telemann was godfather to one of Bach's children. In 1721 he was appointed music director in Hamburg, remaining there for the rest of his long life. The gradual emergence of Telemann's reputation has revealed that, among other things, he produced what is in effect the first German comic opera. He wrote some 45 operas in all, but apart from *Pimpinone* little is heard of them.

Pimpinone
Intermezzo in 1 Act.
Text by Johann Philipp Praetorius.
First performance: Hamburg September 27, 1725.

Notes:
This lively little work preceded Gay's » *The Beggar's Opera* by two years and Pergolesi's » *La serva padrona*, which it more or less resembles, by eight years. Telemann's characteristic style, based upon German counterpoint and Italian aria, is here deployed with a light touch. The story concerns only two characters, a foolish old man and an alert serving wench. The plot makes the familiar point that there is no fool like an old fool. Pimpinone is at the mercy of the servant girl, Vespetta, who twists him round her little finger: after a few hilarious incidents, she marries him and takes control of the purse-strings. It is all enormous fun.

RECORDINGS:
Turnabout TV34124S ●
Stuttgart Bach Collegium
c. Helmuth Rilling

Pimpinone (bs)	Erich Wenk
Vespetta (s)	Yvonne Ciannella

Philips SAL3598 (d) ●
Berlin State Orchestra/Chamber
Ensemble
c. Helmut Koch

Pimpinone (bs)	Reiner Süss
Vespetta (s)	Erna Roscher

Telefunken 2635285 (2) ●
Telefunken 2635285 (2) (US)
Floregium Musicum
c. Hans Ludwig Hirsch

Pimpinone (bs)	Siegmund Nimsgern
Vespetta (s)	Uta Spreckelsen

Below: *Georg Philipp Telemann, composer of some 40 operas.*

AMBROISE THOMAS

(b. Metz 5.8.1811; d. Paris 12.2.1896)

As a child, Thomas began to study music with his father. He entered the Paris Conservatoire in 1828 and won the first prize for piano in 1829 and the Prix de Rome in 1832. On returning from Rome he began to gain success in Paris at the Opéra-Comique and later at the Opéra. He wrote a little non-operatic music, including two masses and some instrumental pieces, but his fame rests upon his operas, and on *Mignon* in particular. However, like some other French composers, he had ambitions beyond his creative means: he would tackle subjects from Shakespeare, Dante and Goethe instead of concentrating on the lighter, melodious type of work for which his talents best fitted him. Thomas was appointed Chevalier of the Legion of Honour in 1845 and received the Grand Cross in 1894. He became professor of composition at the Conservatoire in 1852 and Director in 1871.

Le Caïd

Opera in 2 Acts.
Text by Thomas Sauvage.
First performance: Paris (Opéra-Comique) January 3, 1849.

RECORDING:
Decca SXL6637 □
London 26379 (US)
Je comprends que la belle aime le militaire
Joseph Rouleau (bs)

Raymond, ou le Secret de la Reine

Opera in 3 Acts.
Text by Adolphe de Leuven and Joseph Bernard Rosier.
First performance: Paris (Opéra-Comique) June 5, 1851.

RECORDING:
CBS 61748 □
Columbia MS-6743 (US)
Overture
c. Leonard Bernstein

Mignon

Opera in 3 Acts.
Text by Jules Barbier and Michel Carré based on Goethe's 'Wilhelm Meister'.
First performance: Paris (Opéra-Comique) November 17, 1866. New York 1871; London (Sadler's Wells) 1932.

Synopsis:

Scene: Germany and Italy. Time: late 18th century.
Act 1 The elderly minstrel Lothario and the strolling players Laerte and Philine meet at a German inn. Lothario and Wilhelm, a travelling student, rescue Mignon from the gypsy leader Jarno. Although Wilhelm is attracted to Philine, he buys Mignon's freedom and, after she tells him how she was abducted as a child, is reluctant to let her go with Lothario.

Below: Mignon *at the Opéra-Comique in 1963, conducted by Hartemann.*

Act 2 The famous Gavotte forms the entr'acte. Mignon is furiously jealous of Philine's love for Wilhelm, who tells Mignon that they must part. The theatrical troupe are performing *A Midsummer Night's Dream* at a castle. Mignon hears Philine's performance and then, in the conservatory, tells Lothario that she wishes the building would burn down. Lothario, a little senile, takes her at her word, The conservatory bursts into flames with Mignon inside, and Wilhelm risks his life to rescue her.
Act 3 Mignon has been ill and Wilhelm has bought her an old Italian castle. Lothario is confused, but at last recognises the castle as his former home, from which his child was abducted. Mignon is, of course, his long-lost daughter.

Notes:

Mignon has lost a good deal of its one-time popularity, though its charms can still excite admiration. Its decline has been largely brought about by over-exposure of its famous set numbers, which are numerous. Alternative endings have been used, one tragic.

Well-known arias:

Act 1   Connais-tu le pays? (Mignon)
Legères hirondelles (Mignon and Lothario)
Act 2   Je crois entendre les doux compliments (Philine)
Je connais un pauvre enfant (Mignon)
Me voici dans son boudoir (Frédéric)
Adieu, Mignon, courage (Wilhelm)
Elle est là, près de lui? (Mignon)
As-tu souffert? As-tu pleuré? (Mignon and Lothario)
Je suis Titania (Philine)
Act 3   Je suis heureuse, l'air m'enivre (Mignon and Wilhelm)
Elle ne croyait pas (Wilhelm)

RECORDINGS:
CBS 79401 (4) ●
Columbia M4-34590 (4) (US)
Ambrosian Opera Chorus/Philharmonia
Orchestra
c. Antonio de Almeida
Mignon (m-s) Marilyn Horne
Wilhelm (t)   Alain Vanzo
Lothario (bs) Nicolai Zaccaria
Philine (s)   Ruth Welting
Laerte (t)   André Battedou
Frédéric (m-s) Frederica von Stade

CBS 61748 □
Columbia MS-6743 (US)
Overture
c. Leonard Bernstein

DG 2548 260 □
DG 2548 260 (US)
Overture
c. Louis Frémaux

CBS 76522 □
Columbia M-34206 (US)
Connais-tu le pays?
Frederica von Stade (m-s)

HMV SLS5105 (3) □
Angel S-3736 (3) (US)
Adieu, Mignon, courage
Elle ne croyait pas
Nicolai Gedda (t)
(Massenet: *Werther*)

Above: *Marie Roze as Mignon with the Carl Rosa Company in 1883.*

Hamlet

Opera in 5 Acts.
Text by Jules Barbier and Michel Carré based on Shakespeare.
First performance: Paris (Opéra) March 9, 1868.

RECORDING:
Decca SXL2256/7 □
London 25232/3 or 1214 (US)
A vos yeux . . . Partagez mes fleurs
Joan Sutherland (s)

VIRGIL THOMSON
(b. Kansas City 25.11.1896)

Virgil Thomson has written music of every conceivable form and style—much of it full of a simple charm too long absent from serious music. He has drawn inspiration from many popular sources, notably from Cajun folksong, to the wider fields of American folk song and jazz. He studied music with Nadia Boulanger at Harvard, where he was also Assistant Instructor from 1920-25. He was organist and choirmaster at King's Chapel, Boston, 1922-23, and in 1925 went to live in Paris where he stayed for 15 years. He became a friend of Satie, who influenced his music, and of Gertrude Stein, who wrote the libretti for two of his operas, *Four Saints in Three Acts* (1934) and *The Mother of Us All* (1946). On his return to America in 1940, Thomson became chief music critic of the *New York Herald Tribune*, where he remained until 1954, writing in an entertaining and penetrating style. In general, Thomson's perceptive knowledge of music produces a sense of timelessness in his operas, always with that sure touch of the Thomson hand: at once tender and wry, sentimental and humorous. He is particularly successful in capturing the essence of American speech in his music.

Four Saints in Three Acts
Opera in 4 Acts.
Text by Gertrude Stein.
First (stage) performance: Hartford, Connecticut (Avery Memorial Theater) February 8, 1934. New York 1934 and 1952; Paris 1952.

Notes:
The composer has said: 'Please do not try to construe the works of this opera literally or to seek in it any abstruse symbolism. If, by means of the poet's liberties with logic and the composer's constant use of the simplest elements in our musical vernacular, something is here evoked of the child-like gaiety and mystical strength of lives devoted in common to a non-materialistic end, the authors will consider their message to have been communicated'. The four saints of the title are Saint Teresa of Avila, Saint Ignatius Loyola of 16th-century Spain, and their confidants, invented characters, Saint Settlement and Saint Chavez. A male and female compère, a small chorus of named saints and a larger chorus of un-named saints completes the cast. The compères talk to the audience about the progress of the opera, where the figures move in a landscape giving a 'panoramic view of sainthood'. From all this arises what Gilbert Chase has described as 'a lovely work—a masterpiece in originality and invention'. There is little or no logic in Stein's libretto but Thomson brings the language to life with great clarity and precision.

RECORDING:
RCA Victor LM-2756 *or* LCT-1139 (d) (US) ○
Chorus and Orchestra
c. Virgil Thomson
Beatrice Robinson-Wayne (s)
Ruby Green (c)
Inez Mathews (s)
Edward Mathews (b)
Charles Holland (t)
David Bethea (t)
Randolph Robinson (b)
Altnoell Hines (m-s)
Abner Dorsey (b)

Right: *The American composer Virgil Thomson wrote his operas with the help of Gertrude Stein.*

The Mother of Us All
Opera in 2 Acts.
Text by Gertrude Stein.
First performance: New York (Brander Matthews Hall, Columbia University) May 7, 1947.

Notes:
The theme of the opera is the struggle for women's rights in America centred round the figure of Susan B. Anthony, who wrote a four-volume 'History of Women's Suffrage' and, around the 1870s, led women's marches and was frequently arrested. The opera deals with Susan B. Anthony's history and draws in such diverse characters as Daniel Webster, Andrew Johnson (17th President), John Quincy Adams (6th President), stage star Lillian Russell and Ulysses Grant (who mentions Eisenhower). These people debate the issues in a series of *non sequiturs* that defeat any synopsis. As in *Four Saints in Three Acts* there are two compères who discuss the whole proceeding; in this case two characters called Gertrude S. and Virgil T. Again the simple charms of Thomson's music make the score one of outstanding beauty and clarity.

RECORDINGS:
New World Records NW288/9 (US) ●
The Santa Fe Opera
c. Raymond Leppard
Susan B. Anthony   Mignon Dunn
Anne   Batyah Godfrey
Gertrude S.   Aviva Orvath
Virgil T.   Gene Ives
Daniel Webster   Philip Booth
Jo the Loiterer   James Atherton
(and 22 other characters)

Columbia ML-4468 (d) (US) □
Orchestral Suite
c. Werner Janssen

(Sir) MICHAEL TIPPETT
(b. London 2.1.1905)

The most visionary of living English composers and a profound musical and metaphysical thinker, Tippett's achievement is remarkable by any standards. Biographical details are few and totally unostentatious. He studied at the Royal College under R. O. Morris and Charles Wood, then worked in the music department of London County Council and was music director at Morley College, where his performances of Purcell's »church music were extremely important, both for Purcell's reputation and for his own. Indeed, his artistic nature polarises on an ardent and individual vein of lyricism and polyphonic complexity. This has sometimes led to stylistic dichotomy; but the internal tensions which result have also produced extremely stimulating and potent music. This is frequently difficult, not because it is wilfully obscure, but in the sense in which Shelley said of Plato that he is obscure only because he is profound. Some of Tippett's earlier music was in danger of being 'difficult' beyond its profundity; but as he evolved his personal idiom and worked out his personal problems, his music clarified—although it did not necessarily become 'easy listening'. Each of his three operas is a key work in his development, and each is paralleled by other

kinds of music. An ardent pacifist and a man of great spiritual insight, Sir Michael Tippett is a deeply enriching individual in everything he says or does.

The Midsummer Marriage
Opera in 3 Acts.
Text by Tippett.
First performance: London (Covent Garden) January 27, 1955.

Synopsis:
Act 1   Mark and Jenifer, who are to be married, meet with friends to greet the rising sun: Mark urges the dancers in the magical rites to create a new dance for his wedding. The dancer Strephon is injured by the He-Ancient and the party is ordered back to the temple. Jenifer, dressed for a journey rather than a wedding, announces that she seeks truth rather than love: she mounts a staircase and passes from view. Mark feigns indifference, but follows her after hearing the voice of the tycoon King Fisher, Jenifer's father. With his secretary, Bella, King Fisher organises a search for Jenifer. The Ancients obstruct him, so he calls on Jack,

Above: *Tippett's* The Midsummer Marriage *at the Royal Opera House.*

Bella's boyfriend, to break through the gates. Jenifer and Mark appear at the top of the stairs in a state of exaltation.

Act 2 Strephon leads a dance as the chorus hymns Midsummer Day. Bella speaks to Jack of marriage. They enter a wood and there begins the sequence of ritual dances: in three symbolic actions, the Hound chases the Hare; the Otter chases the Fish; and the Hawk chases the Bird. Bella, somewhat shaken, applies makeup as she tells Jack of King Fisher's plans.

Act 3 King Fisher brings in the clairvoyante Madame Sosostris to find Jenifer. Madame Sosostris prophesies the marriage of Mark and Jenifer in both physical and symbolic terms: furious, King Fisher orders Jack to expose the clairvoyante as an impostor. In an ensemble, King Fisher, Bella and Jack, and two Ancients manoeuvre for advantage; then Jack throws down his symbols of office for King Fisher to take up. King Fisher's unmasking of Sosostris reveals huge lotus petals enfolding a transfigured Jenifer and Mark; and when King Fisher utters threats, the two turn to him and he falls dead. More ritual dancing follows, headed by Strephon, in which carnal love and fertility are celebrated. As the ritual fire dance proceeds, Mark, Jenifer and Strephon are drawn into the lotus petals, which close around them as darkness falls. As light returns, Mark and Jenifer are heard in their human forms, proclaiming that they have found truth.

Notes:

Tippett describes *The Midsummer Marriage* as a 'Quest' opera, in the manner of *The Magic Flute*. The text was written under the influence of T. S. Eliot's poetic drama. Mark and Jenifer, with their overtones of ancient history and mythology, are contrasted with the more earthy Jack and Bella—the 'marvellous' couple and the 'everyday' couple. When it first appeared the opera excited differing responses: the complexity of the libretto which, it was suggested, even Tippett himself did not fully understand, was contrasted with the luminous beauty of the music. The music itself was related to Tippett's contemporary works in other forms, including the Piano Concerto and the First Piano Sonata.

RECORDINGS:

Philips 6703 027 (3) ●
Philips 6703 027 (3) (US)
Chorus and Orchestra of Royal Opera House, Covent Garden
c. Colin Davis

Mark (t)	Alberto Remedios
Jenifer (s)	Joan Carlyle
King Fisher (b)	Raimund Herincx
Bella (s)	Elizabeth Harwood
Jack (t)	Stuart Burrows
Madame Sosostris (c)	Helen Watts

Philips 6580 093 □
Philips 6580 093 (US)
Orchestra of Royal Opera House, Covent Garden
c. Colin Davis
4 Ritual Dances
(from above)

Decca DPA571/2 □
Orchestra of Royal Opera House, Covent Garden
c. John Pritchard
(*A Child of Our Time*)

King Priam

Opera in 3 Acts.
Text by Tippett.
First performance: Coventry, May 29, 1962. London (Covent Garden) 1962; Karlsruhe 1963.

Notes:

As *The Midsummer Marriage* is related musically to the Piano Concerto and other works of a similar nature, so *King Priam* was related to such works as the Concerto for Orchestra and the Second Piano Sonata in a further evolution of the composer's creative force, now requiring a curbing of the former lyricism and a hardening of the structural and expressive edges.

RECORDING:
Decca SET392/3 □
O rich-soiled land
Richard Lewis (t)

The Knot Garden

Opera in 3 Acts.
Text by Tippett.
First performance: London (Covent Garden) December 2, 1970.

Synopsis:

Act 1 Thea tends the flowers in the garden; the help offered by the analyst Mangus is not needed. Flora enters screaming, pursued by Faber, Thea's husband and Flora's ward. Thea sends Flora away with Mangus and admonishes the bewildered Faber. Flora, told by Thea to try flower therapy, announces that Thea's sister, Denise, is expected. Mel, a Negro musician, and Dov, a writer, arrive in fancy dress, perform a charade and sing a nonsense song. Mangus, who has been thinking of himself as Prospero in *The Tempest*, now sees the others as potential members of the cast. A confusion of identities alarms Faber, but is resolved. Flora screams again, for Denise displays marks of torture incurred in her efforts to right the world's wrongs. Mel sings a blues which evolves into an ensemble.

Act 2 Thea and Denise are in different parts of the Knot Garden. Faber approaches Denise but is taken away by Fora and is again admonished by Thea. Dov commiserates with Faber over the humiliations inflicted by women: the two are attracted to each other, but Faber departs when Mel enters. Mel and Dov share a jazz interlude of self-discovery. Denise addresses Mel on race and social oppression. Alone together, Flora and Dov move towards a love scene, but are interrupted by Mel.

Act 3 Mangus initiates a series of charades based on *The Tempest*. Then Thea sings an aria affirming the sanctity of marriage. In a mock trial, Dov (Ariel) and Mel (Caliban) are acquitted. Mel leaves with Denise and Dov wishes to follow Flora, but she goes alone. Thea and Faber, reconciled, remain together in the garden.

Notes:

The structure, metaphysical as well as musical, is delineated in the subheadings of the three Acts: Confrontation—Labyrinth—Charade. The opera is again complex, though in a totally different manner from *The Midsummer Marriage*. It is a play in the true sense: that is: a 'thing in itself', a self-contained piece of drama with an independent existence, not a simulation of 'real life'. The subtleties and complexities are clarified at several points in the recording, where certain effects and intentions can be realised in a way not wholly possible in the theatre. This is not an unusual situation. The influence of T. S. Eliot, whom Tippett has described as 'my artistic father', is again apparent.

RECORDING:
Philips 6700 063 (2) ●
Philips 6700 063 (2) (US)
Orchestra of Royal Opera House, Covent Garden
c. Colin Davis

Faber (b)	Raimond Herincx
Thea (m-s)	Yvonne Minton
Flora (s)	Jill Gomez
Denise (s)	Josephine Barstow
Mel (b)	Thomas Carey
Dov (t)	Robert Tear
Mangus (b)	Thomas Hemsley

RALPH VAUGHAN WILLIAMS
(b. Down Ampney, Glos., 12.10.1872; d. London 26.8.1958)

Vaughan Williams was born in Gloucestershire, son of a clergyman, educated at Charterhouse and Cambridge, and studied music at the Royal College. Later he went to Europe to study with Max Bruch and, briefly, with Maurice Ravel ». He developed slowly, forging an individual style and technique out of various elements, the most important being English folk song and Tudor church music. He served in the army in World War I (while on active service in France, he first conceived his Pastoral symphony, often regarded as his most inwardly English work), and afterwards became professor of composition at the Royal College. Otherwise, he held no major official position, though he was always active in the organisation and encouragement of festivals and other public and private musical events. He composed a great deal of vocal music, solo and choral, and six operas. Although he was not, perhaps, a natural composer of opera, he could adapt himself to it when necessary. He represents in its purest form in music the poet W. B. Yeat's description of the English mind as 'meditative, rich, deliberate'. His first operatic piece, *The Shepherds of the Delectable Mountains*, called a 'pastoral episode', was later incorporated into his masterpiece *The Pilgrim's Progress*, both being derived from John Bunyan's book.

Hugh the Drover
Ballad opera in 2 Acts.
Text by Harold Child.
First performance: London (RCM) July 11, 1922. London (His Majesty's) 1924; Toronto 1932; New York 1952.

Notes:
Besides original, folk-song based material, Vaughan Williams incorporated a number of English folk songs direct into his score. The story, which takes place at a country fair at a small town in Gloucestershire during the time of the Napoleonic wars, concerns Hugh's love for Mary, who is already engaged to John; John's accusation, after a fight, that Hugh is a French spy; Hugh's arrest; Mary's abortive attempt to release him; the soldiers' recognition of Hugh as a well-known patriot; and the release of Hugh and Mary to enjoy freedom and love.

RECORDINGS:
HMV SLS5162 (2)●
St Paul's Cathedral Choir/Ambrosian Opera Chorus/Royal Philharmonic Orchestra
c. Sir Charles Groves
Hugh (t)   Robert Tear
Mary (s)   Sheila Armstrong
John (bs)   Michael Rippon
Aunt Jane (c)   Helen Watts

Pearl GEM128 (m) (r. 1924) ○
Orchestra and Chorus
c. Sir Malcolm Sargent
Hugh (t)   Tudor Davies
Mary (s)   Mary Lewis
John (b)   Frederic Collier
Constable (b)   William Anderson
Sergeant (b)   Peter Dawson
(This is the cast that gave the 1924 performance at His Majesty's Theatre, London. About half the music is included)

Sir John in Love
Opera in 4 Acts.
Text from Shakespeare's 'The Merry Wives of Windsor'.
First performance: London (RCM) March 21, 1929.

Notes:
Shakespeare's *Merry Wives* and the 'fat knight' (Vaughan Williams's original title for his opera) have afforded much grist to the operatic mill. As well as the famous productions of Verdi » and Nicolai », there are a number of others, less famous but not all deserving oblivion. Vaughan Williams bends the emphasis to his own ends here and there, and incorporates some English folk songs and Elizabethan songs, the most famous example being the use of 'Greensleeves' at the beginning of Act 2. He omits the basket-ducking episode and makes the climax the discovery of Mistress Page behind the arras. He also places more emphasis than does Verdi on the love between Ann and Fenton. Vaughan Williams wrote the opera 'for his own enjoyment', according to his widow, and as 'the height of impertinence', according to himself. For further plot details, see under Nicolai and Verdi.

RECORDING:
HMV SLS980 (3) ●
Angel SX-3822 (3) (US)
John Alldis Choir/New Philharmonia Orchestra
c. Meredith Davies
Sir John Falstaff (b)   Raimund Herincx
Mistress Page (s)   Felicity Palmer
Ann Page (s)   Wendy Eathorne
Page (b)   John Noble
Mistress Ford (m-s)   Elizabeth Bainbridge
Fenton (t)   Robert Tear
Mistress Quickly (c)   Helen Watts
Ford (bs)   Robert Lloyd

The Poisoned Kiss (or The Empress and the Necromancer)
Opera in 3 Acts.
Text by Evelyn Sharp after Richard Garnett and Nathaniel Hawthorne.
First performance: Cambridge May 12, 1936. London 1936.

RECORDING:
DG 2383 359 □
Overture
Bournemouth Sinfonietta
c. George Hurst

Riders to the Sea
Opera in 1 Act.
Text from play by J. M. Synge.
First performance: London (RCM) November 30, 1937. Cambridge (Arts Theatre) 1938.

Synopsis:
In a cottage on an island off the west coast of Ireland, Nora and her sister Cathleen are spinning. Clothes taken from a drowned man have been brought so that they may decide whether they are those of their brother, Michael, who has disappeared at sea, like his father and four brothers. The sisters conceal the clothes from Maurya, their mother. Bartley, the only remaining son, is to take horses to Galway Fair. Although warned that the wind is adverse, he declares that he will go, riding the red mare, with the grey pony running with him. Maurya fails to give Bartley her blessing; his sisters run after him with bread. Maurya has had a vision of Bartley on the red horse, with Michael riding behind on the grey pony. Told that Michael is dead—the sisters have identified the clothing—she knows that Bartley is also doomed. Old women enter with Bartley's body: the grey pony has knocked him into the sea. Reflecting that no man lives forever, Maurya invokes God's blessing on all the living as she kneels beside the bier. The wind blows open the door and the sound of the sea is heard; a soprano voice fades into the distance.

Notes:
The text is an almost verbatim rendering of Synge's drama, which was inspired by an incident he witnessed on the Irish coast. It is Vaughan Williams's most successful operatic work, a small masterpiece of music drama, at once poetic and realistic.

RECORDING:
HMV ASD2699 (d) ●
Angel S-36819 (US)
Women's voices of Ambrosian Singers/Orchestra Nova of London
c. Meredith Davies
Nora (s)   Norma Burrowes
Cathleen (s)   Margaret Price
Maurya (c)   Helen Watts
Bartley (b)   Benjamin Luxon
A Woman (m-s)   Pauline Stevens

The Pilgrim's Progress
Morality in Prologue, 4 Acts and Epilogue.
Text by John Bunyan.
First performance: London (Covent Garden) April 26, 1951.

Synopsis:
Prologue Bunyan is writing in his cell in Bedford jail. Pilgrim appears, asking 'What shall I do to be saved?'

Act 1 Pilgrim is directed by the Evangelist to the Wicket Gate and told to bear his burden until he reaches the place of deliverance. Four neighbours try to deflect him; but he is resolute in search of eternal life. The Evangelist points the way and the Pilgrim sets out upon his journey. At the House Beautiful, three Shining Ones relieve him of his burden and he enters, after the Interpreter has placed the mark of the seal on his forehead.

An optional Nocturne leads to the Second Act: Watchful the porter sings a blessing on those who rest within.

Act 2 The Herald asks who will go on the King's Highway. Pilgrim accepts and is given armour. In the Valley of Humiliation he encounters the Doleful Creatures and is hailed by Apollyon, whom he conquers in a fierce fight. Weak from wounds, he is succoured by two Heavenly Beings who bring him leaves of the Tree of Life and drink from the Water of Life. The Evangelist now prophesies moral trials for Pilgrim: he is enjoined to be faithful unto death and is given the Staff of Salvation, the Roll of the Word and the Key of Promise.

Act 3 At Vanity Fair, where all worldly goods are on sale, Pilgrim is under pressure to buy. Madam Bubble and Madam Wanton tempt him, but Pilgrim says only: 'I buy truth'. The crowd set on him. The judge, Lord Hate-Good, condemns Pilgrim. Alone in prison, awaiting death, Pilgrim gives way to despair—but the doors fly open and he is free to set off again on his journey.

Act 4 Pilgrim asks a woodcutter's boy how far it is to the Celestial City. Mr and Mrs By-Ends, two half-hearted pilgrims, provide a diversion. Pilgrim reaches the Delectable Mountains and is met by the shepherds, who offer him refreshment. The Celestial Messenger comes to summon Pilgrim to the Celestial City, where the Master calls for him. But before he can reach the Celestial City, Pilgrim must cross the River of Death. The shepherds pray for his safe passage. The sound of a trumpet is heard and a vision of the Celestial City emerges into light: Pilgrim is seen slowly mounting the steps.

Epilogue The vision fades. John Bunyan is seen again in his cell with his book, which he offers to his hearers.

Notes:

The Pilgrim's Progress, together with the Fifth symphony, to which it is thematically related, is absolutely central to Vaughan Williams's life work. It took more than 40 years to complete and when it was coolly received at its first performance, Vaughan Williams said that although people did not like it, and perhaps never would, it was the kind of opera he wanted to write. Although it was regarded as more or less unstageable, he was adamant that it was a work for the theatre—not the cathedral or concert hall. Vaughan Williams said that he used the name 'Pilgrim', rather than Bunyan's 'Christian', because he wanted the work to address itself to all men of all beliefs, not to Christians only. In this he followed in the footsteps of Elgar, who declared that *The Dream of Gerontius* was not to be considered in any sense sectarian.

RECORDINGS:
HMV SLS959 (3) ●
Angel S-3785 (3) (US)
London Philharmonic Choir/London
Philharmonic Orchestra
c. Sir Adrian Boult

Pilgrim (b)	John Noble
John Bunyan (b)	Raimund Herincx
Evangelist (b)	John Carol Case
Interpreter (t)	Ian Partridge
Watchful (b)	John Shirley-Quirk
Apollyon (b)	Robert Lloyd
Lord Lechery (t)	Joseph Ward
Madam Wanton (s)	Marie Hayward
Madam Bubble (m-s)	Delia Wallis

HMV SEOM15 □
Nocturne
London Philharmonic Orchestra
c. Sir Adrian Boult

GIUSEPPE VERDI
(b. Le Roncole, Busseto 10.10.1813; d. Milan 27.1.1901)

Italy's greatest opera composer came of poor peasant stock. He had his first lessons from the parish priest and heard his first music in the church where he became a choirboy and later organist. He was 11 when he was sent to school in Busetto, where he was befriended by Antonio Barezzi, a wealthy merchant, who took the boy into his house and promoted his further musical studies, most notably under the *maestro di cappella* at the church of San Bartolomeo. He was already beginning to compose and had several pieces performed. In 1832 he was sent to Milan but was rejected by the Conservatoire. In 1836 he married Barezzi's daughter Margherita, but during the two years 1838-40 she and her two children died. In 1839, Verdi's first opera, *Oberto*, was produced. From then on he composed opera after opera but then, duly honoured, he apparently ceased to compose for the theatre. During 1873/4 he wrote his great *Messa da Requiem* for the first anniversary of the death of the poet-patriot Alessandro Manzoni. Then, in his old age, with an astonishing burst of rejuvenated creativity, he produced his two operatic masterpieces, *Otello* and *Falstaff*.

Above: *Verdi wrote his first opera in 1836 and his last in 1889.*

Oberto, Conte di San Bonifacio
Opera in 2 Acts.
Text by Antonio Piazza, Bartolommeo Merelli and Temistocle Solera.
First performance: Milan (La Scala) November 17, 1839.

Synopsis:
Scene: Bassano. Time: 1228.

Act 1 Leonora, disowned daughter of Oberto, seeks revenge on her former lover Riccardo, now betrothed to Cuniza. Leonora and her father, reconciled, tell Cuniza that her fiancé is faithless, and all three confront Riccardo.

Act 2 Cuniza says that Riccardo must marry Leonora, but Oberto challenges him to a duel. Taunted by Oberto and Cuniza, Riccardo fights the old man and kills him. Ashamed, Riccardo flees, leaving his property to the desolate Leonora.

RECORDINGS:
Italia ITL70001 (3) ●
Chorus and Orchestra of Teatro Communale, Bologna
c. Zoltán Peskó
Oberto (bs) Simon Estes
Cuniza (m-s) Viorica Cortez
Riccardo (t) Umberto Grilli
Leonora (s) Angeles Gulin
Imelda (m-s) Maria Grazia Piolatto

DG 2707 090 (2) □
DG 2707 090 (2) (US)
Overture
c. Herbert von Karajan
(This recording contains Verdi's complete overtures and preludes)

Decca SXL6501 □
Ah! sgombro il loco alfin . . . Sotto il paterno tetto
Huguette Tourangeau (m-s)

Un Giorno di Regno

Opera in 2 Acts.
Text by Felice Romani.
First performance: Milan (La Scala) August 5, 1840.

Synopsis:
Scene: A castle near Brest. Time: 1733.
Act 1 Baron Kelbar insists that his daughter, Giulietta, marry La Rocca, although she loves Edoardo. The Marchesa believes that her fiancé, Belfiore, has jilted her, and plans to marry Count Ivrea. Belfiore, who is posing as the King of Poland to protect the real monach, hears of the Marchesa's plan and seeks to 'abdicate', while attempting to aid Edoardo and Giulietta by offering La Rocca a rich Polish bride.
Act 2 'King' Belfiore obtains Kelbar's permission for the marriage of Edoardo and Giulietta, although the Marchesa remains obdurate. But within an hour of her marriage to La Rocca, word comes that the real King is safe in Warsaw and Belfiore may at last 'abdicate'.

Notes:
A pretty impossible story. But even here, in his second opera, Verdi makes all that is to be made of it—and the result when well produced is certainly diverting.

RECORDINGS:
Philips 6703 055 (3) ●
Philips 6703 055 (3) (US)
Ambrosian Singers/Royal Philharmonic Orchestra
c. Lamberto Gardelli
Baron Kelbar (bs) Wladimiro Ganzarolli
Giulietta (s) Jessye Norman
Edoardo (t) José Carreras
Cavalier Belfiore (b) Ingvar Wixell
Marchesa (s) Fiorenza Cossotto

Philips 6570 066 ■
(from above)

Nabucodonosor (Nabucco)

Opera in 4 Acts.
Text by Temistocle Solera.
First performance: Milan (La Scala) March 9, 1842. London 1846; New York 1848.

Synopsis:
Scene: Jerusalem and Babylon. Time: 586 BC.
Act 1 In Jerusalem, the Hebrews lament the victory of Nabucco (Nebuchadnezzar), King of Babylon. Fenena, Nabucco's daughter, is held prisoner by Ismaele, nephew of the Hebrew King. Ismaele loves Fenena, but he is desired by Abigaille, also Nabucco's daughter, who breaks in with soldiers and demands his allegiance. When Nabucco desecrates the Temple, the High Priest Zaccaria threatens to kill Fenena, but she is saved by Ismaele while Nabucco plunders the Temple.
Act 2 *'L'empio' (The Evil Man).* Fenena reigns in Babylon while Nabucco is at war. She frees the Hebrew prisoners, and Zaccaria incites a rebellion. Abigaille, learning she is an adopted slave and not Nabucco's true daughter, tries to depose Fenena. Nabucco, returning from war, proclaims himself a God: he is blasted by lightning and becomes insane.
Act 3 *'La profezia' (The Prophecy).* Abigaille is enthroned in the Hanging Gardens. She tells Nabucco that she will only reign for the duration of his illness and persuades him to ratify death sentences on the Hebrews—and Fenena. By the Euphrates, Zaccaria chides the despondent Hebrews and predicts the fall of Babylon.
Act 4 *'L'idolo infranto' (The Broken Idol).* Seeing Fenena led to execution, Nabucco prays to the Hebrew God. His sanity is restored and he hastens to rescue her. He orders the destruction of the Temple of Baal, the release of the Hebrews and the betrothal of Ismaele and Fenena. Abigaille takes poison, praying for forgiveness as she dies.

Notes:
The famous Hebrew Chorus, 'Va, pensiero', was taken up as a national theme of liberation.

Well-known arias:
Act 1 D'Egitto la sui lidi (Zaccaria)
Act 2 Anch'io dischiuso un giorno (Abigaille)
Act 3 Va, pensiero (Chorus)

RECORDINGS:
Decca SET298/300 ★●
London 1382 (3) (US)
Vienna State Opera Chorus and Orchestra
c. Lamberto Gardelli
Nabucco (b) Tito Gobbi
Abigaille (s) Elena Suliotis
Fenena (s) Dora Carral
Zaccaria (bs) Carlo Cava
Ismaele (t) Bruno Prevedi

Decca SET367 ■
London 26059 (US)
(from above)

HMV SLS5132 (3) ●
Angel SCLX3865 (3) (US)
Ambrosian Opera Chorus/Philharmonia Orchestra
c. Riccardo Muti
Nabucco (bs) Matteo Manuguerra
Abigaille (s) Renata Scotto
Fenena (m-s) Elena Obraztsova
Ismaele (t) Veriano Luchetti
Zaccaria (bs) Nicolai Ghiaurov

Cetra Opera Live L016 (3) (m) (r. 1949) ●
Chorus and Orchestra of Teatro San Carlo
c. Vittorio Gui
Nabucco (b) Gino Bechi
Abigaille (s) Maria Callas

Above: *A production of* I Lombardi *by the Budapest State Opera.*

I Lombardi alla Prima Crociata

Opera in 4 Acts.
Text by Temistocle Solera based on a romance by Tommaso Gossi.
First performance: Milan (La Scala) February 11, 1843.

Synopsis:
Scene: Milan and Antioch. Time: 1099.
Act 1 *'La Vendetta'.* Pagano, banished from Milan for trying to kill his brother, Arvino, who won from him the hand of Viclinda, returns and feigns friendship with Arvino, now leader of the Lombard Crusaders. Trying to abduct Viclinda, Pagano inadvertently kills his father, but is restrained from committing suicide by Arvino.
Act 2 *'L'uomo della caverna' (The Man in the Cave).* Pagano has become a Christian Hermit at Antioch. Arvino arrives to sack the palace, where Acciano holds prisoner his daughter,

Giselda. Acciano is killed and his son, Oronte, who loves Giselda, wounded. Giselda rebels, but her father's attempt to kill her is prevented by The Hermit.

Act 3 'La conversione' (The Conversion). Giselda is reunited with the dying Oronte, who is baptised by The Hermit. The furious Arvino learns that Pagano is in the vicinity.

Act 4 'Il santo sepolcro' (The Holy Sepulchre). In a dream, Oronte tells Giselda that the Crusaders will find water at the fountain of Siloam. Arvino leads the refreshed Crusaders to the attack. The Hermit, wounded in battle, reveals his identity and dies within sight of Jerusalem.

Notes:

In 1847 Verdi visited Paris on his way home from London. He was asked to write an opera, and decided to adapt *I Lombardi*. A new French libretto was written by Gustave Vaëz and Alphonse Royer, and the opera was presented as *Jérusalem* at the Opéra on November 26, 1847. The story was considerably altered and the setting moved from Lombardy to Toulouse.

Well-known arias:

Act 2 La mia letizia (Oronte)
Act 4 Dal tetto natio (Chorus)

RECORDINGS:
Philips 6703 032 (3) ●
Philips 6703 032 (3) (US)
Ambrosian Singers/Royal Philharmonic Orchestra
c. Lamberto Gardelli
Giselda (s) Cristina Deutekom
Oronte (t) Placido Domingo
Pagano (bs) Ruggero Raimondi
Arvino (t) Jerome Monaco

Philips 6570 065 ■
(from above)

Ernani

Opera in 4 Acts.
Text by Francesco Maria Piave after Victor Hugo's 'Hernani'.
First performance: Venice (Teatro La Fenice) March 9, 1844. London 1845; New York 1847.

Synopsis:
Scene: Spain. Time: 1519.

Act 1 Elvira is being forced to marry the aged Don Ruy Gomez de Silva, but the bandit Ernani loves her and plans to abduct her. Don Carlos, King of Castile, also desires Elvira, and thus loses the loyalty of de Silva.

Act 2 Ernani sees Elvira in her bridal gown, loses hope, and throws himself on the mercy of de Silva, who protects him. The King abducts Elvira and Ernani proposes that he and de Silva join to rescue her: afterwards, his life will be forfeit to de Silva, upon the sound of his hunting horn.

Act 3 Ernani is chosen by lot to kill the King. De Silva wishes to be the assassin and offers to release Ernani from their pact, but he refuses. Proclaimed Emperor, Don Carlos forgives his enemies and says Ernani may marry Elvira.

Act 4 As Ernani and Elvira sing of their love, a horn sounds. Confronted by de Silva, Ernani stabs himself to death.

Well-known arias:

Act 1 Ernani, involami (Elvira)

RECORDINGS:
Cetra Opera Live L012 (3) (m) (r. 1956) ●
Chorus and Orchestra of Metropolitan Opera House, New York
c. Dimitri Mitropoulos
Ernani (t) Mario del Monaco
Elvira (t) Zinka Milanov
Don Carlos (b) Leonard Warren
Don Ruy Gomez de Silva (bs) Cesare Siepi

RCA SER5572/4 (d) ●
RCA LSC-3035 (3) (US)
RCA Italiana Chorus and Orchestra
c. Thomas Schippers
Ernani (t) Carlo Bergonzi
Elvira (s) Leontyne Price
Don Carlos (b) Mario Sereni
Don Ruy Gomez de Silva (bs) Ezio Flagello

RCA LSC-3035 (US) ■
(from above)

I Due Foscari

Opera in 3 Acts.
Text by Francesco Maria Piave based on Byron's 'The Two Foscari'.
First performance: Rome (Teatro Argentina) November 3, 1844. London 1847.

Synopsis:
Scene: Venice. Time: 1457.

Act 1 Jacopo Foscari, son of the Doge, is sentenced to exile by the Council of Ten. His wife, Lucrezia, upbraids the Doge for condemning his son, but he must do his duty.

Act 2 Lucrezia tells Jacopo, who is weak from torture, of the sentence, and he parts sorrowfully from his father. Lucrezia and her children plead in vain with the Council.

Act 3 While a carnival is held in St Mark's Square, Jacopo bids farewell to Lucrezia. The Doge learns that a dying man has confessed to Jacopo's crime—but Lucrezia brings word that Jacopo has fallen dead while boarding the ship. The Council asks the aged Doge to abdicate: he agrees, collapses and dies.

RECORDING:
Philips 6700 105 (2) ●
Philips 6700 105 (US)
Austrian Radio Chorus and Symphony Orchestra
c. Lamberto Gardelli

Francesco Foscari
  (Doge) (b) Piero Cappuccilli
Jacopo Foscari (t) José Carreras
Lucrezia (s) Katia Ricciarelli

Giovanna d'Arco

Opera in Prologue and 3 Acts.
Text by Temistocle Solera based on Schiller's 'Jungfrau von Orleans'.
First performance: Milan (La Scala) February 15, 1845.

Synopsis:
Scene: France. Time: c. 1429.

Prologue Charles VII of France has dreamed that the Virgin orders him to lay his arms in front of an oak tree. In Domrémy Forest, Joan asks the Virgin to let her fight against the English. She sleeps, but, when Charles comes with his arms, wakes with the words 'I am ready'. She urges Charles to continue the fight. Her father, Jacques, overhears.

Act 1 Joan has inspired a French victory, but Jacques, believing her a witch, offers to betray her to the English. Joan longs for home, but Charles begs her to remain and declares his love, against which she is warned by spirit voices. She leads the procession to the coronation.

Act 2 The coronation is held at Rheims. Jacques accuses the King of blasphemy and Joan of a pact with Satan. In spite of Charles's support, Joan is stricken by feelings of guilt.

Act 3 Joan is captured and a scaffold is built. Jacques, repentant, begs her forgiveness and releases her. Once again she inspires a French victory, but is mortally wounded. Asking for the battle ensign to take with her to heaven, she dies.

Notes:

Verdi's setting is closer to Schiller than Tchaikovsky's » but even farther from history.

RECORDING:
HMV SLS967 (3) ●
Angel S-3791 (3) (US)
Ambrosian Opera Chorus/London Symphony Orchestra
c. James Levine
Giovanna (Joan) (s) Montserrat Caballé
Carlo VII (Charles) (t) Placido Domingo
Giacomo (Jacques) (b) Sherrill Milnes

Alzira

Opera in Prologue and 2 Acts.
Text by Salvatore Cammarano based on Voltaire's play.
First performance: Naples (Teatro San Carlo) August 12, 1845.

RECORDING:
Decca SXL6429 ☐
London 25282 (US)
Irene lungi ancor dovrei
Mario del Monaco (t)

Attila

Opera in Prologue and 3 Acts.
Text by Temistocle Solera based on Zacharias Werner's play.
First performance: Venice (Teatro La Fenice) March 17, 1846. London 1848; New York 1910.

Synopsis:

Scene: Italy. Time: 454 AD.

Prologue Odabella, whose father has been killed in the fall of Aquileia, so impresses Attila, King of the Huns, that he gives her his sword. Odabella swears to avenge her father with it. Ezio, the Roman envoy, proposes to divide Italy with Attila, who rejects such treachery and prepares to march on Rome. Survivors from Aquileia reach the Adriatic, where Foresto laments Odabella's fate.

Act 1 Foresto arrives at Attila's camp and accuses Odabella of treachery, but she tells him of her plan to kill Attila. Attila dreams of disaster, but still rallies his forces to march on Rome. Pilgrims approach, led by Bishop (later Pope) Leo. Recognising Leo from his dream, Attila is terrified.

Act 2 Slaves sent by Attila come to Enzio's camp, among them Foresto, who plots with Enzio against Attila. At a banquet, Odabella, determined that Attila shall die by her hand, foils Foresto's attempt to poison the Hun. Attila, still planning to march on Rome, announces that he will wed Odabella.

Act 3 Ezio and Foresto plan to ambush Attila, and Foresto again accuses Odabella of treachery. All three are surprised by Attila, who hears the Romans approaching and realises that he has been betrayed. Odabella kills him with his own sword.

RECORDINGS:
Philips 6700 056 (2) ●
Philips 6700 056 (2) (US)
Ambrosian Singers/Finchley Children's
Music Group/Royal Philharmonic
Orchestra
c. Lamberto Gardelli
Attila (bs) Ruggero Raimondi

Odabella (s) Cristina Deutekom
Ezio (b) Sherrill Milnes
Foresto (t) Carlo Bergonzi

Philips 6570 064 ■
(from above)

Macbeth

Opera in 4 Acts.
Text by Piave and Andrea Maffei based on Shakespeare's play.
First performance: Florence (Teatro della Pergola) March 14, 1847. New York 1850; Dublin 1859.

Synopsis:

Scene: Scotland. Time: 1040.

Act 1 Witches prophesy that Macbeth will be King and, urged on by Lady Macbeth, he murders King Duncan.

Below: *Sherrill Milnes as Macbeth in Verdi's first Shakespearian opera, which has recently regained popularity.*

Act 2 To ensure his succession, Macbeth hires assassins to kill Banquo, whose son, Fleance, escapes. Banquo's ghost appears to Macbeth at a banquet.

Act 3 The Witches prophesy that Macbeth will die at Dunsinane and that Banquo's line will be Kings.

Act 4 The armies of Macbeth and Malcolm meet at Birnam Wood. Told of his wife's death, Macbeth fights on in the belief that no man born of woman can vanquish him. But he is killed by Macduff, who was taken prematurely from his mother's womb.

Notes:

The opera was a favourite of Verdi's, who took great pains over everything: libretto, composition, production. It fell from public favour for some years, but has lately made a strong comeback. It was not the first Shakespeare play Verdi considered; a project for *King Lear* was one of the few major plans that did not materialise. A French version of *Macbeth* was produced in Paris at the Théâtre-Lyrique in 1865, with a new text by Charles Nuitter and A. Beaumont.

RECORDINGS:
Decca SETB510/2 ●
London 13102 (3) (US)
Ambrosian Opera Chorus/London
Philharmonic Orchestra
c. Lamberto Gardelli
Macbeth (b) Dietrich
    Fischer-Dieskau
Lady Macbeth (s) Elena Suliotis
Banquo (bs) Nicolai Ghiaurov
Macduff (t) Luciano Pavarotti

Decca SET539 ■
(from above)

DG 2709 062 (3) ★●
DG 2709 062 (3) (US)
Chorus and Orchestra of La Scala, Milan
c. Claudio Abbado
Macbeth (b) Piero Cappuccilli
Lady Macbeth (s) Shirley Verrett
Banquo (bs) Nicolai Ghiaurov
Macduff (t) Placido Domingo

HMV SLS 992 (3) ●
Angel SX3833 (3) (US)
Ambrosian Opera Chorus/New
Philharmonic Orchestra
c. Riccardo Muti
Macbeth (b) Sherrill Milnes
Lady Macbeth (s) Fiorenza Cossotto
Banquo (bs) Ruggero Raimondi
Macduff (t) José Carreras

Decca SET282/4 ○
London 1380 (3) (US)
Chorus and Orchestra of the Accademia

di Santa Cecilia, Rome
c. Thomas Schippers
Macbeth (b) Giuseppe Taddei
Lady Macbeth (s) Birgit Nilsson
Banquo (bs) Giovanni Fioani
Macduff (t) Bruno Prevedi

Decca SET409 ■
(from above)

RCA VICS-6121 (3) (US) ●
Metropolitan Opera Chorus and
Orchestra
c. Erich Leinsdorf
Macbeth (b) Leonard Warren
Lady Macbeth (s) Leonie Rysanek
Banquo (bs) Jerome Hines
Macduff (t) Carlo Bergonzi

I Masnadieri

Opera in 4 Acts.
Text by Andrea Maffei based on Schiller's 'Die Räuber'.
First performance: London (Her Majesty's) July 22, 1847.

Synopsis:

Scene: Germany. Time: early 18th century.

Act 1 Carlo, elder son of Count Massimiliano Moor, is now a bandit. His letter imploring his father's forgiveness is intercepted by his brother, Francesco. Telling Carlo not to return, Francesco informs the Count that Carlo is dead and that his last wish was for the Count's niece, Amalia, to marry Francesco. The Count collapses and, supposedly, dies.

Act 2 Amalia, who loves Carlo, is told of Francesco's plot by a servant, Arminio. She rejects Francesco and flees. Carlo rescues the brigand Rolla from prison and burns a town.

Act 3 Amalia, hiding in the forest, encounters the bandits. She tells Carlo of Francesco's treachery. Carlo considers suicide, but Arminio reveals that the Count is not dead, but in hiding. Carlo sends his men to apprehend Francesco.

Act 4 Francesco is troubled by a dream of the Day of

209

Judgement, but is refused absolution. The Count fails to recognise Carlo, whose men bring word of Francesco's escape. Carlo confesses to his father and Amalia that he is the bandit chief and, rather than have Amalia dishonoured by association with him, stabs her and departs for the gallows.

Notes:

After the production of *Attila* in Venice, Verdi was supposed to go to London to produce an opera for the impresario Benjamin Lumley. But he was ill, and was ordered complete rest. He produced *Macbeth* in Florence before returning to complete *I Masnadieri* for Lumley. He was still not well, and the English climate did him no good. But the opera was produced at the command of Queen Victoria, who attended the first night with Prince Albert, Prince Louis Bonaparte and the Duke of Wellington. It was a successful evening, but it did not last and Lumley himself seems to have been disappointed.

RECORDINGS:

Philips 6703 064 (3) ●	**Carlo** (t)	Carlo Bergonzi
Philips 6703 064 (3) (US)	**Francesco** (bs)	Piero Cappuccilli
Ambrosian Singers/New Philharmonia	**Amalia** (s)	Montserrat Caballé
Orchestra		
c. Lamberto Gardelli	Philips 6570 067 ■	
Massimiliano,	(from above)	
Count Moor (bs) Ruggero Raimondi		

Il Corsaro

Opera in 3 Acts.
Text by Piave based on Byron's poem.
First performance: Trieste (Teatro Grande) October 25, 1848.

Synopsis:

Act 1 On an Aegean island, the pirate chief Corrado plans to attack the Pasha Seid in his city of Corone. Corrado's sweetheart, Medora, tries in vain to restrain him.

Act 2 Corrado attacks Corone and fires the Pasha's harem. But the pirates delay to rescue Gulnara, the Pasha's favourite, and the other women, and are captured.

Act 3 Gulnara falls in love with Corrado, kills the Pasha, and flees with the pirate. On the island, Medora, believing Corrado dead, takes poison and is dying when his ship arrives. Gulnara assures Medora that Corrado still loves her alone, and when Medora dies in Corrado's arms, he drowns himself.

Notes:

After Verdi had seen the production of *Jérusalem* through, he decided to stay on awhile in Paris, and while there wrote *Il Corsaro*, originally for Francesco Lucca to publish and Lumley to stage in London. But it was given first at Trieste. Much has been made of the fact that Verdi did not attend the première: in fact he was otherwise engaged with his attentions to Giuseppina Strepponi (the singer he lived with for some years, and eventually married in 1859), with political matters, and also he had a bad cold.

RECORDING:

Philips 6700 098 (2) ●	**Medora** (s)	Jessye Norman
Philips 6700 092 (2) (US)	**Gulnara** (s)	Montserrat Caballé
Ambrosian Singers/New Philharmonia	**Pasha Seid** (b)	Gian-Piero Mastromei
Orchestra		
c. Lamberto Gardelli	Philips 6570 068 ▣	
Corrado (t) José Carreras	(from above)	

La Battaglia di Legnano

Opera in 4 Acts.
Text by Salvatore Cammarano.
First performance: Rome (Teatro Argentina) January 27, 1849.

Synopsis:

Scene: Milan and Como. Time: 1176.

Act 1 *'Egli vive!' (He lives!).* The Lombard League convenes in Milan to fight Frederick Barbarossa. Rolando, the Milanese leader, meets his friend Arrigo, the Veronese leader, whom he had thought dead. Lida, Rolando's wife, laments the death in

war of her parents and brothers. Arrigo, previously betrothed to Lida, arrives with Rolando and accuses her of disloyalty.

Act 2 *'Barbarossa'.* Arrigo and Rolando ask the leaders of Como to join the League. Rolando denounces Como's treaty with Barbarossa, who appears in person and excites mutual vows of a fight to the death.

Act 3 *'L'infamia' (Disgrace).* Lida's letter imploring Arrigo to see her before going to war is intercepted by a rejected suitor: he shows it to Rolando, who believes his wife to be unfaithful and swears vengeance. Lida goes to Arrigo's room, where he tells her they must forget their former love. When Rolando approaches, she hides, but is discovered. Rolando threatens to kill Arrigo, then decides to dishonour him: he locks the door and leaves. Determined to join his men, who have sworn to free Italy or die, Arrigo leaps from the balcony with a cry of *'Viva Italia!'*

Act 4 *'Morire per la patria' (To die for one's country).* A great victory is announced in Milan: Arrigo has slain Barbarossa, but is mortally wounded. Assuring Rolando that he has not betrayed him, he dies to the sound of a *Te Deum*.

Notes:

This was another of Verdi's patriotic operas, written during the years of Italy's struggle for freedom from foreign domination. The cry 'Viva Italia!' was bound to produce a spirited reaction. It did: 'Viva Verdi!'

RECORDING:

Philips 6700 120 (2) ●	**Arrigo** (t)	José Carreras
Philips 6700 120 (2) (US)	**Rolando** (b)	Matteo Manuguerra
Austrian Radio Chorus and Orchestra	**Lida** (s)	Katia Ricciarelli
c. Lamberto Gardelli		

Luisa Miller

Opera in 3 Acts.
Text by Cammarano based on Schiller's 'Kabale und Liebe'.
First performance: Naples (Teatro San Carlo) December 8, 1849. New York 1852; London 1858.

Synopsis:

Scene: the Tyrol. Time: early 17th century.

Act 1 *'L'amore'.* Luisa Miller loves Carlo, a stranger. Wurm, who desires Luisa, reveals that Carlo is really Rodolfo, son of Count Walter, who intends him to marry Federica. Rodolfo declares his love for Luisa, but the Count provokes the Millers and then orders their arrest. Rodolfo tries to restrain him by threatening to reveal a family secret.

Act 2 *'L'intrigo'.* The Count has Miller arrested: unless Luisa writes a declaration of love for Wurm, her father will die. The Count and Wurm recall the murder that ensured the Count's title — the secret known to Rodolfo. After seeing Luisa's letter to Wurm, Rodolfo agrees to marry Federica.

Act 3 *'Il veleno' (Poison).* When Luisa tells her father of the trick, he restrains her from suicide. Rodolfo brings in poisoned water: Luisa asks for a glass, and both drink. Told by Rodolfo of the poison, she reveals the truth. As the lovers are dying, the Count and Wurm enter, and Rodolfo summons the last of his strength to cut down the treacherous Wurm.

Well-known arias:

Act 2 Tu puniscimi, o signore (Luisa and Wurm)
Quando le sere (Rodolfo)

RECORDINGS:

RCA SER5713/5 ◉		Decca SET606/8 ★◉	
RCA LSC 6168 (3) (US)		London 13114 (3) (US)	
RCA Italiana Opera Chorus and		London Opera Chorus/National	
Orchestra		Philharmonic Orchestra	
c. Fausto Cleva		c. Peter Maag	
Luisa (s)	Anna Moffo	**Luisa** (s)	Montserrat Caballé
Federica (m-s)	Shirley Verrett	**Federica** (m-s)	Anna Reynolds
Rodolfo (t)	Carlo Bergonzi	**Rodolfo** (t)	Luciano Pavarotti
Miller (b)	Cornell MacNeil	**Miller** (b)	Sherrill Milnes
Count Walter (bs)	Giorgio Tozzi	**Count Walter** (bs)	Bonaldo Giaiotti
Wurm (bs)	Ezio Flagello	**Wurm** (bs)	Richard van Allan

Rigoletto

Opera in 3 Acts.
Text by Piave based on Victor Hugo's 'Le Roi s'amuse'.
First performance: Venice (Teatro La Fenice) March 11, 1851. London (Covent Garden) 1853; New York 1857.

Synopsis:

Scene: Mantua. Time: 16th century.

Act 1 While the Duke of Mantua dallies with the Countess Ceprano, his jester, Rigoletto, taunts her husband. But he provokes a father's curse when he mocks Count Monterone, who protests at the Duke's seduction of his daughter. Disturbed, Rigoletto returns to his own daughter, Gilda, meeting Sparafucile, an assassin, on the way. Rigoletto warns Gilda against straying, but she confesses to her Nurse that a young man is wooing her. The Duke, disguised, serenades Gilda. Count Ceprano, seeking revenge and believing Gilda is Rigoletto's mistress, has her abducted—and Rigoletto remembers Monterone's curse.

Act 2 The Duke learns that Gilda is in the palace, and seeks her out, while Rigoletto tells the jeering courtiers she is his daughter. He vows vengeance on the Duke.

Act 3 Gilda claims that the Duke loves her, but Rigoletto takes her to Sparafucile's inn to observe the Duke wooing the assassin's sister, Maddalena. Sparafucile agrees to murder the Duke but, when Maddalena intercedes, says that the victim will be the next caller at the inn. Gilda, overhearing, decides to save the Duke: she enters the inn in male attire and is stabbed. Her body, in a sack, is given to Rigoletto, who is about to throw it into the river when he hears the Duke's song. He finds Gilda dying in the sack: the curse is fulfilled.

Notes:

Rigoletto was the first opera of Verdi's 'middle period' which produced his most popular works. Its combination of melodic richness and dramatic, sometimes melodramatic, effectiveness has proved irresistible. It is hardly subtle; but it is entirely memorable, and has, from the very first performance, always achieved great popularity.

Well-known arias:

Act 1 Questa o quella (Duke)
       Pari siamo (Rigoletto)
       Caro nome (Gilda)

Above: *Luciano Pavarotti, in a scene from Luisa Miller.*

Above: *Sherrill Milnes in the title role of Verdi's Rigoletto.*

Act 2 Piangi, fanciulla (Gilda, Rigoletto)
Act 3 La donna è mobile (Duke)
Bella figlia dell'amore (Duke, Gilda, Maddalena, Rigoletto)

RECORDINGS:
HMV SLS5018 (3) ★●
Columbia MWS817 (3) (d) (US)
Chorus and Orchestra of La Scala, Milan
c. Tullio Serafin
Gilda (s) Maria Callas
Rigoletto (b) Tito Gobbi
Duke of Mantua (t) Giuseppe di Stefano
Sparafucile (bs) Nicolai Zaccaria

Decca SET542/4 ★●
London 13105 (3) (US)
Ambrosian Opera Chorus/London
Symphony Orchestra
c. Richard Bonynge
Gilda (s) Joan Sutherland
Rigoletto (b) Sherrill Milnes
Duke of Mantua (t) Luciano Pavarotti
Sparafucile (bs) Martti Talvela

Decca SET580 ■
London 26401 (US)
(from above)

DG 2709 014 (3) ●
DG 2709 014 (3) (US)
Chorus and Orchestra of La Scala, Milan
c. Rafael Kubelik
Gilda (s) Renata Scotto
Rigoletto (b) Dietrich
Fischer-Dieskau
Duke of Mantua (t) Carlo Bergonzi
Sparafucile (bs) Ivo Vinco

DG 922-017 (US) ■
(from above)

Decca 1332 (3) (US) ●
London 1332 (3) (US)
Chorus and Orchestra of Accademia di
Santa Cecilia di Roma
c. Nino Sanzogno
Gilda (s) Joan Sutherland
Rigoletto (b) Cornell MacNeil
Duke of Mantua (t) Renato Cioni
Sparafucile (bs) Cesare Siepi

London 25710 (US) ■
(from above)

HMV SLS933 (3) (d) ●
Angel S-3718 (3) (US)
Chorus and Orchestra of the Opera
House, Rome
c. Francesco Molinari-Pradelli
Gilda (s) Reri Grist
Rigoletto (b) Cornell MacNeil
Duke of Mantua (t) Nicolai Gedda
Sparafucile (bs) Agostino Ferrin

RCA SER5516/7 ●
RCA LSC-7027 (2) (US)
RCA Italiana Chorus and Orchestra
c. Sir Georg Solti
Gilda (s) Anna Moffo
Rigoletto (b) Robert Merrill
Duke of Mantua (t) Alfredo Kraus
Sparafucile (bs) Ezio Flagello

RCA LSC-2837 (US) ■
(from above)

Everest/Cetra 470 (3) (US) ●
Chorus and Orchestra of Maggio
Musicale Fiorentino
c. Gianandrea Gavazzeni
Gilda (s) Renata Scotto
Rigoletto (b) Ettore Bastianini
Duke of Mantua (t) Alfredo Kraus
Sparafucile (bs) Ivo Vinco
Maddalena (s) Fiorenza Cossotto

Il Trovatore

Opera in 4 Acts.
Text by Cammarano based on Antonio García Gutiérrez's play 'El trovador'.
First performance: Rome (Teatro Apollo) January 19, 1853. New York 1855;
London (Covent Garden) 1855.

Synopsis:
Scene: Vizcaya and Aragon. Time: early 15th century.
Act 1 'Il duello' (The Duel). Count di Luna has ordered
Ferrando to apprehend the troubadour who has been serenading
Leonora. Ferrando tells his men how the Count's father burned a
gypsy witch, whose daughter abducted one of his sons in
revenge. The old Count charged the present Count to seek his
lost brother. Leonora awaits her troubadour, but the Count
appears also. The troubadour reveals himself as Manrico, and
the Count challenges him to a duel.
Act 2 'La zingara' (The Gypsy). Manrico has won the duel but
has spared the Count's life. Azucena, Manrico's mother, tells of
her own mother's burning, and of how she threw her own child
into the flames instead of the Count's son. Ruiz tells Manrico
that Leonora, believing him dead, will enter a convent. The
Count tries to abduct her, but Manrico intervenes.
Act 3 'Il figlio della zingara' (The Gypsy's Son). The Count has
captured Azucena, whom Ferrando recognises as the baby-
snatcher. As Manrico and Leonora prepare to wed, Manrico is
told that Azucena is to be burned, and goes to rescue her.
Act 4 'Il supplizio' (The Penalty). Manrico is imprisoned with
Azucena in the Count's castle. Leonora offers herself to the

Above: *Fiorenza Cossotto in* Il Trovatore *at Covent Garden.*

Count to save Manrico, but when she tells Manrico he is free, he
is suspicious and repulses her. She takes poison. The Count has
Manrico executed—and Azucena reveals that he has killed his
own brother. Her mother is avenged.

Notes:
Il Trovatore is generally thought to be absurd and incomprehensible in terms of its libretto. This is compounded by the fact
that apparently the music exists virtually without reference to
the dramatic situations. The sheer vitality and infectious verve
of Verdi's music puts most ungenerous thoughts out of mind.

Well-known arias:
Act 1 Tacea la notte (Leonora)
Deserto sulla terra (Manrico)
Act 2 Anvil Chorus
Stride la vampa (Azucena)
Mal reggendo all'aspiro assalto (Manrico, Azucena)
Il balen del suo sorriso: Per me ora fatale (Count)
Nun's Chorus
Act 3 Ah sì, ben mio, coll'essere (Manrico)
Act 4 Miserere (Chorus, Leonora, Manrico)
Ai nostri monti (Azucena, Manrico)

RECORDINGS:
RCA SER5586/8 ★●
Victor LSC6194 (3) (US)
Ambrosian Opera Chorus/New
Philharmonia Orchestra
c. Zubin Mehta
Leonora (s) Leontyne Price
Manrico (t) Placido Domingo
Count di Luna (b) Sherrill Milnes
Azucena (m-s) Fiorenza Cossotto

RCA LSC-3203 (US) ■
(from above)

HMV SLS869 (3) ●
Chorus and Orchestra of La Scala, Milan
c. Herbert von Karajan
Leonora (s) Maria Callas
Manrico (t) Giuseppe di Stefano
Count di Luna (b) Rolando Panerai
Azucena (m-s) Fedora Barbieri
(This recording also contains a Callas
recital)

Decca D82D3 (3) ●
London 13124 (3) (US)
London Opera Chorus/National
Philharmonic Orchestra
c. Richard Bonynge
Leonora (s) Joan Sutherland
Manrico (t) Luciano Pavarotti
Count di Luna (b) Ingvar Wixell
Azucena (m-s) Marilyn Horne

DG 2728 088 (3) ●
Chorus and Orchestra of La Scala, Milan
c. Tullio Serafin
Leonora (s) Antonietta Stella
Manrico (t) Carlo Bergonzi
Count di Luna (b) Ettore Bastianini
Azucena (m-s) Fiorenza Cossotto

HMV SLS5111 (3) ●
Angel SXLX3855 (3) (US)
German Opera Chorus/Berlin
Philharmonic Orchestra
c. Herbert von Karajan
Leonora (s) Leontyne Price
Manrico (t) Franco Bonisolli
Count di Luna (b) Piero Cappuccilli
Azucena (m-s) Elena Obraztsova

Decca GOS614/6 ●
London 1304 (3) (US)
Chorus and Orchestra of Maggio
Musicale Fiorentino
c. Alberto Erede
Leonora (s) Renata Tebaldi
Manrico (t) Mario del Monaco
Count di Luna (b) Ugo Savarese
Azucena (m-s) Giulietta Simionato

Cetra Opera Live L029 (2) (m) (r. 1951) ●
Chorus and Orchestra of Teatro San
Carlo, Naples
c. Tullio Serafin

Leonora (s) Maria Callas
Manrico (t) Giacomo Lauri Volpi
Count di Luna (b) Paolo Silveri
Azucena (m-s) Cloe Elmo

Cetra Opera Live L035 (3) (m) (r. 1953) ●
Chorus and Orchestra of La Scala, Milan
c. Antonio Votto
Leonora (s) Maria Callas
Manrico (t) Gino Penno
Count di Luna (b) Carlo Tagliabue

Cetra Opera Live L071 (3) (m) (r. 1941) ●
Chorus and Orchestra of Metropolitan
Opera, New York
c. Ferruccio Calusio
Leonora (s) Norina Greco
Manrico (t) Jussi Björling
Count di Luna (b) Frank Valentino
Azucena (m-s) Bruna Castagna

HMV SLS916 (3) (d) ●
Angel S-3653 (3) (US)
Chorus and Orchestra of the Teatro
dell'Opera di Roma
c. Thomas Schippers
Leonora (s) Gabriella Tucci
Manrico (t) Franco Corelli
Count di Luna (b) Robert Merrill
Azucena (m-s) Giulietta Simionato

HMV ASD2395 ■
Angel S-36404 (US)
(from above)

RCA LSC-6150 (3) (US) ●
Chorus and Orchestra of the Rome
Opera
c. Arturo Basile
Leonora (s) Leontyne Price
Manrico (t) Richard Tucker
Count di Luna (b) Leonard Warren
Azucena (m-s) Rosalind Elias

RCA LSC-2617 ■
(from above)

Below: *Joan Sutherland as Violetta in* La Traviata *at Covent Garden.*

La Traviata
Opera in 3 Acts.
Text by Piave based on Alexandre Dumas's 'La Dame aux camélias'
First performance: Venice (Teatro La Fenice) March 6, 1853. London (Her Majesty's) 1856; New York 1856.

Synopsis:
Scene: Paris. Time: c. 1850.
Act 1 Alfredo Germont meets Violetta and confesses that he has long loved her from afar. Although she is moved, Violetta, a consumptive whose days are numbered, has renounced romantic love. She dismisses Alfredo, giving him a camellia and telling him to return when it fades.
Act 2 Violetta and Alfredo are living together, poor but happy. Giorgio, Alfredo's father, begs Violetta to end the scandalous liaison. She reluctantly agrees, but Alfredo thinks she has returned to a former lover and, encountering her at a party, publicly insults her. Giorgio reproaches him, and Violetta says that he does not realise the extent of her love.
Act 3 The dying Violetta has received a letter from Giorgio: Alfredo, who is abroad, now knows the truth and will come to her. He arrives and begs forgiveness, inspiring Violetta with renewed desire for life. A doctor arrives; but it is too late.

Notes:
This great and enduringly popular opera had the worst possible first performance. The singers had no confidence in the opera,

and thought it ridiculously 'avant-garde'. Nothing went right. Even Verdi himself suspected what would happen if the arrangements were not changed; but he was powerless to do anything about it. It was not long, however, before *La Traviata* found its rightful place in the international repertoire. Violetta is based on Dumas's Marguerite Gautier, herself based on the Parisian courtesan Marie Duplessis who died of consumption at the age of 23. Verdi saw Dumas's play in 1852, in Paris, and *La Traviata* remained a particular favourite of its composer.

Well-known arias:
Act 1 Libiamo (Alfredo)
  Un dì felice (Alfredo, Violetta)
  Ah! fors' è lui (Violetta)
  Sempre libera (Violetta)
Act 2 De' miei bollenti spiriti (Alfredo)
  Dite alla giovine (Violetta, Germont)
  Di Provenza il mar (Germont)
Act 3 Addio del passato (Violetta)
  Parigi, o cara (Alfredo)
The two orchestral Preludes (Act 1 and 3) are also among the best known and most frequently played extracts.

RECORDINGS:
DG 2707 103 (2) ★●
DG 2707 103 (2) (US)
Chorus and Orchestra of Bavarian
State Opera House, Munich
c. Carlos Kleiber
Violetta (s) Ileana Cotrubas
Alfredo Germont (t) Placido Domingo
Giorgio Germont (b) Sherrill Milnes
Annina (s) Helena Jungwirth

RCA SER5564/6 ●
Victor LSC6180 (3) (US)
RCA Italian Opera Chorus and Orchestra
c. Georges Prêtre
Violetta (s) Montserrat Caballé
Alfredo Germont (t) Carlo Bergonzi
Giorgio Germont (b) Sherrill Milnes
Annina (s) Nancy Stokes

RCA SB6779 ■
Victor LSC3036 (US)
(from above)

Decca SET249/51 ●
London 1366 (3) (US)
Maggio Musicale Fiorentino
c. John Pritchard
Violetta (s) Joan Sutherland
Alfredo Germont (t) Carlo Bergonzi
Giorgio Germont (b) Robert Merrill
Annina (s) Dora Carral

Decca SXL6127 ■
London 25886 (US)
(from above)

RCA AT202 (2) (m) (r. 1946) ●
NBC Symphony Orchestra and Chorus
c. Arturo Toscanini
Violetta (s) Licia Albanese
Alfredo Germont (t) Jan Peerce
Giorgio Germont (b) Robert Merrill
Annina (s) Johanna Moreland

Ember GVC2345 (3) (m) ●
Turin Radio Chorus and Orchestra
c. Gabriele Santini
Violetta (s) Maria Callas
Alfredo Germont (t) Giuseppe di Stefano
Giorgio Germont (b) Ettore Bastianini

HMV SLS960 (3) ●
Angel SX3780 (3) (US)
John Alldis Choir/Royal Philharmonic
Orchestra
c. Aldo Ceccato
Violetta (s) Beverly Sills
Alfredo Germont (t) Nicolai Gedda
Giorgio Germont (b) Rolando Panerai
Annina (s) Mirelle Fiorentino

Angel S-36925 (US) ■
(from above)

HMV SLS5097 (3) ●
Angel S-3623 (3) (US)
Chorus and Orchestra of Rome Opera
House
c. Tullio Serafin
Violetta (s) Victoria de los Angeles
Alfredo Germont (t) Carlo del Monte
Giorgio Germont (b) Mario Sereni
Annina (s) Silvia Bertona

Angel S-35822 (US) ■
(from above)

DG 2726 049 (2) ●
DG 337 1004 (3) (US)
Chorus and Orchestra of La Scala, Milan
c. Antonio Votto
Violetta (s) Renata Scotto
Alfredo Germont (t) Gianni Raimondi
Giorgio Germont (b) Ettore Bastianini

DG 922021 (US) ■
(from above)

Decca SET401/2 ●
London 1279 (2) (US)
Chorus and Orchestra of German Opera,
Berlin
c. Lorin Maazel
Violetta (s) Pilar Lorengar
Alfredo Germont (t) Giacomo Aragall
Giorgio Germont (b) Dietrich Fischer-Dieskau

Decca SET483 ■
London 26193 (US)
(from above)

Decca ECS726/8 (d) ●
Chorus and Orchestra of Accademia di
Santa Cecilia di Roma
c. Francesco Molinari-Pradelli

Violetta (s)	Renata Tebaldi	
Alfredo Germont (t)	Gianni Poggi	
Giorgio Germont (b)	Aldo Protti	

Decca ECS777 ■
(from above)

RCA LSC-6154 (3) (US) ●
Chorus and Orchestra of the Opera
House, Rome
c. Fernando Previtali

Violetta (s)	Anna Moffo
Alfredo Germont (t)	Richard Tucker
Giorgio Germont (b)	Robert Merrill

RCA LSC-2561 (US) ■
(from above)

Acanta JB21.644 (3) (film version)
(1973) ●
Berlin State Opera Chorus/Staatskapelle
Orchestra, Berlin
c. Lamberto Gardelli

Violetta (s)	Mirella Freni
Alfredo Germont (t)	Franco Bonisolli
Giorgio Germont (b)	Sesto Bruscantini
Annina (s)	Gudrun Schäfer

Note: Among the plethora of recordings of *La Traviata* some guidance may be helpful. First, the matter of editions. The Caballé/Prêtre (RCA), the Sutherland/Pritchard (Decca) and the Sills/Ceccato (HMV) give the complete score that Verdi wrote. Most of the others make cuts of one sort or another, in line with older practice and lazy theatre 'traditions'. All the Callas sets are old and in mono only; but the artistry is not to be missed. The even older Toscanini version might seem to be hard driven and the singers cramped, but he scrupulously observes Verdi's musical structure, giving it an integrity it has sometimes lost. For the rest, choice will probably depend upon affection for the Violettas: Ileana Cotrubas, Beverly Sills, Montserrat Caballé, Victoria de los Angeles, Joan Sutherland are all excellent and will delight their respective admirers, and each is well served by their colleagues, both musical and technical.
Sadler's Wells highlights in English is also available on HMV CSD1556.

Les Vêpres Siciliennes (The Sicilian Vespers)
Opera in 5 Acts.
Text by Eugène Scribe and Charles Duveyrier.
First performance: Paris (Opéra) June 13, 1855.

I Vespri Siciliani
(Originally 'Giovanna di Guzman': Italian version of 'Les Vêpres siciliennes)
Opera in 5 Acts.
Italian text by A. Fusinato.
First performance: Parma, December 26, 1855. London (Drury Lane) 1859; New York 1859.

Synopsis:
Scene: Palermo. Time: 1282.
Act 1 Duchess Elena mourns her brother, executed by the French, who occupy Sicily. Ordered to sing for French officers, she provokes a riot with a patriotic air. It is quelled by Monforte, the French Governor, who overhears a seditious conversation between Elena and Arrigo, a suspected rebel, who refuses Monforte's offer of service with the French.
Act 2 Giovanni da Procida returns from exile. Arrigo, having promised to avenge Elena's mother, is captured. Hoping that it will rouse the Sicilians to revolt, Procida inspires the abduction of Sicilian women by French soldiers.
Act 3 Monforte is told by a former mistress that Arrigo is his son, but Arrigo refuses to acknowledge the relationship. Elena and Procida tell Arrigo of plots to assassinate Monforte and, torn between patriotism and filial duty, he warns Monforte and is denounced as a traitor by the Sicilians.
Act 4 Elena and Procida await execution; Arrigo pleads with Monforte for their lives. He publicly acknowledges Monforte as his father and is given permission to wed Elena.
Act 5 Procida tells Elena that the sound of her wedding bells will signal the massacre of the French. She tries to halt the ceremony but is overruled by Monforte: the bells ring and the massacre begins.

Notes:
Verdi wrote the *Vespers* to a commission from the Paris Opéra for a work to be performed during the Great Exhibition of 1855. Both subject and librettist were pre-determined. The opera would be in the style still favoured in Paris: the kind of spectacular Grand Opera on which Meyerbeer » had risen to fame and fortune. Verdi was not happy from the start. To begin with the unscrupulous Scribe gave him a crude text barely altered from one he had sold Donizetti » and the composer had set as *Il Duca d'Alba*. But as usual, Verdi overcame the limitations of his text and poured some glorious music into his setting. The original French version was translated and played throughout Italy, reaching La Scala, Milan on February 4, 1856. Thereafter it faded from favour somewhat. The Italian version is the one nowadays usually played (and recorded), though a good case can be made for a revival of the original French.

Well-known arias:
Act 2 O tu, Palermo (Procida)
  The Four Seasons (Ballet)
Act 3 In braccio alle dovizie (Monforte)
Act 4 Giorno di pianto (Arrigo)
Act 5 Mercè, dilette amiche (Elena)

RECORDINGS:
RCA ARL4 0370 (4) ●
RCA ARL4 0370 (4) (US)
John Alldis Choir/New Philharmonia
Orchestra
c. James Levine

Duchess Elena (s)	Martina Arroyo
Arrigo (t)	Placido Domingo
Guido di Monforte (b)	Sherrill Milnes
Giovanni da Procida (bs)	Ruggero Raimondi

Cetra Opera Live L05 (3) (m) (r. 1951)●
Chorus and Orchestra of Teatro
Comunale, Florence
c. Erich Kleiber

Duchess Elena (s)	Maria Callas
Arrigo (t)	Giorgio Kokolios
Guido di Monforte (b)	Enzo Mascherini
Giovanni da Procida (bs)	Boris Christoff

Simon Boccanegra
Opera in Prologue and 3 Acts.
Text by Piave based on the play by Antonio Garcia Gutiérrez.
First performance: Venice (Teatro La Fenice) March 12, 1857. New York 1932.

Synopsis:
Scene: Genoa. Time: 14th century.
Prologue Simon Boccanegra is the plebeian party's candidate for the Doge's office. He hopes to marry Maria, daughter of the former Doge Jacopo Fiesco, but the child he has already had by her has disappeared and Fiesco demands its return. In the Fiesco palace, Boccanegra finds Maria dead, and emerges to hear himself proclaimed as Doge.
Act 1 Twenty-five years have passed. Unknown to all, Fiesco's foster-daughter, Amelia Grimaldi, is Boccanegra's child. She tells her lover, Gabriele Adorno, that Fiesco plots against the Doge. Boccanegra asks Amelia to marry the plebeian Paolo, but changes his mind when he recognises a portrait of her mother. Paolo and his friend Pietro plan to abduct Amelia. Adorno's killing of Lorenzino, another plotter, provokes a riot between plebeians and patricians. Adorno accuses the Doge of complicity, but Boccanegra suspects Paolo.
Act 2 Paolo puts a slow-acting poison in Boccanegra's water, but fails to persuade Fiesco to murder the Doge. Adorno, told by Paolo that Amelia is Boccanegra's mistress, confronts her, but hides when Boccanegra enters. Amelia pleads for Adorno and then leaves: Boccanegra drinks the poisoned water and sleeps. Adorno's attempt to stab him is thwarted by Amelia and, told that she is Boccanegra's daughter, Adorno vows loyalty.
Act 3 The plebeians are victorious. Boccanegra pardons all save Paolo, who tells him they have condemned each other. Weak from poison, the Doge calls Fiesco and reveals to him that Amelia is his grand-daughter. Naming Adorno as his successor, Boccanegra dies.

Notes:
In 1880, 23 years after its première, Verdi took *Simon Boccanegra* in hand and re-worked a good deal of it in conjunction with his then librettist, Arrigo Boito ».

Well-known arias:
Act 1 Come in quest'ora bruna (Amelia)
  Figlia! A tal nome palpito (Simon)

RECORDINGS:
DG 2709 071 (3) ★ ●
DG 2709 071 (3) (US)
Chorus and Orchestra of La Scala, Milan
c. Claudio Abbado

Simon Boccanegra (b)	Piero Cappuccilli
Amelia/Maria (s)	Mirella Freni
Jacopo Fiesco (bs)	Nicolai Ghiaurov
Gabriele Adorno (t)	José Carreras

DG 2537 046 ■
(from above)

HMV SLS5090 (3) ●
Chorus and Orchestra of Rome Opera
House
c. Gabriele Santini
Simon Boccanegra (b) Tito Gobbi
Amelia/Maria (s) Victoria de los
Angeles
Jacopo Fiesco (bs) Boris Christoff
Gabriele Adorno (t) Giuseppe
Campora

RCA SER5696/8 (3) ●
RCA ARL-3 0564 (3) (US)
RCA Italiana Chorus and Orchestra
c. Gianandrea Gavazzeni
Simon Boccanegra (b) Piero Cappuccilli
Amelia/Maria (s) Katia Riccarelli
Jacopo Fiesco (bs) Ruggero
Raimondi
Gabriele Adorno (t) Placido Domingo

Aroldo

Opera in 4 Acts.
Text by Piave.
First performance: Rimini, August 16, 1857.

Notes:

Aroldo is, in fact, another version of the opera *Stiffelio*, which
Verdi wrote at Piave's suggestion on a text based on a French
play *Le Pasteur* by Emile Souvestre and Eugène Bourgeois and
which was produced in Trieste on November 16, 1850. The plots
are virtually identical until the last Act, though the situations
are changed. Act 3 of *Stiffelio* is cut short in *Aroldo* and a fourth
Act added.

RECORDINGS:

DG 2707 090 (2) □
DG 2707 090 (US)
Overture
Berlin Philharmonic Orchestra
c. Herbert von Karajan

Decca SXL6429 □
Sotto il sol
Mario del Monaco (t)

Un Ballo in Maschera (A Masked Ball)

Opera in 3 Acts (original title 'Gustavo III').
Text by Antonio Somma based on Eugène Scribe's play.
First performance: Rome (Teatro Apollo) February 17, 1859. New York 1861;
London 1861.

Synopsis:

Scene: Boston, America. Time: late 17th century.
Act 1 Riccardo, Governor of Boston, loves Amelia, wife of his
secretary and friend Renato. He refuses to heed Renato's
warning of an assassination plot. When Oscar the page ushers in
the Chief Justice with a petition for the banishment of a fortune-
teller, Ulrica, Riccardo suggests that they all visit Ulrica. He is
delighted to overhear Amelia tell Ulrica of her secret love for the
Governor. Ulrica prescribes a herb to dispel the guilty passion.
Riccardo, disguised, is warned by Ulrica that he will be killed by
the next man whose hand he shakes. All decline his hand until
Renato enters, unknowing, and accepts Riccardo's proffered
handshake.
Act 2 Riccardo meets Amelia as she seeks the prescribed herb,
and they sing of their love. Renato comes with a warning of an
ambush: the men exchange cloaks and Riccardo tells Renato to
escort the heavily-veiled lady. The conspirators intercept
Renato and unveil Amelia. Shocked to recognise his wife,
Renato vows vengeance on Riccardo.
Act 3 Amelia denies infidelity and Renato cannot bear to
harm her, but he makes her draw the lot to decide who shall kill
Riccardo at the masked ball. Renato is chosen. Having decided
to post Renato abroad with Amelia, Riccardo ignores a warning
note and leaves for the ball, where Renato learns the Governor's
disguise from Oscar. While dancing, Amelia begs Riccardo to
leave; he tells her of his decision and they bid farewell. But
Renato stabs Riccardo, who dies forgiving him.

Notes:

The story is based on the assassination of King Gustavus III of
Sweden in 1792, at a masked ball. Verdi originally set the opera
in Stockholm with a Swedish cast. But political unrest made the
Italian authorities jib at an opera depicting the assassination of a
king. They allowed its performance only provided the setting
and characters were transferred to Boston, and the cast made
English. In fact, an assassination attempt was made against
Napoleon III when *Ballo* was to be produced in Naples; and
again the cry went up—*Viva Verdi!* But it was not only the
musical acumen of the crowd that was implied: the call was also
a political acrostic—Vittorio Emmanuele, Re D'Italia. Nowadays

Below: Un Ballo in Maschera *at the Royal Opera House, Covent Garden.*

some opera houses revert to the original Swedish version, but we have retained the Italian since all the recordings use that form. The music remains splendidly the same.

Well-known arias:

Act 1 Volta la terra (Oscar)
Act 2 Ma dall' arido stelo divulsa (Amelia)
O qual soave (Riccardo and Amelia)
Act 3 Morrò, ma prima in grazia (Amelia)
Eri tu che macchiavi quell' anima (Renato)

RECORDINGS:
RCA SER5710/12 ★●
RCA LSC 6179 (3) (US)
RCA Italiana Opera Chorus and Orchestra
c. Erich Leinsdorf
Riccardo (t) Carlo Bergonzi
Renato (b) Robert Merrill
Amelia (s) Leontyne Price
Ulrica (m-s) Shirley Verrett
Oscar (s) Reri Grist

RCA LSC-3034 (US) ■
(from above)

HMV SLS984 (3) ●
Angel SX-3762 (3) (US)
Chorus of Royal Opera House, Covent Garden/New Philharmonia Orchestra
c. Riccardo Muti
Riccardo (t) Placido Domingo
Renato (b) Piero Cappuccilli
Amelia (s) Martina Arroyo
Ulrica (m-s) Fiorenza Cossotto
Oscar (s) Reri Grist

Decca SET484/6 ●
London OSA-1398 (3) (US)
Chorus and Orchestra of Accademia di Santa Cecilia di Roma
c. Bruno Bartoletti
Riccardo (t) Luciano Pavarotti
Renato (b) Sherrill Milnes
Amelia (s) Renata Tebaldi
Ulrica (m-s) Regina Resnik
Oscar (s) Helen Donath

Decca SET538 ■
London 26278 (US)
(from above)

Decca SET215/7 ●
London OSA-1328 (3) (US)
Chorus and Orchestra of Accademia di Santa Cecilia di Roma
c. Sir Georg Solti
Riccardo (t) Carlo Bergonzi
Renato (b) Cornell MacNeil
Amelia (s) Birgit Nilsson
Ulrica (m-s) Giulietta Simionato
Oscar (s) Sylvia Stahlmann

RCA AT300 (3) (m) (r. 1949) ●
Robert Shaw Chorale/NBC Symphony Orchestra
c. Arturo Toscanini
Riccardo (t) Jan Peerce
Renato (b) Robert Merrill
Amelia (s) Herva Nelli
Ulrica (m-s) Claramae Turner

Oscar (s) Vera Haskins

Cetra Opera Live L04 (3) (m) (r. 1955) ●
Metropolitan Opera Chorus and Orchestra
c. Dimitri Mitropoulos
Riccardo (t) Richard Tucker
Renato (b) Josef Metternich
Amelia (s) Zinka Milanov
Ulrica (m-s) Jean Madeira
Oscar (s) Roberta Peters

Cetra Opera Live L055 (3) (m) (r. 1957) ●
Chorus and Orchestra of La Scala, Milan
c. Gianandrea Gavazzeni
Riccardo (t) Giuseppe di Stefano
Renato (b) Ettore Bastianini
Amelia (s) Maria Callas
Ulrica (m-s) Giulietta Simionato
Oscar (s) Eugenia Ratti

HMV RLS736 (3) (m) ●
Angel C/L-3557 (3) (m) (US)
La Scala Chorus and Orchestra
c. Antonio Votto
Riccardo (t) Giuseppe di Stefano
Renato (b) Tito Gobbi
Amelia (s) Maria Callas
Ulrica (m-s) Fedora Barbieri
Oscar (s) Eugenia Ratti

World Records SH131/2 (m) (r. 1943) ●
Seraphim 1136026 (2) (US)
Chorus and Orchestra of Rome Opera House
c. Tullio Serafin
Riccardo (t) Beniamino Gigli
Renato (b) Gino Becchi
Amelia (s) Maria Caniglia
Ulrica (m-s) Fedora Barbieri
Oscar (s) Elda Ribetti

La Forza del Destino (The Force of Destiny)

Opera in 4 Acts.
Text by Piave based on the play 'Don Alvaro, o La fuerza de sino' by Angelo Pérez de Saavedra, Duke of Rivas.
First performance: St Petersburg (Court Opera) November 10, 1862. New York 1865; London (Her Majesty's) 1867.

Synopsis:

Scene: Spain and Italy. Time: mid-18th century.
Act 1 The Marquis of Calatrava opposes the marriage of his daughter Leonora and Don Alvaro, who plan to elope. Alvaro accidentally kills the Marquis, who dies cursing Leonora.
Act 2 In a tavern, Leonora, in man's attire, recognises her brother, Carlo, who means to avenge his father. The gypsy Preziosilla foretells tragedy for Carlo. At a monastery, Leonora

asks Fra Mellitone to call Father Guardian: she tells her story and is granted refuge in a hermit's cave nearby.
Act 3 Believing Leonora dead, Alvaro is fighting in Italy. He saves Carlo from marauders and, not knowing each other, they swear friendship. Badly wounded, Alvaro gives Carlo a package to be destroyed if he dies. Carlo, already suspicious, finds Leonora's picture and swears to kill Alvaro. Revealing that Leonora lives, Carlo fights Alvaro but is restrained.
Act 4 Fra Mellitone and Father Raffaello (the disguised Alvaro) distribute food, but Carlo arrives and challenges Alvaro again. Carlo is mortally wounded and Alvaro, seeking a confessor, finds Leonora. Carlo, unforgiving, stabs her as he dies. Leonora dies in Father Guardians's arms.

Notes:

La Forza is a big sprawling opera of tremendous dramatic and musical force. Verdi wrote it for the Imperial Opera in St Petersburg for their 1861/2 season. At first he proposed to use Victor Hugo's *Ruy Blas*, but decided in favour of the Spanish play, which Piave adapted with additions from Schiller's *Wallenstein's Camp*. At the end of 1869 he revised the score with the help of the librettist Antonio Ghislanzoni. It was from this revised version that the overture, one of the most popular and extended in all Verdi, was written. It is a stirring piece, often played in concerts.

Well-known arias:

Act 1 Me pellegrina (Leonora)
Act 2 Madre, pietosa Vergine (Prayer) (Leonora)
La Vergine degli angeli (Melitone)
Act 3 Solenne in quest'ora (Alvaro and Carlo)
Rataplan (Preziosilla)
Act 4 Pace, pace, mio Dio (Leonora)
Non imprecare (Melitone, Alvaro and Leonora)

RECORDINGS:
RCA RL01864 (4) ★●
RCA ARL4-1864 (US)
John Alldis Choir/London Symphony Orchestra
c. James Levine
Leonora (s) Leontyne Price
Don Alvaro (t) Placido Domingo
Don Carlo (b) Sherrill Milnes
Preziosilla (m-s) Fiorenza Cossotto
Guardian (bs) Bonaldo Giaiotti
Fra Melitone (b) Gabriel Bacquier

HMV SLS948 (4) ●
Angel S-3765 (4) (US)
Ambrosian Opera Chorus/Royal Philharmonic Orchestra
c. Lamberto Gardelli
Leonora (s) Martina Arroyo
Don Alvaro (t) Carlo Bergonzi
Don Carlo (b) Piero Cappuccilli
Preziosilla (m-s) Bianca Maria Casoni
Guardian (bs) Ruggero Raimondi
Fra Melitone (b) Sir Geraint Evans

Angel S-36828 (US) ■
(from above)

Decca GOS597/9 ●
London OSA-1405 (4) (US)
Chorus and Orchestra of Accademia di Santa Cecilia di Roma
c. Francesco Molinari-Pradelli
Leonora (s) Renata Tebaldi
Don Alvaro (t) Mario del Monaco
Don Carlo (b) Ettore Bastianini
Preziosilla (m-s) Giulietta Simionato
Guardian (bs) Cesare Siepi
Fra Melitone (b) Fernando Corena

Decca SDD262 ■
London 25085 (US)
(from above)

HMV SLS5120 (3) ●
Angel 3531C (m) (US)
Chorus and Orchestra of La Scala, Milan

c. Tullio Serafin
Leonora (s) Maria Callas
Don Alvaro (t) Richard Tucker
Don Carlo (b) Cesare Tagliabue
Preziosilla (m-s) Elean Nicolai

Decca GOS660/2 ●
London OSA-13122 (3) (US)
Chorus and Orchestra of Accademia di Santa Cecilia di Roma
c. Fernando Previtali
Leonora (s) Zinka Milanov
Don Alvaro (t) Giuseppe di Stefano
Don Carlo (b) Leonard Warren
Preziosilla (m-s) Rosalind Elias

Cetra Opera Live L017 (3) (m) (r. 1953) ●
Maggio Musicale Fiorentino di Firenze
c. Dimitri Mitropoulos
Leonora (s) Renata Tebaldi
Don Alvaro (t) Mario del Monaco
Don Carlo (b) Aldo Protti
Preziosilla (m-s) Fedora Barbieri

RCA SER5527/30 (d) ●
RCA LSC-6413 (4) (US)
Chorus and Orchestra of RCA Italiana
c. Thomas Schippers
Leonora (s) Leontyne Price
Don Alvaro (t) Richard Tucker
Don Carlo (b) Robert Merrill
Preziosilla (m-s) Shirley Verrett

RCA LSC-2838 (US) ■
(from above)

HMV ASD3366 □
Angel S-37407 (US)
Overture
c. Riccardo Muti

Philips 6833 033 □
Philips 6833 033 (US)
Overture
Concertgebouw Orchestra
c. Bernard Haitink

Don Carlos

Opera in 5 Acts.
Text by François Joseph Méry and Camille du Locle based on Schiller's play.
(Italian translation by Achille de Luazières and Angelo Zanardini.)
First performance: Paris (Opéra) March 11, 1867. London (Covent Garden) 1867; New York 1877.

Don Carlo

Opera in 4 Acts (revised Italian version of above).
Text revised by Antonio Ghislanzoni.
First performance: Milan (La Scala) January 10, 1884.

Synopsis:

Scene: Fontainebleau and Spain. Time: 16th century.

Act 1   While hunting at Fontainebleau, Don Carlos, Infante of Spain and son of Philip II, meets Elisabeth de Valois, daughter of the King of France, whom he must marry for political reasons. They fall in love, but news comes that Philip himself now intends to marry Elisabeth.

Above: Don Carlos *at the Royal Opera House, Covent Garden.*

Act 2   At a monastery in Madrid, Carlos tells Rodrigo of his love for Elisabeth, now his stepmother. Rodrigo asks him to attempt to relieve Spanish oppression of Flanders. Carlos asks Elisabeth to make him Governor of Flanders, but then declares his love and is repulsed. Rodrigo pleads with King Philip to moderate his Flemish policy: the King warns him against the Grand Inquisitor and speaks of his suspicions concerning Carlos and Elisabeth.

Act 3   Princess Eboli, who loves Carlos and has guessed he loves Elisabeth, is angry when he rejects her. Carlos gives Rodrigo secret papers concerning the Flemish rebels. He begs the King for mercy for the Flemings and, rebuffed, draws his sword. Rodrigo disarms him and is ennobled by the King.

Act 4   Philip mourns because Elisabeth does not love him. The Grand Inquisitor presses him to hand over Carlos to the Inquisition for death. Eboli takes Elisabeth's jewel box to Philip, who finds Carlos's portrait in it. Remorseful, Eboli confesses to Elisabeth that she loves Carlos but has been seduced by Philip: Elisabeth banishes her. Rodrigo, incriminated by the secret papers, is assassinated by the Inquisition. Dying, he tells Carlos that Elisabeth wishes to see him, and charges him to free

Flanders. Carlos denounces Philip as a murderer, and is helped by Eboli to escape.

Act 5   At the tomb of Charles V, Carlos and Elisabeth declare their mutual but doomed love. Philip and the Inquisitor come to arrest them, but the tomb opens and a monk-like wraith carries Carlos away.

Notes:

Don Carlos, like the *Sicilian Vespers*, was written for the Paris Opéra and was designed also on a scale to meet that city's taste. Seventeen years later, Verdi took the opera in hand and refashioned it. He suppressed the first Act, retaining only Carlos's aria, so that the new Italian version emerged with four Acts instead of five, not entirely to its advantage. The original French version is virtually never heard these days, but the four-Act revision is often performed. The most intelligent and most frequent compromise, however, is to restore the first Act to the later revision.

Well-known arias:

Act 1   Io la vidi (Don Carlos)
Act 2   Dio, che nell'alma infondere (Rodrigo and Carlos)
Canzone del velo (Song of the Veil) (Eboli)
Act 4   O don fatale (Eboli)
O Carlo, ascolta (Rodrigo and Carlos)
Act 5   Tu che le vanità (Elisabeth)

RECORDINGS:
HMV SLS956 (4) (5-Act version) ★●
Angel S-3774 (4) (US)
Ambrosian Opera Chorus/Orchestra
of Royal Opera House, Covent Garden
c. Carlo Maria Giulini
Don Carlos (t)   Placido Domingo
King Philip II (bs) Ruggero Raimondi
Elisabeth (s)   Montserrat Caballé
Rodrigo (b)   Sherrill Milnes
Princess
  Eboli (m-s)   Shirley Verrett

Angel S-36918 (US) ■
(from above)

Decca SET305/8 (5-Act version)●
London OSA-1432 (4) (US)
Chorus and Orchestra of Royal Opera
House, Covent Garden
c. Sir Georg Solti
Don Carlo (t)   Carlo Bergonzi
King Philip II (bs) Nicolai Ghiaurov
Elisabeth (s)   Renata Tebaldi
Rodrigo (b)   Dietrich
                        Fischer-Dieskau

Princess
  Eboli (m-s)   Grace Bumbry

Decca SET353 ■
(from above)

Aida

Opera in 4 Acts.
Text by Camille du Locle after synopsis by Auguste Mariette (Bey) translated into Italian by Antonio Ghislanzoni.
First performance: Cairo (Opéra House) December 24, 1871. Milan (La Scala) 1872; New York 1873; London (Covent Garden) 1876.

Synopsis:

Scene: Memphis and Thebes. Time: of the Pharaohs.

Act 1   General Radames loves the captive Aida, not knowing she is the daughter of Egypt's enemy, Amonasro, and that she is tormented by divided loyalties. Amneris, daughter of the Egyptian King, desires Radames and is jealous of Aida. The armies are consecrated to victory in the Temple of Ptah.

Act 2   Amneris untruthfully tells Aida that the victorious Radames is dead and, when Aida expresses desolation, is confirmed in her jealousy. A Grand March celebrates the victory. Among the captives is Amonasro, who warns Aida not to reveal his identity and pleads for mercy. The Egyptian King grants amnesty, but the priests demand the retention of Aida and Amonasro. The King announces that Radames will wed Amneris.

Act 3   While Aida awaits Radames by the Nile, Amonasro asks her to betray the Egyptian army into an ambush. Radames tells

Aida he will reveal their love to the King, but Aida begs him to flee with her. All are surprised by Amneris: Radames gives himself up while Aida and Amonasro escape.

Act 4 Radames, sentenced to be buried alive, refuses to let Amneris save him. Entombed in the Temple, he finds that Aida has entered unobserved to share his fate. Amneris prays for peace while, below, Aida dies in Radames's arms.

Notes:

Verdi wrote *Aida* to a commission from the Khedive of Egypt for a work to open the new Cairo Opera House. It was not in fact used for that occasion, but found its place there as a grand opera of great colour and power. It has been argued that the story of *Aida* was borrowed from a libretto by Metastasio entitled *Nitteti*.

Well-known arias:

Act 1 Celeste Aida (Radames)
Ritorna vincitor (Aida)
Nume, custode e vindici (Temple Scene)
Act 2 Gloria all'Egitto and Grand March (Chorus)
Act 3 O patria mia (Aida)
Act 4 La fatal pietra (Radames and Aida)
O terra addio (Radames and Aida)

RECORDINGS:

Decca SET427/9 ●
London OSA-1393 (3) (US)
Chorus and Orchestra of Rome Opera House
c. Sir Georg Solti
Aida (s) Leontyne Price
Radames (t) Jon Vickers
Amneris (m-s) Rita Gorr
Amonasro (b) Robert Merrill
King of Egypt (bs) Giorgio Tozzi

HMV SLS977 (3) ●
Angel SX-3815 (3) (US)
Chorus of Royal Opera House, Covent Garden/New Philharmonia Orchestra
c. Riccardo Muti
Aida (s) Montserrat Caballé
Radames (t) Placido Domingo
Amneris (m-s) Fiorenza Cossotto
Amonasro (b) Piero Cappuccilli
King of Egypt (bs) Nicolai Ghiaurov

HMV ASD3292 ■
Angel S-37228 (US)
(from above)

RCA SER5609/11 ●
Victor LSC-6198 (3) (US)
John Alldis Choir/London Symphony Orchestra
c. Erich Leinsdorf
Aida (s) Leontyne Price
Radames (t) Placido Domingo
Amneris (m-s) Grace Bumbry
Amonasro (b) Sherrill Milnes
King of Egypt (bs) Ruggero Raimondi

RCA LSC-3275 (US) ■
(from above)

Decca SXL2167/9 ★●
London 1313 (3) (US)
Vienna Gesellschaft/Vienna Philharmonic Orchestra
c. Herbert von Karajan
Aida (s) Renata Tebaldi
Radames (t) Carlo Bergonzi
Amneris (m-s) Giulietta Simionato
Amonasro (b) Cornell MacNeil
King of Egypt (bs) Fernando Corena

Decca SXL2242 ■
London 25206 (US)
(from above)

RCA AT302 (3) (m) (r. 1949) ●
Victrola VICS-6113 (3) (d) (US)
NBC Chorus and Symphony Orchestra
c. Arturo Toscanini
Aida (s) Herva Nelli

Radames (t) Richard Tucker
Amneris (m-s) Eva Gustavison
Amonasro (b) Giuseppe Valdengo

HMV SLS929 (3) (d) ●
Angel S-3716 (3) (US)
Rome Opera Chorus and Orchestra
c. Zubin Mehta
Aida (s) Birgit Nilsson
Radames (t) Fernando Corelli
Amneris (m-s) Grace Bumbry
Amonasro (b) Mario Sereni

Angel S-36566 (US) ■
(from above)

HMV SLS5108 (3) ●
Angel 3525C (3) (m) (US)
Chorus and Orchestra of La Scala, Milan
c. Tullio Serafin
Aida (s) Maria Callas
Radames (t) Richard Tucker
Amneris (m-s) Fedora Barbieri
Amonasro (b) Tito Gobbi

Decca D47D3 (3) ●
Richmond RS63004 (m) (d) (US)
Chorus and Orchestra of Accademia di Santa Cecilia di Roma
c. Alberto Erede
Aida (s) Renata Tebaldi
Radames (t) Mario del Monaco
Amneris (m-s) Ebe Stignani
Amonasro (b) Alfredo Protti

World Records SH153/5 (m) (r. 1943) ●
Seraphim IC6008 (3) (m) (d) (US)
Chorus and Orchestra of Rome Opera House
c. Tullio Serafin
Aida (s) Maria Caniglia
Radames (t) Beniamino Gigli
Amneris (m-s) Ebe Stignani
Amonasro (b) Gino Bechi

Cetra Opera Live L026 (3) (m) (r. 1943) ●
Chorus and Orchestra of Metropolitan Opera, New York
c. Wilfrid Pelletier
Aida (s) Zinka Milanov
Radames (t) Giovanni Martinelli
Amneris (m-s) Bruna Castagna
Amonasro (b) Richard Bonelli

Otello

Opera in 4 Acts.
Text by Arrigo Boito based on Shakespeare's play.
First performance: Milan (La Scala) February 5, 1887. New York 1888; London (Lyceum Theatre) 1889.

Synopsis:

Scene: Cyprus. Time: late 15th century.
Act 1 The Moorish general Otello, Governor of Cyprus, lands victorious to great acclaim. But Iago hates Otello and plans to use Cassio, whom Otello has promoted above Iago, to destroy him. He tricks Cassio into a drunken brawl which results in Cassio's dismissal by the Moor.
Act 2 Iago advises Cassio to seek the intercession of Desdemona, Otello's wife. He then tells Otello that Cassio has Desdemona's handkerchief, which Iago has himself obtained through Emilia, Desdemona's maid and Iago's wife.
Act 3 Otello demands the handkerchief, but Desdemona says that she does not have it with her—and again requests Cassio's reprieve. She denies Otello's charge of infidelity. Iago arranges for Otello to see Cassio with the handkerchief and to overhear talk of Cassio's amours. When Venetian diplomats recall Otello, appointing Cassio in his place, the Moor says he will kill Desdemona. Iago, triumphant; counsels him to strangle her, offering to deal with Cassio himself.
Act 4 After singing her sorrowful Willow Song and her prayer, Desdemona retires. Otello enters and, ignoring her protestations of innocence, strangles her. Cassio brings help too late. Iago flees, while Otello stabs himself.

Notes:

After *Aida* Verdi wrote no more operas for several years. It seemed, as he himself said, that his account was closed. But a meeting was arranged with Boito » who was anxious to work with Verdi on a Shakespeare project (Boito having already written a Shakespeare libretto, on *Hamlet*, for Franco Faccio). Verdi became interested, and his miraculous late burst of creativity was set in motion. Boito's texts for *Otello* and *Falstaff* are generally considered the best ever provided for an Italian composer.

Well-known arias:

Act 1 Esultate! (Otello)
Beva con me (Iago)
Già nella notte (Otello and Desdemona)
Act 2 Credo on un Dio crudele (Iago)
Ora e per sempre addio (Otello)
Act 3 Dio, mi potevi scagliar tutti i mali miseria (Otello)
Act 4 Piangea cantando (Willow Song) (Desdemona)
Ave Maria (Desdemona)

RECORDINGS:

RCA RL02951 (3) ●
Ambrosian Opera Chorus/National Philharmonic Orchestra
c. James Levine
Otello (t) Placido Domingo
Iago (b) Sherrill Milnes
Cassio (t) Frank Little
Desdemona (s) Renata Scotto

Decca D55D3 (3) ●
London OSA-1324 (3) (US)
Vienna State Opera Chorus/Vienna Grisstadtkinderchor/Vienna Philharmonic Orchestra
c. Herbert von Karajan
Otello (s) Mario del Monaco
Iago (b) Aldo Protti
Cassio (t) Nello Romanato
Desdemona (s) Renata Tebaldi

London 25701 (US) ■
(from above)

HMV SLS975 (3) ★●
Angel SX-3809 (3) (US)

Chorus of German Opera/Berlin Philharmonic Orchestra
c. Herbert von Karajan
Otello (t) Jon Vickers
Iago (b) Peter Glossop
Cassio (t) Aldo Bottion
Desdemona (s) Mirella Freni

Decca SXL2314 ■
London 25701 (US)
(from above)

Decca D102D3 (3) ●
Vienna Boys' Choir/Vienna State Opera Chorus/Vienna Philharmonic Orchestra
c. Sir Georg Solti
Otello (t) Carlo Cossutta
Iago (b) Gabriel Bacquier
Cassio (t) Peter Dvorský
Desdemona (s) Margaret Price

RCA SER5646/8 ●
Victor AGL-3 1969 (3) (US)
Chorus and Orchestra of Rome Opera House

c. Tullio Serafin
Otello (t)   Jon Vickers
Iago (b)   Tito Gobbi
Cassio (t)   Fiorindo Anreolli
Desdemona (s)   Leonie Rysanek

Decca ECS732/4 ●
Richmond RS63004 (m) (3) (US)
Chorus and Orchestra of Accademia di
Santa Cecilia
c. Alberto Erede
Otello (t)   Mario del Monaco
Iago (b)   Aldo Protti
Desdemona (s)   Renata Tebaldi

RCA AT303 (3) (m) (d) (r. 1951) ●
RCA Victrola VICS6120 (3) (d) (US)
NBC Chorus and Symphony Orchestra
c. Arturo Toscanini
Otello (t)   Ramon Vinay
Iago (b)   Giuseppe Valdengo
Cassio (t)   Virginio Assandri
Desdemona (s)   Herva Nelli

HMV SLS940 (3) (d) ★●
Angel S-3742 (3) (US)
Ambrosian Chorus/New Philharmonia
Orchestra
c. Sir John Barbirolli
Otello (t)   James McCracken
Iago (b)   Dietrich Fischer-Dieskau
Cassio (t)   Piero de Palma
Desdemona (s)   Gwyneth Jones

Cetra Opera Live L06 (3) (m) (r. 1951) ●
Chorus of Vienna State Opera/Vienna
Philharmonic Orchestra
c. Wilhelm Furtwängler
Otello (t)   Ramon Vinay
Iago (b)   Paul Schöffler
Cassio (t)   Anton Dermota
Desdemona (s)   Dragica Martinis

(Note: Two classic recordings—Toscanini
(RCA) and Barbirolli (HMV) are
temporarily out of circulation. Both are
so good, so totally Verdian, that they
should be sought.)

Falstaff

Opera in 3 Acts.
Text by Arrigo Boito based on Shakespeare's 'Merry Wives of Windsor' and
'Henry IV'.
First performance: Milan (La Scala) February 9, 1893. London (Covent Garden)
1894; New York 1895.

Synopsis:

Scene: Windsor. Time: King Henry IV's reign.
Act 1 Dr Caius complains that he has been wronged by
Falstaff and robbed by Bardolph and Pistol, but Falstaff blusters
his way out of trouble. The impecunious Falstaff decides to woo
the wealthy Mistress Alice Ford and Mistress Meg Page. They
discover that he has written them identical letters and, aided by
Alice's daughter, Nanetta, and Mistress Quickly, they plan
retaliation. Bardolph and Pistol warn Ford of Falstaff's plan.
Fenton and Nanetta, in love, exchange clandestine kisses.
Act 2 Mistress Quickly tells Falstaff that Alice's husband is
away and that she will receive him. Ford, posing as 'Brook', an
unrequited lover of Alice, offers Falstaff money for his aid.
Nanetta complains that her father intends her to marry Dr
Caius. Falstaff, wooing Alice, is warned by Mistress Quickly of
Ford's approach, and hides in a laundry basket. Ford and his
helpers surprise Fenton and Nanetta in an embrace. Alice orders
the laundry basket to be thrown into the river.
Act 3 As Falstaff restores his dampened spirits with wine,
Mistress Quickly brings a note from Alice asking him to meet
her at Herne's Oak in Windsor Forest, disguised as the phantom
huntsman. Falstaff arrives, disguised, at midnight, and is set on
by masked tormentors. When his adversaries unmask, he learns
that 'Brook' is Alice's husband. But it is Falstaff's turn to laugh
when Ford is tricked into blessing the betrothal of Fenton and
Nanetta. All ends in the best of humour.

Notes:

Apart from the early and unsuccessful *Un giorno di regno*, Verdi
wrote no comedy until *Falstaff*. There were one or two comic
scenes in his operas, but nothing to suggest that he had in him a
great comic masterpiece. His life's work up to *Otello* appeared
as a long succession of tragic dramas, frequently magnificent in
power and expressiveness. Then Boito put this into his hands: he
recognised it as unusual, and set to work, at first saying he was
writing it simply for his private pleasure. He led Italian opera
forward into new domains. He created a marvellous conversa-

tional style and found a declamation in which the Italian
language was matched with its perfect musical equivalent.

Well-known arias:
Act 1 L'Onore (Falstaff)
Act 2 E sogno? o realtá (Ford)
Act 3 Dal labbro il canto estasiato vola (Fenton)

RECORDINGS:
RCA AT301 (3) (m) (r. 1950) ●
Robert Shaw Chorale/NBC Symphony
Orchestra
c. Arturo Toscanini
Falstaff (b)   Giuseppe Valdengo
Fenton (t)   Antonio Madasi
Ford (b)   Frank Guarrera
Mistress Ford (s)   Herva Nelli
Nanetta (s)   Teresa Stich-
     Randall
Mistress Page (m-s) Nan Merriman
Mistress
  Quickly (m-s)   Cloe Elmo

HMV SLS5037 (3) ★●
Angel S-3552 (3) (US)
Philharmonia Chorus and Orchestra
c. Herbert von Karajan
Falstaff (b)   Tito Gobbi
Fenton (t)   Luigi Alva
Ford (b)   Rolando Panerai
Mistress Ford (s)   Elisabeth
     Schwarzkopf
Nanetta (s)   Anna Moffo
Mistress Page (m-s) Nan Merriman
Mistress
  Quickly (m-s)   Fedora Barbieri

Decca 2BB104/6 ●
London 1395 (3) (US)
RCA Italiana Opera Chorus and
Orchestra
c. Sir Georg Solti
Falstaff (b)   Sir Geraint Evans
Fenton (t)   Alfredo Krauss
Ford (b)   Robert Merrill
Mistress Ford (s)   Ilva Ligabue
Nanetta (s)   Mirella Freni
Mistress Page (m-s) Rosalind Elias

Mistress
  Quickly (m-s)   Giulietta Simionato

London 26387 (US) ■
(from above)

CBS 77392 (3) ●
Columbia M3S750 (3) (US)
Vienna State Opera Chorus/Vienna
Philharmonic Orchestra
c. Leonard Bernstein
Falstaff (b)   Dietrich
     Fischer-Dieskau
Fenton (t)   Juan Oncina
Ford (b)   Rolando Panerai
Mistress Ford (s)   Ilva Ligabue
Nanetta (s)   Graziella Sciutti
Mistress Page (m-s) Hilde Rössl-Majdan
Mistress
  Quickly (m-s)   Regina Resnik

Cetra Opera Live L046 (2) (m) (r. 1937) ○
Vienna State Opera Chorus/Vienna
Philharmonic Orchestra
c. Arturo Toscanini
Falstaff (b)   Mariano Stabile
Fenton (t)   Dino Borgiolo
Ford (b)   Piero Biasini
Mistress Ford (s)   Augusta Oltrabella
Mistress Page (m-s) Angelica
     Cravcemco

Cetra Opera Live L014 (3) (m) (r. 1951) ●
Chorus and Orchestra of La Scala, Milan
c. Victor de Sabata
Falstaff (b)   Mariano Stabile
Fenton (t)   Cesare Valletti
Ford (b)   Paolo Silveri
Mistress Ford (s)   Renata Tebaldi
Mistress Page (m-s) Cloe Elmo

RECITALS
Decca DPA555/6
Arias, duets, choruses
Various artists

Decca SPA447
'The world of Verdi'
Various artists

Philips 6747 193 (3)
Philips 6747 193 (3) (US)
Tenor arias
Carlo Bergonzi (t)

Philips 6580 150
(Selection from above)

RCA DPS2001 A/B (2)
RCA VCS-7063 (2)
'Heroines'
Leontyne Price (s)

Decca SXL6605
Verdi arias
Maria Chiara (s)

Decca SXL6190
London 25939 (US)
Verdi arias
Joan Sutherland (s)

Decca SXL6443
London 26146 (US)
'Great Scenes'
Nicolai Ghiaurov (bs)

CBS76426
Columbia M-33516 (US)
Verdi arias
Renata Scotto (s)

Philips 6580 171
Philips 6580 171 (US)
Verdi arias
Ingvar Wixell (b)

DG 2530 549
DG 2530 549 (US)
Verdi opera choruses
Chorus and Orchestra of La Scala, Milan
c. Claudio Abbado

ORCHESTRAL
DG 2707 090 (2)
DG 2707 090 (2) (US)
Complete overtures and preludes
c. Herbert von Karajan

DG 2531 145
(from above)

Decca SXL6726
London 6945 (US)
Ballet music from *I Vespri siciliani, Don*

Carlos, Otello
c. Lorin Maazel

Philips 6747 093 (2)
Philips 6747 093 (US)
Ballet music from *I Vespri siciliani, Don
Carlos, I Lombardi, Macbeth, Otello,
Il trovatore*
c. Antonio de Almeida

Philips 6580 264
(from above)

ANTONIO VIVALDI

(b. Venice 4.3.1678; d. Vienna ?.7.1841)

For much of his life, Vivaldi was music director of the Conservatore dell'Ospidale della Pieta in Venice, a music school for girls, where he produced a great profusion of instrumental works. He himself had his early training from his father and later from Giovanni Legrenzi in Venice. He took holy orders in 1703 and because of his red hair became known as *'il prete rosso'* ('red priest'). Later in his life he travelled much in Europe; but his last years were not happy. He allowed ambitious schemes to distort his judgement and in the end he died in poverty in Vienna where he had settled in 1839, hopeful of making a great success but finding time and circumstance against him. As an opera composer, Vivaldi does not occupy anything approaching the position he holds in the instrumental field. He was prolific and ambitious, and his operas were produced in many Italian cities; but those that survive today—a scant 18 or so—are patchy, and too often marked by haste and careless workmanship, sometimes imposed by the demands of his patrons. Their chief merit, however, lies in their splendid individual numbers.

Handel » (*Alcina* and *Orlando*) and Haydn ». Though *Orlando* has virtually nothing to do with its predecessors some use is made of the same recitatives. It is the arias which carry the musical burden. Even so, the recording interpolates a Vivaldi chamber cantata to bolster *Orlando's* music. Like many Baroque opera plots the storyline is largely incomprehensible.

RECORDING:
RCA Erato STU71138 (3) ●
I Solisti Veneti
c. Claudio Scimone
Orlando (m-s)   Marilyn Horne
Angelica (s)   Victoria de los Angeles
Alcina (m-s)   Lucia Valentini-Terrani
Bradamante (c)   Carmen Gonzales
Medoro (t)   Lajos Kozma
Ruggiero (b)   Sesto Bruscantini
Astolfo (bs)   Nicolai Zaccaria

La Fida Ninfa
Opera in 3 Acts.
Text by Scipione Maffei.
First performance: Verona (Teatro Filarmonico) January 6, 1732.

Notes:
This is the only Vivaldi opera in print; the MS is in Turin. It is not a particularly attractive work, containing few musical plums. The recording (no longer available) is heavily cut, containing *da capo* arias, duet, trio and choral finale, plus the overture. The conventional plot concerns pirates and lovers and reunitings after hard times.

RECORDING:
Turnabout TV34066S (d) ○
Vox SVBX-5210 (3) (US)
Chamber Orchestra of La Scala, Milan
c. Raffaello Monterosso
Oralto/Eolo (bs)   Alfred Giacomotti
Elpina (s)   Mafalda Masini
Osmino/Giunome (c)   Vittoria Calma

Tito Manlio
Opera in 3 Acts.
Text by Matteo Noris.
First performance: Not known.

Notes:
No dates of composition or performance are on record for this opera. There are two manuscripts in Turin, on one of which is written in Vivaldi's own hand *'fatta in 5 giorni'* (written in 5 days). It is now thought that the work dates from around 1719 and was written in Mantua. Like many of Vivaldi's works some parts are borrowed from other compositions. Thus the final chorus is appropriated from Vivaldi's oratorio *Juditha triumphans devicta Holofernis barbarie* with a text of Jacopo Cassetti, which was sung at the Pietà in 1716 (Hungaroton SLPX11359/60). The text of *Tito Manlio* concerns the usual squabble between factions (in this case the Romans and the Italians and their allies) and the usual love entanglements. Vivaldi, the master of the concerto, can be discerned behind several of the arias where the instrumental texture and *obligati* are more interesting than the vocal line. The recording is nearly complete (but for some cut recitatives) and is certainly the best version of a Vivaldi opera yet put onto disc.

RECORDING:
Philips 6769 004 (5) ●
Philips 6769 004 (5) (US)
Berlin Radio Choir/Berlin Chamber Orchestra
c. Vittorio Negri
Tito Manlio (bs) Giancarlo Luccardi
Vitellia (c)   Birgit Finnilä
Lucio (s)   Margaret Marshall
Decio (m-s)   Norma Lerer
Lindo (b)   Domenico Trimarchi

Above: *Antonio Vivaldi, nicknamed 'il prete rosso'.*

Orlando
Opera in 3 Acts.
Text by Grazio Braccioli.
First performance: Venice (Teatro Sant' Angelo) Autumn 1727.

Notes:
Vivaldi had two shots at the Orlando subject, though the operas, separated by 13 years, have nothing in common bar the loosest link of theme. *Orlando finto pazzo* failed when it was produced in Venice in 1714, and when Vivaldi returned to the subject in 1727 he took a quite different line, though using the same librettist, Grazio Braccioli. *Orlando* was originally named *Orlando furioso* (the title on the MS in Turin), but subsequently Vivaldi dropped the *'furioso'*. The text is taken from Ariosto's poem which fed so many Baroque operas, including two by

RICHARD WAGNER

(b. Leipzig 22.5.1813; d. Venice 13.2.1883)

More books have probably been written about Wagner and more controversy aroused by him than by any other composer. His legal father died when he was six months old and his mother married a Jewish actor named Ludwig Geyer, who may have been his true father. Although as a child he moved in artistic circles he did not decide to become a composer until he was 15 years old, when he was shaken into activity by hearing Beethoven's » *Choral* symphony and *Fidelio*; the Ninth Symphony especially remained his musical ideal and model and he described it as "the redemption of music from out of her peculiar element into the realm of universal art". From then on, he saw himself as a musical Messiah. Totally self-centred, like many men of short stature, he had a frighteningly powerful personality, and behaved as one who knew he was a supreme genius; selfish, arrogant and full of prejudices, demanding that the world should support him — "I can't live on a miserable organist's pittance like Bach . . . the world owes me what I need . . . brilliance, beauty and light!" He worked with unrelenting dedication, wrote volumes about himself and his music and established at Bayreuth a theatre where his music could be worshipped. All this would have been ludicrous in a man of lesser ability; fortunately his genius was as great as he presumed it was, and his music was a tremendously powerful influence on those who followed. After his life and work, opera could never be the same again. His first operas were comparatively conventional and not very successful. The tremendous effort he put into works like *Rienzi*, *Der fliegende Holländer* and *Lohengrin* left him impoverished and his life in a turmoil. In various conducting posts that he held he antagonised those with whom he worked, and those whom he played for. But gradually the operas made their mark, forever arousing extremes of hostility and devotion. With *Tristan und Isolde* and the great *Ring* cycle he found his true form, matching words, music and imagination in a glory of sound and olympian drama.

Above: *Wagner founded a theatre for his operas at Bayreuth in 1872.*

Die Feen

Opera in 3 Acts.
Text based on Gozzi's 'La donna serpente'.
First performance: Munich, June 29, 1888.

Notes:

Wagner's second opera (the first, *Die Hochzeit*, was never completed) was not produced until after his death. It declares its allegiances to the German Romantic operas of Weber » and Marschner.

RECORDINGS:
Philips 6500 294 □
Philips 6500 294 (US)
Weh mirm so nah
Birgit Nilsson (s)

HMV ASD2837 (d) □
Angel S-36879 (US)
Overture
c. Marek Janowski

Das Liebesverbot, oder Die Novize von Palermo

Opera in 2 Acts.
Text by Wagner based on Shakespeare's 'Measure for Measure'.
First performance: Magdeburg, March 29, 1836.

Notes:

Das Liebesverbot is quite unlike anything else that Wagner wrote: he seemed to go against all his professional ideals and wrote in a simulation of the Italian style of Donizetti ». The overture, which is really all that survives, has castanets and tambourines, and is full of Latin gaieties. But then the whole work was written in a spirit of youthful hedonism through which it is necessary for spirited young men — even Wagner — to pass.

RECORDING:
HMV ASD2837 (d) □
Angel S-36879 (US)
Overture
c. Marek Janowski

Rienzi, der letze der Tribunen

Opera in 5 Acts.
Text by Wagner based on the novel by Bulwer-Lytton.
First performance: Dresden (Court Opera) October 20, 1842. New York 1878; London 1879.

Synopsis:

Scene: Rome. Time: Mid-14th century.

Act 1 The followers of Paolo Orsini attempt to abduct Rienzi's sister Irene; Steffano Colonna protects her. Rienzi arrives and restores order. The people hail him and urge him to rise against the tyrant nobles. Irene and Adriano, son of Colonna, declare their love. The people swear loyalty to Rienzi as their tribune.

Act 2 Rienzi is successful in his fight against the nobles. All are obliged to offer him homage; but the nobles plan to kill Rienzi. Adriano warns him, although his own father is one of the conspirators. During peace celebrations Orsini attempts to stab Rienzi but fails. The conspirators are condemned and are to be executed, but Adriano and Irene plead with Rienzi for pardon for them. Rienzi yields to the pleas.

Act 3 The nobles re-form their forces and march against Rienzi. Adriano tries to dissuade Rienzi, but the tribune leads his forces out and wins. After the battle Steffano Colonna's body is brought in and Adriano swears vengeance against Rienzi for his father's death.

Act 4 Adriano organises another rising against Rienzi. The people blame Rienzi for the deaths that occur in the fight which they believe he caused by his leniency. He enters the church for a Te Deum, but is renounced and the Pope has excommunicated him. Only Irene remains faithful.

Act 5 Rienzi prays to God for help. Irene prepares to stand by him unto death; even Adriano cannot make her desert her brother. The people attack the palace where Rienzi and Irene stand alone upon the balcony. Adriano tries to enter the burning building, but it collapses and all three are buried in the ruins.

Notes:

Rienzi was written as a Grand Opera for Paris, with all the trappings of fashionable Parisian opera. It was an attempt to out-Meyerbeer Meyerbeer », and asserted the firm Wagnerian principle that if you can't join them, beat them. He suffered humiliations in Paris, and *Rienzi* was produced eventually in Dresden. There are many hints in the score of the Wagner to come, as well as a good deal of noisy theatrical emptiness.

RECORDINGS:

HMV (SQ)SLS990 (5) ●		HMV ASD2695 □	
Angel SX-3818 (5) (US)		Angel S-36187 or S-3610 (2) (US)	
Leipzig Radio Chorus/Dresden State		Overture	
Opera Chorus/Dresden State Orchestra		c. Otto Klemperer	
c. Heinrich Hollreiser			
Cola Rienzi (t)	René Kollo	Philips 6500 294 □	
Irene (s)	Siv Wennberg	Philips 6500 294 (US)	
Adriano (m-s)	Janis Martin	Gerechter Gott — In seiner Blut	
Paolo Orsini (bs)	Theo Adam	**Birgit Nilsson** (s)	
Steffano Colonna (bs)	Nikolaus Hillebrand		

Decca SET227 □
London 6782 (US)
Overture
c. Sir Georg Solti

Der fliegende Holländer (The Flying Dutchman)

Opera in 3 Acts.
Text by Wagner based on an episode in Heine's 'Memoiren des von Schnabelewopski'.
First performance: Dresden (Court Opera) January 2, 1843. London (Drury Lane) 1870; Philadelphia 1876.

Synopsis:

Scene: Norwegian coast. Time: 18th century.

Act 1   Daland is obliged by a storm to drop anchor in the bay of his home port. He sets watch and goes below. A phantom ship materialises. It is the Dutchman (known as Vanderdecken) who has challenged the Devil and is condemned to sail the seas forever until he finds a woman who truly loves him. He may put into port every seven years to look for such a woman. He asks Daland for hospitality and also if he has a daughter, then tells him of his treasures, and Daland takes him to his house.

Act 2   In Daland's house the girls are spinning and singing cheerfully. All except Daland's daughter Senta, who broods on a picture of the Dutchman. She is engaged to the hunter Erik, but is clearly obsessed by the Dutchman legend. Erik enters and is distressed by Senta's behaviour; he tells her of a dream he has had in which he sees her embracing the Dutchman and falling with him into the sea. Erik leaves, and there stands the Dutchman, exactly as in the picture. Senta at once falls under his spell.

Act 3   The Norwegian and Dutch ships are moored close to each other. On the Norwegian vessel, the sailors dance and sing, in contrast to the ominous silence of the adjacent ship. A weird song is suddenly heard. The Norwegians are scared and try to cheer themselves up. There is mocking laughter from the Dutchmen. The Norwegians make the sign of the cross and go below. In the house Erik begs Senta to return to him. The Dutchman, overhearing, thinks he has again lost his chance. Dismissing Senta's protests he orders his ship made ready to sail. The Dutch ship sails; Senta, frantic, throws herself off the cliffs into the sea. At once the Dutchman's ship founders; he is free at last and may find peace. The sun breaks through the clouds.

Notes:

The Flying Dutchman was the first opera in which Wagner found his true voice. It is a work of passionate genius; and if it still has its immaturities, it tingles with life. Both dramatically and musically it spreads out both ways from its pivot point, Senta's ballad. The sea music, so vividly created, came to Wagner while he was on a small ship on his journey from Riga to Paris, and was caught in a violent storm and forced into port, where the sailors' songs gave him his clue for the sailors' chorus.

Well-known arias:

Act 1   Die Frist is um (Dutchman's monologue)
Act 2   Senta's Ballad.

RECORDINGS:

Decca D97D3 (3) ●		**Dutchman** (b)	Norman Bailey
Richmond 63519 (3) (US)		**Daland** (bs)	Martti Telvela
1955 Bayreuth Festival Chorus and		**Senta** (s)	Janis Martin
Orchestra		**Erik** (t)	René Kollo
c. Joseph Keilberth			
Dutchman (b)	Hermann Uhde	DG 2720 052 (3) ●	
Daland (bs)	Ludwig Weber	DG 2709 040 (3) (US)	
Senta (s)	Astrid Varnay	1971 Bayreuth Festival Chorus and	
Erik (t)	Rudolf Lustig	Orchestra	
		c. Karl Böhm	
Cetra Opera Live L051 (3) (m) ●		**Dutchman** (b)	Karl Ridderbusch
1955 Bayreuth Festival Chorus and		**Daland** (bs)	Thomas Stewart
Orchestra		**Senta** (s)	Gwyneth Jones
c. Hans Knappertsbusch		**Erik** (t)	Hermann Esser
Dutchman (b)	Hermann Uhde		
Daland (bs)	Ludwig Weber	Decca 2BB109/11 ●	
Senta (s)	Astrid Varnay	London 1399 (3) (US)	
Erik (t)	Wolfgang Windgassen	Chorus and Orchestra of Royal Opera	
		House, Covent Garden	
HMV SLS934 (3)		c. Antal Dorati	
Angel S-3730 (3) (US) ●		**Dutchman** (b)	George London
BBC Chorus/New Philharmonia		**Daland** (bs)	Giorgio Tozzi
Orchestra		**Senta** (s)	Leonie Rysanek
c. Otto Klemperer		**Erik** (t)	Karl Liebl
Dutchman (b)	Theo Adam		
Daland (bs)	Martti Talvela	Decca Ace of Diamonds SDD439 ■	
Senta (s)	Anja Silja	(from above)	
Erik (t)	Ernst Kozub		
		(Note: There are many recordings of the	
Decca D24D3 (3) ●		famous overture, including ones by	
London 13119 (3) (US)		Klemperer (HMV ASD2695), von	
Chicago Symphony Chorus and		Karajan (HMV ASD3160 and	
Orchestra		SXLP30210), Szell (CBS 61263) and	
c. Sir Georg Solti		Furtwängler (in Unicorn WFS2-3))	

Tannhäuser und der Sängerkrieg auf Wartburg

Opera in 3 Acts.
Text by Wagner.
First performance: Dresden (Court Opera) October 19, 1845. New York 1859; London (Covent Garden) 1876; Paris (revised version) 1861.

Synopsis:

Scene: Thuringia. Time: 13th century.

Act 1   Tannhäuser is discontented with sensual luxury on the Venusberg. He tells Venus he wants to return to normal human life. She exercises her seductive wiles to keep him, but he calls on the Holy Virgin and Venus and the Venusberg disappear. He finds himself in a valley near Wartburg. A band of pilgrims appear on their way to Rome and the shepherd wishes them well. Tannhäuser kneels in prayer. Soon the sound of a hunting party is heard. It is the Landgrave and his knights. Wolfram von Eschenbach recognises him and all welcome him home. They urge him to return to them; he is reluctant until Wolfram mentions Elisabeth, the Landgrave's niece, who according to Wolfram still loves Tannhäuser; and he agrees to go with them.

Act 2   In Wartburg, Elisabeth greets the Hall of Song which she associates with Tannhäuser (the knights are all minstrels, or minnesingers). Wolfram brings in Tannhäuser; Elisabeth is at first uncertain; she asks him about his long absence and he answers evasively. But she then tells him her feelings for him, first aroused by his singing. There is to be a contest of song with Elisabeth's hand in marriage the possible prize. Wolfram sings of love, inspired by Elisabeth. Walther sings, insisting on purity and chastity. Tannhäuser, in rising scorn, sings of sensual delights and, after interjections, continues in a kind of delirium, with a paean to profane love and to Venus. All are outraged and only Elisabeth's intervention saves him from death. She tells him that he must find salvation in repentance. The Landgrave sends him to join a second band of pilgrims on the road to Rome.

Act 3   Elisabeth is praying for Tannhäuser's redemption and return, watched by the faithful Wolfram. The pilgrims are heard returning from Rome; but Tannhäuser is not one of them. Wolfram offers to escort her, and when she declines sings his love for her. A straggler comes in, and Wolfram recognises

Tannhäuser, seeking the way to the Venusberg. When Wolfram asks him if he has been to Rome he bursts out that when he presented himself before the Pope, he was told that for such a sin redemption would be his only when the Papal staff put forth green shoots. Tannhäuser hears the voice of Venus and Wolfram tries to restrain him. A funeral cortège comes near, bearing Elisabeth's body: she has died of grief. Tannhäuser kneels beside the bier, and dies. Then news arrives that the Pope's staff has miraculously sprouted green leaves. Tannhäuser is redeemed.

Notes:

In *Tannhäuser* Wagner made further progress in pursuit of his artistic ideal and objective. It has probably more of the faults of crudeness and banality of which Wagner is frequently accused than any other of his works. But no doubt they had to be worked through anyway; and he recognised it. When he came to prepare a production for Paris in 1861, he substantially revised the score. Wagner, at this stage, was a more mature composer altogether, with the first two sections of *The Ring* and *Tristan und Isolde* behind him. Evidences of this can be seen in *Tannhäuser's* rewritten parts, with their greater flexibility and freedom. Some say the later version shows too many creative seams; but these days it is the preferred edition. Of the two complete recordings, the Decca/Solti used the Paris version, the Konwitschny/HMV the original Dresden text. Tannhäuser himself was a historical character from the 13th century, as were the minnesingers.

Well-known excerpts:

Overture and Venusberg Music
Act 1 Dich, teure Halle (Elisabeth's Greeting)
Dir Göttin der Liebe (Tannhäuser)
Act 3 Allmächt'ge Jungfrau (Elisabeth's Prayer)
O du mein holder Abendstern (O star of eve) (Wolfram)
Pilgrim's Chorus

RECORDINGS:
Decca SET506/9 (Paris version) ●
London 1438 (4) (US)
Vienna State Opera Chorus/Vienna
Philharmonic Orchestra
c. Sir Georg Solti
Tannhäuser (t) René Kollo
Elisabeth (s) Helga Dernesch
Landgrave (bs) Hans Sotin
Wolfram (b) Victor Braun
Venus (s) Christa Ludwig

Elisabeth (s) Elisabeth Grümmer
Landgrave (bs) Gottlob Frick
Wolfram (b) Dietrich Fischer-Dieskau
Venus (s) Marianne Schech

Decca SET556 ■
London 26299 (US)
(from above)

HMV SLS775 (4) (d) ●
Angel S-3620 (4) (US)
Chorus and Orchestra of German State
Opera
c. Franz Konwitschny
Tannhäuser (t) Hans Hopf

Lohengrin

Opera in 3 Acts.
Text by Wagner.
First performance: Weimar (Court Opera) August 28, 1850. London (Covent Garden) 1875; New York 1871.

Synopsis:

Scene: Antwerp. Time: First half of 10th century.
Act 1 King Henry the Fowler calls the people of Brabant to arms to fight the Hungarian invaders. But there are domestic matters to be settled first. Telramund accuses Elsa of having murdered her brother to secure the dukedom herself. He therefore married Ortrud instead. The King requires a contest between Telramund and any champion ready to step forward for Elsa. Elsa has related a dream in which a knight in armour appears as her champion. Then, a strange sight is seen: a knight

in armour approaches in a boat drawn by a white swan. He steps ashore, and offers to be Elsa's champion, but on one condition—that she never asks his name. She agrees: the knight and Telramund fight; the knight wins but spares Telramund.
Act 2 Telramund and Ortrud quarrel. He blames her because she is a sorceress; she says the only way to put things right is to make Elsa ask the knight's name. It is publicly announced that Telramund is banished and the knight is to marry Elsa: Ortrud taunts Elsa with not even knowing who her bridegroom is. Elsa replies that she has total trust in him. The knight dismisses Telramund's requests to reveal his name, saying only Elsa can make him speak. Elsa begins to have doubts.
Act 3 After the bridal procession Elsa and her knight are left alone. They sing of their love; but Elsa is troubled and finally asks him outright. That moment, Telramund appears with four friends. The knight kills him and the four kneel before him; but for the knight and Elsa happiness is over. Before the assembled King and knights the body of Telramund is brought in, followed by the sorrowing Elsa. The knight upbraids her and reveals himself as Lohengrin, Knight of the Holy Grail and son of Parsifal. Now that his identity is known, Lohengrin's power is lost and he must return whence he came. The swan towing an empty boat appears. Lohengrin bids farewell to Elsa, handing her his sword, helmet and ring for her brother should he ever return. Ortrud triumphantly says that the swan is in fact Elsa's brother, Gottfried, whom she has transformed by magic: he might have been redeemed but now it is too late. As Lohengrin kneels in prayer; the swan turns into Gottfried. The Brabantians kneel before him, knowing he will fulfil Lohengrin's prophecy and lead them to victory. Overhead a dove descends: it tows the boat away with Lohengrin. Elsa dies in her brother's arms.

Notes:

In *Lohengrin*, following *Tannhäuser*, Wagner approached the evolving of his mature style from the opposite end. Whereas *Tannhäuser* with its central theme of the contest of song and the minnesingers looks forward to *Die Meistersinger von Nürnberg*, so *Lohengrin* with its Holy Grail motif can be seen, in the retrospect of Wagner's total life and achievement, to have thrown a rainbow bridge across the years to *Parsifal*. Each opera in its way prepares the ground for what is to come; for the fully fledged music drama. Because of his political involvements and consequent banishment, Wagner himself did not hear *Lohengrin* until 1861, and it was first produced in Germany at the insistence of Liszt, who staged it at Weimar.

Well-known excerpts:

Act 1 Prelude
Einsam in trüben Tagen (Elsa's dream)
Act 2 Euch Lüften (Elsa)
Act 3 Prelude and Bridal Chorus
Im fernen Land (Lohengrin's narration)
Lohengrin's Farewell (Swan song)

RECORDINGS:
HMV SLS5071 (5) ●
Angel S-3641 (5) (US)
Vienna State Opera Chorus/Vienna
Philharmonic Orchestra
c. Rudolf Kempe
Lohengrin (t) Jess Thomas
Elsa (s) Elisabeth Grümmer
Telramund (b) Dietrich
Fischer-Dieskau
Ortrud (m-s) Christa Ludwig
King Henry (bs) Gottlob Frick

Angel S-36313 (US) ■
(from above)

Philips 6747 241 (4) ●
Philips 6747 241 (4) (US)
1962 Bayreuth Festival Chorus and
Orchestra
c. Wolfgang Sawallisch

Lohengrin (t) Jess Thomas
Elsa (s) Anja Silja
Telramund (b) Ramon Vinay
Ortrud (m-s) Astrid Varnay
King Henry (bs) Franz Crass

(above also available in Philips 6747
243 (14) with *Tristan und Isolde* and *Die
Meistersinger*)
Decca D12D5 (5) (m) ●
1953 Bayreuth Festival Chorus and
Orchestra
c. Joseph Keilberth
Lohengrin (t)   Wolfgang Windgassen
Elsa (s)   Eleanor Steber
Telramund (b)   Hermann Uhde
Ortrud (m-s)   Astrid Varnay
King Henry (bs)   Josef Greindl

RCA RVL5 9046 (5) ●
Boston Pro Music Chorus/Boston
Symphony Orchestra
c. Erich Leinsdorf
Lohengrin (t)   Sándor Kónya
Elsa (s)   Lucine Amara
Telramund (b)   William Dooley
Ortrud (m-s)   Rita Gorr
King Henry (bs)   Jerome Hines
(extra disc included with discussion of
the recording between Leinsdorf and
producer George Marek)

Der Ring des Nibelungen (The Ring of the Nibelungs)

A Stage Festival Play for Three Days and a Preliminary Evening.
Text by Wagner based on the Nibelung Saga.
First performance (complete): Bayreuth, August 13, 14, 16 and 17, 1878.

1. Prologue: Das Rheingold
Synopsis:

Scene 1   The bed of the Rhine. The Nibelung dwarf Alberich, being rejected by the three Rhinemaidens, renounces love and steals the maidens' Rhinegold.

Scene 2   The giants Fafner and Fasolt have built Valhalla, home of the Gods; for reward Wotan, ruler of the Gods, has promised the giants Freia, sister of his wife, Fricka. Wotan is reluctant to keep the bargain, so Loge, god of Magic, hatches a plan to wrest the Rhinegold from Alberich and give it to the giants instead of Freia.

Scene 3   Down in Nibelheim, Alberich has fashioned a Ring from the gold: a Ring that gives him great power. He has also devised a magic helmet, the Tarnhelm, that makes its wearer invisible or transforms him into any shape. Alberich tyrannises the Nibelungs, including his brother, the weak but scheming Mime. Wotan and Loge then trick the unsuspecting Alberich into turning himself into a toad; they capture him and carry him up to the world above.

Scene 4   Alberich surrenders the gold, but as Wotan wrests the Ring from his finger, Alberich lays a curse on it. The gold is piled up for the giants, but they also want the Ring, much to Wotan's anger. Freia is returned to the gods, but the giants fight and Fasolt is killed by Fafner: Alberich's curse has struck. Wotan leads the Gods over the Rainbow Bridge into Valhalla as the Rhinemaidens are heard lamenting the loss of their gold.

2. Die Walküre (The Valkyrie)

Act 1   The forest hut of Hunding and his wife Sieglinde. Siegmund has arrived, exhausted from fleeing his enemies through a storm. Sieglinde gives him water and the two are attracted to each other. Hunding enters and, over supper, his suspicions are realised: the mysterious Siegmund is his enemy. He gives him shelter for the night but warns him they will fight the next morning. Left alone, Siegmund recalls that his father had promised him a weapon for use in his hour of need; he catches sight of a sword, buried in an ash tree. Sieglinde returns, having drugged Hunding, and recounts the story of the sword, buried in the tree on her wedding feast, by a mysterious stranger, who said only a hero can withdraw it. The door flies open; outside it is a beautiful Spring night. Siegmund withdraws the sword and together he and Sieglinde, hitherto unknown to each other as brother and sister and now passionately in love, go out into the night, at last aware of their identities.

Act 2   Wotan instructs his Valkyrie daughter, Brünnhilde, to help Siegmund win his fight against Hunding. But Fricka, the goddess of marriage, objects and Wotan swears to her he will change his mind, and tells Brünnhilde accordingly. She warns Siegmund of his fate, but when he tells her he would rather stay and die with Sieglinde than go with Brünnhilde to Valhalla, she is tremendously moved and helps him in the fight. Wotan places his spear between the contestants and Siegmund falls. Brünnhilde gathers up the broken sword, pulls Sieglinde across her saddle

and gallops off. Wotan strikes Hunding dead and strides off in search of his disobedient daughter.

Act 3   The Valkyries assemble as Brünnhilde arrives with Sieglinde. No one dares to help, and Brünnhilde sends Sieglinde on her way, saying she bears a child who will be a great hero. Wotan storms in, and condemns his daughter to sleep on a mountain top surrounded by Loge's magic fire until someone fearless enough to breach the flames comes to wake her. He bids her a tender farewell and lays her to rest.

3. Siegfried
Before the action begins, Mime, brother of Alberich, has found the pregnant Sieglinde in the forest, clutching the pieces of Siegmund's sword. She gives birth to a son and dies. Mime brings up the young Siegfried, knowing he is the key to killing the giant Fafner, who has transformed himself into a dragon, so that Mime can gain the Rhinegold and the Ring for himself.

Act 1   Mime is fruitlessly attempting to forge a sword which Siegfried can't shatter. Only the pieces of Siegmund's sword 'Nothung' will work, but Mime is unable to mend it. Wotan, disguised as The Wanderer, tells Mime that only Siegfried is able to forge the sword. Siegfried returns and, tiring of Mime's hapless attempts, forges a new sword from Nothung's pieces and, to test it, splits the anvil.

Act 2   Outside Fafner's cave. The Wanderer is recognised as Wotan by Alberich, who taunts him, saying he will reclaim the Ring and destroy Valhalla. Wotan says a young hero who knows no fear will kill Fafner. Siegfried arrives, tries to impersonate the bird's song on a pipe, then sounds a call on his horn, wakes Fafner and finally kills him. Before dying, the dragon warns Siegfried of Mime's treachery. Siefried sucks Fafner's blood from his fingers and discovers he can understand what the Woodbird is singing: it tells him of the Ring and the Tarnhelm, which he fetches while Mime and Alberich argue over the gold. Siegfried is able to understand Mime's thoughts, and kills him. He then hears from the Woodbird of a sleeping bride who can be woken only by he who knows no fear. He follows the Woodbird.

Act 3   The Wanderer consults the Erda, the Earth Goddess, but is finally reconciled to the downfall of the Gods. He stands in Siegfried's way, in one last attempt to gain the Ring; but Siegfried shatters his spear, and Wotan tells him to go on, he cannot prevent him. Siegfried fearlessly passes through the flames to find the sleeping Brünnhilde. He feels strange emotion, and has learnt fear, through woman. He awakens Brünnhilde and claims her as his bride. After some hesitation she yields.

4. Götterdämmerung (Twilight of the Gods)
Prologue   The three Norns, daughters of Erda, spin the golden rope of Destiny. They recount how Wotan's spear was shattered and foretell the doom of the Gods. The Norns' skein breaks and they vanish. As dawn breaks, Siegfried and Brünnhilde sing of their love. He gives her the Ring in return for her horse, Grane, on which he sets off on his journey down the Rhine.

Act 1   The Gibichung Hall. Gunther, the weak but noble King of the Gibichungs, and his sister Gutrune wish to marry but cannot find suitable partners. Hagen, Alberich's son and half-brother to Gunther and Gutrune, plots to marry them off and recover the Ring. Siegfried is welcomed to the Hall and is given a potion which makes him forget Brünnhilde and fall in love with Gutrune. Swearing blood-brotherhood with Gunther, he agrees to fetch Brünnhilde (using the Tarnhelm to change him into Gunther). Back on Brünnhilde's rock, she refuses to surrender the Ring to her Valkyrie sister, Waltraute, who flies off in despair. The disguised Siegfried comes through the flames, and wrenches the Ring from her finger. Brünnhilde, defenceless, capitulates.

Act 2   Hagen is warned by his father, Alberich, not to let the Ring slip away from him. The double wedding is about to take place, and Hagen summons the Vassals. Brünnhilde, shocked,

sees Siegfried about to wed Gutrune, then spies the Ring on his finger. Still under the influence of the potion, Siegfried swears that he has not betrayed her. She swears the opposite, then plots with Hagen and Gunther to kill Siegfried during the next day's hunt, revealing that Siegfried's weak spot is his back.

Act 3 The Rhinemaidens, still lamenting the loss of their Ring, try to coax Siegfried to return it to them. He refuses, and the Rhinemaidens leave him to his fate. Siegfried is joined by the rest of the hunting party, and Hagen, slipping him a memory-reviving herb, persuades him to tell his story. As Siegfried's memories of his beloved Brünnhilde return, Hagen plunges his spear into his back. Siegfried dies, Brünnhilde's name on his lips. His body is borne back to the Gibichung Hall, where the Ring's curse strikes again, as Hagen kills Gunther. As he tries to take the Ring off the dead Siegfried's hand, it rises up to ward him off. Brünnhilde commands that a massive pyre be built and, placing the Ring on her finger, rides Grane into the flames. The fire increases, the Rhine overflows and floods the Hall. Hagen is drowned by the Rhinemaidens, who at last claim the Ring back. A glow appears in the distant sky as Valhalla burns.

Notes:

The *Ring* tetralogy is so vast, so complex in motive and meaning that no synopsis can do more than follow out the main story line. In 1848 Wagner finished a libretto for an opera *The Death of Siegfried*. He decided that it was necessary to go back to tell the story of Siegfried himself, then back again to his origins, then back once again to explain the overall context. Thus it came out as four complete works. The complete libretti were published in 1853, and Wagner set to work on the music. He wrote *Das Rheingold*, *Die Walküre*, and the first two-and-a-half acts of *Siegfried*. He then broke off for 12 years, during which he wrote *Tristan und Isolde* and *Die Meistersinger*, before completing *Siegfried* and *Götterdämmerung*. *Rheingold* and *Walküre* were produced independently in Munich, but the whole cycle was first presented in Wagner's own festival opera house at Bayreuth in south Germany, in 1876. The first half of the *Ring* cycle represents Wagner's technique of music drama with its complex of *leitmotiven* at its strictest and most 'pure'; when he returned to it after the 12-year break, he was a composer with the experience of *Tristan* behind him. Thus, the latter part of the *Ring* contains new subtleties of harmony and melody added to the earlier style and in several respects modifying it.

Well-known excerpts:
See below under the separate works.

RECORDINGS (complete cycles):
Decca D100D19 (19) ●
London RING S (19) (US)
Vienna State Opera Chorus/Vienna Philharmonic Orchestra
c. Sir Georg Solti
Wotan/
  Wanderer (b)   George London/
                              Hans Hotter
Siegfried (t)   Wolfgang Windgassen
Brünnhilde (s)   Birgit Nilsson
Alberich (bs)   Gustav Neidlinger
Mime (t)   Gerhard Stolze
Fricka (s)   Kirsten Flagstad/
                              Christa Ludwig
Fafner (bs)   Kurt Boehme

Decca SET406/8 □
London RDNS1 (US)
Introduction to the *Ring* by the late Deryck Cooke with music examples
Vienna Boys' Choir and Philharmonic Orchestra
c. Sir Georg Solti

London 1440 (4) (US) ■
(from above)

DG 2720 051 (19) ●
DG 2720 051 (19) (US)
German Opera Chorus/Berlin Philharmonic Orchestra

c. Herbert von Karajan
Wotan/
  Wanderer (b)   Dietrich Fischer-Dieskau/
                              Thomas Stewart
Siegfried (t)   Helge Brilioth/
                              Wolfgang
                              Windgassen
Brünnhilde (s)   Régine Crespin/
                              Helga Dernesch
Alberich (b)   Zoltan Keleman
Mime (t)   Gerhard Stolze
Fricka (s)   Josephine Veasey
Fafner (bs)   Karl Ridderbusch

Philips 6747 037 (16) ●
Philips 6747 037 (16) (US)
1966/67 Bayreuth Festival Chorus and Orchestra
c. Karl Böhm
Wotan/
  Wanderer (b)   Theo Adam
Siegfried (t)   Wolfgang Windgassen
Brünnhilde (s)   Birgit Nilsson
Alberich (b)   Gustav Neidlinger
Mime (t)   Erwin Wohlfahrt
Fricka (s)   Annelies Burmeister
Fafner (bs)   Kurt Boehme

HMV RLS702 (18) (m) (r. 1953) ●
Chorus of RAI and Rome Symphony Orchestra

c. Wilhelm Furtwängler
Wotan/
  Wanderer (b)   Ferdinand Frantz
Siegfried (t)   Ludwig Suthaus
Brünnhilde (s)   Martha Mödl
Alberich (b)   Gustav Neidlinger/
                              Alois Pernerstorfer
Mime (t)   Julius Patzak
Fricka (s)   Ira Malaniuk/
                              Elsa Cavelti
Fafner (bs)   Gottlob Frick/
                              Josef Greindl

Peerless 94077 (11) (m) (r. 1950) ●
Murray Hill 940477 (11) (US)
Chorus and Orchestra of La Scala, Milan
c. Wilhelm Furtwängler
Wotan/
  Wanderer (b)   Ferdinand Frantz/
                              Josef Herrmann
Siegfried (t)   Set Svanholm/
                              Max Lorenz
Brünnhilde (s)   Kirsten Flagstad
Alberich (b)   Alois Pernerstorfer
Mime (t)   Peter Markworth
Fricka (s)   Elisabeth Höngen
Fafner (bs)   Albert

Cetra Opera Live L058/61 (18) (m) (r. 1957) ●
1957 Bayreuth Festival Chorus and Orchestra
c. Hans Knappertsbusch

Wotan/
  Wanderer (b)   Hans Hotter
Siegfried (t)   Bernd Aldenhoff/
                              Wolfgang
                              Windgassen
Brünnhilde (s)   Astrid Varnay
Alberich (b)   Gustav Neidlinger
Mime (t)   Paul Kuen
Fricka (s)   Georgine von
                              Milinkovic
Fafner (bs)   Josef Greindl

HMV SLS5146 (20) (in English) ●
English National Opera Company/Sadler's Wells Orchestra
c. Reginald Goodall
Wotan/
  Wanderer (b)   Norman Bailey
Siegfried (t)   Alberto Remedios
Brünnhilde (s)   Rita Hunter
Alberich (b)   Derek Hammond-
                              Stroud
Mime (t)   Gregory Dempsey
Fricka (s)   Katherine Pring
Fafner (b)   Clifford Grant

Das Rheingold
Prologue in 1 Act.
Text by Wagner.
First performance: Munich, September 22, 1869.

Well-known excerpts:
Scene 2 Wotan, Gemahl
Scene 4 Entry of the Gods into Valhalla

RECORDINGS:
Decca SET382/4 (No 1 of complete cycle) ●
London 1309 (3) (US)
c. Sir Georg Solti

Decca SET 482 ■
London 25126 (US)
(from above)

DG 2740 145 (3) (No 1 of complete cycle) ●
DG 2709 023 (3) (US)
c. Herbert von Karajan

DG 2535 239 ■
(from above)

Cetra Opera Live L058 (m) (No 1 of complete cycle) ●
c. Hans Knappertsbusch

HMV SLS5032 (4) (in English—No 1 of complete cycle) ●
Angel SDC-3825 (4) (US)
c. Reginald Goodall

Die Walküre
Music drama in 3 Acts.
Text by Wagner.
First performance: Munich, June 26, 1870.

Well-known excerpts:
Act 2 *Todesverkündigung* (Death announcement scene)
Act 3 Ride of the Valkyries
  Wotan's Farewell
  Magic Fire Music

RECORDINGS:
Decca SET312/6 (No 2 of complete cycle) ●
London 1509 (5) (US)
c. Sir Georg Solti

Decca SET390 ■
London 26085 (US)
(from above)

DG 2740 146 (5) (No 2 of complete cycle) ●

DG 2713 002 (5) (US)
c. Herbert von Karajan

DG 2535 239 ■
DG 2535 239 (US)
c. Herbert von Karajan
(from above)

Cetra Opera Live L059 (5) (m) (No 2 of complete cycle) ●
c. Hans Knappertsbusch

HMV SLS5063 (5) (No 2 of complete
cycle) ●
Angel SX-3826 (5) (US)
c. Reginald Goodall

Decca 7BB 125/9 ●
London 1511 (US)
London Symphony Orchestra
c. Erich Leinsdorf
Wotan (b)   George London
Siegmund (t)   Jon Vickers
Sieglinde (s)   Grė Brouwenstein
Brünnhilde (s)   Birgit Nilsson
Fricka (m-s)   Rita Gorr

Decca Ace of Diamonds SDD430 ■
(from above)

Siegfried

Music drama in 3 Acts.
Text by Wagner.
First performance: Bayreuth, August 16, 1876.

Well-known excerpts:
Act 1   Nothung! Nothung!
Act 3   Forest Murmurs

RECORDINGS:
Decca SET242/6 (No 3 of complete
cycle) ●
London 1508 (5) (US)
c. Sir Georg Solti

Decca SXL6142 □
London 25898 (US)
(from above)

DG 2740 147 (5) (No 3 of complete
cycle) ●

DG 2713 003 (5) (US) ●
c. Herbert von Karajan

Cetra Opera Live L060 (5) (No 3 of
complete cycle) ●
c. Hans Knappertsbusch

HMV SLS875 (5) (in English—No 3 of
complete cycle) ●
c. Reginald Goodall

Götterdämmerung

Music drama in Prologue and 3 Acts.
Text by Wagner.
First performance: Bayreuth, August 17, 1876.

Well-known excerpts:
Prologue   Dawn and Siegfried's Rhine Journey

RECORDINGS:
Decca SET292/7 (No 4 of complete
cycle) ●
London 1604 (6) (US)
c. Sir Georg Solti

Decca SXL6220 ■
London 25991 (US)
(from above)

DG 2740 148 (6) (No 4 of complete
cycle) ●

DG 2716 001 (6) (US) ●
c. Herbert von Karajan

Cetra Opera Live L061 (5) (m) (No 4 of
complete cycle) ●
c. Hans Knappertsbusch

HMV SLS5118 (6) (No 4 of complete
cycle) ●
c. Reginald Goodall

Tristan und Isolde

Music drama in 3 Acts.
Text by Wagner.
*First performance: Munich (Court Opera) June 19, 1865. London (Drury Lane)
1882; New York (Metropolitan) 1886.*

Synopsis:
Scene: Coast of Cornwall. Time: Legendary.
Act 1   On the ship which is bearing Isolde to her marriage with
King Marke, Tristan is in command. Tristan and Isolde are
already in love; she does not love Marke, and there is
considerable tension as each is aware of the situation. A sailor is
heard singing a love song. Isolde plans to poison herself and
Tristan, but Brangäne, her attendant, puts a love potion in the
drinking cup instead of the poison. As the ship nears land, Isolde
summons Tristan. They both drink from the cup, but instead of
being poisoned both are thrown into paroxysms of ecstatic love.
Act 2   Tristan and Isolde meet in a garden by King Marke's
castle while the King is away on a hunting party. Brangäne

keeps watch. They sing a great love duet and inveigh against the
revealing day and welcome enshrouding night. At the height
Brangäne's warning is heard, the hunting party is returning; but
the lovers take no heed. King Marke and Melot enter. Marke
delivers a long complaint against Tristan's treachery, and Melot
fights with Tristan and wounds him.
Act 3   Tristan has retired to his castle and waits for Isolde to
come to him. Kurwenal attends him in touching faithfulness.
Suddenly Isolde's ship is sighted, and Kurwenal is sent to fetch
her. Delirious, Tristan tears the bandages from his wound.
Isolde arrives: Tristan collapses in her arms—and dies. Isolde
flings herself on his body. Meanwhile a second ship is sighted. It
is King Marke and his train. Kurwenal prepares to defend the
castle. He fights with Melot and kills him, but is slain himself.
Brangäne says that King Marke has come in peace, having been
told about the love potion. Isolde sings her great Liebestod and
finally sinks lifeless into Brangäne's arms.

Notes:
Tristan is music's great testament to sexual love. Wagner himself
was perfectly clear about it. It is also perhaps the most perfectly
realised music drama, in which subtlety of leading motif, of
chromatic harmony and of 'endless melody' are so closely
interwoven that it is virtually impossible to tell them apart.
Wagner wrote *Tristan* while staying near Zürich, at the house of
his friend, Otto Wesendonck. At the time he was having an
affair with Wesendonck's wife, Mathilde—a union which also
produced the five *Wesendonck Lieder*.

Well-known excerpts:
       Prelude and Liebestod (orchestra)
Act 1   Isolde's Narration
Act 2   Isolde!—Tristan! geliebter (Love duet)
Act 3   Mild und leise (Liebestod) (Isolde)

RECORDINGS:
HMV RLS684 (5) (m) (r. 1952) ★ ●
Chorus of Royal Opera House, Covent
Garden/Philharmonia Orchestra
c. Wilhelm Furtwängler
Isolde (s)   Kirsten Flagstad
Tristan (t)   Ludwig Suthaus
Brangäne (m-s)   Blanche Thebom
Kurwenal (b)   Dietrich Fischer-
               Dieskau
King Marke (bs)   Josef Greindl

HMV SLS963 (5) ●
Angel S-3777 (5) (US)
Chorus of German Opera, Berlin/Berlin
Philharmonic Orchestra
c. Herbert von Karajan
Tristan (t)   Jon Vickers
Isolde (s)   Helga Dernesch
Brangäne (m-s)   Christa Ludwig
Kurwenal (b)   Walter Berry
King Marke (bs)   Karl Ridderbusch

HMV ASD3354 □
(from above)

DG 2740 144 (5) ●
DG 2713 001 (5) (US)
1966 Chorus and Orchestra of Bayreuth
Festival
c. Karl Böhm
Tristan (t)   Wolfgang Windgassen
Isolde (s)   Birgit Nilsson
Brangäne (m-s)   Christa Ludwig
Kurwenal (b)   Eberhard Waechter
King Marke (bs)   Martti Talvela

DG 2535 243 ●
DG 136 433 (US)
(from above)

Decca D41D5 (5) ●
London 1502 (5) (US)
Vienna Singverein/Vienna Philharmonic
Orchestra

c. Sir Georg Solti
Tristan (t)   Fritz Uhl
Isolde (s)   Birgit Nilsson
Brangäne (m-s)   Régina Resnik
Kurwenal (b)   Tom Krause
King Marke (bs)   Arnold van Mill

Decca SXL6178 ■
London 25938 (US)
(from above)

Cetra Opera Live L073 (4) ●
Chorus and Orchestra of La Scala, Milan
c. Victor de Sabata
Tristan (t)   Max Lorenz
Isolde (s)   Gertrude Grob-Prandl
Brangäne (m-s)   Elsa Cavetti
Kurwenal (b)   Siegurd Bjoerling

Cetra Opera Live L047 (5) (m) (r. 1952) ●
Bayreuth Festival Chorus and Orchestra
c. Herbert von Karajan.
Tristan (t)   Ramon Vinay
Isolde (s)   Martha Mödl
Brangäne (m-s)   Ira Malaniuk
Kurwenal (b)   Hans Hotter
King Marke (bs)   Ludwig Weber

Die Meistersinger von Nürnberg

Music drama in 3 Acts.
Text by Wagner.
First performance: Munich (Court Opera) June 21, 1868. London (Drury Lane)
1882; New York (Metropolitan) 1886.

Synopsis:

Scene: Nuremberg. Time: 16th century.

Act 1 St Katherine's Church. The service has just ended and the knight, Walther von Stolzing speaks with Eva, learning from her nurse Magdalena that she is to be the prize in a song contest the next day. Determined to win, Walther listens to the complex rules, as explained by Magdalena's fiancé David, apprentice to Hans Sachs, Mastersinger and cobbler. The Mastersingers assemble and Pogner announces his intention of awarding his daughter, Eva, as prize. Walther sings his Trial Song. Beckmesser, the finicky Town Clerk, also a contestant for Eva's hand, acts as marker—and treats Walther viciously. Although Sachs sees some merit in Walther's song, the rest dismiss it.

Act 2 Outside Sachs's house; opposite is Pogner's. Sachs is trying to work but is distracted by Walther's song. Eva joins him and learns of the knight's failure. Sachs, who is tempted to bid for Eva's hand himself, realises that she loves Walther. Just then

Above: Die Meistersinger von Nürnberg *at Covent Garden.*

the knight arrives, as does Beckmesser to serenade Eva, who is impersonated by Magdalena. Sachs acts as marker for the hapless clerk, banging his last with every mistake, of which there are plenty. The din wakes the town and Beckmesser is attacked by David, who recognises Magdalena. Sachs pushes Walther into his house, thwarting his elopement plans, as the Night Watchman completes his rounds.

Act 3 Scene 1: Inside Sachs's house next morning. David serenades his master and goes out. Sachs ruminates on the madness of the world. Walther enters and tells the cobbler of a song that has come to him in a dream. Together they perfect it, and Sachs writes it down. Beckmesser enters, somewhat dishevelled, to collect his shoes and, alone in the room, finds the song. Sachs tells him he has no intention of entering the contest, and gives him the song. A delighted Beckmesser hurries off. Eva comes in on the pretext of a badly fitting shoe; she sees Walther and weeps on Sachs's shoulder with gratitude. David and Magdalena enter and Sachs, boxing him on the ears, promotes him to journeyman. All sing of their feelings in the great Quintet. Scene 2: A meadow outside the city. After dancing and general roistering, the Mastersingers arrive in a solemn procession.

Beckmesser, failing to understand his song, is made a laughing stock. Then Walter sings it properly—to the delight and appreciation of the crowd. Eva declares him the winner: but Walther disdainfully refuses entry to the Masters' Guild. Sachs, extolling the beauty and value of German art, persuades the knight to accept. The opera ends with a chorus of praise to Hans.

Notes:

Die Meistersinger von Nürnberg is as different from *Tristan und Isolde* as day is from night. Indeed, as *Tristan* celebrates the enfolding powers of night so *Meistersinger* extols the colour and luminosity of day. Between them they reveal and inhabit the dark and light sides of Wagner's genius, and are complementary; the saturated chromatic tragedy of *Tristan* being the obverse of the diatonic comedy of *Meistersinger*. But *Meistersinger* is not all and only comedy; originally the opera was intended as a frontal attack on crabbed criticism; Beckmesser being called Hans Lick (a direct jibe at Wagner's sworn enemy, the powerful Viennese critic Eduard Hanslick). But from such crude beginnings, warmth and humanity took over and triumphed. Hans Sachs was a historical figure, like Tannhäuser; and just as that earlier opera dealt with the aristocratic minstrels, known as the minnesingers, so the later opera deals with the essentially bourgeois, but also historical, Guild of Masters.

Well-known excerpts:

Act 1 Prelude (Overture)
Pogner's Address
Im stillen Herd (Walther)

Act 2 Wie duftet doch der Flieder (Sachs)
Jerum! Jerum! (Cobbler's song) (Sachs)

Act 3 Prelude
Wahn, Wahn, überall, Wahn! (Sachs)
Dance of the Apprentices and Entry of the Masters
Selig, wie die Sohne (quintet)
Morgenlich Leuchtend (Prize song) (Walther)

RECORDINGS:

DG 2740 149 (5) ●
DG 2713 011 (US)
Chorus and Orchestra of German Opera, Berlin
c. Eugen Jochum
Hans Sachs (b) Dietrich Fischer-Dieskau
Walther von Stolzing (t) Placido Domingo
Eva (s) Caterina Ligendza
David (t) Horst Laubenthal
Beckmesser (b) Roland Hermann
Magdalena (m-s) Christa Ludwig

DG 2537 041 ■
(from above)

HMV SLS957 (5) ●
Angel S-3776 (US)
Leipzig Radio Chorus/Dresden State Opera Chorus and Orchestra
c. Herbert von Karajan
Hans Sachs (b) Theo Adam
Walther von Stolzing (t) René Kollo
Eva (s) Helen Donath
David (t) Peter Schreier
Beckmesser (b) Sir Geraint Evans
Magdalena (m-s) Ruth Hesse

Angel S-36922 (US) ■
(from above)

Decca D13D5 (5) ●
London 1512 (US)
Gumpoldskirchner Spatzen/Vienna State Opera Chorus/Vienna Philharmonic Orchestra
c. Sir Georg Solti
Hans Sachs (b) Norman Bailey
Walther von Stolzing (t) René Kollo
Eva (s) Hannelore Bode

David (t) Adolf Dallapozza
Beckmesser (b) Bernd Weikl
Magdalena (m-s) Julia Hamari

Decca SET625 ■
(from above)

Philips 6747 243 (5) ●
Philips 6747 167 (US)
1974 Bayreuth Festival Chorus and Orchestra
c. Silvio Varviso
Hans Sachs (b) Karl Ridderbusch
Walther von Stolzing (t) Jean Cox
Eva (s) Hannelore Bode
David (t) Friedrich Stricker
Beckmesser (b) Klaus Hirte
Magdalena (m-s) Anna Reynolds

IC181-01 797/801 (5) (m) (r. 1943) ●
Bayreuth Festival Chorus and Orchestra
c. Wilhelm Furtwängler
Hans Sachs (b) Jaro Prohaska
Walther von Stolzing (t) Max Lorenz
Eva (s) Maria Müller
David (t) Erich Zimmermann
Beckmesser (bs) Eugen Fuchs
Magdalena (m-s) Camilla Kallab

Decca Ace of Diamonds GOM535/9 (m) (d) ●
Chorus of Vienna State Opera/Vienna Philharmonic Orchestra
c. Hans Knappertsbusch
Hans Sachs (bs-b) Paul Schoeffler
Walther von Stolzing (t) Günther Treptow
Eva (s) Hilde Gueden
David (t) Anton Dermota
Beckmesser (b) Karl Dönch
Magdalena (m-s) Else Schürhoff

Parsifal

Sacred music drama in 3 Acts.
Text by Wagner based on the legends of the Holy Grail.
First performance: Bayreuth, July 26, 1882. New York (Metropolitan) 1903;
London (Covent Garden) 1914.

Synopsis:

Scene: Spain. Time: 10th century.

Act 1 Gurnemanz, a senior knight of the Grail, is praying by a forest lake at Montsalvat. Amfortas is borne in on a litter to bathe his wound. Kundry, an exotic, mysterious figure, brings Amfortas some balsam, but the wound will still not heal, and Amfortas is carried away. Gurnemanz explains to his knights and esquires how Titurel, father of Amfortas, founded the brotherhood to guard the Sacred Spear and the Holy Grail, and how Klingsor, failing to gain admittance to the Brotherhood, trapped Amfortas in a garden of seduction and wrested the Spear from him, inflicting on Amfortas a terrible wound. The only person who can restore the Spear to its rightful place is a 'Holy Fool'. Just then the knights bring in a stranger who has shot down a swan; he doesn't know who he is. Gurnemanz takes him to the castle to witness the ceremony of the uncovering of the Holy Grail. Still, the stranger professes to understand nothing, and Gurnemanz angrily sends him away.

Act 2 Klingsor then summons Kundry, and instructs her to seduce Parsifal. In Klingsor's Magic Garden, his Flower Maidens frolic round Parsifal, trying to tempt him. They vanish when Kundry calls to him, and she tells him of his mother. When she kisses him, Parsifal remembers Amfortas and the wound and banishes all thoughts of temptation. Kundry pleads with Parsifal, still he resists, and she calls for help to Klingsor, who hurls the Sacred Spear at Parsifal. He catches it in mid-flight and makes the sign of the Cross. Klingsor's castle and garden disintegrate. Parsifal departs with the Spear, telling Kundry she knows where he is going.

Act 3 A forest, several years later. Gurnemanz is living as a hermit. He finds Kundry, who tells him she wants to serve the knights. Just then, a knight in black armour enters; it is Parsifal with the Sacred Spear. Gurnemanz sees the redeemer of the brotherhood of the Grail, and anoints him while Kundry washes his feet. It is Good Friday, with all nature in serene peace. In the Great Hall of the Grail, Titurel has died and Amfortas prays for death. Parsifal enters and touches the wound with the Spear. It instantly heals. Parsifal orders the Grail uncovered and blesses the knights, as Kundry sinks to the ground and dies absolved.

Notes:

Parsifal was a subject long in Wagner's mind: it appears in *Lohengrin* (who is Parsifal's son) and he saw at one time the 'sin' of Tannhäuser passing through Tristan to rest in Amfortas. When he came finally to write *Parsifal*, Wagner was old and exhausted. Despite the opera's musical subtleties and the stamp of genius on its best pages, some saw signs that Wagner was worn out and defeated. Wagner called *Parsifal* a Sacred Festival Play, and he wanted it played only at Bayreuth; a wish his widow Cosima obstinately tried to carry out. But inevitably the opera went out into the world. It is perhaps the most controversial of Wagner's mature works: there is a religioso atmosphere about which frequently offends, but for many it represents Wagner at his most subtle and profound.

(Note: The origins and historical background to all Wagner's operas are both complex and important. They are brilliantly uncovered and analysed in Ernest Newman's *Wagner Nights* (Putnam, London), a book that is essential for a full understanding of Wagner's mind and work.)

Well-known excerpts:

Prelude and Good Friday Music.

RECORDINGS:

Philips 6747 250 (5) ●
Philips 6747 250 (5) (US)
1963 Bayreuth Festival Chorus and Orchestra
c. Hans Knappertsbusch
Parsifal (t) Jess Thomas
Gurnemanz (bs) Hans Hotter
Amfortas (b) George London
Kundry (s) Irene Dallis
Klingsor (bs) Gustav Neidlinger

Decca SET550/4 ●
London 1510 (5) (US)
Vienna Boys' Choir/Vienna State Opera Chorus/Vienna Philharmonic Orchestra
c. Sir Georg Solti
Parsifal (t) René Kollo
Gurnemanz (bs) Gottlob Frick
Amfortas (b) Dietrich Fischer-Dieskau
Kundry (s) Christa Ludwig
Klingsor (bs) Zoltan Kelemen

Decca SET574 ■
(from above)

DG 2713 004 (5) (d) ●
DG 2713 004 (US)
1970 Bayreuth Festival Chorus and Orchestra
c. Pierre Boulez
Parsifal (t) James King
Gurnemanz (bs) Franz Crass

Amfortas (b) Thomas Stewart
Kundry (s) Gwyneth Jones
Klingsor (bs) Donald McIntyre

DG 2536 023 (d) ■
(from above)

Decca Ace of Diamonds GOM504/8 (m) ●
1951 Bayreuth Festival Chorus and Orchestra
c. Hans Knappertsbusch
Parsifal (t) Wolfgang Windgassen
Gurnemanz (bs) Ludwig Weber
Amfortas (b) George London
Kundry (s) Martha Mödl
Klingsor (bs) Hermann Uhde

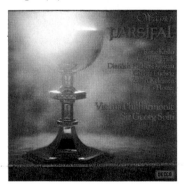

VINCENT WALLACE

(b. Waterford 11.3.1812; d. Château de Haget, Haut-Pyrénées, 12.10.1865)

Son of an Irish Army bandmaster, Wallace lived an adventurous life. As well as being a prolific composer, he was a travelling virtuoso of the violin and had many escapades around the world, including encounters with cannibals, a tiger and an exploding steamer. In 1831 he went to Australia, became involved in a number of enterprises, lost money, and left 'in a clandestine manner'. He married one of his piano pupils, Isabella Kelly, in Dublin, then lived with and later married (bigamously) another pianist, American Hélène Stoepel. Wallace had gone to America in 1850, intending to become an American citizen, but returned to Europe and finally settled in France. He wrote many operas, for London and Paris, of which *Maritana* is the only one significantly remembered.

Maritana

Opera in 3 Acts.
Text by Edward Fitzball based on Adolphe d'Ennery's play 'Don César de Bazan'.
First performance: London (Drury Lane) November 15, 1845. Philadelphia 1846; Vienna 1848.

RECORDINGS:

HMV CSD3651 ■
Veronica Dunne (s)
Uel Deane (t)
Erich Hinds (b)
c. Havelock Nelson
(Balfe/Benedict)

Decca SXL6235 □
London 6486 (US)
Overture
c. Richard Bonynge

Decca SET247/8 □
London 1254 (2) (US)
Scenes that are brightest
Joan Sutherland (s)

EMI EMD5528 □
Yes, let me like a soldier fall
Robert Tear (t)
Benjamin Luxon (b)

Above: *19th century opera was publicised by arrangements for piano.*

(Sir) WILLIAM WALTON
(b. Oldham 29.3.1902)

The senior and one of the most important of the 'middle generation' of English music's 'renaissance' began his musical life at home and at the age of 10 went to Christ Church Cathedral Choir School in Oxford where, among other benefits, he was introduced to Sir Hugh Allen. It is said that Walton is largely self-taught, but there is no doubt he had a thorough grounding in music upon which he was able to build his highly individual talent. He began composing early; but most of his youthful compositions were destroyed, and thereafter he composed and published only at longish intervals and after much deep thought. A major event in Walton's life was his meeting with the Sitwell family at Oxford which led to a long association and the inspiration for several works, the most notable being *Façade*, an Entertainment for speaker and small orchestra to poems by Edith Sitwell. Like that other, older and very different genius of English music, Sir Thomas Beecham, Walton was born and has remained a Lancastrian, with the typical Lancashire directness and honesty of speech and attitude. Walton has written two operas, the full scale *Troilus and Cressida* and the one-act comedy *The Bear*.

Troilus and Cressida
Opera in 3 Acts.
Text by Christopher Hassall based on Chaucer.
First performance: London (Covent Garden) December 3, 1954. San Francisco 1954.

Synopsis:
Scene: Troy. Time: Trojan Wars.
Act 1   The Trojans are at prayer before the temple, to the Virgin of Troas. Calkas, High Priest of Pallas and father of Cressida, tries to persuade the people that the Delphic Oracle has advised surrender to the Greeks. Antenor accuses Calkas of being in the pay of the Greeks, but Troilus, who loves Cressida, stands up for the High Priest. Pandarus, overhearing that his brother Calkas is planning to desert to the Greeks, attempts to console Cressida, and tells her she has the love of a notable prince. Antenor has been taken prisoner, and Troilus swears to release his friend by force of arms, or bring pressure to bear on his father, King Priam, to agree to an exchange of prisoners. It is noticed that Calkas has disappeared, and Pandarus persuades Cressida to give Troilus her scarf. Troilus, ignoring the fact that she is the daughter of a traitor, is exultant.
Act 2   Pandarus has invited Cressida and others to supper in his house. A storm is brewing, and Pandarus has sent for Troilus, and finally brings the two lovers together again. Troilus and Cressida watch the break of dawn. Pandarus hides them, as the Greek commander, Diomede, enters on a mission of state: the exchange of prisoners. He explains that Calkas has served the Greeks well and as reward requires his daughter brought to him, while Priam requires the release of Antenor. Diomede discovers Cressida in hiding and orders her to prepare for the journey. Troilus, in despair, returns Cressida her scarf and promises to smuggle messages to her.
Act 3   Ten weeks later. At the Greek camp, Cressida has had no word from Troilus. She sends her servant Evadne to watch again for a messenger. Diomede enters, and the despairing Cressida submits to him. Evadne destroys the last message from Troilus which, like all the others, she has withheld in obedience to Calkas's orders. Troilus and Pandarus arrive to arrange for Cressida's ransom. But she tells them it is too late. Diomede enters wearing Cressida's red scarf. Troilus sees it and demands Cressida as his own. Diomede, ordering her to renounce Troilus, throws the scarf to the ground. Troilus draws his sword but is mortally wounded. Calkas is sent back to Troy, but Cressida cheats the Greeks by committing suicide.

Notes:
The text is not from Shakespeare (or the *Iliad*) but Chaucer — though with some changes of emphasis. The opera is written in a

kind of post-19th century style, with the major operatic conventions observed, and re-charged. Walton's lineage in English music is via Elgar rather than Vaughan Williams ». Although he was a provocative 'modernist' in his early works, he later evolved a personal style which could be called typical English compromise: making use of serial techniques from a wholly individual standpoint, yet giving an overall traditional impression. So it is with *Troilus and Cressida*. The recording was taken from the 1976 revival of the opera.

RECORDINGS:
HMV SLS997 (3) ●
Chorus and Orchestra of Royal Opera House, Covent Garden
c. Lawrence Foster
Troilus (t)   Richard Cassilly
Cressida (m-s) Janet Baker
Calkas (bs)   Richard Van Allan
Pandarus (t)   Gerald English
Diomede (b)   Benjamin Luxon

Decca SET392/3 □
How can I sleep?
Marie Collier (s)

The Bear
Comic opera (Extravaganza) in 1 Act.
Text by Paul Dehn based on Chekhov.
First performance: Aldeburgh Festival, June 3, 1967.

Notes:
The plot is taken from the most successful of the five short 1-Act plays Chekhov issued under the name 'vaudevilles'. It concerns the fortunes and misfortunes of Madam Popova, still mourning the death of her dear departed husband, and the wealthy landowner who comes to collect an outstanding debt. They quarrel, but in the end, things sort themselves out and the bereaved lady capitulates to the insistent and rich, if boorish, suitor.

RECORDING:
HMV SAN192 (d) ●
English Chamber Orchestra
c. James Lockhart
Madame Popova (m-s) Monica Sinclair
G. S. Smirnov (b)   John Shaw
Luka (bs)   Norman Lumsden
(Note: The recording was made by the cast of the first performance at Aldeburgh.)

Below: *Sir William Walton's one-act opera* The Bear *was first performed by the English Opera Group in 1967.*

ROBERT WARD
(b. Cleveland, Ohio 13.9.1917)

Ward studied at the Eastman School of Music under Howard Hanson and Aaron Copland » and taught at Juilliard, where he was assistant to the president in 1954-56. He was music director of the Third Street Music Settlement School 1952-56, and then became an executive in music-publishing. A regular conductor, his works include four symphonies and various orchestral and choral pieces. His best-known work is his opera *The Crucible* (1961), a very effective piece of writing for the theatre. He also wrote the opera *The Lady from Colorado* with a libretto by Bernard Stambler in 1964, and *He Who Gets Slapped* (an opera based on the play by Leonid Andreyev) which was produced by the New York City Opera in 1959.

The Crucible
Opera in 4 Acts.
Text by Bernard Stambler, based on the play by Arthur Miller.
First performance: New York (City Center of Music and Drama) October 26, 1961.

Notes:
The opera's four acts follow closely the action of Miller's play, set in Salem, Massachusetts in 1692. The plot centres around the notorious witch-hunts of the period and their terrible effect on the community—notably planter John Proctor and his family.

RECORDING:
Composers Recordings SD168 (2) (US) ●
New York City Opera Orchestra
c. Emerson Buckley

John Proctor (b)	Chester Ludgin
Elizabeth Proctor (s)	Frances Bible
Abigail Williams (s)	Patricia Brooks
Rev. Samuel Parns (t)	Norman Kelley
Rev. John Hale (bs)	John McCurdy

CARL MARIA VON WEBER
(b. Eutin, Lübeck 18.11.1786; d. London 5.6.1826)

Weber played a major part in the establishment of German Romantic opera. He was the link between Mozart » (*The Magic Flute*), Beethoven » (*Fidelio*) and the massive achievement of Wagner ». He took opera into enchanted fields first explored by Schubert » in symphony and song, yet he remained a composer with a distinctive voice of his own, in instrumental music as well as opera. The son of a travelling musician, he learnt his first music from his father, and at the age of 10 began to study with Michael Haydn. His operatic career began with *Peter Schmoll und seine Nachbarn* in 1803. After that he held a number of appointments in Germany (including the conductorship of the German theatre in Prague in 1813) and in 1816 took over directorship of the Dresden Court Opera, where he did much to consolidate the emergent German opera. *Der Freischütz* was produced in Berlin in 1821 and *Euryanthe* in Vienna in 1823. He was commissioned by Covent Garden to produce an opera in

Below: *Carl Maria von Weber, whose works helped to establish German national opera.*

English and he studied the language closely before undertaking the task. The result was *Oberon*, which appeared in 1826, but by then he was already in declining health and he died in London at the house of his friend Sir George Smart.

Abu Hassan
Singspiel in 1 Act.
Text by Franz Carl Heimer.
First performance: Munich, June 4, 1811.

Synopsis:
Scene: Bagdad. Time: Legendary.
Hopelessly in debt, Abu Hassan, poet and favourite of the Caliph, has had to give up the high life and be content with singing about it with his wife Fatima. Abu tries to do a deal with Omar, the money changer, while he and Fatima both tell the Caliph that the other is dead in the hope of having the debts discharged. Omar is paying unwelcome attention to Fatima who terrifies him with tales of Abu Hassan's wild jealousy. The Caliph eventually arrives with his own wife, Zobeide, to see for himself—and finds both Abu and Fatima lying stretched out. The Caliph offers money to anyone who will tell him who died first, whereupon Abu jumps up and says it was him. The Caliph laughs at the audacity and pays up, solving Abu's problem.

RECORDING:
RCA LRL15125 (d) ●   c. Heinz Rogner
Dresden State Opera Chorus/Gerhart
Wüstner Student Chorus/Dresden State
Orchestra

Abu Hassan (t)	Peter Schreier
Fatima (s)	Ingebourg Hallstein
Omar (bs)	Theo Adam

Der Freischütz
Opera in 3 Acts.
Text by Friedrich Kind based on Apel and Laun's 'Gespensterbuch'.
First performance: Berlin (Schauspielhaus) June 18, 1821.

Synopsis:
Scene: Bohemia. Time: Mid-18th century.
Act 1 Max has been beaten by Kilian in a shooting contest and must win the final trial or else forfeit the hand of Agathe, daughter of Kuno the forester. Left alone, Max is approached by Kaspar who hands him a gun and sees him shoot down an eagle. Kaspar explains that it was a magic bullet, and Max agrees to allow Kaspar to help him win on the morrow. He must meet Kaspar in the Wolf's Glen at midnight to receive the bullets.
Act 2 Agathe is waiting in her room with her cousin Ännchen. She is troubled by premonitions of danger and by a warning she has received from an old Hermit. She is not reassured when Max arrives late and hurries off, saying he has to collect a stag he has shot in the Wolf's Glen. In the Glen, Kaspar is trying to bargain

with Samiel, the Wild Huntsman, for his soul, promising a new victim. Max appears and is deeply troubled when he sees a ghost of his dead mother and another he takes to be Agathe. But he is determined to continue with the plan. Kaspar casts seven magic bullets; six will hit the target, the seventh will kill Agathe, as sacrifice.

Act 3   After a short entr'acte we are back in Agathe's room, where she is telling Ännchen of a dream; Ännchen tries to console and divert her. Agathe decides to wear the white roses given her by the Hermit the previous day. In the Prince's camp the contest is about to begin. After the hunting chorus, Max comes in, full of confidence. He has used up six of his magic bullets; now the Prince orders him to shoot a white dove as the final trial. Agathe comes out from behind a tree imploring Max not to shoot, but it is too late: she falls wounded. But the bullet has also mortally wounded Kaspar, who dies cursing the world. The Prince orders Max's banishment, but the Hermit intervenes, and Agathe recovers. There is general rejoicing as the Prince countermands the order.

Notes:

This is the most famous German Romantic opera before Wagner ». In it are several innovations: the first, the overture which not only introduces the principal melodies of the opera but is carefully fashioned into a complete tone poem in a way Wagner was to follow up in *The Flying Dutchman*, *Tannhäuser* and *Die Meistersinger*. Secondly, it introduces that note of magic, the supernatural and the fantastic-mysterious that was also to be a Wagnerian leading motif. It is the early German Romantic opera *par excellence*.

Well-known arias:
      Overture
Act 1   Durch die Wälder (Max)
Act 2   Leise, leise (Agathe)
Act 3   Und ob di Wolke (Agathe)
      Hunting chorus

RECORDINGS:
DG 2720 071 (3) ●
DG 2709 046 (US)
Leipzig Radio Chorus/Dresden State Orchestra
c. Carlos Kleiber
Max (t)   Peter Schreier
Agathe (s)   Gundula Janowitz
Kaspar (b)   Theo Adam
Ännchen (s)   Edith Mathis
Hermit (bs)   Franz Crass

DG Privilege 2726 061 (2) ●
Bavarian Radio Chorus and Symphony Orchestra
c. Eugen Jochum
Max (t)   Richard Holm
Agathe (s)   Irmgard Seefried
Kaspar (s)   Kurt Boehme
Ännchen (s)   Rita Streich
Hermit (b)   Walther Kreppel

Cetra Opera Live L042 (3) (m) (r. 1955) ●
Cologne Radio Chorus and Orchestra
c. Erich Kleiber
Max (t)   Hans Hopf
Agathe (s)   Elisabeth Grümmer
Kaspar (bs)   Max Proebstl
Ännchen (s)   Rita Streich

Hermit (bs) Kurt Boehme
(Speaking parts are taken by actors and actresses. Ännchen's Act 3 aria is omitted.)

DG 2530 661 ■
(from above)

Cetra Opera Live L021 (3) ●
Vienna State Opera Chorus/Vienna Philharmonic Orchestra
c. Wilhelm Furtwängler
Max (t)   Hans Hopf
Agathe (s)   Elisabeth Grümmer
Kaspar (bs)   Kurt Boehme
Ännchen (s)   Rita Streich

Decca SXL6077 □
London 25807 (US)
Leise, leise
Birgit Nilsson (s)

Decca SXL6525 □
London 26246 (US)
Leise, leise
Pilar Lorengar (s)

Euryanthe
Opera in 3 Acts.
Text by Helmine von Chézy.
First performance: Vienna (Kärntnertor Theatre) October 25, 1823. London (Covent Garden) 1833; New York (Metropolitan) 1887.

Synopsis:
Scene: France. Time: 12th century.
Act 1   During peace celebrations Adolar sings of Euryanthe's fidelity but Lysiart takes a bet he can destroy it. In the gardens of the Palace of Nevers, Euryanthe is near the tomb of Adolar's sister Emma, who killed herself after her lover had been killed.

Below: *Weber's Die Freischütz was first performed in Berlin in 1821, and by 1884 had been performed there over 500 times.*

She has sworn never to reveal the secret, but Eglantine, who also loves Adolar, discovers it from her.

Act 2 Lysiart has failed to breach Euryanthe's innocence. But Eglantine shows him the ring she has taken from Emma's tomb, proving that Euryanthe has broken her pledge. This he shows to the King in the presence of Adolar and Euryanthe, and although she protests her innocence she cannot deny she broke her promise. Adolar surrenders all that he has to Lysiart in payment of the bet.

Act 3 Adolar is resolved to kill Euryanthe and then himself. But a serpent appears and she throws herself between them, saving Adolar's life. Moved by her courage he kills the serpent and goes off leaving her unharmed. The King and his retinue enter and he promises to help Euryanthe. At the wedding of Lysiart and Eglantine, Adolar appears in black armour. Eglantine confesses her part in betraying Euryanthe. Adolar challenges Lysiart to a duel, but the King forbids it. Then Lysiart stabs Eglantine to death and Euryanthe, whom the King had pronounced dead as punishment for Adolar, reappears and the lovers are reunited.

Notes:

This is one of those operas which are alleged to be unstageable because of the lunacies of the plot. But the music of *Euryanthe* is quite good enough to keep it going. The subject of medieval romance and ladies in distress was near to the heart of the Romantic generations.

RECORDING:
HMV SLS983 (4) (d) ●
Angel S-3764 (4) (US)
Leipzig Radio Chorus/Dresden State Orchestra
c. Marek Janowski
Euryanthe (s) Jessye Norman
Adolar (t) Nicolai Gedda
Eglantine (s) Rita Hunter
Lysiart (b) Tom Krause
King (bs) Siegfried Vogel

Oberon, or The Elf King's Oath
Opera in 3 Acts.
Text by James Robinson Planché based on Sotheby's translation of Wieland's 'Oberon' and earlier French sources.
First performance: London (Covent Garden) April 12, 1826. New York 1828.

Synopsis:

Scene: France, Bagdad, Tunis. Time: Early 9th century.

Act 1 Oberon and Titania are quarrelling, and swear not to be reconciled until Oberon can find a couple who can remain faithful through all trials and temptations. Puck tells him of one Huon de Bordeaux who has been sent to Bagdad to kill the man seated on the Caliph's left and bring the Caliph's daughter back to France as his bride. By magic Oberon summons Huon and his squire Sherasmin and shows in a dream a vision of the Caliph's daughter Reiza resisting an unwanted suitor; he then wafts the pair to Bagdad, Huon equipped with a magic horn. Reiza awaits her rescuer with some impatience, for she has also been party to a magic dream.

Act 2 Huon forces entry into the Caliph's palace and claims Reiza with a kiss. Joined by Sherasmin and Reiza's attendant Fatima, the four make their escape. Now comes the series of tests that will satisfy Oberon. First, Puck produces a shipwreck. Huon and Reiza are stranded on a desert island. Reiza is seized by pirates while Huon is off looking for help, and when he returns he himself is attacked and left to die.

Act 3 Next, Oberon condemns Huon to seven days' sleep, then has Puck take him to Tunis where Sherasmim and Fatima have been sold off as slaves and Reiza is on offer to the Emir's harem. The Emir makes Reiza his wife. Roshana seeks Huon's help to murder her husband. He refuses, so she hands him over to the Emir who has been rejected by Reiza. The pair are condemned to burnt to death. Sherasmin blows on the magic horn summoning Oberon to the rescue. They are all transported back to France, to general reconciliations and thanksgiving.

Notes:

The libretto of *Oberon* is even more complicated than usual; but again Weber poured into the opera some of his finest and most eloquent music, beginning with another magical overture. Much of the trouble lies in the way the music is continually interrupted by pantomime spoken dialogue. The opera was, of course, originally in English, but *Oberon*'s proper place is in the German Romantic theatre and that is where it now abides, in the German translation.

Well-known arias:

Overture
Act 1 Von jugend auf in dem Kampfgefild (Huon)
Act 1 Ozean, zu Ungeheuer! (Ocean! Thou mighty monster!) (Reiza)

RECORDINGS:
DG 2726 052 (2) ●
Bavarian Radio Chorus and Symphony Orchestra
c. Rafael Kubelik
Oberon (t) Donald Grobe
Huon (t) Placido Domingo
Reiza (s) Birgit Nilsson
Sherasmin (b) Hermann Prey
Fatima (s) Julia Hamari
(Note: The above is a reissue of a more complete version containing the spoken dialogue (DG 2709 035 (3) (d)). Unless one has fluent German there is little point in seeking out the previous set and paying for the extra disc. The music remains intact on the later one.)

Decca SET247/8 □
London 1254 (2) (US)
Ocean! Thou mighty monster!
Joan Sutherland (s)

Decca SXL6077 □
London 25807 (US)
Ozean, zu Ungeheuer!
Birgit Nilsson (s)

Die drei Pintos
Opera (unfinished by Weber, completed by Gustav Mahler).
Text by Theodor Hell, based on Carl Ludwig Seidel's 'Der Brautkampf'.
First performance: Leipzig (Municipal Theatre) January 20, 1888.

Notes:

This is something of a curiosity. Weber began it in 1820 but for some reason never adequately explained, abandoned it in 1821. After his death his widow handed the sketches to Meyerbeer », who kept them for a number of years and left them untouched. In 1852, after trying to interest the young Wagner » in the task of completion, she reclaimed them. In the end they came into Gustav Mahler's hands, and he worked out a 'completion' using Weber's original sketches, which consisted of a first Act and the initial part of a second, plus other material from Weber's works. Thus it is hardly a Weber opera in any full sense; but it is still worth attention. The plot, such as it is, concerns Don Gaston Viratos who decides to impersonate Don Pinto de Fonesca who is travelling to Madrid to claim Clarissa as his bride. Don Pinto himself also goes along—and the third Pinto is Clarissa's lover Don Gomez de Freiros. All pretty preposterous.

RECORDINGS:
RCA PRL3 9063 (3) ●
RCA Victor PRL3-9063 (3) (US)
Netherlands Vocal Ensemble/Munich Philharmonic Orchestra
c. Gary Bertini
Don Pinto (bs) Kurt Moll
Don Gaston (t) Werner Hollweg
Don Gomez (t) Heinz Kruse
Clarissa (s) Lucia Popp
Ambrosio (b) Hermann Prey

OVERTURES:
DG Privilege 2535 136 □
DG 2535 136 (US)
c. Rafael Kubelik

DG 2530 315 □
DG 2530 315 (US)
c. Herbert von Karajan

Decca Eclipse ECS645 □
London STS15056 (US)
c. Ernest Ansermet

KURT WEILL
(b. Dessau 2.3.1900; d. New York 3.4.1950)

Like many composers caught in the confusing cross-currents of 20th century music, Weill seemed to follow many paths. Like many young intellectual musicians, following musical studies with Humperdinck » and Busoni », he might well have continued to write the rather serious Germanic music, represented by works like his early Violin Concerto, written for Szigeti. The strains of Stravinsky » and Hindemith » found here were always with Weill's work but, as he turned to the stage, and wrote his first opera *Der Protagonist*, he was becoming aware of the universal call of folk-music, popular music and jazz. By the time he wrote his first great success *Die Dreigroschenoper* in 1928, these popular elements had been absorbed and intermingled with the academic German strains to produce a unique style—a strange mixture of the humorous, sardonic, sentimental and the sinister. His association with Bertolt Brecht confirmed his socialist beliefs and his duty to write music for the people. In their modernisation of *The Beggar's Opera* story, exactly the right libretto emerged to bring out the best of Weill's music. In the morally and politically slanted operas that followed, he continued to mix the ingredients into a product that was romantic entirely in the contemporary terms of a world torn by one World War and preparing for the next. He found in the voice of Lotte Lenya, whom he married in 1926, the perfect interpreter of his music. After 1933, Weill's works were banned in Germany, and he and his wife fled first to Paris and then to New York where he settled for life. So sensitive to contemporary life, it was impossible for him to write the same music in America that a German background had produced. Many have been disappointed that another *Dreisgroschenoper* did not materialise. Instead we must accept that Weill was not a one-work composer and discover the width of his achievement and the unique qualities that have left their mark on the contemporary musical theatre.

Der Protagonist
Opera in 1 Act.
Text by Georg Kaiser, based on his tragedy of the same title.
First performance: Dresden, March 27, 1926.

RECORDING:
DG 2740 153 (3) ■
DG 2709 064 (3) (US)
The London Sinfonietta
c. David Atherton

Girl (m-s)   Mary Thomas
Husband (t)   Ian Partridge
Wife (b)   Benjamin Luxon
Monk (bs)   Michael Rippon

Mahagonny-Songspiel
Songspiel in 1 Act.
Text by Bertolt Brecht.
First performance: Baden-Baden (Deutsche Kammermusikfest) July 18, 1927.

Notes:
Weill was commissioned to produce a short opera for a festival of modern German chamber music. His first idea was to set a scene from *King Lear* or *Antigone*, but as he and Bertolt Brecht were already working on the *Mahagonny* opera they decided to compile the songspiel, a 'style study' of the work of an incidental nature which gave Weill an opportunity to try his hand at writing for opera singers.

RECORDINGS:
DG 2740 153 (3) or 2530 897 ●
DG 2709 064 (3) (US)
The London Sinfonietta
c. David Atherton
Philip Langridge (t)
Ian Partridge (t)
Benjamin Luxon (b)
Michael Rippon (bs)

Meriel Dickinson (m-s)
Mary Thomas (m-s)

Turnabout 34675 (US) ○
Jerusalem Symphony
c. Lukas Foss
Soloists
(with *Kleine Dreigroschenmusik*)

Die Dreigroschenoper
Opera in a Prologue and Eight Scenes (later in 3 Acts).
Text by Bertolt Brecht, based on Hauptmann's translation of 'The Beggar's Opera'.
First performance: Berlin (Theater an Schiffbauerdamm) August 31, 1928. New York 1933. American version by Marc Blitzstein, New York, 1954 (The Threepenny Opera); London 1956.

Synopsis:
The story is partly narrated by a Street Singer who first tells the story of Macheath, now known as Mack the Knife, in a penny-dreadful ballad at the Fair in Soho. Mr Peachum, who runs a seedy shop frequented by beggars, and Mrs Peachum have slightly romantic thoughts; while in Soho, Mack the Knife celebrates his marriage to their daughter Polly. Later Mr and Mrs Peachum advise their daughter that marriage should not be merely for love in the hard world of necessity. Macheath has to flee from the law and the Peachums plan to betray him to make Polly a wealthy widow. Mrs Peachum bribes the prostitute Jenny who signals the police to enter the brothel when Macheath makes a visit there. He is arrested and thrown into jail at the Old Bailey. Polly and Lucy, another girl friend, quarrel over Macheath, but Macheath is now rather more taken with Jenny. Macheath is on his way to the gallows but is pardoned by the Queen in view of the coming Coronation and, moreover raised to the peerage and given a yearly income of £10,000, so even the Peachums are happy in the end.

Notes:
The opera is broadly based on Gay's » piece but spends far more time moralising in long vocal sections as opposed to the short snippets of folksong used by Gay. In view of the pervading gloom that precedes it the pardon comes as a curious ending and less effective than Gay's (see *The Beggar's Opera*).

Well-known arias:
Moritat (Mack the Knife) (Streetsinger)
Kanonensong (Macheath and Chief of Police)
Barbara Song (Polly)
Die Seeräuber-Jenny (Pirate-Jenny) (Jenny)
Salomon-Song (Jenny)

RECORDINGS:
CBS 78279 (2) ●
Odyssey Y2-32977 (2) (US)
Chorus and Orchestra
c. Wilhelm Brückner-Rüggeberg
Street Singer   Wolfgang Neuss
Mr Peachum   Willy Trenk-Trebitsch
Mrs Peachum   Trude Hesterberg
Macheath   Erich Schellow
Polly   Johanna von Koczian
Jenny   Lotte Lenya
(with Lenya: Theatre Songs)

Telefunken AJ6.41911 (r. 1930) ■
(original cast)
Lewis-Ruth-Band-Jazzorchester
c. Theo Mackeben
Street Singer   Kurt Gerron
Mr Peachum   Erich Ponto
Mrs Peachum   Erika Helmke
Macheath   Willy Trenk-Trebitsch
Polly   Lotte Lenya
(with excerpts from film version of 1930)

(Also available recently was a performance by the Frankfurt Opera under Wolfgang Rennert on Fontana SFL14077/8 (d))

Decca PFS4280 □
London 21077 (US)
Orchestral selection
c. Bernard Herrmann

DG 2740 153 (3) or 2530 897 □
DG 2709 064 (3) (US)
Kleine Dreigroschenmusik
c. David Atherton

HMV SXLP 30226 □
Kleine Dreigroschenmusik
c. Otto Klemperer

Candide CE 31089 (US) □
Kleine Dreigroschenmusik (with *Kurka*)
c. Siegfried Landau

Nonesuch H-71281 □
Nonesuch H-71281 (US)
Kleine Dreigroschenmusik
c. Arthur Weisberg

Turnabout 34675 (US) □
Kleine Dreigroschenmusik
c. Siegfried Landau

(Note: The *Kleine Dreigroschenmusik* was arranged by Weill himself in late 1928 some four months after the performance of the opera. It was first performed under Otto Klemperer in February 1929. For 12 wind instruments, piano, percussion, banjo and guitar, it is not a mere selection from the opera but a well-integrated work based on the opera's themes with an inventive finale.)

Happy End
Play with music.
Text by Bertolt Brecht.
First performance: Berlin (Theater an Schiffbauerdamm) September 2, 1929.

Notes:

Not strictly an opera but so close in style to *Die Dreigroschenoper* and not far removed from it in form that it is worth mentioning in the list of Weill's vocal works. The song *Surabya Johnny* is a remarkably close relative to the earlier *Moritat*, and the musical score is a substantial part of the entertainment.

RECORDING:
DG 2740 153 (3) ●
DG 2709 064 (3) (US)
The London Sinfonietta
c. David Atherton
Mary Thomas (m-s)
Philip Langridge (t)
Ian Partridge (t)
Benjamin Luxon (b)
Meriel Dickinson (m-s)

CBS 73463
Columbia COS-2032 (US)
Chorus and Orchestra
c. Wilhelm Brückner-Rüggeberg
Lotte Lenya

CBS78279 (2) □
Lotte Lenya
(with *Dreigroschenoper*)

Below: *David Atherton directs Kurt Weill's* Happy End.

Aufstieg und Fall der Stadt Mahagonny

Opera in 3 Acts.
Text by Bertolt Brecht.
First performance: Leipzig, March 9, 1930. London 1963.

Synopsis:

A general summary of a strange and detailed plot is as follows: The City of Mahagonny is a 'symbolic caricature of freedom', a legendary city where everyone can live as they please, situated somewhere in the gold rush areas of North America. Jenny and her friends are the girls found and brought there by Jimmy and his lumberjack friends on the spree. The standards of Mahagonny are very much based on hard cash as well as sentiment. A hurricane threatens the city at one time, indicated on a map with arrows, but it miraculously misses the city. The gods of Gluttony, Love, Violence and Drink are all worshipped in Mahagonny and their activities are carried on to excess. In the end, Jimmy, unable to pay for his drinks, is tried by Mahagonny law which lets him off lightly for murder, gives a four-year sentence for seduction, and the death penalty for not paying his bill.

RECORDINGS:
CBS 77341 (3) ●
NDRT Chorus/Orchestra
c. Wilhelm Brückner-Rüggeberg
Jenny Lotte Lenya
Mrs Begbick Gisela Litz
Trinity Moses Horst Günter
Pennybank Bill Georg Mund
Jake & Toby Fritz Göllnitz
Alaska-Wolf-
  Joe Sigmund Roth

Fatty the
  Bookkeeper Peter Markwort
Jimmy
  Mahoney Heinz Saverbaum
(Note: It is well worth trying to find a 2-record set called 'Berlin to Broadway with Kurt Weill' (Paramount SPSP29) which gives a good coverage of all Weill's opera and theatre music.)

JAROMIR WEINBERGER

(b. Prague 8.1.1896; d. St Petersburg, Fla., 8.8.1967)

Czech composer, chiefly remembered for his vivacious opera *Schwanda the Bagpiper*, he studied first in Prague and then with Max Reger in Germany. He taught for a year in America (1922-23) then returned to Czechoslovakia where he held some official posts. His compositions did not make much progress until *Schwanda* was produced in 1927. It achieved a huge international success not repeated by his later operas. Weinberger settled finally in the United States in 1939.

Schwanda the Bagpiper (Švanda Dudák)

Opera in 2 Acts.
Text by Miloš Kareš.
First performance: Prague (Czech Theatre) April 27, 1927. New York (Metropolitan) 1931; London (Covent Garden) 1934.

RECORDINGS:
Decca Eclipse ECS632 □
Polka and Fugue
c. Jean Martinon

RCA Victrola VICS-1424 (US) □
Polka and Fugue
c. Fritz Reiner

Decca SXL6484 □
Polka and Fugue
Bracha Eden
Alexander Tamir (pno)

Seraphim S-60098 (US) □
Polka and Fugue
c. Rudolf Kempe

ERMANNO WOLF-FERRARI

(b. Venice 12.1.1876; d. Venice 21.1.1948)

The son of a German father and an Italian mother, Wolf-Ferrari was first apprenticed, in Rome, as a painter: his father's profession. But his musical proclivities soon became apparent, and he studied in Munich with Rheinberger. On his return to his native Venice in 1899, he was sufficiently proficient in composition to have an oratorio produced by the Philharmonic Society. He wrote a number of instrumental works, but it was his operas that brought him principal fame. His first was produced in 1900 on the familiar Cinderella theme (*Cenerentola*); but it failed to impress in Venice and made a better showing in Bremen in 1902. Henceforward many of his operas were given first in Germany—the last of all being presented in Hanover in June, 1943. His most lasting opera is his little masterpiece *Il Segreto di Susanna*. Apart from this work it is the sparkling overtures to the others that claim our principal attention.

I Quattro Rusteghi (The Four Rustics)

Opera buffa in 3 Acts.
Text by Giuseppe Pizzolato based on Goldoni's comedy.
First performance: Munich (as 'Die vier Grobiane') March 19, 1906. Milan (La Scala) 1914.

Notes:

A production of this opera was presented by Sadler's Wells, London, in 1946, under the title *The School for Fathers* in a translation by the late Edward J. Dent.

RECORDING:
Decca Ace of Diamonds SDD452 □
London STS-15362 (US)
Prelude; Intermezzo
c. Nello Santi

(Note: A complete recording was available on Cetra OLPC 1239 (3) (US) conducted by Alfredo Simonetto.)

Pickwick PDA036 (2) □
Intermezzo
c. Vilem Tausky

Il Segreto di Susanna (Susanna's Secret)

Comedy in 1 Act.
Text by Enrico Golisciani.
First performance: Munich (as 'Susannens Geheimnis') December 4, 1909. New York 1911; London (Covent Garden) 1911.

Synopsis:

Susanna is a secret smoker. Her husband Count Gil smells tobacco about the house and suspects she has a lover; enraged, he leaves her. When he has gone, Susanna lights a cigarette. Gil returns and she tries to hide it, but the smell lingers on and he is sure now that the secret lover is around—and a tobacco addict.

He notices that Susanna is hiding something behind her back, makes a grab for it and burns his fingers. The discovery that it is only his wife who is indulging the dreadful habit, and not a lover, at once mollifies him. He relents, and all is forgiven.

Notes:
This little *jeux* could be seen as a linear successor to Bach's 'Coffee' Cantata, which has a go at the then new coffee craze rather than the smoking habit. But there, the connection ends.

RECORDINGS:
Decca SET617 ●
London 1169 (US)
Orchestra of Royal Opera House,
Covent Garden
c. Lamberto Gardelli
Susanna (s)   Maria Chiara
Count Gil (b) Bernd Weikl

World Records OH119 (m) (d) ●
Cetra OLPC 1249 (d) (US)
Orchestra of Radiotelevisione Italiana,
Turin
c. Angelo Questa
Susanna (s)   Elena Rizzieri
Count Gil (b) Giuseppe Valdengo

Decca Ace of Diamonds SDD452 □
London STS15362 (US)
Overture
c. Nello Santi

I Gioielli della Madonna (The Jewels of the Madonna)
Opera in 3 Acts.
Text by Golisciani and Carlo Zangarini.
First performance: Berlin (Kurfürsten-Oper) (as 'Der Schmuck der Madonna')
December 23, 1911. London (Covent Garden) 1912.

RECORDING:
Decca Ace of Diamonds SDD452 □
London STS15362 (US)
Orchestral suite
c. Nello Santi

Il Campiello
Opera in 3 Acts.
Text by Mario Ghisalberti based on a comedy by Goldoni.
First performance: Milan (La Scala)
February 12, 1936.

RECORDING:
Decca Ace of Diamonds SDD452 □
London STS15362 (US)
Intermezzo/Ritornella
c. Nello Santi

La Dama Boba
Opera in 3 Acts.
Text by Ghisalberti based on a comedy by Lope de Vega.
First performance: Milan (La Scala) February 1, 1939.

RECORDING:
Decca Ace of Diamonds SDD452 □
London STS15362 (US)
Overture
c. Nello Santi

Below: *Ermanno Wolf-Ferrari, German-Italian composer of elegant opera.*

RICCARDO ZANDONAI
(b. Sacco, Trentino, 28.5.1883; d. Pesaro 5.6.1944)

Another Italian opera composer in the *verismo* line of post-Puccini », Zandonai studied under Mascagni » at the Liceo Musicale de Pesaro where he took his diploma in 1902. Thirty-seven years later he became the Liceo's director, and remained so until his death. He had an individual lyric vein of melody but only a nominal dramatic gift. But his operas make good theatre and are a positive contribution to Italian music. His non-operatic music is unimpressive and infrequently heard. Of his ten operas the most successful were *Francesca da Rimini* and *Giulietta e Romeo*.

Francesca da Rimini
Opera in 4 Acts.
Text by Tito Ricordi based on D'Annunzio's tragedy drawn from Dante.
First performance: Turin (Teatro Regio) February 19, 1914. London (Covent Garden) 1914; New York (Metropolitan) 1916.

RECORDINGS:
Decca SET422 (d) ■
London 26121 (US)
Monte Carlo Opera Orchestra
c. Nicola Rescigno
Magda Olivero (s)
Mario del Monaco (t)

Decca SXL6585 □
London 25729 (US)
No, Smaragdi, no . . . Inghiriandata di
Violette
Renata Tebaldi (s)

(Note: Several Zandonai operas have been previously available on the Cetra label, notably *Conchita*—OLPC55029, *Francesca da Rimini*—OLPC1229 (3) and *Giulietta e Romeo*—OLPC1266 (2).)

A biographical guide to
100 leading opera singers
of the post-war and LP era

THEO ADAM
Bass

Born in Dresden on August 1, 1926, Adam sang there as a boy chorister in the Church of the Holy Cross. When his voice broke he began serious study with Rudolf Dittrich and made his début at the Dresden Staatsoper in 1949. He appeared with the Berlin Staatsoper from 1952 onwards and made his Bayreuth début in 1952 as King Henry the Fowler in *Lohengrin*, returning there annually for such roles as Titurel, and later Amfortas, in *Parsifal*, Wotan and Fafner in the *Ring* cycle and Hans Sachs in *Die Meistersinger*. He sang Baron Ochs in *Der Rosenkavalier* at Salzburg in 1969 and in 1967 made his début at Covent Garden as Wotan. His dark-hued bass-baritone voice and his dominating stage personality are best-suited to the heroic Wagnerian bass-baritone roles, but he is also an eminent oratorio singer. Apart from Wagnerian roles, his recordings include Bach cantatas, Mozart arias, and the bass part in Beethoven's *Ninth Symphony*.

LUIGI ALVA
Tenor

Born in Lima, Peru, on April 10, 1927, Alva studied singing there with Rosa Mercedes, making his

concert début in 1949. Three years later he made his operatic début, also in Lima, as Alfredo in *La Traviata*. Afterwards he continued his studies in Italy, appearing at the Teatro Nuovo, Milan, in 1954, again as Alfredo. He sang at the Piccola Scala, Milan, in 1957 in *Il Matrimonio Segreto* by Cimarosa, singing in the same opera at the Edinburgh Festival later the same year. He was engaged for the Salzburg Festivals of 1957 and 1958, playing the part of Fenton in Verdi's *Falstaff*, and has also appeared at Covent Garden, Aix-en-Provence, Glyndebourne and the Metropolitan Opera, New York, where he made his début in 1964. His career has indeed been world-wide. He has a lyric tenor voice of fine quality and his training was so good that he is able to surmount the tremendous difficulties of the *coloratura* tenor roles in many Rossini operas with great distinction. He has also become well known for his singing of Mozart roles, and has made a number of excellent recordings.

VICTORIA DE LOS ANGELES
Soprano

Born in Barcelona on November 1, 1923, Victoria de los Angeles studied at the Conservatoire in her native city. While still a student, she sang in Monteverdi's *Orfeo* and then made her first professional appearance at a concert in 1944. In the following year she sang the role of the Countess in *Le Nozze di Figaro* at the Teatro Liceo, Barcelona, and in 1948 went to London to sing in a radio broadcast of Falla's *La Vida Breve*. When she first sang the role of Marguerite in *Faust* at the Paris Opéra, she created a sensation. Her lyric soprano voice had a warmth and a crystalline purity which made her an ideal interpreter of the role, and her charming

appearance and stage bearing added greatly to the power of her characterisation. She followed this with an equally successful Mimi in *La Bohème* at Covent Garden in 1950 and appeared at La Scala, Milan, in the same year in *Ariadne auf Naxos*. Her Metropolitan Opera début was again as Marguerite in *Faust*, and from that time her career has been a series of triumphs. In 1961-62 she sang the role of Elisabeth in *Tannhäuser* at Bayreuth. Other parts in which she has achieved particular success include the title role in Massenet's *Manon*, Rosina in *Il Barbiere di Siviglia* and Charlotte in Massenet's *Werther*. She has been equally successful as a concert artist and in her many recordings; in her prime, she undoubtedly possessed one of the most beautiful soprano voices of this century.

IRINA ARKHIPOVA
Mezzo-soprano

Born in Moscow on December 2, 1925, Arkhipova sang with the Sverdlovsk Opera Company for some years, joining the Bolshoi Company in 1956 and making her début in Moscow as Carmen in the same year. She sang leading roles in Moscow and other principal Eastern European operatic centres for some years before she was known to Western audiences: it was not until she sang the part of Amneris in *Aida* at Orange in 1972, with Montserrat Caballé in the title role, that she attracted much attention in the West. She sang at Covent Garden in 1975, again making her début as Amneris, and made a profound impression with her fine voice and powerful dramatic presence. Apart from leading roles in Russian operas, she has also appeared as Princess Eboli in *Don Carlos* and Charlotte in *Werther*. Recently she has made extended tours in Europe and the US and is everywhere recognised as an artist of exceptional merit.

She has a fine mezzo-soprano voice of great power and unusual range and is also an actress of impressive ability.

GABRIEL BACQUIER
Baritone

Born at Béziers, France, on May 17, 1924, Bacquier studied in Paris and made his début in Nice in 1951. From there he went to the Théâtre de la Monnaie, Brussels, in 1953, and three years later was engaged to sing at the Opéra Comique in Paris. In 1958 he joined the company of the Paris Opéra and in 1960 sang at the Festival at Aix-en-Provence. He was at Glyndebourne in 1962, and made his Covent Garden début in 1964. He has also sung with great success at the Metropolitan Opera, New York, the Teatro Colón, Buenos Aires, and La Scala, Milan. His warm baritone voice is used with the refinement and clarity of diction typical of the best French singers, and he is a forceful dramatic actor. In recent years he has added lighter roles, such as that of Dr Malatesta in *Don Pasquale*, which he sang at Covent Garden in 1973.

NORMAN BAILEY
Baritone

Born in Birmingham on March 23, 1933, Bailey studied locally

and then in Vienna, where he made his operatic début in *La Cambiale di Matrimonio* by Rossini. In the following years he gained experience in the standard repertoire of the operatic baritone, singing such roles as Rigoletto, Il Conte (the Count) di Luna in *Il Trovatore* and Scarpia in *Tosca*, but he is now esteemed particularly in the German repertoire, above all as Wagner's Wotan, a role which he has sung with the English National Opera with enormous success. Another favourite role is Hans Sachs in *Die Meistersinger von Nürnberg*, which he has sung at Covent Garden and in many leading continental opera houses, including Bayreuth in 1969. He now sings regularly in both London opera houses and is also engaged for guest appearances throughout Europe. His voice is a fine, evenly-produced bass baritone, and his interpretations of both German opera and *lieder* have been a notable feature of his highly successful career.

JANET BAKER
Mezzo-soprano

Born in Hatfield, Yorkshire, on August 21, 1933, Baker first studied singing locally and then in London, where her principal teacher was Helene Isepp. She was also coached by Meriel St Clair. She won the *Daily Mail* Kathleen Ferrier Award in 1956 and pursued further studies in Salzburg. She made her operatic début with the Oxford University Opera Club in 1956 in Smetana's *The Secret* and, after appearances in various parts of the UK, she first sang at Glyndebourne as Dido in *Dido & Aeneas* in 1965. She has had enormous success there as Diana in *La Calisto* and Penelope in *Il Ritorno d'Ulisse in Patria*. Her Scottish Opera début was in 1967, as Dorabella in *Così fan tutte*, and she returned in 1969 to sing Dido in *Les Troyens*. Her first appearance at Covent Garden was as Hermia in *A Midsummer Night's Dream* and later she achieved a striking success there in *Les Troyens*. Her success has been world-wide and she was created a Dame of the British Empire in 1976. Her voice is a mezzo-soprano of wide range and her vocal technique is impeccable. Apart from her operatic work, she has been equally successful in

oratorio and concert and has made many fine recordings.

ETTORE BASTIANINI
Baritone

Born in Siena on September 24, 1922, Bastianini originally trained as a bass and made his début as Colline in *La Bohème* in 1945 in Ravenna. For some years he sang bass roles without attracting much attention; then his teacher, Ricciana Bettarini, decided to train him as a baritone. He first sang in this register in 1951, as Giorgio Germont in *La Traviata*. His talents were obviously more talents were obviously more suited to the baritone register and he soon came to the fore, appearing at La Scala in 1953 and also singing in the first staged performance of Prokofiev's *War and Peace*, as Prince Andrei, at the Florence Festival in the same year. He made his début at the Metropolitan Opera, New York, in 1953 as Giorgio Germont, and appeared at Salzburg in 1960-61 singing the Count di Luna in *Il Trovatore*. He made his Covent Garden début in 1962 as Renato in *Un Ballo in Maschera* and was welcomed as one of the first post-war Italian baritones. His warm, rich voice and his easy production made him one of the most admired Verdi baritones of his day and his success was international. He made some fine recordings before his early death in Sirmione on January 25, 1967.

TERESA BERGANZA
Mezzo-soprano

Born in Madrid on March 16, 1935, Berganza studied with Lola Rodrigues Aragon in her native town. She had at first intended to be a pianist, but she won all the available prizes for singing at the

Madrid Conservatoire and as a result decided upon a singing career. Her début was at the Ateneo, Madrid, in 1955, but her first important engagement was at Aix-en-Provence, where she sang the role of Dorabella in *Così fan tutte* in 1957. In 1958 she went to the US, where she made her début in Dallas as Neris in *Médée* with Callas in the title role, and in the same year she sang at La Scala, Milan, and at Glyndebourne, first appearing as Cherubino in *Le Nozze di Figaro* and in the following year creating a sensation with her superb *coloratura* singing in *La Cenerentola*. Covent Garden first heard her in 1960, when she sang Rosina in *Il Barbiere di Siviglia*: again, her charming personality and wonderful singing brought her instant success. Since then her career has been international, with guest appearances in all the principal operatic centres. She is one of the few mezzo-sopranos, since the later Conchita Supervia, able to cope successfully with the elaborate *roulades* of the Rossini comic operas, and this, allied to her warm personality and innate musicianship, has made her one of the most interesting operatic artistes of her generation. She has recorded her principal operatic roles and also many recitals of Spanish music.

CARLO BERGONZI
Tenor

Born in Parma on July 13, 1924, Bergonzi studied at the Conservatoire there before making his début as a baritone, singing Figaro in *Il Barbiere di Siviglia*, in Lecce in 1948. He soon became aware that his high baritone voice was changing to a tenor and after further study he made a second début, this time as a tenor, in *Andrea Chénier* at Bari in 1951. His rise was very rapid: in 1953 he went to London to sing in a season at the Stoll Theatre, where he first appeared as Alvaro in *La Forza del Destino*. In 1955 he sang for the first time in America, making his début at the Chicago Opera, and in the following year he made his bow at the Metropolitan Opera as Radames in *Aida*. He was at Covent Garden in 1962, again singing the role of Alvaro, and since then his career

has been world-wide and brilliantly successful. His fine tenor voice is heard at its best in lyrico dramatic roles and his stylish singing has placed him in the forefront of contemporary tenors. He phrases with an eloquence and an absence of mannerisms which more than compensate for his moderate ability as an actor.

WALTER BERRY
Bass

Born in Vienna on April 8, 1929, Berry studied singing in his native town with Hermann Gallos. He joined the Vienna Staatsoper, singing only minor roles until he appeared as Masetto in *Don Giovanni* in 1953. He later sang Figaro in *Le Nozze di Figaro* and other leading roles in Mozart operas. He went to England in 1954 with the Vienna company, singing the role of Antonio in *Le Nozze di Figaro*, and made his American début in 1958 in Chicago, singing the title role in the same opera. He is an amazingly versatile artist and his roles cover works as divergent as Berg's *Wozzeck*, the operas of Mozart, and even light operas like Johann Strauss's *Die Fledermaus*. He is a brilliant Papageno in *Die Zauberflöte* and an excellent all-round actor. His well-produced bass baritone voice and his warm personality have made him a very popular figure wherever he appears.

JUSSI BJÖRLING
Tenor

Born in Stora Tuna, Sweden, on February 5, 1911, Björling was the

son of an operatic tenor and a pianist, and received his first singing lessons from his father at the age of five. One year later he toured the US with the Björling quartet, consisting of his father and two brothers. Afterwards he settled down to serious study: apart from his father, his principal teacher was the famous baritone John Forsell. He made his first appearance at the Royal Opera House, Stockholm, as the Lamplighter in Puccini's *Manon Lescaut* in 1930, but his official début was as Don Ottavio in *Don Giovanni*, on August 20 in the same year. For the next four years he sang in Sweden: his first important engagement outside his native country was in 1935, when he sang Radames in *Aida* at the Vienna Staatsoper. In 1937 he appeared at Salzburg as Don Ottavio, sang at the Queen's Hall, London, and, two months later, made his adult début in the US, in Chicago, as the Duke of Mantua in *Rigoletto*. On November 24, 1938, he went to the Metropolitan Opera, New York, to sing Rodolfo in *La Bohème*: he was to appear there regularly for the rest of his life. In 1939 he made his début at Covent Garden as Manrico in *Il Trovatore*, receiving glowing notices. For the next 20 years, Björling's performances were among the highlights of the seasons at all the great operatic centres, and when he returned to Covent Garden in March 1960 — a few months before his death in Stockholm on September 9, 1960 — his powers were undiminished. He undoubtedly had one of the most beautiful tenor voices of this century and his immaculate phrasing and unfailing musicianship are fortunately preserved in his many recordings.

KIM BORG
Bass

Born in Helsinki on August 7, 1919, Borg first worked as an engineer. He studied singing at the Sibelius Academy, Helsinki, with Heikki Teittinen and later in Copenhagen with Magnus Andersson and Stockholm with Adelaide von Skilondz. His stage début

was at Aarhus in 1951 and was quickly followed by appearances in Stockholm; he went to Glyndebourne in 1956 and made his début at the Metropolitan Opera, New York, in 1959. He has sung extensively in Eastern Europe and the Scandinavian countries, as well as in Salzburg and Hamburg. His dark-timbred and voluminous voice was ideal for such parts as Sarastro in *Die Zauberflöte* and Osmin in *Die Entführung aus dem Serail*, but he later turned to baritone parts. He has made recordings of operas and oratorios, including the *Requiems* of both Verdi and Mozart.

JAMES BOWMAN
Counter-tenor

Born in Oxford on November 6, 1941, Bowman began his musical career as a boy chorister at Ely Cathedral, where he was trained by Michael Howard. In 1967 he made his début with the English Opera Group, singing the role of Oberon in Britten's *A Midsummer Night's Dream* at the Aldeburgh Festival with great success. Later the production was taken to America; Bowman went with the company and made his American début in San Francisco, following this with visits to Montreal, Paris and Brussels. His counter-tenor voice is particularly suited to early operatic works and he has distinguished himself in the operas of Handel: he made his Sadler's Wells début in 1970 in *Semele* and in the same year sang Endymion in *La Calisto* by Cavalli at Glyndebourne. He followed this by singing in Monteverdi's *L'Incoronazione di Poppea* at the Nederlandse Opera in 1971, and made his Covent Garden début in 1972 in *Taverner* by Peter Maxwell Davies. His full-toned counter-tenor has great carrying power and this, allied to his acting ability and general musicianship, has ensured him well-deserved international success.

GRACE BUMBRY
Contralto

Born in St Louis, Mo., on January 4, 1937, Bumbry studied at Boston University, Northwestern University and the Music Academy of the West at Santa Barbara, where her teacher was Lotte Lehmann. Later she was coached in the French repertoire by Pierre Barnac in Paris. She made her début in 1958 in Basel, after being the joint winner of the Metropolitan Opera Auditions earlier in the year, and sang at the Paris Opéra in 1960 in the title role of *Carmen* and as Amneris in *Aida*. In 1961 she sang Venus in *Tannhäuser* at Bayreuth — the first black singer to appear there. Her début at Covent Garden was in 1963 as Princess Eboli in *Don Carlos*, and in 1964 and 1965 she visited Salzburg, where her Lady Macbeth was outstandingly successful. She reached the Metropolitan Opera, New York, in 1965, again making her début as Princess Eboli, and shortly afterwards began singing soprano roles, including Salome, which she sang at Covent Garden in 1970, and Tosca, at the Metropolitan Opera in 1971. More recently she shared the title role in *Norma* with Montserrat Caballé, having previously sung Adalgisa to Caballé's Norma. She has a large voice of extensive range and has sung with success all over the world; she has also made a number of interesting recordings.

STUART BURROWS
Tenor

Born in Cilfynydd, Wales, in 1933, Burrows worked for a time as a school teacher, but when he won

first prize in the National Eisteddfod in 1959, he decided to become a professional singer. His début was with the Welsh National Opera in 1963, when he sang the role of Ismaele in *Nabucco* in Cardiff, and he was heard at Covent Garden for the first time in 1967 as the First Prisoner in *Fidelio*, although later in the same season he was entrusted with more important parts. He first appeared in the US in 1967, when he sang Tamino in *Die Zauberflöte* in San Francisco. He made his début at the Metropolitan Opera, New York, in 1969, since when he has sung there every season. He sang at the Paris Opéra in 1965, as Don Ottavio in *Don Giovanni*, and appears regularly at the Salzburg Festivals and at the Vienna Staatsoper. He is particularly admirable in Mozart roles and in the lyric tenor roles of Donizetti, Verdi and Puccini. His voice is a fine tenor of beautiful quality and his smooth and polished *legato* singing has been much admired. He has already made a number of recordings of complete operas and also of solo recitals.

MONTSERRAT CABALLÉ
Soprano

Born in Barcelona on April 12, 1933, Caballé studied at the Conservatoire there. Her first engagement was at the Municipal Theatre in Basel, where she made her début in 1957, followed by a period in Bremen, beginning in 1960, during which time she also sang as a guest artist at many opera houses, including La Scala, Milan, where she appeared as a Flower Maiden in *Parsifal*. She made her first professional appearance in Barcelona in 1963, but it was not until her sensational début in a concert performance of Donizetti's *Lucrezia Borgia*, for the American Opera Society in New York in April 1965, that she achieved international recognition. In the same year she appeared as the Marschallin in *Der Rosenkavalier* and the Countess in *Le Nozze di Figaro* at Glyndebourne, and as Marguerite in *Faust* at the Metropolitan Opera, New York. Since then she has been acknowledged as one of the world's greatest sopranos, excelling both in the *bel canto* repertoire and in dramatic *coloratura* roles like

Violetta in *La Traviata*, in which she made her Covent Garden début in 1972. More recently she has added *verismo* roles like Tosca to her repertoire, but her forte undoubtedly lies in *bel canto* roles, where she is unsurpassed, her *pianissimo* singing in the upper register being particularly beautiful. She has made many recordings, including complete operas and arias from rarely performed works by Rossini, Bellini and Donizetti.

MARIA CALLAS
Soprano

Born in New York on December 4, 1923, Callas showed promise at an extremely early age: she was taken to Athens and, quite exceptionally, was accepted at the age of only 13 by the Athens Conservatoire, where she studied with the famous *coloratura* soprano Elvira de Hidalgo. She sang in a student performance of *Cavalleria Rusticana* in the role of Santuzza and made her professional début when she was 16, singing the role of Beatrice in *Boccaccio* at the Athens opera, where she appeared until 1944. After the war she returned to America, but was unable to find engagements; it was not until 1947, when she sang the title role in *La Gioconda* at the arena in Verona, that she received wide recognition. She appeared as Norma at Covent Garden in 1952, having previously made her début at La Scala, Milan, in 1951, and quickly established herself as the leading soprano of her generation, particularly in the early 19th century operas of Bellini and Donizetti. She sang in Chicago in 1954 and finally reached the Metropolitan Opera, New York, in the 1956 season, singing in *Norma*, *Tosca* and *Lucia di Lammermoor*. Thereafter, her career was truly international, for she combined singing of great virtuosity with dramatic talent of a very high order. She was indeed the greatest singing actress of her time, and was responsible for the revival of interest in dramatic *coloratura* roles which had long been neglected and into which she infused new life. She died in Paris in 1977.

PIERO CAPPUCCILLI
Baritone

Born in Trieste on November 9, 1929, Cappuccilli made his début at the Teatro Nuovo, Milan, in 1957 as Tonio in *I Pagliacci*. After singing for some years in opera houses throughout Italy, he was engaged to sing at the Metropolitan Opera House, New York, where he first appeared in 1960 as Giorgio Germont in *La Traviata*. He returned to Milan to sing at La Scala, as Enrico in *Lucia di Lammermoor*, in 1964. In 1967 he made a successful Covent Garden début as Giorgio Germont, and later returned to sing in *Otello* and *Un Ballo in Maschera*. He has appeared at Salzburg and in all the leading opera houses of Western Europe and is now considered to be one of the foremost Italian baritones of the day. His recordings include roles in many operas. His voice is a fine, rather dark-timbred baritone of considerable power and extended range, and he is particularly at home in the great Verdian baritone roles.

JOSÉ CARRERAS
Tenor

Born in Barcelona in 1946, Carreras began singing at a very early age: before his voice broke he sang the boy's part in Falla's *El Retablo de Maese Pedro*, with José Iturbi as conductor, in the Teatro Liceo, Barcelona. After his voice broke, he continued to study in his native city. He made his début in 1970 as Gennaro in Donizetti's *Lucrezia*

Borgia, again at the Liceo, and later in the same season sang the part of Flavio in *Norma*, with Montserrat Caballé in the title role: she was highly impressed by his singing and did all she could to help the young tenor. One year later he came to London to sing in a concert performance of *Maria Stuarda*, again with Caballé, and made a most successful début. He next visited the United States, first appearing with the New York City Opera as Pinkerton in *Madama Butterfly* and also singing in *Lucia di Lammermoor*, *La Bohème*, *La Traviata* and *Rigoletto* in the 1971-72 season. In 1973 he was in San Francisco for a highly acclaimed Rodolfo in *La Bohème*, and then made his first appearance at the Teatro Colón, Buenos Aires, as Alfredo in *La Traviata*, before going on to the Metropolitan Opera House, New York, to make his début as Cavaradossi in *Tosca*. His Covent Garden début was in 1974, as Alfredo, and since then he has been a regular visitor, singing in operas by Verdi, Puccini and Donizetti. He has also sung at the Salzburg Festival, at La Scala, Milan, and other great operatic centres, and is already regarded as one of the foremost tenors of his day. His voice is a superbly resonant lyric tenor which he uses with great taste; his fine breath control and phrasing are evidence of his excellent training. His striking appearance and his dramatic gifts combine to make him an operatic singer of quite exceptional merit. He has already made many fine recordings.

LISA DELLA CASA
Soprano

Born on February 2, 1919, near Berne, Lisa della Casa made her début as Cio-Cio-San in *Madama Butterfly* in 1941 in Solothurn-Biel. She was a permanent member of the Stadttheater Zürich, from 1943 until 1947, while making many guest appearances at leading operatic centres. After 1947 she became a regular member of the Vienna Staatsoper and the Bavarian Staatsoper in Munich. She made her Glyndebourne début in 1951 as the Countess in *Le Nozze di Figaro*, sang Eva in *Die Meistersinger* at Bayreuth the following year, and appeared at Covent

Garden with the Bavarian Opera Company in 1953, appearing first in the title role in *Arabella*. She also sang at the Metropolitan Opera, New York, in the season of 1953-4. Her greatest successes have been in operas by Mozart and Richard Strauss, where her beautiful lyric soprano voice and her immaculate technique have earned her an enviable reputation among the greatest artists of her generation. Her smoothly-modulated *legato* singing has made her performances of *lieder* quite memorable, and her singing of such roles as Arabella and the Countess in *Capriccio* has never been surpassed.

MARIA CHIARA
Soprano

Born in Oderzo near Venice on November 24, 1939, Chiara studied singing in Venice at the Conservatorio Benedetto Marcello with Maria Carbone. She made her début in Venice as Desdemona in *Otello* in 1965 opposite Mario del Monaco, during a Festival production in the Doge's Palace. After a North American début in Toronto in 1966, as Violetta in *La Traviata*, she sang as guest artist in the leading operatic centres of Europe. She made a highly successful appearance as Liu in *Turandot* in 1969 in the Arena at Verona, and in 1972 finally reached La Scala, Milan, where she made her début as Micaela in *Carmen*. In 1973 she went to Covent Garden to sing the role of Liu once more, and shortly afterwards appeared at the Chicago Opera House, as Manon in Puccini's *Manon Lescaut*, and at the Metropolitan Opera, New York, where she made her first appearance in the role of Violetta in *La Traviata*. She returned to Covent Garden in 1978 and was highly praised for her sensitive singing as Desdemona in *Otello*, with Carlo Cossutta in the title role. Her voice is a lyric soprano of beautiful quality, which she uses with great skill, and her musical phrasing and fine *legato* singing have been widely acclaimed. Chiara is now in great demand at all the leading opera houses.

BORIS CHRISTOFF
Bass

Born on May 18, 1918, in Plovdiv, Bulgaria, Christoff originally intended to be a lawyer. While singing in the Gussla Choir, Sofia, he was heard by King Boris, who was so impressed that he arranged for Christoff to go on a scholarship to Milan to study with Riccardo Stracciari. He also studied in Salzburg, and in 1946 made his début in Rome as Colline in *La Bohème*. His fame soon spread: he made his Covent Garden début on November 19, 1949, in the title role in *Boris Godunov*, having already appeared as Varlaam and Pimen in the same opera at La Scala, Milan, where he sang the title role later in 1949 to a tumultuous reception. He first sang the role of King Philip II of Spain in *Don Carlos*, which was to become one of his greatest successes, in Florence in 1950. He was invited to sing in the US in the same year, but visa difficulties kept him away until 1956, when he sang Boris in San Francisco. Since then he has been acknowledged as one of the truly great singing actors of the post-war period. He returned to Covent Garden early in 1979 to sing in *Don Carlos* and the critics were warm in their praise of the veteran artist. His voice is a resonant, dark-coloured *basso cantante*; even after 33 years on the operatic stage it still retains much of its original beauty. He has made many recordings of Russian and Italian operas, and also of Russian songs, and these convey much of the personal magnetism which has made his performances so memorable.

FRANCO CORELLI
Tenor

Born in Ancona on April 8, 1923, Corelli considered a civil service appointment before deciding to make singing his career. He studied first in Pesaro and afterwards in Milan, making his début in 1951 in Spoleto, as Don José in *Carmen*. For the next two or three years he sang in the smaller Italian opera houses, but his remarkable heroic tenor voice soon brought him to the notice of the leading impresarios: he sang at La Scala, Milan, for the first time in 1954, as Licinio in *La Vestale*. He made a very successful Covent Garden début in 1957, as Cavaradossi in *Tosca*, and became very popular at the Metropolitan Opera, New York, where he first sang in 1961 as Manrico in *Il Trovatore*, a role which he repeated at the Salzburg Festival a year later. From that time onwards his career was international. His voice in its prime had a splendid heroic ring and his personal appearance and stage bearing were fully in keeping with his vocal qualities. He has made a number of fine recordings in such roles as Calaf in *Turandot*, in which he was unsurpassed.

FERNANDO CORENA
Bass

Born in Geneva on December 22, 1916, Corena was the child of a Turkish father and Italian mother. He studied theology for a time, but his voice was then heard by Vittorio Gui, who encouraged him to take up singing as a career. He studied with Enrico Romani in Milan and made his début in 1947 in Trieste, as Varlaam in *Boris Godunov*. He sang for some years in Italian opera houses and in 1953 appeared with great success at the Edinburgh Festival in the title role in Verdi's *Falstaff*. He travelled to the US in the same year and made his début at the Metropolitan Opera, New York, in the 1953-54 season, being quickly acknowledged as a superb *buffo* artist and the legitimate successor to Salvatore Baccaloni. Since then he has given more than 350 performances at the Metropolitan Opera and has also made numerous guest appearances in other theatres, including a début at Covent Garden as Dr Bartolo in *Il Barbiere di Siviglia* in 1960. He sang at the Salzburg Festival as Osmin in *Die Entführung aus dem Serail*, but it is above all as a *buffo* artist that he will be remembered. His resonant and flexible bass voice, fine diction and talent for comedy have made him an operatic performer of distinction. He has made many records of his greatest roles, particularly of the Rossini operas.

FIORENZA COSSOTTO
Mezzo-soprano

Born near Turin on April 22, 1935, Cossotto studied at the Turin Conservatoire. She went to La Scala, Milan, as a student and for a time sang small roles there. She also made guest appearances abroad, and in 1958 sang Maddalena in *Rigoletto* at the Vienna Staatsoper, following this with a Preziosilla in *La Forza del Destino* in 1959 at Verona. In the same year she made her Covent Garden début, singing the role of Neris in *Médée*. However her major breakthrough came when she sang at La Scala in 1962, appearing as Leonora in *La Favorita* and scoring an immediate triumph. She went to the Metropolitan Opera, New York, in 1968, appearing first as Amneris in *Aida*, and since then her career has been truly international. She has a rich mezzo-soprano voice of considerable power and extended range and is a fine dramatic artist.

CARLO COSSUTTA
Tenor

Born in Trieste on May 8, 1932, Cossutta went with his family to Argentina, where he studied singing, making his début in one of the smaller opera houses there in 1956 as Alfredo in *La Traviata*. Two years later he appeared at the Teatro Colón, Buenos Aires, as Cassio in *Otello*. Shortly afterwards he returned to Europe, appearing at Covent Garden for the first time in 1964, as the Duke of Mantua in *Rigoletto*, and thereafter singing there in more than 100 performances. He has appeared at almost all the leading operatic centres, including La Scala, Milan, the Arena in Verona, the Vienna Staatsoper and the Paris Opéra. He made his début at the Metropolitan Opera, New York, in 1973 as Pollione in *Norma* and in 1974 went to Moscow with the La Scala company to appear as Radames in *Aida*. He is justly celebrated for his performances in the title role of Verdi's *Otello*, for which his powerful *tenore robusto* is admirably suited. He has recently recorded this role with Sir Georg Solti as conductor and has also sung the tenor solos in Verdi's *Requiem* under the baton of Herbert von Karajan.

ILEANA COTRUBAS
Soprano

Born in Galatà, Romania, on June 9, 1939, Cotrubas studied in Bucharest and Vienna. She made her début in Bucharest as Yniold in *Pelléas et Mélisande* in 1964, and in 1968 signed a three-year contract with the Frankfurt Opera also singing at the Salzburg Festival in the same year. Her first appearance in England was as Mélisande at Glyndebourne in 1969 and she returned there to sing Pamina in *Die Zauberflöte*, Susanna in *Le Nozze di Figaro* and the title role in *La Calisto*. In 1970 she sang in Berlin and at the Vienna Staatsoper, where she is now a permanent member. Her Covent Garden début was in 1971 as Tatyana in *Eugene Onegin*, since when she has sung many roles there, including Violetta in *La Traviata*, Gilda in *Rigoletto* and Adina in *L'Elisir d'amore*. Her début at La Scala, Milan, was in 1975, as a last-minute replacement for Mirella Freni in the role of Mimi in *La Bohème*, and she visited the US with the La Scala company in 1976. Her initial role at the Metropolitan Opera in 1977

was again Mimi, and she repeated this in San Francisco in 1978. She won universal approval for her Norina in *Don Pasquale* when it was revived at Covent Garden in 1979. Ileana Cotrubas has a lyric soprano voice of extended range and fine quality and her *coloratura* singing is notable for its neatness and accuracy.

RÉGINE CRESPIN
Soprano

Régine Crespin was born on March 23, 1927, in Marseilles. Realising that she had a most promising voice, she went to Paris to study with Suzanne Cesbron Viseur and, later, with Georges Jouatte. Her début, in 1950 at Mulhouse, was as Elsa in *Lohengrin*. In 1951 she went to Paris and first appeared at the Opéra Comique in *Tosca*, following this with a much-praised Elsa at the Opéra. This was the beginning of a great international career, and although she remained a principal dramatic soprano at the Opéra she made many guest appearances in the major operatic centres, including La Scala, Covent Garden and the Metropolitan Opera, New York, where she made her début in 1962 as the Marschallin in *Der Rosenkavalier*, a role which she had previously sung with conspicuous success at Glyndebourne. She has also appeared at Bayreuth as Kundry in *Parsifal* and has made many excellent recordings. Her voice is a true dramatic soprano of extensive range, ample power and warm colour, and she is also an accomplished actress.

MARIO DEL MONACO
Tenor

Born in Florence on July 27, 1915, Mario del Monaco studied for a short time in Rome, but was dissatisfied with his progress and decided to teach himself by listening to recordings of the great singers of the past. A period in the army hampered his early career, although he sang Turiddu in *Cavalleria Rusticana* at Pesaro in 1939. The end of the war furthered his rise to prominence: in 1946 he went to London with the San Carlo Opera Company, making his début at Covent Garden as Cavaradossi in *Tosca*. In the same year he was sensationally successful at the Verona Arena as Radames in *Aida*, and from that time onwards concentrated on the more robust tenor roles. He was one of the most popular and highly-paid artists at the Metropolitan Opera, New York, from 1951 to 1959; his handsome appearance and intensely dramatic singing made him a tremendous success. His voice was one of the finest robust tenors to be heard since the war, with a warm, almost baritonal quality in the lower register and ringing high notes of tremendous power. His Otello was justly celebrated and he was at his best in heroic parts: in more lyrical roles, the absence of any subtlety and the almost unrelieved *forte* with which he was inclined to sing made him less successful. He made many recordings, among which his *Otello* and *La Fanciulla del West* can be particularly recommended.

ANTON DERMOTA
Tenor

Born in Kropa (now Yugoslavia) on June 4, 1910, Dermota studied singing with Elisabeth Rado in Vienna. He made his début in 1936 at the Vienna Staatsoper as Don Ottavio in *Don Giovanni* and was immediately recognised as a most promising Mozart singer. He sang an admirable Lenski there in *Eugene Onegin* in 1937 and in 1938 sang at the Salzburg Festival, again as Don Ottavio. During his long career he has remained a permanent member of the Vienna company, but has also made many guest appearances in all the leading opera houses, including Covent Garden, where he sang Don Ottavio, Ferrando in *Così fan tutte* and Narraboth in Richard Strauss's *Salome* in 1947. His singing has always been remarkable for refinement of style and sound musicianship, and his many recordings, particularly of Mozart, are rightly held in high esteem. Upon his retirement from the stage he became a well-known teacher in Vienna.

GIUSEPPE DI STEFANO
Tenor

Born at Molta, near Catania, Sicily, on July 24, 1921, Giuseppe di Stefano studied in Milan with Luigi Montesanto. He made his début in 1946 at Reggio Emilia as Des Grieux in Puccini's *Manon Lescaut* and a year later sang in Rome at the Teatro dell'Opera, following this with his début at La Scala, Milan, in 1948. He went to the Metropolitan Opera, New York in 1948, appearing there for the first time as the Duke of Mantua in *Rigoletto*: his success was instantaneous and complete. He sang at the Metropolitan for the next few years, and also appeared all over the world in the lighter lyric roles in which he was unsurpassed. He made his Covent Garden début in 1961 as Cavaradossi in *Tosca*. In his prime, his voice was quite superb; but later, when he began to sing more dramatic roles, his voice began to deteriorate. His last appearances in London were with Maria Callas in 1973 when she returned to sing in concert, but by then his voice was only a shadow of what it had been. He made many excellent recordings while in his prime.

PLACIDO DOMINGO
Tenor

Born in Madrid on January 21, 1941, Domingo emigrated to Mexico with his parents, who were *zarzuela* singers, in 1950. He attended the Conservatoire in Mexico City, where he studied piano, singing and conducting, and made his operatic début as a baritone in *I Pagliacci*. He very soon realised that his voice was changing to a tenor and made his first appearance as such with the Mexican National Opera in 1961, as Alfredo in *La Traviata*. Other engagements soon followed: he sang later in 1961 as Lord Arthur Buckley in *Lucia di Lammermoor*, with Joan Sutherland in the title role, at the Dallas Civic Opera. Two years in Israel followed, as a member of the National Opera; while there he gained valuable experience and learned 12 new roles. In 1966 he was again in the United States to create the title role in Alberto Ginastera's *Don Rodrigo* at the New York City Opera, and in 1967 he sang in Hamburg, Vienna and Berlin. His début at the Metropolitan Opera, New York, was in 1968 as Maurizio in *Adriana Lecouvreur*; he also sang as Calaf in *Turandot*. Appearances at La Scala, Milan, followed in 1969 and he made his début at Covent Garden in 1971 as Cavaradossi in *Tosca*. Since then he has been in constant demand all over the world: he has recently concentrated on heroic roles, including Canio in *I Pagliacci* and Dick Johnson in *La Fanciulla del West*. His voice combines a warm lower register with a powerful ringing top, and his convincing acting and fine phrasing allied to excellent diction have placed him in the forefront of contemporary tenors. He has made many excellent recordings.

GERAINT EVANS
Baritone

Born in Pontypridd, Wales, on February 16, 1922, Evans studied at the Guildhall School of Music, London, with Walter Hyde, in Hamburg with Theo Hermann, and in Geneva with Fernando Carpi. He made his début at Covent Garden in 1948, singing the Nightwatchman in *Die Meistersinger von Nürnberg*, and gradually developed into a fine operatic singer, scoring great successes as Figaro in *Le Nozze di Figaro* and in other leading roles. From 1950

onwards he sang at Glyndebourne in Mozart operas, with memorable performances as Papageno in *Die Zauberflöte* and Leporello in *Don Giovanni*. His successes abroad have been too numerous to mention in detail: he sang at La Scala, Milan, in 1960, in *Il Barbiere di Siviglia* and was an outstanding *Falstaff*, in which role he made his Metropolitan Opera début in 1963. He is also well known at the Salzburg Festivals and at the Vienna Staatsoper. Recently he has sung *buffo* roles like Dulcamara in *L'Elisir d'amore* and his fine sense of characterisation has made him brilliantly successful in such parts. His voice is a well-produced baritone of warm quality, and his fine diction and engaging stage presence have made him popular wherever he sings. He has recently taken up opera production and has also given master classes for students.

KATHLEEN FERRIER
Contralto

Born at Higher Walton, Lancashire, on April 22, 1912, Ferrier originally intended to be a pianist. She worked for a time as a telephonist, and it was not until she won a prize in a Music Festival at Carlisle in 1937 that she thought of a singing career. She studied first with Dr Hutchinson in Carlisle and then went to London, where her singing teacher was Roy Henderson. After working for some years as a concert artist with ever-increasing success, she made her operatic début at Glynde-bourne, singing the title role in the world première of Britten's *The Rape of Lucretia*, in 1946. The following year she returned to Glyndebourne to sing the role of Orfeo in Gluck's *Orfeo ed Euridice*. She repeated this role at Covent Garden in 1953, although she was seriously ill with cancer and could manage only two performances. She died on October 8, 1953. Although her appearances in opera were so few, she has left an indelible memory of great artistry. her voice was a true contralto of superlative quality which she produced with consummate technique; the radiance of her personality shone through everything she did. Fortunately in the few years of her professional career: the spiritual quality which she possessed in such full measure is apparent in all her work.

DIETRICH FISCHER-DIESKAU
Baritone

Born in Berlin on May 28, 1925, Fischer-Dieskau studied while very young with Georg Walter in Berlin. After serving in the army during World War II he returned to Berlin, where he resumed his studies, this time with Hermann Weissenborn. He made his operatic début in 1948 with the Berlin Staatsoper as Rodrigo, Marquis of Posa, in Verdi's *Don Carlos*. He was soon appearing at other theatres in Munich and Vienna and in 1954 went to Bayreuth to sing such roles as Wolfram in *Tannhäuser*, the Herald in *Lohengrin* and Amfortas in *Parsifal*. He was at Salzburg in 1957, and went to London, where he was already well known for his concert work, to sing at Covent Garden in 1965, making a tremendous impression as Mandryka in Richard Strauss's *Arabella*. He is an extremely versatile operatic artist and has sung leading roles in German, French, Italian and Russian operas, being particularly admired in Mozart. His fine baritone voice and superb technical command, together with his outstanding musicianship, have made him one of the greatest singers of the era, and he is equally distinguished as a *lieder* singer and a concert artist. He has recorded prolifically in all kinds of vocal music.

KIRSTEN FLAGSTAD
Soprano

Born on July 12, 1895, in Hamar, Norway, Flagstad made her début as Nuri in *Tiefland* when she was only 18, but did not attract much notice. After further study she appeared for some years in operetta, and also sang such roles as Aida and Tosca. She was engaged for Bayreuth in 1933 and again in 1934 and then made a sensational début at the Metropolitan Opera, New York, as Sieglinde in *Die Walküre* in 1935. This opened the way to a truly international career and Flagstad was soon acknowledged to be the greatest dramatic soprano of her generation. Her voice had a warmth and at the same time a brilliance which made her unique and she seemed tireless, able to sing the longest roles and remain fresh to the end. Apart from Wagnerian operas, she sang a magnificent Leonora in *Fidelio* at Salzburg in 1949-50, and a Dido at the Mermaid Theatre, London, in 1951. She retired officially in 1955, but retained much of her vocal power until her death, in Oslo on December 8, 1962.

MIRELLA FRENI
Soprano

Born in Modena on February 27, 1935, Freni made an early début in her home town in 1956 in the role of Micaela in *Carmen*. She married shortly afterwards and retired for a short time, but after the birth of a child she decided to resume her career after a further period of study. She won the first prize at the Concorso Vercelli in 1958 and was soon in great demand at the leading European opera houses. She appeared with great success at Glyndebourne as Zerlina in *Don Giovanni* in 1960, returning in 1962 to sing Susanna in *Le Nozze di Figaro* and Adina in *L'Elisir d'amore*, and in 1961 made her début at Covent Garden, singing Zerlina and Nanetta (*Falstaff*). One of her greatest triumphs was when she first sang at La Scala, Milan, in *La Bohème* in Zeffirelli's 1963 production, conducted by Herbert von Karajan. She made her Metropolitan Opera début in 1965 and is now at the height of her fame. Her voice is a very beautiful lyric soprano which she uses with consummate skill and she is a charming and vivacious actress. She has made many recordings and has also appeared in films and in a recent television production of *Madama Butterfly*, with Placido Domingo as Pinkerton and Herbert von Karajan conducting.

GOTTLOB FRICK
Bass

Born in Ölbronn, Germany, on July 28, 1906, Frick sang for a time in the chorus of the Stuttgart opera. His début as a soloist was in 1934 in Coburg, and from 1940 to 1950 he was a permanent member of the Dresden Opera, singing in guest performances in Berlin, Munich and Dresden. In 1950 he took up an engagement with the Berlin Staatsoper. He sang in the 1950-51 season at Covent Garden, making his début as Fafner in the *Ring* cycle with immense success. After 1953 he was based mainly in Munich and Vienna but continued to make many guest appearances. He created a highly favourable impression at the Metropolitan Opera, New York, in 1962. His splendid, resonant *basso profundo* was at its best in the Wagnerian music dramas, but from time to time he sang lighter roles. He recorded in the complete *Ring* cycle, conducted by Sir Georg Solti, as well as in many other operas.

NICOLAI GEDDA
Tenor

Born in Stockholm of Russian parentage on July 11, 1925, Gedda spent his youth in Leipzig, where his father sang professionally as a bass in the Russian Orthodox Church. At the age of nine he returned with his family to Sweden and later, when it was discovered that he had the makings of a fine tenor voice, he was taken to study with Carl Martin Öhmann. He made a very successful début in

Stockholm in 1952 in *Le Postillon de Longjumeau* and was immediately engaged for La Scala, Milan, where he sang in 1953 in the première of Orff's *Il Trionfo d'Afrodite*, conducted by Herbert von Karajan. A début at Covent Garden followed in 1954, when he sang the Duke of Mantua in *Rigoletto*, and he repeated his success at the Paris Opéra in the same year. In 1957 he was at the Metropolitan Opera, New York, and later that year sang at the Salzburg Festival. He has an enormous repertoire, ranging from modern operas like *Vanessa* by Samuel Barber to the established classics by Rossini and Verdi, and is particularly at home in the French repertoire. His singing is notable for consummate musicianship and great refinement of style, and he is also a most accomplished linguist. All his recordings of classical and modern operas can be recommended.

NICOLAI GHIAUROV
Bass

Born in Velingrad on September 13, 1939, Ghiaurov studied singing in Sofia and Moscow. He made his operatic début in Sofia in 1955 as Don Basilio in *Il Barbiere di Siviglia* and in 1958 appeared for the first time at the Bolshoi Theatre, Moscow, as Méphistophélès in *Faust*. In 1960 he went to La Scala, Milan, to sing the role of Varlaam in *Boris Godunov*, and sang in the Verdi *Requiem* in Salzburg in 1962. In the same year he made his Covent Garden début as Padre Guardiano in *La Forza del Destino* and made his first appearance in North America, in Chicago, again as Méphistophélès. He first sang at the Metropolitan Opera, New York, in 1965 and is now in constant demand at all leading opera houses. He has a wide repertoire, encompassing leading bass roles in many Russian, French and Italian operas. His intelligent use of his fine voice and his great dramatic ability have brought him to the forefront of contemporary basses, and he has recorded some of his greatest roles.

BENIAMINO GIGLI
Tenor

Born at Recanati on March 20, 1890, Gigli studied at the Accademia di Santa Cecilia in Rome, where his principal teachers were Antonio Cotogni and Enrico Rosati. He made his début at Rovigo in 1914 as Enzo in *La Gioconda*, but World War I limited his career to Italian theatres for a few years. He sang at La Scala as Faust in Boito's *Mefistofele* in 1918, and in 1920 sang the same role for his début at the Metropolitan Opera House, New York, where he was soon considered to be the legitimate successor to Caruso. Thereafter he sang all over the world, making his Covent Garden début in 1930 in the title role of *Andrea Chénier*. He died in Rome on November 30, 1957. Gigli was generally considered the most famous tenor of his age, for his voice was one of quite exceptional beauty, although his musical taste was sometimes criticised. His vocal control and his *mezza voce* singing were quite superb, and despite his lack of acting ability he was idolised wherever he sang. His many recordings do full justice to the golden quality of his magnificent voice.

TITO GOBBI
Baritone

Born in Bassana del Grappa, near Venice, on October 24, 1915, Gobbi thought for a time of becoming a lawyer. He then began to study voice with the tenor Giulio Crimi in Rome, and made his début in that city in 1938 as Giorgio Germont in *La Traviata*. In 1939 he scored his first great success in the same role at the Teatro dell'Opera, Rome. The war limited his singing activities to Italy: he sang much in Rome and other cities, making his début at La Scala, Milan, in 1942. With the end of hostilities he began his international career, making his first appearance at Covent Garden in 1950 as Belcore in *L'Elisir d'amore* and singing Ford in Verdi's *Falstaff* in the same season. In Florence in 1951 he sang the title role in *Falstaff*: this was to become one of his most famous impersonations. He sang in San Francisco in 1948, in Chicago in 1954 and subsequently, and made his début at the Metropolitan Opera, New York, as Scarpia in *Tosca* in 1953. His career took him to all the leading music centres of the world: he was undoubtedly the most famous Italian baritone of his era. His resonant, well-produced voice, his great ability as an actor, and his most intelligent approach to all his work, combined to make him a great singing actor. Although he has now retired as a singer, he is still actively engaged in producing operas and giving master classes. His autobiography has recently been published.

RITA GORR
Mezzo-soprano

Born in Ghent on February 18, 1926, Gorr studied first in her home town before going to Brussels. She made her début in Antwerp in 1949 as Fricka in the *Ring* cycle and then accepted an engagement at the Strasbourg Opera, where she stayed from 1949 to 1952. In the latter year she went to Paris and stayed at the Opéra there until 1957, when she resigned and accepted guest appearances in various European capitals. In 1957 she was engaged at Bayreuth, where she again made her début as Fricka, and in the following year she sang at La Scala, Milan, first as Santuzza in *Cavalleria Rusticana* and later as Kundry in *Parsifal*. She sang the role of Amneris in *Aida* at Covent Garden for her début in 1959 and two years later appeared at the Edinburgh Festival as Iphigénie in Gluck's *Iphigénie en Tauride*. In 1962 she joined the Metropolitan Opera Company, New York, and also sang as a guest at the Chicago Opera. She has a rich, powerful mezzo-soprano voice of wide range, enabling her to sing roles like Saint-Saëns' Dalila and Ortrud in *Lohengrin*, but also permitting her to cope with a soprano part like Santuzza. Her recordings, particularly some unusual items from the French repertoire, are of great interest.

HILDE GUEDEN
Soprano

Born in Vienna on September 15, 1917, Gueden studied singing at the Vienna Music Academy. She made her début in 1939 in Zürich, singing the role of Cherubino in *Le Nozze di Figaro*. She spent five years in Munich from 1941 and during this period made many guest appearances in Italy and also sang at the Salzburg Festival in 1946, where her Zerlina in *Don Giovanni* was widely acclaimed. In 1947 she became a member of the Vienna Staatsoper and in the same year made her début at Covent Garden with the Vienna Company, singing a superb Zerlina in a cast which included Elisabeth Schwarzkopf as Donna Elvira, Maria Cebotari as Donna Anna and Anton Dermota as Don Ottavio. Later in the season she sang an equally outstanding Cherubino. She made her Metropolitan Opera début in 1950 and became a regular member of the company in 1952, especially delighting audiences as Rosalinde in *Die Fledermaus*. Another great success was her appearance at Salzburg in 1954 as Zerbinetta in *Ariadne auf Naxos*, for although most often heard in light soprano roles, she was a fine *coloratura* singer and coped easily with the fiendish difficulties of the part. Her successes have indeed been world-wide. Apart from her finely-trained and beautiful soprano voice, she is an actress of great personal charm. Fortunately she has made many records, including some of her most celebrated roles.

HEATHER HARPER
Soprano

Born in Belfast on May 8, 1930, Harper studied pianoforte at Trinity College, London. Having realised, however, that she had an exceptional voice, she turned to singing as her principal study, and made her début in 1954 with the Oxford University Opera Club, singing the role of Verdi's Lady Macbeth. Following this she appeared in television productions, including the roles of Violetta in *La Traviata* in 1956 and Mimi in *La Bohème* in 1957. In the latter year she sang the First Lady in *Die Zauberflöte* at Glyndebourne. In 1962 she went to Covent Garden, where she sang the role of Helena in Britten's *Midsummer Night's Dream*, and followed this with an engagement at Bayreuth, appearing as Elsa in *Lohengrin* in 1967. She appeared in Buenos Aires in 1971 and in the same year created the role of Mrs Coyle in Britten's *Owen Wingrave* for BBC Television, repeating the role at Covent Garden in 1973. Her voice is a lyric soprano of most sympathetic quality and she has great power of *sostenuto* in the upper register, while her warm personality makes her particularly fine in character roles like that of Ellen Orford in *Peter Grimes*. She is also an accomplished concert artist and has sung in oratorio with great distinction.

MARILYN HORNE
Mezzo-soprano

Born in Bradford, Penn., on January 16, 1934, Horne was brought up in Los Angeles, where the family moved shortly after her birth, and received her early training at the hands of her father, a tenor. Later she won a scholarship to study at the University of Southern California and was trained by William Vennard. She made her début in Los Angeles as Hata in *The Bartered Bride* and soon afterwards, in 1954, her voice was used for the title role on the soundtrack of the film *Carmen Jones*. At about this time, Stravinsky heard her and encouraged her to go to Europe, where she sang at the Venice Festival and was later given her first contract with the Gelsenkirchen Municipal Opera Company. She returned to the US and sang very successfully in *Wozzeck* in San Francisco in 1960, appearing also in Chicago. She sang at Covent Garden in 1964, at La Scala in 1969, and at the Metropolitan Opera, New York, in 1970. She had an outstanding success in 1963 when she sang with Joan Sutherland in *Norma* and followed this with a concert performance of *Semiramide*: her recording of this work, with Joan Sutherland in the title role, reveals her as a really great Rossini singer. Her mezzo-soprano voice has a phenomenal range and her great facility in *coloratura* has enabled her to sing the *bravura* roles in operas by Rossini and Meyerbeer.

HANS HOTTER
Baritone

Born in Offenbach-am-Main on January 19, 1909, Hotter worked for some time as an organist and choirmaster. He then decided to study singing seriously and went to Matthaeus Roemer, a pupil of Jean de Reszke, for vocal training. He made his début as The Speaker in *Die Zauberflöte* at Opava in 1929, following this with engagements at the leading German opera houses, including Hamburg and Munich. He was first heard in London in 1947 with the company of the Vienna Staatsoper, singing the role of Count Almaviva in *Le Nozze di Figaro* and the title role in *Don Giovanni*. He sang at the Metropolitan Opera, New York, from 1950 to 1954, and from 1952 onwards was a dominating figure at Bayreuth, where his Wotan and his Dutchman in *Der Fliegende Holländer* were considered to be the finest since the days of Friedrich Schorr. He was an imposing figure on the stage, and his fine acting, coupled with his resonant and powerful bass-baritone voice, made him the leading exponent of the major Wagnerian baritone roles. He decided to concentrate upon opera production in the late 1960s, but continued for a time to give *lieder* recitals and undertake other concert work. He created two characters in operas by Richard Strauss—the Kommandant in *Friedenstag* and Olivier in *Capriccio*—and recorded his Wotan in the Solti recording of *Die Walküre*, although by that time (1959/60) he was a little past his vocal prime.

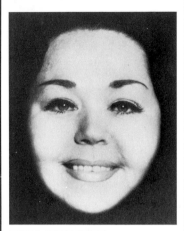

RITA HUNTER
Soprano

Born in Wallasey, England, on August 15, 1933, Hunter first studied singing locally, later moving to London and working for a while with Dame Eva Turner. She began singing with the Carl Rosa Opera Company in 1957 and in the following year was engaged at Sadler's Wells, where she sang small parts without immediately attracting much attention. In 1963 she sang the Third Norn in *Götterdämmerung* at Covent Garden and a year later sang the roles of Senta in Wagner's *Der Fliegende Holländer* and Odabella in Verdi's *Attila* at Sadler's Wells. In 1968 the company moved to the London Coliseum, and the larger theatre revealed her great gifts as a dramatic soprano. She sang the major Wagnerian dramatic soprano roles with distinction and as a result was engaged to sing Brünnhilde at the Metropolitan Opera, New York, in 1972. The following year she was brilliantly successful when the complete *Ring* cycle was given in English at the London Coliseum and also appeared as Leonora in *Il Trovatore*, Amelia in *Un Ballo in Maschera* and Elisabeth de Valois in *Don Carlos*. Her most recent part was the title role in *Turandot*, which she sang in 1979 for the Welsh National Opera. Her voice is a powerful dramatic soprano with a most exciting upper register of great brilliance.

GUNDULA JANOWITZ
Soprano

Born in Berlin on August 2, 1937, Janowitz studied singing in Graz with Hubert Thony and came to the notice of Herbert von Karajan, who engaged her for the Vienna Staatsoper, where she made her début in 1959 as Barbarina in *Le Nozze di Figaro*. She immediately attracted attention and in 1960 was engaged to sing at Bayreuth, where she appeared as a Flower Maiden in *Parsifal*. Since then she has sung in most of the major European opera houses. She sang at Glyndebourne in 1964 and three years later made her début at the Metropolitan Opera as Sieglinde in *Die Walküre*. Her voice is a lyric soprano of unusually beautiful timbre and her vocal technique and fine breath control make her *legato* singing unsurpassed in line and phrasing. She is particularly admired as a Mozart singer, and among her recordings is an outstandingly fine performance as Pamina in *Die Zauberflöte*.

SENA JURINAC
Soprano

Born in Travnik, Yugoslavia, on October 24, 1921, Jurinac studied at the Zagreb Conservatoire. She made her début in 1942 in Zagreb as Mimi in *La Bohème*, but the war interfered with her career and although engaged by the Vienna Staatsoper she was unable to appear there until 1945, when she

made a highly successful début as Cherubino in *Le Nozze di Figaro*. Shortly afterwards she appeared at Glyndebourne, where her performance of Mozart roles excited the enthusiasm of connoisseurs. Since then she has sung in all the leading operatic centres. Her voice is a particularly warm lyric soprano and her immaculate phrasing and intensely musical approach have made her a truly great artist. She has made many very fine recordings and has also had tremendous success as a concert singer.

KIRI TE KANAWA
Soprano

Born in Gisborne, New Zealand, on March 6, 1944, Kiri Te Kanawa studied in England at the London Opera Centre and later with Vera Rosza. She first sang with the Chelsea Opera Group and then joined the Covent Garden Company in 1970, singing small parts in *Parsifal* and *Boris Godunov*. Her début in a leading role was at Covent Garden in 1971, when she sang the role of the Countess Almaviva in *Le Nozze di Figaro*, and she followed this with appearances as Amelia in *Simon Boccanegra*, Donna Elvira in *Don Giovanni*, Micaela in *Carmen*, Desdemona in *Otello* and Marguerite in *Faust*. She sang at Glyndebourne in 1973, again as Countess Almaviva, and a year later made her début at the Metropolitan Opera, New York, as Desdemona. In 1975 she was at the Paris Opéra, singing Donna Elvira, and since then her career has been international. She has recently added the role of Mimi in *La Bohème* to her repertoire and won unstinted praise from many critics when she sang it at Covent Garden in 1976. Her voice is a lyric soprano of great purity and considerable power and her beautiful *legato* singing, fine vocal control, and graceful stage bearing have made her one of the leading exponents of such roles as Countess Almaviva, Desdemona and Micaela. She recently recorded the latter role in a performance which included Placido Domingo as Don José and Tatiana Troyanos as Carmen.

ALEXANDER KIPNIS
Bass

Born in Zhitomir, Ukraine, on February 1, 1891, Kipnis studied music in Warsaw, where he graduated as a military bandmaster. Later he turned to singing and studied in Berlin with Grenzebach. He made his operatic début in Hamburg in 1915: although, as a Russian, he was classed as an enemy alien, he was allowed to continue his career. In 1916 he joined the opera company at Wiesbaden, where he stayed until the end of the war, and then went to Berlin, where he sang for seven seasons. He joined the Chicago Opera Company in 1923 and first sang in England at Covent Garden, as Marcel in *Les Huguenots*, in 1927. He was Sarastro in the 1936 production of *Die Zauberflöte* at Glyndebourne and made a rather belated début at the Metropolitan Opera, New York, in 1939. He sang at all the world's great opera houses and his repertoire was unusually wide, embracing Wagnerian roles, Mozart operas, and even such parts as Nilakantha in Delibes' *Lakmé* and Arkel in Debussy's *Pelléas et Mélisande*, as well as the most celebrated operas of his native Russia. His warm, rich voice and his great nobility of style made him unique in his day. After leaving Hitler's Germany, he became a naturalised American citizen and later taught singing at the New York College of Music.

ALFREDO KRAUS
Tenor

Born in Las Palmas, Canary Islands, in 1927, Kraus studied in Barcelona and Milan. He made his début in *Rigoletto* as the Duke of Mantua at the Cairo Opera House in 1956 and first appeared in London at the Stoll Theatre with a visiting Italian company as Alfredo in *La Traviata*. He made his Covent Garden début in 1959 as Edgardo in *Lucia di Lammermoor* and was first heard at La Scala, Milan, in the following year as Elvino in *La Sonnambula*. He was then engaged to sing with the Chicago Lyric Opera Company as Nemorino in *L'Elisir d'amore*. His début at the Metropolitan Opera, New York, was in 1965 as the Duke of Mantua and in the same year he sang Don Ottavio in *Don Giovanni* at the Salzburg Festival, with Herbert von Karajan conducting. His fine lyrical tenor voice has been beautifully trained and his singing is always polished and elegant in style. His many recordings include an excellent *Rigoletto* conducted by Sir Georg Solti and a *Lucrezia Borgia* with Montserrat Caballé in the title role.

EVELYN LEAR
Soprano

Born in New York in 1931, Lear studied piano and French horn before devoting herself to singing and training at the Juilliard School of Music, New York. After making an early début as a concert singer in the US, she went to Germany and continued her training in Berlin. In 1959 she was engaged to sing Richard Strauss's *Four Last Songs* at the Royal Festival Hall, London, and shortly afterwards made her first operatic appearance, as the Composer in *Ariadne auf Naxos* at the Berlin Staatsoper. From that time onward she was in much demand in Germany and also sang as guest artist at the Vienna Staatsoper, the Hofoper in Munich, the Salzburg Festivals and the San Francisco Opera. She made her début at the Metropolitan Opera, New York, in 1966 as Rosina in *Il Barbiere di Siviglia*, but it is above all as a Mozart singer that she is likely to be remembered, although she has appeared with success in the more recent works of Richard Strauss and in Berg's *Wozzeck*.

GEORGE LONDON
Bass

Born in Montreal on May 30, 1920, London moved to Los Angeles with his family and studied singing there. For a time he worked in musical comedy and toured with Mario Lanza and a soprano in a trio. His operatic début was made in 1949, as Amonasro in *Aida* with the Vienna Staatsoper. He appeared at Glyndebourne in 1950 in the role of Figaro in *Le Nozze di Figaro* and in 1951 began a long association with Bayreuth, where his principal roles were Amfortas in *Parsifal* and The Dutchman in *Der Fliegende Holländer*. He was first heard at the Metropolitan Opera, New York, in 1951 as Amonasro and also sang there in the title roles of *Don Giovanni* and *Boris Godunov*. He first appeared in London in 1954 at the Festival Hall, in *Don Giovanni* with the Vienna Staatsoper. In 1968 he became an administrator with the Center of Performing Arts, Washington, DC, and in 1971 went in a similar capacity to Los Angeles. His firm, well resonated bass-baritone voice and his unusual acting ability made him a great favourite in all leading musical centres.

PILAR LORENGAR
Soprano

Born in Saragossa in 1928, Lorengar, like Victoria de los Angeles, studied at the Conservatoire in Barcelona. Originally she sang as a mezzo-soprano and

made her first appearance as such in 1949. In 1951 she won first prize in a singing competition in Barcelona and thereafter found that she was happier in the soprano register, soon appearing as Violetta in *La Traviata* at Covent Garden in 1955. In 1957 she was a much-admired Pamina in *Die Zauberflöte* at Glyndebourne, returning for the two following seasons to sing the Countess in *Le Nozze di Figaro*. Her international career was now firmly established and she became a permanent member of the Berlin Staatsoper in 1959, also appearing at Salzburg in *Idomeneo* and *Die Zauberflöte* and making other guest appearances in most of the leading European opera houses. In 1966 she made her Metropolitan Opera début as Donna Elvira in *Don Giovanni*. Her lyric soprano voice has a gloriously vibrant quality and she is a talented actress.

CHRISTA LUDWIG
Mezzo-soprano

Born in Berlin on March 16, 1928, Ludwig received her early training from her mother and subsequently studied at the Music School in Frankfurt. It was at Frankfurt that she made her début as Orlofsky in *Die Fledermaus* in 1946; she remained with the Frankfurt company until 1952 and then sang in Darmstadt and Hanover before being taken on the roster of the Vienna Staatsoper in 1955. She sang as guest artist in many centres, including Salzburg, where she was enthusiastically received in 1956, first as Dorabella in *Così fan tutte* and later as Cherubino in *Le Nozze di Figaro* and Octavian in *Der Rosenkavalier*. She made her début at the Metropolitan Opera House, New York, in 1959, and since then has been heard in dramatic soprano roles as well as the mezzo-soprano parts which she originally sang. Her voice is, in fact, a combination of mezzo-soprano and dramatic soprano and her roles cover an enormous range, including Rosina in *Il Barbiere di Siviglia*, the title role in *Le Cenerentola*, Ortrud in *Lohengrin*, Amneris in *Aida* and Lady Macbeth, while her Leonora in *Fidelio* has been widely praised. Her many recordings are justly celebrated and include most of her best-known roles. She is also a most accomplished concert artist.

BENJAMIN LUXON
Baritone

Born in Redruth, Cornwall, on March 24, 1937, Luxon sang locally as a boy and then studied at the Guildhall School of Music, London. He joined the English Opera Group in 1963 and toured Russia with them, singing Sid in *Albert Herring* and Tarquinius in *The Rape of Lucretia*, making further tours of Canada and Australia with the same company. He sang the title role in *Owen Wingrave* when Britten's opera was first televised in 1970 and created the part on stage at Covent Garden in 1972, also singing in Peter Maxwell Davies' *Taverner*. He was first heard at Glyndebourne in the same year, singing the title role in Monteverdi's *Il Ritorno d'Ulisse*, and sang in Geneva as Cyrus in Handel's *Belshazzar*. He sang the title role in *Eugene Onegin* at Covent Garden in 1973 and repeated the role with the Glyndebourne Touring Company. Other parts in which he has distinguished himself are Count Almaviva in *Le Nozze de Figaro* at Glyndebourne and Rodrigo, Marquis of Posa, in *Don Carlos*, with the English National Opera. In addition to his operatic work he has appeared recently in a popular television series and has recorded an album of Wolf *Lieder* and made several records of Victorian ballads and duets with Robert Tear. His voice is a high baritone of sympathetic quality; he is an actor of ability and in every way a most versatile artist.

EDITH MATHIS
Soprano

Born in Lucerne on February 11, 1938, Mathis studied at the Conservatoire in her home town, making her début there as the Second Boy in *Die Zauberflöte* in 1956. She was a permanent member of the Cologne Opera from 1959 to 1963 and then moved to the Berlin Staatsoper. She was at Glyndebourne in 1962 to sing the role of Cherubino in *Le Nozze di Figaro*, returned in 1963 to sing the same role, and two years later appeared there as Sophie in *Der Rosenkavalier*. She has been frequently engaged to sing at the Salzburg and Munich Festivals. Her outstanding roles have included Susanna in *Le Nozze di Figaro*, Pamina in *Die Zauberflöte* and Mélisande in Debussy's *Pelléas et Mélisande*. She has a light soprano voice of unusually attractive timbre and is both a most accomplished musician and an actress of great ability. She has made many excellent recordings of operatic roles and *lieder*.

ROBERT MERRILL
Baritone

Born in Brooklyn on June 4, 1917, Merrill was trained by his mother and afterwards by Samuel Margolis in New York. He sang popular music for a short while, including broadcasts on Radio City Music Hall in 1943, and made his operatic début as Amonasro in *Aida* in Trenton, NJ, in 1944. In the following year he won a competition run by the Metropolitan Opera and as a result made his début there in 1945 as Giorgio Germont in *La Traviata*. When Rudolf Bing became general manager of the Metropolitan Opera in 1950, Merrill sang the role of Rodrigo, Marquis of Posa, in *Don Carlos* on the opening night, but he was dismissed in 1951 when his Hollywood filming commitments clashed with a Metropolitan Opera Company tour. Later he was reinstated and was chosen by Toscanini to sing the leading baritone roles in *La Traviata* and *Un Ballo in Maschera* when these were broadcast by the great conductor. He has had tremendous success in his guest appearances in Italy, singing in Milan and Venice, and also with an American company at the Odéon Theatre, Paris, but he is principally known for his work with the Metropolitan Opera Company, where he was regarded as the legitimate successor of Lawrence Tibbett and Leonard Warren. He is the possessor of a fine, resonant baritone voice with ringing top notes, and his technical control and diction are exemplary. He has made a number of recordings of his greatest operatic roles.

SHERRILL MILNES
Baritone

Born in Dourren Grove, Ill., on January 10, 1935, Milnes intended originally to be a music teacher and for a time sang in the Chicago Symphony Chorus. Then, finding that he was developing a voice 'worthy of a professional career', as he put it, he joined the Goldovsky Grand Opera Touring Company, remaining with them from 1959 to 1964. In 1964 he won the American Opera Auditions and was offered engagements in Italy, singing in *Il Barbiere di Siviglia*. In the meantime he made his début as Valentine in *Faust* at the New York City Opera, which in turn led to his going to the Metropolitan Opera, where he first appeared in 1965, again as Valentine, with Montserrat Caballé as Marguerite. In 1966 Tito Gobbi fell ill and Milnes was asked by Rudolf Bing to take over Gobbi's roles, which included five he had never sung before. His immediate success set the seal on his career: he became the leading baritone at the Metropolitan Opera House, the most recent in a long succession which included Tibbett, Warren, Merrill and MacNeil. European engagements soon followed: he made his British début in a concert performance of *La Gioconda* at Drury Lane in 1969, went on to the Vienna Staatsoper to appear in the title role of *Macbeth*, and returned to London to sing at Covent Garden in 1971 as Renato in *Un Ballo in Maschera*. He has since sung at Covent Garden in *La Forza del Destino*, *Il Trovatore* and *Macbeth*. Other important débuts were at the Paris Opéra in *Il Trovatore* in 1975, and Buenos Aires, where he sang at the Teatro Colón in *Rigoletto*. He has a powerful, warm baritone voice of extended range, is a first-class

musician, and has an imposing stage presence. He has taken part in many operatic recordings and in recitals of operatic arias and duets, and is now considered one of the finest of contemporary baritones.

YVONNE MINTON
Contralto

Born in Sydney, Australia, on December 4, 1938, Minton studied first at the Conservatoire in her native town. She then went to London and made her début at Covent Garden in 1965. At first she sang small parts, but her unusual talent quickly attracted attention and she was soon appearing in such roles as Octavian in *Der Rosenkavalier*, Dorabella in *Così fan tutte* and Sesto in *La Clemenza di Tito*. She was with the Cologne Opera in 1969 and in 1970 made her American début in Chicago as Octavian. In 1972 she went to the Israel festival, where she sang Dalila in *Samson et Dalila*. She chose Octavian for her first appearance at the Metropolitan Opera, New York, in 1973, and in 1974 was engaged at Bayreuth, where she appeared as Brangäne in *Tristan und Isolde*. She created the part of Thea in *The Knot Garden* by Michael Tippett at Covent Garden in 1970 and is now considered to be among the most promising contraltos or mezzo-sopranos of the present generation. Her voice has a beautifully warm timbre and she is a distinguished actress, equally at home in the classical operas of Mozart and in modern works.

MARTHA MÖDL
Soprano

Born in Nuremberg on March 22, 1912, Mödl did not begin serious vocal studies until she was 28,

when she attended the Conservatoire in her native town. She first appeared as Hänsel in *Hänsel und Gretel* at Remscheid in 1943 and was engaged as a contralto at the Düsseldorf Opera from 1945 to 1949. Gradually her voice extended upwards and she became a dramatic soprano; then, when she went to the Hamburg Opera in 1949, she began to sing soprano roles. She first appeared at Covent Garden in 1949 as Carmen, and in 1951 sang the role of Kundry in *Parsifal* at Bayreuth. She was engaged as a permanent member of the Vienna Staatsoper in 1952 and sang a highly impressive Leonora in *Fidelio* at the re-opening of the new opera house in Vienna in 1955. She combined a glorious dramatic soprano voice with considerable powers as an actress, and with the retirement of Flagstad in 1955 she was rivalled only by Birgit Nilsson in such roles as Brünnhilde and Isolde. She made many excellent recordings of the great dramatic soprano roles.

ANNA MOFFO
Soprano

Born in Wayne, Pa., on June 27, 1932, Moffo studied in Philadelphia, New York and Rome. She appeared on Italian television before her début in 1955 at the Rome Opera, which was followed by appearances in Naples, Milan and Vienna. In 1957 she sang Alice Ford in Falstaff at the Salzburg Opera, followed by her first appearance at the Metropolitan Opera, New York, as Violetta in *La Traviata*. She was enormously successful and was acclaimed also in Chicago and San Francisco. She made her début at Covent Garden in 1964 as Gilda in *Rigoletto* and since then has sung all over the world with continued success. Her voice is a soprano *leggiero* of lovely quality and extended range and her *coloratura* singing is remarkable for its effortless ease and fine control. She has made many excellent recordings, her Gilda in *Rigoletto* and the title role in *Luisa Miller* being especially noteworthy.

BIRGIT NILSSON
Soprano

Born near Karup, Sweden, on May 17, 1918, Nilsson studied singing in Stockholm with Joseph Hislop and joined the Swedish Royal Opera company. She first appeared in 1944, although her first major role, as Agathe in *Der Freischütz*, did not materialise until 1946. At this time she was singing lyric soprano roles, and in her first important overseas engagement, at Glyndebourne in 1951, she sang the role of Electra in *Idomeneo*, creating a sensation. She was at Bayreuth in 1954 to sing Elsa in *Lohengrin* and followed this with appearances in Munich, where her Brünnhilde was much admired. The same role served for her Covent Garden début in 1957. She sang the title role in Richard Strauss's *Salome* at La Scala, Milan, and appeared at the Metropolitan Opera, New York, as Isolde in 1959. Since then she has been acknowledged as the true successor to Kirsten Flagstad. Her voice is brilliant throughout its range and her *legato* singing is admirable, while she has a commanding stage presence. Apart from her Wagnerian roles, she has achieved tremendous success as Leonora in *Fidelio*, as Turandot, and as Salome. She has made excellent recordings of all her principal roles.

JESSYE NORMAN
Soprano

Born in Augusta, Ga., in 1935, Norman won awards as a student and then travelled to Europe, where she won first prize in a Bavarian Radio International Competition. She sang in Munich in 1968 and in 1969 became a member of the Berlin Staatsoper, where she made her début as Elisabeth in *Tannhäuser*. In 1971 she sang at the Maggio Musicale in Florence, where she was a striking Selika in Meyerbeer's

L'Africaine, and shortly afterwards went to La Scala to sing the title role in *Aida*. Her Covent Garden début was as Cassandre in *Les Troyens* by Berlioz. She is particularly at home in the French repertoire, which she studied in the US with Pierre Bernac, in addition to which her *lieder* singing, and her concert work generally, have been as distinguished as her operatic appearances. Her voice is a generous lyrico-dramatic soprano of wide range and she is now acknowledged everywhere as a particularly sensitive and intelligent artist.

ROLANDO PANERAI
Baritone

Born in Ciampi Bisenzio, near Florence, on October 17, 1924, Panerai studied first in Florence with Frazzi and subsequently in Milan with Armani and Giulia Tess. He made his début in *Mosé in Egitto* by Rossini at the Teatro San Carlo, Naples, in the 1947-48 season, and in 1951 went to La Scala, appearing with such success that he remained for many years one of the leading baritones there. He sang Figaro in *Il Barbiere di Siviglia* at Covent Garden in 1960, and has had a fine international career, appearing in Spain, where he was particularly successful in Barcelona, and also at the Festival in Aix-en-Provence. His voice is a well-produced, sympathetic, high baritone and he is an actor of distinction. He has made a number of recordings, including *I Pagliacci* and *Cavalleria Rusticana*, both with Maria Callas.

LUCIANO PAVAROTTI
Tenor

Born at Carpi near Modena, on October 12, 1935, Pavarotti, although he had a beautiful natural

voice, at first studied to be a teacher, and in fact taught for two years. He then decided to become a professional singer and studied with Arrigo Pola and Campogalliani. He made his début in Reggio Emilia in 1961 as Rodolfo in *La Bohème* and his success was immediate: engagements in leading Italian theatres soon followed. In 1963 he sang in Amsterdam, Vienna and Zürich, and in September of that year went to Covent Garden to sing Rodolfo. In 1964 he sang the role of Idamante in *Idomeneo* at Glyndebourne, and in 1965 made his North American début with Joan Sutherland in *Lucia di Lammermoor* in Miami, following this with a tour of Australia with the Sutherland-Williamson Company. He first appeared at La Scala, Milan, in 1966 in Bellini's *I Capuleti ed i Montecchi*, returning to the US in 1967 to sing Edgardo in *Lucia di Lammermoor* in San Francisco. In 1968 he made his début at the Metropolitan Opera, New York, as Rodolfo. His fine lyrical voice, with its powerful and extended upper register, and his musical approach to all his roles have placed him in the forefront of contemporary tenors and he has made many fine recordings of complete operas and solo recitals.

PETER PEARS
Tenor

Born in Farnham, Surrey, on June 22, 1910, Pears studied singing at the Royal College of Music, London, and also with Elena Gerhardt and Julius Gutmann. He joined the BBC Chorus and the chorus at Glyndebourne in 1938, and made his début as a soloist in *Les Contes d'Hoffmann* in 1942 at the Strand Theatre, London. He then joined the Sadler's Wells Company, appearing as Ferrando in *Così fan tutte*, the Duke of Mantua in *Rigoletto*, Vašek in *The Bartered Bride* and Tamino in *Die Zauberflöte*. On June 7, 1945, he created the title role in Britten's *Peter Grimes* and was immediately recognised as the unique interpreter of this difficult character. In the succeeding years he created leading roles in many operas by Britten and, apart from his work with the English Opera Group, gave guest performances all over Europe and in America. In addition to his operatic work he is noted as an artist of great

intelligence, who has always set himself immaculate standards as a *lieder* singer and recitalist. His highly individual tenor voice is under perfect control, enabling him to give full play to his intelligent and musical approach to everything he does. He has made many fine recordings, particularly of works by Britten, in many of which he is accompanied by the composer.

IVAN PETROV
Bass

Born in Irkutsk on February 29, 1920, Petrov went at the age of 16 to the Glazunov School of Music, Moscow, where he studied singing with Miniiev. He made his début with the Bolshoi Company in 1943: at first he was entrusted only with small parts, but very soon he was singing leading roles and was looked upon as the successor to Chaliapin. After World War II, he toured extensively in Western Europe and enjoyed a great personal triumph after his début at the Paris Opéra. In his own country he was honoured by the award of the Stalin Prize and the title 'People's Artist of the USSR'. He was considered the leading exponent of the great bass roles in Russian operas but was equally at home in such parts as Don Basilio in *Il Barbiere di Siviglia*. His rich, dark voice was typical of the best Russian basses and his striking appearance and great talent as an actor combined to make him the most popular Russian bass of his day. He made recordings for the Russian State Record Trust.

LUCIA POPP
Soprano

Born in Bratislava on November 12, 1939, Popp studied in her

native town and in Prague. Her first engagement was at the Theater an der Wien in 1963 and in the same year she was given a contract by the Vienna Staatsoper, where she has remained ever since. She has also made many guest appearances; she went to Covent Garden in 1966, appearing first as Oscar in *Un Ballo in Maschera* and then as Despina in *Così fan tutte*, Sophie in *Rosenkavalier* and Gilda in *Rigoletto*. In 1967 she went to the Metropolitan Opera, New York, to appear as the Queen of the Night in *Die Zauberflöte*, and on her return to Europe sang in most of the great musical centres. She is particularly popular in Germany and Austria, where her singing of most roles in the *coloratura* soprano repertoire has been much admired. She has also made many recordings, including the role of the Queen of the Night. Her voice is a very high soprano of fine quality and her flexible and agile singing is of unusual excellence.

HERMANN PREY
Baritone

Born in Berlin on July 11, 1929, Prey studied in Berlin with Gunther Baum and Harry Gottschalk. In 1952 he won a radio singing competition and later in the same year made his début in Wiesbaden. He then began an engagement with the Hamburg Opera and was soon singing as a guest in the principal German opera houses, where he was immensely popular, and also at the Vienna Staatsoper. His début in Bayreuth was as Wolfram in *Tannhäuser* in 1956; he made his début at the Metropolitan Opera, New York, in 1960, in the same role. He had previously made an extended tour of the US and was much admired there as a *lieder* singer. He first appeared at Covent Garden in 1973 as Figaro in *Il Barbiere di Siviglia* and has also sung with great success at La Scala, Milan, the Salzburg Festivals, where his Mozart roles are much appreciated, and in other centres throughout Europe. He has a particularly fine baritone voice which he uses with great polish and technical skill, and his diction is remarkable. He has made many fine recordings.

LEONTYNE PRICE
Soprano

Born in Laurel, Miss., on February 10, 1927, Price studied at the Juilliard School of Music, New York, and with Florence Page Kimball in the same city. After singing in concerts in 1951, she appeared in *Four Saints in Three Acts* by Virgil Thomson, but her operatic career really began when she toured Europe in *Porgy and Bess*, singing with her husband, the baritone William Warfield. Later, the same company returned to the US to continue the tour. Her performance in the title role of *Aida* won her acclaim throughout Italy in 1957 and 1958, including La Scala, Milan, and the Arena at Verona, and also in England at Covent Garden, where she first appeared in 1958. In the same year she went to the Vienna Staatsoper and became a protégé of Herbert von Karajan. She sang Donna Anna in *Don Giovanni* at the Salzburg Festival of 1960, and in 1961 made her début at the Metropolitan Opera, New York, as Leonora in *Il Trovatore*. She created the role of Cleopatra in Samuel Barber's *Antony and Cleopatra* when it had its world première at the opening of the new Metropolitan Opera House in the Lincoln Center, New York, in 1966. She is the possessor of a particularly warm lyric soprano voice which is beautifully trained and of extensive range and she is an intelligent and striking actress. Her many recordings include her highly acclaimed Aida, and her Leonora in *Il Trovatore*.

MARGARET PRICE
Soprano

Born in Blackwood, Wales, on April 13, 1941, Price studied

singing at the Trinity College of Music, London, and made an early début with the Welsh National Opera in 1961, as Cherubino in *Le Nozze di Figaro*. One year later she made an unexpected début at Covent Garden in the same role, replacing an indisposed Teresa Berganza. She joined the English Opera Group in 1967 and first sang at Glyndebourne in 1968 as Constanze in *Die Entführung aus dem Serail*. She is now accepted as one of the finest interpreters of the leading soprano roles in the Mozart operas and has sung them at Covent Garden and other major European opera houses. She appeared at Salzburg for the first time in 1975 as Constanze, and although she is especially associated with the works of Mozart she has also been highly successful in operas by Verdi, singing in Paris as Desdemona in *Otello* and as Amelia in *Simon Boccanegra*. Her voice is a warm lyric soprano with an even scale and extended compass and her singing is always beautifully phrased and intensely musical. She has made some fine recordings of operatic works and *lieder*.

RUGGERO RAIMONDI
Bass

Born on October 3, 1941, in Bologna, Raimondi studied in Rome, first with Teresa Pediconi and later with Maestro Piervenanzi, making his début as Colline in *La Bohème* at Spoleto in 1962. A little later he sang in Rome, taking the part of Procida in *I Vespri Siciliani*; this was followed by a series of engagements at the major Italian theatres. He appeared at the Wiesbaden Festival in 1965, as Roger in *Jérusalem* by Verdi, and sang the title role in *Don Giovanni* at Glyndebourne in 1969. He first appeared at La Scala, Milan, in 1970, again as Procida, and in the same year sang at the Metropolitan Opera, New York, as de Silva in *Ernani*. He went to the Royal Festival Hall, London, in 1968, to sing in a concert performance of *Lucrezia Borgia* and made his Covent Garden début in 1972 as Fiesco in *Simon Boccanegra*. He has a beautifully controlled, full-toned bass voice and his acting ability and fine presence have

brought him rapidly to the fore. He has made some excellent recordings, including a quite outstanding Philip II in *Don Carlos*.

REGINA RESNIK
Mezzo-soprano

Born in New York on August 30, 1922, Resnik studied in her native city with Rosalie Miller. Her début was in 1942 at the Brooklyn Academy of Music, with the New Opera Company, as Lady Macbeth, and in 1944 she sang at the Metropolitan Opera as Leonora in *Il Trovatore*. For the next ten years she sang leading soprano roles there, creating the role of Delilah in Bernard Rogers' *The Warrior* at its world première in 1945. Her European début was at Bayreuth in 1953, when she sang Sieglinde in *Die Walküre*. Two years later she changed to mezzosoprano and contralto roles, first appearing as a mezzo as Amneris in *Aida* at Cincinnati. She was a very successful Carmen at Covent Garden in 1957 and equally well-received when she appeared at the Salzburg Festival as Princess Eboli in *Don Carlos* in 1960. In 1961 she was again at Bayreuth, this time to sing Fricka in the *Ring* cycle, and she celebrated her 25th season at the Metropolitan Opera by singing the title role in *Carmen* in 1970. More recently she has turned to production. Her rich mezzosoprano or contralto voice is of considerable power, with an extended upper register, and she is a fine actress with a particularly powerful personality.

KARL RIDDERBUSCH
Bass

Born in Recklinghausen, Germany, in 1932, Ridderbusch decided to become an actor but, discovering

that he had an exceptional voice, studied singing at the Folkwang School, Essen. After completing his studies he sang in various German theatres, gaining valuable experience, and in 1965 joined the opera company in Düsseldorf. Two years later he made his début in Bayreuth, singing King Henry in *Lohengrin* and Fasolt in the *Ring* cycle; since then he has appeared there regularly. He went to Covent Garden in 1971 and was immediately recognised as one of the leading German basses of the day, making his début as Fasolt and thereafter appearing in other Wagnerian roles. He went to the Metropolitan Opera, New York, in 1967 and made a deep impression with his singing of Hunding in *Die Walküre*. He is the possessor of a rich bass voice of unusual range, enabling him to cope with the higher *tessitura* of parts like Hans Sachs in *Die Meistersinger von Nürnberg*, a role which he has sung at Bayreuth. He is now a popular figure in all leading opera houses.

ANNELIESE ROTHENBERGER
Soprano

Born in Mannheim on June 19, 1924, Rothenberger studied at the Academy of Music in her home town. She made an early début at Koblenz and then joined the Hamburg Opera Company, with which she stayed until 1956. While at Hamburg, she made guest appearances at the Edinburgh Festival of 1953 and, after 1956, went to Düsseldorf. Following a number of guest appearances with the Vienna Staatsoper, she became a regular member there in 1958. She first appeared at Salzburg in 1954, and in 1957 created there the part of Agnes in *Die Schule der Frauen*. In 1960 she sang at the Metropolitan Opera, New York, and in the same year made her début at La Scala, Milan. In 1959-60 she was at the Glyndebourne Festival to sing Sophie in *Der Rosenkavalier*. Her career has taken her all over the world to sing in opera and concert and also in operetta roles. She is a charming and vivacious actress with a delightful personality and a well-trained light soprano voice.

LEONIE RYSANEK
Soprano

Born in Vienna on November 14, 1926, Rysanek studied at the Vienna Academy of Music with Alfred Jerger and Rudolf Grossmann and made her début at Innsbruck, as Agathe in *Der Freischütz*, in 1949. She was engaged at Saarbrücken from 1950 to 1952 and then sang for two years in Munich. She first appeared at Bayreuth as Sieglinde in *Die Walküre* in 1951 and became a regular member of the Vienna Staatsoper from 1954. In 1953 she appeared in London with the Bavarian Staatsoper, returning in 1955, when her Sieglinde was particularly successful. She first sang at the Metropolitan Opera, New York, in 1955 and was acclaimed there in 1959, when she took over the role of Lady Macbeth from an indisposed Callas. While in New York she sang many *lyrico dramatic* roles, including Amelia in *Un Ballo in Maschera*, Leonora in *Fidelio* and the Empress in *Die Frau ohne Schatten*. She has a large voice, particularly brilliant in the upper register, and is an excellent actress. Besides her operatic career she has had universal success as a concert artist and has made many recordings.

SYLVIA SASS
Soprano

Born in Budapest, Sass studied there at the Franz Liszt Academy. On completion of her studies she was engaged in 1972 to undertake principal roles with the Budapest State Opera. In 1973 she won the

Sofia International Singing Competition and was also awarded the Grand Prix of the Bulgarian Musicians' Union. In her short career she has appeared at Covent Garden and at the Metropolitan Opera, New York, where she made her American début in 1977. She first appeared in the UK at the Edinburgh Festival in 1975 and sang in Verdi's *Requiem* at the Albert Hall, London, in the Promenade Season of 1978. She has a voice of radiant beauty, a true lyric soprano, and she has recently undertaken roles which demand great vocal stamina and superb technique, such as Lady Macbeth and Norma. She has made recordings of interesting recitals and is already enjoying a highly successful international career.

PETER SCHREIER
Tenor

Born in Meissen, on July 25, 1935, Schreier studied in Leipzig and Dresden. He made his official début in 1961 at the Dresden Opera and was engaged as a permanent member of the Berlin Staatsoper company in 1962. In the same year he also sang with the Hamburg Opera, travelling with the company to London for a season at Sadler's Wells. Other engagements followed, including guest appearances at the Teatro dell'Opera in Rome, the Salzburg Festival, the Teatro Colón, Buenos Aires, and La Scala, Milan; finally he was engaged for the Metropolitan Opera, New York, where he made his début in 1968. He has specialised in lyric tenor roles and in particular the operas of Mozart, but he has also appeared as Count Almaviva in *Il Barbiere di Siviglia* by Rossini and Jacquino in *Fidelio*. He has a most sympathetic lyric tenor voice with a finely focused upper register and he has wisely restricted himself so far to lighter roles, avoiding more heroic parts. In addition to his operatic work, Schreier is a most distinguished *lieder* singer, having recently recorded Wolf's *Spanisches Liederbuch* with the soprano Edith Mathis.

ELISABETH SCHWARZKOPF
Soprano

Born at Jarocin, near Poznan, on December 9, 1915, Schwarzkopf studied with Lulu Mysz-Gmeiner and with Maria Ivogün in Vienna, making her début in Berlin in 1938 as a Flower Maiden in *Parsifal*. In 1942 she was engaged by the Vienna Staatsoper, where she first appeared as Zerbinetta in *Ariadne auf Naxos*. She joined the Covent Garden Company in 1948, remaining there until 1952. For many years she was a great favourite at the Salzburg Festival, where she sang the Countess in *Le Nozze di Figaro* under the baton of Herbert von Karajan in 1948, repeating her success in the same year at La Scala, Milan. She created the role of Anne Trulove in the world première of *The Rake's Progress* by Stravinsky at the Teatro Fenice, Venice, in 1951, and first appeared in the US in San Francisco in 1955 as the Marschallin in *Der Rosenkavalier*. She chose the same role for her début at the Metropolitan Opera in 1964. Schwarzkopf has sung in all the principal musical centres of the world and has everywhere been acclaimed as one of the great post-war sopranos. Originally she sang *coloratura* roles, but by 1947 she had changed to the lyric soprano repertoire and it is as a lyric soprano that she will be chiefly remembered. Her Mozart singing has been especially praised and she has won general acclaim as a *lieder* singer. Her voice is a true soprano of exquisite quality and her training under two distinguished teachers gave her an enviable technique. She has made many excellent recordings, ranging from grand opera and operetta to *lieder*.

RENATA SCOTTO
Soprano

Born on February 24, 1933, in Savona, Scotto studied singing in Milan, where she made her début

at the Teatro Nazionale in 1953 as Violetta in *La Traviata*. Within a year she was singing at La Scala, where she first appeared as Walter in *La Wally* by Catalani. She sang with an Italian company at the Stoll Theatre, London, in 1957, making her début as Mimi in *La Bohème* and appearing also as Adina in *L'Elisir d'Amore*, Violetta, and Donna Elvira in *Don Giovanni* in the same season. She was immensely successful when she first appeared at the Edinburgh Festival, as a replacement for an indisposed Callas, as Amina in *La Sonnambula*, and appeared at Covent Garden in 1962, singing *coloratura* and lyric roles. She made her début at the Metropolitan Opera, New York in 1965, as Cio-Cio-San in *Madama Butterfly*, and more recently has begun to undertake rather heavier roles, including Elena in *I Vespri Siciliani* and Amelia in *Simon Boccanegra*. Her voice is a warm lyric soprano which she uses with great intelligence and excellent technical control. Her phrasing is immaculate and her *piano* singing has a soft radiance which she uses to great dramatic effect. Her *forte* high notes now tend to harden a little occasionally, but she is certainly one of the most interesting sopranos to be heard since the retirement of Callas.

BEVERLY SILLS
Soprano

Born in Brooklyn on May 25, 1929, Sills studied with the late Estelle Liebling from the age of nine. Even before that she had been a child performer in a weekly children's radio programme, but she did not make her official début until 1947, when she was 18. On that occasion she sang the role of Frasquita in *Carmen* in Philadelphia. In 1953 she sang in San Francisco, following this with some appearances with the New York City Opera, which she joined in 1957. She sang there in more than 60 operas, including the three soprano roles in *Les Contes d'Hoffmann*, Zerbinetta in *Ariadne*

auf Naxos, the title role in Massenet's *Manon*, Cleopatra in Handel's *Giulio Cesare in Egitto* and Philine in Thomas's *Mignon*, but it was not until her sensational success with the New York City Opera in *Lucia di Lammermoor* that she reached her zenith. She sang at La Scala, Milan, in Rossini's *L'Assedio di Corinto* in 1969 and returned there to sing Lucia in the following year. She made her Covent Garden dèbut, again as Lucia, in 1970, but strangely enough did not appear at the Metropolitan Opera, New York, until 1975, singing the role of Pamira in *L'Assedio di Corinto*. It is indeed in the *coloratura* roles of Rossini and Donizetti that she makes the greatest impression. Her voice is not a large one, but her light soprano is capable of extraordinary agility in *coloratura* and she moves well on the stage. Her many recordings include *Lucia di Lammermoor* and *Maria Stuarda*.

GIULIETTA SIMIONATO
Mezzo-soprano

Born in Forli on December 15, 1910, Simionato studied at Rovigo. In 1933 she won first prize in the Florence Bel Canto competition and for the next few years sang minor roles in various Italian opera houses. Her first leading part was that of the mother in Ildebrando Pizzetti's *L'Orseleo* at the Teatro Communale, Florence, in 1938. The next year she sang at La Scala, Milan, where she had a great success in 1942 as Rosina in *Il Barbiere di Siviglia*. Wartime restrictions confined her to appearances in Italy, and it was only after 1945 that she became internationally famous. She sang the role of Asteria in *Nerone* in 1948 in a performance conducted by Toscanini, having made a British début in 1947 as Cherubino in *Le Nozze di Figaro* at the Edinburgh Festival. She made her first appearance at Covent Garden in the Coronation Season of 1953, singing Adalgisa in *Norma*, Amneris in *Aida* and Azucena in *Il Trovatore*, and in the same year

made her début in the US as Charlotte in *Werther*. She went to the Metropolitan Opera, New York, in 1959, first appearing as Azucena, and following this with successes as Rosina, Santuzza in *Cavalleria Rusticana* and Dalila in *Samson et Dalila*. Her voice was a mezzo-soprano of unusual range: in 1962 she actually sang the lyric soprano role of Valentine in *Les Huguenots* at La Scala. Her warm, beautifully trained voice and her fine acting ability made her a great favourite until she retired in 1966. She made many recordings, including *coloratura* roles in Rossini's comic operas as well as more dramatic parts in which she was equally at home.

ELISABETH SÖDERSTRÖM
Soprano

Born in Stockholm on May 7, 1926, Söderström studied at the Royal Academy of Music in her native town. She made her début at the Drottningholm Court Theatre in 1947 in *Bastien und Bastienne* and in 1950 became a member of the Swedish Royal Opera Company. In 1955 she was engaged at Salzburg and two years later scored a great success at the Glyndebourne Festival, where she sang the role of the Composer in *Ariadne auf Naxos*. In 1959 she appeared at the Edinburgh Festival and also at the Metropolitan Opera, New York, where she made her début as Sophie in *Der Rosenkavalier*. Her first Covent Garden appearance was as Daisy Doodle in *Aniara* by the Swedish composer Karl-Birger Blomdahl, and she is now a great favourite in all the great operatic and musical centres. Her roles include Tatyana (*Onegin*), Marie (*Wozzeck*), Marguerite (*Faust*), Violetta (*La Traviata*), all three soprano parts in *Der Rosenkavalier*, Elisabeth in Henze's *Elegy for Young Lovers*, and The Governess in Britten's *The Turn of the Screw*. She is a fine musician and an excellent linguist and she uses her fresh lyric soprano voice with great charm.

FREDERICA VON STADE
Mezzo-soprano

Born in Somerville, NJ, on June 1, 1946, von Stade studied at the Mannes College of Music, New York. She entered the Metropolitan National Auditions in 1969 and was immediately engaged by Rudolf Bing to sing at the Metropolitan Opera House, where she made her début in 1970 as one of the Three Genii in *Die Zauberflöte*. For three years she remained with the company, gaining experience, and then began a series of guest appearances in many cities, including San Francisco and Paris. She was acclaimed as a major star in the operatic firmament when she returned to New York to sing Rosina in *Il Barbiere di Siviglia* at the Metropolitan Opera, and is now in great demand in Europe and America. She has recently made an interesting record of arias by Mozart and Rossini and obviously has a very bright future ahead of her.

JOAN SUTHERLAND
Soprano

Born in Sydney, Australia, on November 7, 1926, Sutherland studied first in her home town and then in London with Clive Carey. Her first roles were as a lyric soprano and she made her début at Covent Garden in 1952 as the First Lady in *Die Zauberflöte*. Thereafter she sang successfully in such roles as Agathe in *Der Freischütz*, Micaela in *Carmen*, Eva in *Die Meistersinger*, Gilda in *Rigoletto* and Desdemona in *Otello*, but it was not until her sensational appearance in the title role of *Lucia di Lammermoor* at Covent Garden, on February 17, 1959, that she reached her full potential. With the encouragement

and coaching of her husband, Richard Bonynge, her lyric soprano voice had acquired a facility in *coloratura* which captivated her audiences, and the production by Franco Zeffirelli was a brilliant success. She quickly conquered audiences world-wide and her enormous success in Bellini's *Beatrice di Tenda* and in her début role of Lucia at La Scala in 1961 earned her the title of 'La Stupenda'. She was by now in enormous demand at all the principal opera houses of the world and her first appearance at the Metropolitan Opera, New York, in November 1961 was met with almost unparalleled enthusiasm. She unites the warmth of the lyric soprano with the brilliance and range of the *coloratura* and for almost 20 years she has been virtually unrivalled in many of her roles. Her numerous recordings give an excellent account of the great singer: this is particularly true of her Lucia, which remains unequalled for sheer beauty of timbre and vocal virtuosity.

MARTTI TALVELA
Bass

Born in Hiitola, Finland, on February 4, 1935, Talvela was originally an elementary school-teacher, but studied singing in Lahti and later went to Stockholm, where his teacher was Carl Martin Öhmann. He progressed rapidly and made his operatic début in Stockholm as Sparafucile in *Rigoletto*. He appeared with the Royal Opera in Stockholm until 1962, when he was given a contract by the Berlin Staatsoper. He first sang at Bayreuth in 1962, as Titurel in *Parsifal*, and thereafter appeared there regularly. He sang Hunding in *Die Walküre*, with Herbert von Karajan conducting, at Salzburg in 1969, and appeared in the same year at the Metropolitan Opera, New York, as the Grand Inquisitor in *Don Carlos*. He has sung at Covent Garden since his début there in 1970, in such roles as Fasolt in *Das Rheingold* and Hunding, and has also appeared most successfully at La Scala, Milan, and other leading opera houses. His great height and his rich bass voice have combined to make him a dominating personality on the operatic stage. He now directs

and takes part in a festival every year at Savonlinna in Finland, and also appears as a guest artist in leading opera houses.

ROBERT TEAR
Tenor

Born in Barry, South Wales, on March 8, 1939, Tear sang as a boy in the choir of St Paul's Cathedral, London. After a period of singing in oratorio and concert, he made his operatic début in 1964 with the English Opera Group, as Peter Quint in Britten's *The Turn of the Screw*, and has since sung with distinction in many modern operas. He made his début at Covent Garden in 1970 as Dov, in the world première of Michael Tippett's *The Knot Garden*, and has sung in works ranging from the operas of Monteverdi to those of Britten and Tippett. His voice is a lyric tenor which he uses with great intelligence, and his wide-ranging ability and fine musicianship have made him much in demand for both opera and concert work.

RENATA TEBALDI
Soprano

Born in Pesaro on February 1, 1922, Tebaldi studied at the Conservatoire in Parma, and later privately with Carmen Melis. She made her début in Rovigo in 1944, as Elena in Boito's *Mefistofele*, and shortly afterwards was heard by Toscanini, who engaged her for the re-opening of La Scala, Milan, in 1946. From 1949 to 1955 she was one of the leading sopranos at La Scala and was the only possible rival in popularity to Maria Callas, although their repertoires were very different

and Tebaldi did not attempt the Bellini and Donizetti roles in which Callas was unique. She was most successful in *verismo* works, where her exquisite lyrico-dramatic voice was heard at its best. From 1950 she began a truly international career, singing Desdemona in *Otello* when the La Scala Company appeared at Covent Garden in 1950 and following this with appearances in San Francisco as Aida. She reached the Metropolitan Opera, New York, in 1955, again making her début as Desdemona, and for many years she appeared regularly there, as well as making guest appearances in all the leading operatic centres. Her supremely stylish singing and her dramatic gifts made her an almost ideal interpreter of the operas of Puccini and the later Verdi: in *Madama Butterfly*, she was said by many critics to be the finest exponent of the role of Cio-Cio-San since the days of Emmy Destinn. Fortunately, Tebaldi recorded this role and many others, including Desdemona and Aida, and these give a very fair idea of her singing at the height of her powers.

TATIANA TROYANOS
Mezzo-soprano

Born in New York of Greek parentage, Troyanos studied at the Juilliard School of Music. Upon leaving, she was engaged by the New York City Center Opera and stayed with them from 1963 to 1965. In the latter year she was engaged by the Hamburg Staatsoper, where she made her début as Preziosilla in *La Forza del Destino*. She made various guest appearances in other centres while with the Hamburg Company and was particularly successful when she sang the role of the Composer in *Ariadne auf Naxos* at the Aix-en-Provence Festival in 1966. In 1967 she made her début at the Metropolitan Opera, New York, as Baba the Turk in *The Rake's Progress* and in 1968 she sang Octavian in *Der Rosenkavalier* at Covent Garden. She created the part of Sister Jeanne in *The Devils of Loudun* by Krzysztof Penderecki in Hamburg in 1969. Troyanos is a fine musician, encompassing a wide variety of

roles, and has recorded one of her favourite parts—that of Carmen —with Placido Domingo as Don José. Her voice is a true mezzo-soprano of considerable power and she is an intelligent and striking actress.

SHIRLEY VERRETT
Mezzo-soprano

Born in New Orleans in 1933, Verrett studied singing in Los Angeles for a very short time before winning a scholarship to the Juilliard School of Music, New York. In 1957 she made her début as Lucretia in Britten's *The Rape of Lucretia* at a Festival in Yellow Springs and then, after some experience in lesser roles, came to the fore after her portrayal of Carmen at the Spoleto Festival of 1962. She sang in the USSR, notably in Moscow and Kiev with great success, again as Carmen, and chose the same role for her début at La Scala, Milan, in 1966. In the same year she sang Ulrica in *Un Ballo in Maschera* at Covent Garden and later appeared in other roles there. She began singing parts which are generally considered to be the prerogative of sopranos, including Selika in *L'Africaine*, and in these she was equally successful. Her voice is a luscious mezzo-soprano with an unusually brilliant head register and she is an accomplished actress. In addition to her operatic work she has had a distinguished concert career and has made many excellent recordings.

JON VICKERS
Tenor

Born in Prince Albert, Canada, on October 29, 1926, Vickers

studied with George Lambert at the Toronto Conservatoire. He sang for a time in oratorio and concert, making his operatic début as Don José in *Carmen* at the Stratford Festival, and then went to England, first singing at Covent Garden in 1957 as Riccardo in *Un Ballo in Maschera*. He was an immediate success and his popularity increased even more when he sang the part of Aeneas in *Les Troyens* by Berlioz. He went to Bayreuth in 1958 to sing Siegmund in *Die Walküre* and followed this with appearances in Vienna, Milan, San Francisco and other leading centres, finally making his début at the Metropolitan Opera, New York, as Canio in *I Pagliacci* in 1960. He is now recognised as one of the finest heroic tenors to be heard since the war. In 1974 he sang Herod in Richard Strauss's *Salome* and Pollione in *Norma* at the open air festival in the arena at Orange and his recent performances as Otello at Covent Garden and elsewhere have been widely praised. His powerful heroic voice, his vocal stamina and his fine acting have combined to make him one of the most popular tenors of his generation, and he had recorded many of his best roles.

GALINA VISHNEVSKAYA
Soprano

Born in Kronstadt on October 25, 1926, Vishnevskaya started singing professionally immediately she left school, taking parts in operettas with the Leningrad Operetta Theatre, and soon found that her exceptional talents brought engagements in more serious music. She studied privately with Vera Garina and in 1953 became a member of the Bolshoi company in Moscow. Her first roles were minor ones, such as the Page in *Rigoletto*, but she was soon singing major parts: her Tatyana in *Eugene Onegin* established her as the leading Russian lyrico-dramatic soprano of her day. Tours followed in Finland, Italy, Germany and England; she visited the

US in 1960 and made her début at the Metropolitan Opera, New York, in the title role of *Aida* in 1961, also singing Cio-Cio-San in *Madama Butterfly* in the same season. Covent Garden welcomed her in 1962, again as Aida, and she made her first appearance in La Scala, Milan, as Liu in *Turandot* in 1964. Her most recent appearances at Covent Garden were as Tosca in 1977. Vishnevskaya is married to the cellist Mstislav Rostropovich and they have toured together extensively. Her voice is a powerful soprano of fine quality and she is a striking dramatic actress. She has made a number of recordings for the Russian Stage Record Trust, and has also recorded the soprano part in Britten's *War Requiem* for Decca.

HELEN WATTS
Contralto

Born in Pembrokeshire in 1927, Watts studied singing at the Royal Academy of Music, London, with Caroline Hatchard and Frederick Jackson. She originally intended to be a concert singer and joined the BBC Chorus. In 1953 she sang the role of Orfeo in a broadcast performance of Gluck's *Orfeo ed Euridice* and was shortly afterwards engaged to sing in recordings of Handel's operas, in which she was extremely successful. As a result, she made her stage début in 1958, when the Handel Society produced *Theodora* in London, and since then has had a most successful career as an operatic artist. She sang in Handel's *Radamisto* at Sadler's Wells in 1961 and has appeared in many Wagnerian music dramas at Covent Garden. In 1964 she toured the USSR with the English Opera Group, singing Lucretia in Britten's *The Rape of Lucretia*, with the composer conducting. She sang the role of Sosostris in Tippett's *The Midsummer Marriage* in 1968 and two years later appeared in the same role at Covent Garden. Her voice is a true contralto which has been beautifully trained, and she uses it with the intelligence and taste of a cultured musician.

WOLFGANG WINDGASSEN
Tenor

Born at Annemasse, France, of German parents on June 26, 1914, Windgassen was the son of an operatic tenor and a *coloratura* soprano. He studied with his father and also at the Music High School, Stuttgart, and made his début in Pforzheim in 1939 as Alvaro in *La Forza del Destino*, but was then conscripted into the army. After the war he was engaged at Stuttgart, where he sang regularly for the rest of his life, making frequent guest appearances at the Vienna Staatsoper, where he was first heard in 1953, and Covent Garden, where he made his début in 1954 as Tristan. He was also heard from 1951 until 1970 in Bayreuth, where he was considered to be the finest German heroic tenor since the war. He was equally acclaimed at the Metropolitan Opera, New York, which he first visited in 1957. He was singing up to the time of his death (in Stuttgart on September 5, 1974), although he was past his prime, and made his last stage appearance in Stuttgart only a week before he died, as Florestan in *Fidelio*. His voice was a finely-controlled heroic tenor of beautiful quality with ringing high notes, and his moving acting and superb general musicianship made him unrivalled in the major Wagnerian tenor roles when he was in his prime. He recorded many of his greatest roles and they have set a standard which will not easily be surpassed.

INGVAR WIXELL
Baritone

Born in Stockholm, Wixell studied at the Music Academy and the Opera School there, before making his début with the Stockholm Opera Company in 1955, as Papageno in *Die Zauberflöte*,

remaining a permanent member of the company until 1968. He sang as a guest in Berlin for the first time in 1962, at the Staatsoper, and in the same year made his Glyndebourne début as Guglielmo in *Così fan tutte*. He has also sung at the Salzburg Festival, at the Vienna Staatsoper, in Bayreuth and at La Scala, Milan, and has frequently appeared in the US, notably in Chicago, where he sang Belcore in *L'Elisir d'amore*, in San Francisco, and at the Metropolitan Opera, New York, where he made his début in 1973 in the title role of *Rigoletto*. He appeared at Covent Garden with the Stockholm Opera Company in 1960, as a guest artist in *Simon Boccanegra* in 1972, and in 1977 in *L'Elisir d'amore*, *Tosca* and *Arabella*. He has a resonant, well-focused, high baritone voice and is a powerful actor. He has recorded a number of operas with Colin Davis conducting.

FRITZ WUNDERLICH
Tenor

Born at Kusel on September 26, 1930, Wunderlich studied privately and at the Municipal Theatre in Freiburg, making his operatic début there as Tamino in *Die Zauberflöte*. From 1955 until his death at the tragically early age of 35, on September 17, 1966, he was a member of the Stuttgart Opera, and later also of the opera houses in Frankfurt and Hamburg, making guest appearances in many other centres. He was first heard at the Salzburg Festival in 1959, as Henry Morosus in *Die Schweigsame Frau* by Richard Strauss and later sang there in many Mozart roles, for which he was admirably suited. He made his Covent Garden début in 1965 as Don Ottavio in *Don Giovanni*. His engagement at the Metropolitan Opera, New York, in November 1966 was prevented by his untimely death. His voice was a pure, easily-produced tenor which he used with charm and distinction; he was equally at home in the classical works of Mozart and in lighter works like *La Dame Blanche* of Boïeldieu. Fortunately, he made several records which do him full justice.

254